HANDBOOK
OF ADULT EDUCATION
IN THE UNITED STATES

HANDBOOK
OF ADULT EDUCATION
IN THE UNITED STATES

Malcolm S. Knowles
Editor

ADULT EDUCATION ASSOCIATION OF THE U.S.A.
743 North Wabash Avenue
Chicago 11, Illinois
1960

Inscribed to those pioneers in the adult education movement so warmly remembered as having brought the spirit and the program of adult education in this country to its flourishing present.

TABLE OF CONTENTS

PART IV: PROGRAM AREAS IN ADULT EDUCATION

PART V: THE FUTURE OF ADULT EDUCATION IN AMERICA

PART VI: NATIONAL ORGANIZATIONS, ASSOCIATIONS, AND AGENCIES IN ADULT EDUCATION

FOREWORD

It has been my privilege—and a strange quirk of fate—to have been president of the Adult Education Association of the U.S.A. during this milestone year when a new edition of the *Handbook* has been in preparation.

The experience of watching in awe as the book was first outlined in broad strokes by several skilled hands, then as the many resources were drawn upon, then together—has been an inspiration I wish you all could have shared.

This volume is long overdue. It is a dozen years since the last edition was published and about eight years since its supply was exhausted. Since then, the practitioner in adult education has been forced to use files of professional journals as references—not the worst way to acquire knowledge, but not the handiest nor the most complete.

Much has happened in our country in these intervening years.' Certainly they have brought America closer to its bicentennial. And with this approaching, I have felt a new sense of maturity throughout the country.

As AEA president I have visited dozens of cities and small towns, state capitals and crossroads, where I have talked with groups, rank-and-file members, and leaders.

From them I have gained a strong impression that America is approaching not only a birthday but a new age: the Age of Maturity.

Until now we have been characterized as a youthful nation. Indeed we have prided ourselves on demonstrating the typical characteristics of youth: energetic, adventuresome in spirit, brash, experimental (often crude trial-and-error). But America is now approaching its majority; we are coming of age.

As a nation, we are now accepting greater responsibility not only for our own citizens but for other nations. As a corporate body we are growing up!

As a people, our pursuits are less frivolous and more of them have a long-range purpose. As individuals, we are growing up!

Perhaps the leavening influence is the growing proportion of mature persons in our population. Demographically we are growing older, with maybe 10 per cent of today's Americans 65 or more years old. More attention is being paid to the older person. In our own field, education for mature man and woman, retired or not yet, is commanding more of our resources. It is now a commonplace to recite the sociological changes: more older people with more time on their hands for a longer period of life.

Another factor encouraging our national maturity is that we—even the younger ones—have more leisure time for broadening ourselves. The four-day, thirty-hour work week is just around the corner. What a golden opportunity!

Does it strike you that America in the last half of the Twentieth Century contains the ingredients which produced the Golden Age of Greece? In just these two respects, at least, we are similar: Greece of the Fifth Century B.C. was a society of leisure and led by the elders. And do you recognize the informal education of the young men that occurred in the market place and in homes, where groups met to discuss? Doesn't all of this sound familiar to you?

Need we follow the parallel further to emphasize that here and now American adult educators have an opportunity and a challenge to create America's Golden Age. The conditions are ripe; the blueprint was set out for use twenty-five hundred years ago.

The specific methods and techniques to bring about this transformation are now in your hands as you hold this book. It contains the passwords to a new era. Use it well and you will play an important role in history.

PHILIP KLEIN
President, 1958-59
Adult Education Association of the U.S.A.

EDITOR'S PREFACE

What is a handbook?

Webster defines it as (1) a manual; a guidebook, or (2) a betting book of a bookmaker. As to the second definition, this Handbook qualifies not at all; and as to the first, only partly. It is not a manual, if by this is meant a set of how-to-do-it instructions—although certain chapters, especially those on methods and materials, have practical suggestions. It does, however, profess to be a guidebook. Its ambition is to point out the landmarks of the complicated territory encompassed by the phrase, "adult education," in much the same way the Baedekers guide the tourist through the high spots of exotic foreign lands.

As in the case of the Baedekers, this Handbook is the latest in a series. The first *Handbook of Adult Education in the United States* was published in 1934 by the American Association for Adult Education under the editorship of Dorothy Rowden. Close on its heels, in 1936, appeared a second version by the same editor. Then occurred a long hiatus of twelve years before the 1948 edition was published jointly by the American Association and the Institute of Adult Education at Teachers' College, Columbia University, with Mary L. Ely as editor.

As the format of this series matured it came to be regarded as the basic reference work in the adult education field. It was the instrument for taking stock every few years of the major developments in the field and systematically bringing adult educators—and the public—up to date on these developments. It also served as a current directory of the major organizations providing for the education of adults.

After a hiatus almost as long as the previous one, the Executive Committee of the Adult Education Association of the U.S.A. asked its Committee on Publications to investigate the need for a new Handbook. This committee determined that so many developments have occurred since 1948 that the character of the adult education field is essentially different from the picture presented at that time. It therefore commissioned the publication of a 1960 Handbook, with the assistance of an underwriting grant from the Fund for Adult Education, and defined its purpose as being:

"To provide an overview description of the current nature, characteristics, and trends of the field of adult education in order that adult education workers may be brought up to date about developments since the 1948 Handbook and place themselves and their programs in the context of the whole field."

The committee asked that the Handbook be written with several audiences in mind:

1. Experienced workers and scholars, who could use the book as both a "refresher course" and a basic reference for quickly looking up important facts about different aspects of the field of adult education and about the national organizations in it.

2. Students in pre-service and in-service training, who could find it useful as a textbook.

3. New workers in the field, who could use it for their own orientation.

4. Interested members of the general public, who could use it to get an understanding of what adult education is all about.

The authors have been asked to keep all these audiences in mind as they wrote their chapters, and none has as yet reported a mental breakdown in consequence. They were also told that "Since the central purpose of the Handbook is to provide a maximum amount of information in the briefest possible space, short, simple sentences with a minimum of modifiers and qualifiers are desirable. But the writing should not be cold and impersonal, with all your personal enthusiasm and charm of style squeezed out of it." How well they have succeeded in following these specifications each reader will, of course, judge for himself.

In planning the organization of the Handbook, the editor—with the advice of the Committee on Publications—sought to slice the field of adult education into its most significant current dimensions. Certainly one such dimension is its general background—historical, semantic, and teleological. This dimension is treated in Part I. A second dimension is the issues which are of greatest current concern to adult educators, and these are surveyed in Part II in order from general to specific. A third dimension is the institutional settings and resources for adult education that (1) are of the greatest social significance in the contemporary scene, and (2) have demonstrated the greatest concern, interest, and involvement in adult education as a field of study and practice. These institutional settings are reviewed, in alphabetical order, in Part III. A fourth dimension is the areas of study in which adults engage in these various institutional settings. These "program areas" are surveyed, also in alphabetical order, in Part IV. In an analytical frame of mind, Part V looks back at the current developments and trends in all these dimensions and tries to assess what it all adds up to. Its central question is, "Where does adult education seem to be going in America as it enters the seventh decade of the Twentieth Century?" Finally, Part VI provides a directory of the major national organizations, associations, and agencies which offer programs of adult education. Its purpose is to facilitate intercommunication among the agencies in the field by providing up-to-date information about addresses, program emphases, and publications; but it also gives every reader a bird's-eye view of the adult educational activities of these national organizations.

The only case that can be made for looking at the complex field of adult education in this way is that it seemed to the editor and his advisers that these dimensions reflected the essential realities of the field at this stage of its development better than any other system of categories examined. This Handbook is organized quite differently from the previous Handbooks—perhaps because the field itself has changed in structure since 1948, or perhaps because this editor simply sees it differently from the previous editors.

A number of judgments had to be made in constructing the basic outline of this Handbook, and for these the editor takes full responsibility; that is to say, they are not necessarily the reflection of official policy of the Adult Education Association. For example, the list of common concerns in Part II are those that survived a screening process which involved determining which concerns appeared most frequently in the periodical literature, conferences, and committee deliberations of adult educators. Another process may have produced a different list of concerns, although it is inconceivable that it could be drastically different.

In Part III judgments had to be made about which institutions met the criteria of significance and concern in adult education, and some may have been omitted which should not have been. Also, some institutions, such as museums and art institutes, were grouped together because of their similarity in organization and program; and perhaps some readers may wish that they had been treated separately. Some artistic license was used in pulling the Co-operative Extension Service out of "Government Agencies" and making it a separate chapter; but the size and significance of its adult education work seemed to warrant separate treatment.

In Part IV probably the most questionable judgments of all had to be made, because of the fluid state of the subject areas in adult education. Obviously the boundaries between many of these categories, such as "Creative Arts" and "Recreation" or "Liberal Adult Education" and practically any of the other program areas, are not black and white but shades of gray. Without doubt another editor, with different advisers, would have produced a somewhat different pattern of categories. What this probably means is that while adult education is partly following the traditional arrangement of academic subjects, it is in the process of developing a unique set of organizing principles for its own curriculum. In a sense, adult education's approach to learning is becoming more problem-centered than subject-centered—a phenomenon that is dealt with in chapters 5 and 47.

A further problem was confronted in the relationship between Part III and Part IV, in that it would hardly be possible for an author to describe an institutional setting without saying something about the program areas it covered, and it would hardly be possible for an author to describe a program area without saying something about the institutional settings in which it occurs. Gross overlapping of this sort has been minimized by encouraging authors to exchange outlines and by editing. But it was felt that a certain amount of cross-referencing between institutional settings and program areas would enhance the value of this Handbook, and an attempt has been made to bring relevant cross-references together in the index.

The judgments in Part V are, happily, those of Paul Sheats of the University of California, who was asked to read the galley proofs of the rest of the book "to analyze the trends pointed up in the various chapters and formulate your own synthesis, adding whatever you wish in the way of additional trends, comparisons with other countries, and implications for future strategy." The resulting look at the future of adult education in America is destined to become one of the classics in our literature.

The judgments as to which organizations are included in the directory in Part VI are largely those of the leaders of the various national organizations themselves. An original list of more than two hundred organizations that appeared to have some kind of adult educational program or service was compiled by searching numerous existing directories. The leaders of these organizations were then invited to fill out and return a questionnaire if they wished to be listed in our directory. Most of them responded positively, but a number indicated that they did not feel that it would be appropriate for their organizations to be listed. A few that did return the questionnaire were eliminated when it became apparent that they did not provide direct services or programs in the education of adults. Without doubt there are unfortunate omissions that should be corrected in future editions, but it is certainly the most comprehensive directory of service agencies (as contrasted with resource agencies) in the field of adult education yet compiled.

Once the basic outline of the Handbook was agreed upon the next step was to recruit authors to write the various chapters. The process used involved these phases: (1) A panel of several possible authors was identified for each chapter by the editor in collaboration with the Committee on Publications. (2) These potential authors were arranged in priority order according to the criteria of known competence in a particular specialty, reputation for comprehensiveness of viewpoint regarding the subject under consideration, writing ability, and availability of time and resources. (3) The editor invited the members of each panel, in order, until an author was obtained.

The quality of this Handbook is, in the last analysis, a reflection of the quality of its fifty-four authors. But it should be understood that each one worked under the handicap of a rigid time limit. Most of them had only two months in which to collect new data, prepare a first draft, circulate this draft among colleagues for criticism, and write the final draft. A few authors were given an extra month or more because their chapters required greater data-collection. All authors were volunteers—our budget allowed for only small allocations to them to cover the cost of data-collection. All of us in the field of adult education owe them a deep debt of gratitude for this self-sacrificial contribution to our professional literature.

The role of the editor has been chiefly that of learner, and he would highly recommend a similar assignment to anyone who wants a liberal education in adult education. He is especially grateful for the assistance, advice, and encouragement he has received from the Adult Education Association's officers and executive committee members for 1958-59. His most intimate advisers during this project have been the members of the Committee on Publications, including Philip Klein and Margaret Monroe—the chairmen during the planning and execution phases—Kenneth Benne, Joseph Matthews, Nicholas Mitchell, David Rauch, James Rietmulder, Thurman White, and Coolie Verner. They share with him all the credit for what is excellent and none of the blame for what is poor. The editor wishes to express particular appreciation, on behalf of both the Adult Education Association and himself, to the Fund for Adult Education and its president, C. Scott Fletcher, for both helpful advice and financial underwriting of the preparation of this Handbook.

A few final words are reserved for the readers. We hope that you will find this Handbook useful, but we realize that it will not fulfill all of your expectations. Read it tolerantly, with the understanding that those of us who are dedicating our lives to the education of adults tend to have the myopia of missionaries, the enthusiasm of pioneers, and—perhaps in some measure—the vision of prophets. But read it critically and, remembering that there will be future Handbooks, let us know how it could have been better.

January, 1960

Malcolm S. Knowles
Boston, Massachusetts

PART I

BACKGROUND AND OVERVIEW

CHAPTER 1

WHAT IS ADULT EDUCATION?

ROBERT J. BLAKELY
Vice President
Fund for Adult Education

Definitions of adult education in the United States are as multitudinous as the autumn leaves, yet none satisfies many persons engaged in it. The difficulties are in both the phrase and the reality.

Education, by its root, implies a "leading out." The meaning is clear when the relationships are between mature persons and immature persons. The meaning is not clear when the relationships are between mature persons in a world where the present changes before we can grasp it and the only safe prediction is that the future will be different.

And what is an *adult?* On the one hand, we draft young men before we give them the vote. On the other hand, a genius like Einstein expressing unpopular opinions is liable to be called "immature."

Put the two words together, and you have the semantics of adult education.

Now let's glance at the reality.

In complexity, adult education traverses every degree from the most simple to the most advanced. In purpose, adult education traverses every degree from education as an end in itself to education solely as a means to other ends.

Does this sound invidious? There is a third dimension.

One of the persons learning the English alphabet is a distinguished refugee from tyranny with a passion to live freely in the United States. One of the persons going beyond the frontiers of knowledge is noted for his ignorance in all fields except his specialty. Another going beyond the frontiers in his own field is simultaneously studying the rudiments in a second field.

One person learning for the sake of learning is neglecting his family; another is doing so to keep his balance amid the impact of practical

3

affairs. One of the persons learning as a means for doing a better job is a counterfeiter; another is a member of Congress.

Even this isn't all. Some activities are called adult education which should not be, and some of the best examples of adult education are not so regarded by those engaged in them.

How can one say "should not be"? Well, surely there are limits. I'll suggest two. First, adult education implies purposeful systematic learning, in contrast to random unexamined experience; that is, it contains elements of science and art. Second, adult education implies a respect for the purposes and integrity of the learner, in contrast to attempts to fool, cheat or exploit; that is, is has an ethic.

Thus, adult education cannot be satisfactorily defined, and not even all the major uses of the phrase can be explained in brief compass. Lest this seem deprecatory, let's remind ourselves that the same could be said about other important ideas and practices such as democracy, freedom, and justice.

But there is more to the point.

"All men *by nature* desire to know," Aristotle wrote; we should respect this human essence in all its pilgrimages.

America is the promise of opportunities for all; we should respect all those who create and use opportunities for continued learning.

The pluralism of adult education in the United States reflects American life. Let us look at adult education again, this time with respect to its institutional auspices, subject matter, methods, "teachers," and clientele.

Adult education is carried on by established educational institutions, from elementary schools through universities. Much is formal, but perhaps even more—certainly an increasing percentage—is informal.

Adult education is carried on by informal educational institutions, such as libraries, museums, theaters, orchestras, etc. These are becoming more aggressive and skillful.

Adult education is carried on by our social organizations—corporations, unions, government agencies, etc. Some of this is "within the family," some in co-operation with educational institutions.

Adult education is carried on in the vast skein of voluntary organizations in the United States: churches; neighborhood groups; community committees, clubs, and councils; state, national, and international associations, societies, federations, leagues; and so on—and so on. Increasingly—as issues become more complex, as we become more interdependent, as the currents of change quicken—educational activities for adults (called that or not) are multiplying.

Whatever interests free citizens in a free society is subject matter for adult education.

In every institutional field, evidence can be found of a broadening of concerns to include more than the private or the special interest.

All the ways by which mature persons learn are the methods of adult education.

Three trends can be noted. First, much more attention is being paid to methods of teaching *particularly designed for adults*. Second, *participation* by the adult learner is becoming a keynote. Third, *the media of mass communications* are increasingly being used as tools, either by themselves or with other methods.

What about "teachers"? (The quotes warn us not to transfer too literally the concept from formal schooling to adult education.) Teachers of young people teach adults also. There are those who teach adults only. There are professors of adult education. There are paid educational directors. There are volunteers who lead in adult education as in other activities. Most adult education occurs under their leadership. Lay leaders, properly used, are a potentially inexhaustible supply, because, as more people learn to learn, more learn how to help others learn.

Adult education is the largest and the fastest growing segment of American education.

More important, much of adult education is becoming, not a "making up," but a "keeping up" and a "going ahead."

And beyond this, just as successive waves of immigrants have adopted "the American way of life," so do social groups rising in the "upwardly mobile" society of the United States respond to adult education. More and more people coming into adult education for narrowly personal or group interests follow the upward and broadening development of many of those which preceded them.

With an alloy of hope and confidence we can foresee the day when the clientele of continuing education is the entire American people.

Is this vision so startling, in a society which has given the franchise to all adult citizens?

This is the optimistic side of the coin—the "heads" of both the American society and of American adult education—the advancing goddess of liberty, the rising sun, "In God We Trust."

There is a pessimistic side: the "tails" has a brooding eagle and "E Pluribus Unum." The eagle, we must remember, besides being our national symbol, is also a bird of prey. And pluralism, which can be a source of strength, can also be a force for disintegration.

The *pluralism* of American life is obvious; not so the *one*. Is pluralism an end in itself? Does it add up to anything, particularly to a whole that is greater than the sum of its parts? If it doesn't, can it survive?

If it adds up at all it is to an equation for an opening spiral: better individuals, who will make a better society, which will develop better individuals. . . .

Without primary concern for the worth of the individual, on the one hand, and, on the other, the meaning of our nation, American life is a chaos, and American adult education a reflection of that chaos. With this primary concern, an order is created—however rich its variety and turbulent its energy.

The purpose of American life and of American education, in this light, is seen to be the development of individuals who will fulfill themselves and freely serve the society which values individuals.

And, in this light and with this purpose, the role of adult education becomes something quite different from what it has traditionally been.

Continuing education becomes the growing and the harvest, for which formal schooling is only the planting and the cultivation.

Continuing education becomes a purposeful and systematic use of the opportunity to be a free individual and a responsible citizen. It becomes an ever-cyclical benefiting from the past, employment of the present, and preparation for the future. It becomes a deliberate enterprise to enlarge the role of intelligence, awareness, and knowledge in the arena of decisions and action.

Continuing education becomes a vision of a society in which, not just its schools, but all of its parts—its government, business, unions, and organizations, its homes, neighborhoods, cities, states, and nation—are concerned with helping individuals fulfill themselves. This is the ideal of the *educative* society.

The continuing education of the American people can be an instrument for performing our duties to the other peoples of the world. And it can be an example for other peoples who are striving to be free.

Other peoples have, all peoples will have adult education, more and more of it, for many purposes. But only a self-governing people can have as the goal of education free individuals and a free society. With this as our concern, in the pluralism of adult education we can find our common ground.

CHAPTER 2

HISTORICAL DEVELOPMENT OF THE ADULT EDUCATION MOVEMENT IN THE UNITED STATES

MALCOLM S. KNOWLES

*Associate Professor of Education and General Consultant in
Adult Education
Boston University*

COLONIAL FOUNDATIONS AND ANTECEDENTS

Adult education probably started taking place the day the settlers landed in Jamestown in 1607, for in order to survive these British colonists had to learn about a new environment and its peculiar requirements. The methods they used can be assumed to consist of rather crude observation, trial and error, and exchange of experience.

While adult education during the entire Colonial period was essentially unorganized and primarily vocational, the seeds of certain institutional forms were planted at this time. And certainly the basic spirit of the "American dream"—the notion that every person can get ahead if he is willing and works hard—which has so greatly influenced the growth of adult education in this country, began to develop during this period.

Apprenticeship was adopted as an instrument of vocational training almost immediately after landing, but the first permanent institutional form of education to be created was the university; it seems truly remarkable to us now that sixteen years after the Puritans landed in Massachusetts—in 1636—they founded Harvard College. The foundations of our public school system were also laid soon after the colonies were established—a Massachusetts law of 1642 directed local town governments to hold parents and masters responsible to teach the young to read and write. Private schools—widely advertised in the newspapers of the day and large-

7

ly conducted in the residences of the "masters"—were the chief source of vocational education for adults. A rudimentary form of secondary education was also provided by private schools—first the Latin grammar schools, then the more practical English schools, and finally the private academies.

The single most universal instrument for intellectual activity in these times was the church. Although the subjects of the colonial sermons were overwhelmingly theological, the Puritan clergy justified their injecting a good deal of humanistic learning as being as necessary for development of human reason as revelation and grace were necessary for faith and salvation. The church was also the scene of mid-week lectures on a wide variety of subjects by both clergy and laymen.

The New England town meeting is frequently characterized as an important adult educational instrument, and perhaps it was to the extent that it served as a training ground in the art of self-government for the colonists. But it was essentially a decision-making agency, not an educational institution.

The only uniquely adult educational institution founded in this period that has survived (at least in name) into modern times was the Junto, a discussion club started by Benjamin Franklin and eleven cronies in 1727. Meeting once a week on Friday evenings, this self-educating group discussed such topics as morals, politics, and natural philosophy, over cups of punch. But perhaps in an even more fundamental way than by founding institutions did Franklin influence the eventual development of adult education in this country. Through all his writings and by the example of his life, Franklin ingrained deeply into the American stream of thought a compulsion toward self-improvement which has exerted a dominant influence on the American attitude toward continuing education. "Franklin, beyond all other early American heroes," according to Grattan, "has claim to being a patron saint of adult education."[1]

The embryos of other institutions can be identified. The subscription library—a voluntary association of individuals contributing to a general fund for the purchase of books (the first of which was organized by Franklin in 1731)—demonstrated the feasibility of making books available to the public. The idea of the museum was projected with the founding of the Massachusetts Historical Society in 1790 and the Pennsylvania Academy of Fine Arts in 1791. A theater was built in Williamsburg in 1716 and a "play house" opened in New York in 1733. The newspaper came into being as an important disseminator of information in 1704 with the founding of the Boston *News-Letter*.

THE GROWTH OF A NATION AND ITS QUEST FOR THE DIFFUSION OF KNOWLEDGE

The forces unleashed by independence, westward expansion, the industrial revolution, and the European Enlightenment conspired to produce a compulsion for knowledge never before noted in the annals of history. But the first task of the new nation was to transform an entire people from subjects to citizens—from a people used to being governed by an aristocracy to a people able to govern themselves. Indeed, no undertaking of any society ever staked more on the ability of adults to learn than did the founding of the Republic. The instruments by which this gigantic adult educational undertaking was accomplished were informal, disorganized, and in a sense unconscious. They included committees of correspondence, pamphlets, editorials, books, speeches, poems, and plays which explored the issues and ideas of democracy.

At the same time that the common man was mastering his new role of citizen-ruler, the world of knowledge was being illuminated by the dawn of the age of science. Reports of new discoveries in the natural sciences in Europe whetted intellectual appetites across the country. Concrete evidence of this phenomenon is given by the experience of Professor Benjamin Silliman of Yale College. Anticipating the idea of university extension by three-quarters of a century, Professor Silliman gave a course of popular lectures in natural science for a class of ladies and gentlemen in New Haven in 1830 which proved so popular that he took it to surrounding communities and by 1859 was including in his circuit points as far south and west as Pittsburg, New Orleans, and St. Louis.

New Institutions

This demand for the spread of useful knowledge gave rise to several adult educational institutions.

Mechanics and Mercantile Libraries and Institutes.—The opening of the Mechanics' Apprentices Library in Boston and the New York Mercantile Library in 1820 stimulated the development of similar institutions in most of the larger cities of the country. Fees in these libraries were lower than for the more scholarly subscription libraries and the book collections tended toward the more technical needs of young artisans and mercantile workers. A more continuous and deeper level of educational opportunity was afforded these same groups by the mechanics institutes. Sparked by the founding of the Franklin Institute in Philadelphia in 1824, these institutes provided libraries, lecture series, scientific collections, and periodicals containing up-to-date knowledge.

Lowell Institute and Cooper Union.—In the same spirit, but with broader purposes and programs, were two institutes that have exerted great influence on their respective communities and on the adult education movement as a whole. The Lowell Institute was founded in Boston in 1836 for "the maintenance and support of public lectures, to be delivered in Boston, upon philosophy, natural history, the arts and sciences"; and Cooper Union was established in New York in 1859 "to provide free courses of instruction in the application of Sciences and Art to the practical business of life." Both institutions have contributed many pioneering developments in the methods and substance of adult education and are still thriving institutions today.

The Lyceum Movement.—Perhaps the most spectacular offspring of the hunger for knowledge that characterized this period was the lyceum. The idea of a national network of local study groups, or lyceums, emerged out of the experience of Josiah Holbrook of Derby, Connecticut, as a lecturer before numerous groups in New England. In October, 1826, Holbrook described a full-scale plan for the organization of an educational society which would reach every part of the nation and proceeded to demonstrate that it would work by personally organizing the first town lyceum in Millbury, Connecticut, that same year, and ten more lyceums in neighboring towns during the next year. The movement spread, and by 1835 there were about 3,000 town lyceums, over 100 county lyceums, and fifteen or sixteen state lyceums.

In May, 1831, a meeting was held in New York City for the organization of the National American Lyceum, with delegates present representing 1,000 town lyceums. The new organization adopted as its purpose "the advancement of education, especially in the common schools, and the general diffusion of knowledge." An organizational pattern was formulated consisting of a hierarchy of local, county, and state lyceums, each with representation in the national lyceum. The annual meetings of the national lyceum were poorly attended and ways were never found to get the county and state organizations functioning properly. The national system therefore gradually withered, and no information concerning it after 1839 can be found.

Although the national lyceum ceased to exist, many town and county lyceums continued to operate until about the time of the Civil War. Around 1869 the function of providing popular lecturers for literary societies, women's clubs, and other groups, began to be taken over by commercial speakers' bureaus—often known as "lyceum bureaus."

The lyceum movement left several permanent deposits in the main streams of American culture and, particularly, of adult education. It demonstrated the feasibility of an integrated national system of local groups organized primarily for adult educational purposes—an experience which doubtless influenced the development of such later organizations as the women's clubs, the service clubs, the parent-teacher associations, and even the modern-day Great Books Program. It developed an educational technique—the lecture-forum—which was later to be adopted and extended by such successors as the Chautauqua, university extension, and public forum movements. Its publication of "scientific tracts" for home study foreshadowed the correspondence course. It even suggested the idea of a national popular movement for the advancement of adult education, which only in our time is perhaps beginning to take shape.

Popular reading and public libraries.—Although private libraries multiplied in connection with lyceums, young men's associations, civic groups, and subscription clubs, the idea of free public libraries began to take hold. A free town library was established in Peterborough, New Hampshire, in 1833, supported by a municipal tax. By 1849 the idea had gained such strength that a state law was passed in New Hampshire enabling towns to establish and maintain libraries by taxation. Massachusetts followed suit in 1851, Maine in 1854, Vermont in 1855, and Ohio in 1867. It was with the opening of the Boston Public Library in 1852, however, that the free public library as we know it came into existence. Boston's example was followed shortly by New York, with an Astor gift of half a million dollars, and the other urban centers of the country. It was characteristic of the early public libraries that they were largely urban and were founded under the stimulus of philanthropy. By the beginning of the Civil War the free public library had become established as an integral part of the American cultural and educational system.

Voluntary associations and agencies.—One of the most uniquely American aspects of our culture, and one of the most significant in the future development of adult education—the voluntary association—had already become so visible by 1831 as to draw these often-quoted remarks from a French observer:

> Americans of all ages, all conditions, and all dispositions constantly form associations. They have not only commercial and manufacturing companies, in which all take part, but associations of a thousand other kinds, religious, moral, serious, futile, general or restricted, enormous or diminutive. The Americans make associations to give entertainments, to found seminaries, to build inns, to construct churches, to diffuse books, to send missionaries to the antipodes; in this manner they found hospitals, prisons, and schools. If it is proposed to inculcate some truth or to foster some feeling by the encouragement of a great example, they form a society. Wherever at the head of some new undertaking you see the government in France, or a man of rank in England, in the United States you will be sure to find an association.[2]

Many of these voluntary associations had an action goal to propagandize for, but most of them carried on adult educational programs as their chief activity. Although most of them were narrowly local in their scope and influence, the way was being paved for the formation of the strong national organizations that came to dominate the picture in the second half of the century. The organization of the Young Men's Christian Associations starting in 1851, the United States Agricultural Society in 1852, the Young Women's Christian Associations in 1855, the first industry-wide trade association in the same year, and the National Education Association in 1857, gave an indication of the future direction of voluntary association development in this country.

Churches.—While the Protestant churches were experiencing a rise in lay activity, they were not yet conscious of any substantial role in the secular education of adults. The Sunday School movement began to be transplanted from England in 1785, and in 1824 the American Sunday School Union was founded. The mission of this movement was completely doctrinal and its clientele was exclusively children.

Perhaps one of the most important developments in this era in adult education in religious institutions was the emergence of Reformed Judaism. Of this movement, Meland observes that "having abandoned the racial taboos and practices of the traditional faith which had tended to set the Jew apart from his contemporaries, the Reformed Jew has taken up the task of adapting himself to the environment of modern culture with a zeal not to be exceeded, if, in fact, matched, by other religious adherents. . . This movement in Judaism has been an energetic influence in behalf of enlightened and socialized living in this country for more than a century."[3]

The earliest form of discrete adult educational activity operated by Catholics were reading circles, often founded in connection with parish libraries. An example was the New York City Catholic Library Association, founded in 1854 "with the object of disseminating Catholic truth and useful knowledge and promoting the moral and intellectual culture of its members."[4] By 1860 it had a historical section, a debating club, a mechanics' society, and a library of over 1,000 volumes. Catholic young men's societies also afforded adult educational opportunities.

Agricultural education.—By the early years of the nineteenth century some need was felt for the co-ordination of the agricultural societies, and state boards of agriculture began to emerge. By the middle of the century a definite movement for agricultural education had developed. A United States Agricultural Society was founded in 1852, and by 1860 it reported 941 agricultural organizations in existence in the country. The year 1862 represents a landmark in this development, with the establishment of a federal Department of Agriculture and the passage of the Land Grant Act (often referred to as the "Morrill Act" after the senator from Vermont who fought for it for many years) providing federal support for land grant colleges.

The Shaping of a National Educational System

The period between the American Revolution and the Civil War stands out like a beacon in the history of education, since it was during this time that the basic pattern of our national system of state-supported elementary and secondary schools, state universities, and normal schools took shape. But it was not an easy, automatic process.

While there was little opposition to the idea of universal education, it being widely accepted in principle that everyone in a republic ought to be educated, there was strong opposition to the idea of universal public education supported by taxation. A battle ensued that lasted a generation, from 1825 to 1850, and about which more feeling and bitter antagonism was engendered than has been caused by any issue in America except perhaps slavery. The process by which the battle was won was essentially an adult educational process, strongly flavored with propaganda and social action. Public interest was aroused and citizens were stimulated to study and discuss the issues through the activities of hundreds of school societies, lyceums, and educational associations. Running debates were carried on in the newspapers and magazines. Public-spirited citizens, as well as professional school men like Horace Mann, traveled over the country making addresses to the people and spreading the vision of a national pattern of universal public education. The result of these efforts was that, as Cubberley phrases it, "In 1825 common schools were the distant hope of statesmen and reformers; in 1850 they were becoming an actuality in almost every Northern State."[5]

As battles began to be won in the establishment of free public elementary schools the same forces gradually developed a public demand for the extension upward to the secondary level of a common system of public education. By 1860 there was little doubt that the high school, although still subordinate to the private academy, would become accepted as a part of the public school system.

Evening schools.—The rudiments of an institutional form—the public evening school—which in the next century was to become one of the principal instrumentalities of adult education, appeared during this period. The literature is replete with conflicting dates for the founding of the early evening schools in various cities. The following table illustrates the disparity between two frequently quoted authorities:

FOUNDING DATES OF EVENING SCHOOLS

	By Cubberley[6]	By Mann[7]
Boston	1870	1836
New York City	1866	1847
St. Louis	1856	1859
Chicago	1856	1862
Louisville	1834	1834
Philadelphia	1869	1869

Most of the discrepancies are probably the product of different assumptions and definitions. Some authorities, for example, date the first evening school from the year special courses were offered in the evening for the instruction of children who could not attend during the day, while others restrict the definition of "founding date" to the point at which official action is taken to establish an evening school as a distinct administrative unit. The fact that some early evening schools were publicly supported and others were private may account for further contradictions in founding dates. More fundamentally, the difficulty encountered in identifying precise founding dates suggests that the evening school emerged through an evolutionary process rather than as a carefully planned stroke of policy.

It is clear that these early evening schools would not qualify as programs of adult education in the modern sense. They were established primarily for working youth—in many cases exclusively for boys—and their curriculum was a repetition of the regular academic courses given in the day time. But the fact that evening schools had become an established unit in many public school systems before the Civil War provided the foundation for what was later to become one of the most important institutions for the education of adults in our country.

Colleges and universities.—By 1861 a total of 182 permanent private colleges had been founded which, happily, did not create a dual system of higher education in the aristocratic European tradition, but articulated with the public education system. The development of a state controlled system of higher education came to fruition in 1862 when the Land Grant College Act was passed and signed by President Lincoln, making a grant of 30,000 acres of public land to each state for each senator and representative that state had in Congress, to endow a college of agriculture and mechanic arts. This act laid the foundation for the establishment in the next half-century of a pattern of state land-grant colleges which has become one of the principal jewels on the crown of our public education system and which was later to provide the home base for the most extensive adult education program ever created.

The notion that the universities have a contribution to make to the general community, over and above the training of resident students, was glimpsed but hardly seen during the early nineteenth century. Popular lectures like those of Professor Silliman were not perceived as extensions of the university's services so much as the leisure activity of a public-spirited professor. But evidence that the university extension idea was in the air is contained in the following letter written in 1835 by Dr. William E. Channing to Josiah Quincy, president of Harvard:

> The education of the people seems to me more and more to be the object to which the college should be directed. This institution has always existed, and exists now, for the people. It trains young men, not so much for themselves, as that they may be qualified to render services to the community; and perhaps they render no higher service than by spreading their own intelligence and giving a higher tone to the public mind. Can not the college do more for this end? I hope it may. If it can furnish a course of philosophical instruction, which can be pursued by a greater number than now pass through college; if it can extend the demand for this higher education by supplying its means, and if it can give a rank to those who enjoy this advantage, it will render inestimable service. . . .
>
> Perhaps the most important inquiry for the friends of the college is, How can it become a popular institution, an object of public interest, without narrowing at all its present course of instruction? Its well being requires that the community should look to it as their friend and benefactor.[8]

THE MATURATION OF A NATION AND MULTIPLICATION OF ITS ADULT EDUCATION INSTITUTIONS

During the years between the Civil War and the First World War the United States went through its developmental transition from adolescence to maturity as a nation. This was a period of teen-age effervescence and gangling growth. Wave after wave of immigrants poured into the country from almost every part of the world and helped to swell its population from just over thirty million in 1860 to well over one hundred million by 1920. The integration of these new peoples into a new culture became one of the great adult education challenges of all time. The most phenomenal expansion of all was in economic life. Indeed, during this period the character of the nation changed from essentially an agrarian society to a predominantly industrial and urban society. And with it, the character of American education was forced to change.

While the dominating spirit of the adult education movement up to the Civil War had been the diffusion of knowledge, that of the period between the Civil War and World War I might be characterized as the diffusion of organizations. In this period the penchant for joining which Tocqueville had observed in Americans in the 1830's reached its full force.

Developments in Institutions

In keeping with the general expansiveness and experimentalism of the times, a number of new institutional forms and methods of adult education were created, and many of the older institutions and methods were expanded and transformed.

Chautauqua.—One of the brightest new stars to light the adult educational skies was the Chautauqua Institution. Founded on the shores of Chautauqua Lake in New York in the summer of 1874, Chautauqua was initially conceived as a pan-denominational normal school for Sunday school teachers. This was the sole purpose in the minds of its founding fathers, Dr. John Vincent, secretary of the Methodist Sunday School Union, and Lewis Miller, a businessman and church layman. But the idea of a summer educational program proved so popular that Chautauqua began to attract other participants than Sunday school teachers and began broadening its program to include every aspect of culture.

In 1878 the first integrated core program of adult education organized in this country on a national scale came into being—the Chautauqua Literary and Scientific Circle ("C.L.S.C.") —which provided a four-year program of home reading in history and literature carried on in connection with local reading circles. Chautauqua also initiated a series of summer schools in language, liberal arts, speech, music, library training, and other disciplines, one of whose early directors was William Rainey Harper— who later became the first president of the University of Chicago. As a result of increasing demand for continuation during the winter months of work begun in the summer schools a program of correspondence courses was soon developed under Dr. Harper's direction. Chautauqua also developed an extensive informal program of lecture series, conferences, concerts, plays, and special interest clubs.

Chautauqua Institution was early imitated, with the founding of a scattering of local and regional "chautauquas" which adhered quite faithfully to the principles of their model, and with the founding of a commercial Chautauqua Circuit which brought mostly entertainment but some education in tents to the by-ways of rural America. But these stepchildren have long since passed from the scene, while the sturdy parent lives on.

Correspondence courses.—The success of the home study program at Chautauqua inspired Dr. Harper, when he became president of the University of Chicago in 1892, to establish a correspondence division in the extension department of the new university. The idea quickly spread to other universities and eventually to a number of high schools and junior colleges.

Correspondence study was soon also discovered and exploited by commercial institutions. The first of these began as a course in coal mining instituted by Thomas J. Foster, editor of the *Mining Herald* of Shenandoah, Pennsylvania, as a means of improving mine safety through education. The course met such enthusiastic response that other subjects were added and in 1891 this program became institutionalized into the International Correspondence Schools of Scranton, Pennsylvania. The success of this pioneering venture stimulated literally hundreds of correspondence schools to be formed by private individuals, partnerships, and stock companies. The great preponderance of the offerings by these private schools was vocational, although a few schools specialized in academic high school and college courses. There is no doubt that the commercial correspondence schools brought systematic learning opportunities to more adults by World War I than had any previous institutional form of adult education, but they also introduced practices which cast a shadow across its reputation in many quarters and which set the stage for a wave of reforms in the period ahead.

Agricultural education.—Local and regional agricultural societies, which reached their peak around 1861, began to wane in favor of farmers' institutes sponsored by state boards of agriculture, and by 1899 institutes had been organized in almost every state. Three large voluntary associations of farmers also emerged out of the ferment of rural interaction—the Grange (1867), the Farmers' Union (1902), and the American Farm Bureau Federation (1919).

But the development that was to influence the character of agricultural education perhaps more than any other single event was the origination in 1904 of farmers' co-operative demonstration work by Seaman A. Knapp. Knapp had become convinced that farmers would not change their practices merely by being told to or even by seeing what could be done on farms operated at public expense. Accordingly, he developed the demonstration method, in which farmers were persuaded to change their habits by demonstrating new techniques on their own farms.

The Cooperative Extension Service—the largest single adult education organization ever created—came into being with the passage of the Smith-

Lever Act in 1914. The act provided that each state was to receive $10,000 in federal funds each year, with additional amounts added in proportion to the size of its rural population, upon the presentation of a satisfactory state plan for the operation of an extension division in its land-grant college. By the end of World War I a strong agricultural extension service had been established in every state and the Cooperative Extension Service had become a recognized addition to our national educational system.

Workers' education.—For all practical purposes, the labor movement as we know it did not come into being in this country until after the Civil War. After a succession of attempts to federate local unions had failed, the American Federation of Labor was founded in 1881. The guiding hand of the A.F. of L. was Samuel Gompers, whose own deep distrust of intellectuals probably accounts in large measure for the long reluctance of the A.F. of L. to have anything to do with education. Membership in the A.F. of L. had grown to over half a million by 1900 and it became the established spokesman for the bulk of skilled labor. But it was not until after World War I that it developed a significant interest in education.

The major activities in the field of workers' education during this period were outside the main stream of labor movement development—the establishment of a residential labor college in 1895 at Trenton, Missouri, by the founder of Ruskin College in Oxford, England; the Bread Winners' College in New York City in 1898; and the Rand School of Social Science in New York City in 1906. These were all highly specialized institutions with strong ideological orientation, and they did not produce an extensive development of residential labor colleges such as occurred from similar beginnings in England. More indicative of future trends was the organization of permanent educational departments by the International Ladies Garment Workers' Union in 1916 and by the Amalgamated Clothing Workers' Union three years later.

Colleges and universities.—From the point of view of the advancement of adult education several important developments occurred in the colleges and universities between the Civil War and World War I. Perhaps the most striking was their tremendous growth in numbers—almost tripling the number existing in 1865. While the number of colleges and the size of their enrollments were expanding, so was the curriculum. The undergraduate programs put increasing emphasis on English, the physical sciences, the social sciences, and other "modern studies." Graduate instruction was also introduced. An innovation that was essentially a new adult educational form was the summer session. Although Harvard had started a summer school in 1869 for teachers of marine biology, it was the pioneering work of Chautauqua a decade later that exerted the greatest influence on the universities to move in this direction. By 1910 the summer session, usually of six weeks' duration and attended primarily by teachers, had become common in universities around the country.

But the most significant development was the emergence of the new institutional form, university extension. English universities had begun to engage in extension work early in the nineteenth century, and in 1873 Cambridge University created the first full-fledged extra-mural organization, a Syndicate for Local Lectures. This development greatly impressed American visitors and they stimulated discussion of the idea in this country. In 1887 Herbert B. Adams, Professor of History at Johns Hopkins University, advocated the development of university extension in the United States at a meeting of the American Library Association. The following year Melvil Dewey, then chief librarian of Columbia University, laid the plan before the regents of the University of the State of New York and in 1891 an appropriation of $10,000 was made for the organization of university extension in that state.

At a national meeting of people engaged in extension work held in December, 1891, delegates reported that some kind of extension work had been started in twenty-eight states and territories, and great enthusiasm was expressed for the new movement. But suddenly it went into decline and did not revive until 1906. In that year the extension division of the University of Wisconsin was reorganized under the direction of Dean Louis E. Reber and a new spirit was infused into the idea of extension representing a shift away from an emphasis on academic subjects toward an all-embracing concept of the role of the university in serving all of the people of the state in relation to the full scope of life problems—economic, political, social, cultural, and moral.

The founding of the National University Extension Association in 1915 symbolizes the establishment of general extension as a permanent element of our national system of higher education. By 1916 this association was able to list twenty-two member institutions with more or less formally organized extension divisions.

Libraries.—By the close of the Civil War the free public library movement had gained a firm foothold, especially in the cities of the North and West. But subscription libraries still outnumbered public libraries two to one. In 1875 the state board of education in Rhode Island was given the right to grant sums up to five hundred dollars to existing libraries. Commissions were established in Massachusetts in 1890 and in New Hampshire in 1891 that could make grants of one hundred dollars worth of books to any town library. Within the next decade many other states followed these examples, and under this stimulus many subscription libraries were induced to become public libraries.

The public library movement was thus expanding under its own power when, in the early 1880's it received a stimulant that made previous progress seem static. This stimulant was the contribution of over $41,000,000 to the building of community libraries between 1881 and 1917 by Andrew Carnegie. Having educated himself largely through books and believing that "the true university of these days is a collection of books," Carnegie offered to finance the building of libraries in those communities that would guarantee 10 per cent of the building cost for annual upkeep. By 1917 he had financed the building of 1,679 libraries.

Public schools.—In the development of a national system of elementary and secondary education, the period between the Civil War and World War I was one of expansion and consolidation. Compulsory attendance through the elementary grades, which had been established by two states (Massachusetts and New York) prior to the Civil War, had been extended to all states by 1918. The public high school movement advanced more slowly, but by the end of World War I there were 14,326 public high schools with an enrollment of 1,857,155 students or approximately 29 per cent of the youth of high school age.

A strong factor in the voluntary integration of our national education system was the creation in 1867 of a federal Department of Education "for the purpose of collecting such statistics and facts as shall show the condition and progress of education in the several States and Territories, and of diffusing such information respecting the organization and management of schools and school systems, and methods of teaching as shall aid the people of the United States in the establishment and maintenance of efficient school systems, and otherwise promote the cause of education throughout the country." In 1869 this department became the Bureau of Education within the Department of Interior.

The evening schools during this period began to attract older youths and adults in increasing numbers and increasingly took on the character of an adult education institution. Most superintendents who had tried them reported satisfactory experiences and resolutions supporting the idea of evening schools were passed by conventions of the National Education Association starting as early as 1860. By the turn of the century the evening school had become an established fixture in the American educational scene.

Several trends and developments in the evening schools during this period are worthy of note. Their enrollments rose both in size and age level. Their curriculum broadened in four directions: (1) expansion of "Americanization" programs for immigrants, (2) expansion of vocational courses, especially in trade and commercial subjects, (3) extension into secondary and college level subjects with the opening of evening high schools, and (4) experimental sorties into informal adult education. Although their financial position remained precarious during this entire period, the evening schools had nevertheless become widely established as worthy objects of local tax support, at least in principle, by the end of World War I. State support for evening schools emerged in four stages: (1) permissive legislation, granting local school districts authority to operate adult classes; (2) the passage of various mandatory requirements, such as compulsory subjects (civics) and teacher certification; (3) provision of direct financial aid; and (4) provision of statewide services to local school systems through the state departments of education. The evening schools also began to develop differentiated administrative and teaching operations as their load of administrative responsibilities became too heavy for peripheral handling.

Vocational education became an established element in the curriculum with the passage of the Smith-Hughes Act in 1919 making available federal funds, to be matched by state funds, to promote the teaching of courses in agriculture, home economics, trades, industries, and commerce. Junior colleges made an appearance during this period, providing another institutional base for adult education. And the professional organization of educators was achieved, with the founding of the National Teachers Association in 1857, which became the National Education Association in 1870.

Voluntary associations and agencies.—As if a profusion of seeds had been scattered on richly fertile soil, voluntary organizations of every size, shape, and color sprang into flower in the period between the Civil War and World War I. They followed no set pattern, no prescribed order, no logical design. They involved every conceivable type of person in many different forms of organizational relationship for a wide variety of purposes. Many of them had the education of adults as their primary purpose; others used adult educational processes as means to other ends; and others had no conscious concern with education at all. The distinctive characteristic of the development of voluntary associations following the Civil War was the emergence of national organizations.

The types most directly concerned with the education of adults included: (1) The women's organizations (General Federation of Women's Clubs, American Association of University Women, Junior Leagues, Altrusa, Quota, League of Women Voters, National Council of Jewish Women, and many others), which frequently combined self-improvement with social service and advancement of the status of women. (2) Youth organizations (YMCA, YWCA, YM-YWHA, 4-H Clubs, Boys Clubs, Boy Scouts, Girl Scouts, Campfire Girls, and others), whose adult educational role— except in the case of the "Y's"—was limited almost entirely to the training of thousands of adults recruited to serve as volunteer leaders of groups of boys and girls. (3) Health, welfare, and recreational agencies (American Public Health Association, American Red Cross, National Tuberculosis Association, Family Service Association, National Federation of Settlements, National Jewish Welfare Board, National Conference of Catholic Charities, National Recreation Association, and others), which developed a variety of programs and services ranging from instructional courses to the publication of materials and providing resource personnel to other organizations. (4) Economic organizations (labor unions, agricultural societies, trade associations, the National Association of Manufacturers, the Chamber of Commerce of the United States, co-operative and credit union leagues, and others), most of which carried on active programs of persuasion for particular economic points of view. (5) Fraternal organizations and service clubs (Rotary, Kiwanis, Lions, veterans' organizations, laymen's societies under religious auspices, and others), the programs of which were strongly flavored with fellowship, self-protection, recreation, ritual, and service, but also included strong undertones of self-improvement through educational activities. (6) Parent education organizations (National Congress of Parents and Teachers, Child Study Association, and others), which sought to promote the welfare of children and youth in home, school, church, and community through providing speakers, demonstrations, discussions, school visitations, study groups, literature, and service projects of various sorts. (7) Public affairs education agencies (Carnegie Endowment for International Peace, National Municipal League, Foreign Policy Association, and others), which sought to improve government and develop better understanding of public issues. (8) Intergroup education organizations (American Jewish Committee, National Association for the Advancement of Colored People, Urban League, Anti-Defamation League, American Civil Liberties Union, and others), all of which engaged in action projects but also carried on education through meetings, publications, study groups, speakers' bureaus, and other means. (9) Professional societies (American Medical Association, American Association for the Advancement of Science, National Conference of Social Work, American Bar Association, and a host of others), which typically performed a dual adult educational role—providing in-service educational opportunities to their members and providing educational stimuli and resources to other groups and the general public. (10) Miscellaneous organizations (garden clubs, drama groups, music groups, nationality organizations, agencies for the handicapped, and the like), which engaged in various degrees and types of educational activity.

Churches.—The churches have been engaged in adult education from their very beginnings, but as has been previously indicated, their adult educational role has traditionally been limited largely to indoctrination in the precepts and tenets of particular faiths. And this continued to be its chief characteristic during this period. For example, in the Catholic Church the chief instrument for the education of adults continued to be the pulpit and the liturgy. But MacLellan points out that "from 1885 to 1900 the development of the Reading Circles was rapid and widespread," and in 1889 became formally organized with the founding of the Reading Circle Union. And in 1892 the Catholic Summer School of America was established "to enable those whose occupation did not allow them to attend the University courses regularly to derive as much benefit from the Summer School lecture as from attendance at a regular university. It aimed to arouse in the minds of its students a thinking spirit and an abiding interest in profound questions, mundane and metaphysical, which dealt with man's past, present, and future."[9]

Although the adult educational work of synagogues and temples remained fairly traditional during this period, they did take leadership in many communities in pioneering the development of highly intellectual public forums. The Sinai Temple in Chicago, for example, launched its first series of lectures in the fall of 1914 and rapidly gained a national reputation as a beacon of free speech in the Chicago area.

In the Protestant churches this was a period of only slightly greater creativity. The Sunday school became established during the decades following the Civil War as a universal form, although essentially for children. Interdenominational national conventions of Sunday school leaders had been meeting intermittently since 1832, and at the Fifth National Convention in 1872 a plan for International Uniform Lessons was adopted which had far-reaching consequences in both the expansion and the fixation of religious education in this country.

Museums.—A number of museums were established during this period in the fields of art, history, natural history, and science, since one of the frequent expressions of public spirit by the new class of industrial titans was the endowment of a museum, usually named in honor of the donor. The principal methods developed by the museums for education were the guided tour, exhibitions, publications, loans, talks, and organized classes or lecture series. With the founding of the American Association of Museums in 1906 an instrumentality was created for the continuous improvement of educational practices and the co-ordinated planning of methods of study to meet popular needs.

THE SHAPING OF ADULT EDUCATION IN THE MODERN ERA

A kaleidoscopic view of American society from 1921 to the present shows changing patterns in rising tempo in population, technology, economic conditions, international relations, social arrangements, communications, philosophical and religious ideas, and government. It is an era that moves from crisis to crisis. And it is the era of greatest expansion and innovation in adult education.

The population grew in size by over one-third, became predominantly urban, rose in average age, became better educated, and dropped in ratio of foreign-born from 13.2 per cent in 1920 to 6.9 per cent in 1950. During this era the United States experienced the dislocation of World War I, followed by ten years of unprecedented prosperity, then the ten-year catastrophe of the Great Depression, then the dislocation of World War II, followed by a period of technological development and economic expansion the scope and limits of which are still not discernible.

The central characteristic of the economic trend has been bigness—in industry, in labor, in the national product, in the national debt, in personal wealth, in agriculture, and in government. The social changes with the greatest implications for adult education include a generally higher standard of living, a broader distribution of luxury goods and services.

a more autonomous role for women, greater mobility—both geographical and social, a marked improvement in health conditions, the expansion and co-ordination of welfare and recreational services, and the gradual reduction of racial and religious discrimination. The general character of the intellectual revolution that was taking place is summarized by Commager as follows:

> ... the two generations after 1890 witnessed a transition from certainty to uncertainty, from faith to doubt, from security to insecurity, from seeming order to ostentatious disorder. . . . First evolution, then scientific determinism, profoundly altered the outlook of most Americans. . . . Americans, who had always accepted change in the material realm, were now prepared to accept it in the intellectual and moral as well, and they were less confident than formerly of their power to direct or control the change.[10]

It was in the atmosphere of this dynamic social setting that the institutions of adult education, the foundations of which had been laid by the end of World War I, took their modern shape. Several trends can be discerned in this shaping-up process which will be summarized, not institution-by-institution as previously, but in terms of directions affecting the field as a whole.

Trends in Adult Education's Institutional Development

1. *There has been a pressure toward national integration of adult educational activities.* Until 1924 the term "adult education" was practically unknown in this country; agencies engaged in educating adults were so unrelated they did not even have a common name for what they were doing. But in that year Frederick P. Keppel, the newly elected president of the Carnegie Corporation of New York, returned from an inspection of the national adult education movements of Europe with a vision of an integrated movement in this country. Under his leadership a series of conferences was held with leaders of various agencies which resulted in the founding of the American Association for Adult Education in 1926. During its twenty-five years of existence, the American Association served as a national clearing house for information about adult education. It conducted annual conferences, published a quarterly *Adult Education Journal* (1929-51), sponsored many studies, and published a large library of books—the most notable of which was the series "Studies in the Social Significance of Adult Education." The association was generously financed by the Carnegie Corporation during most of its life and was further supported by modest dues from about 3,000 members.

Five years before the founding of the American Association a Department of Immigrant Education had been established in the National Education Association. Originally composed of administrators and teachers of programs for the foreign-born, it gradually broadened its scope and in 1924 changed its name to the Department of Adult Education. For several years its members were drawn exclusively from the public school field, but in 1927 it amended its constitution to permit any person engaged in teaching, supervising, or administering programs of adult education, under public or private auspices, to join. During the 1930's and 1940's many people from outside the public school field joined the department, participated in its conferences, received its bi-monthly *Adult Education Bulletin,* and obtained other services.

By 1949 the purposes, programs, and memberships of these two national organizations overlapped to such an extent that strong sentiment developed for amalgamating them into a single national organization. A joint committee of the two organizations conducted a series of conferences that resulted in the decision to dissolve these two organizations and to create a totally new unifying national organization. As a result, the Adult Education Association of the U.S.A. was founded at an assembly of over two hundred leaders of adult education at Columbus, Ohio, on May 14, 1951. The purposes and program of this new association are described in Chapter 15.

2. *There has been a drive toward integration of adult education at the local level.* This impulse toward co-ordination and co-operation expressed itself at the local level with the organization of several dozen local, state, and regional adult education councils or associations during this period. There is no uniform pattern of organization or program among these councils, but almost all of them sponsor conferences, information exchanges, directories of agencies, and newsletters. Many of them in addition conduct surveys of community needs, provide counseling services, stimulate joint planning, sponsor training programs, carry on community-wide publicity campaigns, or try out experimental activities.

3. *Large-scale support of adult education by private foundations has developed.* The example set by the Carnegie Corporation in the second quarter of the century of treating the advancement of adult education as a major obligation of private philanthropy has been followed by other foundations, especially the W. K. Kellogg and Ford Foundations, the activities of which are described in Chapter 19.

4. *Governmental support of adult education has been expanding.* At the local and state levels, financial aid and professional services to adult education have grown in volume. By 1953, for example, twenty-five states provided staff services to local schools from their state departments of education and twenty states provided financial aid totalling almost $12,000,000. Total expenditures that year for public school adult education amounted to $79,000,000, as compared with $120,000,000 for public libraries, $97,000,000 for university extension, and $80,100,000 for agricultural extension. As the chapters dealing with these institutional settings indicate, however, tax support for adult education is still unstable—indeed, in times of economic stress, precarious.

At the federal level, the role of government has been largely stimulative and supportive, in contrast to the role of the governments of most of the European countries, where they directly finance or operate many of the programs. During the Great Depression the federal government directly operated a variety of adult educational programs through the Works Progress Administration, the National Youth Administration, and the Civilian Conservation Corps, but these were discontinued with the return of more normal conditions. It has continued its policy of subsidizing vocational and agricultural education, and further indirect financial support was provided in the "G.I. Bill of Rights" following the Second World War and in the more recent Defense Education Act. The creation of an Adult Education Section in the U.S. Office of Education was a hopeful sign, but in spite of recommendations by a succession of presidential commissions, a coherent federal policy for adult education had still to be worked out.

5. *A distinctive body of knowledge and techniques has begun to emerge.* In 1928 Edward L. Thorndike of Columbia University published under the title *Adult Learning* a report of research which proved that the ability of adults to learn declined very little with age. This study highlighted a growing interest on the part of social scientists in the adult learning process, which after World War II shifted to the process of learning in groups. As a result of this growing volume of research and numerous practical experiments, a wide variety of new methods for teaching adults began to be developed. Over-reliance on lectures tended to give way to the use of group discussion, motion pictures and other audio-visual aids, demonstrations, field trips, dramatic techniques, case study, and the like. Participation by the learner in an active role tended to become the dominating concept underlying the new adult educational methodology. Recognition of the fact that adults differ from children in many ways as learners has begun to lead to a differentiated curriculum and methodology for adult education.

6. *The student body of adult education has greatly expanded.* While the unavailability of reliable statistics about adult education has consistently been one of the major obstacles in understanding the field, it is clear that its constituency has grown enormously since World War I. Rough estimates placed the total enrollment units in all forms of adult educational activity at the 15 million level in 1924, around 22 million in 1934, close to 30 million in 1950, and almost 50 million in 1955.[11] These estimates do not account for multiple participations by particular individuals, and they are not based on scientific sampling procedures; but they probably reflect the rate of increase fairly realistically.

7. *Adult education has become a conscious and differentiated function in an increasing number of institutions.* As more and more agencies have come to see that they are performing adult educational roles, they have tended to establish separate administrative units to operate this phase of their programs. This phenomenon occurred early in the public schools and universities. More recently the American Library Association has created an Adult Education Division, a number of industries have insti-

tuted training departments, an increasing number of health and welfare agencies have added adult education specialists to their staff, a large number of national labor unions have appointed adult education directors, most religious denominations now have full-time adult education staffs, and many voluntary associations have fallen in with the trend. This development has led in turn to the emergence of training—both pre-service and in-service—as a major new aspect of the movement, and one which is dealt with in detail in Chapter 10.

While adult education has not yet become established as a unified national social movement and has not yet been recognized as an instrument of national policy, it has demonstrated its potential in both regards. Perhaps the great awakening—that adult education is the most potent instrument for bringing about planned social change—is about to occur.

SOME GENERALIZATIONS FROM HISTORY

In reviewing the historical development of adult education in the United States to date certain generalizations can tentatively be made which may have implications for the planning of future strategy:

1. The institutions of adult education have typically emerged in response to specific needs, rather than as part of a general design for the continuing education of adults.

2. The developmental process of adult education has tended to be more episodic than consistent.

3. Institutional forms for the education of adults have tended to survive to the extent that they become attached to agencies established for other purposes.

4. Adult educational programs have tended to gain stability and permanence as they become increasingly differentiated in administration, finance, curriculum, and methodology.

5. Adult educational programs have emerged with, and continue to occupy, a secondary status in the institutional hierarchy.

6. The institutional segments of the adult education movement have tended to become crystallized without reference to any conception of a general adult education movement.

Footnote References

1C. Hartley Grattan, *In Quest of Knowledge* (New York: Association Press, 1955), p. 140.

2Alexis de Tocqueville, *Democracy in America* (New York: Vintage Books, 1954), Vol. II, p. 114.

3Bernard E. Meland, *The Church and Adult Education* (New York: American Association for Adult Education, 1939), p. 13.

4Malcolm MacLellan, *The Catholic Church and Adult Education* (Washington: Catholic Education Press, 1935), p. 20.

5Ellwood P. Cubberley, *The History of Education* (Boston: Houghton Mifflin Co., 1948), p. 670.

6Ibid., p. 587.

7George C. Mann, "The Development of Public School Adult Education," *Public School Adult Education* (Washington: National Association of Public School Adult Educators, 1956), p. 10.

8Quoted in Herbert B. Adams, "Educational Extension in the United States," *Report of the U.S. Commissioner of Education for 1899-1900* (Washington: U.S. Bureau of Education, 1901), p. 302.

9*The Catholic Church and Adult Education, op. cit.,* p. 21-23.

10Henry Steele Commager, *The American Mind* (New Haven: Yale University Press, 1950) , pp. 407-8.

11Malcolm S. Knowles, "Adult Education in the United States," *Adult Education,* V (1955), 75-76.

Selected Readings

Adam, T. R. *The Museum and Popular Culture.* New York: American Association for Adult Education, 1939.

Adams, Herbert B., "Educational Extension in the United States," *Report of the U.S. Commissioner of Education for 1899-1900.* Washington: U.S. Bureau of Education, 1901.

Adams, James Truslow. *Frontiers of American Culture.* New York: Charles Scribner's Sons, 1944.

Bailey, L. H. *Farmers' Institutes: History and Status in the United States and Canada.* U.S. Department of Agriculture, Office of Experiment Stations, Bulletin 79. Washington: Government Printing Office, 1900.

Bode, Carl. *The American Lyceum.* New York: Oxford University Press, 1956.

Brameld, Theodore. (ed.) . *Workers Education in the United States.* Fifth Yearbook of the John Dewey Society. New York: Harper and Bros., 1941.

Butts, R. Freeman, and Cremin, Lawrence A. *A History of Education in American Culture.* New York: Henry Holt & Co., 1953.

Cartwright, Morse A. *Ten Years of Adult Education.* New York: The Macmillan Company, 1935.

Commager, Henry Steele. *The American Mind.* New Haven: Yale University Press, 1950.

Cubberley, Ellwood P. *The History of Education.* Boston: Houghton Mifflin Co., 1948.

Deffner, Donald L. "The Church's Role in Adult Education." Unpublished Ph.D. dissertation. Graduate Division, University of California, 1956.

Dewhurst, J. Frederic and Associates. *America's Needs and Resources.* New York: The Twentieth Century Fund, 1955.

Eels, Walter C. (ed.) . *American Junior Colleges.* Washington: American Council on Education, 1940.

Ely, Mary L., and Chappel, Eve. *Women in Two Worlds.* New York: American Association for Adult Education, 1938.

Garceau, Oliver. *The Public Library in the Political Process.* New York: Columbia University Press, 1949.

Grattan, C. Hartley. *American Ideas About Adult Education.* New York: Bureau of Publications, Teachers College, Columbia University, 1959.

————. *In Quest of Knowledge.* New York: Association Press, 1955.

Greenberger, Lawrence F. "Adult Education Through Evening High Schools." Unpublished Ph.D. dissertation. University of Pittsburgh, 1936.

Hayes, Cecil B. *The American Lyceum.* U. S. Office of Education Bulletin 12, 1932.

Hill, Frank E. *Educating for Health.* New York: American Association for Adult Education, 1939.

————. *Man-Made Culture.* New York: American Association for Adult Education, 1938.

Houle, Cyril O., *et. al. The Armed Services and Adult Education.* Washington: American Council on Education, 1947.

Hugg, Alan E. "Informal Adult Education in the Y.M.C.A.: A Historical Study." Unpublished Ph.D. dissertation. Faculty of Philosophy, Columbia University, 1950.

Hurlbut, J. L. *The Story of Chautauqua.* New York: G. P. Putnam's Sons, 1921.

Johnson, Alvin. *The Public Library—A People's University.* New York: American Association for Adult Education, 1938.

Kotinsky, Ruth. *Adult Education Councils.* New York: American Association for Adult Education, 1940.

MacLellan, Malcolm. *The Catholic Church and Adult Education.* Washington: Catholic Education Press, 1935.

Meland, Bernard E. *The Church and Adult Education.* New York: American Association for Adult Education, 1939.

Morton, John R. *University Extension in the United States.* University, Ala.: University of Alabama Press, 1953.

National Association of Public School Adult Educators: *Public School Adult Education.* Washington: The Association, 1956.

National Education Association. *A Study of Urban Public School Adult Education Programs.* Washington: The Association, 1952.

Noffsinger, John S. *Correspondence Schools, Lyceums, Chautauquas.* New York: The Macmillan Co., 1926.

Olds, Edward. *Financing Adult Education in America's Public Schools and Community Councils.* Chicago: Adult Education Association of the U.S.A., 1954.

Overstreet, Harry and Bonaro. *Where Children Come First: A Study of the P.T.A. Idea.* Chicago: National Congress of Parents and Teachers, 1949.

Powell, John Walker. *Learning Comes of Age.* New York: Association Press, 1956.

Reeves, F. W., Fansler, T., and Houle, C. O. *Adult Education.* New York: McGraw-Hill Book Co., 1938.

Rosentreter, Frederick M. *The Boundaries of the Campus: A History of the University of Wisconsin Extension Division 1885-1945.* Madison: The University of Wisconsin Press, 1957.

Seybolt, Robert F. *Source Studies in American Colonial Education: The Private School.* Bureau of Educational Research Bulletin No. 28. University of Illinois Bulletin, XXIII, No. 4, 1925.

True, Alfred C. *A History of Agricultural Extension Work in the United States, 1785-1923.* U. S. Department of Agriculture, Miscellaneous Publication No. 15, 1928.

Wright, Louis B. *The Cultural Life of the American Colonies.* New York: Harper & Bros., 1957.

CHAPTER 3

THE FUNCTION AND PLACE OF ADULT EDUCATION IN AMERICAN SOCIETY

WILBUR C. HALLENBECK
Professor Emeritus
Teachers College
Columbia University

A culture always determines the form, the content, and the scope of its organized education.

The history of education in America can be traced in the story of its changing social circumstances. The forms which education takes, the kinds of education and their contents which are offered, and the parts of the population to which educational opportunities are offered are determined by the needs which changes generate. The great expansion of adult education in the mid-twentieth century is the response of American society to new requirements which recent changes have brought about. In the present world adult education is as essential to a properly functioning society as machinery is to the manufacture of automobiles.

Each characteristic of our civilization, both old and new, creates needs for particular knowledges, skills, understandings, and qualities on the part of those who make up the society and keep the civilization in operation. These changing societal needs in turn have their impact, though often belatedly, upon the educational patterns in schools for children and young people. But were this all, the preparation for membership in our society would lag no less than a generation behind its requirements. Under such circumstances those who do the work and carry the responsibilities for organization, leadership, and decision-making could not be qualified, except by fortuitous accidents, for their contemporary tasks. Educational opportunities to help adults meet their contemporary problems and interests become necessary to compensate for the cultural lag which is an ever-present danger in a rapidly changing world.

Change is terribly contemporary. To live confidently and comfortably, to cope with ever-changing problems, and to enjoy the potential satisfactions all about them, people must understand change and its consequences and be able to adapt themselves and their institutions to what is a new world in some respects each day. This requires a flexibility of attitudes, perspectives, values, and relationships. No matter how effective and contemporary schooling may be it can never fully prepare youths to meet the world as it will be when they are adults. The fundamental function of adult education is to keep the balance between people and circumstances in a changing world. One of the axioms of civilization, democracy, and intelligence is that people can control their destinies. This becomes possible only when people can foresee and direct the changes which are the result of their material and social inventions.

SOME CHARACTERISTICS OF AMERICAN CULTURE AND THEIR IMPLICATIONS FOR ADULT EDUCATION

It is difficult to treat any characteristic of American culture separately, because it is the whole complex in which all of the characteristics are inextricably interrelated which makes American culture. Five characteristics of this present world, however, have particular significance for determining the social functions which fall to adult education:

1. *Rapidity of change.*—This is the atmosphere within which men must live in the present day. It is also a very specific problem, because people as individuals and in their associations and organized activities must learn to live with change. It is one thing to live in a world in which change is the exceptional situation amid the "normalcy" of a stable continuity of patterns of living, but it is quite a different thing to live in a world where change is normal and stable patterns do not exist.

Upbringing, tradition, schools, culture tend to assume that things will continue as they are. Such influences lead individuals to expect material, economic, and social surroundings to remain essentially the same while they move on to attain their goals. This expectancy was fitting when people lived in a world where they were likely to continue to dwell in the same community in which they were born, perhaps even in the same houses in which their fathers and grandfathers spent their lives, to belong throughout life to the same churches and other organizations, and to have the same jobs in the same companies. Life was relatively simple under these conditions; whatever changes came were incidental to the security of continuing patterns.

Life, however, is not like this today. Most people find themselves in a world where everything changes. They seldom settle down. They take new jobs in different communities where they often must adjust to a different climate, other patterns of living, new sets of mores and values, where they must make new friends and establish new connections. People also must constantly adapt to the material innovations which bring about alterations in their habits of living, in their responsibilities, and in their relationships. New problems of living together in communities, nation, and world also have their impact upon individuals. The personal equipment required to live in such a world is vastly different from that which made for effective living where things stayed put.

This new world of rapid change is not a disorderly world. The basis of its order, however, is not that things stay as they have been, but that disarrangements have continuity and are related to consequences which can be depended upon. Nor is this an insecure world. Its security, however, is based not on one's confidence that things will not change, but rather on one's confidence that he can understand the changes which will take place and has the knowledge and capacity to meet and take advantage of the changes with the resources at hand. One does not come by this kind of capacity "naturally", nor has it been a product of the tradition-bound curriculum in schools.

It is quite as possible to learn to live in a changing world as it is to learn to live in a static world. When one comes to adulthood and finds that he is prepared to live in one kind of world, but must live in another kind of world, he learns of course, but as we say, "the hard way". But our kind of society can fall to pieces while its individual members are learning "the hard way" to cope with it, keep it in operation, and guide its destiny. Intelligence has to learn "the hard way" only once.

The job of adult education is to help people to understand the basis of order and security in a world of rapid change and to build their goals realistically in fitting terms; and to help people understand their problems, discover the resources which are available to them, and find the way to solve their problems and to reach their goals under current circumstances. Almost all adults need help in some particular at some time. Even when preparation in school is the best, it has become a different world when one reaches adulthood. Adults are different, too, for they live in the midst of responsibility under pressure to make decisions and take action. Adults need contemporary education.

The everchanging requirements of the rapidly changing world continue to show up lacks in the knowledges and skills of people. The opportunities to fill these gaps in order to keep people's equipment adequate to contemporary living must always be available. The changing world also arouses new interests and stimulates new aspirations which will be followed if opportunity exists.

2. *Dominance of technology.*—As knowledge increases it becomes more and more technical—particularly in the areas of production which have their bases in the physical sciences. Development of knowledge is no different—though somewhat slower—in the services which grow out of the social sciences. We not only have better refrigerators, telephones and automobiles, but also better social services, health programs, government,

and education. The inevitable trend in all areas of life and activity is to become more technical; technology dominates our civilization.

This is good, in that it has provided widespread benefits to people—better products, more conveniences, increased services, and more opportunities of all sorts. It has also brought some very serious problems which have not yet been solved. Among these are automation, technological unemployment, vocational instability, and major changes in the vocational pattern of the American economy. These problems are all very closely related.

Technology is bound to move in the direction of automation, for one of its principles is that man power should never be dissipated by being used to do what machines can do, because man power is too costly and too precious. Such a principle, however, cannot be understood nor appreciated by the hundreds and sometimes thousands of workers thrown out of work by technology. Nor does it ease the situation to say that in the long run technology creates more jobs than it destroys and that new kinds of jobs need man power constantly. There is no long run for men who are out of work and are unqualified for any of the new kinds of work.

People have not been prepared for instability of occupations. Technological unemployment is especially hard on those whose jobs disappear, because the jobs requiring lesser training tend to be replaced by machines and the jobs requiring higher training need more workers. The American economy shows a falling off in numbers employed in the occupations of heavy work and a steady and rapid increase in the service occupations. We are more and more doing the hard work, the routine work, the unpleasant work by machines and using our man power for the important work which only people can do.

Foresight, planning, and organization within the economy are required to solve these problems. They can and will be solved when people make up their minds that a solution is desirable and necessary. To help the citizenry understand this need and the function and process of planning, adult education is needed in many forms. To help those who have been thrown out of adjustment in their vocations adult education has made some efforts at three essential points which must be fully developed in the solution of these problems: (1) Developing understanding on the part of people as to why vocational life is and will continue to be unstable and developing attitudes and values related to flexibility and readiness to change. (2) Vocational guidance for adults to help them find future occupations best fitted to their abilities, aptitudes, and interests; to direct them to training programs which will prepare them for rapid readjustment; and to locate the new job possibilities to which they may go. (3) Provision for retraining which takes into full consideration on the one hand the needs, abilities, and interests of people, and on the other hand the jobs which need to be filled and the requirements for getting and keeping these jobs. So long as technology brings changes in vocational patterns—and as far as can be seen that will be always—adult education has important functions to perform to keep the American economy in operation.

3. Intensity of specialization.—Almost everyone is a specialist today. We are familiar with the high degree of specialization in medicine and in engineering, but all occupations are being specialized. Mechanics tend to do one kind of operation. Ditch-diggers spend their lives digging ditches. Farmers usually raise one special crop on their farms and buy their food in stores like everyone else. Institutions are also becoming more and more specialized—stores, hospitals, churches, social agencies, banks, colleges, and on and on—and the workers within these specialized agencies are specialized.

This trend toward more and more intense specialization gives people the opportunity to grow and develop their capacities and knowledge within an area small and narrow enough to make it feasible to become experts, but if anything happens to the specialists' jobs they must seek other positions within the line of their specializations. This greatly narrows their field of possible employment.

As individuals focus their attention, interest, and energy so completely on their specialization, their preoccupation precludes their contacts and association with other specialists; and out of this isolation grows misunderstanding and even inability to communicate. While such concentration of attention makes people more knowledgeable in the area of their activity it makes them less acquainted with the community within which their special services are carried out. This process is self-defeating, because the need which requires the special function and the circumstances within which the specialization must be carried out are in the community.

Such narrowness of interests, inability to communicate with other kinds of people, and limitations on associations create circumstances within which special interests, prejudices, pressure groups, and conflict tend to arise. Under these conditions it is difficult to arouse interest in community problems and get participation in community affairs. Concern for community as the framework for activity and living sinks into the distant background.

Out of the deterioration of co-operative community life has arisen that part of adult education usually called "community development." In many situations it has been very successful not only in solving community problems and making better communities, but also in contributing to the personal development of those who have participated. Out of these activities come learnings of co-operation, how to get things done, the uses and workings of organization, the ways of politics, the appraisal of accomplishments, and the importance of planning. There are also important side effects: broadening of interests—for interests become contagious in the framework of co-operative action where all kinds of people are involved; spreading information about opportunities for the pursuit of various interests—for word-of-mouth is the best publicity for adult education; strengthening of motivation in companionship of common goals—for learning is a lonesome experience for those who have not made it a habit.

These learnings, moreover, are the basic aspects of democracy, best learned within the process of democratic action. While the theory of democracy can be expounded in books, one learns democracy only through experience—through which he feels as well as sees the power and satisfaction of co-operation, the value of respect for others and their opinions, and the effectiveness of organized action.

Circumstances these days are inimical to the operation of democracy in many ways. In spite of all the difficulties, however, the attainment of democracy continues to be an unqualified objective of American society. The responsibility for conditioning and equipping citizens for democratic understanding and participation falls to adult education. It must be instrumental in creating the situations within which people may experience democratic processes in such ways that they will be impressed by its practicality, its effectiveness, and its superiority. Adult education must further be concerned with helping to motivate people to study and understand the current problems of community living, whether local, national, or international, to express intelligent opinions on the issues which face the citizenry for action, and to help people build into their living the values and behavior patterns of democracy.

4. Complexity of human relationships.—An inevitable concomitant of specialization is interdependence. In order to be a specialist, one must rely on many others to provide the materials which his specialty requires, to carry out various operations which are involved in his specialization, to operate other parallel or complementary specializations, and to provide the many goods and services needed by himself and the members of his family.

Some of these interdependencies or co-operations are remote and impersonal, though none-the-less real; others involve direct contacts and constant working together; many fall in between. Every human being experiences a web of human relationships, some of which are enabling and satisfying, others of which may be frustrating and disappointing. Out of them, nevertheless, each must build the co-operations which will enable him to attain the goals to which he is committed. It takes understanding of oneself, of others, and of the principles of human relationships to accomplish this condition. People must make an effort to learn these things and adult education is responsible to teach them.

Some of society's most serious difficulties are in this area of human relations. The members of each new generation of adults find that the kind of relationships in the midst of which they were brought up and to which they have become accustomed are not appropriate amid circumstances within which they must live. Relationships within families, within work situations, within friendship associations, within organizations, within communities have changed and become more difficult. All too few people realize how crucial these relationships are to their welfare and happiness and how important they are in communities. Nor are people sufficiently aware that to fulfill their responsibilities in making constructive and happy relationships takes understanding and careful study. Here again is a continuing function for adult education.

5. *Vastness of opportunity.*—The May, 1959, *Fortune* contains an article entitled, "The New Masses," which relates that job and income changes are transforming U. S. society; blue-collar families are getting the means and leisure to take up middle class life. This is just one further indication that American democracy and its advancing technology are succeeding more and more to make opportunities, which formerly were the possession of a privileged class, available to everyone. Never before have ordinary people had the opportunity to make as many choices as they have in America in the mid-twentieth century.

Of great importance is the fact that the opportunities for the enrichment of his life, the development of his personality, and the extension of his knowledge—which have been designated traditionally as a liberal education—are open to everyone. Opportunities for study in various areas of knowledge, appreciation of the arts, understanding of society and the world, are available through adult schools, university extension, libraries, art galleries, museums, radio, television, theater, concerts, and many other vast resources immediately at hand. It is not enough, however, to bring such great opportunities into existence. People may be surrounded with them and not know that they are there, or that they are there for them, or how to use them. It cannot be assumed that people have interests, appreciations, and aspirations for these things.

The wider the possibilities for choice, the greater are the problems of choosing. To choose without considering the implications of a choice invalidates the advantage of having choice. The seemingly simple decision as to what goods one will purchase involves a knowledge of quality standards and measurements, the relation of quality to use and to price, the importance of style, and the possible alternatives as well as priorities, with reference to family needs. This is a good deal to have to know; where does one get the knowledge? In choosing each particular educational venture one must know whether it fits one's interests and needs as well as level of understanding, whether the goals to be obtained will be worth the effort, time, and money expended, and other like matters. In the service, in entertainment, in hobbies, and in many other things one must know how to choose properly.

The vast opportunities which those in the American society have in the mid-twentieth century call for three continuing functions by adult education. First is to help people to know how to make choices, to obtain the knowledge involved, and to use the knowledge wisely in terms of needs, circumstances, and implications. Second is to create situations within which people can learn new interests and appreciations, to open windows to new vistas of living, to help people understand the values of enriched living and to want these new experiences. Third is to provide opportunities for liberal education accessible to all the people in its manifold dimensions and increasing variety.

FUNCTIONS OF ADULT EDUCATION IN AMERICAN CULTURE

The implications for adult education of the principal characteristics of American culture already indicated can be organized into a pattern of five categories designating the essential functions which the culture presently requires of adult education. There are many other possible patterns of organization. This pattern puts emphasis upon the qualities of individuals which need special attention and consequently infers general objectives toward which adult education should work. Another group of categories might emphasize the content areas of study, another might be in terms of goals, while still another might be expressed specifically in terms of the processes by which functions are carried out. All of these aspects are essential and all are involved in whatever terms the categories are expressed. The important thing is to recognize that there are fundamental functions for adult education to perform in our society.

1. *Expand communication skills.*—Adult education faces the task of increasing the ability of people to communicate in many forms and by many means. Communication is basic to living and operating in our kind of society. Effectiveness of communication involves many things, such as: to be able to read and follow directions; to read with comprehension the material which contains the information required to meet one's obligations or the knowledge to give one pleasure and enlightenment; to listen with understanding and without bias to what one hears; to write and to speak simply and clearly; to observe with accuracy; to recognize differences in meaning growing out of differences in backgrounds. There would also be included acquiring knowledge needed though formerly missed, and skills which changing circumstances require. No one seems ever to have sufficient capabilities in communication.

2. *Develop flexibility.*—Making and keeping adults flexible is another task for adult education in American culture. The ability and willingness to change in a changing world is essential. To change one's job, to change one's locale, to change one's pattern of living, to change one's ideas about various things, to change one's framework of values, are very difficult undertakings which few can accomplish without help. Vocational flexibility is of paramount importance. One person will find it

necessary to concentrate on a narrower specialization, another completely
to change his vocation, another to apply his basic skills in an entirely
different situation. Such adjustments must be facilitated through opportunities for retraining.

3. *Improve human relations.*—Adult education has long given attention to various aspects of human relations in many programs. Some of
the most serious and difficult problems are in this area—family life, industrial peace and productiveness, interracial and intergroup relations, international affairs, community cleavages and conflicts—and all have their
bases in inadequacies and ineptitudes in relationships between human
beings. Problems will always exist here because new patterns of relationships arise out of changes which take place in our society. Continuing
education in human relations should be concerned with at least three
areas of knowledge: (1) the function and significance of human relations, the various types and degrees of relationships, and the requirements for successful co-operation; (2) patterns of group behavior, the
dynamics of groups, the processes of group accomplishment; and (3) the
importance, place, and function of organization for successful co-operative action, and the development of attitudes toward, participation in,
and evaluation of relationships in co-operation.

4. *Facilitate participation.*—Adult education has endeavored in many
ways to help people to be concerned with the responsibilities of citizenship. The involvement of people in the improvement of their communities, understanding of and participation in politics, and effectiveness in
organizational memberships, are things on which democracy hangs.
Democracy could fail because people refuse or forget to play their parts
in the co-operative life of the communities in which they live, or because
they do not take the trouble to understand and express their opinions
with reference to the issues and problems of the community, state, nation
and world to which they belong, or because they do not understand the
meaning and importance of democratic behavior in their own lives. Adult
education can help at this point by providing the situations within which
people can learn participation and by interpreting the principles of
democratic behavior.

5. *Expedite personal growth.*—Adult education has rendered its best
service to people who have well-developed interests and have sought out
places where their curiosities and interests could be fulfilled. As Lyman
Bryson has so often said, however, "Most people do not know what there
is to be interested in." It is difficult for adult educators, who tend to be
people of broad experience, to understand this fact. Radio, television
and other mass media, in recent years more widely distributed, have
stimulated many people. There are still vast numbers, nevertheless, who
wait to have their curiosities aroused and to be motivated to search for
"the good things of life," and to undertake experiences for their own
enrichment. Little is accomplished by providing opportunities for liber-

alizing educational experiences if people do not grasp these opportunities. Adult education will ever be as responsible for helping people to want this kind of education as for providing it.

IN CONCLUSION

The thesis of this chapter has been that this changing world has brought American culture to that state where it depends upon adult education to make its civilization operate successfully. This analysis is in no sense proof of this thesis. The proof is to be found in the inevitable and tremendous expansion of adult education in recent years. In the forthcoming report of the Ford Foundation study of what the United States should spend for education, Professor Harold F. Clark will say that already in the United States several times as much is being spent for the education of adults as for all formal education—public and private—from kindergarten through university. There are also more students in adult education than in all the schools. A large part of this money and a great many of the students are in the educational programs of business and industry, where time and money are not invested in that which is not essential and profitable.

What this analysis has tried to do is to indicate and explain the points at which the culture depends upon adult education, the essential functions in American society which fall to adult education to carry out. These in turn become the ultimate objectives of American adult education, in reference to which its structure is developed and its program is planned.

Selected Readings

Brunner, Edmund deS., and Hallenbeck, Wilbur C. *American Society: Urban and Rural Patterns.* New York: Harper & Bros., 1955. Especially Chapter 24.

Bryson, Lyman. *Adult Education.* New York: American Book Co., 1936. Chapter III.

Chase, Stuart. *The Proper Study of Mankind.* Revised Edition. New York: Harper & Bros., 1956.

———. *Roads to Agreement.* New York: Harper & Bros., 1951.

Clark, Harold F., and Sloan, Harold S. *Classrooms in the Factories.* Rutherford, New Jersey: Institute of Research, Fairleigh Dickinson University, 1958.

Clark, Harold F., and others. *The Pursuit of Solvency for Higher Education in the U. S. A.* New York: McGraw Hill Book Co., 1959.

Hallenbeck, Wilbur C. *American Urban Communities.* New York: Harper & Bros., 1951. Especially Chapters 18, 23, 29.

Lundberg, George A. *Can Science Save Us?* New York: Longmans Green and Co., 1947.

Wiener, Norbert. *The Human Use of Human Beings; Cybernetics and Society.* Second Edition Revised. Garden City, New York: Doubleday & Co., Inc., 1956.

PART II

SOME COMMON CONCERNS
OF ADULT EDUCATORS

CHAPTER 4

PHILOSOPHIES OF ADULT EDUCATION

JOHN WALKER POWELL

Consultant in Adult Education and Lecturer
Teachers College, Columbia University

with the collaboration of

KENNETH D. BENNE
Director, Human Relations Center
Boston University

PHILOSOPHY, PHILOSOPHIES, AND PHILOSOPHIZING

As the possession of spoken language distinguishes man from the brutes, so the awareness of his philosophy can be said to distinguish the adult educator from the worker in adult education. But the word "philosophy" has two common usages. In one, it represents the more or less unspoken assumptions and values *implicit* in a certain approach to acting and way of acting. In the other, it means an *explicit* and systematic articulation of concepts and principles that have been tested for inner coherence and for adequacy of reference to the events it is intended to make meaningful.

If we were to adopt the first usage, there would be as many "philosophies" of adult education as there are varieties of method and practice —perhaps indeed as many as there are adult educators. If we took the second view, we should find little in the literature that meets these criteria; and this chapter might be a very short one. There have, it is true, been many creeds and professions of belief, stated by adult educators about their own work. But these are only the raw material for philosophy, as the observations and rules-of-thumb of a craft may be raw material for a scientific hypothesis.

The truth is that people in this field of endeavor have done much more educating than philosophizing about it. This is probably as it should be in a growing enterprise, and it is certainly characteristic of the American way of getting things done. But there arise critical occasions, critical times, when disorder will not serve; when choices must be made,

41

with the enhancement or degradation of important human values hanging upon the choice. Then, the kind of philosophizing that examines the competing assumptions, the value-consequences of alternative decisions, that seeks objectivity in the critical scrutiny of one's own beliefs as vigorously as in that of others', becomes a vital concern of the adult educator.

The myriad differences of activity and emphasis in adult education do not, of themselves, imply differences of underlying theory. Fundamental, vocational, avocational, and professional education, the completion of degrees, the pursuit of cultural interests, can all be seen as situational preferences, parts of one potentially harmonious whole of effort. Attempts to impart certain tenets of belief—as in courses in religion, Henry George economics, or organic gardening—or to improve organizational loyalty and performance, through trade union programs and management institutes, are equally tolerated as coming within the limits of personal election in a pluralistic society. Many of the fractional concerns within adult education—literacy education, Americanization, rehabilitation, and so on—have their analogues in fields like health: the Heart, Cancer, Tuberculosis, and Mental Health Associations are devoted each to the elimination of one special kind of illness; and these areas of education are dedicated to removing one or another kind of ignorance.

Philosophical theories, therefore, have little conscious effect upon the hundreds of thousands of learning activities now being pursued by millions of Americans. The vast bulk of school, college, extension, library, and organizational programs simply pursue the main lines of their own traditions of practice; and, when called on for a statement of "objectives," dutifully repeat the resounding platitudes that are the stock in trade of us all. Many unrecognized assumptions do lie behind these activities; but perhaps the proportion of this chapter within the whole scope of this book might represent the fraction of the ideological iceberg that shows above the surface of the educational waters.

To deal with these often unspoken assumptions, one has to straddle the line between a formal philosophy and the many working creeds. This chapter will cite some explicit statements and will try to articulate the assumptions behind a few of the major doctrinal differences that currently divide adult educators into at least verbal camps. This may result in putting forward some interpretations that they themselves would reject. But in so doing they will themselves have joined in the process which is, in itself, far more important than the achievement of any single philosophy of adult education: that is, the process of *continuous philosophizing about it*. The lack of debate, where it is lacking, is of more concern than the fact of debate when it is present.

To say this is not to take sides on the issue between "process" and "ideas" as substantive values. It is only saying what *all* of us believe: that "whether it be in the field of individual or of social activity, men are not recognizable as men unless, in any given situation, they are using their minds to give direction to their behavior."[1]

This is, itself, part of a philosophy. It could also be said that there is only one basic philosophy about adult education: that it is a good thing, and more of it would be better. But the plurality suggested by the title "Philosophies of Adult Education" goes deeper. To seek its source, we have to look out across the present scene, and back along the path of our own intellectual history.

PHILOSOPHIES AS CULTURAL IMPERATIVES

The phrase "adult education," coined in early 19th century England,[2] is sometimes deplored today as being vague, meager, or redundant. Its detractors overlook the fact that this innocent combination of all-too-common nouns embodies the very core of the vital optimism that made Western civilization. The phrase inherits the dynamic—and debatable—assumptions that underlie centuries of Western effort: that Man is improvable, if not indeed perfectible; that he can by thoughtful effort improve both himself and his circumstances; that society can be changed, and for the better; that knowledge is power, over both self and circumstance; and that men can acquire and use it, throughout life, for their own and the general good.

To the Judaeo-Christian concept of the equality of men in the eyes of God, and the later Christian belief in the uniformity of divine laws throughout nature, Europe had added the prophetic dream of *social* equality, which with industrial opportunity became social mobility; and the idea that men could, by understanding the processes of nature, control them—which became science. Stir these in with the optimism of human improvability, social progress, scientific power, and the dignity of human effort toward all these ends, and the concept of *education* becomes socially dynamic; that of *adult* education, potentially explosive.

This highly-charged complex of ideas developed in, and was in fact integral to, Western culture alone; primarily, the northern Protestant peoples, with their compulsions to industry and productivity. The tradition of the Orient has laid its stress on the grace of acquiescence, and on the discipline of the individual soul in its effort to abbreviate the miserable eternity of its finite existence. The Latin peoples, even today, find "adult education" a chilly substitute for the arts of enjoying from day to day what life offers; evening round-tables in heated rooms, a pale reflection of afternoon talk around the cafe tables.

Even today's world-wide efforts at fundamental education and literacy are primarily a Western export necessitated by the spread of the industrial culture along commercial channels, and by its explosive impact on the national self-image of the peoples of Asia and Africa. The high position of adult education in the USSR and Soviet China is directly connected to their acquisition of Western "effort-optimism." Albert Camus[3] remarked that "Man is the only animal that refuses to be what he is"; but he adds that *rebellion* can be thought of only where the idea of equality confronts a kind of inequality-in-fact that can be changed by man's own effort. Once attenuated by individuals, rebellion is now the task of whole peoples. In countries trying to leap-frog a whole population over the centuries between the middle ages and modern times, this effort requires massive central controls; rebellion is a *national* effort. So adult education, in their terms, is a tool and an extension of national control. There, the chief virtue of a citizen is *reliability*. The pacesetting peoples of the West, however, have most need now for creative initiative, by individuals and groups and associations; and the chief virtue of the citizen is *responsibility*. Our adult education will therefore take different forms and serve different values.

The revolutionary demand by "colonial" peoples for self-determination, self-government, and a share in the 20th century, together with the counter-revolutionary attempts of the two dominant socio-political complexes to control this demand in their own interests, have made adult education a prime preoccupation of the entire human world. The "struggle for men's minds" is matched by the struggle *of* men's minds. But American adult education has its own character and history; it must be understood in its own terms, for those terms do not exist outside our own culture. The philosophies we shall describe, therefore, are not those of mankind at large. They are the philosophies that now obtain within the blooming, buzzing confusion that is adult education in the United States.

THE MAIN AMERICAN PHILOSOPHICAL CAMPS

American theories of adult education are polarized (not to say ionized!) around two broad areas of emphasis and method. Each has its spokesmen, each is embodied in actual programs and institutions, and each has its extreme manifestations. Both, to be sure, have a great deal in common, which it would be tempting to discuss. But to stress the overlap and identities at this point would obscure the existence, and the nature, of genuine issues.

For present purposes, we shall distinguish the two major schools as the *developmental* and the *rationalist*. Glib distinctions in terms of one stressing "process" and the other "content" will not serve us here, for it is obvious that both approaches are highly aware of both sides of that educational coin. Other familiar epithets—"scientific" versus "traditional" and so on—are more used in controversy than useful in understanding. The issues will become clearest if we identify some examples of these schools, cite some of their own doctrine, and then examine the meaning of some of the differences. The reader must remember, however, that probably three fourths of all adult learning in America proceeds calmly along its old familiar lines, in school and college classrooms, without much concern—usually, without much comprehension—about the newer outreach of either philosophy or practice.

The most conspicuous camps within the *developmentalist* school are (1) fundamental education, whose principal apex is *community development*; and (2) human relations, whose most intensive focus is *group dynamics*. The *rationalist* camp, since it is the one longest in being and only now being challenged, has never had a name for its own philosophy and practice; but it operates under many banners: liberal arts, reading-discussion, great books, humanities.

The reader might try to sort out the following passages and assign them to their respective philosophies:[4]

(1) "I believe the adult educator should find his central purpose in the cultivation of fitness and excellence of the human mind. He should delight in man thinking, using his mind, and using it well. He should believe that man's dignity as a human being, his self-fulfillment as an individual, his usefulness as a member of society, are all inextricably related to the cultivation of his mind."

(2) "Adult education should have the goal of freeing the individual to reach toward his potentials of growth. . . . Adult education must therefore be concerned with three basic areas: first, with the internal dynamic balance of the individual; second, with his behavior in external situations; and third, with his ability to take membership in his societal unit."

(3) "An educative community is not one filled with instruction. It is one on the move, in action, achieving. Citizens improve as their life together improves. . . . The change in citizens is evidence that a community has become educative. . . . Citizen learning at its best rests upon self-chosen activity in an atmosphere of growth."

(4) "Many educators cling to the notion that their task is to make relevant and accurate ideas, information, and skill available to people. . . . But the contemporary crisis in human relations . . . has penetrated beneath the level of cognition . . . into the inner areas of emotions, attitudes, and values. . . . What is needed is an experimental discipline . . . which moves educative efforts over the traditional lines of 'education' into practices once reserved for 'therapeutic' treatment of persons and groups radically alienated from the main streams of community life. . . . Leadership in such achievement belongs to adult educators who accept re-education of adults in their human relations as a central and continuing concern. . . ."

The list could be extended; the literature grows daily, in both quantity and excitement. But there is enough here not only to indicate the common vocabulary of value references, but also to suggest the main areas of conflict.

The liberal arts, of course, represent the older tradition. But as the term is used in today's adult programs, that tradition shows some marked modifications. The emphasis is still on content; but the goal has shifted from the acquisition of knowledge to the sharpening of judgment, and from scholarship as such to an understanding of ideas and values in relation to social and personal goals in living. Methods have changed accordingly: there is still the classroom and the lecture, but they are retreating before less formal situations and more experimental methods, ranging from weekly discussions based on common reading, through intensive residential seminars of from three days to three weeks, to planned programs of shared experience of theatre, museums, and travel accompanied by discussion of values in the arts and in the life of the city. Throughout, the dominant matrix is the continuing group; and non-academic discussion leaders are carrying an increasing share of the teaching.

The motivation underlying all this activity has been beautifully stated by Wayne Leys:

> There is another kind of interest that is not an interest in knowledge for its own sake . . . it is an interest in *rationality*. It is the interest that the group-discussion people build on. . . . I refer to the adult's desire to talk things over. This desire has been misrepresented as a desire to learn something in the ordinary sense of learning. It is not that. The adults want to clarify their thoughts, but not as scholars clarify things. They want to talk out their worries and untangle their deliberations. . . .
>
> Adults need to become objective, but this is not the scientists' objectivity of disinterestedness. It is objectivity in the sense of a control over passions that have been aroused by strenuous interpersonal conflicts. It is objectivity in the sense of a remembrance of important considerations forgotten in the heat of battle. It is objectivity in the sense of the mobilizing of all relevant knowledge that one has previously acquired and bringing it to bear upon the immediate problem. It is seeing all of the angles. It is *focused study*. . . .
>
> Specific learnings are only an incidental product of this kind of mental activity; mainly it is a struggle with passion, a practical deliberation, a consultation . . . functions . . . vital to the well-being and sanity of society.[5]

The basic method is discourse about ideas, meanings, issues both as they have been formulated by major thinkers and as they become reformulated in the group; on appreciation and insight, analysis and reflection. The learning situation is controlled by these goals. The word "teacher" is still in use here, while it has been discarded altogether in the alternative kinds of program; and his task is to communicate enthusiasm for these concerns, to develop taste for them as well as in them. His standards are those of the intellectual process itself: discrimination, critical independence, logical responsibility, connection of principle with personal instance and of ideas with personal actuality. The experience offered to the group is that of the enjoyment and mastery of the printed word, the spoken word, and the visible and audible communications of the arts, translated into general categories and expressed as personal values.

The opposing camps, equally concerned with communication, recognition, and reassessment of values, find these ends more powerfully served by *action* and by *interaction*. So, along with whatever other content is deemed necessary, *experience with others is the primary content* to be studied, analyzed, reflected on and experimented with. Whether in community action to solve a troublesome problem, or in the open consideration by a group of its members' roles and responses, the *process* is a major part of the content for study. The skills of the mind are focused on the task of analyzing and reshaping the elements of that process.

"Content" is a word that evidently troubles the spokesmen for these schools. William Biddle, a principal statesman of community development, said in a conference in Indiana in 1959 that he preferred not to think of the "issue" before a working group as its content. For example, if the group believes its problem is how to persuade its town to put in new sidewalks, that is still not its *real* problem. What it is really trying to find out is whether the democratic process works. But to make this the explicit "content" of their study would have an inhibiting effect on their attack upon the problem of sidewalks, which is the experience by which they test the democratic process and learn how to play a creative role within it. Action is the source of learning; understanding is its goal; but understanding through conceptualization in advance may short-circuit the very action from which understanding and freedom come.

Another approach to content is voiced by Kenneth Benne on behalf of the human relations-group-dynamics philosophers:

> Stressing as they do, along with Socrates, understanding and discipline of the self as the central instrument of continuing learning and education, and recognizing the weight of scientific evidence that the self emerges and develops through social interaction, they are suspicious of learning situations that leave examination and re-examination of the self out of account, if the aim is to achieve learnings that lead to changed ways of behaving within the actual situations of life.
>
> The content studied may be various—as various as may be required by the problems confronting the learner, as these become clarified in the process of learning. No part of the cultural heritage—cognitive, aesthetic, moral or spiritual—is ruled out as a possible resource in problem clarification and solution. But no part of the cultural heritage is considered essential to be communicated prior to the discovery of the here-and-now problem to be confronted and clarified.
>
> Moreover, the help of others is essential to a learner in finding what his problem uniquely and actually is. Each person has many motivations and resources to avoid facing the problems which he alone must learn to face and resolve, the choices which he alone must learn to accept responsibility for and learn to resolve ideally with as much intelligence as possible. And this is true whether the problem or the choice is uniquely personal or collective in character. Others, if they become disciplined to the responsibility, can point out self-deceptions and avoidances, even as they learn to accept the same sort of painful help from others. A learning group can develop standards of seeking to face present realities which support all members in the learning situation

in learning to live in the only place where lives can be lived—the present, however informed by the past and oriented to the future this present may be or may become.[6]

To use an oversimplified illustration, suppose that three groups set out to consider the problem of *authority* in human relations. The rationalist group has many helpers: Plato and Aristotle, Machiavelli and Rousseau, Marx and Freud, Camus and Sartre. It can unravel the question into threads of scientific authority, artistic authority, political authority; can follow it into anthropology or psychiatry or literature; and it can trace all these threads back into, and test their strength against, the lives and experience of the group members. And it can open up the question at any point, and continue considering it for as long as the members stay interested.

The community development group would not encourage encounter with the problem in so abstract a form. It would confront a fact: the safety of school children requires a new grade-crossing, and there are in the town government those who can cause or prevent its building. The group's task is first to overcome its own timidity and apathy—the defeatism that so often characterizes our citizens; next, to analyze the conditions of the situation and determine the locus of authority; and then to set in motion the processes that lead from talk to consultation to public notice, to conference and pressure or persuasion, and finally to the initiation of definite action. In this process, the group members will have discovered that "authority" is people, that people act according to the forces in the situation—including the force of reason; and that even the lay citizen has the authority to create new situations that alter the old responses of "those in power." Shared initiative has bred new awareness of meanings-in-action, new insights, new confidence and capacity for leadership in further action.

The Group Dynamics approach would be different from both the others. The word "authority" is only a shorthand clue to a welter of feelings accumulated through lifelong personal experiences with those who wield power over one: parent and teachers, policemen and tax-collectors, wives and children, bosses and labor unions. Authority as a word can be analyzed till the Kingdom come without more than glancing off the surface of these accumulated resentments, envies, fears, hopes, and distortions; so communication tends to stay on the surface, not reaching the real currents of feeling and of growth. But by the very nature of the group structure, the *role* of authority is inevitably imbedded in it. The educational experience is therefore one precipitated when the authority-situation becomes visible within the group. The task is to identify it, bring it out into the open, and explore the feelings about it and responses to it of the group's own members. Devices such as role-playing, which gets the members to identify their own feelings with one or another aspect of a situation, are to be preferred to generalized discussion. The kind of discussion that does help begins with what the members actually did and felt, in themselves and toward each other, and what alternative responses would have been possible and preferable in the structuring of the relationships around the authority-figure.

Obviously, this process could be carried all the way into group-analytic psychotherapy; but this would lie beyond the purposes of a learning group. Its ends are served by practice in becoming aware of patterns of relational response within its members' own developing experience. Their communication is most useful if it is confined to experience that has been shared, rather than delving back into private individual pasts. It is not to be assumed that intellectual formulations, literary parallels, and logical criticisms are taboo. Rather, "they are introduced only when they can make a direct contribution to the group's development of analytic sensitivity, and their introduction is not encouraged when it appears to serve as an escape from, or denial of, the stresses inherent in this painful effort. The immediate aim is to learn to grapple with authority problems in a present and confronting reality situation. The educational goal is to generalize this learning for use in thinking, choosing, and acting more intelligently in future authority-situations."[7]

E PLURIBUS UNUM

In conclusion, now, let us examine the ways in which these approaches differ, the ways in which they agree, and the answers they propose to the challenge of our world and the tensions of our times.

One marked difference is in the regard which the two broadly opposed camps pay to cultural continuity with the past. Where the stress is on "the wisdom of the mind," acquaintance with the Great Conversation of the centuries becomes of contemporary utility and value; the obligation to values of the spirit dictates respect for the embodiments of those values, in all forms of human expression; the compulsion to rationality requires assimilation of the great ideas and issues about which, from age to age, man's mind has had to rally all the reason it could command.

On the other hand, where the stress is on organic growth of integrated personalities fully in communication with their fellows, and applying problem-solving intelligence to present needs, the uses of the past become optional; the uses of scientific methods, from psychology and sociology, become paramount; and *new* truths, *new* values, are sought through novel procedures, and are tested in part by scientific means and in part by the "consensual validation" of those who share in the experience.

The three programmatic schools differ again, though less sharply, in the way they conceive the role of the educational leader. In the academic pattern, he is still a "teacher" who professes his learning while his disciples acquire it. In adult liberal education, however, the growth of informal methods has moved him closer to the position of "learners' helper"

—whether expert or layman, rigidly trained in self-exclusion or flexibly permitted to be part of the learning group. Indeed, less *expertise* is required of the idea-discussion leader these days than of the community-development consultant or the therapy-minded relation-process analyst. Perhaps the difference lies in a belief that dealing with concepts and judgments is easier and more familiar, and indeed that only those who have some skill along these lines will be motivated to take up the liberal learnings; while the discovery of patterns of civic action, and the recognition of personal difficulties in relationship, are regarded as more difficult and more sensitive areas of guidance, but open to and needed by *every* kind of person.

The use to which the learning situation should be put thus forms the principal field of controversy. The spectrum of its uses might be projected as a great arc, with purely intellectual analysis at one end, purely emotional analysis at the other, and in the center a span of effectual personal and civic action which forms *one* of the goals of those at both extremes, and is the central goal of the fundamental educationists.

But this figure of the spectrum leads directly to the discovery of the vitally significant beliefs shared in common by all three schools, and related directly to the historical situation in which their work is done.

First, none of the three would disagree that "there is an adult mind, different from those of the youth and the undergraduate; that the adult has a qualitatively different way of using his mind, of relating ideas to experience," and that "it is for this distinctively grown-up mind that education in maturity is now, increasingly, being planned."[8] Second, they would emphatically agree that "education is concerned with the guidance and understanding of action," and what is just as "characteristically American, . . . that education itself is not a possession but an activity, a *method* of action and of modifying other actions in desirable directions."[9] Thus education is seen by all of them as primarily a *learning* rather than a teaching. In the words of Carl Rogers, "It seems to me that anything that can be *taught* to another is relatively inconsequential, and has little or no significant influence on behavior. . . . I am only interested in learnings which significantly influence behavior"; and this has to be "self-appropriated." But "truth that has been personally appropriated and assimilated . . . cannot be directly communicated to another" or "it becomes teaching, and its results are inconsequential. . . . I find that the best . . . way for me to learn is to . . . try to understand the way in which his experience seems and feels to the other person," and "to state my own uncertainties, to try and clarify my own puzzlements, and thus get closer to the meaning that my experience actually seems to have . . . as I try to understand at least the current meaning of that experience."[10]

Except at the extremes, academic at one end and therapeutic at the other, there would also be general agreement about the interplay of intellectual and emotional elements in all personal learning. "Education and therapy are complementary phases of a single process—the learning process as directed to the achievement of effective maturity. [Their relationship] has been obscured by their more salient differences in emphasis: the one upon mastery in the handling of *judgments*, the other in the handling of *feelings*. By an oversimplified aphorism, we could say that education teaches the individual how to *examine what he thinks* about what he feels important; therapy, to *examine how he feels* about what he thinks important. . . . Group discussion, which lies between the two, thus has both a manifest and a latent content. It is, if you like, precisely *because* man's emotions and his judgments are interwoven that such groups are effective; perhaps, even, that learning in its most vital sense is possible at all."[11]

Fourth, for all three schools the most effective matrix for individual learning is membership in a continuing face-to-face group. On one side lies individual self-directed learning, by reading or other evocative reflection upon experience. On the other stand lectures and the mass media, which are admitted to have value in communicating knowledge and understanding. But the favorite vehicle of adult learning activity is the group—to such an extent, indeed, that a number of educational philosophers have felt it necessary to challenge this over-reliance and to point out its own inherent dangers to independence and responsibility of learning.

Fifth, however, under all the group and community emphases, there is a strong and vital agreement on *the individual* as the learner, the agent of learning and of judgment and acting, the goal and test of all the learning-situations that educators can devise. It can be argued that "individual and group," "individual and society," are false dichotomies, since neither exists without the other and they must be defined in terms of each other. Nevertheless, the American philosopher has not relinquished the individual as the touchstone of his major values. In the stirring analogy of a sports writer, "There is no such thing as group pitching. . . . For their craft, like the very act of thinking, is a solitary pursuit."[12] It is the individual adult who is trying to "find himself" in the fluid society from which he is so easily alienated; to "relate himself" to his fellows; to "express himself" in the arts, or "assert himself" in civic action; and in all the shared uses of his mind upon his memberships and relationships to "become visible to himself," *self*-creative.

All the schools of adult education are activated by a hardy variety of *optimism*. "The true end of community development, as of all adult education," Cyril Houle writes, "is to make life better by changing people in desirable ways."[13] But this optimism is spread across the whole front of adult life; it is not confined to a course here or a subject there, because all aspects of individual living in society are inextricably bound up with other aspects. People are not just to become better Baptists or bricklayers or artists; they are to become better adults and better citizens, better parents and better old people. A highly typical two-day conference on city concerns was described in this way: "The traditional subject-matter of the liberal arts and humanities were projected against the specific dynamics of urban life. Basic philosophical, historical, and psychological questions of values were examined and discussed within a framework of parenthood, social problems, economic problems and foreign affairs."[14] Human relations learning is intended similarly to apply to all fields of activity and growth; and liberal arts programs that succeed with adults inevitably cut across a wide range of living interests and concerns.

Finally, all the vital schools share the modern tendency to speak of their own kinds of learning in terms of "skills"—this being the correlative to the notion that education is an activity intended to improve all other activities. But the word "skill" fails to reveal what is most important about the aims of the adult educator: his determination that the skills worth learning shall serve some purposes rather than others: friendship rather than enmity, truth rather than error, comprehensiveness rather than narrowness, creation rather than destruction. They are, as has been said, *skills of implicit commitment*.[15] And it is precisely this implicit commitment that forms the philosophy, supplies the eulogy, and defines the sanctions of the educator of adults.

Against the dwindling of faith in a divine guarantee of human significance, he pits the value of growth and the activities of brotherhood. To the sickness of human alienation he applies the healing arts of relationship; to the dread discovery of man's irrationality, the sciences of shared analysis for the sake of reasonableness. Into the teeth of prejudice and war he flings the challenge of critical intelligence; and to a culture whose intellectual frontiers are out of the reach of laymen, and whose massed collective power is beyond the grasp of personal initiative, he restores the self-respect of the inquiring mind, the "energy of local liberty," the hope of making individuals *count* in both the thinking and the action of the people among whom they move. To the historical forces of what Camus calls injustice, falsehood, and terror, the philosophy of adult education opposes individual and group currents of judgment, investigation, and independence. The differences of sects and schools, the controversies over content and method, pale beside the courageous determination to raise against the threat of silence the challenge of the human assertion. Man may be but barely differentiated from his animal kin, on this small planet near this small sun; but, to borrow a wonderful sentence from Theodore Dreiser, even that "nondescript and indifferent" audience might be "held by the peculiarity of such an unimportant-looking family publicly raising its collective voice against the vast skepticism and apathy of life."[16]

Footnotes

1. Alexander Meiklejohn, *Freedom of Speech* (New York: Harper & Bros., 1948), p. 8.

2. See Robert Peers, *Adult Education: A Comparative Study* (London: Routledge and Kegan Paul, 1958), Part I; C. Hartley Grattan, *In Quest of Knowledge* (New York: Association Press, 1955), Part III, for early association between industrialism, Methodism, and the birth of adult education in Wales and England.

3. Albert Camus, *The Rebel*, tr. Anthony Bower (New York: Vintage Books, 1957), pp. 11, 20.

4. (1) Glen Burch, "Adult Education's Great Purpose." *Adult Leadership*, VII (June, 1958), 34-36.

   (2) Leland P. Bradford, "Toward a Philosophy of Adult Education," *Adult Education* VII (1957), 83-93.

   (3) William W. Biddle, *People Grow in Communities* (Richmond, Ind.: Earlham College, 1956), pp. 3, 10.

   (4) Kenneth D. Benne, "The Re-education of Adults in Their Human Relationships," *Adult Education* VIII (1958), 153-157. The sentences chosen reflect only one of many aspects of thought in this rich statement.

5. Wayne A. R. Leys, "The Two Roles of the University in Adult Education," *Journal of Higher Education*, XXVI, (Jan., 1955).

6,7. Kenneth D. Benne, communication to the author.

8. J. W. Powell, *Learning Comes of Age* (New York: Association Press, 1956), p. 15.

9. ———. *Education for Maturity*, (New York: Hermitage House, 1949), p. 27.

10. From a Harvard Conference on influencing behavior in the classroom. Quoted with the author's permission in J. W. Powell, *Learning Comes of Age, op. cit.*, p. 164.

11. J. W. Powell, Anthony Stone, and Jerome D. Frank, "Group Reading and Group Therapy: A Concurrent Test," *Psychiatry*, XV (1952), pp. 33, 51.

12. Roger Kahn, "Man With the Brainy Arm," *N. Y. Times Magazine*, May 31, 1959.

13. Cyril O. Houle, "The Energy of Local Leadership," *Adult Leadership*, IV (1956), 8-10.

14. Leo Molinaro in *USA Tomorrow*, I (1955) 3.

15. J. W. Powell, "Where Did You Go? Out to Change the World," *Adult Leadership*, VI (1958), 261-63.

16. Theodore Dreiser, *An American Tragedy* (New York: Boni and Liveright, Inc., 1925), p. 4.

Selected Readings

Benne, Kenneth D. *A Conception of Authority*. New York: Teachers College, 1943.

———. "Why I Ran for President of AEA." *Adult Leadership*, IV (1956), 6-8.

Powell, J. W. "Process Analysis as Content." *Journal of Social Issues* VIII (1952), 2. (The whole issue is devoted to group process as seen by 13 authors).

Seeking Common Ground. Monograph #4, 1959. Chicago: Adult Education Association, 1958.

"What Is Adult Education? A Symposium." *Adult Education*, V (1955), 131-45.

CHAPTER 5

LEARNING THEORY IN ADULT EDUCATION

JACK R. GIBB
Director of Research
National Training Laboratories

As adult education becomes professionalized, adult educators become increasingly self-conscious of the bases for professionalization. In taking a long, hard look at how adults learn, adult educators have been forced to look critically at the basic disciplines which provide information relevant to the question of adult learning. Central in this concern is learning theory.

By far the greatest volume of information upon the discipline of human learning comes from the studies of the psychologists. Human learning has been an accelerating concern of experimental psychologists since the pioneering work of Ebbinghaus in 1885. Of recent years, as it has become increasingly apparent that learning is a process that involves the total personality of the learner, and that learning is a social process, the adult educator finds the most penetrating analyses of human learning and the most significant help in understanding the problems of the adult learning situation from the fields of psychotherapy, social anthropology, group psychology, and cultural and organizational sociology. Many disciplines are concerned with the problems of human change and human learning.

THEORIES OF LEARNING

Students of the problem of human learning have taken varied stances in their efforts to understand human change and learning. Their conclusions have been influenced by their initial assumptions, the methods they have used, and the foci of experimental manipulation or observational analysis.

Some students of learning, with a focus upon changes within the organism, have shown that certain neurophysiological and chemical changes can be associated with observed behavioral changes during learning. This promising field of effort holds indication of future application but as yet is of little help to the adult educator.

Other researchers, also looking within the confines of the organism, have centered interest upon phenomenological changes which occur during the course of learning. Of all intra-organismic approaches, this stance perhaps affords greatest immediate hope for the adult teacher. One can get immediate data on how students feel and how they see the world. While these data are subject to many possible vagaries and invalidities, the teacher and the student can communicate directly about such data, feel that they understand them, and obtain a feeling of immediacy. Theorists in this area understandably stress cognitive and perceptual constructs, talk about "insight" and understanding as central mediating mechanisms for what is learned. Cognitive maps and other cognitive structures are built up in the organism by experience and by perceptual restructuring of the world of experience. The conscious participation of the presumably rational learner is solicited by a teacher working with such theories.

Another prominent group of theorists, after looking at the environmental conditions which are associated with motivational variations in the learner, conclude that rewards and punishments are the basic conditions of learning and that learning can be engineered by the educator, and presumably less well by the learner, by manipulating the conditions which reward the learner for responses that for some reason one wishes repeated. This seductively simple model of learning is attractive to adult educators who can then focus human motives and their rewards as a basis for learning. A current logical development of such theories is the memory machine by means of which one can segment the units of learning in appropriate empirically-derived dosages, administer appropriate kinds and amounts of reward, and presumably get whatever kind of response the educator wishes.

What has impressed many students of learning most is the role that repetition and practice seem to play in response acquisition. Students seem to "learn by doing," and the job of the teacher is to help students to select appropriate behaviors and to practice these. Clearly one learns, however, only by doing under certain conditions and usually the practice-oriented teacher-theorist is forced either to stress the selective and differential rewards that come from doing or, on the other hand, to conclude that "doing" is effective only when accompanied by appropriate feedback, knowledge of results, or understandings.

Another group of researchers have centered their interests upon the characteristics of the learner and have given ascendency to conditions of readiness within the learner or to the personality dynamics of the learner as a person. For such theorists there is a fusion of theories of "learning" with theories of "personality." For these students what is important in understanding learning and guiding learners is a better understanding of the learner—his need systems, his defenses against change and learning, his identifications and projections, his total personality. Learning is an adjustment or maladjustment of the organism to its environment. What is significant in understanding the process is a diagnosis of the learner as a person. It is in understanding this view of the learning process that the adult educator can get help from psychotherapy and personality theory as well as from more conventional learning theorists.

Another group of theorists are impressed with the apparent fact that learning is above all a social process, an interaction among learners and teachers, and that significant understanding of the learning process comes from a better understanding of the interpersonal processes that inhibit or facilitate response acquisition and a diagnostic awareness of the groups in which learning interaction occurs. The fact that the next yearbook of the National Society for the Study of Education is devoted to the group *qua* group characteristics of the classroom is an illustration of the ascendency of this point of view. The adult educator can find illumination of the learning process, so defined, in social anthropology, group dynamics, and institutional sociology. Students who have chosen these methods and this focus talk about a climate or atmosphere for learning, the properties of groups that lead to forces inducing or restraining change, the relationships between interpersonal dynamics and group dynamics, and learning as a transaction among people.

THEORY AND PRACTICE

Many difficulties are experienced by the adult educator in applying one or more of the many learning theories to his practice as a professional adult educator. Explicit recognition and analysis of these barriers may be helpful to the educator in his efforts to overcome such obstacles.

1. *Limited populations upon which theories are based.* For excellent methodological reasons most serious students of the learning processes have found for study ontogenetically or phylogenetically simple organisms in order that relevant variables might be more easily manipulated and seen in less ambiguity. The legitimacy of extrapolation of principles so obtained is always open to question.

2. *Overgenerality in statement of the theories.* Highly abstract and general statements of a theory, no matter how theoretically sound the generalizations, are difficult for the practitioner to translate into concrete action steps. Teachers do many and varied things in the name of giving "insights," providing "rewards," or building "climates" in the classroom —actions that have little differential bearing upon the theories that are presumably being applied.

3. *Necessary oversimplification of this stage by theory building.* As

has been mentioned above, each of the major learning theories has been based upon a classic study or paradigm of learning to which the theory applies particularly well. When stretched to include other kinds or instances of learning each theory suffers. Teachers set up rewards that are not rewards to the learner. The spanked child learns to repeat the act for which he was punished. Students do many things when they "know better." Repressive and restrictive climates sometimes seem to cause amazingly effective learning.

4. *Special problems of the adult learner.* Adults often do not respond to the traditional extrinsic rewards of the typical classroom. Many adults require something other than the usual dependency relation between learner and teacher—new relationships for which neither the learner or the teacher are adequately prepared. The typical knowledge-centered curriculum and method has even less perceived relevance for the adult than for the child.

5. *Contradictory and conflicting elements of theories.* The confrontation of difference that is so exciting and necessary for the theorist can be confusing and traumatic to the adult educator. Just as in reading the literature on child rearing, the practitioner can find written justification for almost any methodological option that appears in the adult teaching situation. These contradictions are due to research lags, inadequate data, general and untestable assertions and postulates, obtuse writing, or disparities between problems posed by educators and researchers; whatever the reason they constitute a problem for the teacher.

6. *Mass of writing in scattered sources.* There is both too much and too little writing in the area of learning theory. So many pages are written that even competent researchers do not pretend to "keep up" with the literature. Much helpful material is scattered, and not designated as "learning theory," in such literature as that on psychotherapy, social psychology, personality theory, anthropology, and child psychology. Too little has been done to integrate the understandings from these diverse areas and to translate them into writings directly relevant to the adult educator.

CHANGE PROCESSES

The barriers described above present challenges to the adult educator. In many ways it is highly unfortunate that these barriers are so effective. Adult educators and elementary school teachers—at the ends of the student age scale—have been the most imaginative, inventive, and experimental of all educators. Perhaps because they are perceived as of less consequence, adult and child educators have been more free to experiment than have secondary and college teachers. In addition, the reality demands of adults force change and improvement upon adult educators.

In the newly differentiated area of change theory, the adult educator finds the attempt at a blending of traditional learning theory and the related studies of the dynamics of the individual, the group, and the institution. The institutions that have forced the acceleration of adult education—industry, the military, national organizations, religious groups—have demanded that the student of learning look at the processes that produce behavior change as well as knowledge acquisition. The concern of the traditional schoolroom for knowledge acquisition has blocked the conceptualization of education as process of behavior change. Traditional education has been relatively efficient in producing retention of verbal material but has been woefully ineffective in changing character, personality, marital adjustment, or management skills.

Students of change theory have explicitly devoted themselves to the problem of studying the processes that induce behavior change in persons, groups, and institutions. Early studies of psychological abilities and of behavior change led to the discovery that many apparent changes were illusory—transfer of training, judgment of emotions, formal discipline, acquisition of will power. These reality-based conclusions led to a mass cynicism about all efforts to change significant aspects of personality or character. Recent improvements in training methodology in psychotherapy, human relations training, and management development indicate that this earlier cynicism was unwarranted. What was warranted was the conclusion that education usually *did* not change personality and character, not that it *could* not.

Social psychologists, psychotherapists, and other social scientists, working in relative independence of traditional learning theory, are discovering the conditions under which people may make behavior changes of significance. These conditions include intrinsic determination of goals, emotional participation in the experience of decision making, active involvement in planning the learning experience, expression of feelings and integration of feeling into the learning process, and various forms of person centering.

PRINCIPLES FOR ADULT LEARNING

It is difficult in a small space to summarize a set of principles that would represent the contributions of diverse learning theories to an understanding of the way adults learn. There is no learning theory; there are many learning theories. The list below will be made in an effort to translate some of the basic principles, so often stated in terms that do not imply specific actions on the part of the adult educator, into statements that clearly imply action steps. A functional theory for an adult educator is one which is at a level of generalization that is applicable to the problems about which the adult educator must make decisions. The statements below represent what must be true if learning in an adult setting is to be optimally effective.

1. *Learning must be problem centered.* For the most significant kinds

of learnings that adults do, the problem must be a problem for the learner, not a problem of the teacher. When the learner sees a real problem he is motivated to seek some kind of solution. The teacher cannot "give" another person a problem, cannot expect "read chapter four" to be a guiding problem. In the learning situation the problems must arise in the experiences, perplexities, doubts, and thinkings of the learner. The teacher's obligation is to provide situations in which the learners see a broader and broader range of problems and from which he learns the ability to seek and formulate his own problems. Many educational experiences consist of a fight between the teacher, who sees problems in his frame of reference, and the student who has another set of experiences from which to derive another set of problems.

Learning must be motivated. The problem serves to provide energy, direction, and sustaining force to the activities of the learner. To be maximally effective the motivation must be intrinsic. The problems cannot be imposed from an extrinsic need system: the teacher's ideals, society's demands, the textbook's admonitions, the grading system. The teacher may, of course, help construct bridges between the learner's current problems and the demands of the teacher, society, or the textbook. The teacher must learn to do this in ways that will maximize the tendency of the student to take over the building of such bridges himself—the internalization of responsibility for guiding his own learning process.

2. *Learning must be experience-centered.* All sensory input to the organism is, of course, "experience." The problem for the teacher who is to develop a climate for learning is to help provide the optimal kinds of experiences that will relate to the problems of the learner. The learner must get data upon *his* problem. The data may come from experiments relevant to the problem, from authorities who may tell of their experiences, from logical argument, or from direct sensory experiences of the learner. The learner must get in a stance or posture to allow himself to look at the data. For many problems the learner seems to need hot, compelling, and direct experience in order to satisfy himself. Whenever there is any involvement of the ego in the problem—and any "problem" is by definition a concern of the ego—the individual develops vested interests in certain solutions. This vested interest in the solution prevents a functional "take" of the experience. A joint responsibility of the teacher and the learner is to create a climate which allows the learner to accept the experience as learningful.

3. *Experience must be meaningful to the learner.* The experience that bears upon the problem must be suited to some degree to the learner's innate capacity to perceive, his age, his interests, his readiness, and his capacity to understand. Many theorists have emphasized the role of understanding and insight in the organization of the learning experience. The learner's limitations of experience, background, insight, age, emotionality, and mental ability limit or block his perception of the experi-

ence as meaningful to his problem. Unless the learner sees the relevance of the data to his problem he will be unable to use the data in its solution. The story of the learning process is in part the story of the interaction between the learner and the teacher in an effort to create conditions that minimize the above barriers and that maximize the congruence between the form of the data and the readiness of the learner. The neurotic who fails to see the punishments that people impose upon his behavior; the inventor who cannot see the solution implicit before his eyes; the artist who cannot "see" the better of two designs; all suffer from inability to perceive the relevance of the data to the learner. A shared responsibility of the learner and the teacher is to create a climate in which the learner can see meanings. This is a creative search, both for the learner and the teacher. Meanings do not come passively to a non-participative learner.

4. *The learner must be free to look at the experience.* Much has been written about the appropriate climate for learning. This climate is described in various ways, as permissive, supportive, accepting, free, spontaneous, reality-centered, or person-centered. Learning is a social experience. Learners learn from others in social situations. The learner who is emotionally and psychologically *free* to look at experience is ready to start on the process of acquiring the necessary behavior with which to learn and to grow. The person who *feels* he cannot learn mathematics or languages is not free to exert effort to look at mathematics or language. The student who thinks he is not artistic or is not athletic is incapacitated for certain areas of search for experience. For learning to proceed creatively and optimally the learner must be adjusted emotionally to the learning situation, the teacher, the fellow students, and to the classroom climate.

5. *The goals must be set and the search organized by the learner.* Several experiments indicate that the active learner is a more effective learning organism than the passive learner. In order that problems be problems *to the learner,* it is significant that the goals of the broad learning quest be set *by the learner.* It is also significant that the learner participate in the organization of the total learning situation. His quest for problem solutions must be directed by hypothesis and not by fortuitous or blind impulse. Learning even at the simplest levels is not trial and error. The learner must be free to make errors, to explore alternative solutions to problems, and to participate in decisions about the organization of his learning environment.

For maximum learning the learner must interact with other learners in such a way as to expose his attitudes and gaps in knowledge and skills to himself and to others. His attempts at solution must be a series of provisional tries, which become increasingly effective as he gets feedback on each try and modifies subsequent explorations.

6. *The learner must have feedback about progress toward goals.* Stu-

dents of learning have long emphasized the importance of knowledge of results in acquiring skills. Evaluation of progress toward goals, particularly when goals have been set by the learner, is highly important. Some indication of success or failure, some frame of reference for determining adequacy of problem solution, some corroboration that the alley is not blind, some reality factor with which to assess one's achievement against one's level of aspiration, some knowledge of success or failure—all are necessary in the functional feedback process.

ABOUT THE FUTURE

Certain trends of development in the relationship between adult education and learning theory are apparent. Adult educators are becoming increasingly self-conscious about the methods they use. A growing awareness of the dependence of methodological adequacy upon sound theories of human learning will certainly increase. A weighing of the recent developments in this area, the gaps in our knowledge that must be filled, and the needs of the serious adult gives rise to the following exploratory list of changes that are likely to take place during the next few years in the growing rapprochement between the adult educator and the student of human learning.

1. *A growth in the areas thought of as adult education.* Learning is increasingly seen as a relationship among people. All activities of people are potentially learningful. There is increasing ambiguity in the boundary between formal and informal learning activities. In industry, management development is being increasingly seen as a line function, and as a function that is performed in connection with line activities. This concept of learning requires a learning theory that takes into account the unstructured growth functions of informal activities.

2. *Greater attention to the institutional settings in which learning occurs.* As learning theorists become interested in the climate for learning, many aspects of the institutional situation come under scrutiny. Studies of the educational community shed light upon the learning properties of institutional structures. The architecture of the buildings, the size of class units, the concept of a learning or therapeutic community, the nature of the administrative decision processes, the involvement of the members of the educational community in decisions about educational function, the nature of community forces facilitative and inhibitive to growth and learning—all are examples of the concerns that the learning theorist has about the educational setting. The growth properties of institutions will be of increasing concern to adult educators and to learning theorists building a concept of adult learning.

3. *Further expansion of non-institutional adult education activities.* Not only is adult education being conceived as of broader scope within the institutions where formal adult educational programs are being ex-

panded, but further developments of adult education outside of the formal educational institutions will probably increase. The institutional regulation and control of curricular programs is a mixed blessing. One reason that adult education has been so decidedly experimental and imaginative in some quarters is its relative freedom from centrality of concern of the curriculum builders. When educational activities are essentially voluntary and do not lead to degrees and formal institutional approval, the motivational patterns leading to learning shift radically and impose new demands upon an engineering-learning theory.

4. *Greater integration of learning theory with innovation and invention.* The programming aspects of learning theory demand that a learning theory be an "engineering" as well as a "scientific" theory of change and learning. In order for development to occur in engineering theory a fusion must take place between the innovations of practitioners and the theory building of conceptualizers. Innovations in engineering methodology force expansion and test of basic theoretical notions. For example, the invention of role playing and psychodrama as an educational tool led to demands for role constructs that in turn forced new dynamics into learning theory. A theory of institutional and social forces upon behavior modification will be greatly advanced when administrator-educators invent new forms of institutions which facilitate rather than tolerate human learning. Here theory and practice interact and reciprocally stimulate each other. As adult education advances, greater interaction between theory and practice will occur.

5. *More experimentation with adults in adult settings.* Most learning theory has been based upon experiments with and observations upon children and animals. These findings are highly relevant to adult settings, but will become more so as adults are used more often in laboratory and field studies. Great advances were made in child psychology when researchers ceased to look upon children as miniature adults. Advances will be furthered in adult education when researchers cease to look upon adults simply as grown up children.

6. *More specific study of the problems that adults face, about which they must learn, and for which they must prepare.* We are beginning to build an "adult psychology" and an "adult sociology" to parallel the exciting advances in "child psychology." There may or may not be qualitative differences between child and adult problems, but this issue must be made into an empirical problem, for which research can provide help. For instance, most of the problems that adults face do not have "correct" solutions. Learning theories that predict behavior to correct-solution problems are less relevant to adult learning than to child learning. Adults face problems of sexual adjustment, assessment of moral issues, marital compatibility, handling counter-dependency, and other problems that pose essentially different problems for the learner than some of the problems faced by the child. Skill learning and memorization form a larger

part of the learning demands of the child than of the adult.

7. *Greater development of communication between learning theorists and adult educators.* As communication improves between the two groups each will facilitate development in the other. Learning theorists need to be aware of the problems that face the adult educator. Adult educators need to be aware of the understandings that can come from already available learning theory. Part of this development is a problem of changing the perceptions that each group has of the other.

8. *Increasing development of the social psychology of learning.* As greater insight comes to each group there is a greater merging of the methods, concepts, and conclusions of social psychologists and learning theorists. As learning is seen as a social phenomenon the problems of social change and human learning become overlapping conceptual areas.

9. *Increasing concentration upon the needs of the learner.* There is at present greater and greater overlap and reciprocal stimulation among researchers who think of themselves as working on personality theory and on learning theory. An illustration of this interrelationship is in the study of the problem of dependency. Dependency, a classic personality issue, becomes increasingly relevant to conceptualization of learning theorists. What kind of relationship between learner and teacher must develop for optimal learning to occur? What is the relationship of dependency of social learning? Probably the greatest development in building an adult psychology of learning will come in the relating of personality dynamics to response acquisition.

10. *Closer relationship of therapy to learning theory.* The disciplines studying human development and learning have proceeded in relative isolation. Interdisciplinary trends lead to integration of the efforts of disciplines dealing with learning: psychotherapy, personality theory, character education, management development, educational methodology, child rearing, and learning theory. This is particularly true of the relationships between psychotherapy and human learning. In the 1920's when Muenzinger suggested that psychotherapy be conceived as a problem of learning theory this idea went unnoticed in the other literature. At the present time this is a common notion, the implementation of which will cross-fertilize both disciplines.

11. *Ascendence of theories of cognition and insight over theories of punishment and reward.* Perhaps the most durable and meaningful cleavage among learning theorists is between reinforcement and cognitive conceptions of the learning process. Each body of theory is heuristic, healthy, and growing. Each body of theory has strong adherents among theorists and among practitioners. Just as nondirective therapy found a convivial setting in the democratic ideology of the times, so is cognitive theory finding greater support, deriving in part from the greater apparent congruence between cognitive theory and democratic ideology than between reward theory and democratic ideology. Whether such congru-

ence or lack of congruence exists is of somewhat less social consequence than that practitioners seem to perceive such congruence.

The above trends seem to exist in the cross-fertilization of learning theory and adult education. Whether these trends will continue is an exciting question that will have great effect upon the growth of adult education in our time.

Selected Readings

Bugelski, B. R. *The Psychology of Learning.* New York: Henry Holt, 1956.

Cantor, Nathaniel. *The Learning Process for Managers.* New York: Harper, 1958.

Deese, James. *The Psychology of Learning.* New York: McGraw-Hill, 1958.

Getzels, J. W. *Learning Theory and Classroom Practice in Adult Education.* Presentation at Conference on Instruction, Syracuse University, Sagamore Conference Center. May 1956.

Gibb, Jack R. "A climate for learning," *Adult Education,* IX (Autumn, 1958), 19-21.

Gibb, Jack R., Platts, Grace N., and Miller, Lorraine. *The Dynamics of Participative Groups.* St. Louis: John S. Swift, 1951.

Hilgard, Ernest R. *Theories of Learning.* New York: Appleton-Century-Crofts, 1948.

Kidd, J. R. *How Adults Learn.* New York: Association Press, 1959.

Kingsley, Howard S. *The Nature and Conditions of Learning.* Englewood Cliffs, New Jersey: Prentice-Hall, 1957. (Second edition)

Lippitt, Ronald, Watson, Jeanne, and Westley, Bruce. *The Dynamics of Planned Change.* New York: Harcourt, Brace, 1958.

Miles, Matthew B. *Learning to Work in Groups.* New York: Teachers College, Columbia University, 1959.

Thelen, Herbert. *Learning Theory and its Application to Classroom Teaching.* Presentation at Conference on Instruction, Syracuse University, Sagamore Conference Center, May 1956.

Thorpe, Louis P., and Schmuller, Allen M. *Contemporary Theories of Learning with Applications to Education and Psychology.* New York: Ronald Press, 1954.

CHAPTER 6

PROGRAM DEVELOPMENT
IN ADULT EDUCATION

JACK LONDON

Associate Professor
School of Education
University of California, Berkeley

This chapter makes use of a variety of sources, including general education literature, research studies, and a questionnaire mailed to a selected list of national and local program developers. While some of the findings of this latter study were used in preparing this chapter, limitation of space prohibited reporting them in detail.

DEFINITION

Program is defined in the dictionary as "a brief outline of the order to be pursued, or the subjects embraced in any public exercise, performance, etc." It usually refers to a plan which is undertaken by a group or individual "that has certain ends in view and proposes their orderly achievement." In the field of adult education, "program" is commonly used to describe the type of activities developed by a voluntary association, agency, or non-educational institution for its public. In contrast, formal educational institutions call their programs the curriculum. Generally the curriculum is used to denote the formal credit courses whereas program indicates a more informal, non-credit type of activity. In its usage, program is a more flexible term than curriculum. For example, a university extension division is likely to refer to its campus courses offered in extension as part of its curriculum while referring to more informal, non-credit activities as its program. The more flexible term "program" is preferred by adult educators over "curriculum" because it reflects the need to develop programs especially for adults rather than to carry over, unchanged, the programs developed for children and youth.

The essential difference between program and curriculum can be illustrated by citing two examples which represent the two extremes in programming for adults. One type of program is the activity of an educational nature organized for farm organizations, civic and service clubs, women's clubs, professional associations, libraries, churches, trade unions, etc. The focus of this type of program is on developing attitudes, competency in particular skills, or certain areas of knowledge for an organizational or individual purpose *without regard to credit toward a degree or diploma*. The emphasis of the program is upon flexibility of content so as to meet the needs and interests of participating adults. At the other extreme of the continuum are the credit courses offered by a high school, college, or university which may lead to a diploma, degree, or certificate. Under these circumstances, pressure is exerted upon the adult program to duplicate the exact offerings of the day school, and this is interpreted as meeting the standards of the institution. These two types encompass the extremes of programming in adult education.[1]

PRINCIPLES OF PROGRAM PLANNING

In our study of adult education literature, we found it useful to differentiate between credit- and degree-oriented programs in formal educational institutions and non-credit programs in other institutions or agencies. Similar problems exist in both types of institutions, but the formal educational organization, particularly the evening college and university extension division, is controlled to a large extent by established academic standards. Dyer found that 69 per cent of the evening credit courses must be approved by day school committees. Changes can be instituted more easily in non-credit courses, but there is pressure from students (who tend to be diploma-seekers), as well as the day college faculty, to adhere to traditional material and methods.[2]

The adult education programs which are not under such pressures to conform to traditional curricula are more helpful in discovering the rationale behind uniquely adult education program development. In this regard, there appears to be remarkable consensus among adult educators as to the formal steps in successful program development—whether for a single meeting or a year's program. These can be simply stated:

(1) Determine the needs of the constituents
(2) Enlist their participation in planning
(3) Formulate clear objectives
(4) Design a program plan
(5) Plan and carry out a system of evaluation

Determine the Needs of the Constituents

Because adults do not have to go to school, but undertake adult education courses voluntarily, programs must be based on needs and interests which these students themselves express or which they can be led to recognize. The latter clause is significant, for adult educators almost universally have purposes which go far beyond the offering of courses which a check-list survey of potential participants might indicate would be popular. These adult education goals involve helping adults become more effective persons and citizens, helping enlarge their perspectives, increasing their appreciation, and the like. In order that such goals may be reconciled with the basic premise that "programs should be shaped by those they serve" the concept of adult needs has been expanded. The needs of adults which the educators seek to meet are not just 'felt needs' but also the needs which educators impute when they view the gap between what is and what could be if their students achieved their full potential.

While a valid principle of program development in adult education is to reach adults where they are, a stimulating and imaginative adult educator must develop materials and learning experiences which will enable the participating adults to grow in the breadth and depth of their concerns and interests. A most vital part of every program in adult education, whether of a vocational, avocational, or liberal arts character, is the stimulation of an individual's desire to continue learning throughout life. It is not enough to meet the needs and interests of the adults if that is where they remain after contact with the program activity.

To understand either type of needs, program planners must know their audience and what will stimulate its members to learn.[3] Adult educators urge one another to conduct surveys, analyze census data,[4] quiz community leaders, poll organizations via "self-surveys," and in other ways find out as much as possible about their potential students so that their programs can be adapted, both in content and method, to their needs, abilities, and motivations. Houle and Nelson warn against a generalized 'mass-media approach' and advocate identifying the inattentive, attentive, actively interested, and specialist audiences; program planning for each group will necessarily have to follow different lines.[5]

Enlist Their Participation in Planning

Not only do educators desire to meet with potential students in order to ascertain their desires but there is a universally held view that participation in program planning by community members as well as adult educators is good in itself. The benefits flowing from participation are many. When individual students participate, (1) they have greater responsibility in the enterprise because they have helped in its creation; (2) they may be led to recognize needs which before were not consciously felt; and (3) planning can be as much a learning experience as can direct instruction. The suggestions made in Chapter 7 for involving participants in planning particular activities are easily adapted to the planning of total programs.

Formulate Clear Objectives

General objectives.—The literature is replete with disagreements as to the general objectives of adult education, as described in detail in Chapter 4. Community-group-action versus orthodox-content-classes is but one way to view the most vital area of disagreement as to the proper focus of attention for adult education. Often the problem is seen as involving a three-way split. The question is asked: Should the focus be (1) the development of the individual—social and educational (including vocational)? (2) the development of citizens—with skills and knowledges to meet the challenge of today's world? or (3) the transmission of our cultural heritage—those traditional truths and questions that have been relevant to man's search for meaning throughout history?

The objectives of an educational system are invariably related to the values of the society. In the last analysis, the particular objectives formulated for an educational system are directly related to the existing conception of the "ideal adult" which the society deems appropriate to create. Thus, a major task of the school is to socialize the child into the type of adult model fostered by its society. The concept of socialization covers the different ways in which the culture is transmitted to the child in order to fit him into organized ways of behavior, and it can also be extended to the adult, since socialization continues throughout the life span. In a rapidly changing society, the adult must learn new ways of behavior, participate in new types of institutions, and develop values consonant with the changing society he lives in as well as the good society that he may aspire to develop. For example, raising children, developing greater vocational efficiency, becoming active in civic affairs, and learning new skills, attitudes, and knowledges appropriate to one's personal and societal problems, are continuous aspects of adult socialization. Several pressing current problems, such as increased leisure, retirement, personal identity in a mass society,[6] and the complex international situation impose certain requirements as to what adults must learn to take an effective part in this society.

The Educational Policies Commission of the National Education Association formulated four major areas of educational objectives for our schools. They are: (1) self realization; (2) human relationships; (3) economic efficiency; and (4) civic responsibility.[7] These four areas are inclusive enough to cover education throughout the life span. The only significant difference of opinion among educators is in how these objectives are to be reached and which ones require major emphasis.

Specific objectives.—All educational programs, whether designed for children or adults, require the formulation of specific objectives in order to direct learning toward a desired end. These objectives must indicate the character of change of behavior desired if they are to serve as effective guides to participants, teachers, and administrators in planning, conducting, and evaluating adult education programs.

If an activity has clear and immediate relevance to the participants' own particular needs and interests, it will attract and hold them, and thus bring about the desired changes expressed in the objectives. For example, if an adult takes a course in blue print reading, he obviously must see this course as fulfilling an immediate need in his work—learning a specific skill in order to be upgraded or to secure a new job. The specific objective is related to the broad objective of the school to help to raise the general level of vocational efficiency in its community, and to the goal of his teacher to help him become a more competent craftsman. In a similar fashion, all program activities must be related to both immediate and long run objectives of the participating adults, the teachers or leaders, and sponsoring organizations.

Not all situations will be as clear-cut as the example cited above. Some adults may have motives for engaging in an educational experience totally unrelated to the objectives of the program, such as a need for companionship, to get out of a rut, or to keep up with the Joneses. Once these initial reasons for participating are realized or satisfied to some extent, an adult will develop other objectives—in a good learning situation—which may include the acceptance of some of the broader objectives established by the organization sponsoring the activity.

Since the ultimate end of an adult education program is to change the behavior of adults, the function of specific objectives is to indicate what changes are to be expected as a result of contact with a program. It is not enough to merely state that an objective of a particular program in history is to improve the knowledge of history of the students. Greater specificity must be incorporated in guiding the program through the medium of specific objectives. In other words, a clear-cut definition of specific objectives which spells out the behavioral aspects and the type of subject matter content required to achieve a desired behavioral change serves as an adequate criterion for determining content, suggesting learning activities, selecting methods, etc. Tyler suggests that one test of the clarity of definition of objectives is to determine whether the behavior change expected of the student, as a result of contact with the program, can be easily recognized.[8]

Design a Program Plan

There has been an increased interest in program design by adult educators in recent years. A growing literature has developed in the field and the reader might profitably refer to it in undertaking the design of a program plan.[9] The importance of program design is highlighted by the increasing realization that the design not only establishes a common core of expectations as to outcomes, but also contributes to establishing the "climate" for the entire experience. For example, a lecture series implies a certain method, a particularized or unique relationship between lecturer and audience, and some common expectations about how the lecturer and audience will behave. A clinic suggests a different set of methods, relationships, and behavior.

The lecture and discussion methods represent the two ends of a continuum within which all program designs are formulated. The primary aim of discussion is to promote mastery of a problem, subject matter, or area of knowledge. When the situation requires a need to provide coverage of subject matter rapidly, the lecture is the more appropriate method to utilize. The various program designs will often incorporate elements of discussion and lecture when both coverage and mastery of a subject are desired. The particular objectives of the program will determine whether one method or the other, or a combination of both, will be used.

While there is no agreement on the use of certain descriptive titles for various program forms, the following listing is frequently used in adult education literature:

(1) *The lecture series* is the organization of a series of lectures around a common theme often utilizing different lecturers. The series may extend over a period of weeks and may utilize films, film strips, as well as straight lecturing. A common pattern is to encourage attendance to the entire series although attendance at individual lectures is permitted.

(2) *The convention* is a gathering of representatives from local branches of a parent organization having a common purpose. These representatives meet together to discuss and act upon problems of interest and concern to the entire organization. The convention is often where legislation for the organization is passed.

(3) *The conference* is designed to serve a varying number of persons representing a number of organizations or groups in order to hear different points of view. The purpose of the conference is to discuss mutual problems toward the objective of achieving a reasonable solution. The conference must not be confused with the convention which serves a different purpose.

(4) *The forum* or *panel* is a program design in which two or more specialists in a particular topic or subject-matter area sit on a platform in front of an audience and carry on a discussion on the assigned subject. This design is used frequently to explore a problem, create audience interest, present conflicting points of view, or to examine the advantages and disadvantages of a particular course of action.

(5) *The institute* is a more formal program designed to provide for a series of meetings for a group of individuals to receive instruction and information in a particular field of work. It tends to be a short and intensive training program. The programming for the institute is typically undertaken by a planning staff with the assistance of consultants in particular areas being focused upon in the session.

(6) *The clinic* is designed to serve a homogeneous professional or occupational group to concentrate upon the study of a specialized subject matter area. The focus of the clinic is upon problems, and utilizes the services of consultants to assist participants in gaining understanding of these problems.

(7) *The educational workshop* is designed to bring together individuals with a common interest and background to engage in educational experiences which will aid them in gaining new knowledges, attitudes, and skills as they develop plans and programs of common interest. Consulting experts are used but the primary burden of providing learning experiences is borne by the participants. General sessions and face-to-face discussion groups are used.

(8) *Radio and television*—related programs are designed to organize small discussion groups to listen to radio or television programs as a basis for stimulating discussion in the group. An outstanding example of this type of

design has been the Canada's Farm Radio Forum.[10] A common pattern is to provide some form of feedback from the discussion groups to the radio or television station for guidance in subsequent programming.

(9) *The class* is designed to give the student knowledge, attitudes, and skill in some particular subject matter. The usual pattern is to have a teacher who has mastery of the subject plan and conduct the entire learning experience. This program design specifies a series of learning experiences distributed over a period of several months, with one or two sessions per week.

(10) *The co-ordinated course* is a packaged type of program designed to achieve a specified educational goal through the use of particular content and methods. An important purpose of the co-ordinated course has been to engineer a program to give a large number of people a few basic concepts. The Great Books, World Politics, and the Fund for Adult Education discussion programs are examples of this type of program design.[11]

(11) *The seminar* is composed of a small group of students and a professor or leader who meet together in a face-to-face setting. It is commonly expected that students will prepare reports for presentation to the seminar. Members of the seminar, including the teacher, discuss and analyze the report. The purpose of the seminar is to enable a group of persons to study a subject under the leadership of an expert.

(12) *Action projects* are designed to apply to a wide variety of problems in which educational experiences are utilized to deal with real-life situations. Action projects are an important programming design in community development.

(13) *The training laboratory* is a residential program lasting from a few days to several weeks for the purpose of creating learning experiences which will increase the participant's understanding of human relations skills and to improve his ability to analyze personal and group behavior. There is usually a great deal of opportunity to experiment with new behavioral responses.

(14) *Special interest groups,* such as a Spanish club, parent-education study group, classical music club, etc., often conduct systematic learning programs.

The above program forms are some of the most familiar ones in adult education, but a great deal of experimentation is being undertaken in developing new program designs or combining existing designs. One such experiment is to start a program with a week-end residential institute and continue the program on a weekly basis for a specified number of weeks utilizing a class scheme. Another variation is to combine a residential program for a period of a week with a correspondence course continuing over a period of months. Imaginative program designs are being developed in a variety of situations.

Tyler has described a number of general principles which are useful in determining what learning experiences to include in a program design.[12] These principles are general in character so as to be of value in selecting particular learning experiences in spite of the nature of objectives. They are:

1. The participating adult must gain experience in practicing the type of behavior outlined in the objectives. If the objective is to develop skill in critical thinking, the participant must have an opportunity to practice such skill in the learning situation—the program designs on the discussion end of the continuum may be more useful than those on the lecture end in this case.

2. The particular experience must provide some measure of satisfac-

tion to the participants as they carry out the behavior implied in the objectives. If the learning experience is designed to provide skill in solving civic problems in the community, it is crucial that the participant not only secures experience in solving civic problems but also obtains satisfaction through the experience.

3. The learning experience must start where the participants are in terms of their background, level of experience, perspective, interests, etc. In other words, it must start from the level of interest, understanding, background, and experience of the people concerned. The program must be based on the needs and interests which the participants feel or can be led to recognize. To carry out this principle, the practice of involving representative constituents of a learning program in its planning is one useful method of determining their needs and interests.

4. There are a great variety of learning experiences which can be utilized in a program design to achieve the same objectives. Since there are many alternatives in selecting learning experiences, it is more profitable to select the experience most closely related to the needs and interests of all parties involved in the program. A great deal of experimentation can be undertaken to determine the most appropriate learning experiences for each particular situation.

5. Any learning experience will produce a number of outcomes which can be utilized to achieve more than one objective of the program. While a citizen may be learning how to solve some of the civic problems facing his community, he is also acquiring knowledge about a variety of areas, and may also be developing skill in critical thinking. Or a participant in the Great Books program may be acquiring an interest in international problems at the same time as developing competency in dealing with local community issues or in developing a better understanding of his own opinions and skill in formulating them more clearly. Undesirable outcomes also may be forthcoming, such as the development of an attitude of dislike for a subject or the feeling of apathy developed in the face of an analysis of the complex civic problems facing a community. This tendency of any learning experience to produce a variety of positive and negative outcomes must be considered in program design.

Any learning experience must produce a cumulative effect in order to produce change of behavior. This means that learning experiences must be organized effectively to achieve desired program objectives. The following criteria for effective organization of learning experiences have been suggested by Tyler:[13]

1. The development of *continuity* refers to the need to provide recurring educational experiences which reinforce the development of particular attitudes, knowledges, and skills resulting in changed behavior. For example, in a liberal education program, the objective of developing the ability to make judgments on intelligent bases requires repeated opportunities for practice in making judgments.

2. *Sequence* of learning experiences is related to continuity but goes beyond by the building of a series of successive experiences at increasing levels of difficulty so as to provide broader and deeper treatment. For example, a program to carry out the general objective of acquiring knowledge of the great problems of mankind would start with the immediate problems experienced by the learners and move in steps of increasing complexity toward such age old problems of man as what is freedom, liberty, the nature of man, right and wrong, and the like.

3. The *integration* of educational experiences requires that the participant secures an over-all perspective of the total experience rather than a segmental one. Integration refers to the need of developing educational experiences that utilize and become part of the total capacities of the individual in life, as well as to the need of providing experiences that give unity to the acquisition of knowledges, attitudes, and skills achieved through the educational activities of the program.

Plan and Carry Out a System of Evaluation[14]

An integral part of the process of program development is the formulation of a system of continuous evaluation to ascertain the effectiveness with which the objectives of the program are being realized. Simply stated, evaluation seeks to answer the question, how well are the general and specific goals of the program being accomplished? Some questions that suggest typical indices of evaluation are: Do the students appear to be interested? Do they attend regularly, ask pertinent questions, demonstrate any observable change of behavior?

Evaluation always takes place in one way or another. Often it may be casual, based upon one's own observation or the use of simple questionnaires to secure information from the students. At the other extreme is the formal scientific study which will be discussed at greater length below.

An effective program of evaluation is very difficult to carry out for a variety of reasons, chief of which are the program director's reluctance to face up to the possibility of having to make basic changes in his program,[15] the fear of revealing weaknesses to the potentially critical outsider, lack of clear-cut program objectives, lack of skill in the use of social science research techniques, and complacency arising out of applying the sole criterion of attendance. Adult educators should realize that organizing programs upon the basis of expediency or trial-and-error is expensive of time, money, and the reputation of adult education.

Any educational experience involves the interaction of the instructor (or leader), the students (or participants), and selected subject-matter content designed to produce changes in behavior in accordance with established program objectives. A most effective type of evaluation would include the assessment of all three of these variables in determining the total impact of a program and the extent of its achievement of objectives.

More commonly, evaluation of the content of the program constitutes the major concern of the evaluator. Seldom does a program of evaluation include the quality of the instruction.[16] But the best designed program content cannot be effective if it is not being communicated to students.[17]

In developing criteria of evaluation, the following questions are relevant: Are the general and specific objectives of the program clear? Are these objectives relevant to the needs and interests of the participants? Are the identified needs of students being met by the program? Is the subject matter of each unit appropriate to the objectives of the total program? Are the methods effective in presenting the subject matter and maximizing the learning experience of students? How is the behavior of students being changed by the program? Is such change of behavior in the direction indicated by the agreed upon objectives? What would the evaluator see if the objectives were realized? What kind of measuring devices will be employed and how will the data be recorded for analysis? What theoretical and methodological considerations will be employed in the appraisal of the resulting evidence?[18]

Once the program evaluator develops adequate criteria, he must restate them in behavioral terms so as to be able to determine what behavior changes are expected of participants as a result of experience in the program. As an illustration, some of the behavioral evidences that might serve as a basis for evaluation of the highly abstract goal of developing civic responsibility are: (1) The participant gives more time to thought about civic affairs. (2) He participates more actively in his community. (3) He votes regularly and contributes funds to the political party of his own choosing. (4) He is able to find, use, and evaluate sources of information about civic affairs. (5) He develops his own opinions and makes his own values explicit about issues in his community. (6) He is able to examine and select alternative approaches to civic problems. (7) He is interested in the selection of candidates for public office. (8) He is aware of the complexity of issues, conflict of interests, and value judgments operating in civic affairs.[19]

The next step in the evaluation process is to gather data to determine the extent of achievement of program objectives. Many varieties of the paper and pencil test can be used to test such learnings as political judgment, knowledge of poetry, economic reasoning, or more specific changes in behavior. Other data-collection devices include observational reports, participant observation, interviewing, and scaling devices. The particular device selected will be determined by the character of a program's objectives and the type of data needed to measure behavioral changes demanded by the objectives. Some of the practical ways these techniques can be used include:

(1) compilation of observational reports of student reading habits, attitudes, interests, knowledge, and skills;
(2) the development of a series of interest scales;

(3) utilization of existing standardized achievement tests or the development of new tests;

(4) maintenance of a log of attendance and continued enrollment in further educational activities on an actual or sampling basis;

(5) development of an outline of items that can be used to guide a representative sample of students to keep accurate diaries of their reading and participation in other educational activities over a specified period of time to determine extent of change of behavior;

(6) development of a series of case studies of a representative sample of students to determine extent of change of behavior as a result of contact with the program.[20]

Another approach to gathering data makes use of methods commonly used in social science research. Four methods will be briefly described—the survey, the field study, the experiment in field setting, and the laboratory experiment.

The survey.—When the aim of the survey is simply to provide someone with information, it is a descriptive survey. When a design is formulated to explain rather than describe a situation it is an explanatory survey, and its purpose is to interpret the relationship among a number of identified variables. The relative value of descriptive or explanatory surveys is a hotly debated subject in the social sciences.[21] The value of each type of survey is directly related to the character of the research problem identified for study, with both having some value for different types of problems. The survey requires the systematic collection of data from a sample of population by the use of such techniques as the interview, questionnaire, scaling device, content analysis, and statistical analysis of mass data. It depends upon direct contact with individuals or a sample of individuals whose behavior is to be investigated.

Field study.—While there are many similarities between the survey and field study, the field study permits an intensive investigation of the dynamics of the processes rather than with their distribution in a large population. The focus of study is more likely to be a single group or community than a sample of a larger universe. The relevant ongoing social processes can be studied more directly, and thus provide a more comprehensive explanation of social life than is generally possible through use of the survey method.

Field experiment.—The field experiment is essentially an extension of the field study with the additional use of an experimental design. In the field experiment the experimenter manipulates variables in order to determine causal relationships. The independent variable is manipulated to determine its relation to the dependent variable. The setting for the field experiment is the natural milieu in which the phenomena to be studied are found, in contrast to the artificial environment of the laboratory experiment. The field experiment usually requires the use of a control group. It has the advantage of detecting causal relationships; the field study and survey, on the other hand, only reveal a correlation of variables.

Laboratory experiment.—The laboratory experiment has been borrowed from the physical and natural sciences. The investigator seeks to create the exact conditions existing in the world which he proposed to study by the control of some variables and the manipulation of others in the experimental design. In this way, the researcher studies the impact and measures the extent of change resulting from this manipulation. The laboratory experimental method is the least popular method in social science research largely because of the inadequacy of existing methodological techniques and the nature of human interaction.[22] To validate its results, the laboratory experimental method must be supplemented by studies of real-life situations, and so it is a less useful method for adult education than any of the other methods listed.

Whether to use a simple paper and pencil test or a more detailed research design such as the survey or field experiment will be largely determined by availability of time, expense involved, existence of appropriate research skills, need for and purpose of the findings to be derived from the evaluation research, and the particular conditions under which the study will be undertaken.

Once data have been collected, they must be put into a form appropriate for analysis. This step is called coding. A small number of categories are established to summarize a variety of individual responses. The purpose of coding is to put data into comparable form to make it possible to analyze and interpret the findings. After this step, data are ready to be analyzed through the use of simple comparisons, computation of statistical ratios, content analysis, or use of factor or relational analysis. The essential purpose of analysis is to answer the following questions: What changes of behavior have resulted during the program? Which changes can be identified as resulting from the impact of the program? Which objectives of the program have been achieved? What changes in objectives and programming must be undertaken in light of the analysis? The final step in the evaluation process is the revising of objectives and program activities in accordance with the recommendations arising out of the evaluation.[23]

TRENDS IN PROGRAM DEVELOPMENT

A survey of the opinions of a sample group of leaders in adult education reveals a variety of views on the trends in program development. One dominant trend appears to be in the "liberal" type of adult education programming. Although this trend is primarily reported by respondents of formal education institutions, a substantial number of other agencies show the same shift of interest toward the liberal arts. A university extension dean reports:

> . . . Our greatest area of expansion, however, will be in the liberal arts and cultural programs, including drama, music, art, dance, etc. Precisely because the

university curricula are becoming so highly specialized, as well as because of a sensed general malaise and insecurity among adults, I think they will increasingly be seeking answers in terms of why's and wherefore's of existence and where we are going; as well as the development of leisure time activities that have some substance for them and which can give them more basic satisfactions than their work often tends to give, or rather, not to give.[24]

This trend appears to be an important one because of the growing interest in our society for higher educational attainment, increased specialization, and the search for identity and self-realization, stimulated by the emergence of a mass society. Part of this need for self-realization and the search for identity is exemplified by the growing interest in "psychology, personality development, and other self-analysis courses." An adult educator in religious education states that there is a "greater responsibility for adult education in helping persons to enlarge their vision and their sense of responsibility for the direction of changes in the family, the community and the world."[25] A few respondents report great difficulty in getting adults interested in liberal education programs. A typical reply from this group is that "We find it very hard to get discussion groups or the liberal arts type of course organized."[26] In contrast, several replies show that there is increasing demand for educational experiences beyond the vocational training of such functional groupings as labor, business, farm, and professional associations.

Closely related to this trend is a tendency away from the "cafeteria" style of programming in adult education toward the development of a "core" program that provides a framework for continuing general education. This trend is illustrated by the series of Great Books, World Politics, and Fund for Adult Education packaged program activities. The main difference between this adult education and formal education is that the former does not have prerequisites as a basis for a sequence of courses. It does, however, suggest a closely related theory that an adult program should have a design with continuity, sequence, and integration which is sufficiently flexible to take into account the diverse backgrounds and experiences of adults.

Another trend is a rise in the use of the short course. A public school administrator of adult education reports "a definite shift to short unit courses of 4, 6, or 10 meetings at most. This may be a result of the prevalent rush, rush, rush, and lack of time to do everything one wants to do."[27] Adult educators from a variety of agencies and institutions such as churches, voluntary associations, public libraries, social agencies, and formal education groups report this widespread interest in the short program design.

The short unit courses do not cover the credit-type program in formal education institutions. A considerable number of responses from this source indicate a greater interest than ever in credit-type activities by adults who are interested in securing diplomas, certificates, and degrees. A noted university extension director says:

> To my mind there is great emphasis today on credit courses. In a tuition school such as ours, it is a waste of time to offer non-credit courses. Students feel that they are not receiving anything worthwhile and are not progressing toward their objective in such courses. We offer only those non-credit courses that are preparatory or prerequisite to some credit program. . . . The question may be asked, 'What of the people who have degrees and do not wish any credit?' Strange to say, these students, and there are quite a few, seem to feel that they will receive much more benefit if they enroll for credit. The credit "angle" is a spur, and even if not needed or desired, enrolling for credit brings these students into competition with other students and stimulates them.[28]

The greater emphasis on credit courses appears to be based also upon the growing demand for graduates of high schools and colleges by an increasing number of places of employment. While there is an increase in the credit courses, there is also an increase in enrollment in the non-credit programming. The important element in the development of either type of program appears to be the adult administrator's views on the relative merits of the two.[29]

A variety of other trends are reported, but with less frequency than those already mentioned. One was a reaction to the over-emphasis on group processes. A university dean reports "various conflicting tendencies to suppose that there is a simple solution to problems of program development—for example, blind faith in discussion techniques, group dynamics, methods, community development, etc.—all of which faiths and resultant programs have their places, to be sure, but cannot take care of everything."[30] A few respondents mention the increased use of advisory committees and a greater interest in civic education than in the past. An increase in the number of women enrolled is also cited. A health educator reports increased co-operative activities with other related organizations.

A final important trend is toward the assumption of responsibility for programming of adult education by the people involved in it, rather than by daytime deans and faculty. This view is expressed in a variety of ways by our respondents. One states it as the development of methodology, curriculum, and facilities geared for adults. Another sees this as the replacement of the outworn idea of remedial education for adults by the full implication of a "continuing education." Several others report the development of a concept of programming that does not automatically assume content sequence characteristic of formal educational programs, but a flexible sequence of content more characteristic of the participating adults in the program. This same idea was expressed by Belth and Schueler, who declared that

> . . . in the fields that are closely tied to contemporary events, the establishment of sequences—the building of one course on the content of the preceding one—is unnecessary.[31]

The thesis here, and one increasingly expressed in the literature, is that adult education cannot assume that traditional approaches and content effective in the education of the young will be appropriate for adults.

CONCLUSION

Space limitations prohibited our discussion of the initial step of program development in which an honest appraisal of the circumstances leading to the decision to undertake an adult education program is made. A variety of questions might be raised in starting this appraisal. What are some of the problems that education can help solve? What population grouping can be most effectively served? What time schedule is available for programming and carrying out of proposed activities? What are some of the social characteristics of the public to be reached? What is the nature of the history of the organization in past programming efforts? What are some of the relevant attitudes of the key decision-makers within the organization concerning program development in adult education, and how will this influence program planning? What areas of controversy and conflict may impede the development of effective program activities? These are a few of the questions that should be raised by the program planner prior to developing a program.

The major task of the program developer, in adult education, is to develop educational activities that will be liberalizing in their impact upon adults. The emphasis must be upon providing knowledges, skills, values, attitudes, and habits of mind which help each person continue to grow. To achieve this development, we must combine vocational and liberal arts education as the most effective way of helping the adult realize himself as a person. As our society increasingly becomes a mass society, this responsibility must be a major goal of the adult educator who is seeking to find a place in the sun for adult education.

Footnotes

1A growing literature is calling attention to various elements in the education of adults which differentiates adult education from the education of children and youth. Cf. James B. Whipple, *Especially for Adults* ("Notes and Essays," No. 19; Chicago: Center for the Study of Liberal Education for Adults, 1957) and James W. Harrison, "Designing Courses for Adults," *Adult Education*, VIII (Summer, 1958), 223-30.

2John Dyer, *Ivory Towers in the Market Place* (Indianapolis: The Bobbs-Merrill Co., 1956). Dyer points out that universities do change to meet new needs when they fear that they are losing their importance, although this is a slow process. He sees the evening college as an avenue for the introduction of such changes. Cf. pp. 86-87.

3Ralph W. Tyler, *Basic Principles of Curriculum and Instruction* (Chicago: University of Chicago Press, 1950), pp. 4-17.

4Homer Kempfer, *Adult Education* (New York: McGraw-Hill, 1955), pp. 70-73.

5Cyril O. Houle and Charles A. Nelson, *The University, The Citizen, and World Affairs* (Washington: American Council on Education, 1956).

6Anselm L. Strauss, *Mirrors and Masks: The Search for Identity* (Glencoe, Ill.: The Free Press, 1959).

7Educational Policies Commission, "The Purpose of Education in American Democracy, 1939," Clyde B. Moore and William E. Cole, *Sociology in Educational Practice* (Boston: Houghton Mifflin Co., 1952), pp. 336ff.

8Tyler, *op. cit.*, pp. 28-40.

9Cf. various issues of *Adult Leadership* (Chicago: Adult Education Association); Malcolm Knowles, *Informal Adult Education* (New York: Association Press, 1950); Robert H. Snow, *Community Adult Education* (New York: G. P. Putnam's Sons, 1955); Mildred E. English, *College in the Country* (Athens: University of Georgia Press, 1959); *Public School Adult Education: A guide for Administrators and Teachers* (Washington: National Association of Public School Adult Educators, 1956), etc.

10John Nicol, et al., *Canada's Farm Radio Forum* (Paris: UNESCO, 1954).

11Cyril O. Houle, *Use of Print in Adult Education Agencies*. Offprint from the Fifty-fifth Yearbook of the National Society for the Study of Education, Part II, *Adult Reading* (Chicago: University of Chicago Press, 1956), pp. 169-86.

12Tyler, *op. cit.*, pp. 42-44.

13*Ibid.*, pp. 54-57.

14See the entire issue of Vol. VII, No. 3, 1955, of the *International Social Science Bulletin*, which is devoted to "Evaluation Techniques."

15K. M. Miller, "Evaluation in Adult Education," *International Social Science Bulletin*, Vol. VII, No. 3 (1955), 430-42.

16George Williams, *Some of My Best Friends Are Professors* (New York: Abelard-Schuman, 1958).

17K. M. Miller, *op. cit.*, pp. 432-33.

18*Ibid.* Also Darcie Byrn, et al., *Evaluation in Extension* (Topeka: H. M. Ives & Sons, 1959).

19*Evaluation of Liberal Adult Education*. Conference Report. (Chicago: Center for the Study of Liberal Education for Adults, 1958). (Mimeographed)

20See *ibid.*, for an extension of these suggestions and a discussion of the development of sample devices for use in evaluation.

21Cf. Herbert Hyman, *Survey Design and Analysis* (Glencoe: The Free Press, 1955); C. A. Moser, *Survey Methods in Social Investigation* (New York: Macmillan, 1958); Mary Louise Mark, *Statistics in the Making* (Columbus: Ohio State University, Bureau of Business Research, 1958); and Frederick F. Stephan and Philip J. McCarthy, *Sampling Opinions: An Analysis of Survey Procedures* (New York: John Wiley, 1958).

22George Herbert Mead, *Mind, Self, and Society* (Chicago: University of Chicago Press, 1934); and Anselm L. Strauss, *op. cit.*

23Cf. Edmund deS. Brunner, et. al., *An Overview of Adult Education Research* (Chicago: Adult Education Association, 1959), chapter XIV.

24Questionnaire No. L9.

25Questionnaire No. 49.

26Questionnaire No. 32.

27Questionnaire No. 6.

28Questionnaire No. 16.

29Cf. "Discussion Groups and Lecture-Discussion Groups—Liberal Arts," *University Extension*, Vol. VIII, No. 13 (August 31, 1959), University of California at Los Angeles, for an excellent description of an extensive non-credit program for adults.

30Questionnaire No. L10.

31Marc Belth and Herbert Schueler, *Liberal Education for Adults Re-examined: The Queens College Program* (Chicago: Center for the Study of Liberal Education for Adults, 1959), p. 27.

Selected Readings

Belth, Marc, and Schueler, Herbert. *Liberal Education for Adults Re-examined.* Chicago: Center for the Study of Liberal Education for Adults, 1959.

Blakely, Robert J. *Adult Education in a Free Society.* Toronto: Guardian Bird Publications, 1958.

Brunner, Edmund deS., *et al. An Overview of Adult Education Research.* Chicago: Adult Education Association, 1959. Chapters VII and XIV.

Byrn, Darcie, *et al. Evaluation in Extension.* Topeka: H. M. Ives & Sons, 1959.

Carey, James T. "The Development of the University Evening School in Urban America." Unpublished Ph.D. dissertation, University of Chicago, 1958.

Clark, Burton R. *Adult Education in Transition.* Berkeley: University of California Press, 1956.

Darter, V. W. "County Extension Program Development." Unpublished Doctor of Public Administration thesis, Harvard University, 1955.

A Design for Democracy. New York: Association Press, 1956.

Dyer, John. *Ivory Towers in the Market Place.* Indianapolis: Bobbs-Merrill, 1956.

Evaluation of Liberal Education. Progress Report of Princeton Conference. Chicago: Center for the Study of Liberal Education for Adults, 1958.

Harrison, J. W. "Designing Educational Programs for Adults." Unpublished Ph.D. dissertation, University of Chicago, 1957.

Houle, Cyril O., and Nelson, Charles A. *The University, The Citizen, and World Affairs.* Washington: American Council on Education, 1956.

————. *The Use of Print in Adult Educational Agencies.* Chapter VII in Henry, Nelson B. (ed.) *Adult Reading.* 55th Yearbook, Part II, of the National Society for the Study of Education. (Chicago: University of Chicago Press, 1956), pp. 157-87.

International Social Science Bulletin, Vol. VII, No. 3, 1955. Entire issue devoted to evaluation techniques.

Kempfer, Homer. *Adult Education.* New York: McGraw-Hill, 1955.

Knowles, Malcolm S. *Informal Adult Education.* New York: Association Press, 1950.

Morrow, E. "Long Range Integrated Programming for Adult Education." Unpublished Ph.D. Dissertation, University of Chicago, 1957.

Powell, John Walker. *Learning Comes of Age.* New York: Association Press, 1956. Chapter 3.

Sheats, Paul H., *et al. Adult Education: The Community Approach.* New York: Dryden Press, 1953.

Siegle, Peter E., and Whipple, James B. *New Directions in Programming for University Adult Education.* Chicago: Center for the Study of Liberal Education for Adults, 1957.

Sillars, Robertson (ed.) *Seeking Common Ground in Adult Education.* Monograph No. 4. Chicago: Adult Education Association, 1958.

Snow, Robert H. *Community Adult Education.* New York: G. P. Putnam's Sons, 1955.

Tyler, Ralph W. *Basic Principles of Curriculum and Instruction.* Syllabus for Education 360. Chicago: University of Chicago Press, 1950.

Wandt, Edwin, and Brown, Gerald W. *Essentials of Educational Evaluation.* New York: Henry Holt and Co., 1957.

Whipple, James B. *Especially for Adults.* Notes and Essays No. 19. Chicago: Center for the Study of Liberal Education for Adults, 1957.

CHAPTER 7

METHODS IN ADULT EDUCATION

WARREN H. SCHMIDT
Assistant Director
University Extension, University of California
and
ELWIN V. SVENSON
Associate Director
University Extension, University of California

"What are the conditions which facilitate adult learning?" "Do different educational objectives require different methods?" "How should methods of adult education differ from those of institutionalized elementary, secondary, or higher education?"

More and more adult educators are asking questions like these in their search for more effective methodology. There was a time when adult learning programs used almost exclusively the traditional methods of teaching children and youth. Beginning with the 1920's, however, adult educators developed, discussed, and experimented with methods uniquely designed to facilitate *adult* learning. Throughout World War II and subsequently this quest has continued with increasing intensity and sophistication as educators have explored basic learning theories with researchers and practitioners from many fields—social science as well as education.

From these explorations have come convincing evidence that the adult learner differs from the child learner in several respects which have important implications for adult education methodology:

—The adult learner has more experience and a different quality of experience to contribute to the learning situation.

—The adult learner is ready to learn different things than the youthful learner because he faces different developmental tasks (e.g., parenthood).

—The adult learner tends to be more autonomous and, therefore, less comfortable in a dependent role.

—The adult learner is usually interested in the immediate usefulness of new knowledge.

As adult educators have learned more about their clientele, they have given greater attention to methods and techniques and have made considerable progress toward developing a theory of adult learning. Controversy has raged fiercely among advocates of different kinds of educational methods. Some have argued that adult educators were, in fact, so concerned with methods that they were neglecting to define the broader goals of education.

There is little doubt, however, that experimentation in the areas of methods has been a major dynamic in adult education since the War. It is through this common interest in methodology that an ever increasing number of groups and individuals—professional and volunteer—have come to identify themselves with the adult education movement.

This chapter examines the current thinking and practice in the field of adult education methodology. It approaches this subject from the point of view of the program planner who wants to create an effective learning experience for adults. To accomplish his purpose, he has available as his "ingredients" the learner, the teacher or leader, time, facilities, materials, and perhaps financial resources. The way in which these are combined will determine the nature and effectiveness of the experience. While this chapter discusses briefly many of the methods, techniques, and devices used in adult education, its major objective is to describe an approach to selecting appropriate methods by focusing on the following topics:

Conditions for Adult Learning
Methods for Creating the Conditions for Adult Learning
Steps in Developing an Adult Learning Program
Current Issues and Controversies about Adult Education Methods

CONDITIONS FOR ADULT LEARNING

1. *Understanding and accepting objectives and procedures.*—When the learner understands and accepts the objectives and methods of the program, he is better able to focus his attention on the relevant parts of the learning experience, contribute to it, and integrate the ideas with his previous experience. If he accepts the objectives but does not believe that the methods will contribute toward their achievement, much of his energy may be lost in resisting the learning program rather than taking full advantage of it. One of the responsibilities of planners, leaders, and, in some cases, preparers of materials is to make the learning objectives sufficiently clear so that from the very outset of, and during, the experience the learner feels that he is moving toward a significant and desirable goal.

2. *Making ideas available.*—The process of making ideas and experiences available depends upon both the presence of such ideas within the learning situation and their communication to the learner. The most common source of ideas is an authority (teacher, lecturer, panel of experts, resource person, etc.) who gives a presentation of experiences,

theories, or principles. These ideas and experiences may be in the form of new facts and new observations or the systematic grouping of observations which the learners have had but have not grouped in this particular manner.

A second source of ideas and experiences is the learner himself—the seminar student presenting a paper, the participants in a study-discussion group, the member in an unstructured group. In such situations the planner, teacher, and leader have responsibility for creating a setting which helps the learner to present his ideas and controls the flow of these ideas so that they are relevant to the learning objectives.

A third source of ideas and experiences takes the form of a book, a pamphlet, a film, or some similar kind of "packaged" experience prepared prior to the occurrence of the learning situation. Here, too, the leader has responsibility for effective utilization of the ideas in these materials.

3. *Focusing ideas and experiences.*—Making ideas and experiences available is not enough to ensure learning. To be maximally useful, they must be brought into focus and related to the objectives. This means that the program must be planned so that the learner can see these relationships. The briefing of teachers or leaders, the orientation of the learners, and the periodic assessment of progress all help to produce this focus. While the planner and the program leaders have primary responsibility for focusing ideas and experiences, in many situations it is appropriate for the learners to perform this function. When this occurs, the focusing of the experience is closely associated with the integration of ideas in the learner's experience.

4. *Integration of ideas with the learner's past experience.*—The process of integrating the ideas from a particular program with his previous experience is primarily dependent upon the learner himself. Here the desire to achieve the objectives, general openness to new ideas, and ability to re-examine past experience or previously-held positions become centrally important.

The *planner* can facilitate the integration process by: making sure that the learner's needs and goals are clearly articulated, are central to the program, and are understood by the program performers; providing a design or structure that may be adapted or changed as the experience progresses; and allowing sufficient time for the integration process to take place.

The *teacher* or *leader* can build bridges between new ideas in the situation and the known experience of the learners; he can make sure that learners have an opportunity to participate, and he can evaluate the progress toward integration. But in the final analysis, integration can only be done by the learner.

5. *A facilitating "climate" for learning.*—The adult learner reacts, not only to planned learning experiences, but to the total setting in which the learning takes place. The attitudes of the instructing staff, the friend-

liness of other participants, the formality or informality—as well as many other aspects—of the environment will influence the learner's openness to new ideas and his ability to understand and integrate them.

The program planner who recognizes education as essentially a human transaction—in which feelings, attitudes, and human relationships, as well as ideas, play a crucial role—will pay more careful attention to the many subtle arrangements of the environment which minimize distractions and enable the learner to concentrate fully on the task.

In a similar way, the teacher or leader has a responsibility to help the learner deal with those initial anxieties and embarrassments which adults so often bring to a learning situation.

METHODS FOR CREATING CONDITIONS FOR LEARNING

Methods for Helping the Learners to Understand and Accept the Objectives and Procedures

Many adult educators regard the orientation of the learners to be a key responsibility of the program planner. Even the most carefully-prepared advance material cannot fully prevent individuals from coming to an educational program with widely different expectations. Some methods for developing a more common understanding and acceptance of learning objectives are:

The orientation talk. This initial presentation describes the hoped-for outcomes of the experience, the plan for achieving these objectives, and the roles and responsibilities of both leaders and learners. Such a presentation helps to reassure the participants that the planners have carefully developed a program in a purposeful manner, show how the various parts of the program are related, set the emotional tone of the program, and provide a basic statement which can be referred to later.

Experience has shown that, although such a presentation is valuable, many participants do not hear it or understand its significance. Therefore, important parts of the orientation material are sometimes repeated in later sessions.

Visual aids help—the more clearly the learner can get an overview of the activities which lie ahead, the better able he is to embark upon the experience. Discussion helps, too—particularly in cases where the participants may have markedly different expectations.

Informal orientation sessions. Sometimes a program is best launched by an informal experience. The opening event might be a coffee period, lunch, or dinner, during which program staff can mingle informally and systematically with participants.

The question of how best to begin an educational program still needs exploration. Probably for some time to come educators will be asking: How rapidly can people be inducted into a new learning experience?

How much information should be taken for granted? What kinds of ideas and facts seem to be most difficult to communicate initially?

Methods for Making Ideas and Experience
Available to the Learning Group

Program planners first face the question of whose ideas and experiences shall be highlighted—a single individual, a group of specialists, the participants themselves, or some combination of these? Once this has been decided, the planner can choose from an ever-expanding array of methods.

In choosing methods, the planner is concerned with the quality of the ideas, the effectiveness of the communication, and the active participation of the learning group.

1. When the experience is centered on a *single person:*

The speech or lecture. This is undoubtedly the most widely-used method of presentation—where the teacher in the classroom or the lecturer in the auditorium organizes, polishes, and presents his material. The effectiveness of this method depends on the speaker's grasp of his subject, his communication skills, as well as his sensitivity and ability to modify the presentation in response to audience reaction.

The speech with audience participation. In recent years, increasing attention has been given to ways of improving communication between speaker and listeners. A common method is the *question and answer period* following a speech. This enables members of the audience to get clarification of the speaker's ideas and also to support or dispute his contentions. A period of this kind is most useful when some procedure is used to ensure adequate coverage of questions in a systematic manner.

Audience participation can also be obtained by using *buzz groups.* Here all members of the audience spend a few minutes in small groups (usually from four to seven persons) to share ideas and formulate a question or comment. This method is most effective when the topic given to the buzz group is clear, and when there is adequate time for group discussion, reporting, and speaker reaction. An extension of this method is the *listening team.* Sections of the audience are asked—before the speaker begins—to listen to the presentation from a specified point of view or with some question in mind. Following the presentation, the listening teams meet briefly to compare notes and then give individual or group reaction.

A modified method of audience participation is the *reaction panel.* Four or five people representing different points of view listen to the speech and raise questions designed to improve communication, particularly by clarifying crucial words and concepts. To be successful, speaker and panel members should meet before the program to agree on objectives and "ground rules."

The interview. This has often been used where the speaker does not have time to tailor his ideas to fit the needs of a particular audience. An interviewer who knows both the interests of the audience and the speaker's experience helps the speaker select and organize material by asking questions. Sometimes more than one interviewer is used.

2. When a learning experience calls for the expression of ideas by *more than one person:*

The symposium. This method is used when two or more speakers present different information or differing points of view on some subject. After a moderator sets the stage, they make individual speeches to the audience. The moderator then summarizes key points and may invite questions from the audience.

The panel discussion. Members of the panel usually present brief statements at the outset and then discuss with one another the points which have been raised. A chairman helps to keep the discussion focused. This method permits both the clarification of ideas and the development of new insights. The audience may or may not become involved in the discussion.

3. Sometimes the experience focuses on the *learners themselves* as a major source of program content. This may occur when specialists in the same profession meet to share ideas on how they handle common problems. It may also be appropriate when the purpose of the program is to increase understanding of the discussion process or the development of relationships within the learning group. Some methods for achieving this objective are:

The problem census. This procedure, ordinarily used at the beginning of a program, consists of asking the learning group to identify and establish priorities for the problems, issues, or questions which require study and analysis. This can be accomplished by having participants write problems on cards, by having them call out problems from the audience, or by having them meet in small groups. These questions or problems then guide the development of the learning experience. This method permits the learner to participate actively from the outset and helps to keep the program content relevant and practical.

The dramatic presentation. Variously called "skits," "role-playing," and "socio-drama," these methods are used to stimulate members of a learning group to contribute ideas through analyzing some situation. The situation is acted out before the entire group with either members of the audience or members of a planning group taking the roles. To accomplish a particular objective, this method may be accompanied with the use of a commentator, an "alter ego," role substitution, interrupted episode, and other devices.

The case study. Developed and popularized in the law and business schools, this method is also being used widely in other settings. Individuals in the learning group read the description of a real or simulated problem situation. Through discussion, they share ideas on the key elements of the problem, principles to be followed in solving it, and actions which they would take if confronted by such a situation. The case study provides an opportunity for each individual to articulate his assumptions, attitudes, and theories, and to compare them with those of others in the group.

Analysis of group experience. During any learning experience, the participants are communicating both thoughts and feelings as they react to each other, to ideas, and to other elements of the learning situation. These reactions are the data which are analyzed to produce insights and learnings. The "unstructured" group—an invention of human relations training laboratories—is designed to bring this kind of learning into sharp focus. Such groups usually have no other task than to concentrate on understanding their own feelings, attitudes, and ways of working together.

4. When a program can make use of such other resources as field trips, reading materials, and films, alone or together with the methods described above to provide a varied and significant educational program:

The field trip. This frequently-used device provides a learner with a direct observational experience. A careful briefing before such a trip and follow-up discussion increase the learning.

Reading materials. Ideas which are captured on the printed page "hold still" for inspection and analysis. Unlike listening to a speech, the learner can control the speed with which the ideas pass in review. He can pause, speculate and then return to the author's train of thought.

Films and TV presentations. Films and TV make it possible to bring the resources of top experts and "master teachers" to almost unlimited numbers of individuals and groups separated by large distances. Creative work by film makers has also demonstrated effective ways of portraying complex concepts. Particularly when combined with discussion, such presentations add drama, timeliness, and realism to an educational experience.

Methods for Bringing Ideas and Experiences Into Focus

An educational program should have unity and integrity to make its fullest impact. While these qualities should be sought throughout the total process of planning objectives and methods, special means have been developed or traditional methods have been remodeled to help the learner more directly to bring ideas into focus.

The steering committee. In programs of some length and complexity, new problems and interests are likely to emerge. The steering committee provides a mechanism for noting these developments and modifying the program in the light of unexpected problems and unforeseen interests. Keeping the learning objectives in mind, the committee may alter the pace, content, or sequence of events to ensure focus, continuity and progress toward the goals.

The thread man function. Often one individual—co-ordinator, master of ceremonies, chairman—personifies the over-all unity and purposefulness of the program. He usually describes the purpose and plan of the program at the outset and thereafter points up the relationship of experiences to each other and to the learning objectives. He may also summarize.

The observer-summarizer function. Because an educational program has many dimensions, it can be observed and analyzed from different points of view—the flow of ideas, the shifting patterns of communication, and the underlying assumptions. By assigning one or more individuals to give special attention to them, these aspects of the total experience can be brought to the learning group's attention, helping to give further perspective and meaning.

Informal "psyche" groups. In some residential conference programs, five or six participants make up a "family" group which meets regularly to share impressions of the day's activities. In programs dealing with attitudinal changes, such groups provide a setting in which the learner can express some of his frustrations and anxieties and can get both understanding and better perspective.

Focusing sessions. Though seldom called by this name, some sessions are designed to have the learning group pause to look at the program to that point—recalling the learning objectives and reviewing how the various elements of the program have contributed to those objectives. The test-review session of a class or the mid-point evaluation of a conference program can serve this function.

Methods for Helping the Learner to Integrate Program Ideas Into His Past Experience

In the effort to translate new knowledge and better theory into improved practice, the following methods are commonly used:

Practice activities. Practice activities under supervision enable the learner to try out new ideas or new skills in a setting where failures will not be harmful, but can be analyzed for increased learning. Some kinds of learning require that practice be the major part of the total experience —public speaking, leadership training, interviewing, playing a musical instrument, and the like.

Simulated field situations. These more complex practice activities are used extensively in some programs. The "in-basket" exercise in executive training is an example. Here the learner is asked to spend a period of time filling the position of an executive who has to make decisions about various letters, memos and messages placed in his "in-basket." He is also asked to explain why he made the decisions as he did—and then compares his decisions with those of his colleagues.

Another example is the organization exercise or the "community role play" in which different factions within a simulated community attempt to solve a complex problem.

Projects and field work. These are more complex practice activities designed to help the learner to assess his abilities and sharpen his skills. Projects are usually done by the learner outside the scheduled program time. Field work involves practice in grappling with real—not simulated—problems under supervision. In both cases, much of the value of the experience depends upon the kind of evaluation, analysis, and generalization which follows the activity.

Learner-centered interviews, discussions, and questionnaires. Since one of the best ways to integrate ideas is to articulate them, some programs provide opportunities for each participant to meet with one or two colleagues to share learnings, impressions, and test ideas. This process enables him to clarify his own thinking about what is most relevant to his needs—and how he can best implement his learnings. The self-analysis questionnaire is designed to accomplish a similar purpose.

Time for reflection. Often the program planner can facilitate the learner's integration of ideas by providing time and encouraging the learner to do reflective thinking.

Creating a Climate Which Facilitates Learning

Adults are not always in a mood to learn. The role of student may be strange and uncomfortable. New information or new concepts may be resisted by someone who has developed habit patterns on the basis of outmoded information and concepts. Preoccupation with personal, family and job concerns may make the adult learner less attentive and receptive.

Adult educators have therefore given increasing attention to the physical, intellectual, and psychological environment in which learning is to occur. Some of the factors which contribute to a desirable climate for learning are:

Acceptance and recognition. When an adult feels that it is necessary to protect his own ego, he is less able to concentrate fully on the learning task and make his contribution. If he feels that his behavior is being judged critically, he will tend to tighten up and resist re-examining his present assumptions or attempting new behavior and new integration of information. Part of the teacher's responsibility is to recognize the learner's maturity and experience by both his general manner and his level of presentation.

Inquiry and experimentation. A learning experience can be viewed as a continual process of inquiry and experimentation. New ideas are sought, examined, tried out, perhaps modified again. The "climate" therefore should be one in which this process is accepted and encouraged. It is created, not so much by the use of particular methods as by the attitudes which planners, teachers, and leaders communicate.

Informality—formality. The degree of appropriate formality or informality will differ among programs. The objective is to help the individual to feel at ease and to emphasize that in this setting he is regarded as a human being who is joining with others in the quest for greater knowledge and understanding.

A "cultural island." Some kinds of learning can best occur in a setting where the learner is completely free from the distractions of everyday work pressures. This is particularly true when the learning content involves the re-examination of attitudes, assumptions, and values. Increasingly, therefore, adult educators are scheduling residential conferences and workshops in isolated settings. In such a "cultural island" environment meal and recreational schedules, as well as dinner conversations and informal "bull sessions," tend to reinforce the learning experience.

STEPS IN DEVELOPING AN ADULT LEARNING EXPERIENCE

The development of a high-quality educational experience requires that the planner systematically analyze the various components of the proposed program and make wise choices from among the alternatives. In choosing the methods and sequence of experiences, the planner might ask himself the following questions: 1) How does each activity contribute to making ideas available, focusing them, and integrating them with previous experiences of the learner? 2) What has been done to ensure understanding and acceptance of the objectives and the methods for reaching them? 3) What has been done to make this experience one in which the learner himself takes increasing responsibility for his own education? 4) Is there sufficient flexibility so that the unpredictable reactions and events can be noted and used to influence the remaining part of the program? 5) What has been done to create a favorable "climate" for learning? 6) What has been done to evaluate the program in light of its stated objectives?

The activities described below may be useful as a checklist of suggestions to consider in the building of an educational experience.

1. *Assess needs and state objectives.* A first step in the development of an educational program is to assess and articulate the needs of the prospective learner. This may be done in several ways: making tentative assumptions about the learner's needs, based on previous experience; conducting a survey, oral or written; involving representatives of the potential learning group as participants in the planning phase of the program; conducting a problem census with the learning group; or a combination of the above.

Once the needs are clearly identified, the objectives should be stated in precise terms.

Establishing the objectives clearly in the minds of both the faculty participants and the learners begins with the initial announcement of the program. All communications should give the learner an accurate picture of what to expect from the experience. An attractive theme is a poor substitute for a clear statement of objectives.

2. *Identify available resources and their limits.* Once the needs are identified and the objectives clearly stated, the planner should systematically list all of the available people and material that can be used to accomplish the objectives. This should normally be done within reasonable limits of time and financial resources. However, occasionally the planner should dream, for every now and then he will be able to go beyond what normally would be expected. The process of identifying resources should include not only the listing, but also a ranking, of the people who can be used, considering their ability to communicate effectively.

The same principle applies to any printed or visual materials that may be used. This does not mean that ideas must be presented in the most elementary language possible, but rather in a way that will stretch the mind of the learner.

The perennial limitations faced by the planner are time, money, and physical facilities. It is up to him to get maximum utilization from all the resources available. He should identify all possible physical facilities, be it a classroom, a home, a conference room, a residential center, a lecture hall, a laboratory, an amphitheater. Before deciding on the pattern, he should experiment with a variety of time-schedules, physical facilities, and groupings of activities to determine if different arrangements can accomplish the objectives better.

Once all the alternatives are clearly identified, the planner must pause and decide whether the needs of the learner can effectively be served within the limits prescribed. He should ask himself:

Will the potential learners commit themselves to the minimum time required to accomplish the objectives?

Are there sufficient financial resources to achieve these objectives?

Will the available physical facilities meet the minimum requirements of the objectives?

If the answer to these questions is "Yes," he can move to the next phase.

3. *Select the sources of ideas.* In making selections of people and materials, it is important to keep in mind the *acceptability* of both the ideas and their sources to the learning group. This is not to suggest that unacceptable ideas should not be presented, but rather that they should be presented in such a way that there is enough time for them to be understood and assimilated, or that a different person is selected to present them. It is not sufficient to assume that factual evidence will be persuasive. In selecting a teacher, a leader, a speaker, it is well to consider not only his reputation in his general field of specialization, but also his areas of current interest.

4. *Develop the general design and select methods to accomplish the objectives.* This step involves planning how the flow of ideas and experiences will be initiated and regulated. Both the design of experiences and the methods should be consistent with the objectives to be accomplished. This involves a clear understanding of both the broad goals and the specific objectives.

5. *Orient leaders and learners to the purpose and plan of the learning program.* Once an educational experience has been properly designed and resources (both human and material) selected, the next step is to make sure that the program leaders understand both their task and how it is related to other program activities. Even where there is a single teacher in a class, he should be aware of the responsibilities of both his students and the administration to accomplish the learning objectives. Where there is more than one individual responsible for teaching, speaking, or conducting a discussion, it is particularly important to have a common understanding of how the program is designed to lead toward its stated objectives, and where, within the design, there is opportunity for the assessment and modification of the design.

6. *Plan for evaluation.* The final phase of the cycle in program-building is to develop a procedure for evaluating the experience for purposes of improving subsequent activities. In the use of evaluation procedures, both the leaders and the learners should understand the purposes and the relevancy of the particular instruments to be used. The collection of data should be consistent with the primary objectives of the educational program and should be kept to the minimum needed. (Specific tools for evaluation are given in Chapter 6.)

CURRENT ISSUES AND CONTROVERSIES ABOUT ADULT EDUCATION METHODS

Because adult educators represent widely different backgrounds and experiences, they naturally develop preferences for different methods, program designs and points of emphasis. Some of the major controversial questions are identified below with a capsule presentation of opposing points of view.

What should be the point of departure for a learning experience—people or subject matter?

> *Position A*—Begin with people where they are and move them toward the goal.
> *Position B*—There is a body of knowledge to be learned, and this knowledge should dictate the methods and approach.

Are the major goals in adult education process-centered or information-centered?

> *Position A*—Our major goal is to develop better-informed adults; methods should be used which further this objective.
> *Position B*—Since everyone can't learn everything, methods should be used which help people to understand the processes which are involved in solving any problem.

Is there a single best method for achieving a learning goal, or should adult educators always use several methods?

> Position A—For the goals of this program and within the physical and financial limitations, the "X" method is best. (This may be the Socratic discussion method in the case of studying the Great Books, the lecture method in the case of an American history class, etc.)
>
> Position B—Because of differing experiences and learning patterns of the adults in almost every situation, it is essential to use a variety of methods to ensure that most of the participants will move toward the learning objectives.

To what extent should the responsibility for developing an educational program be shared by the learner, teacher and program planner?

> Position A—The adult learner should be involved to the fullest possible extent in planning the program in order to ensure its meeting his needs.
>
> Position B—The teachers and program planners must plan the program so that experiences will be provided which make learners aware of "unfelt needs" and move more directly toward the learning objectives.

How fully scheduled should a program be?

> Position A—Time is limited, and a great deal of material must be covered; therefore, we should make the learners work hard all the time to accomplish the goal.
>
> Position B—Adults can absorb only a limited amount of material in a given period of time; therefore learning experiences should be spaced with adequate time for reflection and integration.

What constitutes effective and meaningful participation by the learner?

> Position A—The learner is participating most meaningfully when he is articulating his ideas—i.e., participating in the discussion.
>
> Position B—The learner can participate meaningfully by listening to someone who knows his subject matter.

CONCLUSION

The questions and their differing answers point up the continuing need for experimentation and research so that adult educators make crucial decisions on the basis of dependable evidence, rather than on intuition and limited experience.

This quest becomes more urgent as the body of knowledge in every field grows and as the number of education-seeking adults increases. New technical media stand ready to be used in creative ways—making both outstanding experts and significant events immediately available to mass audiences in far places. At the same time, growing evidence supports the view that the learner must participate in more than a viewing-listening experience. Perhaps the great adult education challenge of the near future lies in developing and testing new patterns which combine individual and small group activities with the experience of sitting at the feet (electronically) of the great teachers and using as "case material" the significant discoveries and problems of our time.

Selected References

Bergevin, Paul and Morris, Dwight. *Group Processes for Adult Education.* Community Services in Adult Education, 1804 E. 10 St., Bloomington,

Indiana. Advantages and disadvantages of forums, panels, symposiums and other procedures for large meetings; diagrams show stage arrangements for each procedure.

Brunner, Edmund de S., and others. *An Overview of Adult Education Research.* Chicago: Adult Education Association, 1959.

Houle, Cyril O. "The Use of Print in Adult Educational Agencies," *Adult Reading.* Fifty-fifth Yearbook, Part II, National Society for the Study of Education. Chicago: University of Chicago Press, 1956, p. 157-87. Special attention to methods and materials for "coordinated courses" such as Great Books discussion groups, Liberal Arts discussion groups, etc.

Kelley, Earl J. *The Workshop Way of Learning.* New York: Harper, 1951. The philosophy as well as the methodology of conducting educational workshops.

Leadership Library. New York: Association Press. How to conduct workshops, develop leaders, work with boards and committees, etc.

Leadership Pamphlets. Chicago: Adult Education Assn. of USA. Collected articles from *Adult Leadership* on leading discussion, planning programs, supervising, teaching adults, working with volunteers, etc.

Lippitt, Ronald and others. *The Dynamics of Planned Change.* Harcourt, Brace and Co., 1958. Methods for stimulating change in individuals, groups, organizations and communities.

Liveright, A. A. *Strategies of Leadership in Conducting Adult Education Programs.* New York: Harper, 1959. Survey of methods used in several programs of informal adult education.

Mann, Arthur H. *Bridging the Gap.* Adult Education Division, Department of Public Instruction, Honolulu, Hawaii. This is an excellent brief handbook for teachers of adults.

Miles, Matthew B. *Learning to Work in Groups.* New York: Teachers College, Columbia University, 1959. Describes how a small group, through training, can become a more effective working unit.

The Public School Adult Educator. National Association of Public School Adult Educators. This periodical, issued bi-monthly, has helpful sections on how to teach adults.

UNESCO. *Adult Education Groups and Audio-Visual Techniques.* Reports and Papers on Mass Communication No. 25. Paris: UNESCO, 1958.

Verner, Coolie. "Instructional Methods for Adult Education," *Review of Educational Research* 29, No. 3: 262-68, June, 1959. Review of the research on this topic, with a useful bibliography. Includes attention to bulletins, demonstrations, exhibits, mass media, and meetings.

Whipple, James B. *Especially for Adults.* Notes and Essays on Education for Adults, No. 19. Center for the Study of Liberal Education for Adults, 4819 Greenwood Ave., Chicago 15, Illinois, October, 1957. 70 p. Why and how courses planned for adults should differ from courses planned for youth.

CHAPTER 8

MATERIALS FOR ADULT EDUCATION

GLADYS A. WIGGIN
Professor of Education
University of Maryland

The materials of adult education may be described as aids to learning. They include such printed works as books, pamphlets, and periodicals; and such audio-visual equipment as films, filmstrips, slides, maps, charts, records, and television programs. Ralph C. Preston provides a list of the functions of reading in an age of mass communication which can be so reworded as to apply to all materials and to argue for their proper distribution in adult education enterprises: (a) to provide a "balance in the content of vicarious experience"; (b) to encourage such variety of informational media that a necessary check on authenticity will be provided; (c) "to foster substantial human values" through utilization of all sensory media by which the cultural heritage can be communicated; and (d) "to promote mental and spiritual health" through encouraging the utilization of media for use in public and private hours (3).*

HISTORICAL DEVELOPMENT

There is a paucity of accurate historical data on adult education materials per se. In their absence, the emergence of new and different materials in succeeding decades can be charged to the handy *socioeconomic forces* which are so frequently used to explain the still unexplored. More specifically, such factors as level of literacy and education of the adult population, numbers and kinds of foreign-born, level of development of communication media, and social or economic crises are some of the conditions under which materials designed to educate may emerge.

The increasing number of literate adults in nineteenth century Amer-

*References in this chapter are numbered according to their order in the "Selected Readings" at the end of the chapter.

ica was the stimulus for the development of the penny press, and incidentally, yellow journalism. A purely local crisis, the appalling mine disasters in the 1880's, gave rise to another kind of literature. Thomas J. Foster, proprietor and editor of a newspaper in Shenandoah, attributed the mine difficulties to the ignorance of employers and employees alike. From his vantage point in the publishing business, Foster used his newspapers for exchange of information on mining, and circulated foreign books on preventive measures. The next step was the development of a course covering all aspects of mining. From this small beginning and with interest on the part of thousands not only in mining but in a number of other subjects, there eventually developed the International Correspondence Schools which in a sense deal in nothing but adult education materials (4).

Toward the last of the nineteenth and the beginning of the twentieth centuries, it appeared that this experiment in democracy might be the victim of the social sores spawned by an industrial and a technical development which was outstripping social and political skills needed to cope with it. The robber barons who cornered the gold market and despoiled natural resources, corruption in government, exploitation of the immigrants, the rise of slums, and the consequent increase of both poverty and crime will recall this painful period in American history. In response to these social ills, there came to be found among the sentimental novels and tales of adventure, a few publications designed to educate the public on specific issues. Some readers may recall, for instance, Jacob Riis' *How the Other Half Lives* which was published in 1890. Books on bimetallism and the gold standard (remember the Cross of Gold?) were popular in 1896. Frank Norris' tale of big business and finance, *The Pit,* was third in a list of nonfiction best sellers in 1903; and Mary Antin's *The Promised Land* was first in 1912 (2).

World War I provided the setting for two kinds of adult education literature. The immediate fact of the war gave rise to the Committee on Public Information, which under the chairmanship of George Creel sold the war to American adults partly through a series of specially prepared pamphlets and bulletins. A most pressing and overriding problem, securing the loyalty (or so it was assumed) of the immigrants who had flooded these shores from 1870 to 1920, gave rise to a second kind of literature. For the most part, these millions were peasants who had come from the most rural and unmechanized farms of Europe into the most urban and technologically oriented of American cities. Their problem was that of bridging the gulf between unlike cultures and the chasm of several centuries which lay between the level of their own technical skills and those which Americans used. Many of these people were victimized by overzealous Americanizers. The movement for their assimilation was finally brought under the control of humane procedures of public school and social work agencies which in turn gave rise to one of the more important materials movements in adult education. Aided by the federal government and patriotic agencies, public schools finally wrought out in the period from 1918 through the 1930's an Americanization literature designed particularly for a foreign-speaking and largely illiterate population.

The problem of a literature for an illiterate or a semiliterate adult population has never quite disappeared; but the nature of the clients has changed. By 1940 the median age of the foreign born as reported in the United States census was 51 years. This old population is fast receding in prominence as clients for a special literature, and the refugees who have come to this country in recent years are an educated group for whom there might be improved oral instruction rather than special kinds of materials. At the same time as the foregn-born are becoming less of an adult education problem, however, a group of native Americans is looming large in adult education concerns. The armed forces' rejections for mental deficiency, which as Ginzberg and Bray (1) indicate are a measure of educational deprivation, have highlighted the problem of the millions of functional illiterates. During World War II "The Tales of Private Pete" were developed for use in teaching illiterate inductees to read. The crisis of the war in a society which has not favored a large standing army also incidentally stimulated the development of technical manuals and experimentation in audio-visual aids designed for rapid transformation of a generally-educated to a specially-educated population needed for all branches of the armed services.

In the face of functional illiteracy and the cold war, the remedial function of adult education must continue to engage the attention of adult educators. Confronted with the task of helping adults to tackle a host of socio-economic problems, educators may find that audio-visual rather than simplified reading materials are the more imaginative answer to the materials problem. The long-term solution for remedial education is, of course, a concerted drive to improve and extend education for children and youth.

The repercussions of World War II have resounded in other adult education fields. In a lighter vein, the war-baby crop is reflected in the fact that in the period from 1895 to 1955, the second best seller was Benjamin Spock's 1946 book, *The Common Sense Book of Baby and Child Care* which up to 1955 had sold 7,850,000 copies (2). More seriously, the shock of World War II convinced many Americans that they lived not on a self-contained and barricaded continent, but in a complex of confusing and competing national states; and Sputnik has but reinforced this sentiment. In response to this new outlook, Americans have increased their interest in current affairs, necessitating the development of new materials on current problems and a retooling of such mass media as television. Accelerated technical development may well have the concomitant effects of stimulating a new technical literature and improved visual aids designed for rapid induction of workers into new jobs, and a higher occupational mobility which will in turn require increased output of training aids.

The urgency of the world situation which requires that every American operate at his maximum capacity in all his social and economic tasks would dictate a sharp increase in quality and quantity of adult educational materials. Whether production and demand will equal need is an open question.

SUMMARY OF CURRENT THOUGHT AND PRACTICE

Making due allowance for the lack of reliable information, it can be tentatively proposed that there appear to be four major issues respecting materials. It is quite likely that all of these may be different facets of a single problem as yet unidentified.

The first of these asks the question as to whether adult educators shall accept the materials, particularly reading materials, already at hand, or whether they shall rewrite or develop new material for particular adult groups. The second position has been taken by the Cooperative Extension Service, which provides consultation to state and local agencies in improving the readability of materials particularly for the farm population.

The second issue centers around the question as to whether the educator shall seek materials appropriate to the problems facing the adults with whom he works or whether a group of materials shall be used as the focal point for stimulating inquiry into problems. It will be readily recognized that the Great Books program uses the second approach.

The third issue is addressed to the question of whether the educator shall seek a representative sampling of opinion on public or special issues, or whether he shall use literature with a built-in point of view. The latter is designed to further a point of view or statement of principles or practices of a specific organization.

A fourth desideratum is whether educators shall seek the fuller and more effective utilization of such tried and true materials as the printed word, or whether they shall expend their energies on experimenting with the new media for reaching mass audiences. To support those holding to the former view are the increasing number and variety of paperbacks, offering to adult audiences a fare varying from the classics by whatever definition one cares to use, to how-to-do-it manuals and the lighter sensational novels. To comfort those who believe Americans do not have time nor human resources enough to meet both the impending college bulge and adult education pressures stimulated by the cold war, several universities as well as the armed services and commercial concerns have been experimenting with education via television.

Underlying the above issues—and not as clearly recognized as an issue

—is whether adult educators shall cater to adults already enrolled in their enterprises, or whether they shall develop materials for a group they hope to lure into their programs. Whether it is the finding of a local survey of forum audiences or of a national survey of adult education enrollees, the evidence shows fairly consistently that adult education students are a select group. Except for the illiterates who make their appearance in adult evening schools and armed services programs, those who participate most actively in technical vocational programs, parent education, or current problems and great books programs, are men and women who are a considerable cut above the average American in educational background. The handy grapevine provides the intelligence that some participants in packaged adult education programs have been quite put out with the patronizing and childish presentations of materials. Their largely unrecorded complaints highlight the fact that adult educators have not resolved and perhaps do not recognize the problem of the nature of the group for whom they are actually preparing materials.

SOURCES OF MATERIALS

Although materials especially prepared for adult study groups are relatively limited, sources are legion. In view of the latter, the discussion to follow and the bibliography of sources will be limited to listings and indexes of free or inexpensive materials and to a few developed in recent years for the liberal or political education of adults. Even with these limitations, the bibliography is only suggestive and undoubtedly subject to glaring omissions. It is hoped that it will be suggestive enough to point educators and adult students in the direction of wider exploration of the vast number of indexes and reference works to be found in most libraries.

First Steps

An adult educator in search of materials can do no better than to canvass local and state agencies for assistance. The first stop should be at the local public library. A request for help from this traditional service agency for adult education, in selecting and securing materials, will serve two purposes. First, it may yield immediate help to the adult group. Second, if resources are inadequate as they are in most areas outside of the big cities, the request will provide grist to the mill of the librarian seeking additional funds. There is nothing so impressive to legislators as the complaints of outraged citizens who cannot, for budgetary reasons, secure adequate services from their public agencies.

Next stops might well be the state university (or local private or public college) and the local and state public school systems. A note or call to the director of general university or agricultural extension of the state university may secure assistance in selecting the expert on the faculty who can suggest appropriate materials. Communication with the central office of either the local or state boards of education may yield help from a designated staff person. Adult education services of state departments of education are summarized in a recent bulletin (38) along with a listing of chief state personnel concerned with adult education.

Printed Materials

Those invaluable modern aids to the pocketbook as well as learning, the paperbacks, are indexed in a biannual publication (27). The number of profit and nonprofit agencies which publish these materials, will be a pleasant surprise to the person who is used to seeing the works of only a limited number of publishers on the local drugstore stand. This author and title index, with selective subject guide, lists some "6,000 inexpensive and original editions." The complementary Vertical File Index (41) lists some 3,800 free or inexpensive pamphlets in a subject and title index. The listing is selective and is designed to be of interest to librarians. Descriptive notes are included when titles are not explanatory.

The United States government is a source of printed materials which can be tapped through the regular *Monthly Catalog* (23). However, the largest publishing house in the world, the United States Government Printing Office, issues such a volume of material that the bewildered adult educator needs some guide lines. The latter are provided through such aids as Leidy's guide (21). The educator can also ask to have his name put on a mailing list for regular receipt of any one of a number of special subject price lists some of which are listed in the bibliography (36). Some government agencies publish separate lists of their own materials, and these lists also will be of help because they are limited in scope. Such a list is that of the United States Department of Agriculture (35) which publishes materials largely for farmers and homemakers.

Adults engaged in study of international affairs or problem of foreign nations will want to look at the index to the publications of the United Nations and its specialized agencies (30), and the catalog of publications for the first ten years of the United Nations (29). The index is difficult to use, and the help of a librarian should be secured in using it and finding simpler listings of pertinent subject materials. An example of the latter is the catalog of the United Nations Educational, Scientific, and Cultural Organization (31). This organization, among other things, publishes material in the fields of the arts, communications, the social sciences, travel, trade, and scientific and technical areas. Some free materials can be secured through the United Nations information centers (32, 33). Others can be purchased from the designated sales agency in the United States (20). Some countries, such as England (7), maintain information centers which will supply some free materials. For materials on other countries, designed often for American audiences, one might try the appropriate embassy in Washington. Both the embassies and the information services are often willing to supply materials free of charge. Materials published by any nation for foreign consumption may well have a built-in national bias; and, therefore, adults will be well advised to seek additional materials through the regular periodical and book indexes or other sources noted above. A few such pamphlets are available in the headline series and discussion aids produced by the Foreign Policy Association (15).

The American Library Association has a listing (5) of its own publications which are useful primarily to librarians. Occasionally there will be an item such as *Books for Adult Beginners* (42) which has wide usefulness. Wallace "lists, annotates and grades by reading difficulty over 500 books which have been tested by actual use" for native or foreign-born adults "who read English with difficulty or not at all." Included in this publication, also, are lists of texts and workbooks, and of books on adult education for the librarian or teacher.

Materials on a number of topics in the arts, humanities, and social sciences which have been developed solely for adult discussion groups, are available from the Center for the Study of Liberal Education for Adults (8) and the Fund for Adult Education (16). Readings for eight years of study and discussion along with leaders' guides and readers' aids, can be purchased from the Great Books Foundation (18).

Correspondence courses might be called education by materials. Three organizations which can direct adults to reliable institutions offering such courses are the United States Armed Forces Institute (34), which makes available materials for the personnel in the armed services only; the National University Extension Association (25), which publishes a list of member agencies having such courses; and the National Home Study Council (24), which is the only nationally recognized organization accrediting private home study institutions.

Audio-Visual Materials

There are several guides to free or inexpensive films, including the *Educational Film Guide* (10), which lists 6,326 16mm films alphabetically and by subject and gives a directory of main sources; the *Educators Guide to Free Films* (11) issued annually and giving subject and title index, film lists, and sources; *Films for Classroom Use* (13) listing selected motion picture productions of eight commercial cinema producers; and a guide to United States government films (39) available from all federal agencies for public educational use. The latter indexes 4,500 films and filmstrips by title and subject, and gives information on distribution centers and loan, rental, and purchase regulations. The United States Office of Education has also prepared a directory of 3,300 16mm film libraries (40), through which one can locate libraries closest to him. The *Educators Guide to Free Tapes, Scripts, and Transactions* (12) and the *Filmstrip Guide* (14), which indexes and carries descriptions of 5,882 35mm filmstrips, are handy tools for locating other visual aids. The catalogs of General Motors (17) and New York University (26) illustrate the kinds of film listings which can be secured from individual commercial or educational agencies.

How to use audio-visual materials as well as how to service and where to purchase equipment are always burning questions for adult leaders. Regular texts such as those by Haas (19) and Sands (28) will give aid in use of materials. The United States International Cooperation Administration has published a manual (37) designed to answer questions about agricultural communications. This manual contains a bibliography which includes how-to-use and how-to-construct bibliographies. Mannino has published a manual (22) on projecting and servicing visual aids equipment. The Dent handbook of information for those using audio-visual material (9) is considered a standard reference. Other aids can be found in texts previously cited, many of which also carry commercial source lists of equipment. Illustrative are lists in Wittich (43) and Haas (19). For the person who wishes to go further into the field of audio-visual material, there is a journal (6) carrying articles, notice of new films, research abstracts, and notice of current developments as well as other items.

This hasty foray into the exciting world of materials may indicate the riches to be found by the persistent adult searcher after information.

Selected Readings

A. TEXT REFERENCES

1. Ginzberg, Eli, and Bray, Douglas W. *The Uneducated.* New York: Columbia University Press, 1953.
2. Hackett, Alice Payne. *60 Years of Best Sellers 1895-1955.* New York: R. R. Bowker Company, 1956.
3. National Society for the Study of Education. *Adult Reading.* 55th Yearbook, Part II. Chicago: University of Chicago Press, 1956.
4. Noffsinger, John S. *Correspondence Schools, Lyceums, Chautauquas.* New York: The Macmillan Company, 1926.

B. SOURCES OF MATERIALS

5. American Library Association. *Books and Pamphlets.* Chicago: American Library Association.
6. *Audio-Visual Communication Review,* quarterly journal published by Department of Audio-Visual Instruction. Washington: National Education Association.
7. British Information Services, National Press Building, Washington, D. C.

8. Center for the Study of Liberal Education for Adults, 4819 South Greenwood Avenue, Chicago 15, Ill. *Discussion guides.*

9. Dent, Ellsworth C. *The Audio-Visual Handbook.* Society for Visual Education, Inc., 100 East Ohio Street, Chicago 11, Ill., 1949.

10. *Education Film Guide* 1954-1958. New York: H. W. Wilson Co., 1958.

11. *Educators Guide to Free Films.* Issued each year. Educators Progress Service, Randolph, Wis.; latest, 1958.

12. *Educators Guide to Free Tapes, Scripts, and Transactions.* Fifth edition. Educators Progress Service, Randolph, Wis., 1959.

13. *Films for Classroom Use.* Teaching Film Custodians, Inc., 25 West 43rd Street, New York, April, 1952.

14. *Filmstrip Guide.* Third edition. New York: H. W. Wilson Co., 1954.

15. Foreign Policy Association, 345 East 46th Street, New York 17, N. Y.:
    Headline Series
    Discussion Aids
    Selected Film Lists.

16. Fund for Adult Education, 200 Bloomingdale Road, White Plains, N. Y.
    Study-Discussion Programs:
    Aging in the Modern World
    Looking at Modern Painting
    Great Issues in American Politics
    Ways of Mankind
    The Power to Govern
    Discovering Modern Poetry
    Economic Reasoning
    An Introduction to the Humanities
    Transition and Tension in Southeast Asia
    Jefferson and Our Times
    Parenthood in a Free Nation
    Ways to Justice

17. *General Motors Motion Picture Catalog 1959-1960.* Nineteenth edition. General Motors Corporation, General Motors Building, Detroit 2, Mich.

18. Great Books Foundation, 37 South Wabash Avenue, Chicago 3, Illinois.
    Readings
    Guide for Leaders
    Readers Aids.

19. Haas, Kenneth B., and Packer, Harry Q. *Preparation and Use of Audio-Visual Aids.* New York: Prentice-Hall, Inc., 1950.

20. International Documents Service, Columbia University Press, 2960 Broadway, New York 27, N. Y.

21. Leidy, W. Philip. *A Popular Guide to Government Publications.* New York: Columbia University Press, 1953.

22. Mannino, Philip. *ABC's of Visual Aids* and Projectionists Manual. Revised edition. M. O. Publishers, Box 406, State College, Pa., 1954.

23. *Monthly Catalog of United States Government Publications.* Washington: Government Printing Office.

24. National Home Study Council, 800 18th St., N.W., Washington 5, D. C.

25. National University Extension Association, 1785 Massachusetts Avenue, Washington, D. C.

26. *New York University Film Library Sales Catalogue.* New York University Film Library, 26 Washington Place, New York 3, N. Y.
27. *Paperbound Books in Print.* R. R. Bowker Company, 62 W. 45th Street, New York 36, N. Y.
28. Sands, Lester B. *Audio-Visual Procedures in Teaching.* New York: The Ronald Press, 1956.
29. United Nations, Department of Public Information. *Ten Years of United Nations Publications 1945 to 1955.* A complete catalogue. United Nations, 1955.
30. *United Nations Documents Index.*
31. United Nations Educational, Scientific and Cultural Organization. *Publications General Catalogue, 1954.*
32. United Nations Information Centre, 1908 Q Northwest, Washington, D. C.
33. United Nations Office of Public Information, United Nations, N. Y.
34. United States Armed Forces Institute. *Correspondence Courses* offered by the Colleges and Universities through the United States Armed Forces Institute. USAFI, Washington 25, D. C., December 19, 1958.
35. United States Department of Agriculture. *List of Available Publications.* List No. 11. Washington: Government Printing Office, Revised February, 1958.
36. United States Government Printing Office, Superintendent of Documents, Washington 25, D. C. *Price Lists of Government Publications:*

11.	Home Economics
33.	Labor
35.	National Parks
50.	American History
51.	Health and Hygiene
67.	Immigration and Naturalization
71.	Children's Bureau
72.	Homes
78.	Industrial Workers
81.	Posters and Charts
82.	Radio

37. United States International Cooperation Administration. *Using Visuals in Agricultural Extension Programs.*
38. United States Office of Education. *Adult Education Services* of State Departments of Education. Misc. No. 31. Washington: Government Printing Office, 1959.
39. United States Office of Education. *U. S. Government Films* for Public Educational Use. Bulletin 1955, No. 1. Washington: Government Printing Office, 1958.
40. United States Office of Education. *A Directory of 3,300 16mm Film Libraries.* Bulletin 1956, No. 12. Washington: Government Printing Office, 1956.
41. *Vertical File Index.* The H. W. Wilson Company, 950 University Avenue, New York 52, N. Y.
42. Wallace, Viola. *Books for Adult Beginners.* Third edition. Chicago: American Library Association, 1954.
43. Wittich, Walter Arno, and Schuller, Charles Francis. *Audio-Visual Materials* Their Nature and Use. Second edition. New York: Harper & Brothers, 1957.

CHAPTER 9

RESEARCH IN ADULT EDUCATION

BURTON W. KREITLOW
Professor of Education and
Agriculture and Extension Education
University of Wisconsin

KINDS OF RESEARCH IN ADULT EDUCATION

In 1942 Kurt Lewin reported on the results of a study designed to determine whether food habits could be changed more effectively by the lecture or the discussion method. The problem was to change food habits in the direction of the less popular, more easily obtainable and nutritious foods, and was related to the early World War II war efforts. In this group he used adult women from high-, medium-, and low-income levels. In each income level group, half of the women were given a half-hour lecture by a nutritionist and the lecture was followed by a 15-minute question period. The other half of the women were involved in 45 minutes of group discussion with the nutritionist present as a resource person. In this particular experiment Lewin reported that about ten times as many women from discussion groups tried the recommended foods as did those from the lecture groups.[1] A careful review of the Lewin reports shows that it is a controlled experiment in adult education of a kind that meets the research criteria in any discipline.

In 1956 Wilkening reported on the results of a carefully designed study identifying the adult farmer's perception of the sources of information used in making agricultural decisions. He reported that both form and content are associated with the nature of the communicating agent as a social system with its set of functions, norms, and operational features.[2]

In 1953 the report by Riesman and his colleagues on the impact of an urbanized society upon the American character was made readily available.[3] In the same year Owens reported in *Genetic Psychology Monographs* that adults retested thirty years after taking the Army Alpha Intelligence Test showed gains in both total score and in seven of the eight subtests. The differences were particularly important where the nature of items were vocabulary, disarranged sentences, common sense analogies, and general information.[4]

Although the above four studies and many others reported by sociologists and psychologists are accomplished in corollary disciplines, they are nonetheless research in adult education, and they meet the criteria of research normally accepted by sociologists and psychologists.

In 1958 the first major effort to obtain quantitative data on participation in formal classes was reported. This report was on the collaboration between the U. S. Office of Education and the Bureau of Census in a sample survey of the participation of adults in group or class activity.[5] This was the first real step away from the traditional guesswork on participation in adult education. Summaries of participation in public school adult education and in the Cooperative Extension Service appear annually in reports of the U. S. Office of Education and the United States Department of Agriculture. In the journal, *Adult Education*, Wheeler and Anderson reported on the increase in reading speed of the members in an adult class.[6] Reports like the above are often considered to be research in adult education. Certainly census reports relating to adults, participation of adults in organizations and agencies, and checking on the reading speed of adult classes are related to adult education. There is considerable doubt, however, whether or not studies such as these are based upon a sufficiently standardized scientific procedure to qualify them to be called research.

The seven studies identified above include an experiment by Lewin which would qualify for research in any discipline, reports by two sociologists and a psychologist which meet the scientific standards of research in sociology and psychology and which are useful in adult education, and three reports in adult education which are very useful but leave some doubt as to whether they meet the criterion of research. Brunner writes in his *Overview of Adult Education Research* that "Any examination of research in adult education reveals a rather chaotic situation. A few pertinent areas, such as adult learning, have been explored far more thoroughly than others. Some have received almost no research attention. Where any considerable body of effective research is available, other than in the field of methods, typically it has been conducted not by adult educators but by social scientists who had available a considerable body of theory, generalizations and methodologies developed by their discipline, which could be applied to the problems of adult education. Thus, the movement has benefited much from the work of psychologists and to a considerable but lesser extent from that of social psychologists and sociologists."[7]

There is considerable evidence that the quantity of research in adult education has increased markedly in the several years preceding publication of this *Handbook*. There is perhaps no two-year period in which more adult education research has been reported than between 1958 and 1960. The Brunner "Overview" was a major milestone. The June, 1959, issue of *The Review of Educational Research* provided a much more optimistic outlook on research in adult education than did similar reviews in 1953 and 1950. *The Encyclopedia of Educational Research* published in January, 1960, included very important summaries of research in general adult education and in adult education through university and co-operative extension services. In addition, the summer issues of *Adult Education* have for six years carried research reviews which show a year-by-year improvement in the level of research competency.

The studies included in these reviews of research go all the way from controlled experimentation—of which there are indeed few—through comparative analysis to descriptions of single programs. In an area of developing research such as adult education, one should perhaps not be too critical of descriptions of single programs. One can, however, object to descriptions of single programs where they are descriptions only and where no attempt is made to identify implications of findings for program improvement or to provide hypotheses which can be tested in other settings.

There is a place for description, for comparative analysis, and for controlled experimentation in adult education. Adult educators need to describe programs to get a general picture of what is going on in the field. These data about individual programs and the programs of agencies and organizations need to be ordered and compared, and from these and other sources hypotheses need to be established and designs developed so that these hypotheses can be tested experimentally. At this point in its development, adult education research cannot be compared with research in physics or even sociology. At the same time, unless the improvement of research continues as it has in the past decade, too long a time may ensue before we know some of the answers that administrators of adult programs, teachers in adult programs, and the citizens who support the programs, need to know.

THE ADULT EDUCATOR'S CONCERN FOR RESEARCH

The increase in the amount of research and the improvement in the quality of research over the last decade supports the concern of the educator with getting answers to questions which can be resolved through research. But often the emphasis of the educator of adults is on operation, and many times his reaction to research is somewhat naive. Often his evaluations are based upon numbers of participants only, and he tends to rate the relative effectiveness of the program by saying, "It works, doesn't it?" Actually the question is not whether it works, but whether it works better than something else, and whether it is the most effective means of accomplishing the objective set. An equally useful question is, does it also broaden the horizon of both the adult and adult educator so that new and more significant objectives can be identified and pursued?

The voluntary nature of the program is an important element in determining the research attitude of the profession. Because the adult educator is dealing with volunteers, there is a normal tendency to use numbers as the sole basis of evaluation. Many who believe their program effective because they have participants, live with a false security. Others who are competing in the adult education market place and who find that they have small numbers of participants in their program, live with a false insecurity. Thus, to provide a base upon which to make judgments in a voluntary program, research is probably even more necessary than it is in the compulsory level of public school education or in educational programs with youth where the social pressures make it compulsory.

WHERE RESEARCH IS BEING ACCOMPLISHED

National and state headquarters of adult education agencies are accomplishing some research, although their major emphasis seems to be the organization and ordering of existing data, such as the U. S. Office of Education's report on the census of adult participation and its summaries of state programs. Another example is the reports of adult education divisions in various states, such as the Florida State Board of Education reports on the numbers of teachers, classes, and participants. These data provide a basis for more rigorous research and exploration. The Cooperative Extension Service has summarized data from the fifty states and put it into usable descriptive form, and has begun making certain comparative analyses of data. Reports by Crile, Wilson, and Gallup take special aspects of the work of the Cooperative Extension Service and summarize research from the various states and from the federal office.[8] The review of research relating to method compiled by Wilson and Gallup goes well beyond the mere ordering of data.[9]

College and university adult education programs have just begun to research some of the problems facing them. The Center for the Study of Liberal Education for Adults, working closely with these groups, plays a useful role in summarizing and reporting studies. Historical research and descriptions of the development of these programs have been accomplished by such researchers and historians as Grattan, Hart, Rosentreter, and Stockton. The observer of research in adult education might well ask why research in college and university programs has not taken the leadership in the research responsibility in adult education. The question perhaps can be answered with the same logic with which one could answer the same question about other adult education institutions. University extension and college evening programs have been so concerned with the day-to-day and night-to-night operation, and have been so handicapped by the administrative requirements that their programs be self-supporting that they have not taken the time or money to answer basic questions related to their work.

The research accomplished in subject-matter departments in universities has provided some of the more basic information needed in the development of the field. The studies coming out of departments of sociology, psychology, communications, and education often go well beyond description and comparative analysis, and into the at least beginnings of experimentation with adults. The writings of Beal, Rogers, and Bohlen in Iowa showing how theoretical models are tested relating to the adoption of new practices, have given new insight into programs of Cooperative Extension as well as useful concepts to all areas of adult education.[10] The community development film study at the University of Wisconsin shattered some sacred cows relating to the use of films by experts.[11]

The expanding graduate training programs in adult education will provide, in addition to a more highly trained adult educator, the necessary manpower to accomplish more research. Although most of the studies in Master's or Doctor's degree programs are somewhat limited, there is a tendency in these programs as they mature in any institution to move from descriptive studies to the resolution of hypotheses and finally to experimental programs and longitudinal studies carried on by permanent staff of the institution. It is in these programs that some graduate students will select special segments for their own investigation. Summaries of the research from the institutions now providing graduate training in adult education will undoubtedly increase in the next decade.

Some of the best stimulation for research—and indeed research itself—is being accomplished by special organizations and foundations. The Center for the Study of Liberal Education for Adults provides copies of important research documents to professional adult educators. It organizes and develops bibliographies of research, reviews important research documents for university extension and evening colleges, identifies areas of needed research, and has staff members continually seeking ways in which they can help research projects in organizations and institutions. Important contributions have been made by the Fund for Adult Education—both by grants to other institutions and by the publication of documents stimulating research—and by the Kellogg Foundation, with its special grants for conference centers and institutional training programs. The Adult Education Association of the U.S.A. has added to the research being done both through special studies and self surveys. A rising volume of research findings with special relevance to adult learning in groups, leadership development, and community change, has been flowing from the research centers in group dynamics which have been established in about a dozen universities. Both the military services and industry have supported much of this research while carrying on important research of their own.

AREAS OF RESEARCH KNOWLEDGE

A review of the research accomplished in adult education as it appears in the documents during the past decade indicates what adult education researchers have considered the areas in which research knowledge is necessary. Outside the much-criticized "counting" studies, the focus has been on the adult and on learning, exploring such questions as: Who is the adult taking part in adult education? What are his characteristics? What changes take place in the speed with which the adult accomplishes tasks as he ages? What changes occur in his physical capacities—to see, to hear, and to participate actively? What is the nature of the emotional development of the adult as it relates to his developmental needs? The psychological area has also been researched heavily in the past decade, with special concern for learning curves and whether or not the power of adult learning actually holds steady or declines. The motivations of adults and their attitudes and interests are just beginning to be identified in such a way that the professional worker can see order coming out of the reports being presented.

A description of the adult as he relates to the changing nature of our society is developed more from the work of the sociologists describing society than the work of the educators or psychologists describing the adult's adjustment to that society. Yet the sociological research in this area has great value for the adult educator. A perusal of the June, 1959, issue of *The Review of Educational Research* shows that research on organization and administration is indeed limited and is making a good start in only one or two of the agencies of adult education. Yet considerable research on organization and administration within the field of political science, public administration, and public school administration provides a useful frame of reference for the adult educator.

Finally, the area of methods and techniques of teaching adults has received some research attention. But at the moment we are learning more from studies related to adult education coming from sociology and from psychology than we are from studies from within adult education itself. Although these studies are most helpful, the important questions can probably be better resolved by research organized, administered, and conducted by those who understand the nature of adult education.

STATUS OF ADULT EDUCATION RESEARCH

Much of what has been said identifies by inference the status of research in adult education. It is not at a high level, either in amount or quality.

It moves all the way from areas in which recent research both in amount and quality is encouraging to areas in which both the amount and the quality are practically nil. For example, the amount and quality of research in the psychology of learning and the ability of adults to learn are encouraging. Yet there is practically nothing in these and other areas that are longitudinal and experimental in nature.

No body of systematic research exists in the area of methods used in adult education. The U.S.D.A. has provided general data on methods coming from the reports of extension agents and attempts have been made to classify methods according to use. Cartwright and Zander attempted to integrate theory and empirical findings in the area of group dynamics.[12] Gibb summarized research on learning in the adult group and although he noted an increasing interest in research to determine conditions under which learning may become more effective, he cautioned that most of these studies used young people rather than adults as subjects.[13] Experimentation with methods has been limited even where it would be most appropriate.

We note in a number of researches related to method that the emphasis is placed on the opinion, feeling, and attitude of the learner rather than on whether or not learning takes place.

The last two decades of adult education research might be identified as "the age of description." One should not be too pessimistic about what the age of description has done for the future outlook in adult education research. It has provided an important basis for further study. For example in the Cooperative Extension Service, where research appears to be more prevalent than in some of the other areas of adult education, researchers are now moving to projects that become more than description. Studies are underway dealing with the conceptual roles of the extension agents and supervisors; the morale of the "teaching staff"; the identification of principles of program planning and the testing of hypotheses about principles as they operate in program planning; the assessment of training needs; and testing of plans for follow-up of outcomes after attempts have been made to meet these needs.

However, when it comes to comprehensive research on methodology, there are some real gaps. There are even some gaps in descriptive knowledge which may need to be filled before emphasis can be placed on more sophisticated research.

CURRENT PROBLEMS AND ISSUES IN ADULT
EDUCATION RESEARCH

Current problems and issues in adult education research can be classified according to the six categories below. Issues and problems identified under each of these six categories will be stated in the form of questions. There are partial answers to some of these questions coming from present research data, but for the most part we have only begun the development of scientific, standardized procedures of description, analysis, and experimentation which will lead to answers to these questions.

1. *Needs and wants of individuals and groups*

What particular mental, physical, and emotional needs are important to adults in the community? What determines what the adults want from adult education agencies? Can adult educators help develop adult wants so that they are closely allied to high priority adult needs? What needs of individuals and of community groups are within the realm of agency concern? What do we know about adults in general? How do adults differ—in different social settings, with different economic backgrounds? How should educators and institutions adjust to these differences? Is there a framework among agencies of adult education that identifies some agencies more closely with certain kinds of adult needs than others? Are the agencies concerned with the most vital adult needs?

2. *Plans and purposes of the adult education agency*

Is the agency's program directed toward meeting specific or general needs of the community? Does the program actually do in practice what it says it proposes to do on paper? Should agency goals and objectives be established so that they mirror the goals of special community groups? What is the role of the agency clientele in determining agency objectives? What is the relationship between goals of community adults and goals of the agency?

3. *The resources of adult education and the community*

Are community resources being effectively used in meeting agency goals? In what ways are the resources of the agency an aid to total community development? How does the agency provide resources that aid adult learning? How can this be done for the individual? For the group? What can the agency do to gain for itself a reputation as being an integral part of community life? What are the most effective ways to survey community resources? What characteristics of the sociological make-up of the community influence the adult education agency? In what ways is this influence felt?

4. *The operations of the adult education agency*

How do different administrative structures affect the educational program? What should be the relationship between the instructional program of the agency and the nature of the community? To what extent should operations of one agency be co-ordinated with those of another? What differences does co-ordination make? Under what conditions should an agency run an independent operation? Do adults learn more in a setting in which agencies are co-operating or in one where agencies are competing? How costly are varying programs per unit of achievement?

5. *Methods of teaching adults*

It is often assumed that there is no difference in the use and effectiveness of methods for various age groups. Is this assumption valid? To what extent are selected methods useful in formal and informal learning situations? What are the relationships between characteristics of the instructor and effective use of selected methods? How do the psycho-social factors identified in research on the group influence outcomes of teaching for understanding, for the learning of a skill, for the development of attitudes, and for the adoption of new practices? What is the relationship of group size to the effectiveness of selected methods? What is the comparative effectiveness of the teaching of a professional educator and of a volunteer who teaches after a short period of "leader training"? When are television, radio, and bulletins most useful? Which methods are most effective with adults of high educational level, which with those of limited educational background? Might differences found here account for the limited participation of certain groups of adults?

6. *The outcomes of adult education.*

To start with a particular agency, what questions should cooperative extension researchers be asking? Should it change more than countable farm practices? What has it done in the lives of the people? Should it deal in the improvement of human relationships? Should it take a position on matters of long-time public policy? Has rural citizenship been improved because of participation in cooperative extension programs? Has the rural citizen's participation in government affairs increased or decreased or remained the same because of or in spite of work of the Cooperative Extension Service? Which segment of society is the most resistant to change in the structure of local government? If the answer is rural society, then is it because of the Cooperative Extension Service or in spite of it? How mature are rural understandings and positions on international relations? Has the Cooperative Extension Service had anything to do with this maturity?

These kinds of questions could be asked about the individual and groups with which other agencies work. Yet for most agencies of adult education, their shots toward vague objectives are so scattered that they find it impossible to take credit or blame for any of the outcomes. Do different methods aimed at the same objective provide different outcomes? Or, are our outcomes so generalized that they cannot be validly identified? This lack of definitiveness produces two key problems for research: what are the objectives of adult education and what are the outcomes?

As in any profession, adult education problems and issues are resolved in many ways, including discussion within the profession and by the constant accrual of new facts and understanding. It is in the latter area that research is invaluable. Research will provide the base for intelligent discussion.

Harry Miller, writing in the June, 1959, issue of *The Review of Educational Research,* identified the following issues: (1) the conflict between ideas and action—should adult education have a liberal or a vocational theme, and (2) should emphasis be on content or method? Other writers have identified longer lists of issues, many of which are specific to certain agencies, such as the issue of whether university and college adult education should provide other than delayed academic college level education. In the libraries there is the issue as to whether the library should provide service to adult groups in addition to book service to individuals. In labor education there is the issue of the extent to which unions and universities should work together.

Finally, we must ask in a field as diverse as adult education, whether it is possible to build a cohesive body of research. Is it possible that the diversity of the field of adult education is such that the research must always be borrowed from another field, or at least have the bulk of it come from other disciplines? This may be true until such time as there is more clarity as to what adult education actually is. It is only through a common frame of reference that adult educators can see each other's research as adding to the central core of the field. It is possible and very likely that in the future we shall look back at this period of trial and error in adult education research and in view of what occurs ask, "Why couldn't someone have seen it this way then?" What this final outcome might be is only conjecture at this point. Is it a foundation in the disciplines of social science with an interpretation of their implications for adult education? Is it a concentration of research by adult educators with but small concern for research in the related fields? Is it a base in the fields of sociology, psychology, communications, and political science with selective but critical descriptive, analytical, and experimental research in the "adult classroom"? Whatever it might be, within a reasonably short time research must be developed to gain the knowledge needed to improve adult education and adult learning.

There comes a time in a developing professional area when the parts add up to an identifiable whole or it is recognized that the area is not as independent as its well-wishers thought. It is recognized that clarification of the parts and the potential identification of the whole comes from research rather than from wishing. If the parts are not clarified, they may fall apart rather than fall together.

It is the judgment of this writer that we are fast approaching the period in adult education when we must organize and examine the parts. On the basis of this examination adult education will be a stronger professional area or it will be absorbed into the related professions.

Footnotes

[1]Kurt Lewin, *The Relative Effectiveness of a Lecture Method and a Method of Group Discussion for Changing Food Habits* (Washington: National Research Council, 1942), pp. 459-73.

[2]Eugene A. Wilkening, "Roles of Communicating Agents in Technological Change," *Social Forces*, XXXIV (May, 1956), 361-67.

3David Riesman, Nathan Glazer, and Reuel Denney, *The Lonely Crowd: A Study of the Changing American Character*, abridgment (New York: Doubleday Anchor Books, 1953).

4W. A. Owens, Jr., "Age and Mental Abilities; A Longitudinal Study," *Genetic Psychology Monograph*, XLVIII (1953), 3-54.

5John B. Holden, "A Survey of Participation in Adult Education Classes," *Adult Leadership*, VI (April 1958), 258-61.

6D. K. Wheeler and A. W. Anderson, "Increasing Adult Reading Speed," *Adult Education*, IX (Autumn 1958), 25-30.

7Edmund deS. Brunner *et al.*, *An Overview of Adult Education Research* (Chicago: Adult Education Association, 1959), p. 2.

8Lucinda Crile, *Findings From Research on Meetings*. U. S. Department of Agricultre Extension Service Circular No. 507 (Washington: U. S. Government Printing Office, 1956).

9Meridith C. Wilson and Gladys Gallup, *Extension Teaching Methods*. U. S. Department of Agriculture Extension Service Circular No. 495 (Washington: U. S. Government Printing Office, 1955).

10George M. Beal, Everett M. Rogers, and Joe M. Bohlen, "Validity of the Concept of Stages in the Adoption Process," *Rural Sociology*, XXII (June, 1957), 166-68.

11*The Influence of Four Film Use Methods on Community Planning*. (Madison: University of Wisconsin Extension Division, 1955).

12Darwin Cartwright and Alvin Zander, *Group Dynamics, Research and Theory* (Evanston, Illinois: Row, Peterson and Co., 1953).

13Jack R. Gibb, "Learning in the Adult Group," *Review of Educational Research*, XXIX, (June, 1959), 256-61.

Selected Readings

Brunner, Edmund deS., *et al. An Overview of Adult Education Research*. Chicago: Adult Education Association of the U.S.A., 1959.

Kaplan, Abbott. "Research Review," *Adult Education* V, No. 2 and 4; VI, VII, VIII, and IX, No. 4.

Proceedings of Research Planning Conference of the National Agricultural Extension Center For Advanced Study. "Cooperative Extension Administration—Suggested Areas for Research." Madison: the Center, September, 1956.

Review of Educational Research XX (1950), XXIII (1953), and XXIX (1959).

Riesman, David, Glazer, Nathan, and Denney, Reuel. *The Lonely Crowd: A Study of the Changing American Character*. New York: Doubleday Anchor Books, 1953.

The Encyclopedia of Educational Research. Edited by Chester Harris. Washington: American Educational Research Association, 1960.

Ward, Betty. *Education on the Aging. A Selected Bibliography*. U.S. Office of Education Bulletin No. 11. Washington: Government Printing Office, 1958.

Wechsler, David. *The Measurement and Appraisal of Adult Intelligence*. Baltimore: The Williams and Wilkins Company, 1958.

CHAPTER 10

THE EDUCATION OF ADULT EDUCATIONAL LEADERS[1]

CYRIL O. HOULE
Professor of Education
The University of Chicago

At the heart of the educative process is the student, but he cannot go far in his quest for knowledge without some kind of teacher. This fact has always been as true of the education of adults as of children. The conscious effort of individuals to improve themselves, the sense of mission which causes leaders to take their message to others, and the collaborative effort of groups to increase their understanding are familiar themes throughout recorded history. But in the present century, the effort to provide adult education has grown into a much more highly organized movement, and the location and training of capable and inspiring leaders has emerged as a central problem which has had to be solved in countless ways.

Most adult learning takes place spontaneously and naturally, as men and women decide they want to learn something and proceed to do so by their own efforts. Wherever adult education takes on social form, however, two groups of people are differentiated: those who accept responsibility for providing focus and direction and those whose activities are thereby shaped and led. This duality has many patterns: the teacher and the student; the leader and the participant; the counselor and the person counseled; the administrator and the staff; and the planner and the person who is guided by plans. A certain awkwardness of phraseology grows out of this diversity, but, in an arbitrary fashion, we may give to the first party in each of these pairs the generic term "leader" or "educator of adults." It is in preparing such a person for his role that the need for adequate training arises.

THE PRESENT STATUS OF TRAINING

Most leadership training, like most adult education, is self-directed. An individual confronted with the responsibility of becoming an educator of adults learns partly by the process of participation and partly by his own examination of that process. He studies books or pamphlets or manuals, he talks with others in a similar situation, he goes to meetings, he asks for supervisory assistance, he visits other programs, or he analyzes his own performance in terms of a standard which he has developed himself or adopted from some source. The quality of his learning depends in essence upon his capacity to teach himself.

The largest volume of organized (as distinguished from self-directed) training of adult educational leaders occurs within the institutions which sponsor programs, such as the public schools, the Cooperative Extension Service, and the voluntary associations. Some of these agencies have clear-cut patterns of advancement up the ladder of professional responsibility, and training is a prerequisite for taking each step. Among the techniques used are: constructive and continuing assistance by supervisors; internship; regular or occasional short courses, conferences, and workshops; continuing staff seminars; collaborative training with other agencies; and the deliberate use of decision-making processes in such a way as to broaden the horizons of staff members (as when program-planning is done by a group rather than by the head of the agency acting alone.)

Since organized adult education is still in a relatively primitive state, it does not have such complete systems as have been developed for the preparation of teachers or administrators of childhood education or for such established professions as law, medicine, or the ministry. Any comprehensive plan calls for the use of certain major procedural steps: 1. The definition of the traits of the successful practitioner. 2. The recruitment and selection of promising candidates. 3. The training of these people in such a way that they will gain competence in the duties they are expected to perform. (This is usually called "pre-service training.") 4. The adjustment of the new worker to his first position. ("Induction training.") 5. The continuing education of the worker to keep his capacities at a high level, to equip him with new knowledge, or to enable him to meet new responsibilities. ("In-service training.") While individual institutions of adult education have developed excellent special approaches to one or more of these tasks, no large-scale adult educational program, with the possible exception of the Cooperative Extension Service, has yet worked out and put into effect a comprehensive plan for training its leaders. A number of ambitious efforts are now being made, however.

The most important single influence on the training of educators of adults since the end of World War II has been the study of group behavior. Some of the psychologists and sociologists who have pioneered in this field have been interested only in theoretical studies, but others have been concerned with the development of techniques which would permit groups to work more intelligently and flexibly and to analyze their own processes. The most notable example of what might be called "pure" group relations training has been the annual summer program operated by the National Training Laboratory at Gould Academy in Bethel, Maine, but other activities of like nature are now conducted throughout the country. Even more important, perhaps, has been the gradual incorporation of group concepts or group techniques into virtually all training practice in adult education. While most programs are not centrally group-oriented, and perhaps never will be, it would be hard to find any training program which had not been influenced, however subtly, by the group dynamics movement.

THE PYRAMID OF LEADERSHIP

Insofar as a pattern may be discerned amid the bewildering variety of forms of leadership in adult education, it takes the general shape of a pyramid. This pyramid is divided horizontally into three levels which are essentially different, although at their edges they blend into one another, so that no sharp lines can be drawn to differentiate them. Let us look first at the whole pyramid and then turn back to examine each of its three levels.

At the base of the pyramid is the largest group of people, those who serve as volunteers. Their number is legion and their influence is enormous. There is no brief way to indicate the scope and diversity of volunteer leadership but its nature can at least be suggested by listing the groups which Liveright studied in his comparative analysis of voluntary adult leadership: the county educational program of the Montana Farmers Union; the educational program of the St. Louis Mental Health Association; the home demonstration program of the Cooperative Extension Service; the program of training for supervisors in human relations and problem solving sponsored by the Elgin National Watch Company; the parent education program of a branch of the P.T.A.; the discussion programs of a state League of Women Voters; the steward training program of a local union; the program of training in basic economics provided for the supervisors of the American Viscose Company; the Great Books Program; the World Politics Program; the Presbyterian Bible School Program; the Lutheran Bible School Program; the discussion program of the Henry George School of Social Studies; and the first-aid program of the American Red Cross.[2]

At the intermediate level of the pyramid is a smaller group of persons who, as part of their paid employment, combine adult educational functions with the other duties which they perform. They include: general staff members in public libraries, museums, and settlement houses; school, college, and university faculty members who teach both young people and adults; educational officers in the armed services; personnel workers in government and industry; and persons employed in mass media of communication.

At the apex of the pyramid is the smallest group. It is composed of specialists who have a primary concern for adult education and basic career expectations in that field. They include: those who direct the adult educational activities of public schools, universities, libraries, museums, social settlements, prisons, and other institutions; professors of adult education and others who provide training; those who concentrate on adult education and others who provide training; those who concentrate on adult education on the staffs of voluntary associations or agencies concerned with health, safety, or other special interests; directors of training in government, industry, or labor unions; and most of the staff of the Cooperative Extension Service.

These three groups of leaders are intimately interrelated. A strong program of lay leadership requires the leadership of specialists or part-time workers. These latter groups, in turn, may be isolated or ineffective if lay leaders do not help them carry knowledge to the community. Some volunteer and part-time leaders become intrigued with their adult educational responsibilities and extend their range of knowledge and competence, thereby moving up in the pyramid. Also, while the content of the training program must be pitched at the appropriate level of each of the three groups, there are at least some common elements; certain fundamental principles must be drawn, for example, from the intensive training of the specialist to be included in the briefer training of the lay leader. Certain skills (such as the nature of group processes and the technique of leading a discussion) may also be common to all three.

THE TRAINING OF LAY LEADERS

Lay leaders for the most part require specialized, brief, and clear-cut training to give them the immediate skills they need to carry out their responsibilities. They learn to lead a series of discussions, to demonstrate a technique, to plan a program, to discharge an elective or appointive office, or to conduct a campaign. Their concern is with the task at hand and how to perform it well.

A great deal of thoughtful work has been done in lay leadership development. The large-scale organizations which rely heavily on volunteer assistance—such as the American Red Cross and the various youth-serving organizations—usually employ training specialists and publish extensive libraries of manuals and special aids. Most of these national programs concentrate their efforts on the pre-service aspects of leadership training.

The central task in training lay leaders is to help them understand the appropriate principles of action which seem significant in the light of their experience. This result cannot be brought about by experience alone. As Cardinal Newman pointed out, "If experience were all that is significant in this world, you would expect sailors to be the wisest of men, for they travel around and see everything. But the multiplicity of external objects which they have encountered forms no symmetrical and consistent pattern upon their imagination."[3] And so it is with potential lay leaders. They have had much experience with groups but lack sufficient insight to be able to lead them.

The leadership of a group is a complex process which can never be analyzed and understood in a simple and uncomplicated way. But a training program which sets out to teach a potential leader something about the whole range and complexity of the interpenetration of adult minds will usually end by frightening him and destroying his confidence in himself. He needs, instead, the assurance which comes from understanding the central rules for effective group behavior, the core principles which will cover most of the situations with which he must deal. Given these, he will ordinarily succeed reasonably well. Later, as he gains experience, he will realize that these rules are not enough and that he must move beyond them. He will begin to understand the subtleties of the group process and, in his constant re-examination of his own experience, he will move toward deeper levels of understanding thereby increasing his competence as a leader.

The in-service growth of leaders should not, however, be left to chance or self-direction. One weakness of many programs of lay leadership development is that they are based on the assumption that an initial training period is enough. Ways must be found to encourage potential leaders to realize that, while they are having the experience of leadership, they must also think about it and try to discover ways of improving their own performance. Machinery must be set up to assist that process: advanced courses, friendly supervision, visitation of other groups, guided reading, and meetings with other leaders to talk about the group process.

Inherent within the very idea of lay leadership is the concept that the leader will not want to continue the same task forever. One who leads a specific course several times will gradually discover that it is losing its interest and appeal for him. He will want to go on to some other course —or, indeed, to some other form of leadership. This desire is normal and natural, and anyone who is concerned with the establishment of training programs must realize that he will have a continuing responsibility to replenish the supply of new leaders.

The other aspects of a comprehensive training—identification of leader traits, recruitment, and entrance training—should receive more attention than they normally do. Unfortunately, the directors of many programs find that they cannot secure an adequate supply of prospective leaders and therefore must accept those who are available. Also those who operate leadership training programs are often so hard-pressed for time that they feel they can provide nothing more than pre-service education. As more adequate resources become available for adult education, the breadth and caliber of training plans will improve.

The use of lay leaders for adult education has always been a matter of controversy. There are two major areas of disagreement.

The first has to do with the suitability of using lay people to lead discussions which have to do with highly complex subject matter. To a professor who has made a lifelong study of Plato, international relations, economics, or literature, it may seem preposterous that someone with no specialized subject-matter competence should be allowed to lead a discussion of the "Apology," sovereignty, the gross national product, or "The Wasteland." The dangers are even greater if the subject matter deals with such emotion-laden topics as parent-child relationships, marital adjustment, or mental health. To specialists in these fields, it sometimes seems perilous to trust the handling of such matters to "blundering amateurs."

The advocates of lay leadership make a number of responses which may be summarized as follows: (1) It is the function of lay leaders to help many people gain a few central concepts; if these concepts are carefully chosen and presented in pamphlets, films, recordings, or other media prepared by specialists, the lay leader can be an indispensable means of reaching large numbers of people. (2) There are not enough specialists to handle the mass job which is required. (3) Even if there were enough experts, there is not an adequate public interest in the lengthy and detailed study, which requires expert teaching, whereas, in most fields, a fairly large number of people can be interested in a briefer and more general approach. (4) The role of a lay leader is carefully defined so that he acts not as a specialist but as first among equals in the exploration of the work of specialists. The study materials provided are the teachers and he is merely the leader of a discussion about them. (5) A lay leader deals only with normal situations; part of his training should equip him to know when he is dealing with some problem which goes beyond his own capacity to handle it.

Such arguments as these, and others which might be added, have been advanced for many years, but the debate still rages, partly because lay leadership training is still not as effective as it should be.

The other major area of controversy has to do with the nature of the training provided to lay leaders. Here there are many points of disagreement. Is it possible to have generalized leadership training or must training always be specific to each program? Or can there be general elements which apply to all programs but which can be supplemented by the special requirements of each program? Should the training of leaders concentrate on the materials they are to teach or the methods they are to use? If the latter, should the potential leaders be taught careful rules for performing such functions as discussion leadership or is it better to try to focus directly on the group process? Such questions as these have been discussed for a good many years but little agreement has yet been produced, perhaps because the proponents for any given point of view tend to insist that their own solutions are universally applicable.

Actually, *no* solution is universally applicable. Adult education is so richly diversified that no single approach to lay leadership is possible. Liveright[4] has performed a service in analyzing a number of groups and developing a typology. He analyzes programs in terms of two different factors. The first has to do with whether a program is basically concerned with changing attitudes, understandings, or skills. The second factor has to do with whether it is appropriate for the group to have high, intermediate, or low group cohesion. The comparison of these elements thus produces a typology in terms of which it is possible to define appropriate leadership styles and to establish training programs for them.

PART-TIME LEADERS

There is a rapid increase in the number of people who earn part of their total compensation by teaching adults. Many school teachers, librarians, group workers, health educators, personnel directors, labor union officials, and others find that they are drawn in some fashion into adult educational activities. Usually they make such adjustment to the situation as seems to them appropriate, and do their work without any formal training for it.

As the number of such people increases, the need for some kind of systematic pre-service instruction in how to teach or lead adults becomes more apparent. Teachers' colleges have begun to introduce courses or units on adult instruction. In the fields in which adult classes are frequently found (such as vocational agriculture or home economics) special courses on the teaching of adults are now being initiated on a number of campuses. Methods courses for those who may go into the Cooperative Extension Service are also becoming common in colleges of agriculture and home economics. Librarians (particularly those who expect to serve in public libraries) are sometimes given a special introduction to adult services. Similar activities have been initiated in other professional fields.

The theory of what might be done, however, has far outrun practice. In many fields of adult education, there has been much committee and conference work, often at a national level, and a number of useful books and pamphlets have been published, pointing the way to a better understanding of adult education by its part-time workers. It is doubtful, however, whether actual practice during pre-service training programs has yet been widely influenced.

Nor is the situation very much better so far as the in-service education of part-time workers is concerned. University professors and high school teachers, for example, usually do not believe that they need special assistance when they turn from adolescent to mature audiences. A few extension deans and evening school principals have ingeniously met this situation by developing such special techniques as invitational week-end conferences, manuals, or workshops. These activities are not widespread, however, even in universities and schools, and in many of the other situations in which adult education occurs little or nothing is done to provide in-service training for the part-time leader.

SPECIALISTS IN ADULT EDUCATION

The specialists in adult education, as has already been pointed out, are chiefly identified by the crude test that they earn their living and expect to continue earning their living by teaching adults or by administering such instruction. Often the word "professional" is used instead of "specialist" but such usage probably obscures the situation more than it clarifies it. Certainly the group of present practitioners of adult education cannot yet meet such accepted canons of a profession as: universal social recognition; a highly complex body of verified and widely accepted knowledge; and the existence of a corps of persons trained in a rigorous discipline and organized in such a way as to enforce conformity to its standards of behavior.

Even more important, the traditional pattern of professional training has little relevance to present practices in preparing specialists in adult education. In the ministry, in law, in medicine, and in all the other occupations whose practitioners are educated at universities, patterns of selection, pre-service, induction, and in-service training are followed in a reasonably clear-cut fashion from the time the boy or girl is selected for the professional school until the accomplished professional returns for his last refresher course. Most educators of adults do not prepare for their responsibilities in the field during their youth, but acquire an interest in it only after they have become mature. The young man who wrote George Bernard Shaw for advice on how to become a drama critic got the answer: "There is no way of becoming a drama critic. It happens by accident." When the educators of adults talk about their own entry into the field, it is clear that in their case, too, accident has played a large part. They came in, they usually say, "by the back door"; the comment is made so often as to raise the speculation that there is no front door.

University Training in Adult Education

But there are, at any rate, some people who have prepared initially for another occupation, have then found their way into some form of adult education, and who have then decided to undertake organized study in that field. To meet this need, a number of universities have developed courses of various sorts and a few have gone beyond the provision of special offerings to develop complete programs leading to the master's and doctor's degrees. The 1936 *Handbook of Adult Education* identified forty-nine institutions which had offered courses in adult education during the previous year; Teachers' College at Columbia University had already developed degree sequences. Since that time various authors have examined and appraised the extent of training opportunities for specialists. Beginning in 1941, for example, the present writer wrote ten annual articles in the *Adult Education Bulletin* identifying the institutions which were then offering work in adult education and describing various aspects of their work. The latest comprehensive study is that of Svenson, who found that in 1952-53 twelve institutions offered advanced degree programs in adult education and fifty-three institutions offered some kind of professional study in adult education.[5]

Each such institution has its own conception and pattern of instruction but the scope and nature of graduate study in this field are becoming more clear-cut. In large measure this result has been achieved by a series of annual conferences sponsored by the Commission of Professors of Adult Education of the Adult Education Association, with financial assistance provided by the W. K. Kellogg Foundation. At these gatherings, of which there have now been four (including one conference held prior to the receipt of the Kellogg grant), the full-time professors of adult education have been able to examine their own work carefully, decide on common themes, and project desirable courses of action. As of July, 1958, there were twenty-two such full-time professors representing fourteen institutions, one of them in Canada. The report of the commission, which will probably be issued in 1962, should provide much information to those interested in the advanced training of specialists in adult education.

Fund for Adult Education Grants

The intensive education of specialists has also been greatly aided by the Study-Grant Program of the Fund for Adult Education. Acting on the recommendations of a Development Committee of eleven educators, The Fund for Adult Education began, in 1952, to make study and training awards to individuals. These grants had four objectives: (1) to enhance the skills and increase the knowledge of those already in leadership positions in adult education; (2) to recruit and develop persons capable of administering and guiding the operation and growth of programs of liberal adult education; (3) to help strengthen university graduate programs in adult education; and (4) to utilize operating liberal adult education programs as training situations. These interrelated aims remain unchanged.

By January, 1960, nearly three hundred awards had been made to individuals in adult education and the total amount spent was more than one and one-half million dollars. In the main, the FAE Fellowships have gone to persons pursuing careers in the major divisions of the adult education complex: general and agricultural extension; evening colleges; public schools; libraries; and national and local organizations and agencies.

Fellowships have also gone to adult educators working in labor unions, government, industry, and the clergy.

Objectives of Specialist Training

All educators of adults believe in lifelong learning. Therefore, neither the student who comes to the university to learn how to be a specialist nor the professor who teaches him can assume that the graduate program will provide final and complete achievement of the qualities which characterize the outstanding leader of adult education. The objectives of the graduate program may serve, equally as well, for lifelong professional aims. Universities vary in the way in which they define the basic attributes of the outstanding educator of adults and in the emphasis which they place upon each one. Most of them, however, try to help potential specialists work toward the achievement of the following general objectives:

1. *A sound philosophic conception of adult education based on a consideration of its major aims and issues and embodying convictions concerning the basic values which it would seek to achieve.* Since those who become educators of adults usually have no background of study or investigation in the field, they often tend to accept each new plausible suggestion as a fundamental principle of the universe. Experience and inquiry produces a broader viewpoint. The leader of adult education comes to understand the breadth and variety of his field and accept the fact that it includes countless aims and approaches. He also develops his own set of values which enables him to select the activities he wishes to undertake and guides him in building the program for which he is responsible. His philosophic conceptions cannot be imposed by someone else but must grow naturally within him; they are nurtured by reading, study, discussion, reflection, and the analysis of experience.

2. *An understanding of the psychological and social foundations on which all education (and particularly adult education) rests.* Adulthood is not merely one stage or level of life but a general term covering the successive phases of development through which the individual passes from the time he leaves adolescence until he dies. Moreover, his education during maturity is based on the kind and quality of the education which he experienced during childhood. The educator of adults must, therefore, examine closely what is known about the psychological development of the individual in order to understand both the fundamental laws of learning which apply throughout life and the distinctive aspects or principles which are most significant during maturity.

The individual lives in a society which ranges in scope from intimate groups to the world community of nations. Both the goals he seeks and the methods he uses are powerfully conditioned by his immediate social environment. This fact is true throughout life but is particularly significant in maturity, because men and women play a more active part in society than children ever can. The educator of adults must, therefore, study the social sciences in order to understand the ways in which group life influences and is influenced by education.

3. *An understanding of the development, scope, and complexity of the specific agency or program in which he works and the broad field of adult education of which it is a part.* Because most people enter adult education by accident, their initial impressions are largely circumscribed by the specific jobs they undertake. Usually they are not even aware that it is a part of a broader field. Like Moliere's would-be gentleman who was surprised to learn that he had been speaking prose for forty years, they are amazed to discover that their activities could be called "adult education." Many workers in the field have only a limited knowledge even of the history and scope of the very agencies in which they work, but are aware only of local policies and immediate routines.

One of the essential tasks of educating a specialist, therefore, must be to broaden his horizons to reveal the full range of the field. Invariably he finds far more possibilities for growth in his work than he had ever expected. He discovers that others in his own field of service have developed programs which are new and interesting to him. He learns that the basic problems of education are everywhere the same and that those who work in other kinds of agencies have developed principles which have significance for him. He learns, too, something of the historical and current perspectives of the whole field and sees the place of his own work in its larger setting.

4. *An ability to undertake and direct the basic processes of education: the refinement of objectives; the selection and use of methods and content; the training of leaders; the provision of guidance and counseling; the promotion of program; the co-ordination and supervision of activities; and the evaluation of results.* The effective operation of an adult educational program depends on the capacity of those who direct it to understand and use these central processes in a constructive and creative fashion and to realize how each is related to the other. At the graduate level, the student should not be concerned with the mere techniques or with specific procedures. Naturally it is important for him to have such skills and, if he does not, he must take the responsibility to remedy his deficiencies. His advanced instruction, however, must give him the competence to discharge more basic capacities and to supervise and train those whose levels of knowledge and skill are not equal to his own.

5. *Personal effectiveness and leadership in working with other individuals, with groups, and with the general public.* Personal effectiveness is so much a matter of basic personality, as tempered and developed by previous experience, that advanced training can merely reinforce and supplement patterns which were previously established. Within this broad limitation, however, potential specialists can be helped to gain confidence in

themselves, to participate in activities which give them increased competence, and to survey their own capacities and learn how to remedy deficiencies in them.

6. *A constant concern with the continuance of his own education throughout life.* Nobody would deny the importance of lifelong learning but there is a great difference between understanding its significance and putting it into practice. The lawyer is not above the law, the doctor must conform to the rules of health, the priest lives by the laws of his faith, and the educator of adults must continue to learn. More than other men, he should plan and execute a continuous program of self-education. If he fails to do so, the consequences are serious. He limits his own growth, he becomes a sham, his work grows mechanical and perfunctory, and he ceases to have the personal insight he needs into the rewards and the difficulties inherent in the educative process. His professional education must instill in him an awareness of his own need to continue to learn and it should aid him to understand how to do so.

THE FUTURE

Those who occupy positions of responsibility in adult education must operate in a far more complicated pattern than do those who practice a traditional profession. The educators of adults belong potentially not to a single profession but to a family of professions. Moreover, the future is probably one of increased diversification rather than greater simplification.

As the broad field of adult education grows, however, the education of leaders can increasingly be built around a common core of tested knowledge and belief. While the general shape of the field is no longer as obscure as it used to be, it still has many dark corners. Many of the fundamental principles which underlie successful theory and practice have yet to be discovered. It may be hoped, however, that as knowledge grows the future will bring clearer and firmer—as well as more co-ordinated—ways of educating adult educational leaders for their important responsibilities.

Footnotes

1Most of the material in this chapter was adapted from two earlier publications of the present author: "Professional Education for Educators of Adults," *Adult Education,* VI (Spring, 1956), 131-41; and "The Development of Leadership," *Liberal Adult Education* (White Plains: The Fund for Adult Education, 1956), pp. 53-67.

2A. A. Liveright, *Strategies of Leadership* (New York: Harper & Brothers, 1959), pp. xix-xx.

3J. H. Newman, *On the Scope and Nature of University Education* (New York: Dutton, 1933.)

4Liveright, *op. cit.,* pp. 37-46.

5Elwin V. Svenson, "A Review of Professional Preparation Programs," *Adult Education* VI, (Spring, 1956), 162-66.

CHAPTER 11

PUBLIC UNDERSTANDING OF ADULT EDUCATION

THOMAS L. COTTON
*Community Relations and
Research Consultant and
Former President
New York Adult Education Council*

The importance of a chapter devoted to the topic "Public Understanding" is underscored by the response to a request for data sent by this author April 1, 1959, in a questionnaire to 310 people, mostly members of AEA. It was a two-page schedule containing five main questions. It was quickly returned with questions answered by 183 respondents. This amazing response from nearly 60 per cent of the recipients indicated deep interest in the topic—especially so when one considers the length of the answers, which averaged about 20 words each. People do not usually respond so readily if the subject is deemed unimportant.

Although there was no specific request for it, the respondents tried in many ways to paint a picture of twentieth century adult education. Answers to the first three questions in our questionnaire can be reported in chart form as follows:

QUESTION I: IS THE AMERICAN IMAGE OF ADULT EDUCA-
TION PREDOMINANTLY VOCATIONAL? ACA-
DEMIC? CULTURAL? RECREATIONAL?

Answers:

Vocational	Academic	Cultural	Recreational
46%	12%	13%	29%

Nearly half of the respondents think that the general public considers adult education as predominantly vocational, more than one-fourth as recreational, and the remaining one-fourth as either academic or cultural. Obviously these were quick answers or guess-estimates reflecting opinion at the moment, but they seem close to the truth because of the answers to the second question.

QUESTION II. PLEASE CHARACTERIZE THE AMERICAN PUBLIC IMAGE OF ADULT EDUCATION BY DECADES.

(It should be noted here that about one-third of the respondents answered the question in part or not at all.)

	Vocational	Academic	Cultural	Recreational
1910	21%	63%	15%	1%
1920	33	51	12	4
1930	51	28	7	14
1940	52	22	6	20
1950	32	15	21	32
1960	21	11	36	22

Commenting on the figures as they built this chart, most of the respondents characterized the image of the decades of the 1910's and 1920's as preponderantly "citizenship training," "teaching the foreign-born," and "Americanization." From 1930 to 1950 the image emerges strongly as vocational. The academic aspect of adult education seems to decline gradually, as does the cultural—with the exception that this aspect gains a strong position in the 1950 decade, with greater emphasis being projected as probable in the upcoming 1960's.

A few aspects of adult education as foreseen by the respondents make the projected figures for the 1960's more meaningful. They predicted that there will be increased technology, a growing awareness of adult education, better use of leisure time, more community development and action, a growing number of community centers with broad programs for the whole family, increased general education and lifetime learning, a serious exploration of the meaning of life, a trend toward liberal arts programs, and more respect for adult education and interest in it.

QUESTION III. PLEASE RATE AS TO EFFECTIVENESS THE CHIEF MEANS USED BY ADULT EDUCATORS TO CREATE PUBLIC UNDERSTANDING (Not the same as to get students).

	Choice (number of persons)					
	1st	2nd	3d	4th	5th	6th
Advertising	10	9	15	25	23	8
Promotion—literature, publicity	49	50	34	14	1	1
Promotion—face-to-face	75	53	12	10	6	2
Money raising activity	5	2	7	12	18	29
Legislative work	4	2	16	11	28	21
Conferences and meetings	35	39	25	19	2	2
Other means	2	3	3	3	1	0

Many of the respondents did not carry their choices up to six; some gave only one or two, others four and five. Their identification of specific means, especially under "Other," was particularly enlightening: those in discussion groups telling others, summer seminars, radio and TV programs, magazine and newspaper articles, adult education council programs, the best discussion groups of all types, demonstrations and exhibits, encouragement by industry for in-service training, and service to special groups—libraries, clubs, churches, etc.

The chart figures indicate that face-to-face promotion is most effective with adult education concepts as it is with cereal or gadgets. Promotion by literature and publicity got the next highest rating, while conferences and meetings rated third in effectiveness. The least effective means in this rating is legislative activity and the next least effective is money-raising activity.

A general comment regarding the chart might be that adult educators are skeptical of the effectiveness of advertising to sell ideas. They indicate much more confidence in the spoken word as over against the written word. Conferences, discussions, seminars, face-to-face conversations—these are considered to be the most effective means of creating a clear image in the public mind. To get people to desire adult education according to Dr. Paul A. McGhee, "is simply to get them to *experience* it."

QUESTION IV. WHAT ARE THE MAIN OBSTACLES TO THE CREATION OF AN ACCURATE PUBLIC IMAGE OF ADULT EDUCATION IN THE AMERICAN MIND?

The sheer volume of comment elicited by this question is astounding. There were 140 comments ranging all the way from two words designating an obstacle like "poor publicity" to a forty-word statement describing obstacles such as: "American emphasis is that education have practical value, i.e. money, power, social or economic advancement; fear on the part of educators to offend the community power structure; frantic search for entertainment and avoidance of anything that introduces new ideas to challenge or disturb us." Or one not quite so long but having important comment: "Lack of proper understanding of just what 'education' is, namely, the development of a mature mind, a continuous process, a process of *formation,* not just one of information."

A one-word designation of some of the mentioned obstacles would go somewhat as follows:

1. DEFINITION—No *common image* accepted.
2. COST—*Luxury* not *necessity.*
3. PREJUDICE—*Education* is for *children.*
4. MATERIALISM—Vocational interests predominate.

5. APATHY—Spectatoritis, inertia, failure to involve community leaders.
6. CONFUSION—Communication of facts and attitudes lacking.
7. NO REAL CO-ORDINATION—Clearing house of materials needed.
8. RESIST "EDUCATION"—Seek entertainment.
9. LEADERS—Lack interpretive skills.

The answers to Question IV concerning obstacles to the creation of an accurate image of adult education in the American mind can thus be summarized as having their base in confusion and lack of communication. Adult educators do not agree on the image they wish to create and this confusion stymies easy communication between professional and neophyte.

QUESTION IV (Sub-section): WHAT IS BEING DONE ABOUT THIS PROBLEM BY (a) ADULT EDUCATORS (b) BUSINESSMEN (c) THE CLERGY (d) LABOR EDUCATORS AND (e) FARMERS AND CO-OPERATIVES?

(a) *Adult Educators*
Sixty-three respondents were enthusiastic about the adult education movement and the progress it is making in creating a more accurate concept in the mind of the public as to what adult education really is. On the other hand, 15 respondents expressed the idea that little is being done by adult educators to make their activity better understood.

The majority of the 63 answering favorably offered as evidence: better TV and radio programs, conferences and publicity programs and more skillful interpretation of adult education for the general public. A few said that better information is reaching people in all walks of life and this is building motivation for self-improvement, and that universities and schools are offering better courses.

Those who were critical of adult education and the efforts to create a clearer image for the public made such comments as the following:
"We are too busy running programs, too busy talking to each other."
"Our courses are geared to public demand."
"We are bedeviled by administrative problems, limited budgets, differences of opinion."
"We are overshooting the mark by highbrow programs and the ever-present lack of funds."

(b) *Businessmen*
There were 34 comments on programs of businessmen designed to attack the problem of public understanding. An equal number commented that little or nothing is being done by business to meet this difficulty.

Those programs designed to be of real help in this situation were described as in-service training, management training, plant training, and executive training programs. Six people said that business was encouraging and urging employees to participate in adult education programs. Some employers are even providing financial assistance, others are instituting classes for employees and co-operate through advertising support to such classes. Some corporations carry on their own seminars and workshops. Other activities are carried on by chambers of commerce and trade associations which publicize adult education in the community, creating the impression that there is a sense of awareness in industry as to the need of adult education.

Adult Education Week, September 7th to 13th, 1958, in Milwaukee, Wisconsin, is a good illustration of the widest co-operation between the community, its businessmen, its social agencies, its voluntary organizations, and its adult educators. The local newspapers devoted the whole September 7th Sunday supplement to the week's program of educational treats plus fourteen pages of advertising covering adult education courses. Mayor Frank P. Zeidler proclaimed the week, and commercial stations provided radio and TV programs sponsored and co-ordinated by the newly organized Milwaukee Council for Adult Learning.

Adverse comments on activities of businessmen covered the following: very little action in human area; some programs maintained but no sharing of awareness of over-all problems of the movement; they do not seem to understand the term "adult education," confusing it with training; they seem to forget, one respondent suggested, that "training has for its purpose the perpetuation of its own image whereas education aims to give the individual a larger capacity for creative relationship to his life and work"; some businessmen insist on courses for the benefit of the firm rather than the individual or the community.

(c) Clergy

There were 51 who pointed to good work done by the clergy to solve this problem and 22 comments indicating that little was being done by the clergy. Those in favor seemed to feel that religious groups were doing good work in leadership training, broad programming, increased participation in conferences and meetings on the subject of adult education.

Reacting against the clergy, some respondents indicated a lack of motivation for better service to people, failure to identify activities as adult education activities, sacrificing quality for quantity in their adult education programs, and expanding those courses which clearly serve their own interest and religious programs.

(d) Labor Leaders

Fifty spoke favorably of labor programs, and nine indicated that labor leaders were doing little or nothing to clarify the adult education image in the public mind.

The comments favorable to labor programs indicate that the vast majority of respondents feel that labor has good programming and leadership training for workers' education on a broad scale. Publicity through unions to increase interest in adult education is believed to help clarify the public image, as do the sponsoring of school seminars, scholarships, and awards. A good number of the respondents saw an increasing awareness on the part of unions of the value of adult education and others said there was extensive encouragement on the part of unions for people to participate in adult education. Two respondents went further to say that unions were far ahead of any other group in this respect.

On the other hand, there were such disparaging comments as: "Unions recognize the problem of better public understanding but do not contribute towards its solution because there are selfish motives, thus promoting their own interests to the exclusion of anything else."

(e) *Farmers and Co-operatives*

Forty-one remarks on activities of farmers to solve this problem were favorable. Nine said little or nothing was being done by this group. Favorable comments showed that the majority seemed to think well of the programs being sponsored by the Farmers Union, Cooperative Extension Service, and co-operatives. Scholarships, conference participation, use of mass media, and forums dealing with public problems not wholly oriented to agriculture were seen as influencing many adults in the country.

Other respondents felt that farmers and co-operatives were motivated more by profits than anything else; that they stick close to vocational training focused on agricultural skills; that they are stand-patters with not much evidence of relationship to or understanding of adult education.

QUESTION V. WHAT *TRENDS* DO YOU NOTE IN THE AMERICAN CONCEPT OR IMAGE OF ADULT EDUCATION? IS IT MOSTLY CONSIDERED AN ACTIVITY BENEFITING ONESELF ONLY OR IMPROVING THE FAMILY AND THE COMMUNITY?

Of the 183 different statements made by respondents in answer to this question, 72 said that the trend is toward community improvement as a concept. There were 51 comments that the trend is towards benefit of the family as a concept and 60 respondents stuck to the usual concept that adult education, like any other educational effort, is for the individual's benefit.

In addition, there were a large number of combinations of various categories. For example, 31 comments combined the two concepts "community improvement" and "family benefit" to designate trends they spotted in adult education.

Community Improvement Concept

A few quotes from the comments will make clear how the community improvement concept is growing in the image of adult education: "Adult education has been considered a self-improvement activity but current efforts of adult educators may result in public realization that continuing education benefits all of society. Therefore the concept of adult education for community improvement is growing." "It is considered as an activity benefiting the individual but the community development concept seems to be growing." "It is still self-centered but beginning to be seen as an aid to improvement of organizational and community life." "The trend appears toward utilizing opportunities for vocational and professional improvement and possibly toward community improvement." "Adult education broadens horizons, it not only helps the individual do a better job but improves corporate operations and the community as well."

Self Improvement Concept

The ideas contained in the comments listed under this category were about what one would expect, human nature being what it is: "I believe the personal motive predominates with more individuals and at more times with each individual." "It is mostly considered self-beneficial whereas educating the young is for the benefit of society." "Most popular courses are those where students can see a direct personal benefit, either as vocation or avocation." "Our city has one of the largest adult education programs in the country and participation is at least 10 to 1 on the side of individual benefit." "I think adult education is achieving a wholesome balance. It is not being swept off its feet by increasing pressures for social concern, to forget its fundamental and initial appeal for that which is functional in helping each person improve his personal competence to do well that which he has to do in his daily personal experience." "Adult education is, I believe, increasingly being used to denote self improvement and self-initiated educational growth."

Family Improvement

There were over fifty people who found the trend toward interest in better family life. A typical comment was: "I think adult education encompasses both concepts because through personal benefit comes enlargement of viewpoint which goes beyond self and family to the role of the individual as a responsible citizen in the community."

The respondents testified over and over again that adult education starts as an individual betterment idea but inspiring experiences which one has when adult education is at its best, lead one toward an interest in family betterment and community development. This kind of experience is fairly common when modern techniques and methods are used.

This quotation goes a step further to the international idea, as did seven others: "More and more it is coming to be an activity in the human relations field which would not only improve the individual but also family, community, and extend internationally."

There were nearly a dozen comments which brought in the idea that adult education had something to do with the survival of democracy. One person wrote: "There is an earnest effort on the part of the volunteer organizations to move their members beyond an activity or skills program as such, to that of participation in community goals and acceptance of citizenship responsibility in a democratic society." Another commented: "Too often the sales pitch is made at personal betterment. We are now backing into community and group improvement on a basis of improve or perish."

The trend towards *lifelong learning* which was included in many comments seems to have penetrated the minds of adult educators as not only possible but a thing to work, plan, and fight for. There is a tendency in adult education as in most other human activities for the educated to get more education and the uneducated to stay away.

CONCLUSION

The survey indicates that adult education in America is a live, boiling up of aspirations; that if it is separated from the concept of training and viewed as real education which gives the individual a larger capacity for a creative relationship to his life and work, then we begin to get an image of what it is. But the development is so new and our need is so many-faceted that it will be a symbolic concept for years to come. The image is not—nor need it be—deeply etched and crystal clear. America, with her many important voluntary associations, her schools, colleges, and universities is not posturing for the Russians or any one else to note and be impressed. America is deeply involved in self-improvement as she was a hundred years ago when Tocqueville made a note of it. But today there is much more power behind this thing called adult education because of the process which does more than educate—it makes for a more abundant life.

Selected Readings

Damon, Thomas F. "The Effectiveness of Various Practices in disseminating Information About Public School Adult Education in California." Unpublished Ed.D. dissertation, School of Education, Stanford University, 1957.

Deane, Stephen R. "Who Seeks Adult Education and Why," *Adult Education* I (October, 1950), 18-25.

Gallup, George. Periodic opinion-polls on what adults want in adult education. Obtain directly from Dr. George Gallup, Princeton, N.J.

Holden, John B. "Public Relations, Promotion, and Publicity." Chapter IX in *Public School Adult Education*. Washington: National Association of Public School Adult Educators, 1956.

Lindeman, Eduard C. *"The Meaning of Adult Education."* New York: New Republic, Inc., 1926.

Marble, Duane F. "Estimating the Evening Class Registration Potential of Seattle's Census Tracts." Unpublished Ph.D. dissertation, Department of Geography, University of Washington, 1957.

McGhee, Paul A. "Merchandising Adult Education," *Adult Education* V (Spring, 1955), 146-52.

Van Orman, William. "The Opinions of Citizens Relative to the Place of Adult Education in the Public School Programs in Colorado." Unpublished Ed.D. dissertation, University of Denver, 1955.

Verner, Coolie, and Newberry, John S. "The Nature of Adult Participation," *Adult Education* VIII (Summer, 1958), 208-22.

Weiss, Edward H. "What Adults Really Think of Adult Education." Report of a "motivation research" study presented at the 1958 National Conference of AEA. (Mimeographed).

CHAPTER 12

FINANCE, LEGISLATION, AND PUBLIC POLICY FOR ADULT EDUCATION

WILMER V. BELL
Director of Adult Education
Baltimore Public Schools

An adequate adult education program requires adequate financial support; achieving adequate financial support depends upon the education of adults. This cyclic dilemma is basic and common to leaders of adult education in all areas—tax-supported institutions, private agencies, and co-ordinative organizations.

How can public recognition of the value of adult education be developed within the respective constituencies sufficiently to evoke responsible action? The financial and the educational elements of this question are inextricably linked. Each exerts a controlling influence on the other.

Every barrier to realizing the full potential of adult education can be reduced to a monetary common denominator. Henry Adams observed that the "whole problem of education is one of its cost in money." Lack of public understanding can be seen from a monetary viewpoint as either cause or effect. This and the several other factors constitute a spiral: understanding, popularity, support, legislation, funds, beneficial activities; better understanding, greater popularity, firmer support, further legislation, additional funds, broader benefits; etc. Opinions about the limit of this spiral vary according to concepts of the limit of our resources. If this is fixed, at some point further investment will bring no gain. Conversely, if education creates resources, there may be no conceivable limit.

These views affect the degree of warmth with which requests for funds are seen both by others seeking funds and by those guarding the financial reservoirs. If there is to be no compensating inflow, every supplicant is a rival, draining irreparably the available quantity of a vital elixir. On the other hand, if expenditures are for well-boring, each withdrawal is a welcome promise of enriching dividends and co-operation is a virtue.

From another viewpoint, lack of money is not the determinant. Our national financial resources make costs for adult education insignificant (.03 per cent of the gross national product) in relation to our enormous expenditures on frivolous items. The basic trouble lies in public failure to realize the need for and power of adult education. Its cure will come when leaders have presented a picture of adult education sufficiently convincing to bring about the necessary public affirmation, and thus elicit from private and public pockets the sums essential to unleash the ultimate potential of adult education.

Realistically, adult education now faces increasingly serious challenges from competing influences. In simple terms, funds come from one or more of four sources: (1) the general public, through taxes; (2) the interested public, through contributions; (3) the client, through fees for services; and (4) interested and philanthropic organizations, through donations or grants. The degree and manner by which these may be used in combination is a matter of diverse opinion and practice.

Few institutions derive their supporting funds solely from one source, but the major appeals of the three categories are somewhat distinct. Tax-supported adult education institutions—schools, colleges, libraries, museums, and government agencies—must educate governing boards and taxpayers to influence legislative leaders to appropriate funds for the adult education vital to individual and societal welfare. Private agencies having little or no access to public treasuries must convince clients, members, patrons, stockholders, or private philanthropic organizations of the value of the educational program of the agency. Co-ordinative organizations primarily serving the operating agencies from behind the scenes, must convince agency leaders and the community at large of their worth and need.

Who should pay for adult education activities is a question faced by all agencies and answered in a variety of ways as determined by policy and expediency. The effect which financial practices exert upon the nature, scope, and quality of the educational program extends the problem further and makes it more intricate. These are the immediate considerations with which adult educators and adult education must cope.

However, as a nation or a culture, we encounter a more fundamental problem. If, in fact, our civilization is in a race between education and catastrophe, one obvious hurdle in our path is lack of funds for education. Ironically, adult education, of all educational elements widely announced as the speediest competitor to disaster, faces the greatest hurdle. In these terms we must answer two parallel questions: Can we bring the educational level of the enfranchised public to the point where they can make informed decisions in the current constant crisis? Can we educate enough of the public about adult education sufficiently well and soon enough to gain the financial basis required to realize our potential and to fend off the disaster which our ignorance seems to court?

It appears that adult education is the only ready and promising means to its own essential ends. By monetary measures, however, adult education seems to have a low level of significance in the American scene, and thus may lack the means to speak effectively about itself. The general issues seem clearly drawn: Has adult education the virtue its advocates claim? If so, how do its merits compare with those of other programs competing for support? Who bears the responsibility to assess its value? Who bears the responsibility to pay its costs?

Trends in the resolution of these issues are far less clear as will be seen below.

TAX-SUPPORTED INSTITUTIONS

Tax-supported institutions are constantly involved in the competition for the tax dollar. Success in this competition depends upon the public image of the institution and its program, as well as upon the image held by the members of the legislative bodies. In either case the image may be far from reality. Their programs are subject to indirect influence by legislators trying to balance public protests about the costs of public services with the clamor of clients for this service.

A tangle of issues confronts public institutions: Is public educational service to adults supererogatory? If not, what is the extent and nature of the service justifiable from public funds? If public funds are to be supplied, by what political sub-division; state, local or federal? Will programs be limited to well-populated regions? Which program areas have greatest claim upon resources? How will the source and method of administration of funds affect the program? Will finances or philosophy control the program?

The intensity of this interrogation is aggravated by the magnitude of the sums involved and the speed with which definitive answers are reached is hampered by the distance of the controlling bodies from the field of action.

Public Libraries[1]

In general the funds for the adult education services of libraries are not accounted for separately but are a part of the total library budget. The study made by the American Library Association with a grant from the Fund for Adult Education in 1953 makes this statement:

> *Funds for adult education services*—Funds for young adult and adult education activities were essentially part of the library total budgets and there were no special sources. The source of funds for over half of the libraries (52.7 per cent) was generally library budget tax appropriations; about 40 per cent did not answer; about 3 per cent had library endowments or other sources of funds. Less than one per cent had contributions from community groups, individuals, or other

agencies. The percentage of funds used directly for adult education services could not be separated from other expenditures.[2]

It is assumed that the 40 per cent of the libraries which did not respond considered the elements inseparable.

The problem of financing adult education in libraries is part of the problem of financing libraries, which, like schools, find it increasingly difficult to meet the demands of an expanding population which is requiring more and more education of all kinds. It is estimated that the population of the United States has increased 14 per cent since 1950 while library use has increased 27 per cent in the same time. The increase in library budgets has probably not kept pace with inflation which means that they are actually losing ground (see Table 1). For instance, salaries constitute the largest single element of public library budget. As demands for professionally trained personnel increase and salaries rise, along with rising costs of books and building operation, libraries face the dilemma of deteriorating service: reduced staff—quantity and quality—or reduced contemporary books, periodicals, films, etc., or both.

TABLE 1

Public Library Operating Expenditures

Year	No. of library systems reporting	Population served by reporting systems	Operating expenditures, (excluding capital outlay)	Per capita expenditure
1	2	3	4	5
1945	5,799	88,831,966 (1940 census)	$ 61,790.307	$0.70
1950	5,773	113,943,917 (1950 census)	109,776,824	0.96
1956	6,190	117,302,268* (1950 census)	170,223,000	1.45*

*1956 population estimate of approximately 150,000,000 would reduce per capita expenditure to approximately $1.13.

A major development in support for libraries was the passage of the Library Services Act (Public Law 597) in 1956. Since the federal funds provided in this act must be matched by the states, it has also brought about a considerable increase in the funds provided for libraries in the separate states. A fair proportion of these funds go into adult services.[3] This act affords to libraries generally some of the advantages and incentives which foundation grants have provided in limited measure heretofore.

One of the problems facing public libraries is the existence throughout the country of many little libraries serving an area too small to provide adequate support. The American Library Association recommends that libraries band together in order to provide co-operatively better services through their pooled resources. This idea has met with some opposition. However, larger units of service such as county and multi-county libraries, with their broadened base of support, are steadily increasing. The Library Services Act has advanced this development.

Public Schools

The recurrent issue in financing public school adult education is whether, to what degree, or for what activities, the student should bear the costs. Underlying this issue is concern with the relative value of adult education versus education for children and youth. Thus far there has been no federal aid specifically for general adult education. Whatever governmental support it may receive comes from the states or local districts. Policies differ extremely throughout the states, practices advocated in some being forbidden in others.

Public school responsibility for adult education has been acknowledged in practice and law for well over a century. Today all states except Kansas have legislation relating to adult education. Provisions range from prohibiting use of public school funds for general adult education (New Mexico, Vermont, Wyoming), through many intermediate stages, up to making adult education costs a regular part of general budgets and annual appropriations.[4] In 1956-57 more than $8,000,000 was so appropriated in California, $3,500,000 in New York, and $1,300,000 in Florida.

Forty-one states now enable public schools to finance and operate general adult education programs, but in nineteen the use of public funds is subject to specific limitations. Delaware, Maryland, Nevada, Oregon, Pennsylvania, and Utah once provided state aid for general adult education but are currently not doing so, Oregon and Pennsylvania being the most recent defectors.

In 1954 $79,040,000 was spent for public school adult education in some seven thousand urban localities across the nation. This sum amounted to 1.3 per cent of the total public school expenditures of those districts. Eleven thousand other districts, however, had no provision for adult education, and one third of the cities of the United States had no adult education program. In 1956-57 sixteen states allotted $15,474,209 for general adult education. This, however, was only .69 per cent of the public school education budget of those states (versus 2.3 per cent recommended by the National Commission on Adult Education Finance.[5]

Financial policies and practices have an overwhelming impact upon the size of an adult education program. In ten states which gave state aid amounting to from $.35 to $.91 per capita for adult education, three times as many pupils enrolled in proportion to the population of these states as in the non-aid states. In New York between 1945 and 1953, when state aid was raised 500 per cent, enrollments rose 1500 per cent. The National Commission on Adult Education Finance found that school districts supported by state aid served 6.3 per cent of their adult population, those limited to local funds served 3.6 per cent, and schools in districts which relied entirely upon tuition served only 2.7 per cent.

As an issue, tuition fees evoke a wide variety of opinions even among adult educators. Proponents of tuition fees cite (a) the danger of spreading resources too thinly and undermining free public education; (b) the self-respect which adults get from paying for what they want; (c) the ability of adults to pay for what they get; and (d) the increased stability of enrollment which arises from discouraging those without serious or well-formed intention. Opponents of tuition fees emphasize that (a) limitations are placed upon those who most need adult education, and who are most easily discouraged—those with low educational level, with low income, and with low incentive; (b) fees limit the ability of leadership to adjust the nature of the program to public need rather than public demand; and (c) public affairs, community development, literacy education, citizenship education, and elementary and high school courses are unlikely to be sufficiently popular for financial independence. Regardless of the merit of the argument, experience shows that three fourths of the schools which charge fees have enrollments of three hundred students or less.

This discussion illustrates how materially the nature of the program is affected by monetary considerations. Public schools entirely dependent on fees can offer only what the student is willing to pay for. Typically, this is for courses which will permit him to earn more money or gain occupational advancement or for popular craft or semi-recreational activities. Schools in districts which must rely solely on their local resources have theoretically a great amount of flexibility, being unrestricted by state regulations. Ordinarily, however, their financial resources are limited. In states which benefit from state aid schools generally show more flexible schedules, furnish more activities in more subject areas, and use a greater variety of educational procedures.

Fiscal regulations also influence the nature, size, scope, and adaptability of a program. Distribution of state aid by average daily attendance gives preference to large classes with high attendance and to giving the public what it wants. Distribution on an instructional-hour basis permits classes to be of a reasonable size and thus in subjects somewhat less popular. Allocation on the basis of expenditure permits the widest range of subjects and educational approaches.

State and local school systems are facing a critical financial dilemma, and adult education is being sacrificed in many cases. Funds for state aid to adult education in Michigan and New York have been greatly reduced; other states have held even or declined moderately. In California, while funds have tripled in ten years, they have dropped from 2.5 per cent of the public school budget in 1952 to 1.59 per cent in 1957. In 1957 California staved off a major attack upon public school adult education funds while Florida fought back attacks in both 1957 and 1959.

In educational matters, the controlling influence is exerted at the state level. State boards of education hold the key to co-ordination and also to stimulation of the several aspects of public education. The National Association of Public School Adult Educators, through foundation funds, has underwritten in recent years a Division of Adult Education in states willing to venture in this field.

Solution of the financial woes of public school adult education may be a by-product of federal aid to education measures being debated more insistently at each session of Congress.

Adult Vocational Education

Adult vocational education has the unique distinction of receiving aid from federal funds under the Federal Vocational Education Act. In 1956 these funds amounted to $33,180,000 not generally restricted to any age group. This federal program represents the only systematic educational pattern applying in all states.

The extent to which federal funds allotted to states are used for adult aspects of vocational education is left to the discretion of the states and local communities. It is possible to make expenditures for vocational education at the secondary level to earn federal funds to promote and operate adult vocational programs. Certain reallotment provisions make it possible for states receiving additional reallotments of federal funds to use these for adult vocational education. Response from states and local units in 1956 brought to vocational education, including adult vocational education, an average of $4.36 in supplementary funds for every dollar of federal expenditure.

Enrollment of 1,500,000 adults in these programs in 1959 suggests the cumulative impact of the succession of vocational education acts beginning with the Smith-Hughes Act (1917) to the George Barden Act (1946) and its amendments in 1956 for practical nursing training and fisheries industry vocational training. Title VIII (Area Vocational Education and Technician Training) of the 1958 National Defense Education Act provides the first federal vocational services for post-high school education as well as for groups of limited size in sparsely populated areas.

The benefit of these federal funds is shown also in the fact that of the 339 full time professionals in adult education in the states, 292 are workers in adult vocational education and only 47 in general adult education (for which no such aid is available). It is perhaps not immaterial, either, that enrollments in vocational courses account for over 35 per cent of all adult education enrollments, as compared with 14.2 per cent in general education and 12.6 per cent in civic affairs, the next highest categories in the October, 1957, Current Population Survey.

Federal Agencies

A total of $87,220,000 classified as funds for adult education purposes was expended by or within the government agencies in 1956-57, according to a survey by the U. S. Office of Education.[6] At least half of this sum seems to have been used under the direct supervision of federal agencies for such things as Indian health, patient education at the Carville Leprosarium, mines safety training, prisoner education in federal prisons, F. B. I. police training schools, civil defense schools, science education under the National Science Foundation, and short courses under the Small Business Administration. At least $3,485,000 more was spent for in-service training of governmental civilian personnel.

The survey does not list as adult education such legitimate activities as instruction for off-duty military personnel and the adult education fraction of the international education expenditure. The United States Department of Agriculture and the National Bureau of Standards list their graduate schools under higher education. The Veterans Administration lists veterans vocational rehabilitation and veterans education and counselling in the same category. Costs of public school systems of federally administered regions, such as the District of Columbia, the Canal Zone, and the Virgin Islands, are listed under elementary and secondary education, even though they include typical public school adult education programs. The Cooperative Extension Service, which the report classifies under "Research in Educational Institutions," is the most dramatic and probably the oldest direct federal program in adult education. It expended nearly $145,000,000 in 1958-59, of which 44 per cent was federal money, 34 per cent state, and 21 per cent local.

Bringing all these legitimate adult educational expenditures together, one hundred million dollars appears to be a conservative estimate of the investment by the federal government in the direct education of adults in 1956-57.

Colleges and Universities

With the exception of certain municipal universities and junior colleges, public service programs including television and radio, and the federally-financed Cooperative Extension Service, university-level adult education in the United States has tended to be self-supporting—financed from fees and tuition. Class instruction and correspondence study, which for many institutions represent the heart of the adult education program, are ordinarily financed from tuition and fees and very often make very substantial contributions to university overhead.

In public institutions the inclination has been for administrative costs to be financed from tax funds and the cost of instruction to be financed from fees and tuition. In most private universities the evening college's income covers the cost of both administration and instruction and also contributes substantial amounts to the operation of the total university. Because of the complexities of accounting systems it is difficult to estimate the amount of this contribution but in many institutions it will range as high as 40 per cent of the evening college's income.

The obligation of the state to provide university-level adult education at little or no charge has not been fully recognized in this country. And in private universities the adult education unit very seldom attracts gifts and endowments. The prevailing practice is for the adult to pay the full cost of his education.

There is no indication that this method of self-finance is changing. In 1953 John R. Morton wrote that 90 per cent of tuition fees for part-time students ranged between $5 and $10 a credit hour.[8] In the next six years tuition almost doubled. Costs of salaries and general operations have increased but there also seems to be an increasing tendency to use adult education as a means of helping to finance other university operations.

The pressure of a growing volume of students and increasing costs is very great on all universities at the present time. Private universities, unable to finance activities out of gifts and tuition, look increasingly to the evening school as an income producer. State legislators looking for ways to trim the spiraling costs of state government in general, and education in particular, are inclined to cut drastically the appropriations for university extension.

During World War II and the years immediately following, university-level adult education underwent tremendous growth. The Engineering Science and Management War Training Program and the G. I. Bill resulted in a vast expansion in numbers of students, faculty, and staff, and in variety of program. A program which was developed by public subsidy now in many areas faces the necessity of maintaining itself from private sources. The result is a most difficult financial situation.

Because of rising costs and the necessity of meeting these costs with tuition increases, there is a very real chance that university adult education is pricing itself out of a large part of the market. In the past, university extension and evening colleges served as "poor man's universities,"— where a person who had to work for a living could get an education. But there may be some tendency now toward their veering toward the education of a financial and social elite.

PRIVATE AGENCIES

Private agencies, such as proprietary schools, religious institutions, labor organizations, industry, and voluntary associations, typically operate in even more of an "enrollment economy" than the public agencies.

Their program is largely determined by what their students are willing to pay for and how much they are willing to pay, or what the management group perceives to be of value.

Many private agencies devote a considerable amount of their energy to money-raising from outside sources, such as individual contributors and philanthropic agencies. The effect of this financial policy on their educational policies is likely to be two-fold: (1) a large proportion of staff time may be diverted from educational activity to fund-raising, and (2) the interests and doctrines of donors often influence the type of educational offerings for which their contributions can be spent.

Accounting procedures in private agencies, which seldom show expenditures for the education of adults separately, make it impossible to arrive at even a rough estimate of the total adult educational expenditures by this vast segment of the field. There can be no doubt, however, that they exceed the expenditures of all other aspects of the field combined.

Proprietary Schools

In 1953, approximately 5,000,000 students paid $156,000,000 in tuition and fees to commercial, business, and trade schools—including $30,000,000 to correspondence schools.[9] By 1955 nearly 1,500,000 students were paying fees of $63,200,000 to correspondence schools alone.[10]

Operating at the owners' risk, these private independent schools exist and flourish as they meet public need and demand. They have the advantage of immediate response to public interest; at the same time they are vulnerable to rapid changes in public fancy. For greater stability, an increasing number are becoming non-profit corporations.

Adult Religious Education

Catholic, Jewish, and Protestant respondents agree that no great sums are earmarked in parish, congregational, or denominational budgets for adult religious education. Education budgets here, as in public school systems, are reserved primarily for children and youth. For adults, religious institutions seem to rely upon donated facilities and generous teachers. Costs for leadership training, retreats, and conferences are borne generally by the participants, subsidized in many cases by contributions from religious societies within the congregations.

Religious adult education leaders report the general difficulties of competition for funds, rising cost of personnel, materials, and facilities coincident with a broader and keener sense of need, and an insistence on high quality. They are concerned, too, with the relation of fees to the nature and effectiveness of the program. One authority advises "the safest way to finance an adult education program is to make it self-supporting."[11]

Adult Education in Labor Organizations

In most unions funds to carry on adult educational activities come from the general fund of the organization. Sometimes a per capita tax is levied for the purpose. The International Ladies Garment Workers Union, for example, regards local financing for classes as leading to greater autonomy and variety.[12] As is true of other sponsoring agencies, unions attempt to keep the cost for the participant as low as possible—even to paying for work-time lost. Some unions find it difficult to support educational programs, particularly to the degree of reimbursing members for lost time.

Beyond the activities supported from organizational funds, some organized labor groups conduct vocational education programs with employer-contributed funds. In some of the construction trades, for example, the employer has agreed to contribute to an education fund, from a half-cent to one and one-half cents per hour for each journeyman. The union provides secretarial and other housekeeping services for the administration of the fund. A joint committee made up of representatives of management and labor administers the fund. In some instances the funds are given to local school systems to help them provide training. In others the joint committee itself conducts the training program. Co-operation in adult education programs among labor, industry, and school groups is increasingly apparent.

The combining of education and recreation in many union budgets may contribute to the low level of urgency with which adult education is viewed in many quarters.

Business and Industry

In industry today is found the most rapidly growing arena in adult education.[13] In a sense, the great sums spent on this employee education cost business and industry nothing. Preventing turnover reduces expenditures for orientation of new employees (which may be equal to the annual salary in some instances). Similarly, improving skills, raising morale, and utilizing leadership potential, all contribute to operational efficiency offsetting the cost of the programs. In many cases, failure to conduct such programs would be corporate suicide. Dramatically new processes employing the latest in technical and operational research, could not even be undertaken without the education of technicians, operators, and supervisors. From this viewpoint such expenditures may appropriately be charged to operational expense.

Ninety per cent of the major corporations of the country conduct educational programs of some kind,[14] with a number of students equal to the total enrollment of all colleges and universities. Educational budgets of individual corporations are comparable to those of respectable colleges and universities.[15] One major corporation reports expenditures for educational purposes in 1956 of $35,000,000 to $40,000,000 covering 1500 courses and 32,000 enrollees, as well as an additional $1,400,000 in scholarship grants and fellowships.[16]

Financial as well as instructional practices vary widely. Corporations may underwrite expenditures amounting to $12,000 per student. Frequently only the training of apprentices is supported. Some charge tuition of $2.50 to $6.00 per student for classes conducted by the company outside of company time. In addition there may be contracts with educational institutions, tuition refund plans, full or partial company subsidies, work-study programs, loan funds and scholarships, and co-operative activities with labor groups and public school systems.

Voluntary Associations

The wide range of purposes, programs, and structure among voluntary organizations makes any generalization about financial problems and procedures hazardous. One distinction which many share is the close relation between educational activities and promotional appeals. In some cases the very act of giving to the cause is considered to be an educational process; the amount of contributions and the number of contributors may be taken as tokens of the success of these educational programs. As one illustration, the increase in giving to the American Cancer Society from less than a million dollars in 1945 to over thirty million dollars in 1958 is convincing evidence that many people became aware of the significance of this disease and the possibility of its cure. The cumulative impact of such appeals is attested in financial terms also by the 1958 Congressional appropriation of $75,000,000 for the National Cancer Institute. This close relationship between education and fund-raising is shown also by the necessarily great numbers of volunteers recruited throughout the country who must be trained in the basic facts related with the campaign in order to achieve any impressive financial results.

A serious issue among such national voluntary fund-raising organizations is the merit of joining united appeals. One of the major problems is the multiplicity of voluntary organizations and social agencies. In the health field alone there are more than sixty agencies seeking public support nationally. This situation creates public resistance. This is an issue in terms of volunteer time as well as of available money. At the moment there appears to be a hardening of public attitude on this matter as well as a sharpening of the issue and a crystallization of distinct points of view among health organizations.

Adult Education Councils

Councils are primarily dependent organizations. Operating as they do largely behind the scenes assisting the programs of other organizations, they face serious difficulties in educating their sources of revenue sufficiently well to give them the necessary freedom of action to realize their full value. Even among those agencies which benefit most greatly, coordination appears to be hard to sell.

In 1959 the chief sources of support of seven councils with budgets of any significant size were as follows:

Denver	$22,000 from educational institutions
St. Louis & Cincinnati	$10,000 each from community chest
Chattanooga	$ 6,800 from fund-raising campaign
Chicago	$19,000 from publications, advertising and sales
	$22,000 from Speakers Bureau
	$25,000 from contributions
New York City	Gifts and memberships

Some thirty other councils throughout the country operate without the benefit of sufficient funds to support a paid staff. These frequently have a non-financial subsidy in terms of free quarters, free staff service from other agencies, voluntary workers, and donated utilities.

Budgets, in any case, are generally unreliable, and occupy a considerable amount of staff time and energy. For instance, the budget of the Adult Education Council of the Chattanooga Area had varied from $12,150, (almost entirely from the Fund for Adult Education) in 1952, its first year, to a maximum of $23,550 in 1956-57 and down to $9,250 in 1957-58. During a five-year period, $30,700 was raised locally.

Membership dues, foundation grants, community chest participation, service fees, institutional memberships, and grants from public institutions such as boards of education and libraries, in varying proportions comprise the budgets of these councils. Memberships and gifts are the most common—if not greatest in amount. Each arrangement has advantages and disadvantages: raising gifts from individual membership takes great amounts of staff time; community chest participation raises questions about an education-charity emphasis; income largely from organizational or institutional memberships may limit the nature and scope of the program to that of the interests of the contributing organizations; and dependence on service fees may force the organization onto an operating rather than a co-ordinating function. In every case there is danger that the educational effort may become secondary to that of fund-raising.

A co-ordinative organization needs to demonstrate the significance of its function to its potential constituency (not to say the community at large) sufficiently well to justify its contributing participation. The difficulty of this appeal is sometimes aggravated by popular assumptions that foundation generosity makes local effort unnecessary.

In Denver, the annual income was increased from $13,000 in 1955 to $22,000 in 1959, largely through an intensive program of interpretation of the services to member organizations. This effort resulted not only in increased membership (from 98 to 127 agencies), but also in increase in demands for services for which organizations are willing to pay a fee. The Cincinnati and New York Councils also benefited from programs for public understanding of their activities and needs.

Another favorable trend is improved relationship between the co-ordinating councils and the business and industrial leadership of the communities. More businessmen are serving on the boards and committees of local councils.

PUBLIC POLICY

Any assessment of public policy as it affects the financing of adult education must be measured against the stark reality of action: the opening of purse strings, be they those of governmental units, of public philanthropy, of the individual student, or of individual patrons.

To the degree that legislators recognize and crystallize public policy, tangible evidence may be sought in their enactments. By this measure adult education policy is tenuous and confused. The most recent state laws are as contradictory as earlier ones have been shown to be; federal laws generally fail to identify adult education even when they affect it. Federal support for general adult education is wanting—but as Table 2 shows, not only do traditional specialized areas hold their position, but new ones appear with nearly every Congress.

TABLE 2[17]

FEDERAL FUNDS* RELATED TO ADULT EDUCATION
(Thousands)

AREA	1948-49	1950-51	1952-53	1954-55	1956-57	1957-58
Agricultural Extension	30,438	32,141	32,117	39,550	49,700	50,715
Vocational Rehabilitation	18,216	21,101	22,948	24,790	37,786	45,800
Apprenticeship Training	2,599	3,183	3,324	3,160	3,399	3,600
Mines Safety		780	837	850	898	1,000
Bureau of Prisons		389	422	461	530	538
Public Health Trainees			7,438	11,051	30,836	38,077
National Science Foundation			41	316	10,948	11,056
Library Services Act					1,890	5,000
Civil Defense					707	
Practical Nursing					2,000	4,000
Fishery Occupations						228

*Selected List

These represent strongly felt, tangible, readily demonstrable needs, of which an appropriation of $850,000 for a White House Conference on Aging is another illustration.

It would be optimistic to interpret legislation enacted up to the present time as indicating a trend toward federal support for the general field of adult education, but the National Defense Education Act significantly has no restrictions which would preclude public school adult education programs from receiving monies and the Hill-Elliott proposal would support general extension in a manner similar to that provided for agricultural extension. A half-dozen bills for educational television, and the host of education bills jamming congressional committee agenda are additional indicia of growing public concern.

Other tangible evidences rest in the amounts given to volunteer educational agencies, the amounts of tuition which educational institutions can demand, and the reactions of individuals and foundations to pleas for support. Public response to appeals and the popularity of specific adult education programs for which people are willing to pay tuition are uncertain criteria, in that success is contagious and these tokens may be ephemeral.

Another assessment of public policy may be made from the pronouncements of official, professional, and opinion-controlling leaders. On November 7, 1958, at the Convention of the National Association for Public School Educators in Cincinnati, the U. S. Commissioner of Education stated: "Adult Education is a matter of survival, not of choice," adding that in the Soviet Union, education is considered a primary weapon in the cold war, deliberately challenging the United States, and they believe that we will not commit ourselves.

In 1938 President Roosevelt's Advisory Committee on Education strongly recommended federal support for adult education. In 1947 the President's Committee on Higher Education recommended federal money to be distributed through the United States Office of Education to support adult education. This repeated a recommendation made by the Advisory Committee on Education in the thirties. In 1957 the Second Report of the President's Committee on Education Beyond the High School recommended that the Secretary of Health, Education, and Welfare call one or more national conferences to seek ways of solving the problems of adult education.

The President's Science Advisory (Killian) Committee in 1958 stressed the "urgency of providing high grade and plentiful science adult education now" to permit our citizenry to exercise intelligence in decisions which "cannot be postponed while we are improving our present educational system so that its products will constitute a significant fraction of the mature voting population."

The president of the Fund for Adult Education exhorted in the Spring of 1958 that:

> Organizations should offer incentives to actual and potential leaders to take part in (this education)—incentives by paying the tuition and providing "time off" from the job where necessary. If this is not done, the courses will not be offered or taken. It is not a question of being able to bear the cost of the courses—it is a question of not being able to bear the consequence of not preparing our leaders.[18]

In a statement on national policy, the Committee for Economic Development in February, 1958, said:

> Support for education should include needless to say, support for agencies of *self*-education—often the best means of individual improvement. These agencies such as libraries, museums, public lectures, educational television and adult education courses are highly dependent upon public resources. As leisure increases, this healthy impulsion to self-education will no doubt greatly expand and will call for wider effort.

The president of the Carnegie Corporation of New York wrote in 1958:

> Unfortunately the conception of individual fulfillment and life-long learning which animates the commencement speaker finds no adequate reflection in our social institutions. For too long we have paid pious lip service to the idea and trifled with it in practice. If we believe that what we profess concerning the worth of the individual then the idea of individual fulfillment within the framework of moral purpose must become our deepest concern, our national preoccupation, our passion, our obsession.
>
> Aside from formal educational systems there is little evidence of any such preoccupation. Some religious groups are doing excellent work. Our libraries and museums are a legitimate source of pride. Adult education programs have become increasingly effective. Certain of our organizations concerned with social welfare and with mental health play a profoundly important role.[19]

Many references by leaders to our educational problems refer only obliquely, if at all, to adult education. The adult educator may interpret these as support, but it must be assumed that they strike a glancing blow, if any, upon the public—or upon legislators.

The Superintendent of the Baltimore Public Schools, in an address to the National Education Association on February 9, 1959, stated:

> One cannot help wondering whether the policymakers really know how much there is to be done and how little time we have.
>
> We should be naive to consider the power to make policy apart from the power to translate that policy into action. Power to control rests on the power to decide. Modern education can be made effective beyond imagination if we will but . . . decide to use our resources to take advantage of our opportunities.[20]

In terms of action, however, it is apparent that the policy, as expressed by legislation, has not kept up with these far-sighted viewpoints. Less than two-fifths of our states had passed a personal income tax law, even fewer had sales tax provisions, and only nineteen had both, despite the fact that lack of funds for education is so crucial.

Committees of citizens at any level almost invariably call upon education, and obviously adult education, to do something about such problems as housing, juvenile delinquency, human relations, and lack of skilled manpower—even education about the necessity to pay taxes. However, appropriations of private as well as of public bodies provide little or no monetary support for their demands.

Footnotes

[1]The information on which this section is based was provided by Grace T. Stevenson. Deputy Executive Director, American Library Association.

[2]Helen Lyman Smith, *Adult Education Activities in Public Libraries* (Chicago: American Library Association, 1953), p. 58.

[3]Muriel Javelin, *Wilson Library Bulletin,* May, 1958.

[4]For a comprehensive table of "Legal Provisions in the 48 States for Adult Education Programs in the Public Schools, as of December, 1957" see: Charles H. Radcliffe and John B. Holden, "Adults in Public Schools," *School Life,* XL (April, 1958).

[5]Edward B. Olds, *Financing Adult Education* (Chicago: Adult Education Association of the USA, 1954), pp. 16-21.

[6]Albert R. Munse and Edna D. Booher, *Federal Funds for Education 1956-57 and 1957-58.* U. S. Office of Education Bulletin 1959 No. 2 (Washington, D.C.; Government Printing Office, 1959).

[7]The information on which this section is based was provided by Richard Bray, Associate Dean of Administration and Director, Division of General & Special Studies, The American University.

[8]John R. Morton, *University Extension in the United States* (University, Ala.: University of Alabama Press, 1953).

[9]U. S. Department of Commerce, *Survey of Current Business* (Washington, D.C.: Government Printing Office, July, 1953).

[10]*Private Home-Study Schools in the United States* (Washington, D.C.: Home Study Council, October, 1956).

[11]Anthony Salamone, "Setting up an Adult Program," *Handbook for Catholic Adult Education* (Milwaukee: Bruce Publishing Co., 1958), p. 78.

[12]Mark Starr, Report Educational Department ILGWU, 1959. (Mimeographed.)

[13]Burton W. Kreitlow, *Review of Educational Research,* XXIX (June, 1959), 225.

[14]President's Committee on Education Beyond the High School, *Second Report to the President* (Washington, D.C.: Government Printing Office, July, 1957).

[15]William H. White, *The Organization Man* (New York: Simon and Shuster, 1956), p. 120.

[16]Ralph J. Cordiner, Testimony before the Congressional Committee on Automation, October, 1955.

[17]Albert R. Munse, and Edna D. Booher, *Federal Funds for Education 1956-57 and 1957-58, op. cit.,* pp. 18-19.

[18]C. Scott Fletcher, *The Great Awakening* (White Plains, N.Y.: The Fund for Adult Education, 1958), p. 17.

[19]John W. Gardner, *The Servant of All Our Purposes* (New York: The Carnegie Corporation, 1958), pp. 5-6.

[20]John H. Fischer, "Effective Modern Education as the Educator Sees It," *NEA Journal* (March, 1959), 15.

Selected Readings

Clark, Burton R. *Adult Education in Transition.* Berkeley: University of California Press, 1958.

Clark, Harold F., and Sloan, Harold S. *Classrooms in the Factories.* New York: New York University Press, 1958.

A Design for Democracy. An Abridgement of a Report of the Adult Education Committee of the British Ministry of Reconstruction in 1919. New York: Association Press, 1956.

Dyer, John. *Ivory Towers in the Market Place.* Indianapolis: Bobbs-Merrill Co., 1956.

Grattan, C. Hartley. *In Quest of Knowledge: A Historical Perspective on Adult Education.* New York: Association Press, 1955.

Holden, John B. *Adult Education Services of State Departments of Education.* U. S. Office of Education Bulletin No. 31. Washington, D. C.: Government Printing Office, 1959.

————. "Factors Relating to the Financial Support of Continuing Education as Revealed by a Study of Selected Michigan Communities." Unpublished Doctoral Dissertation, Ohio State University, 1955.

Keeler, Sister Jerome. (ed.) *Handbook of Catholic Adult Education.* Milwaukee: Bruce Publishing Co., 1959.

Kempfer, Homer H. *Adult Education.* New York: McGraw-Hill, 1955.

Miller, Leon F. "Statutory Provisions for Adult Education and Their Implementation." Unpublished Doctor's Thesis, Department of Education, University of Chicago, 1950.

Morton, John R. *University Extension in the United States.* University, Ala.: University of Alabama Press, 1953.

Munse, Albert R., and Booher, Edna D. *Federal Funds for Education 1956-57 and 1957-58.* U. S. Office of Education Bulletin No. 2, 1959. Washington, D. C.: Government Printing Office, 1959.

National Association of Public School Adult Educators. *Public School Adult Education: A Guide for Administrators and Teachers.* Washington, D. C.: National Education Association, 1956.

National Education Association, Division of Adult Education Service. *A Study of Urban Public School Adult Education Programs of the United States.* Washington, D. C.: National Education Association, 1952.

Olds, Edward B. *Financing Adult Education in America's Public Schools and Community Councils.* Report of the National Commission on Adult Education Finance. Chicago: Adult Education Association of the U.S.A., 1954.

Powell, John W. *Learning Comes of Age.* Chicago: Adult Education Association of the U.S.A., 1956.

Schad, Edward. *Catholic Adult Education.* Unpublished Master's Thesis, Catholic University, 1955.

Seeley, John R., et al. *Community Chest: A Case Study in Philanthropy.* Toronto: University of Toronto Press, 1957.

Shea, Albert A. (ed.) *Culture in Canada.* Toronto: Canadian Association for Adult Education, 1952.

Sheats, Paul H., et al. *Adult Education.* New York: Dryden Press, 1953.

Steiner, Arch K. *State School Legislation.* U. S. Office of Education Bulletin 1959 No. 10. Washington, D. C.: Government Printing Office, 1959.

U. S. Office of Education. *Administration of Vocational Education.* Vocational Division Bulletin No. 1, 1958. Washington, D. C.: Government Printing Office, 1958.

Digest of Annual Reports of State Boards of Education. Washington, D. C.: Government Printing Office, 1957.

Van Orman, William T. "Did Congress Overlook Adult Education?" *The Public School Adult Educator* II (March, 1959), 51-52.

CHAPTER 13

ARCHITECTURE FOR ADULT EDUCATION

JOHN W. BECKER

*Garriott and Becker
Architects, and Chairman
AEA Commission on Architecture*

In the fall of 1956, under the joint sponsorship of the Adult Education Association of the U.S.A. and the Fund for Adult Education, a group designated as The National Commission on Architecture concluded two years of research into physical facilities for adult education, and published a monograph entitled "Architecture for Adult Education." This was the first effort to treat the subject with discrimination and comprehensiveness; and the commission's work focussed attention on a major phase of what is widely acknowledged as the fastest growing movement in American learning. A number of related conferences and articles followed, culminating (December, 1958) in a conference of national scope based upon "Creating a Favorable Environment for Adult Education."

While preparing the original study, and in subsequent investigation, those interested in coming to conclusions about architecture for adult education had occasion more than once to circulate questionnaires among sponsors, teachers, and learners. They not infrequently inquired as to the individual's likes or dislikes about the physical facilities in which he presently worked, and what he regarded as desirable changes. The replies to these solicitations were often more revealing in what they failed to indicate than in what they disclosed. They showed to what a very large degree adult education procedures in America are still carried on in hand-me-down or makeshift surroundings, an environment so primitive and meager that the creative imagination of the user is almost completely inhibited. Most of the respondents seemed to be contented with suggestions for quite minimal improvement: folding chairs, more conference rooms, adult toilets, adequate heat, reasonable privacy, etc.

The reasons behind so widespread a tolerance for ramshackle accommodation are two-fold. For one thing, its phenomenal growth in the United States has caused adult education in many areas to outrun its facilities. For another, many educational authorities still feel that except for courses in literacy, vocational training, or citizenship, the official underwriting of anything like autonomous adult facilities bears the stigma of "welfare" culture.

ARCHITECTURAL REQUIREMENTS FOR ADULT EDUCATION

However, architecture for adult education is not altogether an architecture of relegation. The older attitudes are crumbling. More and more adult facilities are becoming the province of design, not of afterthought. Where physical planning for adult education has established itself as an integral part of the community's cultural life, its sponsors might be expected to turn over to their architect early in the development of a building project a list of such general requirements as these: (1) accessibility of site to transportation—public as well as private; (2) adequate off-street and on-street parking; (3) level or near-level building approaches—ramps preferred; (4) proximity of facilities to main entrance— upper story occupancy, except by elevator, prohibited; (5) conference- and work-rooms of varying sizes and flexible arrangement—with adult-size furniture, when facilities are shared, close at hand; (6) good lighting and acoustics (since about seven-eighths of adult classes are still taught at night, the importance of the former is obvious); (7) ample storage, including general storage; storage for adult work-in-progress—particularly if the curriculum includes the fine arts, the home arts, crafts, and shop—and storage for instructional materials belonging to adult-faculty members; (8) room for displays and exhibits; (9) administrative space, no matter how limited, reserved exclusively for adult education activity; (10) as many amenities as the budget will afford, such as audio-visual aids—including blackout blinds and soundproofing, snack-bar, extra ventilation to handle smoking-loads, and year-round air conditioning in warm climates.

TYPES OF PHYSICAL FACILITIES

Buildings for adult education may be classified into those in which adult education shares quarters with other types of cultural activity on a part-time, after-hour, or concurrent basis, and those which are designed exclusively for the education of adults. The latter type of facility, usually found on the college campus, is a comparatively recent and extraordinarily interesting development, to which further attention will be directed later in this chapter. The former—the shared facility—is far and away the most prevalent. And in this class, first in popularity in the United States, as might be expected, comes the public school, chiefly the high school;

next, the college and university building; and then libraries, community
centers, religious institutions, buildings for industry, health centers,
recreation centers, and union headquarters. Limitations of space preclude
analysis of all these types of structure here; but since the first four are
used by a considerable variety of adult educational agencies a brief discussion of their typical features and typical problems is essential.

Public Schools

Public schools accommodate a large share of this country's adult education programs. Their non-sectarian character, community ownership,
and neighborhood dispersal will probably continue this ratio indefinitely.
Partly because of adult insistence, the great majority even of elementary
school plans today call for the inclusion of a multi-purpose room—in
itself an elementary but extremely useful adjunct to adult learning. For
maximum usefulness such rooms commonly have a platform or a modest
stage at one end, are frequently divisible into two or three smaller areas
by means of insulated folding partitions, and are provided with storage
space for adult furniture and equipment. If the multi-purpose room
doubles as dining room during daytime hours, there will be a handy
kitchen close by. Sometimes such rooms are found in even more useful
proximity to a library or to a gymnasium—in which case the common
wall between the two areas may become a movable one, and the multi-
purpose room on occasion be expanded for group use rather than subdivided.

A discussion of the elementary school multi-purpose room as a kind
of least common denominator of adult education facilities invariably
triggers a debate about multiple use in general, as well as its corollary,
flexibility. Both rank high as desirable characteristics of buildings for
adult education, along with such other basic practical qualities as economy and ingenuity in planning. And in this debate a good deal of
prejudice against the multi-purpose concept comes to the fore. It is
undoubtedly true that a room cannot be all things to all men, any more
than a man can. An intent to provide universal accommodations in any
given space would obviously end by providing none effectively. But we
are not really concerned here with "all-purpose" facilities, only with
reasonably versatile ones. Furthermore, the parties to this controversy
should soberly reflect that, considering the tight budget for adult education in most American communities and the widespread need for sharing,
the acceptance or rejection of adaptable or convertible facilities will in
countless instances mean the difference between having an adult education program and forgoing one. It is significant that more rather than
fewer such facilities have been incorporated into the architecture of
adult education during the past decade than ever before.

Economy has been cited as a major, if obvious, factor in producing adult education facilities—as indeed it is, to a large extent, in the production of all valid architecture. But some distinctions and extensions of meaning must be recorded here. Economy does not imply niggardliness; no building can serve its public well if it has been built to starvation-level specifications. Again, economy is not only a qualitative term, but an inclusive one. It extends not only to means and materials, but also to function. As many legitimate ways to reduce construction cost can be discovered in a careful reappraisal of program as in the elimination of "waste space." One example is afforded by a recent experience of the writer in designing a large senior high school for a civic-minded school board in the Middle West. Two members envisioned a huge auditorium as the jewel of the plan—an auditorium which would not only hold the entire student body of twelve hundred, but would be "second to none" in a metropolitan area already provided with four or five auditoriums of like capacity, seldom filled. A majority of the board—and the architect—maintained, on the contrary, that what with TV inside and outside the school, and the availability of the big school gym for such rare mass events as graduation, a big auditorium would be a prodigal extravagance. In the end the board wisely decided to pass up prestige for hard sense; and they were rewarded with an auditorium of realistic size (750 auditors) perfectly equipped for dramatics and music, with several added classrooms and a little theater seating 125, thrown in as "bonus." Not incidentally, the "bonus" areas are exceedingly well-adapted to the district's up-and-coming adult education program.

The elementary public school—chiefly by reason of its modest group-room accommodations—is a humble but hardy perennial in the field of adult education. Sometimes, indeed, adult educators prefer it—in rural areas because it lies closer at hand than the secondary school, and in urban areas when the secondary school becomes preoccupied, so to speak, by round-the-clock teenage activity. But by and large it is the high school, among public schools, which has become the preferred base of adult operations. The very diversity of its program has brought about this preference; to say nothing of the near-adult scale of its facilities.

The period since the Second World War has witnessed the consolidation of high school districts on a prodigious scale all over the country. And consolidation has led to a number of interesting developments in the field of secondary school planning, among which are several of real significance to adult education. Bigger plant means, on the whole, lower building costs. Administrators have been encouraged to add to their space-requirements a few modest amenities such as increased library space, audio-visual departments, conference rooms, student centers, and small auditoriums which admirably serve the uses of a collateral adult education program. Where the more favored districts have ventured into "campus-planning," adults will often find concentrated in one or two buildings of the group—in the administration-library-conference unit, for example, or that given over to homemaking, shop, and craft—accommodations made the more congenial by their atmosphere of discreteness and autonomy.

Universities

Many types of campus buildings make room for the myriad adult education programs sponsored today by the American university. They include all sorts of specialized facilities—magnificently equipped auditoriums such as the one at Oberlin; centers for art, music, and the drama, as at the University of Arkansas; innumerable student union buildings, which handle the great bulk of the colleges' informal adult education activities; and an increasing number of buildings in which the university's extension division, impressively enlarged, finds itself in inspired proximity to main libraries, experimental theaters, and the like. Newly constructed examples of the latter are the Purdue Memorial Union, the Baker Memorial at Western Reserve, Kolbe Hall at Akron, and the Rackham Memorial in Detroit, where the two local universities have recently pooled their adult education resources and effort.

Libraries

Providing facilities for the modern library system is a dual problem, particularly in larger urban centers. On the one hand, there is an increasing need for film, recording, TV, conference and lecture facilities at a central plant—not to mention the traditional library facilities per se; on the other, for responding to a very vigorous demand that new branch buildings in suburban locations be prepared to duplicate many of these functions.

Community Buildings

As for the community building, a great number of expanding satellite towns have seized the opportunity, in recent years, of adding to the usual administrative building complex—police, fire, managerial offices, etc.—accommodations for cultural and group activity. A familiar plan for such projects is of the "H" or "C" variety, with protection operating in one parallel bar, civic activities in the other, and administration between.

Adult Education Centers

The second broad class of physical facilities for adult education—buildings erected exclusively for it—may be in turn subdivided. There are those which provide educational facilities only, and those which combine them with residential quarters. Of the former, perhaps the most recent prototype is the Wisconsin Center Building, at the University of Wisconsin. Overlooking Lake Mendota, it provides on the first floor a handsome main lobby and lounge, an auditorium seating approximately two hundred which communicates with an exhibition gallery running along one side; several conference rooms of varied sizes; and an administrative suite. On the floor below is a 200-seat dining room, which may be expanded into exhibition areas adjacent to it. On the second and third floors are a highly versatile pattern of meeting and conference rooms, each distinctively furnished, with a small lounge on each floor close to the registration desk, and a larger lounge commanding the lake view. One very interesting feature of the Wisconsin Center is that no state funds whatever were used to finance it; all money for construction came from private sources, mostly alumni.

Of the buildings which have been called "adult education in residence" two have been completed under the sponsorship of the Kellogg Foundation. One is at Michigan State University, the other at the University of Georgia. At Michigan facilities similar to those at Wisconsin are topped by living accommodations; at Georgia these latter occur in a five-story wing at one end of the building. Three other "Kellogg Centers" are presently under construction. In California a residential center of a less formal type has been developed by the state university at Arrowhead Lake, in a setting of great natural charm.

Children go to school because it is expected of them; adults, on the contrary, because they volunteer. More than in any other type of structure does design for adult education present an exciting challenge: to the learner, whose collaboration is mature, indispensable—and permissive; to the architect and sponsor, who are handling a medium untrammeled by preconceptions and tradition. For all contributors the most vital working principle is simply this: that the successful architectural environment must always be more than the sum total of its parts. Money, good will, and reasonable forethought are likely, in nine situations out of ten, to produce a cluster of workmanlike physical facilities. But these are by no means of and by themselves architecture. For architecture is, after all, a synthesis in four—not three—dimensions; the fourth being the dimension of delight. Inspired design—inspired environment—these are in their own serene and powerful way, and in the highest sense, educative.

Selected Readings

Architecture for Adult Education. Report of the Commission on Architecture. Chicago: Adult Education Association. n.d.

Creating a Climate for Adult Learning. Report of a national conference on architecture for adult education. Chicago: Adult Education Association, 1959.

CHAPTER 14

THE LITERATURE OF
ADULT EDUCATION

COOLIE VERNER
Professor of Adult Education
Florida State University
Tallahassee, Florida

Like the field itself, the literature about adult education ranges widely over a vast array of topics in a highly disorganized manner. Far more has been written about adult education than many people realize and it has been appearing for a very long time. Very little of this material can be classified as great or even highly significant to the field, but all of it has been timely.

FORM

The literature of adult education has appeared at one time or another in all of the forms of presentation common to printed matter. Much of it is ephemeral in nature and, thus, does not survive for long the destructive influences of time.

Books

Books tend to survive more than any other form. They are fairly easy to collect and preserve, so that one might find somewhere a copy of each of the books that have been published about adult education. Some of the earlier books are as scarce as the first volumes printed from movable type, with only one or two copies known to exist—while other items may be found in abundance. Survival alone is not necessarily an indication of quality, of course, but it does measure to some degree a society's perception of the importance of adult education literature. Perhaps less than half a dozen copies of the first separate book to discuss adult education are extant, even though over 2,000 copies were issued only 145 years ago. Only one copy of this book has been located in an American collection.

Pamphlets

Ephemeral material does not survive as well as books. Because of its form, such publications are almost impossible to classify, catalogue, and preserve; therefore, individuals and institutions rarely retain in their collections any substantial number of the many pamphlets, brochures, catalogues, and broadsides that have been issued. Most of this ephemeral material is issued for specific and immediately functional reasons, such as the schedules issued by local programs, which have little permanent value to the field. At the same time, however, there have been many valuable studies, reports, and historically significant documents issued in ephemeral form that should not be wholly discounted and lost.

Periodicals

Articles on adult education constitute the largest segment of the total body of appropriate literature, and they are generally available because of the preservation of the periodicals in which they have appeared. A number of specific periodicals have been devoted exclusively to adult education, but complete runs of these are not always readily available. Some periodicals have ceased publication, such as the *Bulletin* of the World Association for Adult Education. Others have changed their format, sequence of publication, and title, such as the American periodical, *Adult Education*. These specialized periodicals will naturally contain the greatest bulk of the pertinent literature in this form, but they include by no means all of it.

Unpublished Material

There is a very sizeable quantity of literature that does not appear in print which represents some of the best contributions to the field. Among the unpublished literature may be found various types of institutional studies and reports as well as theses and dissertations. These latter items are generally in available form, since they are preserved in their appropriate university libraries or can be secured on microfilm. Theses and dissertations will be listed generally in the appropriate indexes, but the miscellaneous institutional reports and studies are unavailable.

LOCATING THE LITERATURE

The body of material about adult education forms a vast unsystematized mass that is difficult to identify and all but impossible to locate.

No single comprehensive collection of the literature exists either here or abroad in any public or private institution or collection. Furthermore, no single bibliography lists pertinent items and no evaluative guide identifies the significant items that should be collected, preserved, and used. At the end of this chapter is a list of some of the major bibliographic works that may serve as a starting point in the search for material, but none of them either singly or collectively is adequate.

In the search for items in the literature the field is victimized by library practices. The two principal schemes used in cataloguing printed materials are the Library of Congress and the Dewey Decimal systems, neither of which has a general subject heading "Adult Education" into which the appropriate literature is classified. Both systems catalogue some but not all adult education material under the heading *Education of Adults* which cannot accommodate the entire field or its sub-divisions. Most other subject areas and disciplines are provided for under separate headings, but the material about adult education is dispersed illogically throughout the whole structure of the system. The heading "Adult Education" is used as a title entry in the dictionary catalogue for those items in which those words constitute the title. The bulk of the literature about adult education, however, is neither classified nor catalogued under a heading that even remotely resembles the subject.

Through standard library practice, these cataloguing and classifying procedures, more than any other single force, have seriously inhibited the use of relevant literature and retarded the systematic development of knowledge about educating adults. To find the literature about adult education one must be an expert in the field, able to identify, and thus search through all the pertinent institutional and subject headings that constitute aspects of the field.

These inhibiting procedures will not be altered until sufficient demand for change necessitates the modification of existing systems. This will not come about, of course, until the profession uses the literature with sufficient frequency that the need for changes in the system becomes obvious. Perhaps the constructive use of the literature of adult education will increase as the field itself becomes unified and acquires a sense of common identity through which the dispersed parts gain a perception of their relationship to the whole. Certainly the quantity of substantive knowledge about educating adults is accumulating at such a rate that adult educators will be forced to use the literature in order to keep in step with the developments in the field.

EARLY DEVELOPMENTS

Literature about educating adults made its first appearance in 1814 in Bristol, England, when the Philadelphia-born Quaker, Dr. Thomas Pole, published a small volume with the title: *A History of the Origin and Progress of Adult Schools. . . .* The first printing of 2,000 copies was sold very quickly and in 1816 it was augmented and re-issued. This slim volume is almost wholly unknown to the field and only very few copies are extant.

Pole's work performed the same function for adult educators of its day as do many books today, containing a rationale as well as an analysis of administrative and teaching methodology. Dr. Pole set a moralistic stamp on the field that is still influential. He recognized that people could learn at any age, although he reached this conclusion from experiences in teaching people of all ages rather than from systematic study of adult learning. He insisted that society should teach the poor to read so they could study the Bible for themselves and thus improve their moral qualities. While Pole's rationale is of little interest today, his comments on the organization and conduct of adults schools are of current interest. It becomes obvious very shortly upon reading Pole that the field has actually made very little progress in some respects, since the problems he discusses fill the literature of today without much change. It is interesting to read Dr. Pole's book and the latest general work to be published in England, *Adult Education,* by Professor Robert Peers, at the same time—a comparison of the two provides a startling measure of progress in the field.

Pole was followed shortly by other adult educators. At Windsor in 1816 a pamphlet of 149 pages was published under the title: *Account of the Origin, Principles, Proceedings, and Results of an Institution for Teaching Adults to Read, Established in the Contiguous Parts of Bucks and Berks in 1814.* Since this was in effect a case study report of an adult educational activity, it might be considered to be the first report of an experiment in adult education. This item is even scarcer than Pole's book. In 1821 in London, J. E. Winks published a *History of Adult Schools* that is so rare only one copy has been discovered, and its contribution to the field has not been assessed. An essay by Brougham, *Practical Observations upon the Education of the People* . . . published in London in 1825, was probably the most influential piece on adult education at that time; twenty editions were exhausted during its first year.

These earliest works about adult education were largely propagandistic and sought to exhort the reading segments of the society to provide schools for their illiterate neighbors. In the process of presenting their arguments to support the establishment and maintenance of adult schools they provided some data reflecting their experiences with educational programs for adults. Thus, we can get today a fairly complete picture of the early beginnings of organized adult education in western society.

The propaganda function is still a dominant aspect of the literature of adult education; however, there is a conspicuous difference in the nature of the rationale that underlies the propaganda. The early 19th century was individual-centered and influenced by moralistic and theological motivation. Early adult educators were impelled by the urge to save the souls of the illiterates by teaching them to read the Holy Writ and thus augment the work of the local clergy. Sin was equated with illiteracy without any perception of a relationship between sin and poverty or between illiteracy and poverty. The poor were sinful because they were illiterate, not because they were poor; therefore, by teaching the poor to read they could help save themselves from sin without, at the same time, undermining that "cheerful submission to their lot" as poor that was thought characteristic of them. In time, of course, this perception of poverty changed and by the turn of the century the demand for education from the working class in English society grew from a search for power to relieve poverty rather than sin, and the poor were less cheerful in submitting to their lot.

While the literature of adult education today is still dominated by impressionistic propaganda, the rationale is socially- rather than individually-centered. In the present society illiteracy and poverty are equated, and adult educators are motivated by materialistic utility. Continuous education extends beyond illiteracy into the whole fabric of society in order that every person might acquire the knowledge essential to adjustment to change and preserve the social order.

Most of the literature about adult education that is read at all is read by adult educators; and since they are in general agreement on the need for continuous education, such impressionistic propaganda is less important in the present age. Adult educators need less exhortation to justify their existence to themselves and more substantive knowledge so that they can perform their function appropriately. While the public needs continuous exhortation to pursue its own education further, adult educators themselves need to know more about the basic elements of their craft.

AREAS OF CONTENT

History

At some time or other the literature of adult education has included every familiar category of written matter. Among other things and in company with many other branches of knowledge, the literature of adult education includes a generous supply of historical material.

Since adult education is primarily an institution-centered activity, the historical literature tends to be largely institutional—it records the development of adult education within the context of specific institutions. Thus, we have a sizeable collection of material on the Chautauqua, the Lyceum, University Extension, the Moonlight Schools, and similar programs. There are, however, very few studies that weave together into one consistent whole the many varied pieces that constitute the fabric of adult education history. Grattan's *In Quest of Knowledge* is an effort in this direction that achieves a reasonable degree of success.

General histories of any human activity must depend upon an abundance of detailed studies of specialized segments of the past; and while there have been a number of local histories, on either an institutional or area basis, the historical literature of adult education is both irregular and inconsistent in this respect. Some specialized programs have been reported with some distinction; and while it is inappropriate here to attempt a listing of all notable historical studies, a sampling will show the range available to interested adult educators. The Quaker-sponsored adult school movement has been reported by Hudson (1851), Rowntree and Binns (1903), and Martin (1924). University Extension in England has been described by Draper (1923), among others, and the history of the Workers Education Association, by Stocks (1953). Continuation schools in England and elsewhere have been studied by Sadler in his monumental and definitive volume published in 1908. The Folk High School movement in Denmark has received detailed study by Begtrup, Lund, and Manniche in their book, *The Folk High Schools of Denmark,* and Moller and Watson in their *Education in Democracy.*

Not many of these items are well known to many active adult educators, and more the pity. There is much to be learned from the experiences of the past as provided by such detailed histories. Actually, very few libraries—either institutional or private—can boast a representative collection of some of these significant historical studies. Perhaps, in time they will become highly sought after; but, by then, their pecuniary value will place them beyond the reach of the members of the profession whose history they report.

Adult education in America is more thoroughly reported from an historical perspective than elsewhere, but such literature is only fragmentary. There have been a multitude of historical reports from single institutions and single geographical areas. These range from small studies of single phases of an institutional program, such as Stockton's histories of special extension activities in Kansas, to Mann, Getsinger, and Sworders' study of adult education in California. In addition, reports have been published relating to certain aspects of adult education in the public schools, libraries, Cooperative Extension Service, workers education, and university extension, among others. Far too many of these historical studies have been issued in pamphlet form, with the result that they quickly become fugitive and all but lost to the field.

There is accumulating slowly the mass of localized histories that can serve as the basis for generalized historical studies. The localized institutional histories must be consolidated into general institutional histories first and then from these can come the broad overview of adult education as a whole.

Among the historical forms, the biography is the least represented in the literature of adult education. This may be due to a number of factors: either adult educators have not had sufficient prominence in the world at large; biographers have not found the life histories of prominent adult educators of sufficient interest to warrant the labor required to prepare one; or adult education has been such a peripheral activity in the lives of people that it has not received attention. One such biography has appeared recently with the issuance of Kelly's study of George Birkbeck who founded the Working Men's College movement in England and for whom Birkbeck College of the University of London is named. The life histories of some other adult educators have been written but, by and large, not nearly as many as are deserving of the attention of biographers. There is also a need for a checklist of such biographies so that the field might have some perception of its distinguished pioneers.

Surveys

The use of the survey is generally a mark of the initial development of a field from a chance activity to an area for systematic study. In the literature of adult education the survey is well represented. J. W. Hudson should probably receive credit for making the first systematic survey of adult education. In his *The History of Adult Education,* published in London in 1851, he provided data on the number of adult schools then in operation in England, with information on the extent of participation and the many forms of organized adult education. He included Adult and Benevolent Evening Schools, Village and Farmers' Clubs, Young Men's Reformation, Mental Improvement Societies, Adult Poor Schools, Literary and Institutional Unions, Schools of Design, Museums, Factory News Rooms, Public and Itinerating Libraries, and Atheneums.

Among the data Hudson reports are many curious bits of information, such as the fact that in Manchester twenty thousand brochures produced only fifty students—a familiar situation today. In addition to reporting on adult education in England, he also provides data on adult schools in New York and Philadelphia.

In many respects Hudson merely revised Pole's earlier work without paying suitable respects to his progenitor. Even so, Hudson provides more complete data on adult education than had Pole, and thus his work gains adequate status in its own right. The survey pattern initiated by Hudson has been followed many times since, and surveys have become a standard item in the literature.

Surveys perform a very useful function by providing a picture of the field of adult education or its parts at any given moment in time. They may be concerned with the program of a single institution or of a community and when they are repeated over a period of time, they describe the evolving form and pattern of adult education. The effectiveness of the survey is inhibited somewhat by the absence of any consistency or unifying principle in the design and use of it. In general, it is not used as a part of any long range systematic evaluation scheme, so that its real function is minimized and obscured. Furthermore, survey reports rarely gain distribution beyond the initiating agency, thereby reducing their potential contribution to the field as a whole. It is almost impossible to relate one survey in one place to another at a different time in the same place or to other surveys in other places at the same or different times because of this lack of systematic design. There is a very definite need for the formulation of a survey model to provide consistency to the study of local programs so that these, in turn, can be consolidated into regional, national, or international reports of the status of the field.

Research

An analysis and review of research in adult education is contained elsewhere in this volume and, therefore, requires only passing identification as an area of the literature about adult education. Without doubt this is the single most rapidly growing segment of the literature. It is increasing in quality as well as quantity and holds the greatest potential for service to the field.

General Literature

The bulk of the material written about adult education is difficult to classify into neat categories. For the most part it is unimaginative and repetitive. Written by adult educators for adult educators, the material seems unnecessarily defensive rather than presumptive in approach, and the authors repeat time and again the same justifications for their existence. Thus we read about the aging population, increasing urbanization, shifting values, a shrinking world, and technological changes with the resultant social changes. These things justify adult education. Adult educators should be sensitive to the continuous process of change and should not need reminding constantly that they are taking place. It is a rare pleasure to encounter in the literature those items that show imaginative thinking or a creative approach to adult education and its problems. It is even rarer to encounter careful, scholarly synthesis, analysis, and interpretation of social scientific knowledge pertinent to adult education.

Amidst the forest of mediocre literature about adult education a few giants stand out with a timelessness that should make them continuing favorites. Many of these giants are scarce and thus not often read. Two of the earlier American works with lasting value are Bryson's *Adult Education* and Lindeman's *The Meaning of Adult Education*. These two volumes have lost none of their significance in the passing of time.

From British sources have come two of the world's greatest documents about adult education. These are the famous *1919 Report* of the British Ministry of Reconstruction and the earlier *Oxford and Working Class Education* (1908). Fortunately, both of these have been re-issued recently; the former in an edited abridgement under the title, *A Design for Democracy*, and the latter reprinted in its entirety.

Another giant that makes a unique contribution to the literature is Leonard Q. Ross's *The Education of Hyman Kaplan* which, as a work of fiction, faithfully and delightfully mirrors the period of the education of the foreign born with insight and sympathy.

In spite of the vast amount of material written about adult education with little significance or distinction, a leisurely browsing tour through it can be a rewarding experience. The early volumes of the *Journal of Adult Education* are a treasure house with writing of high quality more closely related to that found in a literary quarterly than in a professional journal. Contributions from many noted figures of the era may be found in its pages and it offers leisurely pleasant reading without bothersome facts or dull reports of empirical research. From Britain again has come a distinguished periodical that is, unfortunately, little known in this country. This is the series, published at Oxford University as the *Rewley House Papers*, which does much to provide scholarship status to the literature of the field.

Much valuable literature relating to adult education is not recognized as such because it appears under the auspices of other disciplines. Such of it as may have gotten into the main stream of adult education has arrived there by chance discovery and has enriched the field materially thereby. Sociology, anthropology, psychology, and social psychology have distinguished material of immediate value to adult education that is read far too rarely by adult educators. Among these items can be mentioned Linton's *The Study of Man*, Spicer's *Human Problems in Technological Change*, Lewin's *Resolving Social Conflicts*, the Sherifs' *Groups in Harmony and Tension*, and Cartwright and Zander's *Group Dynamics* among others. Oftentimes such literature from other fields will not mention adult education as such, but this in no way indicates that it has no relevance to adult education. One major contribution of this literature from other disciplines and fields is that it is broadening the horizons of adult education and extending its sphere of interest beyond the narrow limiting concepts that originally delineated the education of adults. Through such an expansion adult education is assuming its rightful place in relation to all other areas of knowledge.

CURRENT SOURCES

In the search for current literature the two major periodicals in adult education provide a starting place. *Adult Leadership* emphasizes the application of knowledge about educating adults while *Adult Education* is more concerned with philosophy, theory, and research. In addition, there are numerous recent books that survey and summarize research or report programs and current practices. Books of this type are too numerous to mention more than some sample titles; such as Sheats, Jaynes, and Spence, *Adult Education;* Knowles, *Informal Adult Education;* Murray and Ross, *New Understanding of Leadership;* Donahue, *Education for Later Maturity;* Brunner's *Overview of Adult Education Research;* and the Peers and Grattan books cited previously.

PROBLEMS

The growing maturity of a field is represented by the changing character of its literature and by the attention it pays to it. The literature of adult education is rapidly moving out of the phase of impressionistic propaganda and intuitive reports into more carefully structured research. This progress has not followed an unbroken evolutionary line, for research studies have appeared intermittently throughout the entire history of the field. The discipline is reaching the point where research is beginning to be structured on prior research so that a consistent body of knowledge is being accumulated. Along with this has come the analysis and synthesis of research and the beginnings of the systematization of knowledge about educating adults with a resultant construction of theory.

The use of the literature has not kept pace with its development. On the whole, adult educators do not read, study, and apply what has been learned about adult education with sufficient regularity to alter materially the organization and conduct of educational activities for adults. This is due in part to human reluctance to acknowledge and accept the results of social scientific research and in part to the fact that much of the pertinent literature just isn't universally available. Since there is no single comprehensive collection of the literature of adult education, this is one of the pressing needs of the field. The value of such a collection may not now be fully appreciated; but in the future, as the field develops, it will become more and more important.

More pressing than a collection of the material itself is the urgent need for a comprehensive and continuing bibliography. At the end of this chapter is a somewhat detailed but by no means definitive listing of bibliographies about adult education. These are, for the most part, selective rather than definitive. Therefore, singly or together they do not present a true picture of the literature. Foundations are willing to spend untold sums on experimental programs of adult education but none of them seems willing to spend any funds on the systematic identification and listing of the literature from which experimental programming can be designed with greater attention to previous experience. The Center for the Study of Liberal Education for Adults has instituted a significant bibliographic project, but this is limited of necessity to a single aspect of the field and, therefore, cannot fulfill the need for a definitive bibliography.

Another pressing need of the field is for the alteration of standard library cataloguing and classification processes so that adult education literature can be identified and located. The architects of such schemes must realize that the literature of adult education is lost to the field when it is distributed among all the areas of knowledge rather than gathered together within its own special class. They can make a significant contribution to the development of the field by re-appraising present practices in light of the changed nature and requirements of adult education both as a field and as an area of academic study.

A final significant need is for adult educators to educate themselves by making a more systematic use of the literature of adult education. They should conduct their activities in continuous education by example as well as by precept and learn to know and to use the vast quantity of literature about their craft. Only then can the full development of adult education occur and its major problems and obstacles be resolved.

Selected Bibliographies

Adult Education Association. "Research Review," *Adult Education* V (Winter, 1955), 114-127; V (Summer, 1955), 240-246; VI (Summer, 1956), 234-243; VII (Summer, 1957), 195-207; VIII (Summer, 1958), 195-206.

Adult Education in the Canadian University: Bibliography. Toronto: The Canadian Association for Adult Education, n.d. Pp. 12. (near-print)

Anderson, Walfred A. *Bibliography of Researches in Rural Sociology.* Rural Sociology Publication No. 52. Ithaca: New York State College of Agriculture, Cornell University, 1957. Pp. 186.

Bass, John. *Functions of Adult Education in Community Development:* Selected Bibliographic Sources with a Selected Bibliography. New York: Institute of Adult Education, Teachers College, Columbia University, 1951. Pp. 12. (Mimeographed)

Beals, Ralph Albert, and Brody, Leon. *The Literature of Adult Education.* New York: American Association for Adult Education, 1941. Pp. 493.

Bibliografia sobre educacuun obrera: obras en espanol e inglis. Washington: Union Panamericana, 1950. Pp. 5.

"Bibliography of Adult Education," *Journal of Adult Education* IV (January, 1932), 100-107.

Bibliography of Reference Material in Group Development and Related Fields. Washington: National Training Laboratory in Group Development, 1951. Pp. 32. (Mimeographed)

Brophy, John M, Shaw, Bradford, and Golub, Fred T. *Industrial Training: A Guide to Selected Readings.* Bulletin No. 20. Ithaca: New York State School of Industrial and Labor Relations, Cornell University, May, 1952. Pp. 62.

Brown, M. Gordon, and Russell, Jane M. *A Bibliography of Materials for the*

Teaching of English to Foreigners. Federal Security Agency, Office of Education, Bulletin No. 20. Washington: Government Printing Office, 1947. Pp. 24.

Brunner, Edmund deS., *et al. An Overview of Adult Education Research.* Chicago: Adult Education Association, 1959. Pp. 279.

California State Department of Education. *Annotated Bibliography on Adult Education.* Los Angeles: California State Department of Education, Division of Adult Continuation Education, 1938. (Mimeographed)

Coleman, A. Lee, *et al. Bibliography of Research on Social Factors in the Adoption of Farm Practices.* North Central Regional Publication No. 1. Ames: Iowa State College, April, 1956. Pp. 8.

Collings, Mary Louise. "Adult Education Studies Reported," *Journal of Home Economics,* XXXVIII (November, 1946), 569-72.

Congdon, Wray H., and Henry, David D. *Adult Education, A Bibliography with Annotations.* Lansing: Michigan School Service Co., 1934. Pp. 40.

Connor, John M., and de Marge, Moncayo. *Bibliografia de la literatura* sobre Educacion de Adultos en la America Latina Bibliographic series, 37. Washington: Departamento de Asuntos Culturales, Union Panamericana. 1952. Pp. 88.

Cook, Katherine M., and Reynolds, Florence E. *Education of Native and Minority Groups: A Bibliography 1923-32.* Education Bulletin No. 12, 1933. Washington: Government Printing Office, 1933. Pp. 57. (Supplement: Education Bulletin 1935 No. 63. Pp. 25.)

Crile, Lucinda. *Bibliography on Extension Research on Administrative Organization and Management and Training Extension Workers.* Washington: U. S. Department of Agriculture, August, 1956. Pp. 17.

————. *Selected Bibliography on the Origin and Development of the Farmers' Cooperative Demonstration Work.* Extension Service Circular 484. Washington: U. S. Department of Agriculture, November, 1952. Pp. 15.

————. *Review of Extension Studies.* Washington: U. S. Department of Agriculture, v.d. v.p. Issues as follows: Extension Service Circular 449, March, 1948; Extension Service Circular 454, July, 1948; Extension Service Circular 456, December, 1948; Extension Service Circular 460, July, 1949; Extension Service Circular 464, January, 1950; Extension Service Circular 470, July, 1950; Extension Service Circular 471, January, 1951; Extension Service Circular 474, July, 1951; Extension Service Circular 480, March, 1952; Extension Service Circular 486, January, 1953; Extension Service Circular 493, January, 1954; Extension Service Circular 497, February, 1955; Extension Service Circular 506, May, 1956; Extension Service Circular 511, June, 1957; Extension Service Circular 518, July, 1958.

————. *Bibliography on Extension Research.* Extension Service Circular 416. Washington: U. S. Department of Agriculture, October, 1944. Pp. 161. (Same: Library List No. 48, July, 1949; Extension Service Circular 489, 1955.)

Dahir, James. *Community Centers as Living War Memorials:* A selected and annotated bibliography of works relating to community centers. New York: Russell Sage Foundation, 1946. Pp. 63.

Dunham, Arthur. *Bibliography on Community Welfare Organization:* A selection and annotated list of works relating to community organization. New York: Association Press, 1951. Pp. 35.

Eaton, Allen, and Harrison, Shelby M. *A Bibliography of Social Surveys.* New York: Russell Sage Foundation, 1930. Pp. 467.

Group Discussion and Its Techniques — A Bibliographical Review. USDA, Bureau of Agricultural Economics. BAE Farmer Discussion Pamphlet D 4. Washington: Government Printing Office, 1942. Pp. 57.

Hendrickson, Andrew. *A Review of Post-War Literature on Public School Adult Education.* Columbus: Bureau of Special and Adult Education, Ohio State University. n.d. Pp. 5. (Mimeographed)

Jenkins, Frederick W. *Adult Education, A Selected Bibliography.* Bulletin No. 83. New York: Russell Sage Foundation, 1927.

Kelly, Thomas. *A Select Bibliography of Adult Education in Great Britain.* London: National Institute of Adult Education, 1952. Pp. 83.

Lado, Robert. *Annotated Bibliography for Teachers of English as a Foreign Language.* U. S. Department of Health, Education and Welfare. Bulletin No. 3, 1955. Washington: Government Printing Office. Pp. 255.

Legge, C. D. *Guide to Studies in Adult Education 1957.* London: National Institute of Adult Education, 1957. (Same: 1956, 1955, 1954, 1953.)

Legge, C. D., and Waller, R. D. *First Handlist of Studies in Adult Education.* London: National Institute of Adult Education, 1952. (Same: *Second Handlist* . . . . . 1953.)

Mann, George C. *Bibliography on Consumer Education.* New York: Harper and Brothers, 1939. Pp. 286.

Manny, Elsie S. *Rural Community Organization.* Miscellaneous Publication No. 729. Washington: U. S. Department of Agriculture, 1956. Pp. 124.

Meziros, J. D., and Berry, Dorothea. *The Literature of Liberal Adult Education, 1945-1957.* New Brunswick, New Jersey: Scarecrow Press, 1959.

Moore, Clarence D., and Hendrickson, Andrew. *Annotated Bibliography of Materials for Teachers of Americanization and Literacy Classes.* Columbus: Division of Adult Education, Bureau of Educational Research and Service, Ohio State University, 1958. Pp. 12.

Morrison, D. G., and Martorana, S. V. *The 2-Year Community College: An Annotated List of Studies and Surveys.* U. S. Department of Health, Education and Welfare. Bulletin 1958, No. 14. Washington: Government Printing Office, 1958. Pp. 33.

Ozanne, Jacques. *Regional Surveys of Adult Education.* New York: American Association for Adult Education, 1934. Pp. 48.

Proctor, W. M. *Annotated Bibliography on Adult Education.* Los Angeles: Printing Department of the Frank Wiggins Trade School, 1934. Pp. 124.

Ranganathan, Shiyali R. *Social Education Literature.* Delhi: Indian Adult Education Association. London: G. Blunt, 1952.

Reiss, Karl deS., and Spivack, Bernard. *Bibliography of Methods and Materials in Adult Education.* New York State Emergency Adult Education Program, Series 2, Research Bulletin No. 5. New York: New York University, 1936. Pp. 18.

"Review of Educational Research," *Adult Education,* Vol. XX, No. 3, June, 1950; Vol. XXIII, No. 3, June, 1953; Vol. XXIX, No. 3, June, 1959.

Rochester Board of Education. *Selected Bibliographies for Commercial Education, Homemaking, Forums, Recreation, General Education, Vocational Worker's Education; Adult Education; In-Service Training.* Rochester, New

York: The Board of Education, 1938. Pp. 106.

Sayers, Frances C. "Landmarks in the Literature of Adult Education," *Religious Education*, XXIV (October, 1929), 746-51.

Select List of References on Evening Schools. Washington: The Library of Congress, 1905.

Selected References on Workers Education. Bibliographical Reference List. No. 28. Geneva: International Labor Office, 1951. Pp. 6.

Shock, Nathan W. *A Classified Bibliography of Gerontology and Geriatrics*. Stanford, California: Stanford University Press, 1951. Pp. 600.

Skarzynska, Janina. *Bibliografia oswaity pozaszkolne j*. Warsaw: Pod redakcja J. Muszkowsiego: H. Radlinskiej, 1929. Pp. 176.

Smith, Faith E. *A Selected List of Books, Pamphlets, and Magazine Articles on Part-time Education*. Bibliography Bulletin No. 71. Albany: New York State Library, 1922, Pp. 28.

Smith, Ralph C. *Bibliography of Museums and Museum Work*. New York: American Association of Museums, 1928. Pp. 302.

Steinbarger, Helen T. *Bibliography of Reading Interests and Habits*, 1930-36. Chicago: American Library Association, 1936. Pp. 22. (Mimeographed)

Thompson, Laura A. "List of References on Worker's Education," *Monthly Labor Review*, XIV (June, 1922), 1273-90.

————. "Recent References on Adult Worker's Education," *Monthly Labor Review*, XIX (September, 1924), 692-705.

U. S. Department of Health, Education, and Welfare, Office of Education, *Summaries of Studies in Agricultural Education. v. d.*

UNESCO. *A Preliminary Survey of Bibliographies on Adult Education*. Education Abstracts, Vol. VI, No. 7 (September, 1954).

UNO. *Selected List of Books, Pamphlets and Periodicals in English on Community Organization and Development*. New York: U. N., March, 1953.

U.S.W.P.A. Division of Education Projects. *Bibliography for Teachers of Adult Education*. Washington: The Division, 1938. Pp. 16. (Mimeographed)

W. P. A. *Books, Pamphlets, and Other Material Recommended for Teachers of Workers Education*. Washington: Works Progress Administration, 1936. Pp. 58.

Ward, Betty Arnett. *Education on the Aging: A Selected Annotated Bibliography*. U. S. Department of Health, Education and Welfare, Office of Education, Bulletin 1958, No. 1. Washington: Government Printing Office, 1958. Pp. 145.

Wiggins, Gladys. "A Bibliography of Studies on Adult Education," *Adult Education Bulletin* IV (October, 1939), 40.

Wisconsin, University of. *Publications List on Community Development*. Madison: Extension Division, University of Wisconsin, May, 1957. Pp. 18. (Mimeographed)

PART III

INSTITUTIONAL PROGRAMS
AND RESOURCES

CHAPTER 15

ADULT EDUCATION ASSOCIATIONS
AND COUNCILS

GLENN S. JENSEN, *Executive Director*
Adult Education Association of the U.S.A.

INTRODUCTION

> A united front depends upon a sense of working together in a great cause with common objectives and a common philosophy. This common denominator of ideas and thinking takes some real work and experience of thinking together, stretching our ideas to a base broad enough so that all can stand upon it. . . .
>
> Activities of adult education take place in a community, the world of first responsibility of people. The responsibility of individuals to their communities or citizenship is an important part of personality development. The community then becomes the point of focus for adult education in order to make its opportunities available to all of the community's people, in order to concern itself with the development of the community, and in order to help increase the expression of citizenship responsibility of individuals and their groups in co-operative action.[1] . . .

There is no apparent disagreement among members of local, state, regional, or national associations of adult education that the real hope of attaining the objectives of a truly successful and worthwhile adult education movement lies in the productivity of local groups. These groups composed of librarians, public school teachers, college professors, administrators, business people, health and social workers, governmental employees, club men and women, and a host of others from all walks of life, are meeting, planning and working together to strengthen local adult education programs. John Walker Powell has said, "It is reasonably clear that the true strength of organization for adult learning rests on local integration. But it is also quite clear that we have not yet found the key that will open that door, and keep it open to its full width."[2]

At the end of its first three and one-half years of existence, the committees and delegate assemblies of the Adult Education Association of the U.S.A. (AEA) identified several areas of development that were urgently required in order to encourage an adult education movement that would meet the needs of our society. The first area cited as carrying high priority was the need to develop an integrated adult education movement in which the agencies of adult education would plan jointly and work co-operatively at the local, state, and national levels, not only for the co-ordination of adult education, but for the co-ordination of a variety of groups concerned with community improvement.

LOCAL COUNCILS

Their Nature and Number

Olds found that there were actually thirty-three adult education councils listed in 1954 but he narrowed this number down to twenty-eight, in that five of them functioned primarily as advisory committees to public school adult education programs. This meant that at that time every eighth city of 50,000 population had a formal adult education council and one-half of the cities of 500,000 or over had such councils.[3]

The AEA records indicate that in 1954 there were thousands of community councils or co-ordinating councils (Olsen reported 11,000) [4] which had as part of their activities some concern for adult education. In small communities (under 50,000) such councils seemed to be functioning in some regard as adult education councils, in that they played an advisory role and to some extent a co-ordinating role to local adult education programs.

One significant development which has given support to local councils is the new movement of community development through adult education. This approach seeks to raise the cultural level of a total community by involving local citizens in an action program based upon intelligent study and co-operative effort. Through community development the individual becomes an active and participating citizen. This development is discussed in detail in Chapter 35.

Ruth Kotinsky indicated that it is impossible to consider adult education councils without treating community councils in their relation to adult education, because adult education councils tend in many instances to shade off into community councils and a problem of relationships frequently arises between the two.[5] In response to the often-asked question as to whether or not the community councils might substitute for the adult education councils, Kotinsky said, "There is no need for an either-or-position, the two types of organization are closely related, but do not substitute the one for the other. Community organization is, in effect, among other things, a program of adult education; the council is an instrument for encouraging the free play of intelligence among adult educators in devising and implementing all the programs of adult education in the community."[6]

Supporting this point, Dorothy Hewitt and Kirtley Mather add:

> Frequently it is desirable to gather together into an organization all persons who are working in any phase of adult education in a given geographic unit. The council plan has proved a satisfactory way to accomplish this desirable result. If a council for adult education does not exist for the community in which a new project is to be launched, one of the early steps may be to call such an organization into being. Its purposes should be the correlation of existing adult education opportunities, the study of the fields in which further adult education opportunities are needed—and they usually are legion—the promotion of increased opportunities, either through existing agencies or through the creation of new ones. It is generally not the function of a council to present a program of its own.
>
> Another valuable function of an Adult Education Council is the gathering and disseminating of information concerning all opportunities available in the community for adults to continue their mental development. An Adult Education Council may also make important contributions to the movement in its embryonic stages by conducting experiments in special phases of adult education.[7]

"The Council is a powerful potential means for exemplifying the democratic process and focusing the adult education movement upon its major social relevance in furthering widespread realization of democratic values. Often there can be no doubt that the task is too great for individuals alone. The body of thought and type of leadership required can arise only in the midst of an on-going process of search and inquiry among those already concerned with the job."[8]

Even though the existence of an effective adult education council seems of the utmost importance to every community, Edmund deS. Brunner pointed out that:

> The studies of adult education programs and institutions suggest that there has been a singular lack of effective co-ordination of adult education at the local community level.
>
> Three basic patterns of co-ordination have emerged: (1) Primary responsibility for co-ordination is vested in a specialized adult education council made up of representatives of the agencies and associations involved and of interested citizens. This approach seems to be best adapted for large urban communities when the need for such an agency is recognized. Even under such conditions, however, the adult education council has seldom been fully successful. (2) Primary responsibility for co-ordination is vested in a general community council responsible for overall community improvement. This approach appears to be suited to smaller communities or to those where adult education has received only limited recognition. (3) Co-ordinative functions are assumed by existing agencies and institutions. This pattern, unsatisfactory as it often is, appears to have achieved the widest measure of acceptance.[9]

Their Financing

Often cited as the major obstacle to the expansion of adult education councils, the problem of financing is of great concern. Olds reported that twelve of the twenty-eight councils in 1954 were part of the "test cities" project of the Fund for Adult Education, which underwrote council expenses on a sliding three-year scale. The basic plan was to provide $24,000 to each council for the three year period. The Fund for Adult Education later extended the period and increased the financial grants where conditions warranted. The project was described as "a co-operative experiment to discover ways by which the mature individual may better improve himself as a person and as a citizen in the widening circle of communities in which he lives, and to provide community laboratories where they can observe programs and processes of adult education, especially liberal adult education, and where they can experiment with new patterns and techniques which may have significance for hundreds of other communities."[10]

Of the remaining sixteen councils, only six had budgets of $5,000 or more per year. Denver, Chicago, and St. Louis had budgets of approximately $12,000, while New York's was about $34,000. Those councils of the test project which still exist, those formed earlier, and those since, have one thing in common, namely, a real lack of money.

Summarizing his findings, Olds recommended that "in communities where much adult education is provided by institutions other than public schools, it is most important to establish planning and co-ordinating councils for adult education, just as most communities now have planning councils for health and welfare services. The pattern for financing adult education councils should be adapted to the particular circumstances in each community."[11]

While the American Association for Adult Education was receiving sizeable grants from the Carnegie Corporation, it aided many local councils and helped a number get under way. But as this support diminished, so did the funds to local councils. The Adult Education Association has, through local project grants and its membership field services, provided financial aid to a number of councils. But during the last two years this aid has diminished to the vanishing point.

Those councils which appear to be doing the most comprehensive job are those which have also developed a plan of diversified financial support. For example, in 1959 Bernard Kashdan of the Cincinnati Adult Education Council made a survey showing that there were seven local adult education councils offering broad community-wide services. These councils were reported in Chicago, Cincinnati, Denver, Chattanooga, St. Louis, New York, and Akron. Approximately twenty councils were reported which had no principal source of support and hence had no staffs.

Of the first group of seven the Adult Education Council of Greater Chicago, which had relied chiefly upon income from its speakers bureau, a college booklet, and membership dues is now developing new sources of support, including fund solicitations. The council expects to raise in 1959 approximately $25,000 from contributions, $22,000 from its speakers bureau and $19,000 from sales and advertising. The Denver Adult

Education Council draws its major support, about $13,000 annually, from the educational institutions in the city, including the public schools. The St. Louis and Cincinnati adult education councils get $10,000 each from the community chests in those cities, Chattanooga expects to raise $6800 in a fund-raising campaign, and New York will raise the majority of its income from gifts and memberships. The Akron Adult Education Council operates as an arm of Akron University, which in turn receives a grant from the Fund for Adult Education for its program of liberal adult education.

All of the local adult education councils are having serious financial difficulties in spite of their great contribution to community improvement. Limited staffs prohibit effective fund-raising campaigns and individual memberships do not provide the necessary means to do a comprehensive job.

If local community organizations for adult education had adequate financial resources, they would be able to do a better job of relating the adult educational resources to the needs of the community, bringing the local agencies providing opportunities for lifelong learning into closer co-operation, keeping the citizens better informed about opportunities for learning, improving the competencies of local lay and professional adult education workers, pioneering new and better ways of providing learning experience, and arousing the interest of the general public in adult education.

Their Organization and Program

There is no great similarity in pattern of organization, program, or administration of local adult education councils, although there are some threads of similarity, namely a clearing-house function and a publicizing of information about adult education opportunities.

The purposes frequently listed by most councils, as described by Kempfer are:

1. To identify and interpret educational needs.
2. To develop new educational approaches and programs.
3. To publicize and promote programs of all agencies.
4. To co-operate on jointly sponsored projects.
5. To co-ordinate adult education activities.
6. To act as a clearing-house of information about adult education activities.
7. To identify and interpret trends.
8. To promote legislation, public interest, and financial support.
9. To represent the adult education movement before the public.[12]

It is apparent that a close working relationship among adult agencies results in better identification of educational needs and interests of adults and a better total community program. Results have shown that programs developed in closest collaboration with others attracted more participants, served more population segments, maintained a more flexible schedule, and utilized a greater number of educational approaches than did programs developed in isolation.

Local adult education councils presently are performing the following types of services in varying ways:

1. Services to "consumers" including counseling, information as to the location of adult learning opportunities, bibliographies, and directories.
2. Services to adult educational leaders, including workshops, conferences, fellowship activities, newsletters, counseling, employment referral service, and information about resources, materials, and techniques.
3. Services to the agencies and organizations providing adult educational opportunities, including bringing them together for joint planning, conducting joint publicity and public relations programs, and providing consultation services.
4. Services to the community at large, including the assessment of changing needs in the community for adult educational services, interpreting adult educational needs and opportunities to the community, integrating the work of adult educational agencies with other elements of the community of life, pioneering in experimental ventures to develop new adult educational activities in the community, and serving as a resource to municipal government, the local mass media, and other agencies of community life regarding adult education in the community.

In spite of the impetus which has been given to strengthening local adult education organizations, there also exists considerable evidence which supports the idea that local councils must look to a changing pattern of service. Some adult education leaders feel that the present organization and structure of most local councils need revamping. For example, Robert A. Luke said in 1954, "That no satisfactory solution to any of the finance questions has been found suggests that the causes of financial insecurity lie not so much in fiscal policy as in the pattern of service adult education councils set out to provide, of the program needs they profess to meet, and of the clientele they strive to serve."[13]

Luke proposed several first steps which might be taken in a community to start co-operative planning:

1. Establishment of an agency committee with membership composed of individuals with administrative program responsibility for formally organized adult education activities. Members would represent themselves, not their agencies.
2. Gradual development by the committee of two consultative groups: (1) a program advisory consultative panel made up of representatives of the voluntary agencies, with an informal relationship to the main committee; (2) a consultative group made up of technicians and specialists of various kinds, acting as a resource pool.
3. The establishment of a pattern of work by the committee must be under-

taken, but no constitution, dues, letterheads, election of officers, or monthly program would be required.

4. A major goal of this adult education committee would be to work toward some level of collaborative and enriched community-wide program planning. Specific activities would include the exchange of information among the program agencies and help in identifying teachers and leaders. The committee might sometime maintain jointly-sponsored common services, such as co-operative advertising, operational fact finding, or program research and evaluation. But the central functions are talking together to find out what are the social forces at work in the community, trying to gain additional information about why things happen as they do, building a growing and responsive philosophy of adult education service, and taking the diagnostic and analytical steps that precede program planning. Out of the discussions, drawing in consultants from many different fields, will begin to emerge the answers to the questions of what is adult education, whom is it for, and how should adult education opportunities be made available.[14]

Adult learning takes place under a wide variety of sponsors and in many different settings in the local community. It is found in public schools, colleges, and universities, labor unions, social agencies, libraries, rural organizations, religious institutions, voluntary organizations, and every other setting conducive to personal growth. The great task facing local communities at this stage in the development of the adult education programs is to integrate these diversified and separate activities so that they make a greater combined impact on community growth and development.

STATE ASSOCIATIONS AND COUNCILS

One of the great challenges facing adult education leaders and participants is to find a satisfactory way in which the many independent groupings of adult education in a given state can be linked together so that they might maintain their autonomy and also support one another's efforts in some systematic way. For example, "In a typical state," Knowles reported in 1955, "one would find a number of state-wide organizations providing a variety of services for the education of adults. Some of them operate programs directly with consumers of adult education, such as university extension divisions, agriculture extension services, and certain health and welfare agencies. Others provide leadership and resources to local operating units, as illustrated by state departments of education, state libraries, and the state headquarters of such voluntary organizations as P.T.A. and the League of Women Voters."[15]

Some leaders of state adult education associations have become increasingly concerned about the lack of relationship which exists among these educational organizations. Some of the issues which have grown out of this situation are: a feeling of competition for time, interests and dollars; a lack of understanding about their respective roles on each level; and, an apparent duplication of adult educational services.

One of the unique potential strengths of a state adult education council or association is the possibility of effectively co-ordinating a wide variety of organizational and institutional resources in an effort to stimulate a more enlightened total adult educational program.

In 1959 thirty-one state associations or councils of adult education were in existence, with little uniformity of pattern in program or organization among them. Some were composed of representatives of organizations or agencies (councils), some were composed of individual members (associations), and some had a combination of these two forms.

A former AEA president, Grace T. Stevenson, said in a letter to the presidents of state and regional adult education associations on September 25, 1958, "One of the most encouraging things I have encountered during my journeys about the country this past year has been the increasing number and the growing strength of the state and regional adult education associations. I firmly believe that this healthy development at the local level will strengthen the national movement also."

Services of State Associations

Upon examination of their constitutions and objectives it is quickly apparent that these associations are attempting to further the development of adult education opportunities throughout each state in a variety of ways. The most common activities are regular conferences involving interested citizens, field consultation, publications—including regular newsletters—and the promotion of training workshops. Each state having an adult education association is attempting to make available knowledge about adult education, to bring agencies of adult education into closer relationship, to make the general public more aware of opportunities and responsibilities in the field, and to help those engaged as teachers and administrators of adult education to improve their competencies. Some states are having more success than others in accomplishing stated objectives but an example of one state, Michigan, may be cited to show the activities and accomplishments of its membership during a one-year period (1958).

The Adult Education Association of Michigan:

1. *Conducted* six district conferences to give adult educators a meeting ground and a place to exchange ideas and experiences.
2. *Distributed* extensively a resource index that lists in detail the services available to adults from fifty-five state-wide organizations.
3. *Sponsored* and convened eleven working committees to consider special interests in adult education.
4. *Gathered* significant data on what cities are doing to develop better community life and distributed the findings to local leaders.
5. *Helped* launch the "Great Discussions" program in Michigan.
6. *Organized* a committee of state agencies and organizations to promote greater co-ordination of educational services for adults.

7. *Published* four issues of "Topics," the regular Michigan Adult Education Association's newsletter.

8. *Carried on research* into the purposes and programs of organizations conducting adult education programs.

9. *Published* an adult education directory.

10. *Began* a systematic action program to inform state government officials of the needs and urgencies of adult education.

11. *Developed* a joint membership plan with the Adult Education Association of the U.S.A.

12. *Began* a program of public forums at the community level.

13. *Completed* plans for a three-day state-wide meeting with the Michigan Library Association and the Public School Adult Educators.

In accomplishing these important tasks most states have been able to get by on a small budget provided largely by dues from their members. The Adult Education Association of the U.S.A. is currently providing some financial assistance, although small, to seventeen states through its joint membership plan. Under this arrangement the Adult Education Association remits twenty per cent of the dues of its members who reside in the state to the state association. In 1958 2,500 members belonged jointly to A.E.A. and state associations under this plan. The AEA's Delegate Assembly has repeatedly expressed its conviction as to the importance of establishing strong relationships among all persons concerned with the education of adults locally and in the states. The joint membership plan is one attempt to accomplish this end.

REGIONAL ASSOCIATIONS

In a further attempt to co-ordinate adult education programs and activities, exchange information, train leaders, and share experiences, four regional adult education associations presently exist. These associations are:

1. Southeastern Adult Education Association, composed of representatives from the states of Alabama, Florida, Georgia, Louisiana, Mississippi, North Carolina, South Carolina, Tennessee, and Virginia.

2. Missouri Valley Adult Education Association, composed of representatives from the states of Iowa, Kansas, Minnesota, Missouri, Nebraska, North Dakota, and South Dakota.

3. Mountain Plains Adult Education Association composed of representatives from the states of Wyoming, Colorado, New Mexico, and Utah.

4. Southwestern Adult Education Association, composed of representatives from the states of Oklahoma, Texas, and Arkansas.

Involved in these four regional associations are twenty-three states.

The influence of the regional organizations upon their constituents varies from year to year and from area to area. Each has, however, encouraged the formation and development of state adult education associations, has promoted an inter-state exchange of ideas, has maintained close contact with the AEA, and has mobilized genuine interest in working co-operatively on adult education problems.

For example, the Southeastern Regional Adult Education Association can trace its beginning back to 1937 to a conference held at Chapel Hill, North Carolina. Twenty-two years later this association is a stable and working organization with a membership from nine states composed of people from a wide variety of backgrounds and interests. Seven of the states represented have their own state associations or councils. The association provides a framework within which its members can come together to gain new insights into the perplexing problems of adult education and co-operatively point the way to new opportunities. It is growing in scope and importance as it takes steps to mobilize interest in providing professional training opportunities in the Southeast for adult educators, and as it attracts more and more members who are aware of the tremendous significance of adult education to our society.

The Mountain-Plains Adult Education Association has completed thirteen annual conferences, although the association has existed for more years than that. Annual meetings are rotated among the four states, (Colorado, New Mexico, Wyoming and Utah), and each state voluntarily assumes the responsibility of publishing one regional quarterly newsletter each year. It is not uncommon for members to meet informally during the year or to call upon those in other states when help is needed on a problem or project. The Mountain Plains Association has extended its membership and improved its financial support significantly in the last several years by conducting annually a leadership training workshop.[16]

The Missouri Valley Adult Education Association and the Southwest Adult Education Association have made strides in becoming influential adult education organizations. The Missouri Valley Association perhaps summed up today's challenge to all adult education associations in its 1958 brochure:

> Some members of the Missouri Valley Adult Education Association are full-time workers in adult education; some of us are concerned with adult education programs as one of our many community projects; still others of us may seem to have only casual or fleeting connections with adult learning activities. Yet we are a highly homogeneous group in our convictions: (1) that our society cannot wait for its problems to be solved by the next generation, (2) that the "good life" continually seeks and finds new, interesting experiences, and (3) that adults can and want to learn.

The regional associations, like the state associations, depend almost completely for income upon dues from members. Much of the operational expense is provided by the institutions or agencies represented in the associations and the clerical work is done by volunteers. These associations play a vital role in the total adult education picture and indications are that other sections of the country may soon look to regional organization.

NATIONAL ASSOCIATIONS

The Adult Education Association

At the national level adult education in 1959 was in the spotlight as never before. The number and types of program sponsors continued to increase, federal support expanded, religious organizations indicated increasing commitments to adult education undertakings, business and industrial establishments expanded educational opportunities for employees, and in general millions of adults participated in programs of their own choosing, indicating an acceptance of and commitment to adult education.

Eight years earlier national leaders in adult education, recognizing the urgency of a new unifying national organization, the need of a forum for the exchange of experiences and ideas, the desirability of eliminating the overlapping which existed between two national associations, met in Columbus, Ohio on May 14, 1951, and founded the Adult Education Association of the U.S.A. It is a non-profit corporation enjoying today the active support of many of the nation's prominent educators, civic, industrial, and labor leaders, social workers, religious leaders, and voluntary association leaders.

The purposes of the AEA are: (1) to help adult educators improve their competencies, (2) to bring the agencies of adult education into closer working relationship and greater unity of purpose, (3) to extend and deepen the knowledge and practice of adult education, (4) to further the development of adult education resources, and (5) to increase public awareness and support of adult education. The association's services include national conferences, a monthly magazine, *Adult Leadership*, a quarterly journal, *Adult Education*, research studies, field consultation, and a public relations program. Affiliated with the AEA is a Council of National Organizations in which ninety agencies plan jointly, and a National Association of Public School Adult Educators, in which over 2,000 members work on problems common to public school adult education programs.

The Council of National Organizations (CNO), although it is a constitutional organ of the AEA, develops its own policies, program, and organization, and determines its operating relationships with the AEA. National organizations meeting the following criteria are eligible to become participating organizations:

  1. Those interested in the general philosophy and basic purposes of the Adult Education Association.

2. Those actively concerned with and contributing to the educational improvement of the adult population.
3. Those dedicated to broadly acceptable social goals.
4. Those which maintain standards of integrity and factual accuracy in their educational materials.
5. Those which are not essentially partisan political organizations.
6. Those which are not established for profit.

The CNO, headquartered in New York, provides consultation services, opportunities for organizational representatives to work together on significant issues, substantive programs on problems of member organizations, and a focus for organizational planning on adult education. An annual operating budget of $30,000 is raised through organizational dues and grants.

The National Association of Public School Adult Educators (NAPSAE) was organized in 1952 with the help of the AEA and the National Education Association. It is a department of the National Education Association, housed in the division of adult education service of NEA in Washington, D.C. NAPSAE is also an affiliate of the AEA and its president is a member ex-officio of the executive committee of AEA. The executive director of NAPSAE is paid by and serves as assistant director of the NEA division of adult education service.

Some of the services offered by the National Association of Public School Adult Educators are:

1. Consultation services to state departments of education.
2. In-service training program for local public school adult education directors.
3. Interpretation of public school adult education to the public.
4. Centralized information service.
5. Sponsorship of annual conferences.
6. Numerous publications designed for membership and interested persons.

Financial support for this association is provided by membership dues, sale of publications, allocations from the National Education Association, and general grants.

Related National Organizations

There are many national associations concerned with adult education specifically and generally and whose members actively support the program of the Adult Education Association of the U.S.A. The National University Extension Association, the Association of University Evening Colleges, the National Association of County Agents, and the American Library Association, are examples of the more than twenty national professional associations in which adult education workers play active professional roles. Although these associations are concerned primarily with the advancement of their institutional programs, they also contribute heavily in leadership to the national adult education movement through the AEA and its affiliates.

Another important area on the national scene is that occupied by the more than two hundred national organizations which carry on some sort of adult educational activity as a means of achieving organizational goals. Approximately half of these are members of the Council of National Organizations. Some national organizations—such as the Congress of Parents and Teachers, the Chamber of Commerce, and the Federation of Womens Clubs—conduct adult education programs through their local affiliates, while others—such as the National Safety Council, the Public Affairs Committee, and the Committee for Economic Development—provide educational resources for other agencies which operate adult education programs. All of these organizations produce extensive educational materials and employ professional workers to administer adult education services.

In addition to these two main groupings is another category composed of groups which participate actively within AEA as special interest sections. These AEA sections are: Aging, Business and Industry, International Affairs, Home and Family Life, Non-English Speaking Adults, Labor, Public Affairs, Music, Literacy, Liberal Adult Education, Research, Rural Adult Education, Community Development, Young Adult Education, and Residential Education. These groups have more than five thousand members within AEA who participate in some way in their activities.

A growing number of adult education workers are employed in federal agencies. Examples are the subject specialist, research workers, field agents, material producers, and trainers in the Department of Agriculture, the U.S. Office of Education, the Department of State, the Atomic Energy Commission, and the Civil Defense Administration. These workers have many interests in common with workers in voluntary organizations, with whom they often work closely. Many of them see themselves as related professionally to the field of adult education.

Many other agencies or groups might be included under national associations concerned with adult education, even though their interests are not primarily directed to that end. This great diversity of individual interests and groupings is the body of the AEA.

Since a voluntary association is absolutely dependent upon the interest, enthusiasm and active co-operation of its membership, and since such an association must continually evaluate its own nature and role in society, the AEA executive committee early in 1958 negotiated with the Bureau of Applied Social Research, Columbia University, to conduct an intensive study of AEA, under the direction of Dr. Edmund deS. Brunner. This study, completed in 1959, was designed to provide answers to three basic questions:

1. What should be the principal objectives and program of a national organization concerned with adult education in relation to the basic problems, needs, and trends?
2. What organizational and administrative pattern or patterns appear desirable to achieve these objectives?
3. What are the causes of the problems and difficulties which the AEA has faced since its founding?

THE FUTURE

The Adult Education Association of the U.S.A. has a unique role to play in helping to develop an over-all philosophy of adult education which encompasses the ideas that the individual is of infinite worth and potentiality, that the most important thing in life is learning, that a free society is the best because it is the most educative, and that our way of life can only be preserved if we give our system of education the attention that we do our personal rights and material welfare.

It must spearhead an effort to help people look at education as a process continuing throughout life and at the role of adult education in helping America chart and sail its course. In the struggle to preserve our freedom we need men and women who know what is happening in the world about them, who attempt to understand our economic and political systems, and who can equal or surpass the knowledge and skills of any other people, friendly or hostile, in the world. There is no task facing us as a nation that cannot be eased or overcome if we can look toward a more productive, better informed, and more vigilant population.

Basic Needs

Much progress has been made in identifying and developing certain areas of need but additional resources are greatly needed for the development of an adult education movement that will meet present day needs of society. These basic needs are:

1. To create greater public awareness of the role and importance of adult education in our national life by an extension of knowledge about adult education in its relation to the total process of human development.
2. To encourage the development of a large core of highly competent adult education practitioners, both professional and volunteer, and to develop certain standards that will raise the general level of practice in the field.
3. To extend and deepen the knowledge about the theory, methods, and organizations of adult education.

In order to realize these needs and goals there must be a strong national adult education organization which can achieve:

1. A clarification and focus of objectives.
2. A more precise statement and interpretation of services to be rendered to individuals and organizations.
3. A better integrated and stronger identification of national adult education organizations, i.e. NUEA, AUEC, ALA, etc.
4. A better integrated administrative organization.
5. A more adequate plant and facilities for servicing individual members and national organizations.
6. A plan for more stable financial support.

The leadership from the following organizations should be involved in attempting to reach the anticipated outcomes:

1. Professional adult education organizations.
2. Voluntary organizations with a principal concern for adult education.
3. National organizations with special interests devoted to adult education.
4. Committees, commissions, and sections of AEA.
5. Federal government organizations with a principal concern about adult education.
6. Adult education councils and associations (local, state and regional).
7. Mass media associations.

Ways of Proceeding

Some of the steps which should be taken if AEA is to accomplish this mission are:

1. Develop a continuous high level campaign of public interpretation as to the need for and opportunities in adult education. Councils, agencies and organizations equipped to help should be solicited and supplied with basic facts and trends.
2. Develop a national resource center of interpretative materials, such as motion pictures, kinescopes, slide films, pamphlets, books, monographs, and tapes which can be made available to interested people. The few things done by AEA in this regard are very promising.
3. Develop and provide to national organizations consultative and material resources to enrich their own in-service training programs.
4. Develop an adult education referral and placement service in AEA headquarters to place qualified adult education workers. The current system now attempted is haphazard but has already demonstrated its usefulness.
5. Stimulate and encourage the interest of research agencies in adult education and the adult learning process.
6. Expand the field services to make possible the stimulation of coordinating councils and agencies of adult education.

7. Provide stimulative funds to the Commission on Legislative Policies, the Professors of Adult Education, and the Committee on International Liaison, enabling each to perform more vigorously.

8. Collect, catalogue, abstract, and report current adult education literature.

9. Plan and develop a significant demonstration center to serve the adult education interests of the nation.

Adult education throughout the nation could look to citizen-involvement, active participation, and co-operation between organizations without parallel with the acceptance of this charge.

Because the AEA was brought into being in 1951 by people in touch with the realities of that time it reflects its own period, has the strengths and weaknesses of other contemporary institutions, and is still in the process of identifying and involving adult educators in meeting the issues of professional development. It has built within its structure a mechanism for evaluation and assigned this to its legislative body, the Delegate Assembly. It has emphasized the collection of information as a means of giving guidance in planning and it has endeavored to find the means of involving its members in making decisions that affect not merely the AEA, but the development and extension of adult education as an instrument of social problem-solving. The hope is that as the functions of adult education grow and develop, the AEA will prove a sufficiently sensitive instrument to recognize, accept, and implement this growth.

Footnotes

[1]Excerpt from the report of the AEA Committee on Social Philosophy. Wilbur C. Hallenbeck, "Building Working Philosophies in Adult Education," *Adult Education*, III (May, 1953), 148-51.

[2]John Walker Powell, *Learning Comes of Age* (New York: Association Press), 1956, p. 89.

[3]Edward B. Olds, *Financing Adult Education in America's Public Schools and Community Councils* (Chicago: Adult Education Association of the U.S.A. 1954), p. 20.

[4]Edward G. Olsen, *School and Community* (New York: Prentiss Hall, 1945), p. 451.

[5]Ruth Kotinsky, *Adult Education Councils* (New York: American Association for Adult Education, 1940), p. 153.

[6]Ibid.

[7]Dorothy Hewitt and Kirtley Mather, *Adult Education: A Dynamic for Democracy* (New York: Appleton-Century, 1937), pp. 37-38.

[8]Ruth Kotinsky, *op. cit.*, p. 167.

[9]Edmund deS. Brunner, *An Overview of Adult Education Research* (Chicago: Adult Education Association of the U.S.A., 1959), p. 238.

[10]Edward B. Olds, *op. cit.*, p. 20.

[11]*Ibid.*, p. 107.

[12]Homer Kempfer, *Adult Education* (New York: McGraw Hill, 1955), p. 83.

[13]Robert A. Luke, "The Community Organization of Adult Education," *Adult Education*, IV (May 1954), 161.

[14]*Ibid.*, pp. 165-67.

[15]Malcolm S. Knowles, "Administrator's Report, A Four Year Assessment of the Adult Education Association," (Chicago: Adult Education Association of the U.S.A., 1955). (Mimeographed).

16The 1958 workshop held in Boulder, Colorado, and planned with the assistance of the Adult Education Association of the U.S.A. staff is described in detail in the November, 1958, issue of *Adult Leadership*.

Selected Readings

Beals, Ralph A., and Brody, Leon. *The Literature of Adult Education*. New York: The American Association for Adult Education, 1941.

Brunner, Edmund deS. and Associates. *An Overview of Adult Education Research*. Chicago: Adult Education Association of the USA, 1959.

Hallenbeck, Wilbur. "Building Working Philosophies in Adult Education," *Adult Education*, III (May, 1953), 148-51.

Hewitt, Dorothy, and Mather, Kirtley. *Adult Education: A Dynamic for Democracy*. New York: Appleton—Century, 1937.

Jensen, Glenn, Lewis, Evelyn, and Hartley, James R. "Adult Education for Adult Educators," *Adult Education*, V (November, 1958).

Kempfer, Homer. *Adult Education*. New York: McGraw Hill, 1955.

Knowles, Malcolm S. "Administrator's Report, A Four Year Assessment of the Adult Education Association," 1955. (Mimeographed)

Kotinsky, Ruth. *Adult Education Councils*. New York: American Association for Adult Education, 1940.

Luke, Robert A. "The Community Organization of Adult Education," *Adult Education*, IV (May, 1954).

Melby, Ernest O. *Administering Community Education*. New York: Prentice Hall, 1955.

Olds, Edward B. *Financing Adult Education in America's Public Schools and Community Councils*. Chicago: Adult Education Association of the USA, 1954.

Olsen, Edward G. *School and Community*. New York: Prentice Hall, 1945.

Powell, John Walker. *Learning Comes of Age*. New York: Association Press, 1956.

Sheats, Paul, Jayne, Clarence, and Spence, Ralph. *Adult Education*. New York: Dryden Press, 1953.

Snow, Robert H. *Community Adult Education*. New York: G. P. Putnam's Sons, 1955.

CHAPTER 16

ADULT EDUCATION IN
BUSINESS AND INDUSTRY

ROBERT F. RISLEY
Assistant Dean and Professor
New York State School of Industrial and Labor Relations
Cornell University

GROWTH OF PROGRAMS

Adult education in business and industry within the United States is a large and expanding area of activity. It is carried on in part by business and industrial organizations themselves and in part by outside agencies. Any attempt to define the magnitude of this activity or its scope is difficult because of the multiplicity of organizations carrying on such activities, the variations of programs among organizations, and the lack of any accurate nationwide data concerning this phase of adult education.

There has been a steady expansion in number of business and industrial organizations conducting adult education activities, in the number of employees of such firms involved in these activities, and in the breadth of the programs offered. At the start of this century apprentice training was the major formal activity and this, together with less formalized learning on the job, seemed to meet the needs. World War I brought an interest in supervisory training and the development of vestibule schools to provide faster and better job training. Formal education requirements were not thought too important and generally the schools, colleges, and universities were expected to provide needed personnel.

World War II created a crisis for which millions of persons had to be prepared to take on new or greater responsibilities. To meet these problems the military organizations developed educational programs in almost every imaginable field. Business and industry likewise found it necessary to undertake large scale educational activities. The "J" programs—Job Instruction Training, Job Methods Training, and Job Relations Training—were developed by the War Manpower Commission as the "Training Within Industry" program. Job skills had to be taught and supervisory personnel had to be developed.

The problems faced during World War II of manpower shortages, changing technology, changing operational methods, and increased organizational and administrative complexities, have continued since the War. The growth of new industries, the changing technology of old, automation, new management techniques, and changing organizational requirements for supervisors, managers, and specialists have continued to face business and industry with problems of obtaining adequately prepared personnel. These pressures have forced business and industry to have a major concern with educational activities. Both management and employees have learned from experience what can be accomplished by means of education.

While no general agreement exists as to what the relative responsibilities should be, it has become clear that schools, colleges, and universities can not be expected to provide all of the people needed. Neither are they able to provide for the retraining or up-grading of persons already employed. The numbers of individuals involved and the variations in the specific job requirements are too great. To meet this need there have evolved expanded educational activities within business and industrial organizations and, at the same time, expanded adult educational programs offered by schools, colleges, universities, and other groups.

SCOPE OF EDUCATION PROGRAMS

The widening of the activities encompassed within adult education programs of business and industry has been indicated in a general way. A recent survey, "Trends in Training and Development, 1930-1957"[1] indicates that little has been dropped during this time but much has been added. A comparison of an older study of training in New York State[2] with the recent findings reported in *Classroom in the Factories*[3] demonstrates the change in the scope of programs and also the increase in the numbers of persons involved in educational activities.

Job Training

Most organizations provide some type of job training, including orientation of new employees and the upgrading of old employees to permit them to do new jobs. The most elaborate job-skill program is the formal apprentice training requiring years of time and involving both planned on-the-job training and off-the-job related instruction. Vestibule schools and special courses as well as on-the-job training of some planned type are more widely used for most job training. Job training takes place at various levels, ranging from unskilled or semiskilled jobs, through skilled jobs and technician training. Programs for skilled workers or technicians are especially likely to involve a considerable amount of off-the-job class instruction in pertinent academic subject matter.[4]

Foreman and Supervisor Training

Most organizations provide some educational program for supervisory personnel. Usually there is an intensive program just before or just after a person moves to a position of first level supervision.[5] In addition, many organizations provide some type of continuous educational activity—regular meetings, conferences, or periodic course offerings. The subject matter included in such programs varies greatly. Basically, the program for new supervisors is designed to equip individuals for the job of managing the work of others; in addition to providing technical knowledge needed, it usually includes material concerned with administrative activities and with problems encountered in dealing with people.[6] Since supervisors are the first line of management, many organizations feel it is important that they become cognizant of company history, policy, and activities generally. Because this group also provides a pool for higher management positions, frequently a variety of programs are offered to prepare them for advancement, ranging from such topics as controlling costs or handling grievances to courses on human relations theory or economics.

Management Development

Many companies have educational programs concerned with the development of executives in their present positions and with preparing them for movement to higher management positions. Some organizations have developed planned programs, similar to those conducted for first-level supervisors. Some of the larger firms have distinguished between various levels of management and have two or more programs for executives at different levels. These programs have grown because the concept of management is changing, the demands made of the managers are changing, and the demand for managers has increased so rapidly. The wide variety of responsibilities of individuals and the lack of clear concepts of what a manager must do and what education and experience he needs have resulted in a maze of programs and approaches.[7] Even in firms which have developed a core program for all management personnel, some effort is made to provide a program based on an appraisal of an individual's needs.

The educational activity at this level tends to include certain areas of administrative and human relations education that are similar to those contained in supervisory programs, but the concern is generally at a more complex and abstract level. The broader range of activities and problems to be dealt with at higher levels of management make it important for those individuals to be more of the generalist and less of the specialist. Considerable work at college course level is included in technical, business administration, and human relations subject areas. To an increasing degree interest has also developed in liberal education.[8]

Technical and Professional

Changing technology and rapid development of new knowledge, together with a shortage of qualified personnel, have led to the necessity for providing education in technical and professional areas. Many firms have found it necessary to conduct such work to keep their people abreast of current developments in their fields. Some firms have specialized work which requires additional training beyond that normally possessed by persons generally competent in a technical area. This type of educational program, like management development, is usually a combination of a core program for all, plus special educational opportunities based on individual need. This work is generally at the college level with much of it at the graduate level. It is provided through a mixture of in-company and out-company educational work.[9]

Special Educational Activities

Some special educational programs are also undertaken by many business and industrial firms. These may be integrated into one or more of the above programs, or they may be offered separately on either a required or optional basis. In addition to the liberal education programs and human relations training previously mentioned, this special catagory includes economic education, programs for developing reading skills, report writing courses, courses in creative thinking, and public speaking courses. The newest and fastest-growing subject is political education.[10]

General Education

Many of the above educational programs are designed to meet needs which are determined primarily in terms of organization appraisal. In addition, some organizations provide a general education program offering a variety of courses which employees and their families may take on a voluntary basis. Such work may be considered personal development, although it may be recorded as part of an employee's education record.

AGENCIES PROVIDING BUSINESS AND INDUSTRY EDUCATION

It is easily apparent from reviewing the description of the educational activities carried on by business and industry that few if any organizations could carry on this total program solely within the organization. Even among the largest firms, geographic decentralization of activities would cause problems even if a complete faculty could be obtained. In smaller organizations the number of individuals requiring certain educational work at the same time would be so few as to make in-company programs not feasible. As a result of these factors, most organizations utilize some combination of in-company and out-of-company education program.

Job training and supervisory training are most likely to be entirely in-company programs; but the company may arrange to bring in personnel from the outside to provide some of the instruction. In management development and technical and professional education it is likely that a substantial part of such programs will consist of out-of-company education or will be accomplished by making arrangements for outside educational organizations to provide such work at the company. Some of the larger organizations have established centralized schools for management or technical training with a permanent faculty. Educational offerings in the special educational activities or general education program may be accomplished by either approach, depending upon availability of qualified instructors and the number of persons involved in the programs.

Out-of-company education, supported by the company, may be basically of two types—credit or non-credit. To an increasing degree many organizations have committed themselves to pay all or part of the tuition costs for persons working for credit. Sometimes this is limited to work approved by the organizations in view of the nature of an individual's employment or with certain other restrictions. In addition, many organizations have developed scholarship or fellowship programs for employees or members of their families. Such programs are usually limited in the number to be supported and involve competition.

A considerable range of non-credit work is available; public schools provide work through adult education classes; colleges and universities offer seminars, courses, and conferences; professional associations offer conferences and seminars; organizations such as the American Management Association and consulting firms conduct courses and seminars; and regional and national trade associations sponsor educational programs. Most of these programs draw persons from different organizations; thus a firm can send one or two persons without all the expense of supporting and staffing its own program. Many of these organizations are also willing to develop a special educational offering if the cost is underwritten by the requesting company.

SUMMARY

It can be seen from the description of the programs carried on in adult education in business and industry, and the range of organizations involved, that the total adult education activities encompassed in this program are of tremendous size. In some of the larger organizations more is spent on education than is spent in many city school systems and colleges. It is likely that more adults are involved in some phase of the business and industry program than in any other type of adult education today.

There is little uniformity in the programs carried on in different companies which have, of course, grown and developed primarily in response to needs as seen by specific organizations. Not much has been done to date in the standardization of program content and teaching methods and techniques. At the same time the question of the relationships between the programs of outside organizations and the programs of individual firms has not been clarified. There is without a doubt considerable overlap and duplication in the activities carried on by these different organizations.

A further problem is the provision of qualified personnel for the responsibilities involved in these educational activities. In a recent report on "Jobs in Employee Relations,"[11] it was reported from a survey of 600 organizations that 9 per cent of those who had the principal responsibility for planning, organizing, and directing training activities had no degree; 36 per cent had a bachelor's degree; and 55 per cent had a master's degree. The second level of individual on the training staff was reported in 77 per cent of the cases to have no more than a bachelor's degree. The nature of the areas of specialization of degree holders varied over a wide range of subject matter. While this picture is encouraging in contrast with earlier studies which indicated less in the way of educational background, it still indicates that there are considerable problems in terms of the qualifications of individuals assuming these responsibilities. Many of those who have not had advanced formal education holding training positions have had opportunity to develop their compentency in this field, however, through professional associations and other advanced training programs.

Nevertheless, the wide range of activity encompassed in the broad program of adult education within business and industry presents real problems in finding individuals whose educational background and experience qualifies them to manage such a program. Some of the larger organizations have attempted to obtain persons from university staffs, from public schools, and elsewhere who have the competency and interest to operate such programs. The supply of such individuals, however, is limited; and, to the extent that business and industrial firms move in this direction, problems and pressures are created in adult education and other educational work elsewhere.

It would appear from the material that the training activities in the business and industrial area are to be expanded at the levels that currently exist as well as extended into new subject-matter areas involving an increasing number of individuals. Currently the most perplexing problems in adult education in business and industry exist in the field of management and executive development and professional and technical training. The very nature of these activities, the flexibility essential to make the programs effective, the level of instruction required, and the consequent qualifications required of those providing it, make these programs more difficult for firms to develop themselves than is true in some of the more traditional types of programs or in some of the more specialized programs.

At one point in time much of what was done in business and industry was considered to be training, which was considered to be something other than respectable adult education. It would seem from a review of these activities now being carried on in business and industry that the aims, the content, and the approach being used warrant their being considered adult education.

Footnotes

1. William R. Spregil, and Virgil A. James, "Trends in Training and Development, 1930-1957," *Personnel,* XXXVI (Jan.-Feb. 1959), 60-63.
2. John M. Brophy, *Training in New York State Industries,* Research Bulletin No. 1, New York State School of Industrial and Labor Relations, Cornell University (Ithaca, New York, 1949), pp. 19-26.
3. Harold F. Clark, and Harold S. Sloan, *Classrooms in the Factories* (New York: New York University Press, 1958), pp. 13-24.
4. A.S.T.D. Committee on Training Trends, "Current Trends in Job Training," *Journal of the American Society of Training Directors,* X (May-June 1956), 6-11.
5. Homer T. Rosenberger, "Your Money's Worth From A One-Week Supervisors' Course," *Journal of the American Society of Training Directors,* XII (April, 1958), 48-56.
6. Robert F. Risley, "Developing Effective Supervisors," *ILR Research,* New York State School of Industrial and Labor Relations, Cornell University, June, 1956, Vol. II, No. 3.
7. Lester F. Zerfors, "Progress in Management Development," *Journal of the American Society of Training Directors,* XI (Nov.-Dec., 1957), 4-7. See other articles in same issue and American Management Association Research Report No. 26.
8. Peter E. Siegle, *New Directions in Liberal Education for Executives* (Chicago: Center for the Study of Liberal Education for Adults, 1958).
9. Ernest G. Walter, "Western Electric's New Approach to Graduate Engineering Training," *Journal of the American Society of Training Directors,* XII (Sept., 1958), 6-12.
10. J. J. Wuerthner, Jr., *The Business Man's Guide to Practical Politics* (Chicago: Henry Regnery Company).
11. Dale Yoder, and Robert J. Nelsen, *Jobs in Employee Relations,* Research Study No. 38, American Management Association, New York, 1959.

CHAPTER 17

ADULT EDUCATION IN COLLEGES AND UNIVERSITIES

A. A. LIVERIGHT*
Director
Center for Study of Liberal Education
for Adults

The past twenty years have been pioneering, exciting ones in the field of college and university adult education. The period has been characterized by growth in the number of institutions active in higher adult education, in the quantity of students enrolled in college and university adult education, in the scope of offerings, and especially in an increase of imaginative innovation. A growing number of persons especially concerned about adult education and trained for it have been attracted to the field; and a new type of student—one who is interested more in continuing higher education than in remedial training—is increasingly welcomed on the evening college campus and in various extension programs.

At the same time that college and university adult education has been characterized by growth, experimentation, and increase in quality, it has also faced a number of serious difficulties. College and university adult educators are still beset by a feeling among institutions that adult education is a peripheral part of higher education; and while there are clarion calls for self-development, for continuing-education and for education for public responsibility at the university level, basic institutional budgets fail to provide for such education. This state of flux—active growth, countered by penetrating questions about the legitimacy of higher adult education and reluctance to finance it—makes for an absence of institutional arteriosclerosis; thus an air of exploration and vitality typifies the field.

This chapter of the *Handbook* will identify some factors responsible

---

*Roger DeCrow, Director of the CSLEA Clearinghouse has rendered invaluable service and assistance in the preparation, editing, and writing of this chapter.

for the development of university and college adult education, will describe the scope of activity now carried on by the institutions of higher education, and will outline some crucial problems now confronting the total field of adult education. Since many aspects of college and university adult education are dealt with elsewhere in this Handbook, this chapter will look only briefly at areas such as methodology and not at all at special programs described in other sections. We also omit reference to agricultural extension, integrally related to the Land Grant Colleges, for this is also dealt with in another chapter.

BACKGROUND

The idea of university adult education is not a new one. It is rooted in the experience of European universities, and especially in extra-mural departments of British universities. In the United States, two great pace-making institutions have been the University of Chicago on the urban scene, and the University of Wisconsin in state-wide extension.

William Rainey Harper, in his first pronouncements at the founding of the University of Chicago in 1892, asserted the importance of adult education to the University. The first class taught in the new university was an evening class, and the university opened its doors with a correspondence study department in operation.

In the field of university extension, the "Wisconsin Idea" early set a bold and vigorous philosophy. Architect and innovator in the pioneering days of extension at the University of Wisconsin was Charles Van Hise, who said:

> "The broadest ideal of service demands that the University, as the best-fitted instrument, shall take up the problems of carrying out knowledge to the people. . . . . It is apparent that this work is one of enormous magnitude and not inferior in importance or in opportunity to the functions of the university earlier recognized—those of instruction and research.
> The crux of the matter is that it is our aim to take out the knowledge, whether the people ask for it or not. It strikes me that in education we ought at least to be as careful as are the brewing interests in the state, and therefore we are not going to wait for the people to come to us, we are going to take our goods to them. We are going out to the people."[1]

A host of other colleges and universities, either in basic policy statements or in more recent statements by administrative officers, emphasize the responsibility of the college and university for continuing education— that is, programs for extending the knowledge and learning of the campus to the members of the community regardless of age.

This feeling of responsibility on the part of institutions of higher education resulted in 30 to 50 million people utilizing one or more university extension or evening college services and approximately 2 million taking part in organized and continuing adult university instructional programs in 1951-52.[2] In addition, it is estimated that some 300,000 were enrolled in adult education programs of junior colleges. The majority of these adults were involved in programs run either by urban evening colleges or by extension divisions of various state universities. A few, however, were enrolled in programs offered by several hundred small liberal arts colleges operating some kind of adult education courses. In addition, and not necessarily included in the above figures, many adults participated in specialized courses offered through professional schools.

OBJECTIVES

Whereas in the past almost total emphasis was placed by evening colleges on vocational or remedial education (including courses which permitted persons unable to attend day classes to work toward a degree or certificate during late afternoons and evenings) and by extension divisions on extending regular campus offerings to persons in rural areas, more emphasis is now placed on the broad idea of continuing education. It would, however, be unfair to suggest that most colleges and universities have abandoned assistance to adults who wish to complete interrupted college training, or that universities have shifted from vocational to personal goals. It is probably more fair to suggest that a large number of these institutions now have two-fold goals: 1) those relating to college education and vocational training; 2) those relating to life-long learning, continuing education for personal development, self-fulfillment, and public responsibility.

Despite this trend toward a more challenging role for higher adult education in modern society, there exists at the present no carefully conceived and generally accepted statement describing the university's role in the continuing education of adults. Lacking such a statement or some general agreement on objectives, institutional objectives vary widely as they reflect the background and attitudes of administrative officers; the power of the adult education director; his own image of what goals should be; the immediate demands of local audiences; and the influence of one or more of the powerful campus departments.

A number of evening colleges and extension divisions are now re-examining objectives[3] in an attempt to make a timely statement about the function of higher adult education. A review of preliminary restatements of objectives by the Universities of California, Wisconsin, Chicago, Syracuse, Boston, and others suggests that these will be prominent among the emerging objectives of institutions:

Intellectual and aesthetic development of the individual adult.

Dissemination of newly discovered knowledge resulting from research activities within the university.

Utilization of university resources to facilitate citizen discussion and decision making in public problems.

Leadership training, program planning, and educational aid to voluntary organizations.

Education about increasing problems of urbanization.

Dissemination of knowledge and information about crucial issues in the fields of local, national, and world affairs.

Stimulating of adults' desire to continue their education on their own.

Upgrading of scientific and technical personnel to meet the country's growing need for professional manpower.

Professional preparation of adult educators, especially for teachers of adults in public schools.

THE INSTITUTIONAL SETTING

Thanks to an intensive study of evening colleges and extension divisions recently completed by James Carey,[4] we have a fairly complete, accurate account of organizational structure and personnel in these two types of institutions. Unfortunately, similar data are lacking for small liberal arts colleges and for junior or community colleges.

Associations

There are two important associations operating in the field of college and university adult education, and they do much to raise sights, improve standards, and provide for effective communication within the field. The National University Extension Association (NUEA), was organized in 1915. Membership in NUEA is restricted to colleges and universities in the United States which direct a variety of extension operations both on campus and away from it. Most institutions belonging to NUEA are the large state universities; in 1959 there were 79 institutional members. The Association of University Evening Colleges (AUEC) includes in its membership almost all urban colleges and universities in the United States (and several in Canada) which offer evening college programs for adults.[5] The AUEC was organized in 1939, and now has a membership of 125 institutions.

Institutions

Eliminating duplications in membership in AUEC and NUEA, we find that there are 173 colleges and universities carrying on recognized evening college or extension activities in 1959. A study conducted in 1953 by James Crimi[6] suggests that another 200 small liberal arts colleges have some kind of education for adults, bringing the total to 373—a figure which does not include junior and community college programs enrolling nearly 300,000 students in offerings designated as adult education.

Most extension divisions (about 52 per cent) were established prior to 1929, but over two-thirds of the separately organized evening colleges were started after that date; about one-third of all evening colleges started between 1947 and 1959. All of the small liberal arts colleges that have special adult education divisions report that these were started after 1929, and that most of them started after 1947. The major surge in the development of evening colleges came immediately after World War II, and growth in small liberal arts colleges still seems to be underway.

Pattern of growth.—Carey identified a definite pattern of growth—or life-cycle, as he called it—in evening colleges and extension departments consisting of (1) *departmental domination*, when adult education is primarily the activity of campus departments with no independent unit for adult education; (2) *autonomous development*, when a separate unit exists and major emphasis is placed on differentiating this unit from regular campus operations; (3) *integration*, when the extension division is not threatened by close ties with the university and becomes an integral part of it; and (4) *assimilation*, when the adult education division, although still separate, becomes fully accepted as an essential element of the university.

This pattern of growth does not, of course, take place in every institution, for one stage may be completely by-passed, or an institution may never move beyond the first or second stage. It is important to emphasize that there is no ideal stage, and that different stages may be appropriate for different institutions; but in general it seems that programs exhibiting the greatest degree of imagination, innovation, and experimentation are those in the third and fourth stages of growth. Those divisions in the second, autonomous, stage appear to be most expendable and insecure.

Autonomy, control and size.—Almost one-fourth of the evening divisions are not separately organized (that is, they are not considered a separate department and have no special dean or director in charge) ; and almost one-half of the small liberal arts colleges are not autonomous. But ninety-five per cent of extension divisions have a separate autonomous organization. These differences are understandable in light of the relative age of these different kinds of institutions.

A similar situation exists in the size of staff and operation. Evening college organization is usually smaller and less complicated than that of extension divisions; a typical evening college usually numbers one or two staff members, and under 10 per cent of them have more than five. About 60 per cent of extension divisions, on the other hand, employ at least five staff members, and many of these organizations are vast and complex. In very few cases is an evening college staff divided into departments operating different kinds of activities and having different kinds of responsibilities, but in extension this is the usual pattern. As for the small liberal arts colleges, an adult education program is largely the part-time responsibility of a regular faculty member; where a special department exists, it is usually a one-man operation.

There are also differences in backgrounds of evening college and extension deans: 58 per cent of the chief administrative officers of extension divisions, and only 27 per cent of evening college directors, have degrees in education. Extension deans and directors have a much longer tenure than evening college directors, who typically stay on the job for five years or less.

Faculty provisions and relationships.—Procurement and compensation of faculty vary widely. Evening colleges, in general, hold to an even balance between faculty recruited from campus and those recruited from the community, while extension divisions secure considerably more than 50 per cent of their faculty from campus. Liberal arts colleges tend likewise to draw the majority of their faculty from regular campus departments.

Five different faculty systems are used by evening deans and extension administrators in staffing their programs:

1. Use of faculty from daytime or residence department at the discretion of the departmental chairman or dean: 27.8 per cent.
2. Use of extra-compensation faculty for overload teaching; responsibility for hiring and firing in the hands of the adult dean or director: 14.4 per cent.
3. Joint appointment system with specified load apportioned between the adult division and regular departments; decision on hiring and firing made jointly: 11.9 per cent.
4. Full-time adult faculty: 1 per cent.
5. Other or mixed systems, not included in the above choices: 42.8 per cent.

According to Carey, there appears to be a definite relationship between the attitudes of deans and directors toward faculty arrangements and their institutions' stage in the pattern of growth. Those departments in the first stage typically use faculty from daytime departments at the discretion of the departmental chairmen; those in the second mix this faculty arrangement with heavy use of extra-compensation faculty; those in the third or integrated stage tend to combine extra-compensation and joint-appointments; those very few in the fourth stage combine full-time adult education faculty with joint-appointment and extra-compensation faculty.

As far as relations with the regular on-campus faculty are concerned, 68.7 per cent of extension divisions report that they have a regular faculty advisory committee, compared with 52.2 per cent of evening colleges with such a committee; only 35 per cent of the small liberal arts colleges have any kind of faculty committee responsible for adult education activities. Generally, those schools with no separate faculty advisors are the more recent arrivals to university adult education.

An increasing number of deans of evening colleges and extension divisions have become concerned with training faculty to a greater understanding of differences between the adult and the undergraduate teaching situations. Although planned programs of faculty development exist in only a minority of institutions, their variety and imaginativeness indicate growing activity in this area. Several universities (including the Universities of Syracuse and Oklahoma) have arranged either annual or continuing seminars during which campus faculty members teaching in adult education programs discuss and plan these programs. Some universities (including University College, University of Chicago) provide new faculty members teaching adults with packets of relevant literature; others (including Northeastern University and the Universities of Cincinnati and Washington) provide for student ratings of professors; and in at least one case a university supplies a teacher-counselor to work with new teaching personnel.

Financing.—University adult education has become a big financial enterprise. Roughly 48 per cent of the AUEC institutions operate on budgets exceeding $100,000; 81 per cent of the NUEA institutions have budgets exceeding this figure. Forty per cent of the NUEA state extension services have budgets exceeding half a million dollars, and a number are multi-million dollar operations.

Extension divisions and evening colleges are generally required to pay their own way or at least to break even. In some well-endowed institutions, adult education acts as a money-making operation for the university as a whole. Frequently a subsidized campus course when transferred to the extension division or evening college is made to pay its own way even though it bears the same title, the same content, and the same instructor.

There are some exceptions to this usual attitude. Since extension division courses are looked upon as "service" programs to the state at large, there is usually some state subsidy for extension activities, varying from 5 per cent in some states to about 50 per cent in others. State aid to extension is, however, likely to be very small as compared with aid to other units of the university. In one of the better state universities, for example, day colleges are expected to make 20 per cent of their budget, and receive 80 per cent subsidy from the state; the situation is exactly reversed in the extension division, where income from fees is expected to cover 80 per cent of the budget.

The policy of "pay-as-you-go" is muddied by inconsistencies regarding allocation of charges to adult education activities. The manner in which overhead is charged, for example, varies enormously: in one or two evening colleges no charge is made for classroom space, administration, or other general overhead items, but in other institutions a large overhead burden is assigned to adult education operations.

As to the availability of risk capital (money which can be expended for experimental programs and projects), 74.5 per cent of state extension divisions report such money available, 66.6 per cent of the municipal evening colleges have such funds; and only 55.2 per cent of private institutions report any risk capital.

The pressure to make money or to break even unquestionably has a deleterious effect on adult education in general and on informal and liberal education programs in particular. First, with very limited experimental funds, the tendency is merely to incorporate courses from the day departments, although these may often not be suited to the adult clientele. Second, the pressure to make money leads to an emphasis on those courses certain to have a large enrollment—thus inevitably de-emphasizing non-credit and liberal education programs.

This attitude toward financing derives both from the marginal status of an adult education function in the university spectrum and from the conviction that employed adults can and should pay their own way. It is possible that this attitude will change as the adult division matures and gains recognition as a legitimate university function deserving subsidy from the parent institution. Also, present active moves to secure support for a federal extension bill providing funds for adult education in state universities will eventually result in greater financial security.

Facilities.—More and more evening colleges are creating on-campus facilities that are more flexible and therefore more suitable for adults than are the usual undergraduate class-rooms. There has been a remarkable increase in the development and use of residential centers for adult education. According to a recent study of continuation centers,[7] sixteen universities owned and operated some kind of residential center either on the campus or at a sylvan spot nearby. Of these institutions, Michigan State University operates two centers and Syracuse University runs three. Only six such facilities were initially planned as residential adult centers; most of the others resulted from an unused building or an estate left to the university which was converted for this purpose.

This development of residential centers (encouraged and directly assisted by grants to five universities from the Kellogg Foundation) emphasizes the idea that adults can more effectively concentrate on education if they are away from their customary surroundings. Nor is the idea of residential education limited to the large universities, for an increasing number of small liberal arts colleges, eager to make maximum use of their facilities and to enlarge their offerings to adults, are offering summer programs in their dormitories for business men, secretaries, and other groups of adults. It seems most likely that this outcropping of residential adult education may be a forerunner of largely expanded residential programs in the future.

THE CLIENTELE OF UNIVERSITY ADULT EDUCATION

In 1959 most people attending adult programs in institutions of higher education are primarily vocationally oriented. Hundreds of thousands of these young men and women are attending evening colleges and extension classes for special programs in business, industry, or engineering, or to complete the bachelor's degree essential for promotion in business and industry. Many teachers take courses to qualify for promotion or to complete state-required certificates. But John Dyer, in *Ivory Towers in the Market Place*, makes the point that there is no typical student: "Perhaps the first characteristic of the evening college is heterogeneity. One finds here many students who already have college degrees and others who have only finished high school. The age range is from eighteen to sixty-five or seventy, with the median age being thirty plus. One-third is under twenty-five; 10 per cent over forty-five."[8] Dyer emphasizes the variety of motivation among these students, but suggests that there are two major ones: one growing from "life space" areas (the non-academic motivation) and the other from "life chance" areas (rational, economic motivations).

John R. Morton, in his study of university extension services, has identified the extension student as one who attends extension classes or resident centers, or one who uses correspondence techniques, conferences, or extension library services. He observes that men constitute a slight majority, with the educational status of all students "considerably above the average for the nation as a whole. Only 5 per cent of the users of university extension services had failed to complete high school, with 37 per cent completing undergraduate college work and more than 10 per cent being engaged in graduate study."[9] Morton further reports that more than three-fourths of participants in extension activities hold full-time jobs. The age of the extension student is near that of the evening college enrollee, with the median age being 34 years, although the older student (median age, 35) is more likely to be enrolled in conference and institute programs while the younger student (25 years median) is more likely to be registered in the correspondence program. Morton reports that one out of three students is a professional educator; the second largest group is composed of workers in business and industry.

Although no comparable data are available we know that many thousands of doctors, lawyers, engineers, teachers, and other professional persons return every year to college campuses for refresher or advanced training. And even though very many of these are not registered in evening college or extension divisions, they represent a sizeable number of people who count upon colleges and universities as sources of continuing education. While comparable figures for the junior college adult clientele are not available, it appears that these people tend to be younger and more directly interested in technical and recreational programs.

As a result of special programs and recruiting efforts, it seems likely that during the next ten or twenty years these institutions will attract an increasing number of older persons interested in continuing their education; professional groups desiring to keep in touch with recent scientific and technical changes; specialists wishing a broader general education; women stimulated to continue the education they abandoned for careers as housewives; and college graduates wishing to continue or renew intellectual interests.

PROGRAM AND METHODS

On the surface, the major methodological change since 1945 has been the more frequent use of discussion and group techniques and the substitution of these methods for more traditional lecture formats.

Beneath the surface (and not unrelated to the change noted above) the most important trend in methods of higher adult education has been concern about what, if anything, is different about the teaching of adults and undergraduates. A new body of literature and some tentative steps toward research about the teaching of adults are gradually emerging, as administrators and faculty members concerned with adult teaching look at the differences between adults and undergraduates and try to determine what implications these differences have for their teaching methods.

The implications of differing characteristics of adults, as noted in some of Havighurst's writings[10] and by James Whipple in his *Especially for Adults*,[11] are just beginning to be examined. Only a few colleges and universities are looking at their teaching methods in the light of adults' special motivations, and experiences. But more and more universities which are developing faculty training programs are concentrating them around problems of special methods for adults.

What constitutes a good teacher of adults and who is best equipped to teach adults are still moot questions, but some research is beginning in this area. That there are some differences in teaching adults and undergraduates cannot be denied, but whether a teacher required to teach adults must be different from the teacher who works with undergraduates has not been reliably determined. Preliminary study suggests, however, that an *outstanding* teacher of undergraduates will also be an excellent teacher of adults, for both cases require sensitivity to the learning situation and to the needs of students.

Another important trend which may within a decade have a real impact on method is a growing interest in defining objectives for adult programs, along with the concurrent development of instruments to measure the achievement of such objectives.[12] Once it is possible to evaluate results, institutions can in fact compare the efficacy of different methods for achieving the same objectives. Cleveland College and Syracuse University have already launched some research to determine the relative effectiveness of residential and "spaced-learning" programs for achieving similar objectives with similar kinds of groups. It seems likely that the interest in this problem will soon provide valuable data.

Looking at the field as a whole, we find that the evening college still depends primarily on the classroom lecture for credit courses, and on the discussion method for informal, non-credit programs. Audio-visual aids are used frequently, and several evening colleges are using television (especially Washington University in St. Louis) on a pioneering and experimental basis.

Extension divisions—as a result of the need to take educational programs to widely scattered areas—use a greater variety of methods. In addition to regular extension classes offered primarily through lecture and discussion, extension divisions use the correspondence method and, in a few cases, experiment with the technique. Important among these experiments is the combination of correspondence study with televised programs: lessons are given over television with papers submitted by students through correspondence. Some correspondence study programs combine group techniques and traditional correspondence methods; these, called "group" or "directed" correspondence study, encourage people to take a course together and then to submit one paper which represents conclusions of the group. The instructor of the course, from the campus, meets occasionally with the group to answer questions and to lead discussion.

Conferences and institutes have increased markedly since 1945. According to the best available figures in 1958, extension divisions offered 1,000 conferences and institutes of three days' or longer duration, as well as numerous shorter meetings—and this figure is undoubtedly conservative. Although a variety of methods are used within these formats, almost all bring a group of adults (usually persons involved in the same profession or association, or with similar occupational interests) to the campus or to a residential center where they live together for a period of from one day to several weeks. Whereas in the past many extension divisions acted either as innkeepers or as middlemen between the group desiring the conference and faculty members, they now assume a much more active educational role; many universities refuse to accept conferences for which they may not help to plan the educational content.

Extension divisions are similarly more active in the field of community development, which is concerned with bringing to bear the resources of appropriate campus departments and faculty members on the problems of a particular community. The community development department, ordinarily a part of extension, makes contacts with the community, helps with a community survey and, when problems have been identified, asks appropriate campus experts to work with the community in solving its problems.

A number of extension divisions also continue to provide field library service, whereby packets of material are sent on request to residents of the state. A large proportion of the material in package-library service is now sent to teachers.

Programs in liberal education, aimed at developing man as a man rather than man as a worker and directed toward his fulfillment as an individual and citizen, have increased materially during the past twenty years. In 1951, the AUEC, knowing of the Fund for Adult Education's interest in higher liberal education, asked for funds to implement the activities of its Committee on Liberal Education. At the same time, the NUEA evidenced interest in experimental programs in liberal education for adults. In response to the AUEC's request, the Center for the Study of Liberal Education for Adults was established and has been working closely with the AUEC since 1951, with the NUEA since 1956, and more recently in a consultative capacity with the Association of American Colleges and the Association of Colleges and Secondary Schools (representing the Negro colleges in the South). Through publications, research activities, field visits, a national clearinghouse in the field of liberal education for adults, and through a number of small grants, the center has co-operated with scores of colleges and universities to stimulate new ideas in programming and in faculty development, and generally to improve the climate supporting liberal adult education. Because of the increasing audience for liberal education programs, and the existence of an organization concentrating attention on this aspect of adult education, an increasing number of institutions are now involved in informal seminars, institutes, and study-discussion and lecture-discussion programs devoted to liberal education. In addition, a few institutions have begun to experiment with special degrees for adults, degrees which emphasize broad generalized education rather than specialized professional training.[13]

CURRENT PROBLEMS AND FUTURE DIRECTIONS

The state of flux in the field of university and college adult education during the recent past is still its most pervasive characteristic and is likely to remain so for the coming decade. A number of pressing problems confront those dedicated to the field of higher adult education, but within each of them are also seeds which, if properly nurtured, can make for a far more vital program than has ever existed in the past. It seems advisable, therefore, to examine a few of the most serious problems and at the same time to suggest those procedures underway, no matter how hesitantly, to solve them.

The first and most widespread problem is the fact that adult education is still considered a peripheral and possibly expendable aspect of the university or college program. To offset this attitude, which is evidenced by many administrations and faculties, some evening college and extension divisions are now making self-surveys and holding meetings with administration and faculty in an effort to re-examine the program and objectives of the adult education arm of the university. It seems likely that this self-examination and review will continue.

A second problem, and one which may become more serious during the next five years, results from increasing demands on faculties, space, and money as daytime enrollments rise. Evening colleges have greater difficulties in attracting top campus faculty, in securing adequate space for classes, and in sharing in the college budget. Therefore, adult education administrators are: (1) trying to achieve joint appointments of faculty who will teach both adults and youth; (2) asking many qualified persons in the community to teach evening classes; (3) eliminating courses which are not university-level and might better be taught by secondary schools; and (4) improving the quality of their offerings. In addition, confronted by pressures for space, some institutions have secured from private individuals and from foundations funds they use to erect buildings specifically designed for the education of adults.

A third problem, which both underscores the existing administrative and faculty attitudes toward adult education and also hampers expansion, is the lack of endowment or government subsidy for adult education. This problem is a most difficult one, because securing either endowment money or the kind of government support which agricultural extension enjoys requires a change in the image of continuing general education. However, the NUEA and the Extension Council of the Association of Land Grant Colleges and Universities are working closely with several federal legislative committees to secure passage of a general extension bill. And at the institutional level, more top administrative officers have become aware of the importance to public relations, to the community, and to alumni of higher adult education, and have thereby been encouraged to upgrade it in the institutional hierarchy.

Other financial aid has come from the foundations. The Fund for Adult Education has been of enormous help since its organization in 1951, especially in assisting universities to launch study-discussion and other liberal education programs; almost all of the institutions which report any sizeable activity in the field of liberal education for adults have been involved in one or more of the FAE's study-discussion activities. At the present time, moves are being made to interest other foundations in special programs and projects.

A fourth problem, and one related to growth-patterns of the evening college and extension organizations, is that many have considerable autonomy without achieving an accompanying integration into the university complex. Therefore, both administrative officers and faculty members look upon the adult education activities as separate and distinct which in time of pressure or financial crisis can be easily dispensed with. Some people in the field believe that the solution to this problem lies in the adult education operation's building up its own constituency and power base, rather than attempting closer integration with the university; and this may well be the answer for a few very secure and profitable operations. By and large, however, other action appears to be more widely effective, as where special faculty and advisory committees, boards of visitors, and special faculty-extension planning groups are set up to increase the communication and integration between adult education and other university concerns.

A fifth problem relates to the fact that some adult courses are not clearly appropriate for a college or university; there has been insufficient examination of what constitutes "university-level". A difficulty involved here is that many of the less impeccable courses academically nonetheless cost very little and bring assured income, an attractive situation for the pay-as-you-go evening operation. However, present offerings are being more carefully scrutinized, faculty committees are assisting in weeding out inappropriate programs, and administrators are meeting with other adult education organizations on city and state-wide bases in an effort to determine which institution should carry on what kind of adult education program.

The sixth and seventh problems are so closely related that we must examine them together: first, there is no clear-cut statement of goals and directions for higher adult education developed by the field itself; and second, the public has no clear-cut image of what adult education can offer to their personal and social welfare.

Some tentative solutions have been tried: conferences concerning themselves with the future role of college and university adult education; meetings to discuss the philosophy of adult education;[14] and self-studies and faculty-administrative seminars to re-examine the role of higher adult education.[15] Several attempts have been made to set up a national commission on adult education, and the recent President's Commission on Education Beyond the High Schools has asked a committee to study both the function and the role of adult education.

Although these stirrings have not yet resulted in a statement of goals and directions of higher adult education, such a statement is clearly needed. Once it has been drafted, we can concentrate upon our public image, one which underscores the vital educational potentialities existing in the field of college and university adult education.

Footnotes

[1]Charles Van Hise, "The University Extension Function in the Modern University," National University Extension Association *Proceedings*, 1915, pp. 7-24.

[2]John R. Morton, *University Extension in the United States* (University, Ala.: University of Alabama Press, 1953). (The above figures are based on a projection of figures cited in the Master Study)

[3]According to a study recently completed by the CSLEA under a grant from the Fund for Adult Education (by James T. Carey, the study is in preparation for publication), only 37 per cent of the evening colleges, 30 per cent of the extension divisions, and 16 per cent of the small liberal arts colleges studied report that a set of formalized objectives exist for the adult education program.

[4]*Ibid.*

[5]One notable exception is the New School for Social Research in New York City, which is not a member.

[6]James E. Crimi, *Adult Education in the Liberal Arts Colleges* (Chicago: Center for the Study of Liberal Education for Adults, 1957).

[7]University of Washington Division of Adult Education and Extension Services, *A Survey of Existing and Planned Continuation Centers of Member Institutions of the National University Extension Association*, 1958.

[8]John Dyer, *Ivory Towers in the Market Place* (Indianapolis: Bobbs-Merrill, 1956), p. 7.

[9]John R. Morton, *op. cit.*, p. 89.

[10]Robert J. Havinghurst and Betty Orr, *Adult Education and Adult Needs* (Chicago: Center for the Study of Liberal Education for Adults, 1956).

[11]James B. Whipple, *Especially for Adults* (Chicago: Center for the Study of Liberal Education for Adults, 1957).

[12]Center for the Study of Liberal Education for Adults, *Conference Report, Evaluation of Liberal Adult Education* (Chicago: The Center, September, 1958).

13New York University, University of Pittsburgh, Syracuse University, Brooklyn College, University of Oklahoma.

14Robertson Sillars, *Seeking Common Ground in Adult Education,* A Report of a Conference on the Philosophy of Adult Education (Chicago: Adult Education Association, 1958).

15*New Directions for Adult Education* (Syracuse: Syracuse University Press, 1959).

Selected Readings

Carey, James T. "The Development of the University Evening School in Urban America: An Aspect of Institutionalization in Higher Education." Unpublished Ph.D. dissertation, Department of Sociology, University of Chicago, 1958.

————. *Legitimacy and Acceptance in a University Milieu: The Problem of Liberal Adult Education.* Chicago: Center for the Study of Liberal Education for Adults, 1959. Preliminary draft.

Center for the Study of Liberal Education for Adults. *Review of 1958.* Chicago: The Center, 1959.

Crimi, James E. *Adult Education in the Liberal Arts Colleges.* Chicago: Center for the Study of Liberal Education for Adults, 1957.

Dyer, John P. *Ivory Towers in the Market Place: The Evening College in Education.* Indianapolis: Bobbs-Merrill, 1956.

Houle, Cyril O. *Major Trends in Higher Adult Education.* Chicago: Center for the Study of Liberal Education for Adults, 1959.

————, and Nelson, Charles A. *The University, the Citizen, and World Affairs.* Washington: American Council on Education, 1956.

Kidd, J. Roby. *Adult Education in the Canadian University.* Toronto: Canadian Association for Adult Education, 1956.

Mezirow, J. D., and Berry, Dorothea. *The Literature of Liberal Adult Education, 1945-57.* New Brunswick, N. J.: Scarecrow Press, 1960.

Morton, John R. *University Extension in the United States.* University, Ala.: University of Alabama Press, 1953.

Neuffer, Frank R. *Administrative Policies and Practices of Evening Colleges.* Chicago: Center for the Study of Liberal Education for Adults, 1953.

Schwertman, John B. *I Want Many Lodestars.* Chicago: Center for the Study of Liberal Education for Adults, 1958.

Siegle, Peter E. *New Directions in Liberal Education for Executives.* Chicago: Center for the Study of Liberal Education for Adults, 1958.

UNESCO. *Universities in Adult Education.* Paris: UNESCO, 1952.

CHAPTER 18

THE COOPERATIVE EXTENSION SERVICE

JOSEPH L. MATTHEWS
Assistant Director
Division of Extension Research and Training
Federal Extension Service
U. S. Department of Agriculture

DEFINITION AND ORIGIN

The Cooperative Extension Service, often referred to as "agricultural extension," has developed under co-operative arrangements between the state land-grant college or university in each state and the United States Department of Agriculture. It was founded when the Smith-Lever Act of 1914 firmly established the grant-in-aid principle. The name "Cooperative Extension Service" was derived from the then unique plan for sharing costs by federal, state, and county governments which requires dollar-for-dollar matching of federal and state funds and contributions of local funds in amounts that may vary among the states and counties.

A definite pattern of events traces from the agricultural revolution in England to our modern agricultural technology, but it would be a mistake to think that this resulted from a single comprehensive plan or agricultural policy. There were, first, such great scientific bodies as the American Philosophical Society, founded in 1743, and the Philadelphia Society for the Promotion of Agriculture, founded in 1785. These set the pattern for the later county agricultural societies, such as the Albemarle Society, whose organizer was Thomas Jefferson. There were the county fairs, horticultural societies, farm newspapers and magazines, the granges, and similar organizations and agencies. All these combined to bring about the establishment of the land-grant colleges in 1862, the agricultural experiment stations in 1887 and, ultimately, the Cooperative Extension Service.

The concept of co-operative demonstration work as a method to provide informal practical education in agriculture for farm families is

218

credited to Dr. Seaman A. Knapp, who was the leader in this type of adult education during the first decade of this century. The report of President Theodore Roosevelt's Commission on Country Life in 1909, which called for a "nation-wide extension" work, was probably most influential in crystallizing opinion favorable to the spate of legislative bills introduced in Congress that resulted finally in passage of the Smith-Lever Act in 1914.

ORGANIZATION AND STRUCTURE

The Cooperative Extension Service is composed of three parts, namely, the federal, state, and county extension services. The heart of the extension service is the land-grant college system, which is unique in higher education in the world. The American Association of Land-Grant Colleges and Universities was formed in 1887 to provide the machinery for the state land-grant institutions to work with one another and the United States Department of Agriculture. It brings together formal teaching, research, and extension to form an integrated system. This unifying arrangement makes possible completely separate, yet co-ordinated, extension programs in fifty states and Puerto Rico. For the United States Department of Agriculture to have completely separate working arrangements with each of the state extension services would require a tremendous staff in the department or one dictated by policies dedicated almost entirely to achieving uniformity and co-ordination. Few state extension services would be able to resist such a centralizing force. The Association of Land-Grant Colleges has no authority over any of its members, but it is effective because its recommendations are made only after careful study and review by its member representatives.

The Federal Extension Service maintains one of the smallest bureau staffs in the Department of Agriculture. In 1958 it had a total of 247 employees. Professional employees included 6 administrative persons, 16 adult program leaders, 7 youth program leaders, 16 agricultural subject-matter specialists, 4 home economics subject-matter specialists, 8 educational research specialists, 8 educational specialists, and 8 information specialists. Subject-matter specialists were employed in animal husbandry, poultry, agronomy, forestry, soil conservation, dairying, horticulture, entomology, plant pathology, agricultural engineering, rural electrification, health education and rural sociology, home management, foods and nutrition, family-life education, and clothing.

The agency serves as the channel though which the research information and educational materials from other agencies and services of the department are passed on to the state extension services. Its administrator represents the Secretary of Agriculture in relations with the state extension services and other parts of the land-grant institutions. Its staff has primary responsibility for and leadership in the educational programs of the department, including administration of the federal laws and regulations involved in co-operative extension. Each staff member has program leadership responsibilities nationally with his state counterparts and with certain related interests outside co-operative extension.

Each state co-operative extension service is one of the three main divisions of the state land-grant institution, along with resident teaching and its experiment station. The Director of Extension, appointed by the governing body of the institution with approval by the Secretary of Agriculture, is the top administrative officer. The categories and number of professional workers on the state staff depend upon the number of counties and the level of state and local financial support; they vary in size from about 16 in the smallest to over 800 professionals in the largest.

Typically, a state organization has one or more assistant directors and state leaders for agricultural, home economics, and 4-H Club programs. Depending upon the size of staff, there may be area supervisors, who report to the director through the appropriate assistant director or state leader. The states employ varying numbers of subject-matter specialists, depending upon need. They serve in much the same subject-matter areas as do the specialists on the Federal Extension Service staff.

Specialists keep themselves informed about new developments and research results in their areas of specialization and aid county workers to do the same in a variety of training situations. They disseminate special materials and reports of the findings from research, assist with program planning, and give some assistance in conducting educational programs. They write bulletins and other pamphlet materials; they contribute to journals and newspapers; they help prepare educational movies and other visual teaching materials; they prepare and appear on radio and television programs; and they present subject-matter materials and lead discussions at meetings.

The county is the basic unit in the Cooperative Extension Service, for it is here that most programs are developed and the teaching is done. A typical county is staffed by an agricultural, a home demonstration, and a youth programs agent. In some states the latter is designated as a 4-H Club agent and in others as assistant agent. It is general practice to increase the size of the county staff by adding associate or assistant agents in any of the three categories. Some counties with highly specialized types of agriculture, when financial resources permit, have subject-matter specialists on their county staffs.

RELATIONSHIPS WITH OTHER ORGANIZATIONS

From the beginning, there has been co-operation with other organizations and with lay groups. The leadership was quick to recognize that involvement in and identification with educational programs promotes both education and public support.

In the early days several states organized associations of farmers on a paid membership basis. At first the sole purpose of these associations was to co-operate with public agencies in the support and management of the county extension service. Thus the county extension services became allied with semi-private farm organizations which the staff had a part in building up.

The Farm Bureau has had the closest working relationship with the county extension services and the most influence in shaping its programs. County units of this organization were first promoted to provide leadership and financial support to extension. When the American Farm Bureau Federation was organized the program was changed from purely educational purposes to include legislative and business activities. This change was followed by separation moves in all but a few states that retain some type of formal relationships with a farm organization. The usual pattern today is to have one or more extension-sponsored advisory groups either with or without official status.

Co-operative relationships are maintained with social service and educational agencies and institutions that have developed to meet special needs. Prominent among the co-operating organizations are the public schools, libraries, health departments, youth organizations, federated women's clubs, civic clubs, community colleges, welfare agencies, and other adult education groups and organizations. A nucleus of staff members has been active in the adult education associations.

POLICY-MAKING

Occasional reinterpretations of the organic act since 1914, including the latest revisions by the Congress in 1954, have had little effect on the basic policies of the Cooperative Extension Service. The law limits its benefits to the people of the United States and prohibits the use of funds appropriated under the act for resident instruction.

Relationships and responsibilities for co-operative extension under the Smith-Lever Act are set forth in a uniform memorandum of agreement, last revised in 1954, between the United States Department of Agriculture and each state land-grant institution. The department agreed to maintain a Federal Extension Service and agreed that its extension work in the states would be planned jointly by the state director and the department. Each state land-grant institution agreed to establish a separate and distinct administration for co-operative extension work with a responsible leader selected by the institution and satisfactory to the department. All state extension agents were to be joint appointees of the institution and the department. Except for certain legal requirements regarding using and accounting for funds, the administrative and operational policies within a state are established under whatever provisions may be set up by the land-grant institution.

In 1905 a formal committee on extension was established that later became the Extension Committee on Organization and Policy, which is recognized as the national policy-making body of the Cooperative Extension Service. The committee is composed of directors and state home demonstration agents, three elected from each of the four regional state directors' groups.

On several occasions since World War II the leaders in the Cooperative Extension Service have reviewed its objectives and programs for the purpose of reaffirming its basic function and adjusting its programs to the social and economic changes affecting the people it serves. The most recent effort of this kind, by the Extension Committee on Organization and Policy, involved staff members from all states in committees and conferences. One result was a declaration of policy entitled "The Cooperative Extension Service Today—a Statement of Scope and Responsibility" (April 1958). Six kinds of changes that affect what the Cooperative Extension Service should do and how it should be done are described. This is followed by a delineation of nine areas of program emphasis for the future. Four have to do mainly with the business of farming and agricultural production, namely; (1) efficiency in agricultural production; (2) efficiency in marketing, distribution, and utilization; (3) conservation, development, and use of natural resources; and (4) management on the farm and in the home. The remaining five are concerned with education of the family members for life in a modern society: (5) family living; (6) youth development; (7) leadership development; (8) community improvement and resource development; and (9) public affairs.

The principle of first responsibility to farm families is recognized in the report, but attention is called to the broader audience being served that includes these general groups: farm families; non-farm rural residents; urban residents; farm, commodity, and related organizations; individuals, firms and organizations which purchase, process, and distribute farm produce and those which provide farm people with essential services and supplies, such as credit, fertilizers, feed, and many others.

FINANCES

The total Cooperative Extension Service budget for 1958-59 was just under $145 million, with about 44 per cent from federal appropriations, 34 per cent from state sources, 21 per cent from county funds, and 1 per cent from non-public sources. This represents an increase of about 90 per cent since 1950. About 1.5 per cent of the total is budgeted for the Federal Extension Service. State funds for co-operative extension are provided by the state appropriating bodies. County workers usually are paid with federal, state and local funds. Local funds are generally from county government sources.

STAFF AND STAFF TRAINING

On July 1, 1958, there were one or more paid workers in each of 3,152 counties in 51 states and territories of the United States—14,812 in all. By general categories the number of paid workers were as shown in Table 1.

TABLE 1

Directors and assistant directors	120
Administrative officers	82
Specialists	2,528
Supervisors	
Agricultural	253
Home economics	230
4-H Club (including state 4-H Club leaders)	264
Agricultural agent (4-H Club included)	7,064
Demonstration agents	4,271
All state workers	14,812

This number of employees represents an increase of 2,170 persons, or about 17 per cent, over comparable figures for 1950. Most of the increase took place in the county staffs.

Staff training, by supervisors to improve the general competence of county workers and by subject-matter specialists to keep county workers abreast of new technology and methods of teaching it, is a never-ending process. Study for professional improvement has increased rapidly during the last decade, largely owing to administrative encouragement and to educational programs designed especially for co-operative extension workers.

Eleven land-grant institutions award Master's or Doctor's degrees in co-operative extension education. To promote professional improvement, 29 states pay a part of the expenses of staff members while on study leave, and 35 allow official time off for study. During 1957 there were 253 staff members on leave for a quarter, semester, or year of graduate study. Most of these persons were enrolled in adult education or social sciences curricula. The National Agricultural Extension Center for Advanced Study at the University of Wisconsin is giving impetus to graduate study in administration and supervision. The graduate study program of the center is supplemented by research on administrative and supervisory problems and short-term educational activities for administrators. Current thinking regarding minimum requirements is that the Ph.D. soon will be a must for state specialists, and the Master's degree a minimum for permanent employment in any position.

OBJECTIVES AND PROGRAM

The primary function of the Cooperative Extension Service is an educational one—to aid the people it serves to achieve efficient agricultural production, adequate incomes, and responsible citizenship and to build wholesome and prosperous communities. It brings to its clientele the latest knowledge gained from research by interpreting and demonstrating its application to their immediate situations, using the most effective methods know to encourage its use in solving problems. Federal legislation authorizing co-operative extension work states that its function is ". . . to aid in diffusing among the people of the United States useful and practical information on subjects relating to agriculture and home economics, and to encourage the application of the same. . . ."

For some time after the Cooperative Extension Service was established, the agricultural colleges carried information to farmers on crop culture, soils, and home and livestock management. Programs were largely predetermined according to assumed wants and needs of farmers and limited to giving advice on the scientific or technical production problems of farming. By the end of World War I rural people were being given an increasing role in local program planning. Extension agents were meeting them in groups assembled in homes, in schoolhouses, and Grange halls to help them study their needs and problems and plan ways of dealing with them. More emphasis came to be placed on gathering facts about local, state, and sometimes national situations as the basis for planning programs.

During the early depression years the Cooperative Extension Service was the only nation-wide agency of government in close contact with the people in rural areas. Consequently, it was called upon by both federal and state governments to manage and operate state emergency rural relief programs and farm programs aimed at correcting national and international social and economic problems. The first to develop were the Agricultural Adjustment Administration crop and livestock production control programs of 1933-35. Almost overnight, these were handed over to the Cooperative Extension Service to be operated by state and county extension employees. After about five years, during which time separate administrative and operating staffs were assembled—drawn heavily from the co-operative extension staff—a separate agency of the department was developed which continues to operate such programs. Other action agencies with specialized functions, such as the Soil Conservation Service, Farmers Home Administration, and Rural Electrification Administration, were launched with much assistance and some staffing at all levels from the Cooperative Extension Service personnel.

World War II brought a second emergency period close on the heels of the depression years. The agents aided in a variety of wartime activities, such as government bond sale promotions, scrap materials drives, and service on a variety of local boards and committees concerned with helping in the war effort. The national farm labor program carried on during the war to supply farm labor during a period of labor shortage and all-out farm production occupied much time and effort of the extension staff. Such emergency programs are significant because they were conducted at the expense of time and effort of personnel that ordinarily would have been devoted to the regular educational functions of the Cooperative Extension Service. Consequently, with the cessation of these activities there followed a period of reorientation of programs and personnel.

By 1950 about half the county staff effort was devoted to agricultural production, marketing, economic problems and conservation of resources. Leadership development and organizing people to participate in extension activities were occupying about one-fifth of the time of county workers. The balance was being used for educational effort on health and nutrition problems, social adjustment, and management of the family farm and home businesses.

Within this third of the agents' time was included a variety of adult education activities incorporating general education content. These activities included observance of United Nations Day, discussions of international relations, discussions of interrelationships of agriculture and other segments of the economy, international fiestas, and citizenship leader training.

The farm and home unit approach initiated on a national scale in 1954 is a family-centered method designed to teach families the principles and applications of good management in their own particular total situations. By 1957 it was being used in 2,300 counties and involved 56,000 families. Extension was also taking a leadership role in initiating and helping to implement rural development—a resource development approach—in 57 pilot counties or trade areas in 25 states. This program enlists the co-operative efforts of government, business, industry, and agriculture to improve the lot of families who live in rural areas with a large amount of underemployment.

Educational programs aimed at reducing marketing costs and expanding market outlets for farm products, which involved providing consumer information to nearly 10 million homemakers, was receiving special attention in 1956. Public affairs education to present facts, help people interpret them, and make sound decisions based upon them involved an estimated 760,000 persons on matters affecting agriculture and rural life nationally and 560,000 on international problems.

PUBLICATIONS

Written materials for the public consist of a wide variety of subject-matter bulletins and leaflets that serve as one medium for channeling the research findings of state experiment stations and the Department of Agriculture to the people who can use it. The Federal Extension Service publishes mainly tool materials consisting of teaching aids, staff training manuals, leaflets, reports, digests and bibliographies of educational research, and its house organ, *Extension Service Review*. Subject-matter and technical publications, for the most part, are prepared and published by the states and the research agencies of the Department of Agriculture. County offices are the local distributors of publications of both kinds.

PLANNING GROUPS

Three basic types of organization are widely used for involving people in the program-planning process: (1) some variation of specialized program and commodity committees; (2) separate agricultural, home economics, and 4-H Club committees or councils; and (3) an over-all committee or council. It is the responsibility of the county extension staff to develop whatever type of organization is to be used. In some states the organizations used in planning and teaching have official status, and in others they have none. Regardless of their status, however, informal participation by individuals and groups in all stages of programing is universal.

EVALUATION OF RESULTS

Systematic evaluation of teaching activities and programs using sound research methods were initiated a few years after the Cooperative Extension Service was founded. Training of staff in evaluation methods and techniques has been carried on to some extent in almost all states. This training in practical methods for use in day-to-day evaluation of educational programs is supplemented by educational research.

Some research involves co-operation of the federal and state personnel to gather and use data regionally or nationally. Other projects consist of intensive experimental or developmental work by means of special resources and specialized technical staff. For example, a five-year action-research project in farm and home development is designed to determine the difference in effectiveness between this and other methods, to determine effective ways of doing farm and home development, and to find out the relative costs of this method as compared with others. Another project involves determining the minimum threshold of knowledge and understanding needed by farmers for efficient production of a particular crop.

To obtain use of findings from educational research, the Federal Extension Service publishes a series of research or special-subject bibliographies and an annual review of extension research and sends quarterly newsletters to counterparts in the states. It publishes special program-trend reports from time to time and brief summaries of significant current extension research.

STATUS AND TRENDS IN PROGRAM,
CLIENTELE, AND METHODS

County extension agents estimated the number of farm families influenced to adopt improved farming or homemaking practices in 1957 at just under 11 million. During the period 1954-57 there was a decrease of about 4 per cent in the number of farm families, an increase of 40 per cent in the urban, and an increase of 24 per cent in non-farm families reached. These changes reflect in part the decreasing number of farm families, the spreading of urban areas, a growing number of rural non-farm residents, and increased program emphasis on marketing and a consumer education with non-farm people—trends that are expected to continue.

The people served included about 270,000 young men and women eighteen to thirty years of age involved in special programs. Membership in 4-H Clubs reached 2.2 million boys and girls, bringing the all-time total number of different boys and girls ever reached by 4-H Clubs to 19.8 million. The number of volunteer leaders increased about 5 per cent from 1954 to 1957 to a total of over 1.1 million men and women and nearly 100,000 older 4-H Club boys and girls.

An over-all or general advisory group was reported to be functioning in 85 per cent of the counties. There were agricultural councils or committees in 85 per cent of the counties; 90 per cent had a group to advise on home demonstration work; an advisory group on 4-H Clubs existed in 96 per cent of the counties; and a young men and women's council had been formed in about one-fifth of the counties. During the four-year period 1953-56, the number of councils or committees increased by 26 per cent to the equivalent of ten per county.

The personal-contact methods used by extension agents resulted in 4 million visits by agents to farms or homes, 8 million visits by individuals in the extension offices, and 10 million telephone conversations between the staff and the people served. The telephone accounted for 45 per cent of the individual contacts made.

Result demonstrations have declined from a peak figure of about ¼ million in 1942 to 187,000 in 1957, reflecting greater dependence on meetings and mass media methods. Attendance at meetings held by extension staff members or volunteer leaders has increased from 25 million in 1930 to 75 million in 1957. Nearly 2.7 million meetings were held by agents or volunteer leaders. About three-fourths of the meetings were conducted or participated in by the agents and one-fourth by volunteer leaders alone. Attendance averaged 39 persons at meetings conducted by professionals and 15 at meetings conducted by volunteer leaders. Meetings for adults were 47 per cent of the total—49 per cent of those by professionals and 42 per cent of those conducted by the leaders. Training meetings for volunteer leaders accounted for one-eighth of all meetings and 7 per cent of the total attendance. Of these, about three-fifths were for adult leaders.

Generally, mass media were the means used to reach urban people and those who do not attend extension meetings. During 1957 about 70 news stories or magazine articles were prepared by each extension agent. The total of about 785,000 newspaper stories represents a decline of about 140,000 since 1950, the year of the highest number. The decrease in the number of news articles published has been accompanied by increased numbers of radio broadcasts and television programs given by extension staff members. Between 1950 and 1957 the number of radio broadcasts has about doubled—from about 140,000 to about 260,000. The first television programs were reported in 1953, and in 1957 just under 17,000 were reported as taking place in 58 per cent of the counties, with an average of eleven television appearances per county.

County extension agents used about 31 million pieces of published materials including bulletins, circulars, and other pamphlets of the state land-grant institutions, the United States Department of Agriculture, and other agencies.

COLLECTION OF STATISTICS

Annual statistics are collected in reports from all county extension workers to the states. County data are summarized by the state in a single report to the Federal Extension Service, where all state reports are combined into an annual statistical report of activities and accomplishments. A form is supplied by the Federal Extension Service that provides for reporting statistical estimates on participation, educational methods, volunteer leadership, organization and program planning, use of time by the professionals, and changes in farming and homemaking practices. Annual statistics are supplemented with trend charts for major items. In addition, the county extension agents prepare an annual narrative report to accompany the statistical report.

UNIQUE CONTRIBUTIONS TO ADULT EDUCATION

In World Wars I and II and the depression the Cooperative Extension Service demonstrated its effectiveness in dealing with emergency social, economic, and disaster situations. These and other examples have shown that adult education can be a powerful instrument of social policy.

Few people would question that the Cooperative Extension Service has played a major role in helping the American farmer to become the most efficient producer of food and fiber in the world. This result reflects the development of an attitude among farm people that management skills and new ideas are the most important resources in farming. It has always been the extension service's purpose to help farm families learn how to make the most of their gains through living a fuller life enjoying cultural and liberalizing educational experiences. Although substantial results have been achieved in some areas, the results have not met expectations generally.

Probably no other adult education organization has so effectively taught its staff members how to simplify technical materials for lay readers. This effort has led to simplification of publications prepared by the state agricultural experiment stations and the U. S. Department of Agriculture.

From the beginning, involvement of the learners has been a basic principle of program building. Although many programs have shown the efficacy of procedures involving the people affected, most administrators continually re-emphasize its importance.

The demonstration method was the basis of the extension service's early work and continues to be the core of many of its educational activities. The Cooperative Extension Service pioneered with materials and methods adapted to the teaching of adults. Visual materials always have been a feature of its teaching activities. It has also made a substantial contribution to new knowledge and methods through educational research and evaluation. The total volume over the years has been larger than that of any adult education organization.

Selected Readings

Bailey, Joseph C., and Knapp, Seaman A. *Schoolmaster of American Agriculture*. New York: Columbia University Press, 1945.

Bliss, R. K., *et al. The Spirit and Philosophy of Extension Work*. Washington: Graduate School, U.S. Department of Agriculture, 1952.

Byrn, Darcie, *et al. Evaluation in Extension*. Topeka, Kan.: H. M. Ives & Sons, Inc., 420 Quincy Street, 1959.

Crile, Lucinda. *Bibliography on Extension Research*. Extension Service Circular No. 416. Washington: Federal Extension Service, U.S. Department of Agriculture, 1944 (and every five years since).

————. *Review of Extension Studies 1946-7*. Washington: Federal Extension Service, U.S. Department of Agriculture, 1948. Semi-annually or annually since.

Kelsey, Lincoln D., and Hearne, Cannon C. *Cooperative Extension Work*. Ithaca: Comstock Publishing Co., 1957.

Loomis, Charles P., *et al. Rural Social Systems and Adult Education*. East Lansing: Michigan State College Press, 1953.

True, Alfred C. *A History of Agricultural Extension Work in the United States*. U.S. Department of Agriculture, Miscellaneous Publication No. 15. Washington: Government Printing Office, 1928.

Wilson, Meredith G., and Gallup, Gladys. *Extension Teaching Methods*. U.S. Department of Agriculture, Extension Service Circular No. 495. Washington: Government Printing Office, August, 1955.

CHAPTER 19

FOUNDATIONS AND ADULT EDUCATION

PAUL L. ESSERT
Professor of Education and Executive Officer
Institute of Adult Education, Teachers College
Columbia University

DEFINITION AND SCOPE

A philanthropic foundation has been defined as "usually a non-governmental, non-profit organization having a principal fund, managed by trustees or directors, and established to maintain or aid social, educational, charitable, religious, or other activities serving the common welfare. There are some 8,000 general research, special purpose, and family foundations. In addition, there are something under 2,000 company foundations, created to disburse corporate contributions."[1]

Any attempt to identify the activities of the numerous foundations which have an indirect impact upon adult education, as contrasted to those whose policies, programs, and budgets directly aid adult education, would be purely arbitrary and subjective. This survey, therefore, will draw its data from the three foundations which have directly supported adult education during the past third of a century: The Carnegie Corporation of New York, the W. K. Kellogg Foundation, and the Ford Foundation.

ORIGINS AND PURPOSES

In 1924 the Carnegie Corporation took the first steps toward adding adult education as a specific category of philanthropy and gave the first major foundation grants to get facts and promote the concept of adult education. Its purpose was to marshal the national and international resources of adult education and focus their energies upon the changing needs of society. In 1941 the Carnegie Corporation terminated its grants to the American Association for Adult Education and gave a ten-year grant to Teachers College, Columbia University, to support an Institute of Adult Education.

In 1939—fifteen years following the first grant of the Carnegie Corporation—the W. K. Kellogg Foundation made a significant revision in its Articles of Association, which had previously designated children and youth as the sole beneficiaries of its services. Because its experience in aiding communities to learn to help themselves through community education had demonstrated that adults and adult institutions were served as well as children and youth, the articles were changed at Mr. Kellogg's suggestion to read, "for the promotion of the health, education, and welfare of mankind."[2] This change gave increased flexibility to the Foundation in the application of its philanthropy to adult education. Its programs, policies, and budgets increasingly used the term "continuing education."

In 1951 the Ford Foundation established the Fund for Adult Education and assigned it a concern with "that part of the total education process which begins when schooling was finished." Its purpose was the expansion of opportunities for all adult men and women to continue their education throughout life in the interest of mature and responsible citizenship.

ORGANIZATION AND STRUCTURE

The adult education operations of the three foundations have been organized somewhat differently. The Carnegie Corporation made its grants primarily to or upon the recommendation of the American Association for Adult Education, and once the grants were made the recipients were relatively independent of the Corporation in carrying out their purposes. The executive committee of the Association was assisted by twenty-six advisory committees in specialized aspects of program in formulating its recommendations to the Corporation.

The W. K. Kellogg Foundation carries on its assistance to continuing education through its general offices in Battle Creek, Michigan, under the direction of its Division of Education. The other divisions of the Foundation (Agriculture, Dentistry, Hospital, Latin America, Medicine and Public Health, and Nursing) contribute ideas to the Division of Education and provide assistance for the continuing education of some professional groups.

The Fund for Adult Education was established by the Ford Foundation as an independent organization separately administered by its own board of directors. It has operated under grants from the Ford Foundation, its current grant extending through 1961. Its offices are housed in a special building which contains both offices and discussion laboratories in White Plains, New York. The Board of Directors of the Fund makes all major decisions regarding the program, policies, and budget, within the limitations of the grant by the Ford Foundation. It often shapes programs on advice of special *ad hoc* committees. The program is executed by a staff consisting of executive officers, specialists, and consultants.

In all cases the foundations have made broad use of conferences of citizens and leaders of international, national, state, and local associations and institutions.

FINANCES

The Carnegie Corporation made $4,500,000 available for adult education grants between 1924 and 1941, and $350,000 more to Teachers College, Columbia University, for the Institute of Adult Education for the period 1941-1951. Average expenditures per year were $300,000 for the first period and $35,000 per year for the Institute grant. Between 1942 and 1958 the Corporation contributed about $4,000,000 for projects in community development, international affairs education, and leadership training.

Between 1945 and 1958 the W. K. Kellogg Foundation has reported appropriations of approximately $13,000,000 in continuing education activities in the U. S. A. and abroad, averaging approximately $1,000,000 per year for this purpose.

The Fund for Adult Education made grants or administered projects under its own staff management amounting to approximately $33,000,000 for adult education projects and for development of educational television and radio between 1951 and 1957. The reports of the Fund recognize explicitly that its undertakings in educational television and radio are "broader than adult education, both in ages served and subject matter concerns." Adult education will continue to be influenced, however, by the $11,666,291 investment of the Fund in educational television and radio between 1951 and 1957. Apart from its television and radio grants, the Fund's expenditures for adult education projects will have averaged $2,300,000 per year by 1961.

Adult education has benefited from an investment by these three major foundations of $41,100,000 over the thirty-five years between 1924 and 1958, averaging well over $1,000,000 per year.

POLICIES

The policies of the Carnegie Corporation and the American Association for Adult Education in regard to adult education were primarily directed toward securing and diffusing information about adult education, sponsoring publications, and promoting co-ordinating conferences of the agencies of adult education. Both the Corporation and the Association had policies against their directly engaging in studies, researches, and experiments, although the Corporation supported a number of experimental programs conducted by other agencies.

The policies of the Kellogg Foundation are, in the main: to promote the use of existing knowledge rather than to further basic research; to favor self-help projects in which the recipients contribute services from their own time and resources; and to keep the Foundation-supported projects flexible and abreast of changing social and economic conditions.

The Board of Directors of the Fund for Adult Education defined its special task to be that of supporting programs of liberal adult education. The subject-matters favored are those of liberal arts and sciences. The methods favored are study and discussion activities and the use of the mass communications media, or combinations of the two.

OBJECTIVES AND PROGRAMS

The objectives of all three foundations in relation to adult education seem to have a common focus: to aid adult education institutions, organizations, and leaders to extend the scope and improve the quality of adult education. The ultimate goal is a more intelligent, mature, and responsible adult citizenship and quality of living.

Their programs have varied. The categories of grants of the Carnegie Corporation, in order of amounts granted over the first ten-year period, are as follows: occupational education; general purpose, including experimentation and support of the American Association for Adult Education; community studies; workers' education; urban organization; radio education; museums; research; rural adult education; university extension; adult elementary education; library adult education; alumni education; international adult education; Negro adult education; drama; parent education; adult science education; and recreation.

While the Carnegie Corporation was concerned with encouragement of adult education activity over a wide front, its program accented the exchange of information and knowledge about adult education, the advancement of its theory and practice, and the achievement of visibility and significance in the American scene. Nevertheless, the Corporation directed part of its efforts toward bold and courageous experimentation in such areas as prison education, the development of Town Hall and the People's Institute in New York, the promotion of local and regional adult education councils, the extension of forum and discussion methods, the establishment of the Readability Laboratory and the Adjustment Service in New York City, and the encouragement and support of the Workers' Education Bureau of America. Its ten-year grant for the Institute of Adult Education at Teachers College was a pioneering experiment in institutionalizing research and graduate education, and its pathway has since been followed by at least seventeen other universities.

The term "continuing education" runs through many of the projects and studies assisted by the W. K. Kellogg Foundation from its inception, in medical educational administration, agricultural education, and other areas of specialization. But by 1945 the Foundation had come to report explicitly certain activities under the category of "continuing education," which it insisted was one form of adult education. The largest proportion of the Kellogg grants has been given to establish facilities and operational funds for centers of continuing education. These grants have been conditional upon the ability of the recipients to match a designated portion of the grants, in keeping with the Foundation's self-help policy. The programs of the centers include adult work conferences; short-term work-study sessions; television, radio, and film follow-up of the center conferences back in the home communities of the participants; research and experimental services in the education of adults. These centers, now five in number, have been built or are being built in the United States at Michigan State University, the University of Georgia, the University of Chicago, the University of Nebraska, and the University of Oklahoma. In other countries smaller centers with somewhat similar program designs are being developed through the Irish Country Women's Association, the Edinburgh Center for Rural Economy, and the Institute of Central America and Panama (which specializes in adult nutrition education).

In addition to the centers for continuing education, the Kellogg Foundation has allocated funds for promotion of continuing education; experimentation and development in fundamental education; continuing education in nursing, journalism, and agricultural reporting; agricultural extension; and the improvement and extension of graduate training in adult education.

In pursuing its objective of advancing the education of adults for responsible citizenship, the Fund for Adult Education has sought to conceptualize and implement a *particular kind* of education which it holds is peculiarly appropriate for the task, — what it has called "liberal adult education." The Fund's aim is to create learning situations in which men "learn how to think, rather than what to think,"[3] through the process of free thought and communication of ideas.

Apart from its early support of educational television and radio, the major emphasis of the program of the Fund between 1951 and 1957 was in advancing liberal adult education through educational institutions and national organizations. This program included what the Fund calls "more sharply focused activities" designed for the liberal education of adults only and "only in situations where individual study is related to meeting in small groups." Grants to institutions and organizations for this purpose have been used to: (1) develop materials, courses of study, audio-visual aids, and experimental procedures in aiding the teaching-learning process in continuing liberal education; (2) assist selected universities, colleges, public schools, public libraries, and national organizations to develop programs of formal and informal continuing liberal education; and (3) carry on experimental programs in continuing liberal education under the direction of the Fund staff. These experiments under the Fund's staff include such projects as its Experimental Discussion Project, through which thirteen courses have been developed, tested, and diffused broadly. This project has produced findings which advance our knowledge regarding the time-span of courses, leadership requirements, and use of materials in liberal education through informal, lay-led discussion groups. Other major areas of concern of the Fund have been: co-ordination of resources and stimulation of ideas in adult education, working through such organizations as the Adult Education Association of the U. S. A. and other national, regional ,and local organizations; provision of scholarships and fellowships for leaders of adult education and the mass media; and fact-finding, research, and publication.

EVALUATION

One fact that is outstanding about the impact of foundations on adult education is that they have made significant contributions to the strengthening of adult education as a national force. They have displayed inventiveness, boldness of design, and willingness to anticipate new national needs beyond what the public has demanded in classes or special services. In brief, the foundations have encouraged experimentation beyond the obvious.

They have also enriched and modified the form, structure, content, and method of adult education. They have built and equipped centers of continuing education. They have supported the training of leaders for classes, discussion groups, and conferences. They have supplied materials, equipment, devices, and encouragement. In doing these things they have tried to reinforce the idea that maturity in government, labor-management relations, race relations, community improvement, parenthood, family management, and worthy use of leisure time are as important in our personal development as competence in our occupations or our ability to read the headlines or the newspaper or the captions under the pictures. The foundations have also appropriated substantial sums to give vigor, vitality, and quality to national, regional, state, and local co-ordination of the vast array of specialized interests in adult education.

It may be true that some of the efforts to establish better communication and co-ordination of the agencies of adult education have missed the mark. It may be true that after thirty years of getting together in adult education in the United States its leaders still lack effective, coherent, and significant national, regional, state, or local expression. Whatever the evidence of lack of progress may be, it can safely be said that much of the positive growth in coherent expression is attributable to the interest and encouragement of the foundations.

Finally, it seems clear that the contributions of these three foundations to adult education over the past thirty-five years have been sufficiently valuable to justify their being continued. But it is also clear that the foundations are increasingly focusing upon a particular quality and kind of adult education: one which will serve the prior needs of the nation in the cultivation of responsible citizenship in a world which is demanding the very best that a mind in action can contribute to our common purposes.

The major weakness of the relationship of foundations to adult education is that thus far they generally subscribe to these purposes and goals but seem uncertain of the power of adult education to make much difference in progress toward them. Even the generous contribution to adult education of the three foundations discussed above is somewhat timid and sporadic as contrasted with their investment in other types of education. This is even more apparent in the hundreds of other foundations with expressed interests in education but no clearly defined policies regarding adult education. Admittedly, this lack of conviction as to the power of adult education to assist in achieving adult educational purposes is no more true of the foundations than it is of national, state, and local governments. So far, in the use of both private and public risk capital for experimentation in adult education, little confidence has been shown in the claims for it by adult educators. Until more foundations and government agencies encourage a wide range of soundly financed, coordinated, and long-term experiments and researches in adult education, adult educators can only hope to make sporadic impacts upon quality living in our nation, only limited tests of the power of wholesome adult education.

Footnotes

[1]*Giving USA: A Compilation of Facts Related to American Philanthropy* (New York: American Association of Fund Raising Counsel, 1959), p. 38.

[2]*The First Twenty-Five Years* (Battle Creek: W. K. Kellogg Foundation, 1955), p. 11.

[3]*Annual Report, 1951* (White Plains, N.Y.: Fund for Adult Education, 1951), p. 13.

Selected Readings

American Association of Fund Raising Counsel, Inc. *Giving USA: A Compilation of Facts Related to American Philanthropy*. New York: The Counsel, 1959.

Andrews, F. Emerson. *Philanthropic Giving*. New York: Russell Sage Foundation, 1950.

Buhl Foundation. *Report for the Period Ended June 30, 1950 and Report for the Period Ended June 30, 1955*. Pittsburgh: The Foundation, 1950 and 1955.

Carnegie Corporation of New York. *Annual Reports*, each year, 1924-1959 New York: The Corporation.

Cartwright, Morse. *Ten Years of Adult Education*. New York: The Macmillan Company, 1935.

Fletcher, C. Scott. *The Great Awakening*. White Plains, N. Y.: The Fund, 1958.

The Ford Foundation. *Annual Report for 1958*. New York: The Foundation.

Fund for Adult Education. *Annual Reports*, 1951, 1952, 1953-54, 1954-55. White Plains, N. Y.: The Fund.

————. *The Challenge of Lifetime Learning Annual Report for 1952-53.*

————. *Continuing Liberal Education Report for 1955-57.*

————. *What It Is and What It Is Doing.*

Journal of Adult Education. Volumes I, II, XII and XIII are particularly useful to get the perspective of the fifteen year span of the most active relationship of the Carnegie Corporation of New York to adult education. These, supplemented by Morse Cartwright's, *Ten Years of Adult Education* and the Carnegie Corporation of New York's Annual Reports since 1924 present the basic sources for that Corporation's involvement in adult education.

W. K. Kellogg Foundation. *Annual Reports* 1955, 1956, 1957, 1958. Battle Creek, Michigan: The Foundation.

————. *The First Twenty-Five Years.* Battle Creek, Michigan: The Foundation, 1955.

New York Foundation. *Two Year Report, 1956-1957.* New York: New York Foundation, 1957. Suggested here, together with Buhl Foundation reference, as illustrative of numerous foundation reports that contain *implied* but no explicit references to "adult education" or "continuing education." The student of this subject should look at the many contributions of foundations not developed in this chapter of the *Handbook*, which have meaning for the education of adults, if not "adult education" or "continuing education."

CHAPTER 20

ADULT EDUCATION ACTIVITIES OF GOVERNMENT AGENCIES

AMBROSE CALIVER, ET AL*
Assistant to the Commissioner and Chief, Adult Education Section
U. S. Office of Education
Department of Health, Education, and Welfare

DEFINITION, ROLE, AND HISTORICAL DEVELOPMENT

The purpose of this chapter is to give some indication of the nature, scope, and extent of adult education activities of government agencies.

Emphasis is placed on federal agencies, and on the general and vocational activities of state agencies as they are related to the federal government. In this chapter adult education is assumed to include all those government-sponsored organized learning activities, of all types and levels, including elementary, secondary, vocational-technical, collegiate, graduate, and professional, which are designed to assist adults to improve themselves and their occupational competencies, after their formal education has either been completed or interrupted.

Historically, education in this country has been a state and local responsibility. However, for a variety of reasons, the federal government has found it necessary to assume an increasing responsibility in this field. Perhaps the chief reason for the growth of federal concern for education in general and adult education in particular is the natural expansion and increasing demands in certain major fields which have always clearly been a federal responsibility. These fields are: (1) assistance to the states, (2) education of persons under federal jurisdiction, (3) scientific research and the collection and dissemination of information regarding education, (4) intellectual and educational co-operation of the United

---

*Other persons assisting in preparing the chapter included: Edward W. Brice, Milton C. Cummings, Roy B. Minnis, and Betty A. Ward, of the staff of the Adult Education Section of the U.S. Office of Education. Many others were helpful in supplying materials and making suggestions, for which acknowledgment is gratefully made.

States with other nations, and (5) the training of persons in the service of the national government. Many of the activities in most of these fields are concerned with adults.

These educational activities started as early as 1779 with the instruction of men in the military service. Using the "General Welfare" clause and others in the Constitution as guides, this was followed by setting aside public lands in 1785 for the endowment of schools. From those early beginnings, federal activities in education for national defense and war have grown to include instruction in practically all subject fields and levels of education from teaching adult illiterates to read and write to post-graduate courses. In addition to provisions for training military personnel, the federal government made provisions for education in the District of Columbia and Alaska in the early 1800's. In 1862 the Congress passed the Morrill Act which aided the states in providing education in certain specialized fields such as agriculture and the mechanic arts. Many of the benefits of this Act clearly had adult education overtones. Other federal programs initiated for such purposes as nautical education (1874), in-service training of government personnel (1876), extension of land-grant education (1892), international education (1906), vocational education in public schools (1917), vocational education of physically disabled persons (1920), apprentice training (1934), and aeronautical education (1939), have been wholly or partially adult education programs. Add to these the emergency education services during the Depression, and the veterans' educational programs of World War I, World War II, and the Korean conflict, and we see an impressive array of federally sponsored or aided programs designed to assist adults in remedying some of their educational deficiencies, adjusting to the changing times, and improving their own personal development.[1]

OVERVIEW OF PRESENT STATUS AND TRENDS IN FEDERAL AGENCIES

The great number and variety of programs in federal agencies which are concerned with some aspect of adult education make it difficult to present a clear, unified, and co-ordinated overview of the status and trends in this area. However, the fact that the federal government is currently spending something over a billion dollars in fields that are directly or indirectly related to adult education indicates that there are probably some broad purposes underlying the provision of these funds.

A review of the legislation providing these funds reveals the following purposes of the federal government: To assist other agencies when it serves the national interest; to discharge its own inherent obligations; to provide education and training essential to national defense; to assist in the education of persons, and of nations both for the national defense and for improved international relationships; to maintain governmental efficiency through employee training; and to advance the general welfare of the nation by promoting research and the preparation of specialists. All these purposes either directly or indirectly are more or less concerned with the continuing education of adults.[2]

These purposes are achieved through many different organizational and operational arrangements. In some cases the federal government controls the program completely, as in the Bureau of Prisons, the Office of Indian Affairs, or certain military training programs. In other cases local, state, and institutional authorities have almost complete autonomy, as, for example, in the veterans education program, or the federally-aided vocational education program. There are many varieties between these two extremes.

There are also a variety of methods of distributing the federal funds which in one way or another benefit adult education. They may be distributed on the basis of land areas, population, flat grants, matching grants, program cost, payments in lieu of taxes, equalization aid, tuition cost, or contract for services.[3] The practices regarding personnel and facilities in like manner vary among the agencies and programs. In some instances the federal agency provides all or most of the teaching personnel and facilities; in others, practically none. There is also a vast difference among the audiences reached. For example, the Bureau of Public Roads operates a training program which reaches approximately fifty individuals a year; whereas other programs such as those of the armed forces, the Veterans Administration, and the Cooperative Extension Service, reach many millions.

Federal programs relating to adult education may be classified into five broad categories:

1. *Direct training programs,* such as those concerned with employee training, education of Indians, education of persons in federal territories and prisons; and civil defense.

2. *Educational services programs,* such as those concerned with collection and dissemination of information and statistics; and with consultation, advice, and leadership. Among the agencies providing such services are the Office of Education, the Public Health Service, the Children's Bureau, the Bureau of Public Assistance, and the Bureau of the Census.

3. *Research programs,* which provide basic information concerning health, education, agriculture, commerce, defense, and many other subjects. Among the agencies carrying on such basic research activities which have relevance to adult education are: The National Health Institutes, the National Science Foundation, the agricultural experiment stations, the Bureau of Standards, the Atomic Energy Commission, and the cooperative research program of the Office of Education.

4. *Grants-in-aid, fellowship, and internship programs,* which provide assistance to school systems and institutions, promote the preparation of leaders in various fields, and improve the work skills of adults. The fed-

eral vocational education program, the library services, and the National Defense Education programs of the Office of Education belong to this category, as well as certain programs sponsored by the Veterans Administration, the Office of Vocational Rehabilitation, and many others.

5. *International programs,* designed to promote communication and public understanding between our citizens and nationals of other countries, and to provide technical assistance to less developed countries. The State Department, the Department of Agriculture, and the International Cooperation Administration are examples of agencies conducting these kinds of activities.

OVERVIEW OF PRESENT STATUS AND TRENDS IN STATE AND LOCAL GOVERNMENTAL AGENCIES

At The State Level

The status and trends of the major governmental agencies concerned with adult education at the state level are dealt with in other chapters—state universities in Chapter 17, agricultural extension in Chapter 18, health organizations in Chapter 21, state library agencies in Chapter 25, and state departments of education in Chapter 29. The aggregate picture presented in these chapters is one of expanding role and services on the part of the state agencies in respect to the continuing education of adults.

But many other state agencies also take part in one way or another in the total state program for the education of adults, including welfare departments, state prisons, park and forest services, recreation departments, conservation departments, the state police, and numerous specialized bureaus and commissions. Their adult educational activities tend to fall into four categories: (1) in-service training for their own employees or inmates, (2) direct training for selected segments of the public (such as the families of inmates of mental institutions), (3) advisory and informational services to local communities and the general public, and (4) research. No comprehensive survey of the adult educational activities of these non-educational state agencies has ever been made, but without question they represent a tremendous adult educational resource.

The contribution that can be made by a state agency is well illustrated by the role of the director of adult education that has been established in the state departments of education in a number of states (see Chapter 29). The role tends to have three aspects: (1) administrative and regulatory, (2) consultative and advisory, and (3) communicative and interpretive. Its major functions include: the collection of statistics; certification of part-time teachers of adults (full-time teachers are certified through regular teacher-certification channels); organizing and conducting conferences; co-operative establishment of standards; accreditation of adult schools; allocation of state funds; operation of state-sponsored programs; stimulating and assisting local school officials with curricula, teaching methods, and organizational problems; preparing and publishing resource materials; advice on budgetary and accounting procedures; development of model policies; assistance in assuring co-operation and co-ordination between agencies and institutions; maintenance of an information clearinghouse; publication and distribution of materials and newsletters; and leadership and participation in meetings, conferences, and workshops. Among the fifty states, twenty-three collect extensive statistical information on adult education in the public schools, eleven provide aid to assure a counseling and testing service for adults, twenty have an advisory committee to the state departments of education concerned with adult education issues, thirty-two grant high school equivalency certificates, and fourteen provide services of an educational nature for the aging.

At The Local Level

The major governmental agencies operating adult educational programs at the local level are the same as those at the state level, and they are described in the same chapters elsewhere in this *Handbook*. But, as at the state level, many of the non-educational arms of local government also play important adult educational roles. For example, almost every local public housing authority has an adult educational specialist on its staff who organizes and supervises a variety of educational programs for the occupants of housing projects. In Chicago the Metropolitan District Police pioneered a program of inter-group education to improve race relations that has been adopted by many other police departments. The park or recreation department of practically every community sponsors instruction in arts and crafts, sports, and other leisure-time activities. And most of the operating departments of local government, especially in the larger cities, have more or less extensive programs of in-service training for their own employees.

ADULT EDUCATION ACTIVITIES IN CERTAIN FEDERAL AGENCIES

Practically every department and independent agency carries on activities which are, by virtue of the needs they are designed to serve, adult education activities. The amount of money expended by the federal government in these adult education activities is one indication of the extent of its programs in this field. According to the latest compilation of statistics of federal funds for education, these activities were both extensive and varied in nature. However, the study reporting these statistics[4] did not claim to list all the adult education activities in operation, nor was it possible to secure complete financial data on some that were listed. Even with these limitations, the study reported a federal expenditure of over \$87 million for adult education in 1956-57. In 1948-49 the amount reported was nearly \$21 million. Descriptions of a few of these major activities are given here to indicate something of the extent and nature of the far-flung federal program in this field.

Department of Health, Education, and Welfare

1. U. S. Office of Education

Adult Education Section.—Within the broad framework of its mandate to promote the cause of education, the Office of Education over the years, has conducted some research and provided some services for adult education. In 1955, in recognition of the growing interest and its own responsibility, it established an Adult Education Section. This section, which is concerned with all education needs of all segments of the adult population, is attempting to achieve the following long-range purposes:

> To help Americans become more aware of the importance of lifelong learning and of what it can do to solve many of their problems.
>
> To assist in identifying national trends and problems that have implications for adult education.
>
> To encourage educators and the public generally to accept adult education as an integral part of the regular educational programs.
>
> To help bring about greater clarity of purpose and policies, more communication and co-operation among adult education groups, and better co-ordination among public and private agencies in the use of resources.

In working toward these purposes the section hopes to develop programs of research, consultive services, and a clearinghouse of information. It is giving special attention to statistics; education of the aging, the foreign-born, young adults, and leaders and teachers of adults; fundamental and literacy education; community development; education for public affairs and leisure time; and intergroup and human relations education.

The section regularly gives consultive services and provides advisory services, as requested, through speeches, articles, individual and group conferences, institutes, and workshops. Recent adult educational publications of the Office of Education include: "Adult Education in American Education Week"; "Fact Book on Adult Education"; "Adult Education Services of State Departments of Education"; "Participation in Adult Education (based on the October 1957 Current Population Survey)"; "Education on Aging: A Selected Annotated Bibliography"; "Television in Education"; and "Homemaking Education Programs for Adults."

The section has assisted in having adult education accepted as a regular topic in American Education Week, and incorporated as a regular feature of the convention programs of the American Association of School Administrators. It has promoted the involvement of education in the considerations of the problems of aging on the federal level, and is currently responsible for planning and conducting the Education Section of the 1961 White House Conference on Aging.

Vocational Education Division.—The program of vocational education operated under the Smith-Hughes and George-Barden Acts serves both youths and adults. In 1956 there were approximately the same number of adults and older out-of-school youth enrolled in vocational programs as high school youths. Vocational instruction for adults under these acts is limited to that which is supplementary to the daily employment of those enrolled. Such instruction may consist of training in new techniques, development of new skills, and related science and mathematics necessary for a better understanding and performance of the trainees in their daily work. Training is given for occupations in the fields of agriculture, distribution, homemaking, trades and industry, practical nursing, and fishing.

Vocational programs are conducted by state education agencies or local boards of education according to state plans prepared by the State Boards for Vocational Education and approved by the U. S. Commissioner of Education. State plans set forth the qualifications of the teachers and other standards for conducting the classes. Federal funds may be used under state plans for salary and travel of teachers of adult classes and for instructional equipment and supplies. Such use is left to the discretion of and is under the control of the state boards. It is a requirement that for each dollar of federal funds used for vocational education a dollar of state and local funds will be spent.

Civil Defense Education Section.—The Office of Education has assumed the responsibility of directing a program of civil defense instruction. A nonmilitary program, it is concerned primarily with employing the educational "know-how" of adult educators to teach the principles of individual, family, and community responsibility and protection. The purpose of this project is to coordinate civil defense adult education at the national level. The program itself will be administered and developed by the states.

Beginning late in 1959, four "pilot" states were chosen in which to initiate the program, after consultation with the Office of Civil and Defense Mobilization and the Adult Education Section of the Office of Education. Contracts with these states provide for the establishment of a program with a full-time state coordinator and one or more instructor-traveling teams consisting of two professional educators. Having received their initial training in civil defense at the OCDM Staff College, the teams will conduct civil defense courses to train selected adult educators as instructors who in turn will conduct civil defense education classes for adults in individual, family, and community protection and responsibility. It is anticipated that appropriate funds will enable the expansion of the civil defense education program to many more states in 1960, and to the rest of the states in 1961.

The Library Services Branch.—A Public Library Specialist provides advisory and consultant services in library adult education to state library agencies, library and other associations, graduate library schools, individual public libraries, government officials, and citizen groups concerned with public library development. This specialist encourages public libraries to serve as community co-ordinating agencies as well as sponsors of adult education programs.

The branch administers the Library Services Act, a federal grant-in-aid program for the extension and development of public library service to rural areas. This program is resulting in the improvement of state and local libraries as effective agencies for informal adult education. Through this act over 300 rural counties across the nation with populations totaling more than 7,500,000 children and adults are receiving new or improved library services.

Educational Statistics Branch.—Basic statistics related to adult education are collected by the Educational Statistics Branch. The program presently planned includes a survey of adult education programs offered by public school systems and, at a later date, surveys of adult education in institutions of higher education, group work agencies, and other major types of sponsoring institutions. Many of the surveys will be conducted on the basis of scientifically selected samples, but the collection of reliable data will depend on the universal standardization of definitions, terms, and concepts in the field of adult education.

Staff members of the Educational Statistics Branch worked with personnel in the Adult Education Section of the Office of Education and with staff members of the Bureau of the Census in planning questions on adult education which were included in the October, 1957, Current Population Survey, conducted by the Bureau of the Census. A statistical analysis of the data was published in 1959.

Other Office of Education Units.—Other units in the Office of Education having more or less concern for some phase of adult education include: Higher Education Division, Elementary and Secondary Education Sections, School Administration Branch, Cooperative Research Branch, and International Education Division. In addition, practically all the titles of the National Defense Education Act have direct or indirect implications for adult education.

2. Social Security Administration

The Social Security Administration carries on a continuing program of staff development not related to specific job training. In addition to regular monthly staff meetings, there are courses of general orientation for new staff members and special sessions organized to meet a specific need—for example, courses in improving reading skill and a pre-retirement seminar.

An extensive public relations program is conducted throughout the Social Security Administration, and its publications frequently form the basic material used in adult education activities carried on by others.

On various occasions, kits of materials have been assembled in response to the particular needs of classes conducted by adult educators.

3. Public Health Service

An important adult educational activity in the Public Health Service is its traineeship for the specialized training of physicians, nurses, sanitary engineers, nutritionists, medical social workers, dentists, health educators, veterinarians, and other health personnel needing upgrading. Another phase of adult education is conducted by the Public Health Education Branch of the service, which provides consultative services in health education techniques to states and communities, to other units of the service and the department, and to voluntary agencies. It conducts a number of research studies in the behavioral sciences which have important relevance to adult education.

Many other units of the Public Health Service engage in or sponsor activities that are significantly related to adult education, such as the program of research in the aging process and workshops for training health personnel.

4. The Children's Bureau

Adult education has been a basic function of the Children's Bureau since it was set up by Congress in 1912 to investigate and report upon conditions of children throughout the nation. Traditionally, the bureau has not only gathered information on the growth and needs of children, but has disseminated such information widely to adults through publications written especially for parents, leaders, and workers in child-serving professions.

Four of the five best-selling government publications are parent publications of the Children's Bureau. Publications like "Homemaker Service" and "Child Welfare" provide background for citizen leaders interested in developing needed services for children. For professional workers, the Bureau produces such titles as "Psychiatric Consultation in a Child Welfare Agency," "Screening School Children for Visual Defects," and "Police Services for Children," plus a bimonthly inter-disciplinary journal, "Children." Other adult education materials published by the bureau include: "Infant Care," "Prenatal Care," "Your Child From One to Six," "Your Child From Six to Twelve," and many other titles.

The Children's Bureau takes part in adult education in other ways, including its administration of three grant programs for maternal and child health, crippled children, and child welfare services; its Division of Social Services; its Division of Juvenile Delinquency; and its Division of International Cooperation. With assistance from Children's Bureau funds, a number of states conduct classes for expectant parents in their local health departments as a part of the over-all maternal and child health programs.

5. Office of Vocational Rehabilitation

In addition to individual counseling and guidance, psychological testing, and the occupational training provided disabled men and women, this office provides the following adult educational services:

> In addition to support of year-round academic training programs for professional personnel, OVR has helped to finance nearly 70 short-term training courses in various aspects of rehabilitation. These courses are intended to raise the level of knowledge and skill for vocational rehabilitation personnel and those in related agencies, so that services may be of higher quality.
>
> The Office's continuing concern for raising the level of performance of the staffs of State vocational rehabilitation agencies has been expressed in a variety of ways: (1) through a series of in-service training grants to state agencies to assist them to organize continuing and comprehensive staff development; (2) conducting orientation courses for newly employed counselors and advanced courses in counseling or other aspects of vocational rehabilitation for experienced counselors; (3) providing seminars on administration for state executive personnel; (4) developing plans for a nationwide program of supervisory training for State agency supervisors; and (5) conducting a course for state medical consultants on administrative and program development.[5]

Department of Agriculture

In addition to the program carried on by the Cooperative Extension Service described in Chapter 18, the Department of Agriculture includes a number of administrative agencies designed to carry out special action programs which by their nature involve considerable adult education. The most important of these agencies are: Farmers Home Administration; Soil Conservation Service; Rural Electrification Administration; Production and Marketing Administration; Farm Credit Administration; and Forest Service. The first two serve to illustrate the range of their work.

Farmers Home Administration supervisors are in charge of 1,619 local county offices, some serving more than one county. Operating loans, long-term farm purchase loans, and special emergency loans are made available under authority derived from the Bankhead-Jones Farm Tenant Act of 1937, and the Farmers Home Administration Act of 1946. The power of review and decision in the hands of a local FHA county committee means adult supervision and education in improved farming methods and investment planning. Study which the local FHA county committees give to financing the business of agriculture with borrowers, and the annual meetings of borrowers, are genuine adult education experiences which broaden the knowledge of farm people about investment potentials, needs, and financial resources.

The Soil Conservation Service gives assistance to farmers and ranchers chiefly through soil conservation districts which the farmers organize and operate under state laws. Over 10,000 locally elected adults who constitute the 2,418 Conservation District Boards study the needs of their localities and assume leadership for accelerating needed conservation practices. Community leadership in the growing conservation education program is a practical type of adult education related to the specific needs of soil and other resources on American farms.

The Graduate School of the Department of Agriculture is unusual in that it is a quasi-official, self-supporting institution. It offers an after-hours program of some 450 courses, most of them designed to help federal employees improve their performance on the job or to qualify for new jobs in government. The teachers are in the main federal officials, usually supervisors of the work they teach. The classrooms are in government buildings. Most of the 6,500 students each year come from federal agencies, although enrollment is open to everybody in Metropolitan Washington. The graduate school does not award degrees. Its work is recognized by the U. S. Civil Service Commission, and many colleges and universities accept its credits. Along with the after-hours program, the graduate school has twenty correspondence courses and a number of courses are taught under contract to government agencies and other groups on official time.

Department of Defense

The education programs for military service are designed to meet specific requirements of the armed forces, upgrade the educational level of military personnel in specialities, and raise the educational level of career personnel. Some of these programs may be classed as adult education. In addition, educational programs are provided for a large number of civilians, many of whom are highly trained professionally but who need additional training in order to keep abreast of changes in their fields of work. Much of this training may be classed as adult education. It is short term and specialized and is usually given at the place of employment. During 1956-57 there were approximately 1800 students enrolled in the programs for civilians, at a cost of $1,883,825.[6]

Besides the full-time training schools, personnel in the armed forces may continue their civilian-type education while fulfilling their military obligations. The armed forces have provided the opportunity for their personnel in off-duty time to take civilian courses at a minimum cost. In 1956-57 a total of 503,787 military personnel participated in off-duty programs at a cost of $10,878,673 in federal funds.

The United States Armed Forces Institute (USAFI) located at Madison, Wisconsin, as a field activity of the Office of Armed Forces Information and Education, is the backbone of the armed forces' voluntary education program. The materials and services of USAFI available to military personnel include correspondence courses and group study; resident center programs; tests of general educational development; achievement tests; subject examinations; and educational and vocational advice. USAFI offers approximately 165 courses to military personnel on active duty. These courses are offered at the elementary, high school, and college levels with credit recommendations made by the Commission on Accreditation of Service Experiences. USAFI also provides 44 technical and vocational courses by correspondence for those individuals in the military who wish to prepare for certain vocations upon their return to civilian life. USAFI has no classrooms but offers its courses by the correspondence, self-teaching, and group study methods.

The Federal Bureau of Prisons

There has been developed in recent years in the federal prisons a comprehensive and diversified program which ranges from classes for the functionally illiterate, through elementary and high school classes, to subjects at the college level. It also includes social education—essentially a "life adjustment" type of program—emphasizes family and community living and occupational and personal adjustment, and correspondence courses (most of which are offered in co-operation with the International Correspondence Schools). Vocational training is offered in practically all trades and occupations, and several institutions have established craft shops to provide training in a variety of arts and crafts as a basis for the development of individual skill and vocational interests. In 1958 slightly more than 12,000 persons enrolled in all programs.

The International Cooperation Administration

The International Cooperation Administration is one of the three operating agencies which administer the mutual security program. It has semiautonomous status within the Department of State. The central purpose of this agency is to provide technical co-operation in the form of training by U. S. technicians, and study grants for foreign technicians in order to help nationals of partner nations acquire skills, knowledge, and abilities needed for economic and social progress. More than 6,000 skilled American technicians are working overseas providing technical knowledge and skills in 58 countries. They have trained more than three million people, a large majority of whom have been adults, who are now passing this training on to others.

Adult education services are channeled mainly through field operating divisions or branches such as agriculture, forestry, and fishery education, industry, health and sanitation, community development, engineering, and public administration. ICA is aiding 55 countries to improve diets and food supplies and thus keep pace with rising populations. In addition, ICA has helped many countries establish farm credit institutions, agricultural extension services, farm organizations, and clubs for out-of-school youth. Much of this service is through adult education.

Thousands of public health workers have been trained in the 40 countries where ICA is co-operating in health work. Adult education programs have been utilized to enlist the support of people in the host country in the worldwide campaign against malaria, cholera, tuberculosis, and the waterborne diseases, which are the greatest killers in some of the countries.

ICA has developed work in community development in a number of countries. These programs are generally adult-centered and they stress ways and means of adapting and using modern production techniques and other methods.

One of the most successful adult services of ICA has been the training program for foreign-born participants who have been trained in the United States or some third country. Since 1955 this activity has provided training for several thousand adults.

It is estimated that approximately 250 million are expended annually by the federal government for educational purposes in other countries, much of which is for adult education services.

Department of Labor

The Bureau of Apprenticeship and Training stimulates and assists industry in the development, expansion, and improvement of apprenticeship programs designed to provide the skills required by an increasingly complex economy. Its principal functions are to encourage the establishment of sound apprenticeship and training programs and to provide technical assistance to industry in setting up such programs. In the performance of these functions, the bureau is guided by the Federal Committee on Apprenticeship, comprised of leaders of management, labor, and vocational education. The bureau works closely with state apprenticeship agencies, trade and industrial education institutions, and management and labor.

The Bureau of Employment Security, through affiliated state employment security agencies, assists job seekers to obtain suitable employment, and helps to maintain income during a period of unemployment through unemployment compensation. One of the special activities of this program has been the development of special services and benefits to older persons. Special research and developmental work are being carried out to enable the local employment offices to provide improved services. This includes: (1) Research studies on the use of tests in serving older workers, (2) development of a case book on desirable employer practices, (3) preparation of technical guides for conducting state and area studies on the problems of older workers, (4) development of guides for conducting labor-management institutes and older worker forums, and (5) preparation of promotional and educational materials on the qualifications of older workers.

The Women's Bureau has as its basic objective the effective utilization of womanpower. It is the duty of the bureau to formulate standards and policies which shall promote the welfare of wage-earning women, improve their working conditions, increase their efficiency, and advance their opportunities for profitable employment. The bureau works with other government agencies; women's and civic groups of this and other countries; personnel groups in industry, government, and schools; unions, employers, and trade associates; and educators, writers, students, and other individuals. Facts that are collected by the bureau with the cooperation of employers and unions are made available to the public. Services are provided to management and labor in the form of consultation, publications, and specially compiled information, as well as articles, assistance on articles, and exhibits. Special programs are developed for occupations in which the shortage is acute.

One of the most effective adult education programs of the bureau is a new approach to finding jobs for mature women—an "Earning Opportunities Forum" which is organized at the community level. The forum focuses attention on the types of jobs available to older women, and the women in the area who are available to fill them. The bureau has found the forums particularly valuable in bringing together community resources, such as employers, unions, voluntary groups, and others to assist their elder citizens.

Veterans Administration

Much of the training provided for veterans under the Servicemen's Readjustment Act of 1944, the Veteran's Readjustment Act of 1952, and the Vocational Rehabilitation Training Programs may be classed as adult education. The readjustment training programs are for the purpose of restoring lost educational or vocational opportunities to veterans whose educational or vocational ambitions had been interrupted or impeded by service in the armed forces. The vocational rehabilitation program is designed to help veterans overcome the handicap of a service-incurred disability. Approximately ten million World War II and Korean War veterans had had training prior to fiscal year 1958 in institutions of higher learning, schools below college grade, job training, and institutional-on-farm training.

The Veterans Administration, like most other government agencies, also has an employee training and development program. This program is carried out on many fronts—administrative, professional and technical. The Veterans Administration also has an adult education program for the orientation of volunteer workers in VA hospitals.

Other Federal Agencies

Many other federal agencies—too numerous to treat separately, provide adult education in the form of in-service training.[7] The programs of the agencies described above serve, however, to illustrate the scope and character of the federal government's role in adult education.

Government Employees Training Program

Perhaps the most significant event, as far as Government activities in adult education are concerned, was the passage by Congress on July 7, 1958 of the Government Employees Training Act (Public Law 85-507, 85th Congress, S 385, July 1, 1958). Section 2 of the Act, on Declaration of Policy says:

(1) That, in order to promote efficiency and economy in the operation of the Government and provide means for the development of maximum proficiency in the performance of official duties by employees thereof, to establish and maintain the highest standards of performance in the transaction of the public business, and to install and utilize effectively the best modern practices and techniques which have been developed, tested, and proved within or outside of the Government, it is necessary and desirable in the public interest that self-education, self-improvement, and self-training by such employees be supplemented and extended by Government sponsored programs. . . .

(2) That such programs shall be designed to lead to (A) improved public service, (B) dollar savings, (C) the building and retention of a permanent cadre of skilled and efficient Government employees, well abreast of scientific, professional, technical, and management developments both in and out of Government, (D) lower turnover of personnel, (E) reasonably uniform administration of training, consistent with the missions of the Government departments and agencies, and (F) fair and equitable treatment of Government employees with respect to training.

On January 20, 1959, the President issued Executive Order 10-800, implementing the Government Employees Training Act. He ordered in Section 2 of the five section Order, that "The head of each department shall, . . . (a) review periodically the immediate and long-range needs of the department for employee training . . . ; (b) formulate plans of action to meet such training needs; (c) establish and maintain, . . . , needed training programs; (d) establish adequate administrative controls . . . ; (e) stimulate and encourage employee self-development and self-training; and (f) utilize the training facilities and services of other departments. . . ."

In the forthcoming amendment of the Civil Service Commission on the Intragency Training Programs there are eighty-six subject-matter listings, grouped under the following broad categories: General Management, Administrative Operations, Supply and Transportation, Personnel Administration, Communications and Languages, Safety and Related Skills, Specialized Agency Programs, The U. S. and World Affairs, and Physical Sciences and Kindred Fields.

MAJOR NEEDS, PROBLEMS, AND ISSUES

As one views the far-flung and complex variety of federal activities that in one way or another impinge upon adult education, one unfamiliar with the situation would expect some unifying principle and consistency of policy. However, such is not the case. In 1931, the National Advisory

Committee on Education stated that "the Federal Government has no inclusive and consistent public policy as to what it should or should not do in the field of education." In 1957, the President's Committee on Education Beyond High School, in reference to this, commented that "this statement is as true today as it was 26 years ago." This committee further stated that "similar statements have been made by a succession of study groups and advisory committees including the Advisory Committee on Education (1936), the President's Commission on Higher Education (1947), and the first Hoover Commission (1949)."[8]

From the foregoing statements it would appear that the major need as far as adult education activities are concerned is for some kind of co-ordinating agency. There is also need for a clearinghouse of information about the various activities relating to public and private adult education. Furthermore, there is need, in the field of adult education generally, for clarification and standardization of definitions, terms, and procedures. These clearly seem to be tasks requiring the assistance and leadership of the federal government.

One of the major problems relating to government's responsibility in adult education on all levels, federal, state, and local, is concerned with lack of adequate and qualified personnel. Another problem is a lack of awareness on the part of our citizenry of the importance, magnitude, and urgency of the adult education needs posed by the accelerating rate of change taking place in the advances of science and technology. Still another problem—resulting largely from the above-mentioned advances—is that of remedying the great "social deficits" in our population.

Two of the major issues or questions faced as these needs and problems are considered are these: To what extent should government, and particularly the federal government, provide leadership and financial assistance in this important and burgeoning field? Should adults be educated at the expense of children? To the first question, the answer is that the problem is national in scope, and therefore no other agency than the federal government is adequately equipped to render the needed assistance. To the second question, the U. S. Commissioner of Education gave an appropriate answer at the opening session of the 1958 NAPSAE convention when he said:

> "As a nation we are not yet sufficiently appreciative of the fact that better informed adults mean richer developmental experiences for children. Thus, providing public funds for adult education should be regarded also as an investment for the children. Our nation certainly does not lack the resources to make additional investments in education. Opportunities are needed for all those who can be upgraded as citizens and who can join the ranks of well-trained manpower. Indeed, in these times we can afford to do not one bit less."[9]

Footnotes

[1]Charles A. Quattlebaum, *Federal Educational Activities and Educational Issues Before Congress.* Library of Congress, The Legislative Reference Service. 82nd Congress, 2nd Session, House Document No. 423 (Washington: U. S. Government Printing Office, 1952), pp. 4-6.

2Albert R. Munse and Edna D. Booher, *Federal Funds for Education, 1956-57 and 1957-58.* Bulletin 1959, No. 2, U. S. Department of Health, Education, and Welfare, Office of Education (Washington: U. S. Government Printing Office, 1959), p. 3.
3*Ibid.*, p. 5-6.
4*Ibid.*
5*U. S. Department of Health, Education, and Welfare Annual Report, 1958* (Washington: U. S. Government Printing Office, 1958).
6Albert R. Munse and Edna D. Booher. *op. cit.*, p. 108.
7For example, see: U. S. Department of Commerce, *Graduate School of the National Bureau of Standards Announcement of Courses for 1958-59* (Washington: Government Printing Office, 1958), p. 2; and U. S. Department of State, *Catalog, School of Foreign Affairs, School of Languages.* Publication 6747, Department and Foreign Service Series 84 (Washington: Government Printing Office, 1959).
8The President's Committee on Education Beyond the High School, *Second Report to the President* (Washington: Government Printing Office, 1957).
9Lawrence G. Derthick, "The Public's Responsibility for Adult Education," *The Public School Adult Educator,* II (January, 1959), 35-36.

Selected Readings

Caliver, Ambrose. "The National Concern for Adult Education." Reprint from *School Life,* May, 1957. Washington: Adult Education Section, Office of Education, Department of Health, Education, and Welfare, 1957.

Carlson, Theodora E., and Williams, Catherine P. *Guide to the National Defense Education Act of 1958.* Office of Education Circular No. 553. Washington: Government Printing Office, 1959.

A Federal Committee Report on Federal Responsibility in the Feld of Education. Report of the U.S. Commission on Intergovernmental Relations, Study Committee on Federal Responsibility in the Field of Education. Washington: Government Printing Office, 1955.

Federal Relations to Education. Report of the National Advisory Committee on Education. Washington: National Capital Press, Inc., 1931.

Holden, John B. *Adult Education Services of State Departments of Education.* Office of Education Miscellaneous No. 31. Washington: Government Printing Office, 1959.

Munse, Albert R., and Booher, Edna D. *Federal Funds for Education, 1956-57 and 1957-58.* Office of Education Bulletin No. 2. Washington: Government Printing Office, 1959.

Olds, Edward B. *Financing Adult Education in America's Public Schools and Community Councils.* Chicago: Adult Education Association of the U.S.A., 1954.

The President's Committee on Education Beyond the High School. *Second Report to the President.* Washington: Government Printing Office, 1957.

Quattlebaum, Charles A. *Federal Educational Activities and Educational Issues Before Congress.* The Library of Congress, The Legislative Reference Service. 82nd Congress, 2nd Session, House Document No. 423. Washington: Government Printing Office, 1952.

Waterman, Alan T., and Kelly, Harry C. *National Science Foundation Programs for Education in the Sciences.* Washington: Government Printing Office, 1959.

CHAPTER 21

ADULT EDUCATION THROUGH VOLUNTARY HEALTH ORGANIZATIONS

LEVITTE MENDEL
Associate Director
National Health Council

Other chapters in this *Handbook* report on adult education in governmental health organizations, in social welfare organizations which often involve education relating to health, and in civic and other organizations which frequently include health activities in a more general program. Principal consideration is given here to the national voluntary health agencies and their state and local affiliates, although it should be recognized that local agencies, hospitals, and other health institutions not organized as units of a national agency also engage in adult education and are, therefore, resources to be considered in community adult education programs.

DEFINITION AND SCOPE

The national voluntary health agency has been defined as a national organization of individuals, or of associations of individuals, the primary purpose of which is health-related in that it is organized to combat a particular disease, disability, or group of diseases and disabilities, or to improve the health of a particular group of people. It is supported primarily by voluntary contributions from members or supporters, rather than from government sources or endowment. It engages in programs of research, education and service to individuals and communities in its particular sphere of interest.[1]

Education is one of three primary functions of the national voluntary health agency, the other two being research and patient or community service. The educational programs of such agencies can usually be classified as directed to: (1) the professions, (2) the patient and his immediate family, and (3) the public at large. In most cases, the educational program of the voluntary health agency is concerned with some phase of health or disease prevention.

Education of professional groups is an important part of the work of most voluntary health agencies and concerns itself with information on new research findings, resources for services and information, and educational materials and techniques. Educational pamphlets, journal articles, films and other visual aids are used as well as the support of fellowships, scholarships or research grants, sponsorship of seminars and conferences, and involvement of professional personnel in the work of the agency.

Educational work aimed at the patient and his immediate family is designed to improve the condition of the patient and, in some instances, to prevent the spread of the disease to other family members. Designed to supply essential knowledge and motivation, such services include distribution of pamphlets or other instructional materials, home or institutional visits by professionals or volunteers, group discussions and other devices to help people understand and to stimulate them to action.

The use of group discussions for patients and for family members—a borrowing in large measure from the field of adult education—is increasingly popular as a technique in the education of patients or family members. The supportive effect of the group is especially valuable with parents whose children are affected by mental retardation, cerebral palsy, muscular dystrophy, or other neurological disabilities. Many of the more recently established national voluntary health agencies have been developed through the joining together of parents' groups which have then expanded to involve others in their work of research, service, or education.

The use of group activity for patients themselves is also increasingly found, both in institutions and in the community. A recent study on the relation of smoking to cancer among teen-agers and their parents provides specific information on teen-age smoking habits, parental attitudes and smoking behavior, and indications of the groupings in which smokers and non-smokers may be classified. The study shows the importance of simultaneous educational programs among high school age youngsters and organizations of parents. As the result of this research, the American Cancer Society is developing an educational program in close cooperation with teachers, leaders of youth organizations, and national organizations such as the National Congress of Parents and Teachers.[2]

In educational work aimed at the public at large, the goal is to stimulate action either for individual or community health improvement. The process is designed to impart information and motivate people so that they will act to promote their own and their families' health, take adequate preventive measures, recognize danger signals, seek competent advice and services, or work together to assure the availability in the community of needed services or facilities.

In many communities health agencies have encouraged citizen groups to study their health problems and to put plans into operation which are based upon their own findings and their own recognition of health needs.

CHANGING CHARACTER OF HEALTH PROBLEMS

Educational efforts of the voluntary health agency are the result of slow growth, development, and change in public health programs as they have occurred in the United States during the past seventy-five years. The earliest public health programs dealt with the control of communicable disease and were chiefly effected through statute or regulation. Even before the health departments were organized in the cities, rules and regulations governed certain health habits of citizens. These laws were usually enforced by police, sanitation officers, or other authorities in the communities. Enforcement of the law was not much concerned with education. People merely were prohibited from carrying out certain acts which contributed to insanitary conditions. As the germ theory of disease became universally accepted and preventive methods for the control of diseases were discovered, a more personal approach to the health of the public began to develop. At this point in health program development the health of the individual became important.

During the past half century medical science has created many changes in our concepts of disease. As these pieces of newer knowledge began to be transformed into practical efforts the present-day approach of meeting community health needs started to develop.

As diseases of early childhood came under control life expectancy of the population tended to increase. Recent population studies show a longer life span for our population and as a result an increase in the amount of chronic disease. This shift in morbidity from the communicable diseases to a high prevalence of chronic diseases has begun to place even higher values upon the educational procedures in the health program both of the voluntary and official health agencies.

A patient recovering from a communicable disease can usually anticipate returning to his normal activities in a reasonably short time, but a patient with a chronic illness, in most instances, must look forward to a change in his daily habits, and frequently in the means for making a living. Because in most cases of chronic illness, such as heart disease, diabetes, and tuberculosis, the effects of the disease itself will be with the patient for the duration of his life, the patient must learn to live with the existing condition.

EDUCATIONAL GOALS

The educational programs of the voluntary health agencies are unique in many ways as compared with educational institutions. Their educational goals are usually defined in terms of the diseases with which they are concerned. Most agencies direct their educational efforts toward prevention, case finding, and dissemination of knowledge about treatment, rehabilitation, and other health services. Health agencies are also concerned with research and transmission of the knowledge gained from research into practical and useful application. Some agencies are concerned with diseases and disabilities for which the cause is not known. In these instances, educational emphasis is on care of the patient, research, and doctor-patient relations. The nature of the disease and the knowledge about it are prime factors for establishing the health agency's objectives for its program and educational goal. In recent years health agencies have expanded their interests to include support of community health services and planning bodies engaged in co-operative efforts for meeting community health needs.

Many voluntary health agencies are accepting a broader approach to their educational efforts. This reflects the newer goals which are now recognized by the health agency. In these larger health goals there is recognition of the relationship between optimum health for the individual and community planning, especially as it relates to raising the health standards of the community.

As the health agencies accept broader and more inclusive responsibilities for health they become more involved in the health problems of the community and the need for better health resources for the community. For example, a local voluntary agency may direct its educational programs so as to provide information on needed resources—hospital and medical centers, rehabilitation and psychological services, and care of the mental patient. As these educational programs become more general the agency becomes involved in wider interests which include larger numbers of people. In many communities the health agencies, official and voluntary, join with other groups and form health councils. Usually the health council includes representatives of wide community interests, such as city planning agencies, school, industry and professional groups, religious and social agencies, as well as individuals. Such health councils constitute a significant facility for joint planning for meeting community health needs and for exchange of information on the work of each agency and new knowledge in the field of health. In the community health council a common meeting ground is provided for co-operative development of the community health program.

HEALTH EDUCATION PRACTICES OF A VOLUNTARY HEALTH AGENCY

In its broadest concepts health education of the public encompasses many things, some of which would not normally be accepted as "education" if considered in the academic setting. For example, community education involves not only reaching an audience but obtaining the audience in the first place. It not only involves teaching the class or student, but frequently means training the teacher. In each instance the activity is carried out as a learning experience, with the ultimate objective of improving community health services or in providing health resources for individuals.

Health education activities of the voluntary health agency involve special education on the subject matter with which the agency is concerned. The educational program of the national and state agency varies somewhat from the local affiliate in that materials of the national agency are used but the additional components inherent in the grass-roots program are built in by the local agency. It is chiefly at the local level of operation that most of the direct contact is made with the recipient to whom health knowledge is directed. In this case the local health agency affiliates establish the educational program directed to special interest groups or to individuals. The Muscular Dystrophy Associations of America's educational program for parents provides an excellent example. Parents of children with muscular dystrophy meet together with physicians, medical social workers, and therapists. They become informed on the nature of illness, where resources are available, preventive methods, if any, long term care, and rehabilitation.

Providing Information

Voluntary agencies usually have well trained, qualified people on their staff. They are not only available for the usual question-answer kind of educational service on the specific disease or service of the agency, but also provide information on the much broader field of community health resources. In addition to serving as an information center, local agencies arrange for film distribution, loan of visual aids, provide for lectures or classroom instruction, exhibitions for special purposes, radio and television scripts, and program planning on health topics. Within the agency's field of operation news articles and health information copy are placed in newspapers, local journals, industrial and club house organs.

Advising and Guidance

Providing information is closely related to the function of advising and guidance. Agency staff often finds itself faced with requests for information when it knows the individual asking questions is seeking advice. To meet this problem many requests for information dealing with medical problems are referred to committee members or medical volunteers who serve agencies in this capacity.

Working With Volunteers

Volunteer participation in the health agency program is a key to the success of the educational effort of the local health agency. The volunteer establishes the grapevine for the information process. The volunteer may be assigned specific jobs of the agency, but is usually very much involved in the "reaching job" of getting health information out to the public. Assistance in program planning almost always involves volunteer training. This training in turn includes a wide scope of activities not always specifically dealing with preventing a disease. How to be a good leader, how to plan a program, techniques of group dynamics, how to get stories in newspapers, are all subject matter for volunteer training. An agency volunteer of long standing receives a broad knowledge of the community, and its resources and cultural patterns. Frequently volunteers include professionally trained experts who contribute to the agency's program from their vast experience, and provide skills which contribute to the quality of the volunteer programs.

Case Finding

Nearly all voluntary health agencies are involved in finding unknown cases of the disease or illness in which the agency is interested. Many agencies have built-in educational experiences in case finding programs. Finding new cases results in educating the public at large, even though the effort is directed to a specifically few people.

In most instances case finding efforts require especially well planned program activity. Such activities include public meetings, door to door home visits, appearances on radio and television. Volunteers are also involved in interviewing other citizens to interest them in the work of a committee or the agency. Hundreds of citizen volunteers are frequently working on case finding projects. (Each volunteer may be tested, if a test is involved. The testing is also an educational experience.)

SPECIALIZED PROGRAMS

Since the beginning of the voluntary health agency movement attention has been given to health education of the adult in his "working environment." A more recent development emphasizes educational efforts concerned with raising the general health standards of the community. These efforts have included school health programs, industrial health programs, professional education, education on legislation, and education to promote and strengthen local health departments and community health services.

School Health Education

Although each agency as it develops its school health program has a specific health interest, its major objectives in school health work is to assist the teacher in developing health education courses which will help the student understand the components of a healthful way of life. To do this, agency staff finds itself working with teachers and school administrators on school health curriculum studies, and in-service education conferences. These efforts involve school work at all grade levels.

Consultation is also given to personnel in teacher training institutions, and to staff in college health service programs. In many ways the agency services do not differ widely from community health education service, in that the same educational techniques (pilot projects, evaluation studies, etc.) are used even though the literature and visual aids are especially designed to meet the school situation.

Industrial Health Education

Working people are difficult to reach through normal channels of communication and frequently special effort must be made to inform the working man or woman at his or her place of employment.

Here again the skills of community organization become an important part of the educational process. To interest or motivate the working man, it is often necessary to promote health committees within the industry. Industry has health problems too and often seeks assistance in working out the solution to these problems. By providing consultation on educational methods and procedures and by supplying material, health agencies have found numerous opportunities to develop health education activities within industry.

Professional Education

Each health agency in its own field of interest has attempted to keep the professional health worker up to date with the latest information. Most of the health and medical specialists and their professional societies are at one time or another involved in educational programs of the voluntary agency. These include physicians, dentists, nurses, laboratory technicians, vocational and employment counselors, guidance workers, health educators, occupational and physical therapists, statisticians, and others who make up the health and medical care team. Subject matter for the professional program varies as to the group involved but mainly it is concerned with developments in prevention, case finding, diagnosis, treatment, rehabilitation, management of the patient and his family, and specific health practices.

Education On Legislation

Many times through the past years legislation on health problems has been the main support for raising the health level of a community and the subsequent improvement of the health of the individual citizen. Frequently agencies have organized groups to study the cause and prevalence of health conditions only to find it necessary to stimulate action programs. With community groups, legislators, and civic officials working together, the needs of the community have frequently been met. A large part of this work is done through education of the public, the legislative bodies, the officials of the communities. It has led to the development and strengthening of health departments and to new laws establishing higher health standards and services for the people and the communities in which they live.

Footnotes

1Philip E. Ryan, "The Role of Voluntary Health Agencies in Planning to Meet the Health Needs of Older Persons," University of Michigan 12th Annual Conference on Aging, Ann Arbor, June 22-24, 1959.

2Daniel Horn, "Report from School Survey in Portland, Oregon." New York: American Cancer Society.

Selected Readings

Cavins, Harold M. *National Health Agencies: A Survey with Especial Reference to Voluntary Associations.* Washington: Public Affairs Press, 1945.

"The Job Ahead in Health Education: Summary of a session at the Mississippi Valley Conference, October 1955." New York: National Tuberculosis Association. (Mimeographed)

Kammeier, C. W. "The Voluntary Health Agency in the American Scheme." The second in a series of Annual Michigan Tuberculosis Association Endowed Lectures delivered at the School of Public Health, University of Michigan, Ann Arbor, Michigan, Dec. 5, 1949. Lansing, Michigan: Michigan Tuberculosis Association, 1950.

Lifson, S. S. "Health Departments in Adult Education," *Adult Education Journal*, (January, 1949), 21-24.

National Tuberculosis Association. "Health Education Opportunities for Tuberculosis Associations." New York: The Association, 1954.

Patterson, Raymond S., and Roberts, Beryl J. *Community Health Education in Action.* St. Louis: The C. V. Mosby Company, 1951.

Ryan, Philip E. "The Role of Voluntary Health Agencies in Planning to Meet the Health Needs of Older Persons." University of Michigan 12th Annual Conference on Aging, Ann Arbor, June 22-24, 1959. New York: National Health Council. (Mimeographed)

———. "Health Education—Whose Job Is It?" A digest of Keynote Address given at the Health Education Workshop sponsored by the West Virginia State Department of Health, Huntington, West Virginia, June 5, 1957. New York: National Health Council. (Mimeographed)

Shryock, Richard Harrison. "National Tuberculosis Association, 1904-1954: A Study of the Voluntary Health Movement in the United States." New York: National Tuberculosis Association, 1957.

"Voluntary Agencies Have Important Health Role," *Bulletin of the Pennsylvania Tuberculosis and Health Society,* February, 1952, pp. 4-5.

CHAPTER 22

ADULT EDUCATION IN INDEPENDENT AND RESIDENTIAL SCHOOLS

HENRY KLEIN
Executive Director
Junto Adult School, Philadelphia

and

ROBERT H. SCHACHT
Assistant Director
Informal Instructional Services
University of Wisconsin Extension Division

It is clear from surrounding chapters that the great bulk of adult education takes place in institutions that were founded primarily for other purposes than the education of adults—public schools, universities, labor unions, business and industry, libraries, and so on. A small but significant fraction of adult education, however, takes place in institutions that were founded expressly for the education of adults and that are completely independent of any larger institutional control. Some of these independent adult schools are located in population centers and provide activities for "commuters." Others, usually located in more sylvan settings, serve students who "live in" for periods ranging from several days to several weeks. This chapter is concerned with both non-residential and residential independent adult centers.

THE INDEPENDENT ADULT SCHOOL

As was pointed out in Chapter 2, the first independent adult school was established in this country in 1727 by Benjamin Franklin. His informal "Junto" was, in fact, the prototype of a long line of independent adult study groups that have dotted the history of our country.

Today's independent adult school bears well the comparison with

American industry's "free enterprise." Such a school usually arises from a local need, is "sparked" by a few civic leaders who rally around them some workers who plan the program, set up faculty and facilities, spread the word, open the doors one night and yell, "Come and get it."

If, like many a small business, the entrepreneurs have guessed wrong about the public's crying need for education, the school joins the business failure rolls. But if it catches on—like the American economy itself—the independent school will sail like Franklin's kite, free as the wind from controls.

Why an independent adult school in a community where there already exists solid coverage of all adult interests, well presented and well attended? Under those rare circumstances—no justification at all for a fifth wheel. But you'll generally find that the independent school fills some educational gap, or presents subjects differently. Otherwise, it either doesn't start or quickly goes out of business.

The structure of the independent adult school varies. In its purest form, a group of civic leaders take out a non-profit educational charter and conduct classes in some public or semi-public building, sometimes in their own quarters. In another form, a well-heeled foundation provides the venture capital. Around the periphery frequently is the public school co-operating with, or co-sponsoring, the citizen-group effort by providing classrooms and faculty.

The Philadelphia area provides a fair cross-section of these various types. The Junto is the extreme independent, with its tailor-made board, faculty, program, and building. Suburban Philadelphia has several other independent schools with their own citizen-boards (including several school district officials ex-officio) but holding classes in the local public school buildings. In another pattern, the Allen's Lane Art Center, the Bryn Mawr Art Center, and the Wallingford Community Arts Center, each has its own board, specialized program, and building.

New Jersey has evolved a formation in which the local citizens form the board of control but conduct the program with the co-operation of the local board of education in public schools. Fees are charged high enough, in most cases, to make the programs self-sustaining, without tax support.

The Mott Foundation supports the Flint, Michigan, Board of Education in a variety of programs, including a summer camp; health and safety education; graduate study and in-service training; recreation; activities for fatherless boys, lonely girls, teenagers, and alcoholics; and college and high school credit courses.

In the Cincinnati area, several PTA's plan and carry out adult programs in the public schools. The Baker-Hunt Foundation offers arts, crafts, and cultural subjects in a former home of the foundation-families. The McCall Industrial School operates vocational courses with funds left to it about forty years ago.

The Watkins Institute is the major source of adult education in Nashville, Tennessee. It has provided tuition-free (with nominal registration fee) courses to over 100,000 adults in the past seventy years. Dependent upon neither tax support nor gifts for its continued existence, it relies on rental income from owned property to cover its $200,000 annual budget. Courses are recreational, vocational, and some for high school credit. Attending classes above a five-and-ten-cent store is no deterrent to some 4,000 adult students annually, because those nickels and dimes are, in effect, paying their tuition.

Boston, in its tradition of Yankee individualism, has four unique independent centers. The Boston Center for Adult Education and the Cambridge Center for Adult Education have provided rich and creative programs of informal courses in charming old mansions since their founding in the depression years. The Prospect Union Educational Exchange was founded in 1923 as a clearing house of information about adult education in the Greater Boston area. It investigates schools for adults and publishes an annual catalog, *Educational Opportunities of Greater Boston*, listing about two hundred approved schools and 4,600 courses every year. It also provides free educational information and counseling for adults, and is wholly supported by endowments and gifts. The youngest independent institution made its appearance in 1958—the Adult Education Institute of New England. It is the first independent school ever established expressly for the training of adult education teachers and group leaders in a non-degree program.

The range of offerings of the independent adult schools follows the public interest. Instead of trying to channel people's curiosity into a pre-set institutional goal, the independent school operates according to the corner grocer's creed: "Give 'em what they want." There are certain moral bounds, of course, and the customer is not always right in demanding courses in Parlor Hypnosis or Tea Leaf Reading. Like the independent proprietor, the independent school must be competitive with other local educational institutions in its tuition fees and faculty "honorarium" (a lofty term to describe a lowly salary).

The advantages and disadvantages of an independent adult school are limited only by the amount of true liberty given to the governing board. On the plus side, there is freedom to hire and fire teachers regardless of state certification, tenure, or family relationship. In subject matter, the independent adult school is not bound to public school district precedents or traditions; no courses are forbidden by higher edict or political scaremongering. There is no prescribed teaching method; indeed, because some of the teachers may come out of the artist's studio or china-mending shop, some of the most effective teaching is done by those who have not had the advantages of a teacher's college. And one of the attractions of the independent school which meets in anything but a public school classroom is just that—adults often hate the thought of going back to the old school and sitting in those same seats which caused them so much misery ten or twenty years ago.

Let us admit the hazards of operating an independent adult school. Most of them boil down to one: finance. This school must depend on its own resources for sustenance, unless subsidized by a foundation or annual public campaign. And so the independent school operates on a lean budget. It must be able to adjust quickly—without time lag—to unwanted or wanted courses and teachers. "Lean and hungry" is not an unapt description of the independent (person as well as school), and who will deny that opportunism is necessary for existence under such circumstances?

The independent adult school therefore is a living, growing organism in the community. It lives by keeping its fingers on the public pulse which, like all human pulses, sometimes beats slower or faster. It lives by experimentation, and by non-conformity—even not conforming to its own past actions. It is in the best spirit of American democracy, free enterprise, and do-it-yourself-ism.

RESIDENTIAL SCHOOLS*

A complete picture of the total range of residential programs, historic and current, would include the Danish folk school movement in the United States; The University of Wisconsin Farm Short Course; The Pocono Peoples College at Henryville, Pennsylvania; The Opportunity School at Berea, Kentucky; The American Peoples Schools at Van Cortland Park, New York; The Shannondale Community House at Gladden, Missouri; The Bryn Mawr Summer School for Women Workers in Industry; The Hudson Shore Labor School; The Opportunity School of South Carolina; The Lisle Fellowship; Goddard College Adult Schools and Conferences; The National Training Laboratory in Group Development at Bethel, Maine; The American Assembly at Arden House; The Institute of Humanistic Studies for Executives at the University of Pennsylvania; The Junto Weekend Residential School, Bryn Mawr, Pennsylvania; The Midwest Seminar on United States Foreign Policy; Residential Seminars on World Affairs; and a growing number of church and union residential programs.

Some of the above programs are no longer operating while others are still in the experimental stage. Most of them have some type of institutional affiliation. It is, however, with the existing unaffiliated residential schools that this section is primarily concerned. The term "unaffiliated"

*One of the few places in which can be found a rather comprehensive picture of the history, variety, status, and possible future of residential adult education in the United States is an unpublished doctoral dissertation by Robert H. Schacht entitled *Residential Adult Education—An Analysis and Interpretation,* University of Wisconsin, 1957. This is available in microfilm from University Microfilms, 313 N. First St., Ann Arbor, Michigan.

is used to denote an autonomous institution which enjoys all the privileges and responsibilities of independence.

Chautauqua Institution, Chautauqua, New York

"Chautauqua" means different things to different people. For many, it meant the non-residential tent Chautauquas which reached up to one-third of the nation's population in 1924 and whose history covered roughly the first third of the twentieth century. For others it meant one of the three hundred pavilions more or less permanently established in as many as thirty states which for six to eight weeks each summer became centers for the dissemination of mass culture for a society yet to feel the impact of radio and television. The generic term does cover these variations on the original but should not be confused with the institution founded in 1874 as a summer institute for the advanced training of Sunday School teachers located on Lake Chautauqua, New York. For there is really only one Chautauqua, although it has been a prototype for a wide variety of adult education programs, as the description of its early history and impact in Chapter 2 demonstrates.

Chautauqua today is a summer community with a wide variety of programs appealing to persons of many different interests. Each year over fifty thousand people from all parts of the United States are drawn to this center of culture, education, and recreation. The amphitheater lecture platform continues to be a classic demonstration of free speech in American democracy. Chautauqua's religious program, while predominantly Protestant, is ecumenical in nature. The typical season includes twenty-eight concerts, six operas, six plays, and numerous film travel lectures. Non-credit courses are offered in a variety of the arts and Syracuse University conducts a fully accredited summer school program.

The original Chautauqua is very much alive although it no longer exerts the influence it once had in the field of adult education nationally. It is much too huge and complex to conform to most of the accepted criteria of a residential center. Its glory lies in its past. But the story of residential adult education in the United States would be incomplete without the acknowledgment of the important contributions Chautauqua has made to the development of this concept.

The John C. Campbell Folk School, Brasstown, North Carolina

In the southwestern corner of North Carolina, near the little community of Brasstown, is one of the few remaining examples of a successful American adaptation of the Danish folk school idea. It was founded in 1925 by Marguerite Butler and Olive Dame Campbell and named in honor of the latter's husband, John C. Campbell. At the time of his death in 1919 he had become one of the best informed individuals in the United

States on the subject of the southern highlander and his homeland. Mrs. Campbell and Miss Butler had come to believe that the best answers to the day-by-day problems of these people lay not in the accredited missionary schools of the area but in something resembling the Danish folk school which they had studied at first hand. The program of the school attempted to enrich the whole content of rural life, to build an enlightened and enlivened citizenship, and to inspire a community life and social order that might be satisfying to the young people of the community. The school is responsible directly to neither church nor state, but co-operates with the activities of both.

The John C. Campbell Folk School is more of a center than a school. In some ways it is a demonstration farm which serves as a cultural and recreational fountainhead for the community. The long winter residential programs have by necessity given way to shorter sessions, from a week end to several weeks held throughout the year. Emphasis is largely on folk arts and handicrafts, manual skills, and vocational improvement.

Its director since 1952 has been Georg Birstrup who joined the staff in 1926 with a background of Danish folk school and farm experience. He is married to Marguerite Butler, so in a sense the school is still run by those who founded it. Only time will tell if it is sufficiently established to continue as an institution beyond the lifetime of those whose enthusiasm and devotion brought it into existence, and if a privately run institution of this type can successfully withstand the competition of publicly supported educational agencies.

Highlander Folk School, Monteagle, Tennessee

Highlander Folk School is an aggregation of buildings around a small lake on a two-hundred acre mountain farm and woodlot in Grundy County, near Monteagle, Tennessee. Highlander is also an idea—a conviction that southern democracy can best be strengthened by undergirding labor unions and co-operatives and by helping both white and colored leaders in these fields to learn how to work together. The current emphasis is upon leadership training in the interests of integration in school and community life.

Highlander is also a man—Myles Horton, one of the two founders of this residential school. Back in 1932, he and Don West were given a building and some land by Dr. Lillian W. Johnson, an outstanding southern liberal. It was their idea to establish a southern people's school for people's problems. Horton disclaims any attempt to transplant the Danish folk school to American life. He has been more concerned with evolving a pattern which would be more appropriate to the needs of the South as he saw them.

This involved bringing leaders of industrial and farm unions, co-operatives, and religious and interracial groups to Highlander to train for leadership in their local communities. As these leaders of both races returned to their homes and attempted to put into practice the kind of living democracy they had developed at Highlander, opposition of varying kinds and degrees has developed. So far, both the school and its director have managed to survive, although attacked in both courts and legislatures.

Highlander's program is also carried out through field services and intensive community programs. The school is co-operatively owned and managed by the teaching staff. It is affiliated with no organization.

Highlander is closely identified with one personality and with a number of unorthodox points of view. It is difficult to predict if such an agency can survive the personality, and what will happen when today's unpopular causes become accepted by the more respectable tax-supported educational agencies.

The Penland School of Handicrafts, Penland, North Carolina

Opportunities for residential adult education in music, art, and handicrafts abound in the United States, especially in the summer and in locations which combine opportunities for vacation with educational experiences in these fields. Cited here as an example of a well-established national center for the learning of more than fifty separate crafts is the Penland School of Handicrafts in western North Carolina.

The present craft center grew out of a country boarding school for boys and girls founded before World War I by Rufus Morgan, a young Episcopal clergyman. Instruction in weaving was introduced partly in order to revive for future generations what was becoming a lost art and partly because hand weaving fitted appropriately into Rufus Morgan's scheme of things in the training of heart, hand, and imagination.

When Rufus Morgan's sister, Miss Lucy Morgan, joined the staff in the early 1920's, she was allowed to spend most of her time teaching craft work to the women of the community in order that they might supplement the family income. In 1923 the first loom was taken into the mountain home of Mrs. Henry Willis, Miss Morgan's first pupil. The financial return of this home project encouraged others and the idea grew. By exploiting every possible market, the sales grew, more equipment was purchased, and a weaving center was built. In 1928, a pottery department was added.

During the following years, Penland became a mecca for craft-loving people from all over the United States. These include amateurs, hobbyists who expect to realize incidental financial returns from their products, and professionals, including teachers and therapists. While the programs are focused upon the crafts, the staff is much concerned with the contributions which can be made by the fine and applied arts to the development of the whole person.

Since there seems to be a recognized place in adult education for the arts and crafts, it would appear that a center for the instruction of these activities would continue to grow and prosper.

Pendle Hill, Wallingford, Pennsylvania

Pendle Hill is located a few miles from Philadelphia on a beautiful campus of seventeen acres which includes six residential buildings. It is not a graduate school, a folk school, a religious house, a wayside inn, or an over-sized family, though in some sense it is all of these and more. It can most appropriately be termed an educational community maintained by members of the Society of Friends. It endeavors to provide the values of a small, intimate, integrated community and the values of an education balanced in a combination of divine, liberal, and useful arts. The direct ancestors of Pendle Hill are Woodbrooke in England, founded in 1903, and still exerting a very wide influence, and the Woolman School in America which operated between 1917 and 1927.

Students come to Pendle Hill for a variety of reasons—to write a book, carry on research, liberalize their specialized education, solve some personal problems, search for a satisfying religion or philosophy of life, or supplement preparation for employment in religious, social, or educational work.

Courses at Pendle Hill present a balance between the inward and the outward aspects of religion and society; international, interracial, and inter-class relations; the Bible; the history of religion; and languages. The resident group begins each day with a period of meditation and worship, following the pattern of the Society of Friends. Each person also takes part in the common tasks of the institution, and in sports and recreation.

Pendle Hill seeks to create within itself the kind of life which it believes should prevail throughout the world. To it can come the creative minority for a period of withdrawal from which it can return to the outer world with greater power and knowledge. Since no grades, credits, or degrees are part of this unique institution, time spent at Pendle Hill must be judged by intrinsic rather than extrinsic values. Its successful history indicates that there is room in the United States for at least one residential center of this type.

The Aspen Institute of Humanistic Studies, Aspen, Colorado

Aspen was "discovered" in 1945 by Walter Paul Paepcke, chairman of the board of Container Corporation of America. He, with the encouragement of Robert M. Hutchins, had been considering the possibility of developing a small community as a year-round resort and cultural center with an opera group, summer study group, a summer repertory theater, and seminars that would interest intellectuals and musicians.

Paepcke decided that skiing could provide an opening wedge for this ambitious venture and in 1946 formed the Aspen Company and the Aspen Ski Corporation. Over one and a quarter million dollars were spent in the next few years acquiring property, restoring the gay nineties flavor to the old mining town, developing winter sport facilities, and publicizing the project to the world.

In 1949, Paepcke arranged for Aspen to be the site of a monumental Goethe Bi-Centennial Festival. He wanted to pay practical tribute to Goethe's belief that life becomes complete only when man pursues the balanced and harmonious development of all his potentialties. The festival was an enormous success and brought unparalleled publicity to Aspen.

During the next few years, the program was developed along two general lines—music and humanistic studies. The physical plant grew with the increased patronage of this new cultural center. By the end of the 1954 season, Paepcke put the grounds and buildings at the disposal of the music faculty who organized a separate corporation to run the Music School and music festivals. He concentrated his interests on The Aspen Institute of Humanistic Studies, where noted specialists in law, politics, art, letters, and business give lectures which are followed by a series of forums and discussions. The music students are encouraged to take part in the humanistic program and the participants in the Institute programs attend the concerts of the Music School. In 1956 Paepcke opened the Aspen Health Center for which he erected a quarter of a million dollar modern plant. The business executives for whom it was primarily established participate in a rugged mixture of Spartan physical development and Athenian culture.

Aspen has demonstrated that a program of liberal adult education of a residential nature can do pretty well if extravagantly subsidized, promoted, and staffed. Walter Paul Paepcke is, however, an unusual man with more influential friends than most adult educators. But he has demonstrated what vision, imagination, and daring can do when supported by considerable amounts of money.

The Cold Spring Institute, Cold Spring-on-Hudson, New York

Sixty miles north of New York City in what was once a spacious and comfortable country home is the site of an unusual experiment in residential living for older persons. Its purposes, as described by the director, Ruth Andrus, are to discover and provide a program of living which meets the needs of persons over fifty-five years of age, to evaluate the different elements of such a program as they contribute to the total development of such persons, and to make such findings available to other groups.

Enrollment for the nine-month season is limited to twenty men and women capable and desirous of making constructive use of their later years. Members of the group set the pattern for a joint adventure in retirement according to their mutual and individual interests. The program includes lectures, discussions, creative-writing opportunities, do-it-yourself activities, musicales, and physical exercise sessions.

Since this is essentially a research program, examinations and tests are given at frequent intervals and comprehensive records are kept which show a substantial improvement in mobility, strength, and energy; creative potential; ability to get along with others; and ability to form satisfying social and emotional contacts.

The Cold Spring Institute may ultimately have an influence far beyond its present size if what is learned can be adapted to homes for the aged.

The Clearing, Ellison Bay, Wisconsin

Out on the tip of beautiful Door County, on one hundred and twenty acres of dense woodland overlooking Green Bay, is a cluster of buildings known as The Clearing. This forest retreat was built in 1935 by Jens Jensen who at the time was one of America's foremost landscape architects. He wanted to build a place to which he could invite those who were interested in sharing with him the strength and understanding that are found close to the roots of living things.

After his death in 1951, five of his friends formed The Clearing Corporation and in 1953 invited the Wisconsin Farm Bureau to assume charge of operations. The program is aimed at developing a greater appreciation of nature, encouraging the arts and crafts, fostering the development of a fuller life, and developing a better understanding between rural and urban people.

A resident adult school was begun in the summer of 1955 with classes in the liberal arts with instructors from the University of Chicago, Lawrence College, and Beloit College. The program has continued with varying degrees of success. Most of the enrollment in the liberal studies has come from the Chicago area and only limited progress has been made in attracting rural people during the busy summer months.

CONCLUSION

Un-affiliated residential centers of adult education in the United States are admittedly few and largely the results of the conviction and devotion of a few individuals. Half of those included in this chapter are in a sense affiliated with a supporting institution or agency: Pendle Hill with a religious group, Aspen with an industrial group, Cold Spring Institute with a foundation, and The Clearing with a farm organization.

Chautauqua is the only example cited which has become an institution

in its own right, so to speak. The John C. Campbell Folk School, Highlander, and Penland are too much a personal possession of their founding
individuals to be considered well-established institutions with a future.

This is not to say that there is no role to be played by the un-affiliated
residential center in adult education. The peculiar nature of the American educational tradition with its lack of federal control and pattern of
autonomous and pluralistic private and local direction will insure continual innovation and experimentation. In some ways, the un-affiliated
institution is more free to experiment and meet minority needs than is
the well-established social organization. But the odds in today's society
seem to be against any major development of residential adult education
which does not have the money, personnel, facilities, and prestige of the
institutionalized agencies of our culture.

CHAPTER 23

INTERNATIONAL ORGANIZATIONS IN ADULT EDUCATION

WILLIAM C. ROGERS

Director, State Organization Service, and
Director, Minnesota World Affairs Center
General Extension Division
University of Minnesota

DEFINITION OF INSTITUTIONAL SETTING

The figures 20 and 100 and 1,000 provide a handy guide for finding one's way through the maze of international organizations in today's world. There are approximately 20 United Nations-affiliated international organizations, including the UN itself and its specialized agencies. There are about 100 other international governmental organizations, and around 1,000 international nongovernmental organizations.[1]

American government agencies engaged in foreign affairs should not be called "international organizations" (although they often are!) since they are the organs of only one government. Some three dozen federal agencies, including the State Department, the Defense Department, the Commerce Department, and the Agriculture Department have foreign programs; yet if they were added to our list of international organizations, one would have to add the foreign ministries and related agencies of each of the eighty-two members of the UN.

American interest in international organization has not been confined to the UN system. The immediate post-war years saw the refurbishing of the Organization of American States and the creation of NATO. Two-thirds of the over one hundred non-UN agencies are indeed regional associations, such as those mentioned above. In Europe, the first true supra-international organizations have been established in the fields of coal and steel production, atomic energy, and trade.

Private citizens, in the western world particularly, have formed voluntary associations for myriad purposes at local and national levels. There are over 5,000 national associations in the United States, many of which are affiliated with international non-governmental organizations. For instance, the American Association for the UN, with branches in many communities, is a member of the World Federation of UN Associations. American youth organizations, health organizations, scientific organizations, and welfare organizations all have ties with world-wide or regional international private organizations.

As the world has shrunk, matters which were formerly considered of purely domestic concern have taken on a strong international complexion. Thus, the number and scale of activities of universal, regional, and non-governmental international organizations has burgeoned in the last fifteen years.

All international organizations may be said to have some concern with adult education. Certainly, all wish to educate the general public and their own special publics about their work. Many of them use adult education techniques in their operations and programs. Yet few have an immediate interest in the subject as a special and conscious discipline. As is true in our own country, many people doing adult education work are not conscious of the fact and would not recognize their work by the label "adult education." In its discussion of the UN and adult education the *International Directory of Adult Education* states:

> The UN is interested in the methods and content of adult education only as far as it helps that organization to achieve its objectives. Several departments of the UN secretariat are concerned with adult education as part of their specialized programs and are interested in contributions which adult education can make in fostering economic and social welfare in the world.[2]

Most adult educators have a special subject-matter interest apart from their technical interest in adult education. There is scarcely a subject matter which is not treated by some international organization. This idea is expressed very simply by a popular UN publication.

> What you want to learn about the United Nations will probably depend fully upon your personal interests and those of the group or groups to which you belong. . . . Whatever your particular interests are, whether farm improvement or a drama club, they can be seen in relation to the wider world. Almost every topic can be shown to have international significance and can be linked to some part of the work of the UN and the specialized agencies.[3]

THE UNITED NATIONS AND ADULT EDUCATION

To the educator the UN may seem to be a vast educational institution trying to teach mankind to live together in a warless world and to improve his material, social, and cultural welfare. Taking the broadest possible definition of adult education—the education of adults!—the United Nations works as an educational institution in three major ways:

(1) it educates statesmen, (2) it educates the general public, (3) it educates the recipients of the social and economic services of the organization.

The UN Educates Statesmen

The delegations of eighty-two nations are in more or less constant attendance at the UN. They all meet formally at the sessions of the General Assembly. The great powers have permanent membership in the Security Council, Economic and Social Council, and Trusteeship Council, but smaller powers also come and go as members of these bodies. There are endless meetings of committees and sub-committees of these and other bodies in New York and in Geneva, where the European office of the UN is located. In addition, there are various regional centers and the headquarters and offices of the specialized agencies scattered around the world. The milieu of the UN is one of co-operation and common problem-solving. The delegates are in constant contact with members of the secretariats—the international civil servants—who see the goals of the UN above national interests. Out of this environment, representatives of nations become aware of the problems of the world as a whole. They learn to modify and shade their national positions to conform where possible with that nebulous thing called "world public opinion." The UN experience is an educational experience for statesmen.

> International organization and international politics may long co-exist. While they do, the art of conducting foreign relations so as to gear national policies into the policies of international organization is the key discipline. . . . The establishment of the United Nations and the Specialized Agencies with thousands of employees devoting themselves to this art and educating the national statesmen, who represent their states in Council and Assembly meetings, in the elements of the art, may provide a leadership for public opinion which will in time develop a sufficient sentiment of internationalism to accommodate the need for world unity with the need for national individuality.[4]

The Education of the General Public

The most obvious educational function of the UN is to tell the world's people about the organization. Ultimately the success of the UN rests on the support it gains from world public opinion. It must have this support to live and grow. "The United Nations cannot achieve the purpose for which it has been created unless the peoples of the world are fully informed of its aims and activities."[5] This basic principle, laid down at the first session of the United Nations General Assembly, imposes an obligation on its member nations and the UN Secretariat.

The UN and its specialized agencies have special sections for information and education. Because the world public consists of over two and one-half billion people and the total budget of the UN is only fifty million dollars, the job would at first sight seem to be impossible. The

UN takes the position that the task is primarily one for the governments and private agencies in each member state and their existing channels of information.

The UN Office of Public Information has a staff of around four hundred and a budget of approximately five million dollars. A third of the operation is devoted to the two dozen information centers scattered around the world. Its major emphasis is on the mass media, in view of the necessity of reaching a large audience with a small budget. The OPI arranges press conferences and briefings, issues press releases, and answers inquiries from the many correspondents accredited to the UN. Its radio section broadcasts in many languages, kinescopes sections of important UN meetings for television broadcasting, and works with TV news and special events correspondents.

The UN has its most direct and probably most effective contact with its world "student body" in the millions of people who visit the UN, most of whom are Americans. Over four million visitors have taken the famous guided tours. Last year programs were arranged for over 3,000 visiting groups. The UN is indeed New York's leading tourist attraction.

The UN also educates by correspondence. Every month it receives some 8,000 inquiries by mail and phone. Since 1946 it has issued and distributed some twelve million copies of pamphlets and brochures about the UN. The present best-seller is *Your United Nations*, the official guidebook. *Basic Facts about the UN* and *Everyman's United Nations* are also popular.

The Un's Social and Economic Educational Services

The UN has four basic purposes: (1) maintaining peace, (2) developing friendly relations among nations, (3) acting as a center for harmonizing the actions of nations, and (4) solving international problems of an economic, social, cultural, or humanitarian character. Aiding the underdeveloped world under the fourth purpose has increasingly absorbed the UN's efforts. Helping peoples and nations to help themselves is certainly basically an adult educational function.

The methods used are quite familiar to most adult educators: (1) technical missions, (2) fellowships for training, and (3) demonstrations. Since many of the nations receiving this assistance are former colonies, some of the work of the UN might be said to be that of running a "school for new nations." The rapid disappearance of the old colonial empires since the war has brought into existence numerous nations which are having considerable difficulties in developing adequate economies and viable administrations. Technical missions from the UN and its specialized agencies assist in scores of fields—government administration, health, formal education, and agricultural problems. Government officials and technicians are sent to more advanced nations for study in many subjects. While few adult educators are sent to assist on

adult education projects as such, the subject-matter specialists who make
up these missions must have many of the skills of successful adult educators. They must be able to communicate, to teach, to understand, and
to inspire. The test of their ability is, of course, how well the local
people are able to carry on their projects after the "teachers" have gone.
As those concerned with the technical assistance programs gain experience, they will no doubt increasingly recognize the contribution which
adult education can make to their work.

UNESCO AND ADULT EDUCATION

Among the UN family of organizations, the United Nations Educational, Scientific, and Cultural Organization particularly has adult education as an important and recognized part of its program. It is the
specialized agency concerned with adult education as a discipline as well
as a method of operation. The opening paragraph of the section on
"Unesco and Adult Education" of the *International Directory* states:

> "By the very nature of its aims and purposes Unesco has to concern
> itself actively with adult education and adult educators. In all parts of
> its programme a double aspect may be found: The technical one, with a
> program designed for specialists on the subject, and a popular or educa-
> tional one. Thus, it may be said that adult educators find themselves
> "technically" represented in a part of the Department of Education, but
> that much of the content and method of their work will be reflected in
> other parts of Unesco's programme.[6]

Development of Unesco's Adult Education Program

The beginnings of UNESCO's adult education program may be traced
to the 1949 International Conference of Adult Educators held in Elsinore, Denmark. Two important early publications resulted directly from
the conference. These were *Adult Education—Current Trends and Practices* (1950) and the *International Directory of Adult Education* (1952),
which devotes its first 72 pages to international governmental and non-
governmental organizations, and over 200 pages to purely national programs of the various member countries. *Universities in Adult Education*
also appeared in 1952, and the name of the *Quarterly Bulletin of Fundamental Education* was changed to *Fundamental and Adult Education*.
In 1953 it was recommended that UNESCO should decentralize its activities and give equal attention to the needs of developed and underdeveloped countries.

With two-thirds of the world underdeveloped and the same proportion
of the population of the world illiterate, it is understandable that Unesco
would devote much of its energy to fundamental education. The series
Monographs on Fundamental Education presents UNESCO's point of
view and activities in this field. The organization has established an

information clearinghouse in the subject and a world-wide network of training centers, the first of which was opened in 1951 in Patzcuaro, Mexico, for leaders from eighteen Latin American states. In 1952 a second was opened in Egypt for six Arab nations. Technical assistance educational projects in many nations are in process of expansion into national training centers.

Education for international understanding is also one of UNESCO's main objectives. Efforts in this area include pamphlets such as those in the series titled "Towards International Understanding," international seminars, and audio-visual aids. The important program of East-West mutual appreciation is a vital world-wide adult education project to which UNESCO is now heavily committed.

The C in UNESCO stands for culture, and the organization has made numerous educational contributions in this field, such as: conferences and publications on the best methods of the teaching of visual arts; an up-to-date catalog of the best colored reproductions of paintings; collections of phonograph records of contemporary music; assistance in publishing the world's classics in philosophy and literature; and work with public libraries and museums.

In the natural sciences, UNESCO publishes materials for science teachers, works in the development of science clubs, and organizes traveling science exhibitions. In the social sciences, its publications on international tensions and race prejudice and its "Way of Life" series on the national character of some of the principal peoples of the world are outstanding contributions of interest to adult educators concerned with international co-operation.

The mass communications program of UNESCO contributes both directly and indirectly to the work of adult education. Its monthly *Courier* is one of the real magazine bargains in the English language whose illustrated articles on education, science, and culture throughout the world are of exceptional interest and quality.

UNESCO's Exchange of Persons Program has made a direct impact on the lives of many Americans who have received and worked with UNESCO fellows visiting this country from many parts of the world. The annual publication *Study Abroad—International Handbook of Fellowships, and Educational Exchange* is of practical value to the increasing number of Americans and nationals of other countries interested in foreign study.

From 1954 to 1958 a series of adult education seminars and other projects (forty-six in number), were held in different regions of the world. At each of these meetings, attended by prominent educators, stress was laid on the role of adult education in a world of rapidly changing technical conditions. All these international projects were organized either by member states or by international nongovernmental organizations with UNESCO participation.[7]

Much of UNESCO's work has been with trade unions which, particularly in Europe, are in the forefront of mass adult education. From 1951 to 1953 an International Workers Education Centre was operated at La Breviere, France. In a list of seminars, study courses, pilot projects and surveys assisted by UNESCO in the last five years, 20 out of 46 projects were related to labor education. Organizational sponsors included the International Confederation of Free Trade Unions, International Federation of Christian Trade Unions, and the International Federation of Workers Educational Association. Co-ops were sponsors of three meetings and such women's groups as the International Alliance of Women, International Federation of University Women, and the World Union of Catholic Women's Organizations sponsored seven conferences. Meetings were held in such widely separated places as Calcutta, Accra, Jamaica, Geneva, Bangkok, Melbourne and Athens.

As this chapter is written, the most important immediate adult education project of UNESCO is the 1960 World Conference on Adult Education. A sequel to the Elsinore conference, it will survey UNESCO's adult education work since 1949 and develop a general out-of-school education policy.

Less distinction will be made in the future between adult and fundamental education programs. A resolution at the 1958 general conference stated:

> The time has come when these artificial distinctions, which in a number of countries, bear no relation to the out-of-school education movement, must be abandoned. . . . During the next six years, Unesco will have to meet the need for "permanent" out-of-school education, which ten years ago was felt in varying degrees but which today is viewed in similar if not identical terms and with equal conviction by the population of the so-called developed countries and by those whose rapid rate of development is transforming their way of life. The best development Unesco can make to this out-of-school education is to aid Member States and appropriate international or national organizations to install the necessary substratum of institutions and services, harmonized and co-ordinated with the basic structure of school education.[8]

UNESCO will thus devote special attention to political, social, civic, scientific, and cultural education, closely linked with technical and vocational training in co-operation with ILO, FAO, and WHO. Also out-of-school education projects will be included in concerted community development programs in co-operation with the UN and other specialized agencies.

Money for the adult education section of UNESCO's department of education has always been inadequate.[9] The staff of the section has usually consisted of only three professional people who have been charged with much of the program described in the preceding pages. From the viewpoint of adult education it is unfortunate that there is no world-wide association of the adult education profession which can work with UNESCO for a larger budget in this special field. National adult education movements and nongovernmental organizations have not been effective in increasing the direct adult education activity of UNESCO, with the exception of work in the workers' education field.

American Interest in UNESCO's Adult Education Program

The United States has been represented at sessions of UNESCO's Consultative Committee on Adult Education which grew out of the Elsinore Conference, and its representatives have consistently promoted the formation of an international adult education body.[10] The Adult Education Association of the U.S.A. has exerted direct influence through its representative on the U.S. National Commission for UNESCO. At its 1958 conference, the association asked that the American delegation at the UNESCO general conference seek full support for the World Conference on Adult Education and expressed interest in the use of the *Bulletin of Fundamental and Adult Education* for the collection and dissemination of more information about adult general education in the member states. The National University Extension Association has also been represented on the U.S. National Commission and has had an active program in support of UNESCO.

The work of the U.S. National Commission for UNESCO has had an important influence on American adult education. Its national conferences have always attracted large numbers of adult educators. Its citizens' consultations on such subjects as the American as traveller and host, East-West mutual understanding, and the teaching of foreign languages, have attracted the interest of adults in many communities. Kansas, Minnesota, and other states have UNESCO committees carrying out UNESCO oriented world affairs adult education activities.

ADULT EDUCATION IN OTHER MAJOR UN SPECIALIZED AGENCIES

While all the specialized agencies do some adult education work, attention here is directed to three of UNESCO's largest sister organizations, the ILO, WHO, and FAO.

The International Labor Organization

Among the objectives stated at the ILO's famous 26th session in 1944, which provided the basis for its post-war program, was listed "The provision of adequate facilities for recreation and culture for the workers of the world." The ILO has not lost sight of the fact that the improvement of the material conditions of the working class should go hand in hand with the raising of their level of education, and it has worked with UNESCO and other international organizations interested in workers' education. Much of the ILO's program has been devoted to vocational training of adults. The monthly *International Labor Review* is the ILO's principal publication of general interest.

Food and Agriculture Organization

The Food and Agriculture Organization is interested in adult education pertaining to the extension of technical knowledge about nutrition, agriculture, and forestry. It seeks to raise nutrition levels, improve standards of living, and contribute to rural welfare. The FAO employs specialists in agricultural extension organization and methods. Some of its basic studies include *Essentials of Rural Welfare, Social Welfare in Rural Communities, Training Rural Leaders, Educational Approaches to Rural Welfare,* and *Rural America and the Extension Service.* It endeavors to develop a sound co-operative movement and has done a great deal of work with co-operatives all over the world. Much of the FAO's work is similar to that of agricultural extension in the U.S. It has concerned itself with such topics as the mechanization of farming, soil conservation, efficient use of fertilizers, nutrition, and home economics.

The World Health Organization

WHO's constitution includes the words, "The extension to all peoples of the benefits of medical, psychological, and related knowledge is essential to the full attainment of health and informed opinion and active cooperation on the part of the public are of the utmost importance in the improvement of the health of the people."

WHO works with other international organizations both governmental and nongovernmental, assists national health administrations in their health education programs, and demonstrates health education techniques and procedures. Like other specialized agencies, it collects data and exchanges information, assists with planning and developing health education projects in various countries, arranges courses, seminars, study groups, and institutes, and gives fellowships and travel grants. WHO has a section on health education of the public in its secretariat. It recognizes that health education is largely adult education, and that it is essential to any successful public health program.

INTERNATIONAL NONGOVERNMENTAL ORGANIZATIONS AND ADULT EDUCATION

There are over 1,000 international nongovernmental organizations (INGO's), most of which have some adult education program.[11] UNESCO's *International Directory of Adult Education* describes briefly the programs of over fifty of these with major projects in the field of

adult education. The mention of a few of these groups will be enough
to indicate the nature of their work:

Associated Countrywomen of the World Association
Educational Cinema and Culture International Committee
International Catholic Commission for Adult Education
International Confederation of Free Trade Unions
International Confederation of Popular Societies of Music
International Cooperative Alliance
International Council of Museums
International Federation of Business and Professional Women
International Federation of Library Associations
International Federation of Workers' Educational Associations
International Theatre Institute
World Alliance of Young Men's Christian Associations
World Federation for Mental Health
World Organization of the Teaching Profession

Cutting across national boundaries but along the lines of national
interests, the thousand INGO's have many millions of members. Combined budgets are in excess of $100,000,000, or nearly that of all the UN
"family" together. Active individual participation is mainly confined to
leaders of national sections with the millions of rank and file members
having limited contact with the rather distant international apex.

The INGO's have both formal and informal contacts with the UN
agencies. Many have consultative status with the UN's Economic and
Social Council and with various specialized agencies. They act as agents
of international understanding, help form world public opinion, and
act as pressure groups for their various causes.

Few INGO's recognize adult education as a special discipline, but most
of them are engaged in some aspect of adult education—such as informing their members and various other publics about their aims and
progress. In the aggregate their influence is significant, and they help to
give an international focus to tens of thousands of local organizations.

U.S. Agencies Interested in International Affairs

More and more adult educators are concerned with programs dealing
with international affairs. Over two hundred AEA members, for instance, indicated an interest in the International Relations Section of the
organization.

American agencies circulate information about the work of the UN
and its specialized agencies in this country in accord with the UN's
policy of decentralizing the enormous task of reaching the world's people.
They also educate people about their own programs in international
affairs, which are very similar in many cases to work done by international organizations. For instance, the Department of State distributes

a great deal of information about the UN and American participation in the UN organizations. The United States has its own unilateral programs of technical assistance which perform work similar to that done by the UN. In many respects the work of the Foreign Agricultural Service of the Department of Agriculture is similar to work done by the FAO. United States government agencies are thus important sources of information about international affairs.

What can be said about American government agencies can also be said about private organizations—they dispense information about international organizations, they carry on adult education projects in international affairs, and many of them carry on overseas projects similar in character to activities of international organizations. American national organizations in international affairs number over 400 and their local branches are active in most American communities.[12]

THE PROSPECT FOR ADULT EDUCATION IN INTERNATIONAL ORGANIZATION

Science and technology and two world wars in a generation have made Americans conscious of the leading role our country plays in world affairs. Nearly a million passports for foreign travel are issued every year. A hundred thousand Americans are working abroad. Adult education about world affairs is a major function of many educational agencies. In this rapidly shrinking world the UN is "a symbol of the urge to civilization" and "man's best hope for peace."

The UN has grown more slowly than its founders and the peoples of the world hoped when the organization was born in 1945. Nevertheless, it has moved forward, particularly in its economic and social work. There is little doubt that the UN will play an important part in helping the new nations of the underdeveloped world become viable states. In this process adult education can be expected to make an increasingly important contribution. The skills of adult education are, in fact, essential to the task.

Footnotes

[1]Bertram Pickard, *The Greater UN* (New York: Carnegie Endowment for International Peace), 1957.

[2]*International Directory of Adult Education* (Paris: UNESCO, 1952), p. 17.

[3]*How to find out about the United Nations* (New York: United Nations Department of Public Information, 1958), p. 6.

[4]Quincy Wright, *The Study of International Relations* (New York: Appleton-Century Crofts, 1955), p. 211.

[5]*The United States Public and the United Nations* (New York: Carnegie Endowment for International Peace, 1958), p. 24 ff. (This valuable publication furnished much of my information about the UN's public information function).

[6]*International Directory of Adult Education*, op. cit., p. 19.

7Much of the above section on Unesco benefited from the information and materials provided to the author by the staff of UNESCO's department of education whose director is W. Harold Loper. The interpretation and appraisal are mine, however, and not his.

8Unesco Document 10C/10 Resolution 11, 1958.

9Paul H. Sheats, "Unesco and World Wide Adult Education," *Adult Leadership,* VI (November, 1957), 129.

10*Ibid.*

11William C. Rogers, "INGO's and Adult Education," *Adult Education,* VII (Winter, 1957), 119-22.

12Katherine C. Garrigue, *U.S. Citizens in World Affairs—A Directory of Non-Governmental Organizations* (New York: Foreign Policy Association, 1953).

Selected Readings

Asher, Robert E., and others. *The United Nations and the Promotion of the General Welfare.* Washington: Brookings Institution, 1957.

Carnegie Endowment for International Peace. *The United States Public and the United Nations.* New York: The Endowment, 1958.

Claude, I. L. *Swords into Plowshares.* New York: Random House, 1959.

Fundamental and Adult Education. Paris: UNESCO, quarterly.

Garrigue, Katherine C. *U. S. Citizens in World Affairs.* New York: Foreign Policy Association, 1953.

Goodrich, L. M. *The United Nations.* New York: Thomas Y. Crowell, 1959.

Hambridge, Gove. *The Story of FAO.* New York: D. Van Nostrand Co., 1955.

How to Find Out About the United Nations. New York: United Nations, 1958.

International Directory of Adult Education. Paris: UNESCO, 1952.

Laves, Walter, and Thomson, Charles A. *Unesco: Purpose, Progress, Prospects.* Bloomington: Indiana University Press, 1957.

Pickard, Bertram. *The Greater United Nations.* New York: Carnegie Endowment for International Peace, 1957.

Rogers, William C. "INGO'S and Adult Education," *Adult Education, VII* (Winter, 1957), 119-22.

Savord, Ruth, and Wasson, Donald. *American Agencies Interested in International Affairs.* New York: Council on Foreign Relations, 1955.

Sharp, Walter R. *International Technical Assistance.* Chicago: Public Administration Service, 1952.

Sheats, Paul H. "Unesco and World Wide Adult Education," *Adult Leadership,* VI (November, 1957), 129-34.

Speeckaert, G. P. *International Institutions and International Organization.* A select bibliography. Brussels: Union of International Associations, 1956.

United Nations, *Annual Report of the Secretary General,* 1946 to Present.

White, Lyman C., and Zocca, Marie R. *International Nongovernmental Organizations.* New Brunswick: Rutgers University Press, 1951.

Wright, Quincy. *The Study of International Relations.* New York: Appleton-Century-Crofts, 1955.

Yearbook of the United Nations. New York: United Nations, 1946 to present.

CHAPTER 24

ADULT EDUCATION IN LABOR UNIONS

JOSEPH MIRE
Executive Director
National Institute of Labor Education

DEFINITION OF INSTITUTIONAL SETTING

Union education deals primarily with the educational needs of workers —manual or white collar—as they arise out of their participation in the labor movement. The institutional setting is the organized labor movement comprised first of an estimated fourteen million members joined together in approximately 75,000 local units of 136 national and international unions, all affiliated with the American Federation of Labor— Congress of Industrial Organizations (AFL-CIO). To these must be added the educational activities carried on by independent unions with a total membership estimated at three to four million.

By any measure, the *labor movement* is by far the *most numerous organized constituency for the dispensation of adult education.*

The operation of unions has become a profession, a complicated and responsible job, requiring training and expert knowledge in a great many fields. Also, since the collective bargaining relationship now extends to almost every aspect of social and economic well being, public issues play a large and increasing role in union policies and in turn, have an important impact on our total living today. Thus, the need for knowledge and training pertains to subjects ranging from the why-and-what-and-how of labor unions, to a great many social, economic, and political issues and to the integration of the worker—and the union—into our society.

To meet the increased responsibilities of unions towards their members and the public, the *union education specialist* has taken his place on the staff of unions side by side with such other experts and technicians as economists, lawyers, industrial engineers, accountants, doctors and other medical personnel, actuaries, journalists, public relations consultants, and political scientists.

HISTORICAL DEVELOPMENTS SINCE 1945

Union education has been profoundly affected by the dynamic changes in unionization and collective bargaining which occurred in the post-war period:

1. The up-swing in union membership—an after-effect of the employment in war industries—resulted in expanded educational activities and for brief periods, also in a return to an emphasis on bread and butter issues. To "unionize the organized" became the major determinant for the scope and content of labor education programs.

2. The passage of the Taft Hartley Act in 1947 brought about a decisive change in the relations between government and labor leading to intensified educational efforts in the political arena. The act also caused a leveling off of union membership, a favorable by-product of which was the opportunity to broaden the scope of labor education so as to include a concern for cultural subject matters and participation in civic affairs on the local, state, federal, and international level.

3. New dimensions in collective bargaining present staggering and complicated new tasks to union educators. Among these are the expansion of health plans, the negotiation of pension agreements, productivity adjustments clauses, guaranteed employment plans, and the very serious problems caused by the accelerated pace of technological change.

4. The momentous merger of the American Federation of Labor and the Congress of Industrial Organizations in December, 1955, eliminated much—although by no means as yet all—of the inter-union rivalry which had tied up much of union efforts and finances. At least some of these resources were freed for union education and much duplication was eliminated by the amalgamation of the departments of education of the two federations. At the state and local level, the merger of the two federations and the pooling of their financial resources has made possible the appointment of a number of full-time education directors where previously neither of the two federations was in a position to do so.

5. The exposures of the McClellan Committee on the misuse of funds in some unions have put unions on the defensive. The labor movement has reacted remarkably firmly and forcefully through the adoption of ethical practices codes, and following through with the expulsion of corrupt unions, setting thereby an example which has yet to be copied by other voluntary organizations faced with like problems of corruption. There is recognition in many quarters, however, that the real answer to racketeering and dishonesty in unions lies in the vastly accelerated program of union education designed to promote mature rank and file participation in union affairs and to recapture the idealism and devotion of the earlier pioneers of the labor movement.

6. There has been a very significant increase in co-operation in the field of education betwen labor and institutions of higher learning. A number of universities have established educational services to labor groups. Classes, lectures, and institutes are sponsored jointly with labor unions. This development is partly a reflection of the heightened interest in education on the part of unions themselves, and partly a recognition of the importance of the labor problem in our industrial society.

An important experiment in labor-universities co-operation was conducted from 1952 to 1953 under the auspices of the Inter-University Labor Education Committee (IULEC), financed by a grant from The Fund for Adult Education. Eight universities participated in the program which was administered by a board of directors composed of eight university and eight labor representatives. The experimental program centered around economic education, international affairs, and education for citizenship.

Encouraged by this experience and in view of the continued and growing interest in labor education of labor and non-labor agencies alike, including some foundations, there followed another historic development in 1957 with the establishment of the National Institute of Labor Education (NILE), which will be described later in this chapter.

PRESENT STATUS AND TRENDS

Objectives

Union education—as distinguished from labor education activities carried on by non-labor agencies—has to serve the needs of the institution, that is, the labor movement. A good part of union education is unashamedly practical—knowledge for use, not for its own sake. But the goal of social changes sought by the labor movement provides the raison d'etre of union education.[1]

As for the definition of union purposes, there are some who feel that they begin and end with the negotiation of collective bargaining contracts with management and others who want the union also to be an effective force in the legislative halls of government. Still others feel that the labor movement should be a force for social, economic, and political reform and want workers' education to provide "movers and shakers" as well as effective shop stewards and union administrators and negotiators.

Any attempt to appraise specifically the needs of workers in the field of education—and consequently the objectives of labor education—requires some acceptable starting place or criterion. Workers have educational needs as individual citizens, as members of functional groups, and as part of the community. We have chosen to examine the needs of workers at the different levels of authority and responsibility which they hold in a functional group—the labor movement. We shall thus distinguish between the needs of line and staff representatives of labor organizations; of local union officers; and of rank and file members.

1. *The executive training of full-time appointed or elected union officers and staff.* This group includes persons charged with the administration of the union, negotiating contracts, presenting arbitration cases, handling appeals before the National Labor Relations Board, administering health and welfare plans, conducting publicity and public relations, and appearing before legislative bodies. In addition to their union duties, these men frequently represent labor on the policy-making bodies of local, national, and international organizations. Because of his growing leadership responsibilities, a union leader must know how to interpret and utilize the studies of industrial engineers, the opinions of lawyers, the conclusions of actuaries, or the advice and findings of economists, political scientists, and sociologists.

2. *The education and training of local union leadership.* The group is not employed by the unions, but assume the duties of local union presidents, financial and recording secretaries, bargaining committee members, shop stewards, and executive board and committee members.

The smooth operation of labor-management relations at the plant level depends to a good measure on the knowledge, training, and maturity of local officers. It is they who must navigate around individual and group resistances that arise in solving the production, seniority, transfer, job classification, and wage incentive problems created by technological change.

3. *The educational needs of rank and file members.* These needs range from vocational training, parliamentary law, and procedure, and knowledge about the labor movement and about working conditions, to the advancement of the workers' social, economic, and cultural interests. The ultimate objective is a mature, wise, and responsible citizen, able to play his part in the union and in a free society and to assure for himself a status of dignity and respect equal to those of other groups and individuals.

Programs

The scope of union education programs is as wide as the interests and needs of the labor movement and of the individual workers who make up the movement. Historically, union education began with the need for apprenticeship training programs. Then came the concern for training on bread-and-butter and tool subjects. Finally, in response to the ever more complicated problems faced by unions, occurred a branching out into broad areas of general liberal education.

Some unions still limit their activities to a concern for apprentice training, although in recent years the curriculum has increasingly included classes on trade union history, collective bargaining, and the like.

Other programs—frequently those of unions which only recently concerned themselves with education—hold strictly to training on such bread-and-butter subjects as parliamentary law, public speaking, handling of grievances, union administration, and collective bargaining. Still others, particularly those with a past history and experience in labor education, have added programs on international affairs, economics, health, community participation, education for retirement, and cultural subjects.

International affairs is a discussion subject that appears almost as a matter of course in many union programs, frequent use being made of people who have been overseas as speakers and discussion leaders.

Health and welfare problems are the subject of widespread study. For example, some local unions have done educational work in setting up a health plan for their members; others have training for stewards and members directed to making their health service programs function more smoothly; some have trained health stewards to process grievances in relation to the health plan; and in a few, health education for union members and their families is carried on through a union health center.

Community relations programs are mainly centered around education on, and relationships with, health and welfare agencies. The Community Activities Division of the AFL-CIO sponsors training programs of union counselors in many cities in the country so that they are able to handle out-of-plant problems of workers. Annual week-long staff conferences are held for local Chest staff and also for training staff people on how to prepare local union leaders for membership duties on boards of social agencies.

A few affiliated unions have also a community affairs department which encourages the training of union counselors to work on all kinds of out-of-plant problems. A Department for Older and Retired Workers has been established by the Auto Workers in order to develop an effective program of education for retirement. The Steelworkers have added to their staff an insurance and pension consultant to make a study of retirement problems, a field in which the Upholsterers have also pioneered.

The problem of effective communication is receiving increased attention. Programs in this area are usually concerned with improving channels of "up and down" communication. Recently the Meat Cutters Union—in cooperation with Roosevelt University—offered to its full-time business representatives courses in "Formal and Informal Writing" and "How to Read Better and Faster."

Some unions have devoted a good part of their education efforts to the promotion of the Union Label. Among these are the Clothing Workers Union, the Hatters, Cigarmakers, Ladies Garment Workers, the Printers, and the Bakery and Confectionery Workers. Assisted by the National Union Label Department, these unions have done promotional work through films, TV programs, and other media.

Special subject matters to meet new conditions are continually being developed. For example, some unions have done much experimentation with the development of approaches to teaching in the field of automation. With the guaranteed annual wage as a major bargaining goal in a number of unions, GAW has appeared in the subject listings of many schools, conferences, and institutes—as has the subject matter of atomic energy. More recently, the maintenance of a full employment economy in the face of rapid technological changes and the relations between science and labor have come in for increased attention. Other areas of recent concern are the management of unions and the use of attitude surveys to gather facts and knowledge about the union member and his views on the union.

There is also a beginning of concern for education which is aimed at development of the human personality rather than specific content or skills. For example, the Ladies Garment Workers Union offers its members classes on sculpture, ceramics, dancing, music appreciation, painting and drawing, swimming, sports, and many other cultural subjects; the AFL-CIO in Cleveland sponsored a music festival; the Steelworkers sponsored free sympony concerts in Pittsburgh; the Automobile Workers Union promoted the Steichen exhibit with its theme of "The Family of Man"; the ILGWU has established a vacation and recreation home for its members; and several unions have begun to look into the matter of promoting group travel for members. Several unions have recently co-operated in experimental liberal arts programs sponsored by three or four universities with the support of the Center for the Study of Liberal Education for Adults. The programs include such subjects as human personality, logic, the mind of America, understanding music, the power of words, public opinion and propaganda, social protest, and the philosophy of unionism.

Finally, as a part of its public relations activities, the AFL-CIO has established a roster of trade union officials who are able and willing to speak on college and university campuses on subjects related to labor problems.

Organizational Structure and Personnel

Operationally, education within the labor movement is carried on at six levels:

1. *The Department of Education of the AFL-CIO*—This agency encourages, assists, and supports educational programs of local unions, trade councils, city central bodies, state central bodies, regional agencies, and national and international unions. It provides organizational support, administrative experience, staff assistance, speakers and resource persons from its own and other headquarters departments, publications, plans, materials, audio-visual aids, and assists in the co-ordination of resources.

It sponsors two national conferences of union education directors a year; publishes a monthly periodical, *Education News and Views,* which features news about labor education activities and carries how-to-do-it articles geared to local union education committees; reviews pamphlets and books; promotes the use of the film library and reviews new films added to it; reports new and unique experiments in workers' education; prepares manuals on a variety of subject matters for use in conferences and schools as well as special exhibits for display at conferences or educational meetings. A labor song album featuring Joe Glazer has also been prepared by the Department.

2. *The Industrial Union Department of the AFL-CIO*—This agency concentrates on staff training programs offered to affiliated organizations on such subjects as wages, productivity and labor costs; bargaining and law; health and welfare bargaining; pension bargaining; supplementary unemployment benefits and employment security; union communications; job evaluation and wage determination; work measurements and incentives; arbitration; and instructors' training.

3. *International and National Unions*—These agencies carry the bulk of union education programs, largely through the estimated seventy-five to eighty-five thousand local units. Over fifty unions have now established a department of education at international headquarters. Educational staff is also employed by a number of district organizations and a few local unions. Many thousands of union members serve on a voluntary basis as members of educational committees.

4. *Regional Organizations*—Three examples of regional pooling of resources for the purpose of education are the Southern and the Rocky Mountain Labor Schools and the Union Leadership Academy. The Southern Labor School is an annual two-week affair participated in by delegates from twelve southern states including representatives from international unions as well as from state and local federations. The Rocky Mountain Labor School sponsors a one week institute annually, attended mostly by state and local city or county union delegates of the eight intermountain states. The labor schools have been instrumental in awakening interest in education in areas which are still largely educationally "underprivileged." The Union Leadership Academy represents the combined efforts of six international unions and three co-operating universities. It sponsors joint programs of a broad and general nature, on a labor-movement-wide basis, and carries on experimentations to develop a program of systematic progression in labor education.

5. *State-wide Organizations*—Some thirty-five state-wide federations affiliated with the AFL-CIO are now sponsoring educational activities. At least fifteen of these—California, Connecticut, Indiana, Iowa, Kentucky, Louisiana, Massachusetts, Michigan, New Jersey, Ohio, Oregon, Pennsylvania, Texas, West Virginia, and Wisconsin—have a full-time person assigned to education. This is considerable progress considering the fact

that only fifteen years ago not one single state federation of labor had a full-time person employed to do educational work. The state education department conducts programs on a state-wide basis, but also assists local federations in developing educational activities.

6. *Local Federations*—An increasing number of the some eight hundred city- or county-wide federations are engaged in some form of educational activities. The nature and extent of the program is determined by the size of the organization, its resources, the assistance available from other unions and universities, leadership, and other factors.

Clientele

Most union education programs are directed at local union officers. Next come programs directed at rank and file members. More recently, the training of staff representatives has received serious attention by many national and international unions and by the Industrial Union Department of the AFL-CIO. Some programs are addressed to apprentices and journeymen and are predominantly of a vocational nature.

The clientele of labor education includes also the general public. Programs designed to educate the public in regard to the labor problem have long been recognized as legitimate and important companion aims of labor education, since the public today is a partner in every major collective bargaining negotiation and industrial dispute.

The stimulation of demands for education is the most crucial of all problems faced by labor educators. Workers' education, like all adult education, lacks any coercive element. The problem is not too serious in regard to the training of staff representatives and union officers. Much more serious—and largely unsolved—is the problem of attracting rank and file members of unions to educational programs. This is partly a problem of finding the vast resources needed to finance a program of education for some eighteen million people, and partly a problem of overcoming apathy, of developing effective methods to reach rank and file members, and of competing successfully with the many other demands on the leisure time of workers.

Financing

Three major sources are available for financing labor education—labor unions, public funds, and private funds.

Labor Unions—The major cost of union education is borne by the unions themselves and their members. The specific amounts available for educational purposes vary, depending upon needs, financial resources, as well as appreciation for education shown by the union officers, or the members themselves. In some unions a definite percentage of the income from dues is set aside for educational purposes.

Some national and international unions, in addition to their own direct expenditures for education, are encouraging local unions to engage in educational activities by offering to match their expenditures either on a dollar for dollar or some other basis. The financing of education programs by state and local bodies rest on a similar basis; that is, the money either comes from appropriations by some authorized body or through definite per capita payments towards an educational fund as, for instance, in Kentucky.

The dollar value of unions' funds and efforts spent on education purposes is considerable and growing. Unfortunately, however, not even estimates are available as to its precise magnitude.

Public Funds—These are three types:

1. Federal.   No direct funds are available for union education at the present time, but some indirect federal support is possible through the use of George-Barden Funds for vocational purposes, and use is made of it by unions in some states through joint programs with universities.

Previously, the federal government has entered into workers' education on two occasions, both of them marked by emergency conditions in the economic life of the country. The first was the *Workers Education Program of the Work Projects Administration (WPA)*, which lasted from 1933 to 1943, reached a total of one million workers, and provided employment for thousands of teachers. The second was undertaken in 1946/47 under the aegis of the Division of Labor Standards of the U. S. Department of Labor. The service assisted unions and non-labor agencies in formulating programs; demonstrating teaching techniques; planning of educational activities; preparation of specific materials, such as course outlines, discussion guides, and pamphlets; and in teacher training. Unfortunately, the appropriation for the division was not continued by Congress.

Hopes that Congress would subsequently set up a permanent extension service administered through the U. S. Department of Labor have not materialized. The labor movement has repeatedly gone on record in favor of such a program. Its most recent action took place at the 1957 Convention when the following resolution was adopted:

> The AFL-CIO reaffirms support of a Labor Extension Service in the Department of Labor to provide service and material comparable to those provided through the Department of Agriculture to farmers, and businessmen through the Department of Commerce, administered at the national and state levels through advisory boards made up of representatives of the organized labor movement and cooperating institutions and agencies.[2]

2. State Funds—The Morrill Act, passed over a hundred years ago, committed the land grant colleges, in return for substantial grants of land, to provide educational services to "agriculture and the industrial classes." While this promise has been fairly kept as far as agriculture is concerned, it has been largely ignored as far as the "industrial classes" are concerned. The exceptions are some fifteen state universities which

have now established departments of labor education, rendering a year-round services to labor groups. In a few states unions are successfully using school buildings and state vocational funds or general adult education funds to underwrite part of the cost of labor education programs.

3. Private Funds—The major private sources for the support of labor education today are foundations. Very important and significant programs in the field of racial discrimination, economics, international affairs, citizenship, community participation and the liberal arts have been made possible through grants from foundations. Unions, universities, and other non-labor organizations have participated in these programs.

Methods and Techniques

The standard device for labor education used to be—and for many unions still is—the classroom session meeting once a week over a period of from six to eight weeks. More and more, however, the devices of one-, two-, and three-day conferences and seminars, and week-end schools are replacing the weekly class.

An interesting combination has been applied by Rutgers to its Union Instructor Candidate School. Students attend weekly three-hour meetings over a period of four weeks, with two all-day conferences on week ends in between. Supplemental tutorial instruction is provided for small groups and personal assistance by a roving county agent is available during and after the program.

Other methods used are: injection of educational content into regular membership meetings; radio and television; role playing; how-to-do-it-yourself workshops; combined education-action projects, particularly on community projects; membership attitude surveys; opinion meters, used to gain information on the effectiveness of programs or on the thinking of the groups—and to stimulate interest and participation; legislative institutes in Washington or state legislatures; trips to UN; clinics; materials distribution; labor press and news services; book clubs; outings; sports; theater groups; concerts; choirs; and musical revues.

A unique device for attracting interest in union education as well as public attention to the problems of the labor movement is the biannual nation-wide education conference sponsored by the Automobile Workers. It usually runs from three to four days and is attended by some 3,000 delegates. The program consists of buzz and panel sessions, speeches by prominent scientists and political leaders, and various cultural activities, such as labor song festivals and historical pageants.

Straight-forward lectures have all but disappeared from the run-of-the-mill workers' education program. They have been replaced by a variety of other techniques, mostly the discussion group.

Correspondence courses, although of great potential value—particularly in outlying areas—have not met with any conspicuous success in labor education. Learning by correspondence courses requires a measure of self-discipline and skills in learning which the ordinary worker did not seem to possess.

Relationship With Other Organizations

Universities.—Co-operation between unions and our institutions of higher learning is pronounced. At this moment there are probably some eighty universities, including about twenty denominational colleges, which render educational services of a kind to labor groups, ranging from occasional conferences and institutes to year-round services by a full-time staffed department.

No uniform pattern exists, however. Some unions have almost no recourse to outside assistance and conduct their educational programs solely under their own auspices and with their own resources. At the most, these unions might be using classroom facilities and living accommodations of universities. On the other hand, some unions operate almost their whole educational program through universities, leaving to them a large measure of discretion in curriculum, course content, and selection of teachers. Probably the majority of unions operate their educational programs on two levels—partly under their own auspices and partly jointly with some university. In the latter case, these unions have worked out a variety of arrangements whereby some precise understanding is reached on course content and selection of faculty, which, quite often, will include some union staff members, who may or may not be placed on the staff of the university for the duration of the program.

Many unsolved problems remain. Not all universities which attempted to develop education services to labor groups have actually succeeded in establishing permanent on-going programs. A few have withdrawn from the field after they found out that in meeting the educational needs of workers they become embroiled in discussions of controversial social and economic problems. Others failed because they operated in a vacuum with no relation to "felt needs" and no proper contacts with the labor movement or concern for institutional channels and jurisdictional boundaries. Other programs proved too costly or failed because the expected financial or moral support from labor did not come through.

Thus, the subject continues to be an insufficiently explored area and the debate goes on, though one notices a significant shift in substantive matter of the discussion. Earlier expressions of suspicion and distrust on the part of labor which questioned the advisability and propriety of university-sponsored labor education activities have now given way to a concern for the most appropriate manner in which universities can serve. Agreement seems to have been reached now on two significant points, namely:

(1) that universities can and should render genuine services to work-

ers, which are in no way inconsistent with the legitimate desire and need of educational institutions to maintain objectivity and academic standards; and

(2) that unions can advantageously use these services without fear that in doing so, they might impair or dilute their own programs or objectives.

Other organizations.—In addition to universities, unions co-operate with a great many private non-profit organizations. The Department of Education of the AFL-CIO is officially represented on the National Institute of Labor Education, the Joint Committee on Library Services of the American Library Association, and the Joint Council on Economic Education.

The National Institute of Labor Education was established in 1957 with the endorsement of the Executive Council of the AFL-CIO. The six labor members of the 14 man board of Directors serve on appointment of the President of the AFL-CIO, and the director of its Department of Education is one of the two Vice Presidents. The major purpose of the National Institute of Labor Education is to expand the scope and volume of labor education and to improve and enlarge the co-operation between labor and non-labor agencies in the field of education. The organization raises funds from both unions and foundations and distributes grants to universities and other non-labor agencies for joint programs with labor unions.

As of May, 1959, NILE was sponsoring two curriculum research studies, one on mental health and the other on pre-retirement education, and a research seminar on comparative labor movements. Other program proposals pertain to economic education, international affairs, education for public responsibilities, long term training opportunities for union staff and officers, and inter-group relations.

The Committee on Library Services to Labor Groups has been established jointly by the AFL-CIO and the American Library Association for the purpose of stimulating the use of library facilities by union staff and rank and file members. The committee holds regional meetings of local librarians and representatives of labor unions. Newsletters keep union education directors and librarians posted on matters of mutual interest.

The Joint Council of Economic Education has had official labor representatives on its board of trustees for a number of years. Unions are also represented on practically every state and regional council of this organization, the major purpose of which is to promote the development of effective programs of economic education, particularly in the secondary schools.

National and international unions and their local units, as well as many state and local bodies, have established some sort of co-operative relationship with a great many non-profit educational organizations. Among these are: American Labor Education Service, Association of

Catholic Trade Unionists, Catholic Labor Alliance, Jewish Labor Committee, Labor Education Association of Philadelphia, National Labor Service, National Religion and Labor Foundation, Negro Labor Committee, Adult Education Association[3], American Civil Liberties Union, Councils of Social Agencies, chapters of the Foreign Policy Association, Institute of International Education, League for Industrial Democracy, National Association for the Advancement of Colored People, National Conference of Christians and Jews, National Planning Association, Social Science Research Council, United Nations Association, Urban League, and local units of the Young Men's and Young Women's Christian Associations.

For most of these organizations the participation in labor education constitutes only a part, and often a very small part, of their general operation—the only exception being the American Labor Education Service, the operation of which is exclusively devoted to labor education.

The American Labor Education Service (ALES) was established in 1940, but goes back to the Byrn Mawr Summer School for Women Workers (1926) and the Affiliated Schools for Workers (1932). The ALES works with unions on a local, state, and national level and co-operates with colleges, universities, and other adult education agencies—currently with emphasis on programs in the area of international affairs. Assisted by grants from the Fund for Adult Education, ALES has conducted one or two week residential schools on international affairs for selected union leaders. It has set up local demonstration centers, of six months to thirty months in duration, to develop long-term study programs, both for rank and file members and secondary union leadership. It has sponsored UN schools which bring labor representatives to week-long or week-end schools in New York and it co-operates with government and private agencies on various exchange programs. The participation of workers and unions in community affairs is also given a good deal of attention, as are the problems of democracy, the impact of science and technology in the modern world, and the art of communication. An annual event is the Washington Birthday Conference which brings together professional workers in labor education from unions, government, public and private educational institutions, for a discussion of current problems in labor education. Another feature is the white-collar workshop, held annually, to deal with organizational and educational problems of white-collar employees.

DEFINITION OF ROLE IN THE GENERAL ADULT EDUCATION FIELD

Workers' education is an integral—though separate—branch of adult education. It has taken its rightful place side by side with other forms of adult education, meeting the specialized educational needs of workers, as other special agencies meet the needs of farmers, businessmen, and others. Its concern is, to use Havighurst's term, the "developmental tasks" which workers face at various times either in the union or in society. It tries to meet these tasks, however, through group action rather than through independent individual efforts.

This description makes labor education a valid part of adult education, but, at the same time, sets it clearly apart from it. There are several important considerations which explain the separateness of labor education:

1. An examination of the developmental tasks of workers leaves little doubt that our general educational institutions are, as a rule, ill equipped to meet these educational needs. Nor are most of the subject matters which make up the bulk of union education programs such that any other audience but union members would be attracted to them.

2. It is largely through labor organizations that workers appear as actual or potential consumers of education. Efforts to reach workers through general adult education groups and programs have, with few exceptions, been unsuccessful. It has now become axiomatic that the best way to reach workers is through their union, since it provides a natural, convenient, and practical channel for educational group contacts.

3. In the union workers meet as a homogeneous group bound together by common problems, common education levels, common experience and training. Using the union as a center of educational activities results in maximum efficiency in the use of educational techniques, materials, personnel, and methods, all of which can be closely geared to the needs of the group.

4. Workers appear to be, comparatively speaking, less "joiners" than other segments of our society. With the possible exception of church affiliation, unions are often the only organization in which workers hold membership.

5. Workers often have less formal education than those they ordinarily meet in adult education classes. Although the program in such classes may be excellent, the presentation as a rule is above the head of many workers. They soon lose self-confidence, feel inferior, and either "clam up" or become aggressive. More frequently they drop out and nothing is accomplished.

MAJOR CURRENT PROBLEMS AND ISSUES

Labor education has made impressive gains since the end of World War II. The number of full-time employed education staff members has risen sharply. In turn, the up-swing of educational activities within unions has stimulated non-labor agencies, primarily universities, to enter the field. Consequently, the number of labor education classes and institutes, and the number of students, have reached all time highs.

Yet, it is this very growth of union education, the sizable increase in funds and efforts expended on education, which makes it necessary to redefine goals and purposes of union education, to pin-point areas of neglect and shortcomings, to determine short- and long-range needs and goals, so as to maximize educational efforts.

Heading the list of current issues is the need to provide better opportunities—or any opportunities at all—for executive training of union officials and staff members.[4] Obviously, this requires a specific curriculum which our institutions of higher learning do not offer today. Nor has the labor movement, until now, seen fit to establish under its own auspices some center where such training might be provided for, the only exception being the Staff Training Institute established by the Ladies' Garment Workers Union.

Especially pressing is the need for training opportunities for union education specialists, few of whom have any theoretical training in the field of education. Most of them came into labor education by accident. They are usually long in knowledge of union structure and union problems and how to deal with workers. They usually also have zeal, devotion, and a strong philosophical commitment to the labor movement. But they are, as a rule, short on educational psychology, human relations, and communications research, various aspects of learning and intelligence of adults, and recent findings concerning the problems of homogeneous groups. The fact that so many of them seem to be doing a fairly good job does not minimize the need for better training, as the education directors themselves would be the first to admit.

Following a close second in terms of urgency is the need for a large pool of well informed union members which could be drawn upon for local and national union leadership in the labor movement. Such a pool cannot come from the present emphasis on short-term institutes but requires the establishment of long-term, possibly residential, training opportunities similar to those which exist in Western Europe and some Scandanavian countries. Brookwood College served such a purpose in this country but it has long ceased to exist. Such centers, whether they are called labor colleges or something else, could also serve as a training center for smaller unions which do not have by themselves sufficient resources—nor sufficient demands—for the operation of separate educational programs.

Third, on the list of current issues is the need to devise some approaches and techniques—perhaps a system of rewards and incentives—which would effectively promote rank and file workers' interest in education. The job on hand here is to discover the real desires and aspirations of workers.

Other current issues concern the continual and increased need for experimentation with new approaches and new materials to provide more effective education for more people with the limited resources on hand;

the more effective and imaginative use of television and radio; and some attempt to deal with the large geographical areas where no significant effort is being made either by unions or non-labor agencies, to meet the educational needs of workers.

Finally, labor education practitioners need to reach among themselves some agreement as to the precise role which they want the federal government to play in workers' education. Several years ago a bill in Congress to provide federal funds for labor education died in committee because of a divergence of opinion among unions as to the administration of the law.

Footnotes

[1]For a similar view on adult education see Paul Sheats, Clarence Jayne, and Ralph Spence, *Adult Education: The Community Approach* (New York: Dryden Press, 1953).

[2]*Labor and Education in 1956 and 1957* (AFL-CIO), p. 43.

[3]Co-operation between workers and adult educators is now a special concern of the Labor Education Section of the AEA. See Alice H. Cook, "New Goals for Labor Education," *Adult Leadership*, VI (October, 1957), 108.

[4]See Russ Allen, "What's Lacking in Labor Education," *IUD Digest*, Fall, 1958; and "Report on a Panel Session on Leadership Education," *Education News and Views*, February, 1959, p. 5.

Selected Readings

Barbash, Jack. *Universities and Unions in Workers' Education*. New York: Harper & Bros., 1955.

Cook, Alice H., and Douty, Agnes. *Labor Education Outside the Union*. Ithaca: Cornell University Press, 1959.

Hardman, J. B. S., and Neufeld, Maurice F. (eds.). *The House of Labor*. New York: Prentice-Hall, Inc., 1951.

Kerrison, Irvine L. H. *Workers Education at the University Level*. New Brunswick: Rutgers University Press, 1951.

Liveright, A. A. *Union Leadership Training*. New York: Harper & Bros., 1951.

Mire, Joseph. *Labor Education*. Madison: Inter-University Labor Education Committee, 1956.

Schwarztrauber, Ernest E. *Workers' Education*. Madison: University of Wisconsin Press, 1942.

Starr, Mark. "Union Education Survey," *Labor and Nation*, VII, No. 4 (1951).

Ware, Caroline F. *Labor Education in Universities*. New York: American Labor Education Service, Inc., 1946.

Workers Education in the United States. Fifth Yearbook of the John Dewey Society. New York: Harper & Bros., 1941.

CHAPTER 25

ADULT EDUCATION IN LIBRARIES

GRACE T. STEVENSON*
*Deputy Executive Director
and Director, Office for Adult Education
American Library Association*

Among the early institutions established in this country for the education of adults was the public library. It had its beginnings in the parish libraries of Maryland and North Carolina in the late seventeenth century, and in the town libraries of New England. An excerpt from the first annual report of the Boston Public Library, written by Edward Everett in 1852, states:

> It has been rightly judged that . . . under political, social, and religious institutions like ours . . . it is of paramount importance that the means of general information should be so diffused that the largest number of persons should be induced to read and understand questions going down to the very foundations of the social order, which are constantly presenting themselves, and which we, as a people, are constantly required to decide either ignorantly or wisely.[1]

Henry Steele Commager, in commenting on this report, says, "The public library is as characteristically American as the public school, and as important a part of the educational system. . . . It was all part of that faith in democracy and the perfectibility of man that was associated with the great reform movement of the 1840's and the 1850's. . . . From these . . . came the library movement which is one of the glories of American civilization."[2] The on-going life of that civilization is reflected immediately in the demands made on libraries.

THE CHANGING ROLE OF THE LIBRARY IN ADULT EDUCATION

Any event of consequence, local, national, or international, brings people to the library seeking further information about it. Our interests,

---

*Prepared with the assistance of the staff of the ALA Office for Adult Education.

our culture, our problems, our fads, are all apparent in the questions asked, the books and other materials borrowed. As one of a number of educational agencies and organizations in a community, the library has three unique functions. It serves as an instrument of continuous self-education for the individual reader; it is a materials resource for other agencies and organizations and their clientele; it assists other agencies and organizations in planning their programs, and sometimes assists in the presentation of those programs by providing personnel, skills, materials, or physical facilities. Many libraries perform a fourth function by presenting educational programs of their own—lectures, concerts, discussion groups—a variety of activities on a wide range of subjects, using many techniques. Some of these services are available in any library serving adults. Because more of them are more generally practiced in public libraries, it is to the public library practices that this chapter will be devoted.

In the early development of the library movement the philosophy of librarianship centered chiefly on building good collections of materials in all subject areas, and arranging these materials for ease of use. The patrons who came to the library were served, but little attempt was made to take the library outside its walls. In the last forty years there has developed the conviction that it is also the library's responsibility to make people aware of what this treasure house of materials they had paid for could mean to them. This is the principle that more and more has taken librarians into the active live of the community. It began with the upsurge of the adult education movement in the United States in the twenties. The American Library Association was very active in the formation of the American Association for Adult Education, and libraries and librarians have been increasingly active as agencies for adult education and as part of the adult education movement.

During the last fifteen years this philosophy of library service has gained wider acceptance. Services to adults have improved and those activities thought of specifically as adult education have increased. New library buildings make provision for these activities with informal, home-like reading rooms, auditoriums, conference and meeting rooms, screening rooms, and listening booths. During this period librarians have extended and improved their adult education knowledge and skills. Out of their interest, experience and everyday practice they are developing a solid body of information and literature that will be a foundation for the future.

LIBRARY OBJECTIVES IN ADULT EDUCATION

The educational objectives set down in that first report of the Trustees of the Boston Public Library more than a hundred years ago were made specific in the revised standards for public libraries adopted by the American Library Association in 1956.[3] The following excerpts from those standards illustrate some of the ways libraries now strive to achieve those objectives:

> The program of each public library should be focused upon clear and specific objectives.
>
> The public library should be closely integrated with the communities it serves.
>
> Continuous and periodic study of its community should be made by the library in order to know people, groups, and institutions thoroughly, and to keep up with developments and changes.
>
> Contact between the library and the constituency served should be a regular, day-to-day occurrence, and not just an academic matter of periodic studies. The community needs regular information about the services and resources of the library and on its side, the staff needs the constant stimulus and insight furnished by community contacts.
>
> Library staff members should participate in the life of the community and be willing to assume responsibilities in its institutions and organizations.
>
> The community-related library should be in regular touch with other agencies, should be informed at all times of the activities of these agencies, and should design its programs in relation to their services.
>
> The public library has a positive program of guidance to individuals in the use of educational, informational and recreational materials.
>
> Each library system should guide and stimulate use of materials by personal consultation, lists of materials, instruction in use of the library, displays, arrangement of the collection, radio and television presentations, and indeed by the whole range of library activities; the library should facilitate the use of materials by verbal, visual, or other interpretative means.
>
> The public library may sponsor or co-sponsor group activities within the framework of its own program.

ALA PROJECTS SUPPORTED BY GRANTS FROM THE FUND FOR ADULT EDUCATION

Office for Adult Education, 1953-61

This is an administrative unit within the headquarters office of ALA. Its function is to coordinate the headquarters activities resulting from project grants in the field of adult education, so as to provide better utilization of the project staffs, and better counseling and advisory services. The grant funds provide staff, and a small amount for special studies and activities of the Adult Services Division of ALA not falling within any of the other projects.

American Heritage Project, 1951-55

The purpose of this project was to assist libraries throughout the United States to provide opportunities for the discussion of the political, social, and economic problems of our time in the light of the basic documents, ideas, and experiences which constitute our American heritage. All discussions were based on readings or films, or a combination of both. Suitable materials were suggested and made available. Local groups, working with their librarian, and assisted by a state project director and a staff member from the ALA office, decided upon the subjects to be discussed (within the areas listed above) and selected materials to study.

After the first experimental year the projects were usually centered in the state library extension agencies which took the responsibility for organizing the program within the state, involving as many libraries as staff and funds would permit. Subgrants provided staff and travel funds at the state agency, materials for the discussion groups, and travel funds for the lay leaders. The staff at national headquarters was responsible for training and counseling the lay leaders, and serving as consultants to the state project directors. National conferences for orientation and training of state project directors were held at least annually.

Besides the seventeen states which received subgrants, sixteen other states participated in the program informally. These states received assistance with materials and consultation from the national office, usually by mail. During the four years of the grant period 1,474 groups were formed in thirty-three states and Guam, with a total of 28,476 participants. Twelve hundred eighty-eight discussion leaders were trained. The grant funds ceased in 1955, but many libraries have continued their discussion groups, though in most cases they are discussing a different subject area. The major publications resulting from this project were:

> Lee, R. E. *Getting the Most out of Discussion, a Guide for Participants.* (Chicago: American Library Association, 1956)
> Lee, R. E. *The Library-Sponsored Discussion Group.* (Chicago: American Library Association, 1957)

Survey of Adult Education in Public Libraries, 1952-53

This survey resulted in the publication of *Adult Education Activities in Public Libraries* by Helen Lyman Smith. This report was used by ALA as a basis for long-range planning to extend and improve the quality of library adult education. Committees of the association studied various aspects of the report and made recommendations, many of which have been acted upon, some of which are still being carried out. The report is used in all library schools and is constantly referred to in library literature.

Adult Education Subgrant Project, 1953-54

The purpose of this project was to stimulate the initiation and devel opment of adult education services to adult—and young adult—community groups through libraries, thereby giving libraries an opportunity to initiate new programs or to develop current ones, and to demonstrate the fitness and ability of libraries to present meaningful and vigorous adult education services to groups. Applications were solicited from libraries all over the country and subgrants were made to twenty libraries in nineteen states. The institutions varied in size and governmental structure, including three college or university libraries, and one graduate library school.

The amount of the awards differed and the individual projects ranged from a program planners' institute presented by a small library in Artesia, New Mexico, to a half-hour book discussion with listening groups presented on a commercial television station by the Seattle Public Library; from a music appreciation series using recordings with commentary and discussion in the Queens Borough, New York, Public Library to a series of group discussions on improved family and community life in the Boonslick, Missouri, Regional Library. The grant to the Graduate School of Library Service, Rutgers University, resulted in Eleanor Phinney's book *Library Adult Education in Action*.

Many articles about this project appeared in library literature. The complete report, *Experimental Projects in Adult Education*, is available from the American Library Association.

Allerton Park Conference, 1954

The need for training more librarians in the philosophy and skills of adult education was established by the survey reported in *Adult Education Activities in Public Libraries*. In response to this need the National Committee on Study Grants of the Fund for Adult Education made a grant to ALA for a conference to discuss appropriate training and learning situations for librarians engaged in adult education activities. Thirty-eight directors and faculty members of university library schools and adult education departments, and administrators of small, medium and large-sized libraries attended the conference. The conference identified attitudes, knowledges and skills necessary for librarians engaged in adult education activities, and made recommendations which could be useful in preparing better-trained librarians in this field. To determine the effects of the conference the ALA Office for Adult Education in 1956 requested the participants to report on ways in which they had carried out the recommendations of the conference, and on other effects they might have observed. In January 1957 the conferees met again to discuss those recommendations of the conference on which little action had been taken.

Publications of this project are:

Asheim, Lester. *Training Needs of Librarians Doing Adult Education Work*. (Chicago: American Library Association, 1955.)

Asheim, Lester and Phinney, Eleanor. "Progress Report on the Allerton Park Conference on Training Needs of Librarians Doing Adult Education Work: a synthesis of reports from participants." (Chicago: American Library Association, 1956.)

"Allerton Park Adult Education Conference Meeting: January 29, 1957." (Chicago: American Library Association, 1957.) (Mimeographed)

Library-Community Project, 1955-60

The project is designed to assist libraries to develop long-term adult education programs based on the analysis of community needs. Grants were made to eight state library extension agencies, each of which developed programs on two levels. On a statewide basis the extension agency provided opportunities for librarians, trustees, and lay people to increase their knowledge and skills in library adult education. Publications, workshops, and institutes were developed for this purpose.

Each of the eight state extension agencies designated one local library as a pilot library to undertake an intensive experiment in community study as the basis of continuing adult education activities. Staff members, trustees, and citizens have studied the needs, interests and educational resources of the community. Together they have interpreted their findings and tried to determine the library's role in the total educative community.

The grants to the first four states came to an end in August 1958. In each case the state library agency reported that activities would continue as part of their regular program of work, and that participation in the project had been a major factor in the development of their ability to improve and extend library adult education in the state. Of the other four states, the grants for two will come to an end in 1959, and for the remaining two in 1960.

A very important part of the Library-Community Project is the consultant service it offers through the state library agencies to the agencies themselves, to library schools, and to library associations all over the country. This service has been used principally in the planning and presentation of workshops and institutes in adult education. Since 1955 the project staff has assisted with fifty-seven institutes and workshops involving librarians, library trustees, and other lay people. The results of this in-service training program may be one of the most widespread and lasting effects of the project.

This project has stimulated many articles in the professional literature. The staff has prepared a great deal of material to be used in a library-community study. The major publications to date are:

> *Focus on Adults* series—Six articles on the Library-Community Project in the *ALA Bulletin*, October and November 1956, and January, February, March and May 1957.
> "Library-Community Study: a basis for the Development of the Library's Role in Adult Education" to be published by the American Library Association. (In preparation).

Effects of Adult Education Projects

In 1957 the Fund requested the ALA Office for Adult Education to make a study of the effects of these projects. This report concluded that "The ALA Adult Education projects supported by the Fund for Adult Education have had far-reaching and significant effects not only upon the libraries which participated in the projects, but upon the entire public library field. The ALA projects have produced more skilled professionals, stronger adult education institutions, and a profession better able to define its role in adult education and more willing to accept the responsibilities in the total adult education field."[4]

STATE LIBRARY EXTENSION AGENCIES

One of the interesting developments in the past few years has been the emergence of the State Library Extension Agency as a force in developing adult education services in libraries. This is the state agency which is charged by law with the extension and development of library services within the state. The agencies are in various stages of development in the different states, and many of them are understaffed and ill-supported. By the nature of their responsibility their major efforts go into helping the smaller libraries, many of which put a disproportionate amount of their funds into services to children and to schools. The grants to state agencies for adult education projects provided them with resources in staff and funds which made it possible for them to guide and encourage local libraries in establishing adult education services. Notable progress has been made through their efforts.

The passage of the Library Services Act in 1956 gave further impetus to the development of adult education through the state library extension agencies. This act, which provides federal aid on a matching basis to rural libraries for five years, is administered through these agencies. A progress report published in January, 1958,[5] indicates that consistently the forty-five states then participating were putting a major emphasis on improvement of services to adults. The most general pattern of development under the Library Services Act is the encouragement of small libraries to co-operate in establishing larger units of service which can command better support. This consolidation, and the increased emphasis on services to adults, will gradually bring about improved library adult education. The state library extension agencies play a key role here.

PROFESSIONAL DEVELOPMENT

The most noticeable gains in professional development have been through in-service training by means of workshops and institutes in adult education. Many of these have been the result of the ALA projects. The state library extension agencies and the library schools have always held workshops on various phases of library services and a number of these have been on library adult education in the past few years. Various combinations of the state library agencies, the state library associations, the library schools, and the ALA Office for Adult Education have co-operated in the presentation of such workshops and institutes. They have used as resource people many non-librarians—library trustees, university faculty members, sociologists, economists, statisticians, and officials of government agencies. They have helped librarians and non-librarians understand the educational role of the library; to see that role vis-a-vis that of other educational agencies in the community; to study the needs and resources of their community; and to plan better programs.

The American Library Association, like many professional associations, consists of a number of subject divisions. In 1926 ALA established an Adult Education Board. In 1952 those members interested in adult education established the Adult Education Section of the Public Libraries Division. In 1956-57 ALA was reorganized and the Adult Education Section achieved division status as the Adult Services Division, incorporating the Adult Education Board, with its own office and executive secretary at ALA Headquarters. A number of the state library associations also have adult education sections or committees.

Librarians of this generation, following in the footsteps of their predecessors of the twenties, have demonstrated their interest and belief in a national adult education movement that draws together adult educators from a variety of institutions and organizations. They took part in the organization of the Adult Education Association of the USA and have been increasingly active in it since. Many of them are also active in the state and regional associations.

THE LIBRARY AS AN EDUCATIONAL FORCE
IN THE COMMUNITY

The first responsibility of a library is to acquire the best collection of materials of all types suited to the needs of the community which it serves. These materials must then be organized to make them easily accessible and usable. Many libraries attempt in various ways to call the reader's attention to books he might otherwise miss. A unique example of this is the Detroit Public Library's system of Reader Interest Classification which arranges books on the shelves, not by the Dewey Classification System common to nearly all public libraries, but in terms of the individual's broad basic interests. After using this arrangement for more than ten years the library staff feels that it has been very successful in terms of reader response and increased use of materials.

Library materials must meet three kinds of needs: the basic or universal need of which the reader may be unaware but which, if appropriate material is supplied, will develop the discriminating reader; the general informational, cultural, and recreational needs common to the continuing education of all adults; and the particular needs of the community served. For instance, when a new city charter was to be voted upon by the citizens of Omaha the public library acquired a quantity of new materials on the subject. Having acquired such materials the library has the further responsibility to let people know they are available. When Grand Rapids, Michigan, planned a series of special events to focus attention on the problems of metropolitan planning the public library—with the League of Women Voters—acquired the needed materials, which were then used in special publicity campaigns and for a variety of group meetings, speeches, panel discussions, and forums.

To obtain material for this chapter the ALA Office for Adult Education sought information about their adult education programs from a selected list of public libraries. The returns showed that almost without exception special materials had been acquired for their programs of adult education. These materials were of all types, printed materials ranking first, films second. They also included recordings, slides, pictures, tapes, maps, and music scores. The variety in subjects programmed, materials used, and methods of presentation was equal to the number of libraries reporting. The Newark, New Jersey, Public Library had presented an arts program using art films, slides and pictures, recordings and live concerts along with books and pamphlets. The Dunklin County, Missouri, Library offered a basic course in French and Spanish using books, recordings, and specially mimeographed materials. The local high school will offer the courses next year. For three years a group has been gathering regularly in the Akron Public Library to read plays, listen to recorded plays, or discuss the ideas in some play they have seen. Over three hundred libraries provide films for their patrons, and many of them have regular showings of films in the library. Music appreciation programs using recordings are fairly common.

Libraries are using television for adult education also, particularly in the larger cities where facilities are available. In practically every city where there is an educational television station the library has worked actively to use it for programming. Some smaller libraries also find it possible to use television for educational purposes. In Jacksonville, Florida, the library is presenting a series on books and ideas. The Osterhout Free Library in Wilkes-Barre, Pennsylvania, presented a series on the countries of Asia, using visitors from Asian countries and suitable costumes, artifacts, and musical instruments. Owing to an unusual situation, which makes special funds available, the Louisville Public Library makes extensive use of the mass media: it is building its own television station and it owns two FM broadcasting stations; it has a large collection of films, recordings, and tapes, and the tapes and recordings are piped into all branch libraries and to universities and colleges within the area.

This kind of cooperation with other organizations and groups is basic to library adult education. The library assists these groups in attaining their objectives and extends its own services farther into the community. The questionnaire returned on the survey mentioned above record cooperation with a lengthy list of organizations as varied as American life itself. The Philadelphia Free Library and the Family Service of Philadelphia presented in branch libraries three discussion series of six sessions each on home and family life; the Richland, Washington, Public Library and the Richland Chapter of the American Association of University Women sponsored a series of speeches, forums and panel discussions on finance and investments.

Cooperation with other governmental agencies ranks even higher than cooperation with the less formal organizations. The public library of Charlotte and Mecklenburg County, North Carolina, cooperated with the State Commission for Aging and the County Committee on Aging in a workshop which resulted in a permanent Committee on Aging being formed by the local Social Planning Council. The Chattanooga Public Library joined with the League of Women Voters and the Mayor's Committee for UN Day in 1951 in the presentation of a series of meetings on the United Nations. The success of these programs resulted in a city-wide increase of adult education services which still continue. In 1953 the Enoch Pratt Free Library, Baltimore, joined with sixteen other organizations and agencies, such as the Baltimore Department of Schools, Department of Police, and the Criminal Justice Commission, in an institute on Crime and the Citizen. The five sessions presented distinguished speakers and panelists from the Eastern Seaboard, and many civic groups and organizations had follow-up meetings. For five years the library in Kendallville, Indiana, has cooperated with Indiana University and Purdue University on a series of town meetings presenting facts and information about community problems to the citizens. Denver Public Library cooperated with the Colorado Expenditures Council and the City Revenue Department on a special forum to discuss community tax problems, during which the recognized authorities brought by the library to the city were consulted by state and municipal officials.

This cooperation with other organizations and agencies often serves another purpose for libraries. It helps them with the choice of materials in particular subject fields. The Rochester, New York, Public Library and the Health Education Committee of the Council of Social Agencies worked together on the selection of films and printed materials in health education. The result is a better collection in the library, more widely used by the community. It is a common practice, particularly in those libraries which have film collections, to ask the advice of the local Mental Health Society, the art museum, or specialists in various scientific fields to advise on the purchase of materials.

That libraries reflect what is going on in their communities as well as in the larger national and international scene is evidenced in the programs they present as well as in the materials they buy. During the International Geophysical Year the Queens Borough, New York, Public Library presented nine lectures, followed by discussion, on nine categories of geophysics. At the same time booklists and exhibits were prepared and special materials of all types purchased. The library in Waukegan, Illinois, recognized the need for information about the city on which to base current city planning, and with the League of Women Voters conducted a survey of the City. Specific community problems presented by the survey and interpreted through programs were met by successful referendums.

In the presentation of their programs libraries lean heavily on community resources, particularly for personnel. They employ every kind of program technique—lectures, panels, demonstrations, role-playing—and often provide for audience participation through buzz groups, work groups, question periods and open forum discussion. Libraries, like other institutions, are too often faced with the lack of personnel trained in these techniques on their own staffs as well among the general public. Some efforts are made to train community leaders though most libraries do not have staff, time, or funds for this undertaking. The most extensive leadership training program in libraries has been carried on under the ALA grant projects, particularly the American Heritage and Library-Community Projects. Several states which began such training under the American Heritage Project have continued it—among them Colorado, Georgia, and Vermont.

One of the commonest forms of leadership training is the program planners' institute, such as that presented by the Carnegie Library of Pittsburgh. The need for this activity was evidenced by the 960 people who attended. This is too large a group to work with, but it was followed by similar institutes on a smaller scale, by many requests for assistance in program planning, and in implementation of suggestions made at these institutes.

The Library as a Community Resource

The services and activities enumerated above underscore the library's major function as an educational agency in the community. The library should be the community's chief resource for materials and for assistance to other agencies and groups in program planning, and if needed, in the presentation of their programs. The library should further assist these groups by publicizing their programs in all ways appropriate.

To fulfill this role competently the library must take an active part in community life. It is not enough for the library to be a child of its time. It must be a maker of its time as well.

Footnotes

[1]Henry Steele Commager, *Living Ideas in America* (New York: Harper & Bros., 1951), p. 575.

[2]*Ibid*, p. 571.

[3]*Public Library Service; A Guide to Evaluation with Minimum Standards.* (Chicago: American Library Association, 1956), pp. 25-31.

[4]Charles H. Hewitt, "Grant Evaluation Study" (Chicago: American Library Association, 1958), p. 178. (Mimeographed).

[5]Muriel C. Javelin, "Adult Services under the Library Services Act," *Wilson Library Bulletin*, XXXII (May 1958), 637-43.

Selected Readings

"Adult Education Issue," *ALA Bulletin* XLVIII (April, 1954), 191-231.

Asheim, Lester. *Training Needs of Librarians Doing Adult Education Work: A Report of the Allerton Park Conference, November 14-16, 1954.* Chicago: American Library Association, 1955.

Experimental Projects in Adult Education; A Report of the ALA Adult Education Subgrant Project. Chicago: ALA Office for Adult Education, 1956.

Houle, Cyril O. *Libraries in Adult and Fundamental Education; the Report of the Malmo Seminar.* Paris: UNESCO, 1951.

Phinney, Eleanor. "ALA Projects Supported by the Fund for Adult Education," *ALA Bulletin L* (October, 1956), 591-95.

————. *Library Adult Education in Action: Five Case Studies.* Chicago: American Library Association, 1956.

Public Library Service: A Guide to Evaluation, with Minimum Standards. Coordinating Committee on Public Library Standards of ALA. Chicago: American Library Association, 1956.

Smith, Hannis S. (ed.). *Informal Education Through Libraries; Proceedings of the Sixth Institute on Public Library Management.* Madison: Wisconsin Free Library Commission, 1954.

————. *Informal Education Through Libraries; Proceedings of the Sixth Institute on Public Library Management. Supplement: The Complete Papers.* Madison: Wisconsin Free Library Commission, 1955.

Smith, Helen Lyman. *Adult Education Activities in Public Libraries; A Report of the ALA Survey of Adult Education Activities in Public Libraries and State Library Extension Agencies of the United States.* Chicago: American Library Association, 1954.

Stevenson, Grace T. "Role of the Public Library in Adult Reading," *Adult Reading.* National Society for the Study of Education. Fifty-Fifth Yearbook, Part II. Chicago: University of Chicago Press, 1956. Chapter 6, p. 114-135.

————. "What is Adult Education?" *ALA Bulletin L* (October, 1956), 578.

Stone, C. Walter. "Adult Education and the Public Library," *Library Trends* I (April, 1953), 437-453.

Thomsen, Carl and others. *Adult Education Activities for Public Libraries.* Paris: UNESCO, 1950.

CHAPTER 26

THE MASS MEDIA AND ADULT EDUCATION

EUGENE I. JOHNSON
Director
Civic Education Center
Washington University

DEFINITION

The mass media of communication comprise the major system for the circulation of information and intellectual stimuli of various kinds in the United States today. The media discussed in this chapter are the broadcast media of radio and television and the printed media of newspapers, popular magazines, and books. There are other media, of course, but broadcasting and print offer unique opportunities for adult education and frequently encompass other media in their operation—movies shown via television, for example.

Educational Broadcast Media

Television has sprung almost fully grown onto the American scene since World War II and educational leaders have marshalled their forces to press vigorously for the development of a separate, non-commercial educational television service. This effort is quite the reverse of the approach taken initially to radio when, in the years before World War II, educators together with leaders in the commercial radio broadcasting field established the Federal Radio Education Committee (FREC) to develop the educational possibilities of commercial radio channels. Educators greeted the formation of the FREC in 1936 as enthusiastically as they later greeted the advent of television; in fact, many of the same phrases were heard, including the reference to radio (and a decade later, to television) as the greatest invention since the printing press. But by 1950 the FREC had disappeared from the scene.

314

During the 1950's, national leadership in developing a separate educational broadcasting service was provided through four major agencies—the Joint Council on Educational Television (JCET), the Committee on Television of the American Council on Education, the National Association of Educational Broadcasters (NAEB), and the National Educational Television and Radio Center (NETRC).

The JCET, organized in 1950 and reconstituted in 1955, represents the full panorama of United States educational and civic interests in matters affecting the development of educational television. It maintains liaison between educators, the Congress, and the Federal Communications Commission and provides services to communities which are in the initial stages of developing educational television channels. The Committee on Television of the American Council, in close touch with educational policy makers, provides opportunities for educational leaders to discuss new developments in education and television other than purely operational matters. These two organizations maintain headquarters in Washington, D. C.

The NAEB is the educational trade organization in the broadcast field. Founded by a small group of educational radio stations in the 1920's, it was greatly strengthened in the early 1950's with financial assistance from the Fund for Adult Education, the Kellogg Foundation, and other sources. The NAEB conducts conferences, offers personnel training, engages in research and publishes significant reports. It has developed the nation-wide "tape network" to which almost 150 educational radio stations belong and makes grants-in-aid to educational radio production centers. (It produced the highly successful *Ways of Mankind* and *Jeffersonian Heritage* radio series which have since been incorporated into adult study-discussion programs.) NAEB maintains headquarters at the University of Illinois in Urbana, Illinois.

The NETRC is the major source of high quality programs for educational television stations in the country today. Moving its headquarters from Ann Arbor, Michigan, to New York City in 1959, the Center has predicted that it will be recognized as the fourth major network in the country within five years.[1] The NET Center has been given a five million dollar terminal grant from the Ford Foundation to be used during the period 1960-1965 for the purpose of establishing a broad base of financial support for good programming, outstanding production, and expansion of the educational television station network.

The Fund for Adult Education was the key element in the design and development of educational television broadcasting from the time of its founding in 1951, by the Ford Foundation, to 1956, when the Ford Foundation itself entered the field. During those six years the Fund financed the initial year of JCET, provided funds for radio program development through NAEB, established (with the professional assistance of NAEB) the Educational Television and Radio Center (which added 'National' to its corporate title in 1959) , and gave construction grants to twenty educational television stations.

The number of educational television and radio stations has expanded considerably in the past decade. There are now nearly 150 radio stations (mainly FM) with educational licenses, the majority controlled by universities and colleges, although libraries (Louisville, for example) and religious institutions also hold FM licenses. The growth of educationally-licensed FM stations is accounted for chiefly by technical improvements developed by Syracuse University and the General Electric Company which made inexpensive 10-watt FM stations feasible, by changes in the regulations of the Federal Communications Commission, and by the leadership of the NAEB.

By the fall of 1959, there were forty-four educational television stations on the air, with the likelihood that this number would reach fifty by the end of the year. The spread of educational television stations has occurred entirely since 1952, when the FCC issued its *Sixth Order and Report*, setting aside 242 channels for educational, non-commercial purposes. Educational stations are operated in various ways—as non-profit community corporations (KETC in St. Louis, KQED in San Francisco, and WQED in Pittsburgh, for example); by colleges and universities (Ohio State University and the University of Nebraska, for example); by public school systems (Cincinnati, Denver, and Milwaukee, for example) ; by a public library (Louisville, which enjoyed the distinction of being the only library to hold an educational license in 1959); and by special state or regional authorities set up especially for that purpose (Alabama, for example, with similar networks planned for Florida and Oklahoma.)

Five commercial stations are operated by colleges and universities, but their programming reflects the thinking prevalent in the commercial field and they are not included with the educational stations.

Aside from stations operated by state universities, the educational channels are all in large metropolitan areas. Paradoxically, however, New York and Los Angeles were still without educational channels in 1959 because the maximum number of VHF channels feasible in any given area was already in use in both of these cities prior to the FCC order setting aside channels for educational purposes. New York City attempted, through the Metropolitan Educational Television Association, to place educational programs on commercial channels, but abandoned this approach in May, 1959.

Television is an expensive medium to put into production. Construction costs for the existing educational channels ranged from a low of $115,000 to a figure surpassing one million dollars for stations with multiple studios.[2] While it has proved possible to raise money for construction purposes, particularly in the larger metropolitan areas, it has proved more difficult to raise the annual operating budget. No educational television station today operates for less than $150,000 a year, while some spend in excess of a half million dollars. These amounts of money are small when compared to commercial operations. Edward R. Murrow, for example, has estimated that it costs about $100,000 to place an hour-long documentary like "Small World" on the air.[3] An educational channel could operate for an entire year, indeed in some cases for several years, on what the commercial networks often spend for a single hour-long program.

The educational stations had not solved the VHF-UHF problem at the close of the decade of the '50's. Most television sets are equipped only to receive programs broadcast on a VHF (very high frequency) band rather than on a UHF (ultra high frequency) band; yet nearly half of the educational stations operate on UHF. Efforts both to popularize low-cost adapters for VHF sets and to open up more VHF channels for educational purposes are now under way but have not been very successful.

Commercial Broadcast Media

There are now three national commercial television and radio networks (ABC, CBS and NBC), with Mutual making the fourth radio network. Although there were 564 commercial television stations in the country in May, 1959, and 3,938 radio stations, FCC regulations permit a national chain to own only five stations outright; others are owned locally, many affiliated with one of the broadcast services.

Educational broadcasting via commercial channels is supervised usually by public affairs departments, on both the national and local level. The geographic distribution of the commercial stations, particularly television, reflects the same concentration in metropolitan areas that holds true for the educational stations.

Printed Media

The University Press movement has reached maturity in the years since World War II, with forty-three university presses in operation, the newest of which is at the University of Missouri. The university presses "continue to publish scholarly monographs and scientific tabulations. But they also . . . are returning to the assumption that publication is an act of immense cultural responsibility. That responsibility is to adults. . . ."[4] It is estimated that one-fourth of the new adult trade non-fiction titles each year now bear a university press imprint.

In the field of book publication, the paperback has won widespread acceptance. In 1958, the total sales of paperbacks exceeded 250 million, almost half of all books bought in that year for general reading. The extraordinary growth in the sale of paperbacks since World War II has resulted not only from the lower price but also from the greater availability of these books throughout the country. Paperbacks are distributed like magazines and can be found in supermarkets, drugstores, bus and railway stations, and other places where hardcover books are not available.

Newspapers reflected a trend toward growing circulation but consolidation of ownership in fewer hands. From 1930 to 1955 the total number of dailies published in the United States declined by 182, from 1,942 to 1,760, while total circulation increased from 39 million to 56 million.[5] Several long-established magazines, such as *Colliers*, ceased publication, while others made their appearance—e.g. *Horizon* and *The Reporter*.

PROGRAM AVAILABILITY

People who live in large metropolitan areas have an enormous advantage over residents of smaller cities, small towns and rural areas in the quantity of mass media offerings to which they have access. Accessibility is roughly equal throughout the country only for magazines and paperback books. As far as newspapers, radio and television are concerned, the city-dweller has a wealth of material on which to draw.

The libraries are a principal agency through which books reach people. There are an estimated 7,500 public library systems in the United States reaching a potential of 123 million people and circulating over 400 million volumes annually.[6] While vigorous efforts by state and county library systems, utilizing such devices as bookmobiles, are making books more available in rural areas than in the past, it is still true that the largest collections, the largest budgets per capita, and the bulk of professionally trained staffs are found in the larger cities.

Bookstores scarcely exist outside of metropolitan areas. According to recent studies there are about 500 bookstores in the United States which can offer an adequate range of materials, while another thousand offer a considerable number of books and can special-order any book.[7] Sixty-two per cent of all bookstore sales are made in twenty-five of the nation's large cities. This concentration appears to be increasing, with there being less likelihood that a town of 10,000 people will have a bookstore today than would have been the case prior to World War II.

The same discouraging picture is repeated in the newspapers. While certain newspapers are mailed in large volume to out-of-town readers, all too few cities have newspapers that provide adequate coverage of the day's local, national, and international news.

Adult educators who wish to utilize the mass media must realize they are reaching essentially the people who live in cities. While radio, magazines, and paperbacks have improved the position of the non-city dweller, he is still at a disadvantage compared to his city cousins.

THE MASS MEDIA AND THE BIG CHANGE
IN THE UNITED STATES

The relative concentration of the mass media in the larger urban centers of the United States points up the peculiar challenge which the adult educator faces at the present time. It is primarily the challenge of metro-politanization, the concentration of the country's population and re-sources in the larger metropolitan areas. As the 1960 census will show, more than ninety per cent of the population growth, through migration and natural increase, is occurring in metropolitan areas, of which there were 174 in 1955. The nation has not yet evolved patterns of govern-mental and social organization to meet this new situation. Our cities and towns and states still operate within patterns worked out for a simpler and more agrarian society. The St. Louis metropolitan area, for example, with a total population of nearly two million, is divided up into parts of two states, six counties and some two hundred incorporated municipal-ities, ninety-eight of which are concentrated in St. Louis County.

The mass media offer unique opportunities to overcome the paralyzing effect of this complexity. If educators can learn to employ the mass media to build common loyalties—a sense of community—among the population splinters of a metropolitan area, to develop more consistent value struc-tures, and bolder and more compelling images of the good life—then they will render a service of incalculable value to the people of this country.

THE MASS MEDIA AS EDUCATORS

Few people will question the sweeping influence of the mass media on the attitudes and behavior of the American people. Interest centers not so much on whether the mass media affect behavior but on how they do, and to what extent the media can be and indeed seek to be deliberate educational agencies in the spectrum of influences to which people are daily exposed. The Study Committee set up by the Ford Foundation in 1949 to recommend policy and program emphases for the Foundation's activities stated the problem in this way:

> The necessity to elevate these media to appropriate educational standards con-stitutes a serious challenge, since democracy may survive and grow only as the people acquire some sane, realistic values and develop a high capacity to reason for themselves.[8]

While adult educators not directly connected with the media can and do use the media to present educational programs, what do the media themselves do?

Newspapers

The educational role of the newspapers is seen most clearly in four of its major activities.

1. *Presentation of the news.*—The first of these is its most obvious edu-cational role—to inform—to report the news, as the Commission on the Freedom of the Press urged, in ways that give people a "truthful, com-prehensive and intelligent account of the day's events in a context that

gives them meaning."⁹ Some measures which newspapers and press services take to improve the adequacy of the daily news are educational in character. For example, the insertion of background material into the news account itself, thereby making its context clearer, is essentially the same educational function the music teacher performs when he relates the breaking of traditional symphonic forms by Beethoven to the revolutionary movement then sweeping Europe. Since few newspapers can give specialized coverage to *all* the news (in the manner of the *New York Times*), each must decide what major focus of interest it will have. The *Minneapolis Star,* for example, provides regular news and feature articles interpreting the activities of the state legislature and economic developments within the state that otherwise would not be covered.

2. *Interpretation of the news.*—The newspapers perform another educational function by *interpreting* the news, helping readers arrive at some conclusions regarding the meaning and significance of major developments. The editorial pages and the special columnists with varying points of view are essentially interpretive services. When it is done well, the editorial page of a high quality daily newspaper is itself an educational force of great significance. For example, the *St. Louis Post Dispatch* editorial page usually includes an editorial, a cartoon, at least one letter to the editor, and reprints of opinions from other leading newspapers or national magazines, all focused on the same topic.

3. *Publication of special educational materials.*—A third educational role is the publication of special materials of educational significance on major issues—a specific foreign crisis, the struggle against urban blight, the nature of metropolitan problems, the state of the arts in a city, for example. The decision to present an educational series of articles is a *voluntary* decision made under fewer of the pressures that operate in the newspaper field than almost any other decision. It represents the editor's priority ranking of major topics on which he feels his readers need more information. When making these decisions the educational role of the newspaper is clearly ascendant. Decisions about special series reveal the issues and value judgments which link the media to other educational agencies in the general adult education movement.

The Foreign Policy Association reports that 140 newspapers co-operated in carrying a series of articles on "Great Decisions of 1958," an educational program focusing on eight major issues the American people faced. *The San Francisco Chronicle,* for example, devoted its entire editorial space once a week for eight weeks to a discussion of the issue of the week.

In 1959 the *Chronicle* again showed its concern with an issue of major importance to most educators, the human needs of the Negro people moving in great numbers to the large cities of the North and West, by publishing a series of thoughtful articles on the Negro population of San Francisco.

Austin C. Wehrwein of *The Milwaukee Journal* won the Pulitzer prize in 1953 for a series of twenty-five articles on Canada. George Beveridge of the *Washington Evening Star* won a Pulitzer prize in 1958 for a series of articles on "Metro, City of Tomorrow: What It Will Be Like." The prize was awarded for local reporting *not* under pressure of deadlines and again represented a deliberate educational decision; it reflected the value judgment of both writer and publisher:

> The *Star* had no sensations to sell, no blast of page I headlines, no crooks to put in jail. . . . Its only purpose was to make its readers think about the problems of growth that were confronting the nation's capital.[10]

4. *Co-operative efforts with other educative agencies.*—Newspapers occasionally fill a fourth educational role by publishing material designed specifically to supplement educational materials carried by other media—radio and television for example. Although wary about losing their independence or giving any advantage to a rival medium, newspapers in such cities as Salt Lake City, San Bernardino, and St. Louis have co-operated in highly significant programs aimed at correlating the educational activity of the newspaper with other influences simultaneously at work in the community. These experiments are reported later.

Finally, the Worthington (Minn.) daily *Globe* provides an interesting illustration of a newspaper in a small community (pop. 10,000) that exercises a major educational influence by focusing its various educational roles on one theme. In 1957, Worthington won the World Brotherhood Award for its efforts to promote international understanding through a 'town affiliation' program with the city of Crailsheim, Germany. In the decade following the close of World War II the people of Worthington, deliberately selecting a formerly hostile area, established contact with the people of Crailsheim. They sent barrels of clothing and household goods; they sent Worthington students to attend schools in Crailsheim and played host to students from Crailsheim. And recently they have sent the local leader of the 'town affiliation' movement on a round-the-world tour, not only to visit Crailsheim, but also India in the course of which he will spend time selecting a community which will become a third in a unique three-way movement of international understanding, uniting East and West. Throughout this experience the *Globe* has been a constant shining light, supporting the movement editorially, interviewing the people going to and coming from Crailsheim, and running frequent background articles which have helped the community gain understanding not only about the former enemy, but about the nature of the problems faced in reducing world tensions today.

Popular Magazines

While the great majority of popular magazines endeavor to entertain their readers, there are two areas in which decisions are made which reflect the educational role of magazines: (1) the selection and organization of content, and (2) the extension of services to readers.

In the organization of content, the educational role is seen most clearly in special supplements or series. *The Atlantic Monthly* with the assistance of Intercultural Publications, Inc. has presented supplements on most of the major countries of the world. These supplements present an interpretation of the entire culture of a country. *Life* has published several memorable series in such fields as religion, the arts and anthropology. The *Saturday Evening Post* inaugurated a series of articles on "Adventures of the Mind" in 1958 which met with such favorable popular response that it has been continued. *The Reporter* and *Saturday Review* in recent years have devoted entire issues, or the major portion of issues, to subjects of world-wide importance. A series of articles in 1955 by Peter Drucker in *Harper's Magazine* on "America's Next Twenty Years" and a recent series in *Fortune* on "The American Market in the Sixties" are examples of presenting significant topics in depth. Occasionally a magazine becomes so convinced of the importance of certain fields of human activity that it may add a new department, such as *Saturday Review's* section on research in science and the humanities.

Many magazines offer various extra services to readers. *Readers Digest* publishes an outstanding series of "Adult Education Readers." *Parents' Magazine* prepares and distributes two discussion series a year, with free discussion guides, for parent study groups throughout the country. *Newsweek* provides aids to the study of major developments in national and international affairs which are widely used in high school classes and adult groups.

Like newspapers, magazines are largely prisoners of the markets they serve and of the pressures of meeting various deadlines. When editors are most free from these influences, the choices they make reflect their value judgments about what it is important for people to know about. Along with careful educational method—respect for fact and logic as opposed to attempts at irrational persuasion—the making of free choices regarding content clearly links the magazine publishing field to the adult education movement.

Commercial Television and Radio

In the broadcast field, educators have directed their energies chiefly to creating a separate radio and television service, and the commercial media have been generally cool, with notable exceptions, to educational agencies. One statement of the ways in which commercial television and radio can serve education stresses three factors:

1. To create an atmosphere of respect for intellect and learning in its entertainment and information programs.
2. To provide a more comprehensive and continuous coverage of educational events and issues of vital concern to America and the free world.

3. To make available to its mass audience programs from schools, colleges and universities, with great teachers sharing their knowledge and wisdom of civilization with all who choose to learn.[11]

One of the most widely respected programs on either television or radio and with one of the longest records of continuous broadcast is CBS Radio's "Invitation to Learning," with Lyman Bryson as moderator. The commercial networks and local stations occasionally present outstanding documentaries (on such subjects as the sun, the heart, and others) but for the most part sustained high quality programming with significant educational content has been confined to the "intellectual ghetto" of Sunday afternoon.[12] Then such programs as "Twentieth Century", "Meet the Press", and "Small World" are aired.

That the standards of the commercial media can be raised was demonstrated by the success of "Omnibus" on CBS. Originally subsidized by the Radio and Television Workshop of the Ford Foundation and carried on sustaining time, "Omnibus" attracted a large audience and eventually a commercial sponsor.

All networks and many local radio and television stations have experimented with formal educational programs, "The University of the Air" being broadcast by radio in the 1930's. Both NBC and CBS television carried successfully college credit courses in 1958 and 1959. "Sunrise Semester," carried by CBS in New York City at 6:30 a.m. attracted a large audience as well as several hundred credit enrollees and created a run on bookstores for textbooks featured in the course. NBC carried "Continental Classroom" in 1959, a high school or early college level course in physics, and announced intentions to continue the highly successful type programming in the future.

HOW ADULT EDUCATORS USE THE MASS MEDIA

By far the most frequent use which the colleges, universities, and public school systems make of the mass media is for formal courses which can be taken for credit, or simply viewed for whatever use the viewer cares to make of them. A survey by Michigan State University revealed that 117 educational institutions offered 464 credit courses in 1958.[13] Nineteen per cent were in the field of Social Science, 14 per cent in English classes and 13 per cent in Physical Sciences. Non-credit enrollment has usually been larger than credit enrollment (by a ratio sometimes as large as 5 to 1). A course in General Psychology at Western Reserve University, for example, attracted 70 adult viewers who enrolled for credit and 451 who paid a small sum for "auditing" the course. The famed Dr. Baxter, when he first offered "Shakespeare" on KNXT in Los Angeles, attracted 242 credit as compared to 1260 non-credit enrollees.[14]

After the novelty of the telecourses had worn off, most educational institutions reported a drop in enrollment from the general adult population. High enrollment figures appear to be related to the outstanding quality of the teacher, the usefulness of the course in a systematic program leading to a degree, or a high level of interest in the subject matter.

The drawing power of high-quality educational programming is illustrated by a "Conference on Science and Human Responsibility," organized by Washington University in St. Louis in 1956-57 and telecast by the local educational channel. An audience estimated at fifty thousand tuned in to watch such figures as Barbara Ward, Julian and Aldous Huxley, Robert Hutchins, Erich Fromm, Harrison Brown and others discuss scientific insights into the nature of man and current developments in the international field.

Speculation about the motives of non-credit adult enrollees in telecourses varies widely, but it appears that a genuine hunger for knowledge lies behind the interest. If so, credit courses that are geared essentially to past patterns of curriculum development and based on performance criteria for undergraduates may not be the best organization of educational offerings for adults. Research is needed to clarify this issue. Telecourses can be expected to continue, however, since both credit and non-credit enrollees in many cities pay some fee for their course and this helps the educational institutions defray production costs and the instructor's salary.

When colleges and universities and public school systems offer programs that depart from the academic course patterns, their motive appears usually to be public relations. The university showcase program is a familiar feature in many cities, with the "Johns Hopkins Science Review," providing an outstanding example. However, the motive may also be strictly educational service, as in the case of the Chelsea Closed Circuit Project in New York City, in which residents of four low-income housing developments are linked by closed circuit television with the Chelsea schools to receive instructional programs for both children and adults.

The fruitful collaboration of educational television stations and the colleges and universities of the country, frequently with the help of the National Educational Television and Radio Center, is the strongest current factor leading to improved programming on educational stations throughout the country. The NETRC is developing, usually through contract with educational television stations and other production centers, program series in six content areas: the arts, the humanities, the social sciences, the natural sciences, public affairs, and children's programs.

Labor has made extensive use of both radio and television in educating its own membership as well as the general public. With several decades of experience, labor has become sophisticated in regard to matters of quality production and attracting and holding an audience. One of its most successful programs is "Eye Opener," a radio program taped and distributed nationally by the United Automobile Workers and presented in many communities at 6:15 a.m.

Public libraries in many cities utilize both radio and television to help local people evaluate best sellers, call attention to good books that might otherwise be overlooked and publicize the resources available in the public library. For example, "Public Conference," presented weekly by the Milwaukee Public Library, features a panel discussion of a major public issue and ends with a review of pertinent materials available from the library. The majority of the library programs, however, feature discussions about books.

For reasons that are entirely understandable, uses of mass media by local and national organizations not exclusively educational in character tend to reflect the special purposes of the organization. Thus the League of Women Voters' sponsors "Face the Issue," the National Conference of Christians and Jews presents "Everybody's Business," an association of savings and loan companies presents an educational series on the activities of those organizations and the Bar Association presents "Law in Your Life." In Memphis, Tennessee, a highly successful series of programs initiated by the Council of Jewish Women and directed toward individuals in need of literacy education has led to the establishment in that city of a world center against illiteracy.

Although most of the informal television and radio offerings of adult education agencies have not been evaluated, three limitations reduce the total impact of their work: (1) prime broadcast time over the commercial stations is not usually available to them; (2) they lack funds to develop content objectives effectively; and (3) they lack sufficient personnel who are experienced and competent in broadcast programming. The potential power of the new broadcast media and the willingness of some station managers to provide time for public service (or in the case of some educational television channels to build community support and fill program voids) has led many inexperienced agencies to offer programs that have been failures.

Educational channels still struggling with the problem of financial survival, do not have the funds to invest in program content, and the commercial channels are too accustomed to passing the cost on to the sponsor. The adult education group without resources, therefore, may not be very effective at present.

> Time, without the means of filling it with suitable program content, is worthless. Educational programming on the commercial facilities, then, is too often inadequately planned (in educational terms) and ineffectively produced (in broadcasting terms) simply because these jobs are left to volunteers or to the least capable and the lowest paid.[15]

Many national organizations attempt to correct for this by producing superior tape or kinescope recordings for later re-issue over the local broadcast stations. The programs are sometimes excellent but they suffer from a lack of adequate local promotion and, since they bring the station no income, may be shown at hours when the adult audience cannot be reached effectively.

REINFORCED AND INTEGRATED EDUCATIONAL PROGRAMS

Most of the educational offerings of the mass media, with or without the participation of other educational programming agencies like the schools, consist of non-reinforced offerings; that is, the total educational offering consists of the television program (or program series) , the newspaper or magazine article (or series) , or the book to be read. While the organizers of these offerings *hope* that people will utilize the information presented or discuss the ideas set forth, they do not plan systematically for this to occur. Sometimes it occurs voluntarily, as in the case of informal study groups that developed around a series of family life television programs, but this is scattered and unsystematic and unpredictable.

Several promising experiments are under way, however, both to reinforce the program offerings of any one mass medium and to relate the program offerings of several mass media to each other. *Parents' Magazine,* as previously reported, produces discussion material for parent groups with the expectation that the other material in the magazine will be valuable background reading for the members. McKune found thirteen educational institutions provided some organized follow-up with telecourse enrollees.[16]

The experimental work of Johnson with radio in San Bernardino and currently with television in St. Louis, of Jarvis in Salt Lake City, and Booth at Antioch College in Yellow Springs, Ohio, furnish dramatic examples of the utilization of several educational media in relation to each other. The essential feature of these efforts is the self-organized "viewing posts" or discussion groups (averaging 12 members) that meet usually in private homes.

The name "St. Louis Metroplex Assembly" has been adopted as the continuing name for a demonstration in that city. The assembly operates twice a year, each time for a period of six to ten weeks. Each evening program consists of three units: (1) a half-hour TV presentation on the issue of the week; (2) a one-hour discussion by the more than two hundred listening groups, the findings and questions of which are telephoned in to the station; and (3) a concluding half-hour television discussion.

The groups are also serviced with discussion guides prepared by the Civic Education Center of Washington University, reading lists of books available from the public library, printed materials (such as fact sheets on the local issue) , and newspaper articles appearing before the television program of the week. A major strength lies in the fact that people of widely different educational, occupational, religious, and social backgrounds participate.

Jarvis in Salt Lake City has developed through the University of Utah Extension a program similar in format and appearing under the title "Peoples Lobby."

In general, the experience of adult educators with mass media has established the fact that no one medium is the complete and final answer to the educational needs of adults. Television may be the most important invention since print, but it is still no substitute for print. Furthermore, the ultimate determination of the value of any educational program lies in what happens to people. The educator who uses the mass media skillfully and with sensitivity to the widely varying needs, interests, and capabilities of the people he seeks to reach will unquestionably make major contributions to the further development of adult education in the United States.

MAJOR ISSUES AND PROBLEMS

The further development of the potential of the mass media for adult education involves the following issues and problems:

1. *Quality of programming.* Mass media offerings will invite failure if the general public comes finally to associate educational programs with low quality. While there is some evidence that most radio and television stations and many educational groups understand this fact, considerable unease arises from the willingness of many educational agencies to seek and sometimes obtain air time for which both planning and production are inadequate. Poor quality will kill the educational potential of the media more rapidly than anything else.

2. *Finance.* The ability of educators to sustain an effective and separate broadcast service rests largely on developing a broad base of financial support in place of complete dependence on one or two major foundations. The financial weakness of local educational television and radio stations hampers their work, while the poverty of many adult education groups desiring to utilize radio or television frequently results in programming of poor quality.

3. *Co-ordination.* Will the different media and the different kinds of adult education groups that seek to utilize the media really develop close communication and co-ordination? Will they be willing and able to perceive the unique qualities of each medium and blend their efforts in a richly integrated approach to common educational goals?

4. *A value structure.* There is tenuous evidence that a value structure may be developing within the media; it is most manifest in the kinds of programming decisions educators make when free from various operational pressures. Will educators seek to make this value structure clear and explicit, providing thereby an educational framework for their efforts? Will there be more deliberate decisions made, for example, by people in different media about the importance of educating people about certain parts of the world or in such major current developments as science?

5. *A sense of direction.* Will educators acquire a sense of direction with respect to the social context in which they work? Particularly, will they

recognize, in time to be effective instruments of change, the metropolitanization of the country now taking place? Will they learn to employ the mass media to develop clear images of the good society in the realistic context of the metropolitan arena within which the living generation must keep its rendezvous with destiny?

Footnotes

[1]*Net News,* (Ann Arbor: National Educational Television and Radio Center, Spring 1959) p. 1.

[2]Richard B. Hull, *Educational Television in the United States, Status Report—1957* (An unpublished report prepared for the Educational Television and Radio Center, the Fund for Adult Education, and The Ohio State University Committee on Telecommunications, Columbus, Ohio, December, 1957), p. 9.

[3]Edward R. Murrow, "The Responsibility of Television," one program in a series, *The Press and the People,* moderated by Louis Lyons and produced by WGBH-TV, Boston, 1958.

[4]Howard Mumford Jones. "The Renaissance Man Today," *Saturday Review* (June 20, 1959), p. 11.

[5]Richard E. Chapin, *Mass Communications* (East Lansing: Michigan State University Press, 1957), p. 9.

[6]David H. Clift and Dan Lacy, "How Books Get to Adult Readers," *Adult Reading,* Fifty-fifth Yearbook of the National Society for the Study of Education (Chicago: NSSE, 1956), p. 191.

[7]*Ibid.,* p. 200.

[8]C. Hartley Grattan, *In Quest of Knowledge* (New York: Association Press, 1955), p. 295, quoting *Report of the Study for the Ford Foundation on Policy and Program* (Detroit, November, 1949).

[9]Robert M. Hutchins and Others, *A Free and Responsible Press* (Chicago: University of Chicago Press, 1947), p. 21.

[10]John Hohenberg, *The Pulitzer Prize Story* (New York: Columbia University Press 1959), p. 37.

[11]Parker Wheatley, Public Affairs Director of KMOX-TV in St. Louis and former director of the educational channel in Boston, WGBH, made this formulation in a conversation with the author.

[12]Murrow, *op. cit.*

[13]*Telecourses for Credit,* Vol. 5 (East Lansing, Michigan: Michigan State University, Continuing Education Service, 1958), foreword.

[14]William K. Cumming, *This Is Educational Television* (Ann Arbor: Edwards Brothers, Inc., 1954), pp. 250 and 258.

[15]Sydney H. Head, *Broadcasting in America* (Boston: Houghton Mifflin Co., 1956), pp. 403-4.

[16]*Telecourses for Credit, op. cit.*

Selected Readings

Books

Barnouw, Erik. *Mass Communication.* New York, Toronto: Rinehart & Company, 1956.

Bogart, Leo. *The Age of Television.* New York: Frederick Ungar Publishing Co., 1956.

Bryson, Lyman (ed.). *The Communication of Ideas.* A series of addresses published by the Institute for Religious and Social Studies. New York: Harper & Bros., 1948.

Callahan, Jennie Waugh. *Television in School, College, and Community.* New York: McGraw-Hill Book Co., 1953.

Chapin, Richard E. *Mass Communications: A Statistical Analysis.* East Lansing: Michigan State University Press, 1957.

Commission on Freedom of the Press. *A Free and Responsible Press.* Chicago: University of Chicago Press, 1947.

Cumming, William Kenneth. *This is Educational Television.* Ann Arbor: Edwards Brothers, 1954.

Elliott, William Y. (ed.). *Television's Impact on American Culture.* East Lansing: Michigan State University Press, 1956.

Head, Sydney W. *Broadcasting in America: A Survey of Television and Radio.* Boston: Houghton Mifflin Co., 1956.

Hohenberg, John (ed.). *The Pulitzer Prize Story.* New York: Columbia University Press, 1959.

Lerner, Daniel. *The Passing of Traditional Society.* Glencoe, Illinois: The Free Press, 1958.

National Society for the Study of Education. *Mass Media and Education,* Fifty-third Yearbook of the National Society for the Study of Education, Part II. Chicago: University of Chicago Press, 1954.

Peterson, Theodore, Schramm, Wilbur, and Siebert, Fred S., *Four Theories of the Press.* Urbana: University of Illinois Press, 1956.

Schramm, Wilbur (ed.). *Mass Communications.* A book of readings selected and edited for the Institute of Communications Research in the University of Illinois. Urbana: University of Illinois Press, 1949.

Articles and Periodicals

Adler, Kenneth P. "Mass Media Responsibility to the Political Elite," *Journal of Communication,* III (Summer, 1958), 51-52.

Educational Television Factsheet. Washington: Joint Council on Educational Television, 1957-59.

Educational Television Newsletter. Washington: American Council on Education, 1957-59.

Fletcher, C. Scott. "Battle of the Curriculum in the Sputnik Age," *Adult Education,* VIII (Winter, 1958), 113-23.

Jones, Howard Mumford. "The Renaissance Man Today," *Saturday Review,* June 20, 1959, 10-12.

Murrow, Edward R. "The Responsibility of Television," *The Press and the People,* Boston: WGBH-TV, 1958.

"Mass Communications—An Atlantic Supplement," *Atlantic,* CC (December, 1957), 79-160.

NET News. Ann Arbor: National Educational Television and Radio Center, 1957-1959.

Reports

Educational Policies Commission. *Mass Communication and Education.* Washington: Government Printing Office, 1958.

Educational Television and Radio Center. *Educational Television Today.* Ann Arbor: The Center, March, 1958.

CHAPTER 27

MUSEUMS AND ART INSTITUTES AND ADULT EDUCATION

CLIFFORD GREGG
Director
Chicago Natural History Museum

WHAT IS A MUSEUM

The word "museum" means many things to many people. This is necessarily so as a museum may include either a single collection of related objects or many collections of related and unrelated objects in many fields of interest. Such museums as the Metropolitan Museum of Art in New York City, the Fine Arts Museum in Boston, the Art Institute of Chicago, and the National Gallery of Art in Washington include many of the finest examples of art objects of many kinds and are of such quality that a visit to any of those cities is justified by a visit to the museums alone. By contrast, a museum may be a lonely and dilapidated building at some remote crossroads where there are housed a few forlorn objects relating to the early history of the local village or to one of its so-called prominent families; but to call such an institution educational would stretch the imagination beyond reasonable limits. It is important, therefore, that we use the word museum in its best sense—a research and educational institution which collects and preserves for study, interpretation, and exhibition appropriate objects within its legitimate field for the purpose of increasing and diffusing knowledge. Collections are the unique feature of museums.

COLLECTIONS AND STAFF

Dictionaries point to the origin of the word "museum" as "a temple sacred to a muse." The housing of collections is also stressed and rightly so, because a museum which fails to assemble and to preserve for posterity objects in the field of its studies is neglecting one of its primary obligations to posterity. But a museum is more than a building, and more than a building which houses collections. As a library houses and classifies books, so a museum houses and classifies its specimens. The museum is a library of specimens. The specimens must be preserved as vital records, to be re-examined and perhaps re-interpreted in the years to come. Knowledge is not static; past knowledge is influenced by continuing observation and study. Only an adequate collection permits the museum curator a reasonable degree of selectivity in the material to be displayed. Further, without adequate collections a museum would be unable to attract to its staff men of outstanding research ability, as such persons would not ally themselves with institutions which failed to provide them opportunity to exercise and improve their scholarship. The staff is essential to interpret the meanings of specimens and to present graphically the stories they have to tell. I am in complete agreement with Dr. Hans Huth's statement that "the museum cannot accomplish its purpose without research by its staff." Neither can it establish its authority without staff members of outstanding quality.

MANY KINDS OF MUSEUMS

It is impossible to define a "typical" museum, as museums vary widely in their objectives and are limited by their resources. Usually, the more specialized institutions are found in the larger cities. For example, the Chicago region has an art museum, a museum of history, two natural-history museums, a planetarium, two zoological gardens, an aquarium, a museum of archaeology, a museum of arms and armor, a scientific and industrial museum, as well as an arboretum and conservatories which display living plants. There are, in addition, many private or teaching collections which may or may not be classified as museums. In some cities, many diverse fields of interest are combined into a single museum. The Los Angeles County Museum and the Carnegie Museum at Pittsburgh are good examples of institutions covering both art and natural history. The excellent Buffalo Museum of Science includes not only natural history collections, but a planetarium and an aquarium as well. In addition, its educational work includes certain of the manual arts. The Smithsonian Institution in Washington, considered by many persons to be a single red stone building south of the Mall, is in fact the holding corporation which included at the end of its first century the following separate units: The U. S. National Museum, the National Gallery of Art, National Collection of Fine Arts, Freer Gallery of Art, Bureau of American Ethnology, Institute of Social Anthropology, International Exchange Service, National Zoological Park, Astrophysical Observatory, and the Divisions of Radiation and Organisms. This institution reflects the concise statement of James Smithson, its founder, who provided funds for "the increase and diffusion of knowledge among men."

When many diverse fields of study are combined in a single institution, there is always the danger of bias with relation to budgets, exhibition space, and opportunities for research. The Smithsonian Institution has avoided this hazard by establishing separate museums to work in different fields of study.

VARIETY OF SUBJECTS

There is no limit to the variety of subjects in museums. In New York state alone, the following institutions are listed among the membership of the American Association of Museums:

> Hall of Fame of the Trotter
> Bell System Historical Museum
> Chase National Bank Museum of Moneys of the World
> Fort Ticonderoga Museum
> Museum of American Comedy
> Corning Museum of Glass
> National Baseball Hall of Fame and Museum
> Wood Library—Museum of Anaesthesiology
> National Museum of Racing

For further variety, we might mention Colonial Williamsburg—which is a collection of buildings restored accurately to their state of greatest usefulness, representing in many buildings a museum of early colonial life in America. The Mariners' Museum at Newport News, Virginia, and the Whaling Museum at New Bedford are institutions of unusual appeal to those interested in the ships that sail, and have sailed, the seas.

Anyone is free to gather the objects that interest him—whether they be matchbook covers, postage stamps, paintings, or porcelains—and to arrange and display them for the interest and edification of his fellow man. Whether such collections remain stored and static or useful and educational depends upon the knowledge and ability of the curator or research scientist to translate hidden values into understandable ideas.

With the variety of objectives and the multiplicity of patterns of organization a clear picture of the museum in education can be brought out only through an understanding of various types of museums. They vary in their fields of study, and in the area they are designed to serve.

A national, state, county or municipal museum may include almost anything, as the adjective applied usually refers only to the authority which governs it. The university museum, however, is normally a distinct educational aid to one or more areas of the university studies, and in some instances the university museum is outstanding in its own right. Typical examples are the University of Pennsylvania Museum and the Oriental Institute of the University of Chicago. The Museum of Comparative Zoology at Harvard, while not designed to attract the general public, has distinguished itself for decades in its research and the training of natural scientists.

CLASSIFICATION OF MUSEUMS

Art-Historical

Classification according to subject matter is vital if a museum is to be an educational institution rather than a warehouse of miscellany.

The art museum came into being through man's desire to surround himself with beautiful things. As time passed, art collections became the basis of the study of the history of art. Today, the art museum may include in its collections all manner of objects in which man has displayed his artistic ingenuity and creativity from Maori war clubs to paintings, statuary, porcelains, textiles, and medals worked in as diverse materials as stone, plaster, metal, wood, cloth, or perhaps any substance. The sand-painting of the American Indian and the grotesque modern art figures of steel wire indicate something of the range of possibilities when man seeks to express himself.

Knowledge of the past may well be a guide to the future. A collection of historical objects, properly interpreted, constitutes a historical museum. Perhaps some of the older museums of this type arose not from a desire to interpret the meaning of the past but rather from the urge to glorify the collector. Certainly, personal glorification was the motive in ancient Egypt when a Pharaoh caused the name of his illustrious predecessor to be chiseled out of a hieroglyphic epic, and his own name substituted.

Even in modern times the museum administrator must be alert to resist the tendency to make his institution a shrine for the famous dead. Enlightened resistance to public pressures is definitely a function of museum administration.

There is inspiration as well as education in the historical museum. Who can view the tiny "Spirit of St. Louis" in which Charles A. Lindbergh made the pioneer solo flight across the Atlantic without a feeling of deep respect for the courage of the man? Yet, the Smithsonian Institution is hardly to be called a Lindbergh shrine. The collection of formal dresses worn by the wives of our Presidents may provoke surprise and laughter; nevertheless one glimpses the march of history as depicted in the evolution of party dresses.

Within the field of historical museums are many whose interests are highly specialized. The Army Museum at West Point, Colonial Williamsburg in Virginia, and countless other institutions focusing on the life of an individual or the development of an area or region fall within this group.

Science Museum and Planetarium

The term "science" is so broad that its application to a museum gives little information as to the scope of that institution. Therefore, in most instances clarification is provided, such as "natural science," "science and industry," or "astronomical museum and observatory" which presents science without that word being mentioned.

The planetarium today is basking in the limelight of space travel, artificial satellites and planned planetary conquest. It is fundamental that we understand as much as we can about the universe in which we occupy such an infinitesimal spot. The first Zeiss planetarium to come from Jena to the United States is the Adler planetarium in Chicago. Others are located now in Los Angeles, New York, Philadelphia, and Pittsburgh. A small "spitz" planetarium is now in the field, and while limited in its operation it has the obvious advantage of being within the price range of many American museums.

Science and Industry

A museum of science and industry seeks to show the application of science in the industrial field. Philadelphia's Franklin Institute is outstanding in this field, showing much of the history of scientific development as well as its modern usages. In varying degree many of the same objectives and applications are to be found in "commercial" museums, "industrial" museums, and museums fostered by manufacturing corporations to tell their own stories. The "economic" exhibits in the natural history museums tend to fall within the same category. Cleveland's Health Museum is an institution which relates science to human welfare rather than to industrial progress. So, too, is the Army Medical Museum in Washington, D. C., although the stark realism of many of its exhibits would tend to repel rather than to attract visitors. The Chicago Museum of Science and Industry has demonstrated that scientific phenomena can be made attractive and understandable by being interpreted rather than merely displayed. All museums of this type emphasize the effects of technological advance on the lives of human beings.

Museums of Natural History

The scope of the natural history museum includes the mineral, vegetable, and animal kingdoms—in other words, every natural thing in the world. Obviously, this is an impossible field for complete presentation, and most natural history museums tend to limit their areas of interest to those which they can accomplish best. Botany is omitted in many institutions due to the difficulty of preparing adequate exhibition material, although the Chicago Natural History Museum includes botany as one of its four scientific departments. The arboretum or botanical garden displays living plants and usually has an adequate study collection of herbarium specimens.

In geology the museum interprets the materials, history, structure, and dynamic forces which are constantly changing the earth. Paleontology, due to its often spectacular exhibition material, sometimes tends to over-shadow the importance of the structure, changes, and composition of the earth itself. Yet the fossil remains are the buried history of prehistoric life, both animal and vegetable, on the earth.

Zoology has a constant appeal to the adult public, whether it be pre-sented in aquariums and zoological gardens or in the museum. Each type of institution has its advantages. The zoo can show the animal as it moves, breathes, eats, drinks and, conducts its life within the narrow confines of its cage or pen. Unfortunately, a lazy, overfed, and damaged living specimen often presents a misimpression of a "wild" animal. A caged eagle is not the same as the one soaring above you in the free air. And many nocturnal mammals in the zoo present an impression of perpetual sleep, except to the night watchman making his rounds.

The museum has the advantage of presenting the animal at its best, in typical natural surroundings, provided there is adequate scholarship available to know the truth, and adequate technical skill to reproduce the proper setting. The museum specimen is always available and holds a pose long enough to give the viewer more than a fleeting glimpse.

Man himself is a popular subject for museum presentation. The anthropologist approaches him through

(1) physical anthropology, the analysis of how he is put together, and how one race or natural group differs physically from another;

(2) archaeology, the study of man's buried history through excavating his buried houses, cities and civilizations, and

(3) ethnology, the study of contemporary primitive man.

In both archaelogy and ethnology, we try to discover how primitive people used the natural objects about them for their own advancement. It is often disconcerting to learn how much development has been accom-plished with so little, while we today accomplish so little with so much of both material and knowledge at hand.

Many objects of art are found among ethnological and archaeological collections as well as in the art museums (which seek to portray the artistic phase of a people's cuture), because ethnologists seek to portray man's entire cultural pattern.

INTERPRETATION

While museums often display rare and curious objects, such displays in themselves contribute little to the educational process. I could not do better than to quote Dr. Robert Maynard Hutchins, then Chancellor of the University of Chicago, speaking at the meeting commemorating the fiftieth anniversary of the (now) Chicago Natural History Museum:

> The characteristic of knowledge is organization, which implies understanding, ordering, and interpretation. A heterogeneous collection of facts is not knowledge;

a heterogeneous collection of objects is not an educational institution. The art of the museum scientist, which is displayed at the highest pitch in this building, lies in the presentation of objects on an organized plan to convey meaning. For it is not the object that is important; it is the meaning of the object. The educated man is not the one whose mind is a waste-basket, or even an Encyclopedia Britannica, of unrelated facts. He is one who grasps the significance of what he sees. An educational institution is one which helps its students to make these interpretations, or at least to learn how to make them.

I have sometimes defined a museum as a collection of descriptive labels illustrated by specimens, because understanding is not to be achieved by merely viewing an object. A strange and unknown animal is still a strange and unknown animal after it has been viewed by someone who has no training or understanding in the field of zoology. However, if this unknown beast is displayed in a scene illustrating its natural habitat and is supported by a label giving information which cannot be gained from the inspection of the specimen itself, the educational process is at work. Inaccurate or inept labeling contributes to misunderstanding and compounds ignorance. A label stating that an animal "lives in the south" may mean in the southern part of the United States, or possibly in the southern part of the state, or even in Central or South America. It is essential, therefore, that in preparing museum labels every word be carefully weighed. To label a rabbit as "a long-eared fur-bearing animal" apparently assumes that the museum visitor will not look at the specimen. But we assume that people visit the museum *in order that they may* view the specimens. We assume, further, that they would like to know what object they are looking at and some of the things which distinguish it from other more or less similar objects.

The exhibition labels are, in effect, the written textbook of the museum. A good label must be short enough to be read and long enough to have meaning. It may refer to a single specimen or to several specimens, and in many instances there must be additional labels covering categories or groups.

Guide books are often general directories to the exhibits or catalogues of educational opportunities, although art museums frequently publish guides or catalogues describing in detail the objects displayed in regular or special exhibitions.

THE MUSEUM IN ADULT EDUCATION

The particular genius of the museum is its ability to present reality rather than theory. A three-dimensional object instantly dispels misinformation and often speaks more clearly and simply than pages of descriptive matter. Many of the stories of Marco Polo were not believed until others had the opportunity to see for themselves the objects he had described. But, not having a captive audience, a museum seeks to present its exhibits attractively as well as logically. The aesthetic appeal is essential, not to the art museum alone, but to all other museums as well. An attractive exhibit invites one to linger and to learn.

A museum as an educational institution may be self-sufficient. Yet, co-operation and outreach multiply educational opportunities. Co-operation with universities combines the realities of the museum with the lecture course, the laboratory, and the library. Knowledge gained from books, lectures, and laboratory experimentation is supplemented and reinforced by contacts with the actual specimens in the museum. What book or photograph can transmit accurately the grandeur of the elephant, the iridescent beauty of the hummingbird or the inspiration of a great painting?

Museum staff members present lectures at or away from the museum, and serve the interested public through radio and television as well. Museum research often begins with expeditions to remote areas of the world, to gather the specimens for future laboratory study. The resulting museum publications serve as authentic bases for education world-wide. Traveling exhibitions such as those sponsored by the Smithsonian Institution take the benefits of the museum to distant points and to those who have no other access to these educational opportunities. Catalogues, bulletins, books, photographs, and news stories from the museums of America serve to inform the intelligent public of new fields of exploration, research, and discovery.

Adult education is well served by discovery and recording of new information in the books and periodicals that become the source material for other studies. Perhaps the most important contribution of the museum in adult education is the fact that it is pioneering—presenting new facts, new ideas, and new source material.

Happy is the museum visitor whose interests are sufficiently developed that he may be selective. Too often the visitor tries to absorb everything that a museum offers in a single visit, just as a small boy approaches his first smorgasbord. Each receives too little of anything, but too much of everything. The all-inclusive museum visit results in mental indigestion and physical exhaustion. Colleges and universities do not suffer from this strange complex. No student at Harvard or the University of Illinois would feel the need of sampling every course, or even every college in the university.

Adult education is not automatic; mere exposure to educational opportunities does not produce a learned man. Serious attention and a desire to learn are prerequisites, but museums do manage to make the learning process easy and pleasant for those who are willing to make the effort. And often the inspiration received from a museum exhibit transforms the casual visitor into a true seeker after knowledge.

The museums of America present a priceless treasury of educational materials arranged, well presented, and available at nominal or no cost to those who have the desire to learn. As automation and long life-expectancy combine to give more leisure time to the people of the United States, the museums will continue to grow in importance in providing educational and inspirational media that will help them to lead richer and fuller lives.

Selected Readings

Adam, T. R. *The Civic Value of Museums.* New York: American Association for Adult Education, 1937.

Adam, T. R. *The Museum and Popular Culture.* New York: American Association for Adult Education, 1939.

Coleman, Lawrence Vail. *College and University Museums: A Message for College and University Presidents.* Washington: The American Association of Museums, 1942.

"Fifty Years of Progress." *Field Museum News,* Vol. 14 (September-October, 1943), 9-10. Chicago: Field Museum of Natural History.

True, Webster P. *The First Hundred Years of the Smithsonian Institution: 1846-1946.* Washington: The Institution, 1946.

CHAPTER 28

ADULT EDUCATION THROUGH PROPRIETARY SCHOOLS

H. D. HOPKINS
Executive Secretary
The Accrediting Commission for Business Schools

The private school is basically an American institution. It is deeply rooted in our whole system of education. In elementary and secondary education it was the early pioneer, but retreated before the development of the public school system; but it is still represented by many excellent schools in these areas.

In general, the emphasis has changed to where private schools now serve specialized fields, providing for educational needs of business and industry, professional training, and many areas of social and cultural nature. They exist and flourish because they meet a public need and demand. They provide an open door to further education which might not otherwise exist. They are not substitutes for, nor in basic competition with, endowed or publicly financed and operated schools.

They carry the general term of "proprietary schools" because they are independently financed and operated, with the operator assuming the risk of loss or gain. In structure, they are single-ownership institutions, partnerships, or incorporated bodies, with an increasing percentage of them now having corporate non-profit status.

Without subsidy or tax support, they meet their operating costs through income from tuitions. They pay taxes in support of other education and are subject to state and local regulations covering their operation. They constitute a very important element of the nation's education, reaching in their major divisions more than 5,000,000 adults annually.

The past history of this field, like that of the high school and college, exhibits lack of over-all unity of program and purpose. Strong, well-qualified educators established individual schools in line with their own personal thinking, and these expanded into chains of schools following the pattern of the pilot institution. The characterizing growth since 1945 has been to attain effectiveness of national organization and the development of a national concept of method and purpose. It marked the growing acceptance of educational responsibility and a clearer concept of the role of the private school. There is a movement away from belief that this is a personal activity, to recognition of public interest and concern. The response has been a realistic broadening of fields of instruction to meet changing business and industrial needs and more positive enforcement of educational standards and control of operational methods.

The major sections are now effectively organized and directed and there is general movement in other sections of the field to perfect for themselves such organization and criteria. In several of these sections this has included the creation and operation of agencies of accreditation, designed to meet in the public interest professional evaluation based on criteria of educational competence and sound operational policies.

The broad areas covered by the proprietary schools are indicated by the following list of types of schools and training programs:

Accounting, advertising, airline personnel, art (commercial and cultural), barbering, beauty, business administration, charm, Dale Carnegie, dancing, dramatic art, design, dental technology, driving schools, electronics, engineering technology, estimating, flight, foremanship, hairdressing, homemaking, insurance, interior design, languages, modeling, music, nursing (home and practical), real estate, secretarial, sewing, switchboard, tailoring, typing and shorthand, voice, and the whole wide area in crafts and trades.

This chapter cannot hope to give adequate attention to all these types in detail. There are, however, certain sections—those in which accreditation is now a working procedure—which merit wider exposition. They are the independent schools of business, the home study or correspondence schools, and the technical schools.

INDEPENDENT SCHOOLS OF BUSINESS

The independent schools of business cover the minor and major office skills, bookkeeping and accounting, business administration, and newly developing techniques in this age of automation.

An exact census of the numbers of these schools is impossible. The field has been reduced in numbers because of the increase in the teaching of these subjects in high school and college, and through normal attrition, consolidation, and the slowing down of veterans' education. But the field is again expanding as demands for this area of education increase. This number includes small schools with limited enrollments, facilities, and personalized instruction. But the heart of this field consists of schools with enrollments of 500 and more, with a few departmentalized institutions with 2,000 students or more. In the main, these institutions require high school completion for enrollment and provide programs which include courses from a few weeks in length to four years. They graduate from certificate or diploma programs 200,000 students annually and reach in total enrollments 600,000 students a year.

Current demand for their graduates exceeds, particularly in the secretarial field, by seven to one the numbers available. A major concern is the tendency of students to leave school before training programs are completed because of the availability of employment even for the inadequately prepared.

The major agency serving the independent colleges of business schools is the National Association and Council of Business Schools. Its function is the promotion of sound educational standards and ethical business practices throughout the business school field. To this end, it works with federal, state, and local educational institutions and authorities. It has served this field since 1912, and in 1951 sponsored The Accrediting Commission for Business Schools. This agency, developed in accordance with criteria established by the U. S. Office of Education, has been recognized by The U. S. Commissioner of Education as a national accrediting agency.

The characteristics of these institutions are:

Resident attendance

Flexibility which permits ready adaptation to changing needs

Specialized programs of study wherein the training is specifically keyed to the field of study, designed to provide maximum coverage with definite time economy

Faculty requirement of adequate educational background plus required experience in the areas taught

Free, continuous placement service to all graduates

Training that is keyed to area and community needs

Reasons for selection of this source of education are:

Economy of time afforded those with financial or other reasons for not acquiring the four-year liberal arts collegiate program

Thoroughness and completeness of training

Personalized attention given to instruction

Responsibility taken by institutions to assist graduates in location of suitable employment

These institutions emphasize adequacy of preparation, and provide minimum requirements for graduation as follows:

Stenographic program	36 weeks
Secretarial program	48 weeks
Junior accountancy program	36 weeks
Executive secretarial program	72 weeks
Professional accounting program	72 weeks
Business administration program	72 weeks

To this general program are added many special developments, both lesser in time and more exacting. In training for general office skills, recommended speeds of 120 words a minute in shorthand and 60 words per minute in typing are in line with seeking to upgrade the capacities of those going into the nation's offices. There is now a growing emphasis on specialized skills in line with automation, both in machine operation and increased efficiency in mathematics, English, and science.

The Accrediting Commission for Business Schools was established in recognition of responsibility to the public and to further emphasize the necessity to meet demands for educational excellence. The commission is autonomous and is composed of eight persons from the independent colleges of business and five persons from the collegiate field and industry.

Essential requirements to accreditation and maintenance of accreditation are:

> All additions or changes in faculty to have baccalaureate degrees or better
> Establishment of a working library under adequate supervision within the school
> Maintenance of a program of student services embracing sound counseling and guidance
> Adequate testing programs
> Proper space and facilities for the job to be done
> Utilization of college calibre texts and audio-visual materials
> Teacher loads and class sizes limited to prevent impairment of quality of teaching
> Inclusion of required general education materials and courses

This branch of training is one wherein the employing public has placed major reliance. It has shown its ability to expand to meet emergency needs, as is evidenced by the more than one million veterans who secured their educational training through these schools.

CORRESPONDENCE SCHOOLS

The correspondence schools have operated since 1890 and have coverage of 1,500,000 students a year. The major agency serving this branch of education in The National Home Study Council.

Unlike the resident business schools, the programs of the correspondence schools are more widely diversified, as shown by the areas of service of their accredited schools:

> Landscaping and gardening, architecture, apprentice training, plumbing, diesel engine, drafting, engineering, business administration, building construction and blueprint reading, surveying, firemanship, mathematics, sheet metal, auto mechanics, commercial art, electronics, radio, TV servicing and broadcasting, auxiliary nursing, voca-

tional rehabilitation subjects, industrial electronics and automation, dressmaking, courses for the blind, business and secretarial subjects, air conditioning, heating, refrigeration, criminal and civil investigation, pre-high school, high school and college subjects, traffic management, hotel management, factory management and executive training, camera repair, floristry, airline training, photography, professional locksmithing, upholstery, real estate.

The need for regulation and supervision in the public interest was recognized by The National Home Study Council, resulting in the creation of an Accrediting Commission for Home Study Schools, which is recognized by the U. S. Commissioner of Education as a national accrediting agency. It operates as an independent body and is comprised of nine members—five from the home study field and four from education and business.

The aim is not to establish an identical mold but to encourage development toward individual excellence. Among the requirements for accreditation are:

Clearly stated educational objectives
Sound instructional methods and materials
Qualified faculties
Adequate financial resources to carry out obligations to students
Screening of students to accept only those who can benefit from the training
Honesty in advertising and promotional materials

TECHNICAL SCHOOLS

The proprietary technical schools operate in the engineering field in development of engineering technical aides and assistants. They are incorporated in the accreditation of The Engineering Council for Professional Development, an agency recognized and listed by the U. S. Office of Education. Institutions affiliated with The National Council of Technical Schools are part of the wider field embracing many collegiate institutions. Approximately 30 per cent of this roster are private institutions and are recognized and accredited by ECPD because of the strength of their professional curricula.

Of note is the specialized system of schools under The Dale Carnegie Corporation, which holds classes in 850 cities. Berlitz Language Schools are located in forty American cities, in addition to their world-wide affiliations.

PROBLEMS AND PROSPECTS

A major problem confronting all these types of schools is the unawareness of the American public of the services these schools are equipped to render. Financing is made more difficult because of the demands for advertising and promotion, but they have capacity which they will utilize to expand facilities and services as necessity arises. Too often they operate without recognition or assistance of educational agencies in the various states and face real difficulties because they must of necessity be entirely self-supporting. They have facility in working to achieve sound legislation in behalf of all education in the belief that each segment of education has obligation to all youth, and believe that the maximum results cannot be achieved until there can be found a common clearinghouse throughout all education for the maximum utilization of our educational resources.

These institutions operate at no cost to the taxpayer. They recognize and operate under proper supervision. They are assets to our total educational effort. In the inventory that each community should make of its educational resources, these should be definitely appraised and assigned such part of the load as is reasonable for them to carry. The future is one fraught with educational demands that either cannot be met or only inadequately met unless all facilities are employed. Here is an area of education capable of expansion, receptive to whatever regulation is in the public interest, willing to meet these regulations, and able to prevent some of our people from being denied the privilege of further education.

CHAPTER 29

PUBLIC SCHOOL ADULT EDUCATION

ROBERT A. LUKE
Assistant Director
Division of Adult Education Service
National Education Association

HISTORICAL BACKGROUND AND SCOPE

The founding of the American system of free public education was in itself an adventure in adult education. One of the chief protagonists for the common school, Horace Mann, was confronted with the task of educating the adult population of his day to the importance of a free education. Contemporary with Horace Mann was the lyceum movement, the main purpose of which was to improve the common schools. As is shown in Chapter 2, the lyceum was one of the first steps in the organized adult education movement in this country.

As the public school adult education movement was getting underway, the concept of the adult education role of the public schools was primarily thought of as offering opportunities for immigrants from abroad to learn English or to enable boys and girls who had to leave school to go to work an opportunity to complete their formal education in night school. These concepts of the role of the public school in adult education remain highly important. The extent of the public school's educational responsibility to these adults is illustrated by the fact that there are an estimated 3,000,000 foreign-born individuals in the United States who have not become citizens and 2,000,000 adults who have not gone to school at all. The 1950 census indicated that there are 10,000,000 functional illiterates in the United States and that 26 per cent of the population twenty-five years of age and above had not graduated from elementary schools. During the year 1950-51, over 16 per cent of all recruits were rejected for military service on the grounds of educational deficiency.

In time, the emphasis of the public school's adult education program was broadened from that of a strictly remedial program to one which made available opportunities for employed adults to study new trades or to increase their skills in their present occupations. Although vocational classes were being offered for adults in most early programs, the passage of the Smith-Hughes Act in 1917 provided great stimulation for adult vocational education across the country.

Along with this development in adult education was the recognition of homemaking as an important vocation, and the public schools began offering educational services designed to help mothers and fathers create a better and more comfortable home for themselves and their children. By 1928 parent classes had been recognized as a responsibility of the New York State Department of Education. California's program of state-sponsored parent education classes was underway during the year 1926. Since then many local school districts—either with or without the stimulation of leadership from the state department of education—have established programs of parent education that are comprehensive and still expanding.

As adult education programming moved into the second half of the twentieth century, the public schools began to address their curriculum for adults toward still another significant area: the systematic and self-conscious provision of opportunities for all adults in the community—including those who already possess a full measure of formal education—to have the opportunities to grow in wisdom and to acquire the skills necessary for making decisions as citizens of a democracy. While this has always been an implicit value and an assumed outcome of all adult education, enrichment of the curriculum to include activities in the arts, sciences, public affairs, and the humanities specifically designed to foster and develop economic, political, and cultural literacies represents a relatively new emphasis.

One of the program resources that has helped public schools move into this area is the study discussion materials of The Fund for Adult Education. Using these as a basic curriculum guide, many communities have planned programs in the area of economic, cultural and political affairs that otherwise would have been difficult for them to develop. Interesting courses in public affairs have also been developed locally. For example, in New York a number of communities have established discussion groups which run concurrently with the state legislature and consider the issues confronting that body. "Know-Your-Candidates" political forums have been held in numerous communities in California and New York. In Minnesota the State Director of Adult Education was responsible for organizing a "Know-Your-State-Government" program for newly elected members of the state legislature.

The modern adult education program is also witnessing a growth in kinds of adult education methods that differ markedly from traditional classroom procedure. Forums, film-forums, lecture series, workshops, conferences, and informal discussion groups are all frequently-used devices.

In addition, in many communities, the public schools are carrying their program to the entire community by means of television. In Washington, D. C., for example, television instruction has been offered by the public schools in shorthand, typewriting, and family finance. A class in basic mathematics was televised by the Milwaukee public schools. The adult education program of the Omaha public schools included a community forum entitled "Private Line" which provided for telephone interaction between groups viewing the program throughout the city and the forum participants in the television studio. In Denver parent education programs are carried by the public schools' television station to various community centers.

CURRICULUM AND PARTICIPATION

A study made in 1951 indicated marked differences in enrollment trends in the large, medium-sized, and small cities.[1] In the metropolitan areas, the most rapid expansion of enrollment was in public affairs, safety and driver education, and remedial education. In middle-sized cities, the greatest increase was in recreational skills, followed by agriculture, with safety and driver education in third place. In the small cities, safety and driver education was in first place followed by recreational skills and parent and family education.

The subjects in order of enrollment in all schools in 1951 were ranked as follows:

1. Civic and public affairs
2. Commercial and distributive education
3. Vocational and technical education
4. General academic education
5. Homemaking education
6. Americanization and elementary education
7. Health and physical education
8. Parent and family-life education
9. Practical arts and crafts
10. Fine arts
11. Recreational skills
12. Safety and driver education
13. Agriculture
14. Personal improvement
15. Remedial education

The subjects in order of greatest increase in enrollment in all schools over the five years, 1946-1951 were ranked as follows:

1. Safety and driver education
2. Civic and public affairs groups
3. Remedial and special education
4. Health and physical education

5. Agriculture
6. Practical arts and crafts
7. Americanization and elementary education
8. Recreational skills
9. Homemaking education
10. Fine arts
11. Personal improvement
12. Parent and family-life education
13. Commercial and distributive education
14. Vocational and technical education
15. General academic education

Although there is no study of the relative proportion of credit to non-credit offerings, the available evidence indicates a gradual shift on the part of public school programs away from credit programs toward relatively informal, non-academic programs. This trend can be predicted to continue as the number of individuals completing high school annually increases and as the concept of life-long learning for all adults gains currency in our national cultural patterns.

The actual number of different people enrolled in public school adult education was shown by the population survey of the U. S. Bureau of the Census in 1957 to be about two million. This study was subject to some limitations in that it restricted responses to those chosen first by the individuals interviewed. Earlier studies set the figure for total enrollments at about three million.

The available research into the characteristics of people served by public school adult education was summarized by Louis K. Mather as follows:

"They come from all age groups—from the retired and aged, from those in the prime of life and productive power, and from young people just out of high school. A quarter of all enrollees are workers, both highly-skilled and otherwise. Another quarter are housewives. One student out of six, it is estimated, is a clerical or business worker. Only one in twenty is a professional person. One participant in every fifty is illiterate. Every thirteenth student is an alien preparing himself through Americanization courses to seek U. S. citizenship. Fewer than one in two hundred is a physically or mentally-handicapped person taking part in remedial education courses."[2]

FINANCIAL PATTERNS

To think of public school adult education as being anything but publicly supported is a contradiction in terms. Most of the discussion as to whether public school adult education should be "free" or "fee" usually revolves around a consideration of whether instructional costs only should be met by fees—seldom as to whether the basic costs of plant operation, maintenance, and administrative leadership should be passed on to the adult student.

The patterns of support for adult education have tended to follow to some degree at least the patterns of support for education generally. At first, the costs of adult education assumed by taxation were generally met entirely by the local school system. Gradually, however, as school equalization needs drove a larger and larger proportion of total school costs to the level of state government, a number of states began to provide financial aid to local systems to support programs of adult education.[3]

Support for adult education on both the state and local school district levels has grown until in 1954 well over $79,000,000 was spent for adult education in urban communities. (No figures are available on the amount of public support in communities of less than 2,500). Of this amount about $16,000,000 was appropriated out of state tax funds and the remainder by local districts.

There is substantial evidence to indicate that where state funds are employed, a far more comprehensive program of adult education develops. In ten states and the District of Columbia[4] which have relatively adequate state aid provisions for adult education, three times as large a proportion of the adult population is engaged in public school adult education activities as in those states with little or no aid. This means that if all states could be persuaded to deal as generously with adult education as do ten states then ten million adults might be taking part in public school adult education rather than but a fifth that number.

Once state aid for general education has been secured the curriculum of an adult evening school also undergoes expansion. This expansion leads mainly toward programs in health and physical education, fine arts, civics and public affairs, remedial special education, parent and family life education, high-school subjects, and practical arts.

With the rising costs of state government and with the pre-emption of many fields of taxation by the federal government, there have been strong pressures on state legislatures to restrict services and keep down taxes. In several states, adult education has been one of the services sacrificed to keep the gap closed between available revenue and total expenditures. In 1957 the Michigan Legislature reduced from $300,000 to $200,000 the annual appropriation available for state aid to adult education. In 1958 the appropriation in New York of approximately four and one-half million dollars was cut in half. On the other hand, during the meetings of the 1959 legislatures, Florida and California staved off attempts to reduce the adult education budget.

ADMINISTRATIVE AND TEACHING PATTERNS

In 1920 California established the first division of adult education within a state department of education and employed a professionally trained adult educator to give it leadership. In the next ten years five additional states—Connecticut, Delaware, Nebraska, Massachusetts, and Pennsylvania—established divisions of adult education and at least nine other state departments of education added full-time or part-time adult educational personnel to their professional staffs.

The significance of the creation of divisions of adult education as a part of the program of the state department of education lies primarily in the fact that trained leadership thus becomes available to give guidance and inspiration to the program throughout the state. A state director of adult education can help communities that have no program begin to make plans for a program and help those that do have a program discover ways of enriching and extending it.

In the years since 1920 there have been some changes in the rollcall of the states providing administrative leadership in adult education. Some states which had this service have dropped it and new states have added it. In 1959 twenty-five states and Puerto Rico had at least a half-time director of adult education.[5]

On the community level similar advances have been made in securing qualified administrative leadership for the adult programs of local school districts. According to a 1952 study, 46.9 per cent of cities over 100,000 and 22 per cent of cities from 30,000 to 100,000 had full-time directors. Two hundred and twenty-five other cities reporting had part-time directors.[6] It is estimated that in 1959 there are about 600 full-time directors of adult education and about 2,000 part-time directors. In numerous communities an adult education program is carried on solely as an additional activity by other administrative personnel in the school. It is significant that recent increases in the number of local directors is greater by far in states that also have full-time administration in state departments of education. Where a local director of adult education is appointed a great leap forward in program development is made. Programs become both larger and more diversified, enrollment rises, and the community begins to invest more public money in the education of its adult citizens.

In some states and in many communities the administrative leadership of the adult education program is complemented by the services of an advisory committee of citizens which helps plan the school's total program for adults and co-ordinates its work with that of other adult education agencies in the community.

There are about 90,000 teachers of adults. Approximately half of these are drawn from the regular day school faculty. In this group usually are found the teachers of both academic and non-academic subjects regularly taught in the secondary schools. In school systems requiring the certification of teachers in adult education, a high proportion of the teachers of adults also teach in the elementary or secondary schools. The remainder of the teaching force is recruited from outside the schools. Teachers and leaders of public affairs programs, practical arts and crafts classes, and many of the general or "liberal" adult education activities tend to be drawn from this group. Two-thirds of the teachers of adults have been trained as teachers of children. Twenty per cent have no training of any kind in education, and only 12 per cent have special training as teachers of adults. There is, therefore, rising demand for increased opportunities for special in-service training for teachers of adults.

PROFESSIONAL ORGANIZATIONS

The full-time professional worker in public school adult education has available to him three major types of professional organizations. As an adult educator he has an interest in an overall adult education organization, such as the Adult Education Association of the U.S.A. or a state adult education association. As an employee of a public school system he has much to gain—and give—as a member of a national teachers' organization such as the National Education Association, or a state education association. Finally, as an adult educator practicing his profession in public schools he has a direct stake in a specialized association of public school adult educators. At the national level, the National Association of Public School Adult Educators seeks to meet the professional interests of adult educators working under the auspices of the public schools; and at the state level state associations of public school adult educators have been organized in California, Michigan, New York, and Florida.

Because adult educators in the public schools are so intimately concerned with the organizational interests of both general adult education and public school education, the National Association of Public School Adult Educators has organizational identification with both the Adult Education Association of the U.S.A. and the National Education Association. The formation of the National Association of Public School Adult Educators was authorized by the Delegate Assembly of the AEA in 1951 and came into formal existence one year later. By action of the Representative Assembly of the NEA, the NAPSAE became a department of the NEA in 1955.

The program of the NAPSAE is divided into two distinct parts. One part—the membership services program—is designed to provide professional assistance by means of publications, conferences, informational services, and the other usual services of a national organization. The national conference of the association is held annually immediately preceding the conference of the Adult Education Association. The association's principal journal, *The Public School Adult Educator,* is the first and only professional magazine designed exclusively for the interests of adult educators working in the public schools.

The second part of the association's program is a complex and interrelated series of projects developed out of grants from The Fund for

Adult Education which are designed to strengthen and extend adult education in the various states. The "public school development program" of the association has three major points of emphasis. The first is the extension of state leadership for adult education into state departments of education. Since 1955, under the terms of one-year grants from NAPSAE to state departments of education, full-time directors of adult education have been added to the staffs of the chief state school officers in Colorado, Oklahoma, Minnesota, Georgia, Iowa, and Utah. As of July, 1959, all six of these are now supported by their respective state departments of education.

A second phase of the development program is the provision of training in the methods and purposes of general and liberal adult education for both newly appointed and veteran state directors of adult education. A three-year program of training institutes began in 1958.

The third major phase of the development program is the provision of training programs for local directors of adult education in those states which can provide sufficient state leadership to co-ordinate, develop, and promote the program. By 1959 training programs or experimental demonstration programs for local directors had been held in Minnesota, Rhode Island, New Jersey, Mississippi, Colorado, Georgia, and Oklahoma and were scheduled in fifteen additional states.

FUTURE TRENDS

Historically, public school adult education has been built on the concept of meeting individual needs. Many early programs were planned to meet needs for remedial education, but others were based on an individual's need for increased vocational or civic competence. There is some evidence now to indicate that the new look in public school adult education will be a look toward an increasing emphasis on meeting community needs.

One obvious and pressing concern of the American community today is achieving and maintaining adequate support for public education and fully involving the public in a thoughtful and educated appraisal of the aims and goals of education. Other community needs—as differentiated from individual needs—are those of maintaining an adequate civil defense structure, providing for long-range social planning, continuously re-examining social values, and diagnosing and understanding the educational implications of such social disorders as crime, delinquency, and family disorganization.

Some indication that public school adult education is beginning to move toward an attack on these problems is found in the influence adult education exercises in some communities in helping to enrich and extend the in-service training programs of teachers within the schools. In Baltimore, Seattle, Trenton, and East Lansing, Michigan, the director of adult

education is called upon to help plan and develop an educational program for teachers which extends beyond the strictly technical aspects of
teaching and includes a well-rounded general education.

A second approach adult educators are taking to meet community needs
is co-operative programming with community institutions and social
agencies. In Highland Park and in Battle Creek, Michigan, classes in
homemaking, family budgeting, and child care are held for mothers of
children committed to the care of the judge of the juvenile court. In
San Francisco, the adult education program of the schools works closely
with the social service volunteer bureau, maintains a parent co-operative
nursery, and operates an education center for older adults and for the
blind. In Flint, Michigan, with the added resources of the Mott Foundation, the public schools have undertaken a comprehensive community-
school educational program which involves adults and children in a wide
range of activities. To cite a single example, regular story hours for preschool children are conducted by the public library. While the children
are listening to the stories their mothers attend activities sponsored by
the adult education program of the Flint Public Schools which help them
learn how to tell stories to children and to introduce children to books.

A third way in which the public school adult education program is
beginning to make a greater impact on the community's total educational
program is by providing consultative help and leadership training in the
methods of adult education to the educational leadership of voluntary
agencies. Program-planning clinics and leadership-training institutes are
sponsored by the public schools in many communities. In many others the
director of adult education is instrumental in involving his own staff or
that of the total school in working with community agencies in consultation on the educational aspects of community problems.

CONCLUSION

In many communities the heart of the adult education enterprise is,
for lack of other facilities, the local public school district. The role of
the public school for this purpose is both logical and obvious. The public
school is, first of all, publicly supported by the same adult population
which requires its service. Second, the public school has existing plant
and trained personnel to teach and administer programs for adults. Third,
the public school is an acceptable and inexpensive facility for all adults.
For example, it has been estimated that one-half of the total adult population of the nation could be provided sufficient educational opportunities using just three percent of the total expenditures for schools today.
Fourth, as a recognized local educational resource, the public school is
able to provide educational leadership to other educational activities for
adults through a variety of partnerships with the multitude of agencies
and interests in the average community.

The public schools of the country thus have a unique opportunity in the total adult education program. They have no monopoly in terms of responsibility and leadership and they must conduct their activities in close co-operation with other community groups and agencies engaged in many other phases of adult education. But among all the educational institutions, the public school reaches more people in more places than any other.

For this opportunity to be fully realized, the public school adult education movement must be extended into the yet unserved school districts. In 1951 two-thirds of the nation's school districts, many of them very small districts in rural areas, had no adult education program. The adult program of the schools also needs to be kept under constant evaluation. While it can draw heavily on the intellectual facilities of the elementary and secondary schools, the program of the adult school must always be seen as a different type of education. It has characteristics that call for a different curriculum, different course content, different materials, different counseling service, and different facilities. In many instances it requires either a different teaching staff or a thorough in-service training program to provide teachers of children with the unique abilities necessary for teachers of adults.

Footnotes

1*A Study in Urban Public School Adult Education Programs* (Washington: National Education Association, 1952), pp. 15-25.

2Louis K. Mather, *The New American School for Adults* (Washington: National Education Association, 1935), p. 11.

3For the early history of state aid, see chapter 2.

4New York, Florida, California, Louisiana, Pennsylvania, Michigan, Massachusetts, Wisconsin, Washington, Connecticut, and the District of Columbia.

5Arkansas

Arkansas	Hawaii	Minnesota	Rhode Island
California	Illinois	Mississippi	South Carolina
Colorado	Iowa	New Jersey	Utah
Connecticut	Louisiana	New York	Wisconsin
Delaware	Maine	Oklahoma	Puerto Rico
Florida	Massachusetts	Oregon	
Georgia	Michigan	Pennsylvania	

6Louis K. Mather, *op. cit.*, pp. 33-36.

Selected Readings

Periodical Publications

The Public School Adult Educator. The National Association of Public School Adult Educators. Quarterly.

Swap Shop for Administrators. The National Association of Public School Adult Educators. Quarterly.

General References

Crabtree, A. P. *Civic Education Programs for Adults.* Curriculum Series No. 1. Washington: National Association of Public School Adult Educators, 1956.

Hand, Samuel E. "Community Study as a Basis for Program Planning in Adult Education." Unpublished Doctor's thesis, Florida State University, 1956.

Holden, John B. *Adult Education Services of State Departments of Education.* U. S. Office of Education Miscellaneous Publication No. 31. Washington: Government Printing Office, 1959.

Kempfer, Homer H. *Adult Education.* New York: McGraw-Hill Book Co., 1955.

Loomis, Charles P., and others. *Rural Social Systems and Adult Education.* East Lansing: Michigan State College, 1953.

Mather, Louis K. *The New American School for Adults.* Washington: National Education Association, Division of Adult Education Service, 1955.

National Education Association, Division of Adult Education Service. *A Study of Urban Public School Adult Education Programs of the United States.* Washington: the Division, 1952.

Olds, Edward B. *Financing Adult Education in America's Public Schools and Community Councils.* Report of the National Commission on Adult Education Finance. Chicago: Adult Education Association, 1954.

Ponitz, Henry J. "The Adult Education Development Program." *The Public School Adult Educator* II (November, 1958), 19-20.

Snow, Robert H. *Community Adult Education.* New York: G. P. Putnam's Sons, 1955.

CHAPTER 30

ADULT EDUCATION IN RELIGIOUS INSTITUTIONS

EDWARD R. MILLER
Director, Continuing Education
Antioch College

The Sunday school movement in Christian groups in the eighteenth century is credited with being the beginning of modern adult religious education. In earlier centuries there were other forms of religious education for adults. Particularly was this true in the Jewish faith from the time of the introduction of the synagogue during the fifth century, B.C.E. So large has adult education in religious institutions grown (an estimated 15,000,000 people in Protestant groups alone taking part in Sunday schools, men's and women's organizations, study clubs for married couples and young adults) that these adult educational undertakings form one of the largest segments of all adult education.

The years since World War II have seen tremendous changes in the philosophies and programs of religious adult education. This chapter is an attempt to summarize these changes. It is written from an awareness of the developments in all three of the major religious institutions in the United States—Jewish, Catholic and Protestant. More than fifty leaders in adult religious education in these three main bodies have been consulted in its preparation.

CHANGES IN THE PHILOSOPHY OF ADULT RELIGIOUS EDUCATION

Up till now the one important item in the religious education of adults has been "content." The discovery of the importance of "method" in adult religious education presents a challenging new dimension which is causing many of the new changes in philosophy. The following are some of the outstanding philosophical changes:

The concept of continuity of learning.—Secular adult education has been increasingly seen as a continuous process, never completed at any one time during an individual's life. Adult religious education, on the other hand, has usually been limited to the rearranging of concepts acquired early in life on a one-dimensional continuum. Consequently, the introduction of a continuous education that involves such concepts as "maturing," "broadening," "deepening," "new horizons," "new relationships" is a new aspect of a philosophy of adult religious education.

It at once makes adult religious education both more challenging and more difficult—more difficult in that easy repetition of doctrinal ideas is not enough, and does not guarantee growth in the adult participant; more challenging in that the adult participants in the educational process are seen to have a new potential.

Discovery of the educability of the adult.—The second outstanding change, and corollary of the first, is the discovery of the educability of the adult and the importance of the adult continuing his education. The assumption in religious circles has been that the children are the important and malleable units. The amount of effort put into the religious education of children by religious institutions makes this point adequately clear. Adult education has been more of an afterthought, and the methods of instruction were only extensions of those used with children.

The realization that adults do continue to learn when the teaching methods are appropriate, when the subject matter meets their needs, and when they are given opportunity to do something about the problem, is a new insight and gives a new dynamic to adult religious education. Here is a whole new, untapped reservoir of ideas, energy, and activity. A good example of this realization is found in such pamphlets as "The Church Educating Adults" and "Ways of Teaching Adults,"[1] which recognize adults as individuals who can not only continue to grow mentally, but also have the right to have such opportunities.

The religious education of the adult has been neglected in part because it was assumed that the adult was already educated from childhood teachings. The newer understanding brings about the realization that without continuous religious education the adult does not (and cannot) necessarily know what ought to be known and that in his ignorance it is he, the adult, that is influencing the children. " 'It is to adults, not children, that we must look for a better future'—such is the conclusion of the Danish Lutheran Bishop H. F. S. Grundtvig. . . ."[2]

The adult as a learner.—The third change in philosophy has to do with the adult as a learner, be he the professional religious leader or the layman. Not only is the adult being rediscovered as a learner, but much is being freshly understood about the conditions under which he learns— that he has his own special conditions, rates, and abilities in learning. One of the most extensive plans for the application of adult learning principles to adult religious education programs is the "Indiana Plan" developed by Paul Bergevin, director of the Bureau of Studies in Adult Education, Indiana and Purdue Universities, and his staff.[3]

CHANGES IN PRACTICES AND PROGRAMS OF ADULT RELIGIOUS EDUCATION

Changes in any philosophy, to be effective, must eventuate in practice —in programs. The theologian (concerned about content) must no longer be at war with the educator (concerned about method). The two must work effectively and creatively together if adult religious education is to become all that it should become. If the tenets of the religious faith are at all important, then they must be effectively learned in all of the increasing maturity of the adult mind. Since the adult has special learning conditions and abilities, they need to be taken into account if anything real is to happen in the religious education of the adult. The following are some of the implications of this fact for the practice of religious adult education.

Architects of learning programs must understand how adults learn.— In understanding how the adult learns, one of the first realizations is that "learning programs should begin and deal with needs which learners recognize as needs."[4] Opportunity must then be provided for the adults to put these insights to work. In considering how the adult learns it is important for programs to recognize the background of "adult experience"; the "emotional meaning" for the adult; the "relatively fixed" nature of adult thought patterns; the "varying time and energy" patterns of adults, and the "complex of motivations" of the adult.

*Teaching methods must be adapted to adults.—*Awareness of how adults learn has a direct influence on teaching methods. The predominant method used with adults has been the lecture, question-answer procedure, which assumes that the participant listens, absorbs, asks some questions for clarification, and believes what is given. The new understanding of what the adult is and how he learns demands a different kind of participation on his part if he is to learn. It demands a recognition of the adult's wealth and variety of experiences, and it demands a different kind of relating of the subject discussed to possible lines of action. This automatically means a different kind of teaching, with a resulting move toward the discussion techniques being widely used in secular education.

There are two requirements in this development: first, the training necessary for teachers to use the discussion method effectively, and second, training on the part of participants to take part in discussions. Several approaches to training have been developed. The training institutes developed by the Indiana center[5] have been used at the national, regional, and local levels by several denominations. The United Presbyterian Church in the U. S. A. has a three-year Church Officers Training Program which has reached most of the ministers, who are in turn expected to develop training programs within their churches. The Southern Baptist Seminaries have developed a unique Seminary Extension Department for continuing the training of the ministers in both content and method. Both the Episcopal and the Methodist denominations have instituted a national network of leadership training workshops, and the National Council of Churches sponsors an annual laboratory in group development at Green Lake, Wisconsin.

This rapid proliferation of programs for training teachers and participants in the discussion method is creating a real revolution in adult religious education. This does not mean that other methods of teaching adults will be or should be abandoned. It does mean that any method of teaching adults in religious education settings will be done with a heightened consciousness of the needs of adults and how they learn.

Variety must be provided in subject matter.—One of the conditions of good learning for adults is the relating of the material to actual adult situations and needs. This calls for the introduction into the adult religious education curriculum of a wide variety of courses. Whereas the older curriculum was marked by uniform courses of study of the Bible and doctrinal problems, the current materials are introducing electives of many kinds and helping the individual relate the religious aspects of the problem to temporal considerations. Even the more traditional courses are being constructed with more breadth. The United Lutheran Publishing House, Pittsburgh, has a "Suggested Two Year Adult Program," while the American Baptist Department of Adult Work and Family Life, Philadelphia, has printed a pamphlet, "Making Use of Electives in Adult Christian Education." Noveck, in his "Toward a Curriculum for Adult Jewish Education,"[6] shows the same trend toward breadth and diversity in the adult Jewish education curriculum.

Courses that deal with the moral implications of what would ordinarily be considered secular subjects are found in many of today's adult curricula for religious education, such as: moral issues in atomic warfare, religion and the United Nations, religion and minority problems, and religion and labor. Some of this kind of course are found in "The Beacon 25 Series," by the Council of Liberal Churches, Boston; in the "Young Adult Idea Book, No. 2," by the United Lutheran Church, Philadelphia, and in "The Bulletin," published by the Association of Universalist Women, Boston. *Adult Jewish Leadership*, published in New York, and the quarterly, *Jewish Heritage*, Washington, D. C. provide similar help in broadening the curriculum in Jewish institutions. The "Educational Outreach" program of the Department of the Church and Economic Life of the National Council of Churches of Christ in the U. S. A. is one of the best specific illustrations of these courses that deal with the moral implications of secular subjects. Its brochures and programs include such topics as "Inflation: Some Economic and Ethical Implications," "Religion and the Day's Work," "The Camel and the Needle's Eye—a study guide for *Ethics in a Business Society*,"[7] and a set of ten study courses under the general title of "The Ethics and Economics of Society."

The very structure of the now famous 1958 Workshop on the Christian Education of Adults, held at the University of Pittsburgh, indicates this breadth of approach to the subjects considered fruitful for adult consideration in the religious education setting. Ten per cent of the group assembled in Pittsburgh were specialists in disciplines rather than Christian Education—economics, sociology, political science, psychology, education, psychiatry.[8]

Family life has also become an important item in adult religious education. Detailed courses of study have been prepared for participants, and resource materials in the form of magazines, hand books, and bibliographies are available from almost all of the religious publishing houses. Jewish Community Centers, Catholic Adult Education Centers, and Protestant parish programs are all showing a greater interest in this aspect of adult religious education. Family camps are becoming increasingly popular as means for combining an opportunity for adult learning to take place, for the family to work together, and for the adults of the family to apply their new knowledge to the immediate life situation.

INSTITUTIONAL CHANGES IN ADULT RELIGIOUS EDUCATION

To develop the changes in philosophy and program in adult religious education that have been listed, there have been some developments in the religious institutions, themselves.

Departments of adult education.—The first such change is at the national level in the development of departments of adult education and the appointment of the necessary staff personnel. For example, there are forty-one denominational directors of adult education on one list available to the writer. Other similar lists could be compiled for other Protestant, Catholic, and Jewish groups. There are now probably several hundred people giving adult educational leadership on the national scene, developing programs, publishing materials, organizing workshops, and generally giving an impetus to adult religious education that it has never had before.

New national and ecumenical organizations and departments.—The recently formed National Catholic Adult Education Commission is a good illustration of the development of a special national organization for adult religious education within one particular faith. The Department of Adult Work, The National Council of Churches of Christ in the U. S. A., is an illustration of such a development in an ecumenical organization. The Department of Adult Jewish Education in the B'nai B'rith is illustrative of a department developed to serve different branches of one faith—in this case the Orthodox, Conservative, and Reformed Jewish congregations. Even such a worldwide organization as the World Council of Christian Education and Sunday School Association has personnel assigned to adult work.

Religiously oriented organizations.—A third institutional development that falls within this area, in that it supports and strengthens the religious institutions, is the development of adult programs in several of the religiously oriented organizations that are outside the immediate sponsorship of any one religious institution. Examples of such organizations are the Religion and Labor Foundation, the National Conference of Christians and Jews, the Y. W. C. A., and the Y. M. C. A. Many of their staff members spend a great amount of time and energy developing programs with direct religious implication for the adults who participate. Adult education has become such an important item in the Y. M. C. A., for example, that various regional and national institutes and workshops are now held especially for those of their staff assigned to adult education.

Local adult religious education centers.—Another significant institutional development is at the local level where a religious institution, or a group of institutions, creates a center for adult religious education. Programs of such centers vary widely: courses that range from religious subjects to social problems to the arts; discussion groups; selected audiovisual materials—movies, slides; lecture series; concerts, and so forth. Illustrative of some of these centers are: Catholic Adult Educational Centers, Chicago; Catholic Community Center, Kansas City; Jewish Community Centers in many cities; and the "University of Life" programs of numerous local Protestant churches.

University co-operation.—A final development in this area is the growth of co-operation between institutions of higher education and religious institutions in the development of programs of adult education. Some of this co-operation is between religious institutions and related colleges and universities, such as the Department of Adult Education, Yeshiva University, New York City; the Southern Baptist Seminaries, Extension Department; and many of the Catholic Colleges. Perhaps an even more significant development is the growth of co-operation between religious institutions and colleges and universities. The contributions by the Bureau of Adult Studies at Indiana and Purdue Universities in research, experimental and pilot programs for training leaders, and publications, and by the University of Pittsburgh 1958 Workshop on the Christian Education of Adults have already been cited. A third example of such co-operation is the help given by Michigan State University to the General Alliance of Unitarian Women in holding their national conference.

The various developments within the organization of the religious institutions, in ecumenical organizations, in religiously oriented organizations, and in both church supported and independent universities, most certainly places at the disposal of those interested in adult religious education a wealth of resources not dreamed of a few years ago.

PRINTED RESOURCES AVAILABLE IN ADULT RELIGIOUS EDUCATION

Almost every group within every religion, and their respective publishing houses, either has or is planning extensive publication of leadership training material and course material for adult religious education. Such resources are illustrated by the Congregational Christian Church's "Study Resources for Adult Groups in the Church" and "A Program of Christian Education for Adults"; "Adult Study Groups," published by the B'nai B'rith; the very excellent *Handbook of Catholic Adult Education*;[9] the Episcopal "Teacher Training Guide" and "Leading Adult Classes: A Handbook"[10]; the Methodist "Adult Teacher"; the Presbyterian "Westminster Adult Leader"; and other publications cited on pages 359-60.

Whereas twenty-five years ago there was very little material other than standard adult Sunday school lessons, there are now handbooks, planning guides, special course materials, and monthly and quarterly adult magazines, all devoted especially to adult religious education problems from "how adults learn" to "what to study." The next ten years will see a continued increase in the volume—and, hopefully—in the quality and depth of such materials.

PROBLEM AREAS NEEDING FURTHER ATTENTION

These new developments in adult religious education by no means imply that all problems are solved. Interest in the field has only really just been aroused, and the magnitude of some of the problems has just been glimpsed. Some of the important problems that still need consideration are:[10]

Poor training of leaders.—In spite of the upsurge of all kinds of training institutes and leadership materials, a great portion of the leaders of adult religious education groups are poorly trained with respect to the problems and needs of adults as learners. Even the professional religious leaders have difficulty in getting specific training for the teaching of adults, although a growing number of theological schools are adding it to the curriculum. The traditional pattern is hard to change because so many of the leaders in the present adult religious education programs have been volunteering their services for many years, and the problems of retraining or replacing them are most complex.

Remoteness of teaching from adult needs and interests.—Much of the teaching is removed from the present interests and needs of adults. The problems of today must be faced and solved by adults if the conditions of life are to be realized for the maximum spiritual growth of each person. Too rarely are contemporary questions considered in adult religious education and too often learning is approached by the religious institutions "handing down" what is to be studied, when it is to be studied, and how the adult is to be taught. Perhaps more application of good adult methods at this point—the involvement of adults in the discovery of their own needs and the search for their own solutions—is needed more than any other thing.

Translation of ideas and ideals into the present day.—A third problem area, closely related to the second, is the need for opportunity in adult religious education to translate the ideas and ideals of "the Faith" into the idiom and the circumstances of the present day. This is a real problem for both Christians and Jews. Otherwise, adults—especially each new generation af adults—feel that "the Faith" has less and less relevance for the times. This problem of relating the ideas and ideals of the religion is one of great immediacy, both for the individual and the religious institution.

This problem takes on an added dimension when the increased age of the population is considered. More people attending the religious institutions are living longer—longer into a new age with ever more and more changes, which their religious education must help them prepare for and understand. This older part of the population presents some very special problems to adult religious education.

Materials for the non-academic reader.—In spite of what seems to be a wealth of adult education material, many leaders feel there is a dearth of materials for the non-academic reader. Authentic books, simply and clearly written, with built-in incentives for discussion, are still lacking in most areas of interest.

Limitations of the Discussion Method.—In the first flush of discovering the discussion method as a new learning technique for adults, one problem is beginning to appear: the substitution of one poorly-used teaching method may be made for another poorly-used teaching method. The major safeguards against this pitfall are the provision of adequate leaders —in training, in motivation, in depth of subject-matter knowledge, and in appreciation of adult problems and the motivation of the adult learners to participate in continuous education. There is no easy answer to adult education, and there is certainly no magic in the use of some one special teaching technique unless it is accompanied by a lot of other things.

The free method of study and discussion.—One final problem, which actually may be a dilemma rather than a problem, is the introduction of the free method of study and discussion into adult religious education. If it is taken seriously by the participants, their creative needs and responses are drawn out in the setting of a religious institution which has certain suggested answers to certain pre-stated questions. Although there is religious freedom in the United States, members of religious institutions have not been noted for tolerating divergent interpretations and ideas within their own sect or congregation. Consequently, adult education leaders in religious institutions will need, sooner or later, to come to terms with the conflict between indoctrination and education and face up to the consequences of providing a type of adult education that is really effective in producing growth within the lives and minds of the adult participants.

If adult religious educators can continue for another twenty-five years in the directions taken in the last quarter century, not only will adult religious education become a most dynamic force in American life, but the religious institutions themselves will become more vital and dynamic.

Footnotes

1Published by the Board of Parish Education, The United Lutheran Publication House, Philadelphia.

2"The Church Educating Adults," The Board of Parish Education, Philadelphia, *ibid.* page 1.

3Paul Bergerin and John McKinley, *Design for Adult Education in the Church* (Greenwich, Conn.: Seabury Press, 1958).

4*Ibid*, p. VIII.

5*Ibid.* Part II and appendices give complete details of an "Indiana Plan" institute and workshop.

6Simon Noveck, *Central Conference American Rabbis Journal:* June, 1957. An off-print.

7M. W. Childs and Douglas Cater (New York: New American Library of World Literature, Inc., 1954).

8For a detailed report of this workshop, see Lawrence C. Little (ed.), "Charting the Future Course of Christian Adult Education in America" (Department of Religious Education, University of Pittsburgh, 1958). (Mimeographed)

9Sister Jerome Keeler (ed.), *Handbook of Catholic Adult Education* (Milwaukee: Bruce Publishing Co., 1959).

10These problems are summarized from the article by Lawrence C. Little, Lily Edelman, and Sister Jerome Keeler, "Where Are We in Adult Religious Education?" *Adult Leadership VII* (February, 1959), 235-40.

Selected Readings

Bergevin, Paul, and McKinley, John. *Design for Adult Education in the Church.* Greenwich, Conn.: The Seabury Press, 1958.

Clemmons, Robert S. *Dynamics of Christian Adult Education.* New York: Abingdon Press, 1958.

Douglas, Paul F. *The Group Workshop Way in the Church.* New York: Association Press, 1956.

Imber, Rebecca, and Cohen, J. J. *The Creative Audience.* Reconstructionist Press, 1954.

International Journal of Religious Education, Vol. XXXV, No. 9 (May 1959). A special issue on "THE CHRISTIAN EDUCATION OF ADULTS".

Jones, Idris W. *Our Church Plans for Adult Education: A Manual on Administration.* Philadelphia: The Judson Press, 1952.

Keeler, Sister Jerome (ed.). *Handbook of Catholic Adult Education.* Milwaukee: The Bruce Publishing Co., 1959.

Knowles, Malcolm S. *Informal Adult Education.* New York: Association Press, 1950.

Lindhorst, Frank A. *Teaching Adults.* New York: Abingdon-Cokesbury Press, 1951.

Little, Lawrence C. (ed.). *Religion and Education for Professional Responsibility.* Pittsburgh: The Department of Religious Education, University of Pittsburgh, 1956.

———— (ed.). *Charting the Future Course of Christian Adult Education in America.* Pittsburgh: Department of Religious Education, University of Pittsburgh. (Mimeographed)

MacClellan, Malcolm. *The Catholic Church and Adult Education.* Washington: Catholic Education Press, 1935.

Noveck, Simon. "Toward a Curriculum for Adult Jewish Education." Off-print from *Central Conference American Rabbi Journal,* June, 1957. Philadelphia: Press of Maurice Jacobs, Inc.

————. *Adult Study Groups.* Washington: B'nai B'rith, n.d.

————. *Adult Jewish Education in the American Synogogue.* New York: National Academy for Adult Jewish Studies, n.d.

————, and Edelman, Lily, *The Laymen's Institute—An Adventure in Jewish Living.* New York: National Academy for Adult Jewish Studies, n.d.

Ostoyee, Edith T. *Teaching Adults.* Philadelphia: Judson Press, 1948.

Suggested Courses for Adult Jewish Study. New York: National Academy for Adult Jewish Studies, n.d.

CHAPTER 31

ADULT EDUCATION IN VOLUNTARY SOCIAL WELFARE ORGANIZATIONS

JOE R. HOFFER
Executive Secretary
National Conference on Social Welfare

SOCIAL WELFARE ORGANIZATIONS AND SETTINGS

Definition of Social Welfare Field

Voluntary social welfare is used in this chapter to describe the field encompassing the community services under non-governmental auspices which exist potentially for each member of a community, without regard to his resources, with the aim of helping toward a mutual adjustment of individuals and their social environment. Within the field defined thus broadly are many agencies and services which are not manned by social workers, but also health educators, teachers, lawyers, ministers, home economists, nurses, doctors, etc., insofar as these latter involve or relate to the problems of individual and group adjustment and social organization. These other professionals bring their technical background and skills to bear upon the social education and emotional problems which are central to social welfare services. These problems and their solutions may even be partly in the field of one or more of the specialties that they represent.

Scope of Social Welfare Services

Social welfare services are found in all rural and urban sections of our country, carried on at all geographic levels—local, state, national, and international—and under governmental, as well as voluntary non-sectarian and sectarian auspices, trade unions, business and industry, and many other agencies, including those where they are the chief activity and those where they are secondary activities.

The network of social welfare services appears on the surface to be less well organized and more haphazard than is actually the case. The largest part of the program is financed and directed by government. It is estimated that in 1955 approximately 80 per cent of the money spent for welfare services and social security came from government funds.[1] While a wide range of services are provided under voluntary auspices, the social welfare system is based to a considerable degree on theories, policies, and lines of responsibility established by law. In spite of the major role of government, the growth of voluntarism in the U. S. has been steady and dynamic since 1945. The reasons for this growth may be attributed to the wide gap between needs and services, the lag between new needs and public programs, and a traditional attitude of resistance in this country to turning things over to government.

An individual who seeks a starting point from which to comprehend the complicated network of social welfare services in a modern community has only to grasp two fundamental ideas:

1. All the agencies and services are concerned with four basic human problems: dependency, ill-health, maladjustments, and recreational needs;

2. These four problems tend to converge, in one combination or another, on the individual, family, and the community, each problem intensifying the destructive consequences of the other.

Definition of Social Work

"Social work" is used to designate the professional core of social welfare. The boundaries of social work have not been defined, and this remains one of the principal tasks of the professional organization (the new National Association of Social Workers), the organization concerned with professional education (the Council on Social Work Education), and other groups within the social welfare field.

Social Welfare Services

The following outline suggests the scope of social welfare services but does not attempt to develop an ideal classification or to include all aspects of the field, and the inclusion of an item does not necessarily reflect its relative importance or frequency. It is based on a cursory analysis of programs of recent Annual Forums of the National Conference on Social Welfare[2] and a partial review of current literature in the field. The reader may consult *The Social Work Yearbook*[3] for definitions and explanations of many of the services and terms included in the outline.

A. Services to individuals and families.—These are direct services to individuals and families provided by such agencies as family service associations, public welfare departments, and in such areas as:

    1. Income maintenance

2. Dependency and protection
3. Correction and prevention
4. Adjustment
5. Health education
6. Medical care
7. Rehabilitation
8. Mental health

B. Services to groups and individuals in groups.—These are direct services to groups provided by such agencies as recreation and informal education agencies, business and industry, trade unions, church-centered agencies, and clinics, in the following areas:

1. Activity skills
2. Clubs
3. Educational courses
4. Provision of facilities
5. Group dynamics training
6. Informal education
7. Camping
8. Recreation
9. Therapy
10. Other group activity

C. Services to agencies and communities.—These are direct services to agencies and communities provided through welfare federations, united funds, conferences, and commissions in the following areas:

1. Budgeting
2. Community planning
3. Consultation and referral
4. Co-ordination and integration
5. Education and promotion
6. Fund raising
7. Forum
8. Inter-agency relations
9. Information and communication
10. Social action, including legislative action
11. Liaison with outside groups
12. Personnel and administration
13. Professional education
14. Public relations and interpretation
15. Social research and studies
16. Inter-group relations

The Educational Component in Social Welfare

It should be evident from the institutional settings which have been described and the illustrations of services given that education is an important ingredient in this field. As far as the author is aware, no classification of educational activities in social welfare exists. The following listing has been developed in an effort to present at least a partial picture of the educational component in the social welfare field.

A. Informal Education.—Many forms of informal education are being carried on under the auspices of social welfare organizations. These include:

1. *Formal instruction in classes:* more or less formal instruction by

specially trained teachers. The primary objective is to impart information or skills, and the participants are chosen on the basis of age or educational status, or they attend by their own choice.

2. *Clubs and special interest groups:* activities carried on primarily for the values to be derived in group association. The activities themselves, whether recreational or educational, are secondary.

B. *Social work.*—Many aspects of the job of the social caseworker, the social group worker, and the community organization worker can be classified as educational. Some examples are:

1. *Social casework:* social caseworkers help individuals with problems by providing supportive treatment and by development of self-awareness.[4] The degree of educational emphasis in this type of activity varies with the needs of individual clients. Agencies providing casework services often give information about availability of community resources, eligibility requirements for financial assistance, and similar matters.

2. *Social group work:* "Social group work like casework, community organization, administration, and research is now recognized as a basic aspect of social work practice. Its distinct characteristics lie in the fact that group work is used in social relationships within group experience as a means to individual growth and development, and that the group worker is concerned in developing social responsibility and active citizenship for the improvement of democratic society."[5] Many educational methods and techniques may be employed by social group workers, but they are directed toward social work objectives.

3. *Community organization for social welfare:* educational and promotional activities form an important part of community organization for social welfare in an effort to achieve some of the following objectives: (1) to spread knowledge about human needs among as wide a public as possible; (2) to stimulate citizen interest in social and health problems and to create motivation for action through participation; and (3) to enhance community understanding and to mobilize support, both moral and financial.

C. *Staff and volunteer development.*—In the broad field of social welfare many positions are filled by paid staff without the desired professional preparation, or by volunteers who need and want special training. For this reason various educational methods for increasing the competence and knowledge of workers and volunteers in the field have always been important activities. These have included:

1. *In-service training:* in addition to the formal supervision which is a regular part of social work practice, social welfare agencies have relied heavily on case conferences, staff meetings, and regular training sessions for staff and volunteers.

2. *Institutes and workshops:* widely used as methods of providing

short-term training for staff and volunteers, these may be under the auspices of state conferences of social welfare, schools of social work, and national agencies in a particular functional field.

3. *Conferences:* although the purposes of conferences in the social welfare field are not exclusively to provide staff and volunteer development or vocational education, this has certainly been one of the major functions. In addition to the Annual Forum of the National Conference on Social Welfare and state conferences, most of the national functional agencies conduct conferences, which, among other things, serve as a useful means for transmitting technical and specialized knowledge to workers and volunteers in the field.

D. *Education of the public.*—Most social welfare organizations consider it to be an important part of their on-going program to inform the public at large about social and health needs and ways of meeting them. The large numbers of volunteers involved in social welfare programs (as board and committee members and in direct service) are regarded as an invaluable link in this general educational process. By becoming familiar with community needs and the nature of specific social welfare programs, they can fill an important role in interpretation to the public at large.

E. *Recreation.*—The primary objective of recreation is to offer an outlet for self-expression. The individual participates from choice because of the personal enjoyment and satisfaction he gains. The educational objective is not a primary one, although many individuals seek improvement of skills through recreation programs.

From this brief analysis it is obvious that educational methods and techniques are widely employed in social welfare and that many of the activities carried on by social welfare organizations can be described as adult education.

HISTORICAL DEVELOPMENTS SINCE 1948

From the world-wide point of view, probably the most significant development since 1948 has been the emerging emphasis on the concept of the well-being of all peoples in the world community. The place that adequate social welfare services play in bringing about the desired improvement is receiving increasing attention.

Of all the changes taking place in today's society and the one which presents the greatest challenge to social welfare, as to so many other fields, is the increasing population, with its altering composition. Not only is the population of this country growing at a quite unanticipated rate, but it is becoming older and it is changing as far as social classes are concerned, with an apparently increasing homogeneity. Mobility of people adds to the problems faced by social welfare agencies, such as inadequate housing, new problems in race relations, unprecedented demands on health facilities, and entire new communities requiring social welfare services. Most writers agree that social welfare services are not adequate to meet these new needs.

There is no doubt, on the other hand, that the field in general and the social work profession in particular have shown considerable growth. In 1930, the first year that the U. S. census listed social workers as a separate category, there were 31,000. By 1940 the number had reached almost 70,000, and it is estimated that at present there are over 125,000 paid workers in the field. Of these between 25,000 and 30,000 probably have some graduate training. Estimates of volunteers in social welfare vary from sixteen to twenty million. These volunteers render service in several hundred capacities in a multitude of social welfare organizations. They bring a variety of skills and experience to the day-to-day job of providing essential social, educational, and health services to people. They work as administrative assistants with responsibility for sharing in policy making and financing of programs. They function as direct service volunteers in family and child care, recreation, education, and health programs. They carry important responsibilities on fact finding and planning to improve the quality of social welfare services.[6]

Recent Trends

Some of the recent trends in the social welfare field which have special implications for adult education are:

1. *The growth of national education, professional, and planning groups.*—National voluntary organizations play a very important role in social welfare. Like the more than 100,000 local organizations in the field, they defy classification. Over 400 of these groups, at least 40 of which have been organized since 1945, serve the total field by providing leadership, education, information, social action, co-ordination, forum, standard-setting, and planning activities on a national scale. In addition, many of them serve as the United States' link with international voluntary organizations in their special fields of interest.

Five new national organizations, organized or reorganized since 1945, deserve special mention:

The National Social Welfare Assembly (NSWA) is the major national planning body for social welfare. Its purpose is to further the concept that social welfare means the well-being of all people and that all parts of social welfare are interrelated through a three-fold partnership of governmental and voluntary, national and local, lay and professional interests. In addition to over sixty-five national and federal government agency affiliates, three autonomous national co-ordinating bodies have a special affiliation—the Council on Social Work Education, the National Health Council, and the National Council on Agricultural Life and Labor. One of the major methods used by the assembly in pursuing its objectives is bringing together in conferences and committees representatives of national agencies and interested citizens to discuss and study common problems and concerns.

The National Association of Social Workers (NASW) was formed in 1955 as the result of a merger of seven separate professional groups in various areas of social work practice. There are approximately 23,000 members of the association at present. The general membership requirement is graduation from a graduate professional school of social work accredited by the Council on Social Work Education. The major purpose of the NASW is to promote activities appropriate to strengthening and unifying the social work profession as a whole and to promote the development of social work practice to meet particular aspects of human needs. To achieve these goals, the Association must be concerned with the ongoing educational needs of its members.

The Council on Social Work Education (CSWE) is the agency with authority to speak and act for the social work profession on all educational matters. It is the official accrediting body of general programs of graduate professional social work education and the specializations within these programs. The constituent membership of the council includes over 60 graduate schools of social work in the U. S. and Canada and more than 90 undergraduate departments, the National Association of Social Workers, and over 36 national employing agencies. It seeks to enlist the understanding and support of the general public as well as those with special interests in professional education in the development of educational programs of high standards which will produce professional workers of competence.

The United States Committee of the International Conference of Social Work (ICSW) is a permanent world organization for individuals and agencies concerned with meeting the social welfare needs of people. It provides an international forum for the discussion of social welfare and related issues. It is non-governmental, non-political, and non-sectarian, and like the National Conference on Social Welfare does not take positions on issues, nor does it have a social action function. In this country the ICSW is represented by a United States Committee, a semi-autonomous body within the National Conference on Social Welfare. The U.S. Committee was last reorganized in 1952 as an autonomous membership body with the Secretariat provided by the National Social Welfare Assembly. However, as of October 1, 1959, the committee membership was consolidated with the NCSW membership and the committee will probably be reconstituted with greater participation by national organizations with major international social welfare interests.

The National Health Council (NHC) is a mechanism established by the national health agencies to assist them to work together in their common interest to promote the health of the nation. Its basic purposes include: to help identify, call attention to, and promote solutions of national health problems, and to promote better state and local health services —governmental and voluntary. The NHC provides a convenient vehicle between social welfare and voluntary health agencies for the exchange of information and activities pertaining to the common problems of individual and group adjustment and social organization.

2. *The growth of international social welfare.*—The phenomenal growth of the international social welfare field has been described in the following words:

> It is only thirteen years ago that international social welfare under official sponsorship began, with the overseas assignments of the first UNRRA workers. In a little more than a decade . . . a myriad of programs contributing to the health and well-being of millions of people around the world have been organized under governmental and intergovernmental auspices, taking their places within the voluntary programs of long tradition.
>
> The story of social welfare has always been one in which past accomplishments are dwarfed by the size of need still to be met, and in this comparatively new field of endeavor the story repeats itself. Yet today, it is an accepted part of programs of the U. S. Government and of the United Nations, as well as those of many voluntary agencies.[7]

This rapid expansion of the field has meant the establishment of many voluntary organizations, some of which combine programs of direct service with educational activities, while others are devoted entirely to educational ends. Generally, these educational activities have been of two kinds: (1) conferences (international and regional), seminars, individual exchange programs, all of which are designed to spread knowledge about more or less technical developments in the field; and (2) use of many devices (meetings, mass media, audio-visual aids, etc.) for the purpose of increasing public understanding of international relations in general and the place of social welfare in improving international understanding.

3. *The increasing number and frequency of forum activities.*—Conferences traditionally have had an important place in our democracy and, particularly, in the social welfare field. As in any developing field, the new departures in thinking and practice in social welfare and its experiments and demonstrations are usually first presented at a forum, then are reflected in proceedings and articles in periodicals, and much later appear in books.

There has been substantial growth in the number and frequency of conferences—national, regional, and state—in the social welfare field. Probably the largest number of new conferences have been on a regional level and in specialized subject areas. Conferences serve a number of purposes in addition to staff and volunteer development, including: building a sense of identity for an organization or a field, general public education (through publicity resulting from conferences) about the interests and concerns of the organization, transmitting specialized knowledge to interested persons from related fields and disciplines, and informing workers in the field about major economic and social issues.[8]

4. *The expansion of family life education.*—Family life education pro-

grams, which are sometimes conducted by social welfare organizations and sometimes by other groups in the community, have expanded at a rapid rate during the period under discussion. Family life education, which in its broadest sense includes all educational efforts designed to prepare people of any age to make the most of family living, "is now reaching a high proportion of the population. Estimates vary from five to fifteen million and upward, depending on what kind of mass media programs are included."[9]

5. *The growth and formalization of parent groups.*—During recent years many groups have been formed by parents of children with a particular handicap. In general, their purpose has been two-fold: (1) to secure more adequate services and facilities for their children and other children with similar handicaps; and (2) to educate the community to the needs of these children and ways for meeting the needs. In many cases members of such groups have also been able to provide emotional support to one another in facing their problems. A number of the national social welfare organizations which now provide professional leadership in a specialized field represent the coming together of scattered local groups of varying degrees of formality. The National Association for Retarded Children is one example of this development.

6. *The increasing use of new educational techniques.*—New techniques developed in the education field are being increasingly employed in adult education activities in social welfare. Many agencies have adopted them for their in-service training programs.

Issues

Some of the current issues in the social welfare field which appear to be directly related to the adult education activities in the field include:

Future of Conferences.—The National Conference on Social Welfare, which is the oldest forum body in the field, is engaged in a study of its future role and structure. Other national agencies are being involved in the study process because the Conference has recognized that the issues it faces could not be solved by a single organization, since they impinge on or are affected by future emphases and programs of other national organizations with major forum activities.

There appears to be general recognition in the field that the problems created by the trend toward multiple independent conferences in social welfare mentioned earlier—a natural response to increasing specialization, both technical and organizational—needs to be examined.

Techniques for Meetings.—As already indicated, there has been some hesitancy about introducing new educational techniques in the social welfare field—whether in conferences, for staff training, or for other purposes. With particular regard to meetings, there is a belief in some quarters that the use of small groups with emphasis on audience participation has been oversold. Many feel that for transmission of technical knowledge and information the large meeting with a presentation by an expert is to be preferred to other methods. What is undoubtedly needed—in both social welfare and adult education—is further study of the purposes of meetings and of the relationship of purpose to types of meeting and the techniques to be employed.

Informal education and social group work.—Within the social work profession there is at the present time a lack of agreement about the nature of social group work, with particular relation to its educational aspects. Clara Kaiser has described the current situation in the following words:

> It is evident from the results of this study that we are far from having accurate knowledge about what distinguishes the practice of individual social group workers from that of other practitioners who work with groups. We are probably not even prepared to articulate a basic conceptual framework of our practice with which all members of our disciplines would agree. . . .
> Associated mainly with informal education and recreation for many years, social group work practice was chiefly practiced in agencies affording leisure-time activities to children and youth. In recent years, however, there has been increasing recognition of the value of social group work as a means for enriching and facilitating services directed toward specific forms of treatment for persons who are suffering from physical, emotional or social disabilities.[10]

Group dynamics and social welfare.—Group dynamics has been receiving increasing attention within the social welfare field but has made little impact on the social work profession.

Grace Coyle has this to say: "The research [in group dynamics] is often of a minute fragment or set up under laboratory conditions so unlike those of the group's social environment as to seem unusable. The absence of a consensus or explicit personality theory used in research on groups or the lack of what appears to social workers to be an understanding of the dynamics of individual behavior makes some of the research seem, as one correspondent put it, mechanical, manipulative and gadgetty."[11]

Other leaders are concerned over the emphasis on the group as the primary creative vehicle and fear that in group-centered leadership[12] the creative and imaginative individual may be submerged. Others criticize about the time required to achieve goals through the use of group-centered leadership. There is also a question as to whether this method is appropriate for many of the group activities in social welfare and for dealing with problems that require immediate solution. Some concern has developed about the danger of the indiscriminate use of role-playing and other techniques by leaders insufficiently trained to deal with a procedure which is apt to bring to the fore emotional aspects, including unconscious materials.

It is the contention of the author that these criticisms have had some basis of fact but that in recent years many of them have been getting attention as the interchange between the behavior sciences and social work has increased. Group dynamics as a relatively new theory developed a technical vocabulary and special meanings to words in social work usage. Group dynamics was held by a few to be a panacea for all human relations problems and a cultist atmosphere may have appeared for a time. It is understandable that a great deal of attention was given to small group theory and little to actual practice. The social science researcher on small groups has been oriented to examining the group process as it functions while the social group worker has concentrated on objectives and on methods to bring about change in group values and behavior. There is evidence that there will be more interchange between these two disciplines.

The National Training Laboratories at Bethel, Maine, and others engaging in recent research on small groups, have made considerable progress in meeting these criticisms. There is growing recognition that social work cannot ignore the findings of research in small group theory and behavior.[13]

CONCLUSIONS

From this survey it becomes clear that adult education and social welfare have much in common and that many adult education activities are conducted by social welfare organizations. The replies to a questionnaire which was sent to a selected group of individuals and a large number of national social welfare agencies reveal that all the types of activities specified by the Adult Education Association as comprising adult education are carried on in social welfare agencies. These include: academic education, programs for aging and preparation for retirement, community development, creative arts, economic education, fundamental and literacy education, general personality development, home and family life education, leadership training, liberal education, public affairs, recreation, and vocational education. In view of this fact it is probably safe to say that one of the most important settings for adult education is provided by the social welfare field.

In view of the confusion of thinking which exists about the nature of the two fields and their relationship to each other, it seems that the time may be ripe for efforts to clarify some of the questions that have been raised in this chapter. At heart both are concerned with inter-personal relationships as the basis of the learning and maturing process and both depend on the dynamics of relationships. Each should be able to learn from the other and to contribute to the enrichment of the other.

Footnotes

[1]Wayne McMillen, "Financing Social Welfare Services," *Social Work Yearbook* (New York: National Association of Social Workers, 1957), p. 264.

[2]*This is the NCSW* (Columbus, Ohio: National Conference on Social Welfare, 1958).

[3]*Social Work Yearbook, op. cit.*

4Florence Hollis, "Personality Diagnosis in Casework," *Ego Psychology and Dynamic Casework* (New York: Family Service Association of America, 1958), pp. 84-85.

5Grace Coyle, "Social Group Work," *Social Work Yearbook* (New York: American Association of Social Workers, 1954), p. 480.

6Robert F. Fenley, "Volunteers in Social Welfare," *Social Work Yearbook*, 1957, *op. cit.*, pp. 592-98.

7Marion Robinson, "The Citizen Looks at International Social Welfare," (New York: National Social Welfare Assembly, 1957).

8For detailed information see Ruth Williams, "Conferences in Social Welfare," *Social Work Yearbook* (New York: National Association of Social Workers, 1960), pp. 191-98.

9Gunnar Dybwad, "Family Life Education," *Social Work Yearbook*, 1957, *op. cit.*, p. 239.

10Clara Kaiser, "Characteristics of Social Group Work," *Social Welfare Forum* (New York: Columbia University Press, 1957), pp. 164-67.

11Grace L. Coyle, *Social Science in the Professional Education of Social Workers* (New York: Council on Social Work Education, 1958), p. 35.

12For a definition of group-centered leadership see Malcolm Knowles, *Informal Adult Education* (New York: Association Press, 1951), p. 60.

13Edgar F. Borgatta, "What Social Science Says About Groups," *Social Welfare Forum*, 1957, *op. cit.*, pp. 212-35.

Selected Readings

Bruno, Frank J., and Towley, Louis. *Trends in Social Work as Reflected in the Proceedings of the National Conference of Social Work, 1874-1956.* New York: Columbia University Press, 1957.

Cloward, Richard S. "Agency Structure as a Variable in Service to Groups," *Group Work and Community Organization, 1956.* Papers presented at the 83rd Annual Forum of the National Conference on Social Welfare. New York: Columbia University Press, 1956.

Fink, Arthur E., Conover, Merrill B., and Wilson, Everett E., *The Field of Social Work.* New York: Henry Holt & Company, 1955.

Friedlander, Walter A. *Introduction to Social Welfare.* New York: Prentiss Hall, 1955.

Green, Helen D. *Social Work Practice in Community Organization.* New York: Whiteside, Inc., 1954.

Hoffer, Joe R., "The State Conference in Social Welfare—Its Future Role." Columbus: National Conference on Social Welfare, 1953. (Mimeographed)

Kaiser, Clara, "Characteristics of Social Group Work," *The Social Welfare Forum*, 1958. New York: Columbia University Press, 1957.

Kasius, Cora (ed.). *New Directions in Social Work.* New York: Harper & Bros., 1954.

McMillen, Wayne. *Community Organization for Social Welfare.* Chicago: University of Chicago Press, 1945.

Ross, Murray G. *Community Organization—Theory and Principles.* New York: Harper and Bros., 1955.

Social Work with Groups—1958-1959. Selected papers from National Conference on Social Welfare. New York: National Association of Social Workers, 1958.

Sills, David. *The Volunteers.* Glencoe, Illinois: Free Press, 1958.

CHAPTER 32

ADULT EDUCATION IN GENERAL VOLUNTARY ORGANIZATIONS

MAX BIRNBAUM
Educational Consultant
American Jewish Committee

THE VOLUNTARY ORGANIZATION—
A NEGLECTED INSTITUTION

The voluntary organization in the education of adults defies precise description, comprising as it does a universe of some 5,000 national organizations with and without local constituencies, with single or multiple purposes, with broad or limited memberships, with federated or corporate organizational structures. There is a wealth of information available concerning the social, political, and economic impact of the voluntary organization; but with the exception of a few out-dated treatments, there is a virtual absence of data on how the organization educates its own membership and what it contributes to the education of the public at large. The sole contemporary exception is the 1954 *Adult Education—A Directory of National Organizations,* published for the Council of National Organizations of the Adult Education Association.

In spite of the peripheral nature of its educational activities, the voluntary organization will inevitably be compared with colleges and universities, libraries, public schools, and proprietary schools, where the educational role is central to organizational purposes. An understanding of its unique roles and functions is therefore necessary to an understanding of the complicated phenomenon of the voluntary organization in the adult education movement.

The following sections have been based largely upon responses to two sets of questionnaires specifically prepared for this *Handbook.* The first was sent to over a hundred organizations, eighty of which responded. A follow-up questionnaire to many of the organizations, seeking information on training and local and national programming, elicited some sixty

378

responses. The CNO publication mentioned above, although somewhat dated, was an invaluable source of additional data. This statement is by way of warning to the reader that the generalizations which follow are based on a crude sample and reflect solely the activities of those organizations which responded to the questionnaires. But since the responses came from organizations of widely divergent types, it is unlikely that an investigation of a larger and more scientifically devised sample would substantially alter the conclusions which follow.

THE NATURE OF ADULT EDUCATION IN VOLUNTARY ORGANIZATIONS

To paraphrase Moliere, most voluntary organizations are surprised to learn that they are providing adult education. Indeed, there is an influential professional group which feels that this surprise is more than justified. The confusion and challenge warrant some critical inquiry into the nature of the adult educational contribution of the voluntary organizations as a group and a comparison of this contribution with that of the more formal institutions.

A basic purpose of adult education, as of education in general, is to help equip the individual with the knowledge, insights, and skills which will enable him to make the wisest decisions in his social, economic, and political life, as well as to contribute to his personal enrichment. The ultimate educational decisions are a matter of individual choice not predetermined by the educative agency. When the educative institution dictates the action or decision, the process is usually not regarded as educational, but as persuasion, propaganda, or manipulation. The educational process, moreover, requires scrupulous attention to objectivity in selection of content, and a minimum of personal bias in presentation of conflicting data. Adult education thus defined would rule out of the field any institutional setting other than those which are classroom-centered or those informal institutions which operate their programs after the classroom-centered model. Organizations such as the Y's, both Christian and Jewish, certain men's and women's organizations which still carry on activities in the tradition of the American Lyceum, and those organizations which feature arts and crafts programs or studies of a semi-vocational or literary character, would be included as legitimate adult education instrumentalities. The more liberally inclined observer might also include parent education groups and organizations in the civic education field which conduct programs in accordance with classroom criteria, such as the PTA's, the Child Study Association, and the League of Women Voters. If the classroom image of adult education were the sole determining criterion, however, very few voluntary organizations would meet the test of acceptability.

In recent years a group of adult educators has challenged the traditional definition of individual-centered education and has argued that community-centered adult education will ultimately be recognized as the field's unique function. Using the community as a setting for the education of adults creates a different classroom and a new professional role with great similarity to both the setting and the behavior of the voluntary organization; in both cases education is a means to an end, not an end in itself. It is precisely this distinctive union of education and action in the community development program that provides the bridge between classroom-centered instruction and voluntary group education. Community development education and organizational education thus share basic similarities, but the two are not synonymous.[1] Although both regard education as instrumental, this common ground must not obscure the real differences that exist between them, nor the unique contribution of the voluntary organization.

The community development specialist has elected to use the community, with its formal and informal groupings, as the natural classroom for the education of adults and the solution of their problems. He still operates with complete objectivity in the helping role—presumably he has no personal judgment concerning which community problems require priority treatment. He is concerned primarily with the procedures of problem solution and the total educative effects of participation in the process of problem-solving. Organizations, on the other hand, are usually committed in advance to a specific cause, and use their educational programs to convince both memberships and public of the importance of the problem and the desirability of a particular solution.

Most voluntary organizations have goals and objectives which, although shared by all or many of their members, are yet independent of any one member. Their educational programs are, therefore, usually organization-centered as distinguished from the individual-centered curricula which characterize the formal educational institutions. The organization usually has a fairly well-defined point of view which is reflected in its educational materials. Respectable educational methods and techniques of every description are employed to inform, motivate, and persuade their target groups to think and act in accordance with this specific point of view. In many cases, an organization will take public positions in support of or in opposition to a given issue, utilizing its educational ammunition to rally support or to justify its action. Professional voluntary organizations may at times act in this fashion when the interests of the profession would appear to be at stake, while carrying on their major role of in-service education for their members and general education for the public at large.

Despite the peculiar nature of the educational process in the voluntary organization setting, it is still considered by many competent observers as *potentially* the single most influential adult educative setting in our society. This belief is founded upon the evidence that the primary group (which meets face-to-face) exerts the most powerful educative force on the individual in our society. Voluntary organizations fulfill primary group needs for millions of adults.

Most American voluntary organizations are predominantly middle-class, with a membership possessing a comparatively high formal educational background. With the near universality of a high school education, it is a safe conjecture that most voluntary group members have been exposed over a significant period of years to formal educational experiences. Indeed, many organizations, including those of the professionals, are composed entirely of the college-educated. The influence an educated membership exerts on the educational programs of the voluntary association must never be underestimated—research findings support the observation that to influence successfully an educated group, care must be taken to give a balanced presentation of the pros and cons of a particular issue.

Organizations do not exist in isolation; multiple influences are constantly being exerted on their members. In view of the fact that most people are affiliated with many organizations where they are exposed to slightly different points of view and have access to information from the mass media of all descriptions, there are few limits on the free market place of ideas to which most members are exposed. All these influences affect the educational programs of specific organizations, making them freer of bias than one might assume to be the case.

Educational programming frequently responds to the interests of the membership, thus promoting activities far from the public image of the organization's goals. The need to maintain the continued allegiance of the members influences many organizations in truly miraculous ways, especially on the local level. The curiosity of members to explore beyond strictly organizational bounds, the pressures on program chairmen to provide interesting meetings, and the disinclination of most Americans to attend purely business meetings, all exert forces which influence the character of local programs.

Finally, many organizations are of the federation-type, as distinguished from the corporative-type, which means that responsibility for educational programs originate in the local units, and this tradition still continues strongly. The PTA's, service clubs (Rotary, Kiwanis, etc.) and the General Federation of Women's Clubs are typical examples of this tradition.

Both national and local programs are indeed a curious mixture of individual-centered and organization-centered activities. If one were to list associational education programs along a continuum, these would extend from the most praiseworthy endeavors, as viewed by the professional adult educator, to those with clear organizations bias. A distribution exercise of this type might confound both the critics and the supporters of the voluntary organization as a setting for adult education.

Although a significant number of organizations by this test would cluster at either extreme, a very large number would have to be distributed, program-wise, along the entire range.

The American Medical Association's *Today's Health*, public exhibits, TV programs, and pamphlets on public health, as well as its programs of professional education and improvement, would clearly meet the test of individual-centered programming. On the other hand, its program material on "Socialized Medicine" would clearly fall within the organization-centered portion of the continuum. Similar analyses of the programs of the Women's Christian Temperance Union or the National Association for the Advancement of Colored People would distribute these on the organization-centered end of the line. The Lions Clubs, the League of Women Voters, or the PTA would cluster more to the individual-centered end, inasmuch as the bulk of their programs are prepared with a minimum of ideological bias, and their general objective is personal improvement without explicit guidance to appropriate action. These groups, however, also conduct programs that can properly be termed organization-centered.

The classification of associational programs as organization-centered does not imply that these have slight educative value. Society and the adult education movement specifically would suffer a serious loss if voluntary groups ceased their organization-centered activities. Moreover, the satisfaction of organizational needs and the gratification of individual needs are inexorably intertwined in the programmatic operations of the voluntary organization, making it impossible to evaluate them separately. As the following overview will demonstrate, it would be neither wise nor accurate to accord one a higher value than the other.

PROGRAM DEVELOPMENT

Programming for educational purposes in voluntary organizations is both national and local in character. The main source of written materials, films, discussion guides, suggestions for speakers, and other program aids, is the national office. Except for programs utilizing national communication media or carried on during annual conventions, the bulk of program operations take place in the community, state, or region. Some service organizations, such as Lions International, inspire local programs from the national level. Most organizations indicate that their local units usually initiated their own programs and that they may or may not be related to national programs.

Those organizations reporting national program emphases list the following typical categories: leadership training, human relations, general personal development, community development, public affairs, creative arts, health and safety, vocational education, economic education and recreation. They report the use of a wide range of methods, including conferences, sysmposia, study groups, workshops, institutes, and correspondence courses. The most frequently employed techniques are oral presentations, visual aids, and dramatizations.

Education in public issues is predominantly inspired by the national office. To a significant degree program materials in foreign affairs, inter-group relations, housing, public education, and problems of atomic energy, are developed on the national level. These problems undoubtedly require a degree of expertness and study which is more easily in reach of the national office. The quality of much of this programming has been questioned by critics. To be sure, these topics are frequently seen through an organizational lens, with minor corrections for inherent astigmatism, but the quality of many programs, considering their controversial character, is surprisingly good. Restricted-membership organizations, such as The National Citizens Council for Better Schools, The Foreign Policy Association, and the Committee on Economic Development, are particularly active in some of these fields. These organizations regard the general public as their target, but spend a good deal of time and energy in servicing specific groups which are sympathetic and often fraternally related to them.

It is in the programs of their local units that voluntary organizations make their greatest contribution to the education of the community. The welter of programs staggers the imagination: fine arts, crafts, civic improvement, religious education, professional improvement—no phase of adult learning appears to be omitted. Organization-centered programs are implemented with modifications suitable to the local climate and combined with locally initiated programs which frequently bear slight resemblance to the public image of the sponsoring organization. American Legion Posts have been known to offer child welfare programs. One Chamber of Commerce, over a five year period, invited members of the Washington Ambassadorial Corps to spend several days speaking and meeting with businessmen and the general public. During the last two years local branches of the local Leagues of Women Voters have distributed their efforts in the following fashion: 376 worked on some phases of planning and zoning; 370 on schools; 225 on taxation and finances; 180 on recreation; 158 on local government surveys; 144 on juvenile problems; and 134 on problems of city- or county-manager government.

Frequently, groups of local constituencies combine to sponsor programs of both local and national significance. Jointly-sponsored local programs have revolved around civic improvement, mental hygiene, foreign affairs, group relations, art exhibits, musical events, and comparable topics. Lists of sponsoring organizations frequently include groups whose organization-centered programs appear to have slight relationship to the co-sponsored activity. But the interests of local members, as well as their need to be associated with activities sanctioned by powerful community figures or organizations, are probably the forces which account for the collaboration. From an adult education point of view the quality of these programs is often excellent, for the compromises necessary to maintain the support of all segments of the sponsoring committee make for a balanced approach. The educational experience for the representative participants is heightened by mutual exposure to opposite points of view.

Many local educational activities have no immediate relevance to any stated organizational goal, either national or local. A common paradox in associational life on the local level is to make use of one's primary memberships to satisfy a variety of personal and social needs, some of which are not logically relevant to the particular organizational locus. To be sure, this diffusion and extension of organization programming does not go on unchallenged either locally or by national staffs. Despite these challenges, however, the local program chairmen continue to be sensitive to local membership needs.

Voluntary organizations still carry on programs that are beyond question in the proud tradition of self-improvement which characterized the programs of their nineteenth century forebears. Speakers, discussions, films, and other program aids devoted to an appreciation of the arts and belles lettres and a better personal understanding of social, political, and economic issues are still the mainstay of much programming for these organizations. But self-understanding on the psychological plane is the twentieth century addition to the basic program shelf from which chairmen select their topics.

TRAINING FOR PARTICIPATION AND LEADERSHIP

The college for training in citizen participation is the voluntary group. The skills and techniques of leadership and membership, once acquired, can be utilized in any group situation. Although the training and experience are provided for organization-centered reasons, the individual is permanently enriched in the process.

Some groups have systematic training programs for both staff and volunteers. A questionnaire item on training reveals that out of thirty-three organizations which responded, twenty-two have training programs. The Association of Junior Leagues, for example, provides a six-month course for their provisional members; and the U. S. Chamber of Commerce offers a three-year sequence of in-service training for its local executives. Board member training, given in conjunction with annual or regional meetings, is provided by most organizations.

Training programs in recent years have emphasized the leadership skills and knowledge of group behavior which are the contributions of "group dynamics." These processes, basically democratic in ideology and practice, have not only enriched adult education methodology, but also have provided a substantial common ground of communication between voluntary organizations and the adult education profession. Confirmation of this assumption is reflected in the vicissitudes encountered by *Adult Leadership* since its inception. When methodology and techniques were the major features of the periodical, voluntary group support was high; with the change of emphasis in recent years, the major loss in circulation has been among this group.

Interest in training for membership, leadership, and staff work is increasing. Recently the Council of National Organizations has inaugurated a successful institute for the discussion of the training needs of national organizations and an annual training laboratory for staff members of voluntary organizations has been initiated by the National Training Laboratories. Both developments augur well for future collaboration in training between educational institutions and voluntary organizations.

PUBLICATIONS

Millions of copies of organizational publications, substantially informative in nature, are published each year. William Rogers cites approximately two million as the total periodical and pamphlet circulation for the state of Minnesota alone.[2] *The Directory of National Organizations,* compiled by the CNO of the AEA, lists a total of 84 official journals reported by 113 national organizations. In addition to their official journals, 75 of these organizations listed other regular periodicals, pamphlets, research reports, study guides, and a host of other publications.

The overwhelming majority of the regular and most of the special publications are prepared for the membership and the general public. Many of these are professional journals of high repute with a considerable reading public beyond the membership, such as *Nation's Business, Child Study, Journal of Home Economics, Commentary, The Foreign Policy Bulletin,* and *Mental Hygiene.* Many voluntary organizations' publications of every description are used in public school adult classes and in university educational activities, as well as by other voluntary groups. Very often the first announcements of research findings relating to such matters of public interest as community improvement and social welfare are published in the official journals and special pamphlets of the voluntary groups. Frequently, publications reflecting conflicting points of view of two different organizations are listed in study guides and bibliographies issued by still a third group.

Organization-sponsored publications appear to be, on the whole, excellent educational resource material. Perhaps because the general public is a major target for the printed materials, they are characterized by considerable objectivity and a patent effort to be persuasive without obvious slanting of facts. Such treatment is a tribute both to the editorial committees' respect for the printed word, as well as to the American public's healthy skepticism toward publications of "special interest" groups. A perusal of some of these publications causes one to question the jaundiced view with which educated Americans generally regard publications bearing an organizational imprint, unless it be one of which they approve. Such summary judgment often discredits many a useful publication whose message could profit the very people who rejected it. A publication which deserves widespread use beyond its designated public is the U.S. Chamber of Commerce's course in practical politics for businessmen.

Conceivably, the Adult Education Association might rescue some of these publications from an unfair oblivion by sponsoring a board of review which could render independent judgment on their quality and utility. Such a "Seal of Approval" might encourage more organizations to edit their general publications with an eye to the circulation value of an objective recommendation. This endorsement would also benefit adult educators who do not have the time to winnow from the mass of publications materials suitable for classroom use.

RESEARCH

The voluntary organization is rarely associated in the public mind with the initiation and subsidization of research. The outstanding exceptions are the research contributions of the major health groups, such as The American Cancer Society, The National Foundation, and similar associations. Despite the public stereotype, a cursory survey of the research interests of a limited sample of organizations reveals that a significant portion of past and current research owes its origin to the program interests of the voluntary groups.

The CNO survey previously mentioned reports that sixty-eight responding organizations reported research accomplished or in progress that was related to adult education or on subjects which were suitable for adult education. Eleven general areas were indicated: education of the public or of organization members, organization program, organization leadership and training, job training, job content, recruitment of workers, community action and participation, and community needs, health, economic affairs, government, politics, world affairs, mass communication, and propaganda. Although an analysis of the original data suggests that the respondents interpreted the term "research" liberally, the responses reflect studies of more than passing significance.

Three examples are illustrative. *The Volunteers,* by David Sills, which has been praised as a major contribution to sociological knowledge and organization theory, was initiated by the National Foundation in order to ascertain the future of its organization in the light of the Salk vaccine. The Cincinnati study of the impact of educational programs on opinion and attitudes regarding the United Nations was sponsored by the American Association for the United Nations pursuant to its own program needs. The implications of the research, however, for the mass media and students of public opinion have been widely recognized, and the study is on its way to becoming a classic in the field. Lastly, the *Authoritarian Personality*, one of the "Studies in Prejudice" sponsored by the American Jewish Committee, is now considered a major contribution to personality theory, with far-reaching implications for research and practice.

Much of the organization-related research is carried on in conjunction with universities—the National Foundation study was undertaken by the Bureau of Applied Research of Columbia University; The Association for the United Nations project was under the direction of a University of Chicago team, and The American Jewish Committee publication was the result of collaboration between University of California social scientists and the organization's Department of Scientific Research. The Committee for Economic Development sponsors studies which are the collaborative effort of businessmen and nationally known economists, as well as books written by outstanding university scholars.

Voluntary organizations, with few exceptions, have not developed research departments whose studies are comparable to those designed and executed for them by social scientists from university centers. Although some studies carried on by organizational departments of research are undoubtedly of the highest calibre, few have been published or distributed for general circulation.

In the opinion of many observers, the most noteworthy contribution of organizations to research is their function of translating into practice and popularizing research data. Organizations such as the Foreign Policy Association, The American Medical Association, the Child Study Association, and the various professional and vocational associations, are especially active in transmitting research results to the general as well as special publics. The research and resource agencies which belong to the CNO of the AEA consider this function their major contribution to adult education.

RELATIONSHIP WITH OTHER ORGANIZATIONS

Often a voluntary organization will co-operate with one or more organizations in order to pursue program objectives. These co-operative relationships may be transitory or long-term, on given issues or on total program objectives. The National Federation of Business and Professional Women's Clubs, for example, reports that its programs for older women workers are carried on in conjunction with other organizations. The American Institute of Cooperation lists land grant colleges, the U. S. Office of Education, National Education Association, and the American Vocational Association as groups with which it collaborates.

So-called "umbrella" or co-ordinating organizations are a common phenomenon of American life and many organizations belong to one or more. Approximately one hundred organizations, representing a cross-section of organizational life, are members of the Council of National Organizations of the Adult Education Association. The creation of a co-ordinating group, clearly identified with the adult education movement, is the decade's most significant development in organizational colla-boration for educational purposes. Under CNO auspices, a rich variety of groups have collaborated in programs and institutes dealing with the uses of TV, the handling of controversial issues, problems of staff and member training, the role of leadership in national organizations, and numerous other areas of common concern. The CNO has maintained its membership despite the presence within its fold of organizations as diverse as business and labor groups, all three major religious denomina-tions, Planned Parenthood, and numerous other organizations clearly competitive with each other, or diametrically opposed in purpose and program.

Similar collaboration on the local level, unfortunately, still does not exist in many communities. National collaboration through the CNO has been strengthened by the professional complexion of the organiza-tional representatives, most of whom have received their original training in education or social work. Such similarity in background appears to be lacking on the local level, where in most cases volunteers represent their local chapters in community enterprises. The great challenge for the CNO in future years is the creation of local counterparts—a development which would not only aid the adult education movement, but also make a major contribution to local communication among groups which now have only slight contact with each other.

VOLUNTARY ORGANIZATIONS AND PROFESSIONAL ADULT EDUCATION

Perhaps the most striking testimony to the desire of voluntary organi-zations to improve their adult education programs is their employment of professional educators. The U. S. Chamber of Commerce, the National Association of Manufacturers, The Association of Junior Leagues, and the National Conference of Christians and Jews, for example, have staff members in charge of adult programming who were originally trained to teach. Few of those presently employed have professional adult educa-tion degrees, although organizations show increasing interest in such trained individuals.

The presence of professionally-trained personnel has facilitated co-operative relationships with college and university sponsored adult educa-tion services. The Adult Education Association of the United States has also stimulated this collaboration by opening its ranks to memberships from voluntary organizations of all types, as well as to college and public school adult educators. For years, the AEA publication, *Adult Leadership*, was widely read and used to improve leadership training, meeting design, group discussion procedures in hundreds of voluntary organizations. Attendance at workshops of the National Training Laboratories, Boston University, the University of Chicago, the University of Texas, the University of Utah, and the University of California, has served also to spread the newer methodologies of adult learning from social science research to the organizational life of the volunteer groups.

A number of university extension departments have not waited to be approached for service by voluntary groups. Their contributions have included helping to design annual meetings, conducting volunteer training, teaching classes composed of members of one or a group of organizations, and arranging conferences for organizational leaders. For example, the University of Wisconsin Extension Division brought together some forty organizations to confer on appropriate educational means for dealing with controversies in local communities. The University of Minnesota, which has had a State Organization Service in existence for some years, has co-operated in numerous ways with state-wide and local organizations. The creation of residential centers[3] has increased considerably the co-operation between voluntary groups and the universities—during the course of a single year Purdue has been the site of dozens of conferences which have involved organizational membership and personnel.

Organizations as diverse as the Credit Union National Association, American Library Association, National School Boards Association, American Dietetic Association, American Bar Association, American Physical Therapy Association, American Medical Association, General Federation of Women's Clubs and others report the regular use of university extension facilities for leadership training. The Cooperative League of the USA uses short courses at Michigan State, the University of Wisconsin, and the University of Minnesota. Other organizations, such as the American Automobile Association, serve universities by preparing courses in auto safety and driving for university use.

FINANCING

Organizational adult education programs are financed in a variety of ways. The major source of support reported is the general budget, which is usually based on membership dues, tuition fees, charges for materials, and contributions. Foundations and local community chest allocations are the second major source of income. Some organizations raise their money directly from the public, including the National Conference of Christians and Jews, The American Cancer Society, and the National Foundation. No information is presently available on how much is spent by voluntary organizations for educational purposes, but the total must reach many millions of dollars.

CURRENT PROBLEMS AND ISSUES

Voluntary organizations desirous of improving their adult education programs must make a number of important decisions during the decade ahead. One of these previously alluded to—the development of local CNO's—is the best instrument for effective deployment of both university and agency resources in the improvement of local participation, leadership and membership training, and educational programming. Success will not be easily achieved in the face of the realities of local competition, conflicts, and estrangement. Experience with collaboration of this type on the national scene and similar success in a few local ventures suggests that concentration on techniques and methodology may be the sole basis for local collaboration for some time to come. Co-operation on other mutual needs will come much later.

A second decision of equal importance is the elimination of communication barriers between professional adult educators and those who serve the function of adult education in voluntary organizations. Agreement on more than a common interest in methodology must be sought, if the interests of both groups and the advancement of adult education in general are to be achieved. The recent decision of the Fund for Adult Education to stress the training of citizen-leaders and to encourage their involvement in community affairs underscores the importance of the voluntary organization as a setting for adult education. More meaningful collaboration between both groups of professionals to improve the education of these citizen-leaders is clearly the test for the future. The adult education movement has been a unique enterprise precisely because it has always included those who teach so that others may act, as well as those who act and teach at the same time.

Footnotes

1For a detailed discussion of community development as a program area in adult education, see Chapter 35.

2William C. Rogers, "Minnesota Voluntary Associations" (Minneapolis: University of Minnesota Extension Division). (Mimeographed, n.d.)

3See Chapter 17.

Selected Readings

Council of National Organizations. *A Directory of National Organizations.* New York: Association Press, 1954.

Ely, Mary L., and Chappell, Eve. *Women In Two Worlds.* New York: American Association for Adult Education, 1938.

Hill, Frank Ernest. *Man-Made Culture.* New York: American Association for Adult Education, 1938.

Sills, David. *The Volunteers.* New York: Columbia University Press, 1958.

PART IV

PROGRAM AREAS IN ADULT EDUCATION

CHAPTER 33

ACADEMIC EDUCATION FOR ADULTS

PETER E. SIEGLE
Research Associate
Center for the Study of Liberal Education for Adults

THE MEANING OF ACADEMIC

In reality "academic" education, properly so-called, refers to education conducted in, around, or by an academic institution. To label certain kinds of education "academic" and others "non-academic" is to cut a line perhaps too fine for the satisfaction of most people. Some might say that academic education is that kind of education which carries with it an appropriate certification of transferable credit. But this would deny all the excellent non-credit work in adult education which is of the highest academic quality and standard, and which makes up a considerable portion of adult education both in the United States and elsewhere.

Yet this chapter is supposed to deal with academic education for adults, and requires a delimitation of the problem. For the purpose of this discussion, therefore, academic education for adults shall be defined as that kind of education which *involves attainment of credit in a number of courses, is systematic and cumulative, and which leads to a certificate or a degree.* Some of these certificates or degrees might carry with them transferable credit; other might be terminal; still others might have transferability or acceptance for further work only in certain institutions. For example, there are certain state universities in this country offering high school equivalency courses by correspondence. The credits received in these institutions are frequently not acceptable for matriculation even in neighboring state universities. Likewise, there are Associate in Arts degrees offered by some universities which are indications of satisfactory completion of a systematic curriculum, but which cannot be applied as credit toward a baccalaureate or any further systematic degree work.

WHY DEGREES AND CERTIFICATES

One might justifiably ask why such programs exist if they do not carry transferable credits. In other words, why should one engage in programs of systematic study leading to a certificate or a terminal degree rather than taking courses at random in accordance with personal needs and satisfaction? To this question there may be no satisfactory answer unless one assumes that in most cases special programs of systematic study have been developed with the specific needs of adults in mind, and by people who hope so to structure an extended learning experience that it adds up to something which leads toward personal integration. Moreover, the granting of a certificate or degree as a symbol of completion of an integrated program of study says to an adult that he has found a place for himself in the main stream of the academic tradition. This is a need which has been met at several different levels.

AT THE HIGH SCHOOL LEVEL

At the high school level adults have for years found it necessary to gain a diploma in order to qualify for appropriate positions in the economic hierarchy. We are all aware of the programs offered by public schools through evening classes leading toward the high school diploma. In addition, however, there has developed a need for high school equivalency work which helps adults move on toward matriculation in colleges and universities. Such needs have been met not only by proprietary home study or correspondence schools, but also by colleges and universities themselves. Several state universities offer high school equivalency certificates by correspondence. The University of Nebraska is a prime example, offering courses to students all over the world whose high school education has been interrupted.

In an urban environment evening classes leading toward college entrance credit are available in universities. New York University maintains what is called an "Academic Department" designed to help the adult student qualify for college entrance. Through this program competent adults may speedily qualify for college entrance even if they now have few or no satisfactory credits. The courses are available to persons who: (1) are 21 years of age or over; (2) are admitted with a condition to one of the colleges of the university; or (3) are high school graduates who need such remedial activity. A qualified academic adviser is available to help students plan a program consistent with the admissions requirements of New York University or some other university of the student's choice. About its own standards, New York University has this to say:

> Because the Academic Department is primarily concerned with preparing mature students for college entrance, it maintains a high academic standard. The passing grade (for college recommendation) is 80. To receive credit for a course, a student must attend at least 80 percent of the regular class meetings.

AT THE COLLEGE OR UNIVERSITY LEVEL

As the high school becomes more and more a part of the attainment of the large majority of the population, the need for high school equivalency programs diminishes. By the same token, however, greater emphasis is placed upon the acquisition of creditable recognition for achievement at the level of higher education. This emphasis has been expressed by our colleges and universities through evening colleges and extension divisions in certificate and degree programs. Some attempt has been made in various places around the country to develop programs leading to a certificate, as well as to such degrees as the *Adjunct in Arts, the Associate in Arts, the Baccalaureate,* and the *M.A. in General Education.*

Certificate Programs

The principle behind the development of certificate programs rather than degree programs is the fact that they offer opportunity for experimentation and individuation of sequences and courses unhampered by the stringent traditionalism of academia, yet organized into some integrated whole. The examples presented here represent a study in contrast between relative freedom of subject matter devised at New York University and the stringently prescribed program at the University of Chicago, both under the rubric of liberal education. They are offered here as examples of full-blown attempts at developing certificate programs which carry no transferable credit.

The Certificate in General Education at New York University.—The basic assumption of this program is that which underlies most of the work at New York University's Division of General Education; namely, the "cafeteria" principle, under which it is assumed that mature people who come to study at the Division of General Education and who take courses of their own choosing, are well on their way to becoming liberally educated. The certificate program further assumes that if these same persons wish to have a certificate, and will go to the division for guidance and counsel, they may work for a certificate which is in no way bound to a credit structure imposed from the outside, but is rather tailored to the needs and requirements of each individual. Designed for the mature mind, the program is adaptable to varied aims of individual students, who pursue studies of their own choice at a rate of advancement best suited to their own capacities.

The purpose of the program is to help the individual mature student gain recognition for having successfully negotiated a highly individualized program of general education. But because the program is so individualized, it aims to provide him with an intellectual or artistic experience that helps him focus his varied studies.

There are no "required" courses. Any courses may be included in a student's program. With the assistance and approval of his designated faculty adviser, each student plans a program in accordance with his abilities, aims, previous training, or practical experience. The resulting program of study should be suitably balanced among the student's special interests, his need for further training in communication skills, and a deepened appreciation of the liberal arts and sciences.

When the student registers for the Certificate Program, or shortly thereafter, he meets his Certificate Program adviser, who helps him to plan his studies in general and to register for specific courses. Later a project adviser is assigned to him. The student is encouraged to seek the assistance of his advisers in connection with any problems pertaining to his studies.

In addition to regularly conducted classroom courses, the program also includes an individual project, in the area of a student's special interest, which he selects with the assistance of a Certificate Program adviser. This project may be a report of the student's special studies in the humanities, a literary or artistic production in the practical arts, or some design or construction in technology. In general this project may serve as a directive for planning the student's individual program.

When his faculty advisers consider the student prepared to begin work on the project described above, an arrangement is made with a faculty member to serve as his special project adviser. As a specialist in the subject matter of the student's project, the project advisor assists the student in developing his project, guides him in his preparatory studies, and gives such special instruction as may be appropriate. This is accomplished through regularly scheduled private conferences of varying duration, according to the adviser's discretion. If the project is not completed during two terms of scheduled conferences, the student may continue to consult his project adviser, provided either that he continues his registration in the Certificate Program or that he has satisfactorily completed all other requirements.

The student may, with the approval of the faculty advisers, select any subject for his project, provided that facilities for its study are available to the Division of General Education. The project, as the student's individual task, may be elementary or advanced or complex, depending on the student's prior training and education.

To qualify for a Certificate in General Education, a student must fulfill the following conditions:

(1) He must complete forty-eight term hours of courses with a grade of Satisfactory or Excellent, including four term hours devoted to project conferences.

(2) His completed project must receive the approval of his project adviser and of the administrator of the Certificate Program.

(3) Within one year of his registration in the Certificate Program he must file with the division satisfactory evidence of his graduation from high school or of his passing a High School Equivalency Examination.

The Basic Program of Liberal Education For Adults at the University of Chicago.—The Basic Program of Liberal Education for Adults has been in operation for ten years. Although enrollments have been relatively small, it is a successful venture in high quality education for adults.

According to one of its bulletins, "the aims of the Program are to help men and women to think more clearly, to talk and write better, to share in discussion more easily, to enjoy works of art more fully; and further to know more about themselves, other people, the major fields of learning, and the great intellectual achievements of the West."

Five different classroom activities are planned to give the student as comprehensive a program in liberal education as possible. Classes meet either once a week or twice a week. The once-a-week plan is less comprehensive and does not include the Social Science Tutorial or the Natural Science Tutorial. Descriptions are taken from a recent bulletin describing the Program:

The Seminar—This class is the heart of the Basic Program. Here the participants and instructor gather around a table and discuss the week's outside reading. Seminar readings consist of great novels, plays, poems, and classic works on politics, economics, ethics, history, and psychology. Textbooks and other secondary sources are avoided on the ground that they oversimplify and distort ideas by isolation and summary. An average time of four or five hours a week is required to do the Seminar readings.

The Humanities Tutorial—This class balances the rapid reading for Seminar with close reading in class. The purpose of the class is to see how works of art, music and poetry, as well as history and philosophy, are constructed. The group analyzes representative works line by line or paragraph by paragraph. This procedure provides invaluable training in methods of reading. In the first year of the Humanities Tutorial the group reads two essays in literary criticism, followed by the close-reading analysis of lyric poems. Little outside preparation is required.

The Social Science Tutorial—The purpose of this class is to apply philosophy to the practical problems of our time. The student writes three papers a year relating a great philosophical work to contemporary problems of ethics, economics, and politics. The factual material necessary for writing the papers is provided. Instruction is given, not by group discussion, but by individual conferences with a teacher. This class does not meet in the first year of the Program, and it is not included in the once-a-week plans of study. It meets only in the second, third, and fourth years of the twice-a-week plan.

The Natural Science Tutorial—Here the group studies the nature of science—what it is, how it goes about solving a problem, and how valid its conclusions are. Short papers by scientists are read in class. The group analyzes the methods of investigation used in solving problems in the various fields of science. No scientific or mathematical background is presupposed; on the other hand, those whose training has been in science will not find this course a duplication of their previous work. The Natural Science Tutorial is not included in the once-a-week programs. Little outside preparation is required.

The Lecture—Once a month, on Friday evenings, a lecture is held to supplement the classroom discussions. Given by distinguished members of the University faculty, the lectures usually discuss texts that are currently being read by first-year students. Basic Program students are admitted to the lectures at a cost of $2.00 for the complete series.

Associate in Arts Degree

Several colleges and universities have been experimenting over the years with something on the order of an AA degree which generally is something less than the baccalaureate, and which usually carries no transfer credit. Such programs have tended to be the equivalent of two years of college work with little attempt to gear the content or the method to the special needs of adults. Recently, however, a few universities have begun to examine the possibilities in special degree programs specifically for adults leading toward the AA degree.

One example of such a program underway at the time of this writing is the *Associate in Arts in General Education* at Syracuse University which was launched in September, 1959. The program is designed to assist adults in four specific areas: (1) increase their skills of critical thinking; (2) further their independent study and learning; (3) enhance an informed sense of responsible citizenship; (4) heighten appreciation in the arts and humanities area.

Consisting of sixty credit hours, the program is designed both in content and procedure for a group of mature people who can work productively together. Such persons might be those who, because of family or economic considerations, have been unable to commence or complete undergraduate or degree work.

Another type of individual who can find the Associate in Ats program valuable is the one who has finished a degree program, particularly in the professional fields, and now has a need for a general studies program to up-date and fill gaps in his previous education.

This program consists of three eight-semester-hour courses required of all students, one each in social science, humanities and science. In addition, there will be nine semester hours of independent study and creative work, fifteen semester hours in a field of special interest, and electives totaling twelve semester hours. The emphasis in each of the courses is upon ideas, concepts, appreciation, and standards of judgment.

The Adjunct in Arts

Of special interest here is the Adjunct in Arts program offered by the Commission on Extension courses, administered by Reginald Phelps of Harvard University and representing Harvard, Tufts, Massachusetts Institute of Technology, Boston College, Boston University, the Boston Museum of Fine Arts, Wellesley, Simmons, Lowell Institute, the Massachusetts Department of Education, and the School Committee of the City of Boston. The courses of the commission are taught by members of the faculties of the universities involved. Any of the courses may be offered for credit toward the Adjunct in Arts at Harvard University.

Candidates for the degree must pass in seventeen full courses with grades of C or better in twelve of the seventeen. This is equivalent to the amount of work required for the Bachelor's degree in many collges. The program must include one full course in English composition and one full course from each of four groups of subjects: (1) Language, Literature, Fine Arts, or Music; (2) Natural Sciences; (3) History or Political and Social Sciences; and (4) Philosophy, Psychology, or Mathematics.

Not more than five of the courses may be in Education, and at least five of the seventeen courses must be offered by Harvard faculty.

Several things distinguish this program from other Associate or Adjunct programs:

(1) Other courses of collegiate grade besides those offered by the commission will in certain cases be accepted for the degree.

(2) Holders of the degree of Adjunct in Arts may be admitted to the Graduate School of Arts and Sciences at Harvard University, based on the quality of the record of the student, a condition which holds for any candidate from an accredited university.

(3) The commission's television courses may be offered toward the fulfillment of the degree requirements.

(4) This is a co-operative endeavor among several accredited universities in the vicinity.

The Bachelor's Degree Especially for Adults

According to a survey conducted by G. Allen Sager of the University of Maryland, there are approximately 150 accredited American colleges and universities offering baccalaureate degree programs entirely through evening study. A very large additional number restrict the number of evening courses which can be offered toward the degree. In virtually all of these schools the evening credit programs meet all the requirements of the day school and very little attempt has been made seriously to consider the special nature of the adult in developing the curriculum.

At the time of this writing, however, several universities are in various stages of planning degree programs especially for adults. The Syracuse AA program has already been mentioned. The University of Oklahoma and Western Reserve University are in the process of careful faculty analysis of plans for baccalaureate degrees which take into account the special needs and abilities of adults.

The Brooklyn Endeavor.—The great break-through in this important endeavor has already been made at Brooklyn College, where a Bachelor's degree program, especially for adults, has been going since 1953. The program began as an experiment to find out how much experience can count toward the achievement of those attributes of a liberal education which are recognized as having been systematized in the regular liberal arts degree.

The underlying assumption of the project is that experience makes possible the achievement of many of the goals of liberal education as recognized by the A.B. Degree. The Brooklyn College program assumes that the goals of a liberal education can be defined so as to make it possible to grant credit for experience and also to devise individual programs for experienced adults which capitalize on life experiences acquired outside the formal academic environment.

After several months of exploration and experimentation, the feasibility of the project was demonstrated. The adults enrolled proved themselves richly endowed with many intellectual, emotional, and social characteristics considered as the desired goals of a liberal education. This was ascertained through counseling and interview techniques as well as through objective tests.

The faculty faced the problem of finding creditable equivalence for the experience-related endowments of the adult students, and were able to develop individual programs and tutorials which make possible an extraordinary acceleration of adults toward the Baccalaureate degree. Instead of spending eight years acquiring the 124 credits necessary for the degree, many of the adults were able to achieve the regular Brooklyn College degree in two or three years or less. Of the first sixteen graduates of the program, fifteen received the Brooklyn A.B. with honors.

The Brooklyn program demonstrates that much of an adult's past and present life experience adds up to a great deal when equated with academic credits. Secondly, it demonstrates that it is possible to teach adults in a manner especially geared to adult rhythms and adult needs. Thirdly, it shows that highly individualized programs for adults can be developed economically. *In fine,* an individualized baccalaureate curriculum for adults has been developed which is different from that of the young undergraduate, which demonstrably achieves the goals of liberal education without in any way lowering standards of scholarship, and which capitalizes on adult experience by both accelerating learning and by stimulating serious motivation to learn.

The Master's Degree

Academic education especially for adults appears to be developing gradually at higher and higher levels. Special adult courses leading to the M.A. degree are being conducted at some colleges, most specifically in general education for teachers. Partial attempts can be found at Hunter College and at Northern Illinois (DeKalb). But one outstanding example of a full degree program is the Graduate Summer School for Teachers at Wesleyan University (Connecticut), established in 1953 for the purpose of providing teachers and school administrators with the opportunity of extending their general education.

No similar opportunity had previously existed. The teacher who wished to go on to a Master's degree had to choose between the M. Ed. and the academic Master's degree in a single subject. Both are admirable degrees of long standing, but many teachers found neither well suited to their needs. The degree in a single subject involves intensive but narrow research; for most public school teachers broad correlative study is more valuable. The M. Ed. involves many courses in education; many teachers feel that their undergraduate courses in education, plus their experience as teachers, make further study of education less valuable than greater command of subject matter.

Wesleyan accordingly established the new degree of *Master of Arts in Liberal Studies* (M.A.L.S.) which gives the candidate an opportunity to work in three or more subjects. In at least one he must take advanced courses, but in the others he may take elementary courses. This makes it possible for teachers to begin the study of new subjects, thereby broadening their general education and making themselves better teachers.

At the most obvious level, they become better teachers by learning new subjects allied to their specialties. At a less obvious level, an important and surprising amount of cross-fertilization occurs when almost any new subject is studied. At the least obvious level, but in some ways the most important, there is abundant evidence that all serious and thoughtful study tends to make a more stimulating, versatile mind—and therefore a better teacher.

What of the teacher who has the Master's degree, wishes to continue his formal education, but finds the specialization and research required for the Ph.D. unsuited to his needs? Should not general education be available to him? Wesleyan believes that it should. The Certificate of Advanced Study (C.A.S.) is therefore now made available to those who wish to pursue an integrated program of not less than thirty hours beyond the Master's degree. Programs leading to the C.A.S. need even more adjustment to individual needs than those leading to the M.A.L.S. because previous study will vary more. A teacher who has taken the M.Ed. has less command of subject matter than one who has taken the M.A.L.S. or the degree in a single subject. He must be encouraged to take courses which make sense for *him,* including elementary courses. The teacher who has gone to the other extreme and taken a research degree in a single subject should usually do no more work in that subject, but devote his attention to others. Whatever his pattern of undergraduate and graduate training, the candidate for the C.A.S. will usually want a program of broad, coherent exploration of one or more subjects in the Liberal Arts curriculum. Wesleyan makes every effort to provide the most rewarding experience possible.

To be eligible, a candidate for the M.A.L.S. must have a Bachelor's degree and be a teacher, librarian, or school or college administrator. The total program must form a coherent pattern in line with the objectives of the program. A candidate for a Certificate of Advanced Study must have a Master's degree and come from the same fields as those in the

M.A.L.S. program. The Certificate is awarded after thirty hours of study beyond the Master's. The nature of the program is planned in conference between the candidate and appropriate university faculty.

SUMMARY

It appears from the foregoing discussion that there is a trend toward extending certificate and degree programs especially for adults upward in the academic hierarchy. In an era of specialization there will undoubtedly be an ever increasing demand for specialized training at higher and higher levels. Concomitantly, however, current trends indicate that there is an increasing search by both academicians and adult students for systematic programs in liberal education. Current explorations such as those taking place at Harvard, Syracuse, Oklahoma, Western Reserve, and Brooklyn would suggest that models of the future are being established which might cause a geometric progression in the number of such programs offered and attended. Television and Home Study have made it possible for students to gain one or two years toward a degree in a regular curriculum. It is possible to obtain the full junior college diploma in Chicago entirely by television. Virtually every major university offers some television credit programs, many of which are developed into systematic sequences, requiring examinations and discussions on campus, or some correspondence study.

There is a restlessness in the air. Universities are seeking ways of liberating themselves from those aspects of the tradition which bind them. What we see as of now is but a small step. With experimentation in method and media, with increased understanding of the sociology and psychology of adulthood, with greater attention to learning theory, perhaps a new pedagogy of adulthood will emerge. But we have seen only the beginnings. If the universities are to succeed in effecting a rapprochement between the demands of the academic tradition and the special needs of adults, there is much hard work ahead.

Selected Readings

Belth, Marc, and Schueler, Herbert. *Liberal Education for Adults Re-Examined: The Queens College Program.* Notes and Essays No. 25. Chicago: Center for the Study of Liberal Education for Adults, 1959.

Blakely, Robert. *Adult Education in a Free Society.* Edited by J. Roby Kidd. Toronto: Guardian Bird Publications, 1958.

Carey, James T. *Legitimacy and Acceptance in a University Milieu: the Problems of Liberal Adult Education.* Chicago: Center for the Study of Liberal Education for Adults, 1959.

Crimi, James E. *Adult Education in the Liberal Arts Colleges.* Notes and Essays No. 17. Chicago: Center for the Study of Liberal Education for Adults, 1957.

Daigneault, George (ed.). *The Changing University*. A Report on the Seventh Annual Leadership Conference. Chicago: Center for the Study of Liberal Education for Adults, 1959.

Demerest, G. Stuart, and Kinnel, Galway. *New Directions for University Adult Education*. "Faculty Organization at Rutgers" and "The Basic Program at Chicago." Notes and Essays No. 11. Chicago: Center for the Study of Liberal Education of Adults, 1955.

Diekhoff, John S. *Schooling for Maturity*. Notes and Essays No. 13. Chicago: Center for the Study of Liberal Education for Adults, 1955.

Houle, Cyril O. *Major Trends in Higher Adult Education*. Notes and Essays No. 24. Chicago: Center for the Study of Liberal Education for Adults, 1959.

Leys, Wayne A. R. "The Terminal Master's Degree," *The Harvard Educational Review*, XXVI (Summer, 1956), 233-40.

McGhee, Paul A. *A School for Optimists*. Notes and Essays No. 6. Chicago: Center for the Study of Liberal Education for Adults, 1953.

Schwertman, John B. *I Want Many Lodestars*. Notes and Essays No. 21. Chicago: Center for the Study of Liberal Education for Adults, 1958.

Siegle, Peter E., and Whipple, James B. *New Directions in Programming for University Adult Education*. Chicago: Center for the Study of Liberal Education for Adults, 1957.

Stern, Bernard H. *How Much Does Adult Experience Count?* A Report of the Brooklyn College Experimental Degree Project. Chicago: Center for the Study of Liberal Education for Adults, 1955.

————. *Adults Grow in Brooklyn*. Chicago: Center for the Study of Liberal Education for Adults, 1955.

Whipple, James B. *Especially for Adults*. Notes and Essays No. 19. Chicago: Center for the Study of Liberal Education for Adults, 1957.

CHAPTER 34

EDUCATION FOR AGING

HERBERT C. HUNSAKER
Assistant Director
Division of Adult Education, Purdue University

and

MARTIN TARCHER
Secretary, Committee on Aging
Health and Welfare Council of Indianapolis

WHY EDUCATION FOR AGING

We devote large resources to preparing young people for a working life which may last for forty or more years. We gladly pay for this preparation and accept it as a basic investment, although the cost of it is usually the biggest single item in the budget of the family and of the community.

But we have also fifteen million people in this country who are aged sixty-five or over and each year increasingly larger numbers of them are retiring from gainful occupations. With an average life expectancy at sixty-five of about fifteen years, the need to pay more attention to education for the retirement, as well as for the working period of life, is self-evident.

The adult educator is engaged in a race against time. Advances in medical science are giving increasingly more people the opportunity to live into old age, and advances in technology are providing free time for possible enjoyment of the added years. But for millions approaching or past retirement age this bonus of time may well prove to be a curse of boredom and uselessness unless they actively prepare for its enjoyment.

The first responsibility of the adult educator is to create learning opportunities, leading to new attitudes and skills. To the extent that he is working with the aging, his task is to give them confidence, to help them to develop skills and talents, and to help them to realize that they are still useful and important citizens. Working with younger persons he has increasingly to remember that he is preparing them for the future as well as the present—so that they may look forward to retirement and the later years of life in the knowledge that these can still be years of purposeful growth and self-fulfillment To do these things, the adult educator must have an insight into the problems and special needs of the aging and an understanding of the social situation of which they are a part. He must be clear in his own mind about the role of education in this situation and of what is being done by other educators and educational institutions.

BASIC PROBLEMS

Because they will affect and be reflected in educational programs, some of the background factors in the current situation should be briefly stated.

1. The technological and social revolutions of the twentieth century have altered the roles, status, and living patterns of older persons. With increasing mobility, family ties have weakened and older folks have been left behind, no longer needed. An adventuresome, fast-moving society always puts a premium on youth. Millions of middle-aged people are finding themselves with twenty-five or thirty years of independence following the maturation of their children and with larger increments of free time as the work-week shortens and retirement becomes more commonplace.

2. Acceleration of technological change particularly affects the economic status of older people. This is evident in difficulties over compulsory retirement without adequate income maintenance; the greater impact of inflation on fixed retirement incomes; discrimination in hiring and greater difficulties of retraining to compensate for obsolete skills. Each of these difficulties raises specific problems with social and educational content: the adequacy of social security legislation and of private retirement benefit schemes; the relative advantages of fixed and flexible retirement ages; the determining of responsibility for retraining; etc.

3. Economic changes and associated changes in social patterns have special consequences for the housing and health of older people. If it is assumed that increasingly older people will not live with and be in part supported by sons and daughters, an entirely new and difficult housing problem is created. An income-deficient section of the population has a social claim for specially-designed housing which will almost certainly not be provided through profit-seeking enterprise. Similarly, the part of the population least able to pay for it from personal income has a greater-than-average need for medical care and treatment.

It is these special factors that justify a separate concept of education for aging. Today's old people and their current problems are the product of past social experience. Whether the aged of tomorrow will look upon their added years of leisure as a curse or a blessing will depend upon their social experience today—of which adult education can be an important part.

EDUCATIONAL OBJECTIVES

The principal objective of education for aging is to help the individual develop new goals and activities in middle life and to anticipate in advance the needs and the problems which he is likely to experience in retirement and old age. This objective concerns not only the individual himself, but also his family, his employer, and the community.

But before considering programs and activities which focus directly on education *for* aging, it is important to point out that much general education *about* aging and the aged helps some people to become aware of problems that they will face themselves, and they may, thereby, be stimulated to think about and plan for their own retirement. There is evidence that those who anticipate and plan in advance for their retirement frequently make the best adjustment to it.[1] Indeed, it can be argued that the best preparation for retirement is a good education and that a *good* education is education for a lifetime.[2]

This presentation, therefore, is concerned not only about education for retirement but even more about education which helps people of all ages to achieve a better understanding of aging as a process, its physical and psychological characteristics, and its consequences for individuals and their communities.

SOME CURRENT PROGRAMS AND ACTIVITIES

Education for a better understanding of aging and the aged is presently being carried on in many different ways, including conferences, institutes, workshops, forums, discussion groups, and regular college courses. Considerable information and informal instruction about aging is being made available by films, radio, newspapers, magazines, and television.

At the national level at least thirty-two national organizations have developed specific programs and many more provide training and educational materials for their local and state affiliates; some of them foster educational programs through the mass media. Notable among national organizations is the National Committee on the Aging of the National Social Welfare Assembly. The Committee assists communities in organizing programs, conducts regional and national conferences, maintains a library, and undertakes projects and studies. Important resource contributions are also made on the national level by the Special Staff on Aging of the U.S. Department of Health, Education, and Welfare, and other federal agencies.

On the state level there are committees and commissions on aging currently functioning in about thirty-two of the fifty states. Most of these state organizations are especially interested in the education of the general public.

In local communities are a growing number of committees and subcommittees and community organizations concerned about aging and the aged. Funds, programs, and services for the benefit of the elderly are also being provided by numerous clubs, sororities, and civic organizations. Public and private agencies in health, education, recreation, employment, and welfare concerned about aging include golden age and senior citizens clubs, arts and crafts shops, community centers, schools, colleges, universities, libraries, and municipal departments of recreation, employment, health, and public welfare. Labor and management organizations are beginning to provide pre-retirement counselling and educational programs for their members and employees and to sponsor activities and services of interest to their retired personnel.

The most difficult educational programs to assess are the informal ones which are being carried on in the "Senior Citizen" and "Golden Age" clubs and centers. Their activities include watching TV, listening to the radio, playing cards, sewing, weaving, wood carving, ceramics, painting, playing in an orchestra, singing, and social and square dancing, as well as direct education for aging. A few of the outstanding programs are to be found at: Little House, Menlo Park, California; Hyde Park Seniors, Chicago; Hodson and Sirovich Centers, New York City; The Golden Age Center, Cleveland; The Wagon Wheel, Syracuse; The Drop In Centers, Detroit; Junior League Center, Detroit; Senior Citizens, Inc., Nashville, Tennessee; San Francisco Senior Citizens Center; The Bartholomew County Retirement Foundation, Columbus, Indiana; and The Senior Citizens Center program conducted by the Park Board of South Bend.

Many of the activities and services of these organizations are educational. Some of the programs which are specially designed to focus attention on and to meet the needs and problems of the aging and the aged include: (1) general adult education courses; (2) in-service training projects for workers with the aged; (3) community self-study and action projects; (4) preparation for retirement programs; and (5) formal instruction in gerontology. A brief description of the nature of some of these programs follows.

General Adult Education

Most general courses on aging are concerned with developing an understanding of the aging process and its impact on the individual, the family, and the community. For example, materials for the use of discussion groups have been prepared under the leadership of the University of Michigan and financed by the Fund for Adult Education under the title, "Aging in the Modern World," which are slanted toward the interests of those who are in or near their middle years.[3]

Under the auspices of some schools, colleges, universities, libraries, community committees on aging, and various other organizations, instruction is being offered on education for and about aging in public lectures and short courses. These lectures and short courses usually deal with one or more aspects of the following subject-matter areas: education for aging; employment and maintenance of income; health (mental and physical) ; housing and living arrangements; personal and social adjustments; religion and retirement problems; and recreation and leisure time. A few school systems and universities employ full-time persons to provide instruction in education for aging.

Among the universities of the nation, the University of Michigan has taken the lead in education and research in social gerontology. Through its Division of Gerontology of the Institute of Human Relations, it has for twelve years conducted an annual institute that has become a conference of national importance. Several other universities have also made significant contributions, notably Teachers College, Columbia; Chicago; Florida; Duke; California; Iowa; and Cornell. Several of them have established institutes of gerontology which engage in teaching and research and conduct annual conferences or institutes to which the public is invited.

Although as yet relatively little instruction is offered about aging, a considerable number of institutions and organizations offer regular formal adult education programs in which older persons participate. According to a survey conducted by the U.S. Office of Education in 1957, 2,428,000 out of 8,270,000 persons enrolled in formal programs were forty-five years of age and older and 515,000 of them were age sixty and over.[4]

Occasionally it is possible to find a general adult education course which is intended specifically for older persons. For example, under the sponsorship of the adult education services department of Seattle Public Library a creative writing class for people over sixty was conducted a few years ago which attracted initially some 150 persons. This project led to the formation of a writers club which continues to meet regularly.

A few institutions and communities now offer their senior citizens free tuition as an inducement to enroll in their regular adult classes. In the main, however, our educational institutions have been slow to adopt and to provide courses, materials, and facilities specially adapted for older persons.

In-Service Training Projects for Workers with the Aging and Aged

Relatively little systematic instruction aimed at preparing professional or lay persons for work with old people is presently available. Most of what is being done is in the form of short-term intensive courses. There are some educational institutions and agencies in Illinois, Pennsylvania, and Indiana which have conducted short courses on the management and administration of institutions for the aged. The University of New Hampshire, through its extension division, conducts courses for the training of community leaders to work with the aged. Some labor unions, particularly the United Automobile Workers, conduct institutes and workshops for their own leaders. An example of this kind of training program is the annual institute on "Preparation for Retirement" conducted by the Division of Adult Education of Purdue University. This institute is planned especially for persons responsible for the administration of personnel policies and pension plans, the counselling of older employees, and the conducting of training programs.

Many of the annual and special conferences on aging conducted by universities, state commissions,[5] and the national organizations whose principal concern is aging (i.e. The National Committee on Aging of the National Social Welfare Assembly and The Gerontological Society) are designed to be helpful to those who are working with elderly persons. Two conferences held at the University of Michigan in June, 1959, are examples. The National Leadership Training Institute for the White House Conference on Aging was held primarily for the purpose of informing and training leaders from various organizations, communities, and states for participation in the studies and conference activities which will precede and follow the Conference in January, 1961, and the annual conference which preceded this institute had as its central concern preparation for retirement.

Community Self-Study and Action Projects

In many states and in an increasing number of local communities, citizens' committees composed of both lay and professional persons are being formed to study problems of aging with a view to promoting community action. Community self-study projects can be found in many sections of the country; two which may be cited are in Bartholomew County, Indiana, and in Peoria, Illinois. Both of these have been reported in recent issues of *Aging*, published by the Department of Health, Education, and Welfare.[6]

The 1961 White House Conference on Aging will undoubtedly do much to encourage community study and action programs in every state in the union. Already (November, 1959) plans are underway for establishing citizens committees in forty-seven of the fifty states, each charged with the responsibility of conducting surveys[7] and holding local and state-wide conferences in advance of the national conference.

Preparation for Retirement Programs

Specific pre-retirement instructional programs are aimed at the individual who is approaching retirement. They are conducted by colleges, universities, schools, employers, labor unions, and other community agencies and made available through institutes, workshops, and seminars. Among the universities currently offering pre-retirement courses are Michigan, Chicago, New York, and Wisconsin.

The objectives of most "Preparation for Retirement" courses are: (1) To develop in the participant an awareness of the need for planning in order to help bring about a satisfactory adjustment to retirement; (2) To study and discuss those areas in which, according to research findings, retired persons have been faced with serious problems of adjustment; (3) To present information which may be of help in planning and in the prevention or solution of problems usually associated with retirement and aging; and (4) To provide an opportunity for participants to exchange ideas and to discuss them with the guidance of a trained discussion leader. These courses commonly include the use of visual aids and selected readings and the participation of resource persons.

One of the most comprehensive "Preparation for Retirement" courses is that developed by the University of Chicago's Industrial Relations Center. This course has been used almost exclusively by certain industrial organizations for their own employees, but in Bartholomew County, Indiana, it has been conducted experimentally for three years on a community-wide scale. Each group meets weekly for two hours over eleven weeks under leaders trained by the university staff. Some ten topics are studied and discussed in each of the groups and specially prepared reading materials are given to each participant a week in advance. Topics considered are: looking ahead to maturity; nutrition and health; physical changes; mental attitudes; financial planning; the meaning of work; getting the most out of leisure; increasing your retirement income; family, friends, and living arrangements; and where to live.

The Bureau of Adult Education of the New York State Education Department has also worked out a special course on preparation for retirement. A manual sets forth eleven teaching units with suggested operating procedures, selected readings, and methods for evaluation.[8]

Several labor unions have been designing pre- and post-retirement courses for their members. Such courses are being conducted by the United Auto Workers, United Steel Workers, International Ladies' Garment Workers, and Upholsterers International Union. A survey of retirement programs conducted in 1958 by a graduate student at Purdue University provides some interesting information about the growing interest of industry in pre- and post-retirement services: "out of 257 companies studied, 31 per cent conducted programs in both the pre- and post-retirement areas. Forty-four per cent conduct programs only in pre-retirement; and 36 per cent conduct only programs for post-retirement."[9]

Formal Instruction in Gerontology

There is a growing demand for trained personnel to administer homes, institutions, and agencies for the aged; to render a variety of education, health, welfare and community services for older people; and to conduct instruction and research in the field of social gerontology. This need exists because workers in gerontology are largely being recruited from other fields and disciplines and comparatively few universities offer special instruction in gerontology. A survey of university instruction and research in gerontology conducted by the University of Michigan in 1957 revealed that fifty colleges and universities were offering seventy-two credit courses or seminars in some aspect of gerontology and fifteen others had courses in prospect.

Probably the most significant contribution to education for aging took place in 1957, when a grant of $205,000 was made to the University of Michigan by the National Institutes of Health in support of the Leadership Training Institute for Social Gerontology. Sixteen universities were invited to become co-operating institutions for the project and an Inter-university Council and Executive Committee were formed by their representatives. Three handbooks have been prepared and will be available for distribution before the end of the year from the University of Chicago Press:

Handbook of Aging and the Individual: Psychological and Biological Aspects, A Handbook of Social Gerontology: Aging and Society, and *Survey of Aging in Western Cultures.*

Teaching aids have also been prepared and published. Five syllabi and annotated bibliographies are now available: *The Economics of An Aging Population, The Psychological Aspects of Aging, Social Welfare and The Aged, Sociological Aspects of Aging,* and *An Interdisciplinary Course in Social Gerontology.*

The National Institutes of Health have also begun to support graduate student training. Programs for specialization in social gerontology were established in the fall of 1959 by the Department of Psychology, Washington University (St. Louis) and by the Committee on Human Development at the University of Chicago. A grant to the Inter-university Council on Social Gerontology made possible the holding of a four-week summer training institute in social gerontology at the University of Connecticut in August, 1958. Fellowships to this institute were awarded to thirty-six full-time college and university teaching faculty members in the social sciences. Following the success of the first institute, the Inter-university Council received an additional grant to continue the project and to hold a second Summer Training Institute in Social Gerontology, at the University of California in Berkeley. Forty fellowships were awarded to full-time teaching faculty, but this time one-fourth were to faculty in medicine, social work, family life, nursing, and public health, and three-fourths were to faculty in the social sciences.

The Training Institutes may be assumed to have laid the basis for a rapid expansion of training in social gerontology. Courses in aging are proliferating in undergraduate colleges, universities, and professional schools. These will lead to the development of organized curricula and possibly to degree programs in aging and social gerontology and to short-term courses and institutes for in-service training of professional personnel in such areas as adult education, recreation, social work, medicine, and public health.

Another logical extension of present programs would be the development of opportunities for research workers just entering the field to obtain training and experience in evaluating current research, delineating crucial research problems in aging in the several fields by the social and psychological sciences, and in developing research designs and methodologies appropriate for the study of these problems.

The work being conducted under the auspices of the Inter-university Council has great significance not only for extending and expanding formal instruction and research in our colleges and universities, but also for adult education. The full value of this unique program will be realized only when these research findings, teaching materials, and the knowledge acquired by the college and university faculty have been communicated to all segments of our society. An important channel of communication is the teacher of adults. It is to be hoped that a further step in the development of this program will be that of providing a specially-designed institute for the training of adult educators.

SOME IMPLICATIONS FOR ADULT EDUCATION

Concern with aging and the aged represents a challenging field for the adult educator. He cannot approach it successfully without enlarging his own education. He must reconsider motivation, review learning theory as it is affected by reduced sensory acuity on the one hand and greater experience of life on the other. He must be aware of new dimensions of social and economic policy, not only in the provision of educational opportunity, but in the improvement of housing and health care, economic security, and other problem areas.

If needs are to be more adequately met, we should move in the following directions:

1. Learn more about the factors which influence adjustment to retirement, through research and experimentation.

2. Provide instruction about the process of aging in our schools and colleges, so that both children and youth may become more aware of the needs and problems associated with the aging and the aged.

3. Help young adults to understand better these needs and problems, so that they may plan more wisely for their later years.

4. Aid adults, particularly during the middle and later years, to develop interests, attitudes, and skills which will help them to make better personal and social adjustments when they retire.

5. Conduct educational activities for the purpose of encouraging community action which looks toward providing programs designed to meet the needs of people in their later and retirement years.

6. Encourage both management and labor to develop and extend pre-retirement information and counselling services.

7. Increase opportunities for the general public to learn about aging, through adult education courses, informal groups, and mass media.

8. Provide an expanded program of adult education and recreation for the steadily increasing number of middle-aged and older persons, in order that they may continue to be active, mentally and physically.

9. Offer vocational training or retraining for middle-aged women who are re-entering the labor force and for workers whose skills have become obsolescent.

If we are to go far along this road we must provide increased opportunities for the teachers of youth and adults to learn about all aspects of aging process, from the point of view of biology, economics, psychology, and sociology; we must make available additional opportunities for the training of persons who work with older persons, whether they be professional personnel or volunteers; and above all there must be increased public understanding and support of these kinds of educational activities at all levels—local, state, and national.

RESOURCES

In addition to earlier references, some of the indispensable sources of information and materials which are now available include:

National organizations directly concerned with education for aging: Gerontological Society, Inc., 660 South Kingshighway Boulevard, St. Louis 10, Missouri; The National Committee on the Aging of the National Social Welfare Assembly, 345 East 46 Street, New York 17, New York; The Council of State Governments, 1313 East 60th Street, Chicago 37, Illinois; The Inter-University Council on Social Gerontology, Institute for Social Gerontology, 1510 Rackham Building, University of Michigan, Ann Arbor, Michigan; and The Adult Education Association of the U.S.A., 743 North Wabash Avenue, Chicago 11, Illinois.

Some programs and publications of federal agencies: A recent summary prepared by the Special Staff on Aging of the Department of Health, Education, and Welfare refers to relevant activities of its own and the following Departments: Agriculture, Treasury, Commerce, Labor, Housing and Home Finance Agency, Veterans Administration, Railroad Retirement Board, Civil Service Commission, and Small Business Administration.

The Cooperative Extension Service of the Department of Agriculture is engaged in research to determine the most practicable adjustments for retired farm families and the degree to which farm people are making provision for their own economic security in the period of retirement. Such research information provides a more adequate basis for the informal education programs conducted jointly by the department and the individual state land-grant colleges. The Extension Service also stresses the development of group activities to provide an opportunity for both social and civic contributions, with particular attention to insuring that persons in rural areas understand the Old-Age and Survivors Insurance program and the steps necessary to enable them to be covered.

Because of the continuing necessity for informing employers and the public regarding the qualifications and abilities of older persons, the Labor Department has been working on informational aids. It has completed a draft of a Leaders' Guide for conducting labor-management institutes on the employment of older workers. Also in process of development are a number of materials for use on TV and radio, as well as exhibits which might be used at meetings and conventions.

The Office of Education emphasizes five major activities or services in the area of education for aging: (1) a clearinghouse of information services; (2) studies of aging programs and adult education in selected communities; (3) consultative services to assist the states and localities; (4) liaison with national organizations and educational groups; and (5) co-ordination of the resources made available by Congress to the states, localities, and educational institutions for research, demonstrations, surveys, services, and experimentation.

In 1956 the Center for Aging Research was established in the National Institutes of Health to encourage research in aging by investigators located in universities and non-federal institutions. It has contributed administrative assistance toward planning and establishing two university-wide, interdisciplinary programs in aging—one at Duke University in 1957 and the second at the Albert Einstein College of Medicine in 1958.

The Special Staff on Aging of the Department of Health, Education, and Welfare keeps aware of the major advances in gerontology and assists in the development of programs designed to provide a favorable environment for middle-aged and older people and to make better use of their experience and skills. Its major activity currently is preparing for the White House Conference on Aging to be held in January, 1961.

Footnotes

1Gordon F. Streib and Wayne E. Thompson, "Personal and Social Adjustment in Retirement," *The New Frontiers of Aging*, Wilma Donahue and Clark Tibbitts, eds. (Ann Arbor: University of Michigan, 1957), pp. 180-97.

2Russell F. W. Smith, "Education for a Lifetime," *The Journal of Educational Sociology*, XXX (January, 1957), 216-20.

3Information about this course may be secured from The Fund for Adult Education, 200 Bloomingdale Road, White Plains, New York. These materials have been republished in a single volume in Clark Tibbitts and Wilma Donahue, *Aging in Today's Society* (New York: Prentice-Hall, 1960).

4Marie D. Wann and Marthine V. Woodward, *Participation in Adult Education*, U. S. Department of Health, Education, and Welfare Office of Education Circular No. 539 (Washington: Government Printing Office, 1959), pp. 29 and 35.

5As examples of state activities and conferences see "Charter for the Aging," the proceedings of the New York State Conference convened by Governor Harriman in 1955; and "Aging in Indiana," edited by Morton Leeds and published by The Indiana State Commission on the Aging and Aged.

6"Indiana's Bartholomew County Action-Study Program," *Aging*, No. 40 (February, 1958); and, "Peoria Reports To The Nation," *Aging*, No. 35 (September, 1957).

7See: "Guide for State Surveys on Aging," prepared by the Staff for the White House Conference on Aging, U. S. Department of Health, Education, and Welfare, 1959.

8"Retirement—A Second Career," Bulletin No. 8 (revised) *Teaching Units on Preparation for Retirement*, published by the University of The State of New York, The State Education Department, Pupil Personnel Services and Adult Education, Bureau of Adult Education, Albany.

9Howland Joseph Reich, Jr., "An analysis of Industrial Program Plans for Retirement and for Retired Employees" (Master's thesis, Purdue University, 1958).

Selected Readings

Community Project for the Aged of the Welfare Council of Metropolitan Chicago. *Community Services for Older People: The Chicago Plan*. Chicago: Wilcox and Follett Co., 1952.

Council on Social Work Education. *Toward Better Understanding of the Aging and Social Work Education for Better Services to the Aging*. New York: The Council, 1959.

Donahue, Wilma (ed.). *Education for Later Maturity*. New York: Whiteside, Inc., and William Morrow & Co., 1955.

Donahue, Wilma, *et al. Free Time: Challenge to Later Maturity*. Ann Arbor: University of Michigan Press, 1958.

Donahue, Wilma and Tibbits, Clark. *Aging in the Modern World*. A Study Discussion Series for Adults. Ann Arbor: University of Michigan Division of Gerontology, 1957.

————. *The New Frontiers of Aging*. Ann Arbor: University of Michigan Press, 1957.

Havighurst, Robert. *Social Roles of the Middle-Aged Person*. Notes and Essays on Education for Adults, No. 4. Chicago: Center for the Study of Liberal Education for Adults, 1953.

Kempfer, Homer. *Education for a Long and Useful Life*. U. S. Office of Education Bulletin 1950 No. 6. Washington: Government Printing Office, 1950.

Moore, Elon H. *The Nature of Retirement*. Ed. G. F. Streib, New York: Macmillan Co., 1959.

Shock, Nathan. *Trends in Gerontology*. Stanford: Stanford University Press, 1957.

U.S. Department of Health, Education, and Welfare. *Selected References on Aging*. An annotated bibliography prepared by the Special Staff on Aging. Washington: Government Printing Office, 1959.

U.S. Senate, Committee on Labor and Public Welfare. *Studies of the Aged and the Aging*. Selected documents; 12 volumes. Washington: Government Printing Office, 1956-57.

U.S. Senate, Subcommittee on Problems of the Aged and Aging. *The Aged and the Aging in the U. S.* Report of the Hearing of the Subcommittee. Washington: Government Printing Office, 1959.

Ward, Betty. *Education on the Aging: A Selected Annotated Bibliography*. U.S. Department of Health, Education, and Welfare, Office of Education Bulletin 1958, No. 11. Washington: Government Printing Office, 1958.

CHAPTER 35

COMMUNITY DEVELOPMENT

HOWARD Y. McCLUSKY
Professor of Educational Psychology
Univeristy of Michigan

INTRODUCTION AND DEFINITION

When one gives full rein to the meaning of the words "community" and "development" he is struck with the scope and audacity of the term which is created by their combination. First of all, community development denotes change. That is, it involves movement from one point to another point in community life. Next, it signifies control. It means that change can be induced or modified and may be the result of measures deliberately contrived to achieve a projected goal. Again, while development may be down as well as up, it usually refers to improvement in the status of the community concerned. It generally means that change occurs from something less good to something better. So far, then, we could define community development as induced change for the achievement of community improvement.

But this is not enough for the adult educator. He will want to go further by stressing the importance of the way community development is achieved. Moreover, he will insist that the ultimate test of community development, both as object (what) and process (how), is what it does to the people who make up the membership of the community being developed.

To be more explicit, the adult educator will say that the community is a teacher or developer of the people who live there. At the same time it should be one of the people's obligations to help the community become a better teacher and, in the process of doing so, themselves become better educated. Community development would then be defined as the induction and educational management of that kind of interaction between the community and its people which leads to the improvement of both. In this context the community would be regarded as external

416

fact of streets, buildings, parks and services, etc., as well as internal experience of ideals and values held in common. It would be regarded as both place and spirit.

Already it begins to appear how scopish and audacious the idea of community development is. As for scope, the word "community" can be rigged up to cover about everything from sewers to art and group identification. As for audacity, the word "development" attributes to some "developer" enormous power over all the forms of community life.

To press the point of audacity, the word "development" is really a word in a hurry. It means that change need no longer be regarded as requiring generations and even centuries to effect, but can now be speeded up to take place within the span of a few years, and more important can be directed to the achievement of some of man's most cherished and long deferred aspirations. It suggests that people are not compelled to accept such limiting circumstances of life as poor education, decrepit housing, ill-health, inadequate employment, and an impoverished spiritual environment as irreversible, but that these limitations can, by deliberate intent, study, and action, be substantially if not completely overcome.

ANTECEDENTS OF COMMUNITY DEVELOPMENT

So many different kinds of agencies are engaged in community development, and agreement as to what kinds of activities community development should include is so loose, that the materials for a clear outline of its history are not available. But it is possible in selected areas of human endeavor to identify several elements of both viewpoint and activity which we now currently associate with the field.

One of these consists of a long history of successful experience on the part of the farm population in strengthening the general conditions of rural living. Not long after the middle of the nineteenth century the holding of conferences designed to acquaint farmers with improvements in agriculture was common practice. In 1904 Seaman Knapp was employed by the U. S. Department of Agriculture to help farmers combat the ravages of the boll weevil which was then threatening to destroy the cotton economy of the South. In 1914 the Congress passed the Smith-Lever Act authorizing the establishment of a national system of county agricultural agents now known as the Cooperative Extension Service. From the beginning this program has been based on local participation in the improvement of homemaking and agricultural production. It has been a gigantic demonstration of 'technical assistance' on the part of government, self-help on the part of the farm family, and co-operation on the part of both.

Many of the features of community development were also foreshadowed in the response of local communities to the depression of the

1930's and World Wars I and II. Sometimes crude in procedure, but often productive in outcome, the federal emergency programs of the depression years often led to substantial achievements which local people could see and enjoy. While not a classic example of community development, the public works of the Works Progress Administration, the projects of the National Youth Administration, and the road building, reforestation, and conservation programs of the Civilian Conservation Corps were demonstrations of the fact that the rank and file citizen could make a substantial contribution to the betterment of the region in which he lived.

The wars of 1917-18 and 1941-45 gave similar proof of the community service a citizen can perform. Defense councils of World War I, and the defense councils, block leaders, air raid wardens, victory gardens and salvage campaigns, etc., of World War II, gave millions of volunteers in thousands of American communities an opportunity to develop skills which were just as important for the protection of the home front in peace as they were in time of war.

Another area of historical overlap with the field of community development is that of community organization. It has been common for American communities to support a number of organizations devoted to the service of the community's interests. In some instances these organizations have been limited to a single sector of community life, and operate more effectively when brought together under some over-all mechanism of co-ordination. Examples are councils of social agencies, welfare councils, and welfare federations, which, in recent years and in medium-sized and large cities, have become more and more prominent in combining agencies in the fields of health and social welfare.

In other instances, usually in smaller communities, several areas of interest, such as recreation, adult education, delinquency prevention, youth welfare, industrial development, and aging, as well as health and social welfare, have been assembled in a general rather than a single effort at co-ordination. This has usually been called a community council. If to the foregoing we add collateral community chests and united funds, councils of churches, advisory committees to schools, libraries, hospitals, and other public and private agencies, as well as the great number of voluntary membership associations such as service clubs, women's clubs, labor unions, farm groups, parent-teacher associations, boards of commerce, etc., the cumulative picture is a comprehensive network of community organizations through which for many years millions of lay and professional persons have made impressive contributions to the strength of American communities.

In concluding this section a brief reference should be made to the area of physical planning and economic development as one of the streams of activity which has contributed to the field of community development. Land-use planning, city planning, urban renewal, industrial development, and related activities are all examples of ways which both volunteer and professional workers have used to strengthen the physical and economic base of the local community.[1]

INSTITUTIONAL SETTING

After considering the range of agencies reviewed in the preceding section, and recalling that most of the programs described there are still active without benefit of the community development label, it should not surprise the reader to learn that there is yet no institutional home for the field of community development. It is usually only one of several programs which the sponsoring agency supports and, whenever it appears, its developmental targets include only a part of the full range of activities which a literal interpretation of the 'entire community' would encompass.[2]

The upshot of the preceding points is that the administrative vehicles of community development are elusive, in fact, so elusive that it could be an unprofitable exercise to devote any time to their delineation in this context. Illustrative programs will appear later in the discussion.

COMMUNITY DEVELOPMENT AS AN EDUCATIONAL METHOD

To return to our original theme, the adult educator is primarily interested in community development as a means of educating the community and the people who live there. For example, if a community sets up a project in improving health and recreational facilities, in the course of doing so there will be an opportunity (often unexploited) to learn a lot of facts about problems of health and recreation. If it conducts a survey of conditions essential for the attraction of new industry, the community should be in a position to acquire a lot of information about town and city planning, and so on for any area of living which it elects to improve. These are the factual learnings which community development may stimulate. At the same time, however, it is also possible to learn about how the community is put together and the methods by which it may achieve its goals. These are the process and contextual learnings of community development. Both kinds can be fruitful, but it is the second kind (process and contextual) which is currently most neglected by other forms of adult education, and to which community development can make a unique contribution.

If we can borrow a term from the field of pedagogy, community development is essentially a direct method of teaching. Instead of standing on the side lines and assuming that instruction done out of context (say in a night class on municipal government) will somehow automatically lead to a productive attack on local problems, community development helps the learner make the connection between his learning and its application directly and without the interference of intervening factors. It may deal with concrete data or concepts and at times be highly intellectual, but in any case *relevance* is the chief characteristic of its approach.

Community development is also a method of teaching adults the use of timing and the sequence of activities in bringing a project through successive stages to an acceptable closure. At the risk of oversimplification, the first stage is essentially exploratory in character, where in the felt and manifest need of either an individual or a group is tentatively shared with others. Included here are also the beginning of diagnosis, and the provisional indentification of other persons and agencies who may enlist in the project after it gets under way. The second stage is basically one of organization and target selection. At this point the permanent leadership will emerge, and additional persons and agencies join the enterprise. The third stage is a combination of study and action. This is not to say that study and action have not occurred before, but now it is better organized and more likely to be goal-directed, and there is more of it. The fourth stage is one of either closure or transition. In the former case the organization will disband, and in the latter it may regroup to work on new projects. In both there may be some time out for evaluation.

The writer makes no claim that the stages just described are an accurate picture of the succession of events which must transpire before a project is dismissed as completed. But they serve to illustrate the flow of activities and decisions which a person must respect, and a sense of timing which he must learn, if he is to attain any degree of success in helping a community to help itself.

One of the conditions with which community development must always contend is the web of inter-relatedness which one encounters as he attempts to work his way through a problem affecting the life of the community. If the four-stage sequence described above may be regarded as the vertical dimension of community development, the web of inter-relatedness may be regarded as its horizontal dimension. If, for example, we start with the problem of providing housing for older people, we will soon encounter problems of health, recreation, and money. Or if we begin with the objective of preventing juvenile delinquency, we will soon run into questions of employment, education, and family relations. This simple fact adds immeasurably to the complexity of the field. But we can't move in the local arena without having to deal with it.

One consequence of this fact is the importance of the structure of community organization and the dynamics produced by the roles which the structure requires. Community development, therefore, teaches a person how to go about setting up an organization and, more important, how to keep it moving toward a productive goal. Another consequence is the necessity of bringing professional workers together in a collaborative approach to diagnosis, understanding, and solution of community problems.

But the most significant lesson which we can learn from having to struggle with the realities of inter-relatedness is the disposition of looking at a problem in its relation to the community as a whole. In some respects, this is the most unique contribution of community development to adult education. No other form of educational experience quite matches it for giving adults a broad view of the community affairs.

COMMUNITY DEVELOPMENT AS AN EDUCATIVE FORCE IN SOCIETY AS A WHOLE

Community development may also be regarded as an educative force in society as a whole. This may sound naive to the realist, but if the habits of community self-help through study and co-operative action could become as much a part of the American scene as political campaigns, vacation travel, school commencements, or sports events, it is possible that new forces would be released which would serve as a healthy check against some of the dominant trends of our time.

Take, for example, the current trend toward the bureaucratization of institutional life. An objective view tells us that bureaucracy is the price we pay for our interdependence and high standard of living. But the flexibility of procedures inherent in the processes of community development is the antithesis of formal regularities and channels of the bureau; the absence of status differences in community development is contrary to the rank order of officialdom; and community development's encouragement of agenda-setting at any point in the organizational network is a contradiction of the bureaucracy's habit of letting the echelon above decide what the echelon below should do and how it shall behave. In fact, the "organization man" in the grey flannel suit may be a good worker for his company, but he would probably run into serious trouble if he insisted on installing the formalities of his organization in an effort to develop the suburb to which he returns from work.

Or take community development as an offset to the centralist trends of modern society. Where transportation and communication transcend all boundaries, some centralization of authority over large consolidations of operation is inevitable and necessary, especially in a specialized and highly interdependent society. But, because of this fact, it is all the more important that control of decisions with respect to the task of everyday living be kept as close to the local community as possible. Community development, conceived as an educational experience, could accomplish a great deal toward offsetting the habits of dependency which the practice of deference to superior economic and political authority tend to encourage. In fact, if community development were an integral part of the American scene, it could well become the soil whereby the spirit of democracy would be constantly replenished.

Perhaps it is really naive to assign community development the task of reordering the structure of American society, but it is possible that a great increase of meaningful interaction across class lines would substantially improve interclass understanding and overcome some current tendencies toward social disorganization by increasing the individual's positive identification with the welfare of his community.

SOME ILLUSTRATIVE PROGRAMS[3]

Although the institutional pattern through which community development operates is elusive, there is some consistency in the activities which in recent years have become an established part of the extramural programs of some universities and colleges.[4]

University of St. Francis Xavier, Antigonish, Nova Scotia

In 1929 the University of St. Francis Xavier at Antigonish, Nova Scotia, established an Extension Department under the direction of Monsignor M. M. Coady. Among other things, the new department took over and expanded the program of self-help through group study and group action earlier set up by Father J. J. Tompkins. In the intervening years it has become an outstanding example of how the education of adults can literally lead to the development of some of the most basic elements of the community. A common procedure consists of setting up study groups in the homes, which at first center on economic questions and from that point move on to other problems of the community. The department at Antigonish deals with needs of both rural and urban communities, has a fairly sizeable staff, and works somewhat apart from the academic departments of the university. It is a well established example of an educational approach to the development of the total community.

University of Wisconsin

The Extension Division of the University of Wisconsin has for many years maintained a Bureau of Community Development. Unique for its stress on economic and industrial development, its basic objectives are (1) to provide communities within Wisconsin with a source of information and advice on problems of community development and redevelopment, (2) to help co-ordinate and channel requests for technical information to appropriate technical departments, and (3) to supply planning information.

It places heavy emphasis on research as basic to planning and technical advice, and regards the teamwork and co-sponsorship of representatives of the local community as an important prerequisite for undertaking a project. As a member of the Wisconsin Community Organization Committee, it has access to the advice and resources of key agencies at the state level. Like all bona fide programs of its kind, it is thoroughly committed to the philosophy not to solve problems for the community, but rather to work with the community as it attempts to solve its own problems.

Southern Illinois University

The department of Community Development of Southern Illinois University had its origins in the work of Baker Brownell and Richard Poston in Montana. As a matter of record, it is worth noting that the Montana program was inaugurated by a philosopher (Brownell) and a journalist (Poston), and received its original subsidy from the Division of Humanities of the General Education Board. Poston transferred his work from Montana to the University of Washington and, after having established a Department of Community Development there, moved to Southern Illinois University where he became director of its newly established Bureau of Community Development.

The Southern Illinois program is distinctive for the intensive use of the study group, the extensive involvement of persons in the community, and the wide range of problems included in the scope of its activities. It began its work first in small towns and cities, but is now spreading its operations to larger urban and industrial areas.

It began originally as an extramural program of the University. It is now in process of setting up closer integration with the offerings of academic departments, and is developing a program for training professional workers in the field.

Earlham College

In addition to the standard features of community development, the program under the direction of William Biddle at Earlham College is unique for its identification with the central curriculum of a small liberal arts college. For one thing, students may enroll in the program as part of their general nonprofessional education. For another thing, it draws freely on the members of the academic staff for the research phases of its program. Another unique feature is the cross-cultural aspect of its activities growing out of its summer program in Puerto Rico.

West Georgia College

Another program of long standing and located in a different region of the U. S. is the "College in the Country" sponsored by the West Georgia College, of Carrolton, Georgia. This program is the outcome of many years of wise and patient work by the members of the college staff. A distinctive feature of its program is its combination of community organization with programs of didactic instruction. Along with attention to the physical and economic base of the community, it sponsors study tours to the United Nations in New York, sets up courses in astronomy and other "impractical" subjects on the theory that one way to develop a community is to deepen the intellectual insight of its people. It is the contention of the writer that the transfer of the results of "impractical" instruction to the enrichment of the climate of the "intellectual" community is much more likely to occur when a program like the "College in the Country" also involves processes of integrating the requirements of the physical, economic and social community.

The University of Michigan

The first activity of what later became the Extension Service of The University of Michigan was a lecture given by a member of the faculty in response to a request from a community in Michigan's upper peninsula for assistance in the solution of one of its urgent problems. This was in 1911. In 1938 the University's Board of Regents set up what was then known as a "Program of Adult Education" and assigned its administration to the office of the Vice President in charge of University Relations. After nine years of semi-autonomous existence, the program, later known as "Community-Adult Education," was expanded by Regential action to continue as an integrated operation, with one section in the School of Education and another section in the Extension Service.

From the beginning the work of the department was committed to a policy that the production of knowledge about community and adult education and the development of a curriculum of studies for training professional workers should be a central objective of its activities. Also from the beginning, and with equal conviction, the department was committed to the objective of using educational procedures in helping communities to improve their level and style of living. Assistance in community self-improvement became the field service component of the over-all program.

In the pursuit of these objectives, a unique outcome of the department's work has been the invention of what has become called an "area conference for community self-help." Designed to attract leaders from communities no farther than an hour's driving distance from the place in which the meetings are held, the area conference has served as a means for initiating a diagnostic look at community affairs, and in creating a new readiness on the part of responsible citizens for attacking the solution of local problems. Other features of the program have been the encouragement of adult participation in self-surveys, the production of discussion courses aimed at a better understanding of community life, and work with citizens' committees and community councils as a means of helping communities develop the machinery and habit of looking at themselves as a whole.

Perhaps the distinctive characteristic of the program of community-adult education at The University of Michigan is its combination of service, research, and instruction in a program aimed at the education of adults and the community.

COMMUNITY DEVELOPMENT ABROAD

No discussion of community development in the second half of the twentieth century would be complete without some reference to the international phase of the subject. One of the most dynamic forces of our times is embodied in the determination of the less developed countries of the world to improve their standard of living, and one of the most impressive educational phenomena of our times is the fact that community development is viewed by these countries as a major instrument for the achievement of this goal.

Some evidence of the place community development occupies in the aspirations of other countries is contained in the attention it receives in the programs of the United Nations. Evidence of its importance for the U. S. A. is revealed by the policies and activities of many overseas programs of this country. As one example, note the work of the Community Development Division of the International Cooperation Administration.

An encouraging feature of community development abroad is the fact that the desire to improve the community in which one lives, and confidence in the ability to do so, may be found in all parts of the world. And it is also significant that the principles which a community uses as a guide in attempting to improve its style of life are equally universal. It is quite possible therefore, that in providing a world-wide experience in the decentralization of initiative, and in strengthening local responsibility for decision making, community development may help create a universal basis for teaching people everywhere the substance of the democratic way of life. Because of this fact, and with proper orientation, community development in the years ahead could well become one of the most powerful and educative forces available to the peoples of the world in their struggles to achieve a better civilization.

THE TASKS AHEAD

In drawing this discussion to a close, brief reference should be made to some of the tasks which confront community development in the years ahead.

First is the formulation of an operational taxonomy which will enable the lay and professional worker to understand those elements which make community development a unique department of the human enterprise.

There can be little advancement in our grasp of the field if "anything anybody does at the local level" is our best definition of community development.

A second task is that of creating a better institutional home from which community development may operate. A better taxonomy should help here because a sharp classification of function makes possible the creation of more useful structures of administration. But, in addition, community development will in the future require more convincing support than it has heretofore received not only from agencies with which it is already identified, but from new agencies that have not yet become involved in the field.

Another task for the future is the adaptation of procedures of community development to conditions of urban living. Much of the current literature in the field is based on work in small cities and towns. As a result, there has been much skepticism in some quarters about the applicability of the principles of community self-help to the large scale problems of a complex metropolitan setting. But, in the judgment of the writer, this skepticism should be qualified if not rejected. For, to cite only a few examples, the work of Thelen in Chicago, Johnson in St. Louis, Wolff in New York, and the success of the Citizens Advisory Committee on School Needs in Detroit, with which, as a participant-observer, the author was associated in 1958-59, indicate that it is possible to apply principles of community development to cities with encouraging results.

But the greatest challenge to the future of community development is basically educational in character. Meeting the challenge will require a twofold effort. One of these would consist of placing greater emphasis on community action as a special means of adult education. And the other would consist of giving greater prominence to the inner (i.e., mental, experiential, or spiritual) dimension of the field. In both instances, outcomes would be tested by the impact which the experience with community development has on the adult, both as a person and citizen. Or, to state the point in slightly different and more general terms, one consequence of this view would be for community development to regard the cultivation of the educative adult in the educative community as the central purpose of its effort.

Footnotes

1As far as the writer knows, Irwin Sanders is the only person who has proposed an explanation for the kind of content that in his judgment may now be included in the field of community development. He says that community development is now a composite of community organization on the one hand and economic development on the other hand.

2There are few, if any, simon-pure instances where *all* the people or representatives thereof participate in the development of *all* possible aspects of community life. Sometimes the friends of the field of community development give the impression that they are doing more than they actually are.

³The programs listed were selected because (a) they are sponsored by institutions of higher learning, (b) they employ educational methods, (c) they or their direct antecedents have a history of at least ten or more years of continuous existence, (d) because documents (published and unpublished) are available describing their programs, and (e) they are now in existence. Other programs fulfill the preceding criteria, but they were omitted for lack of space, and not because of lack of experience.

⁴See Division of Community Development, National University Extension Association.

Selected Readings

Biddle, William W. *The Cultivation of Community Leaders*. New York: Harper and Brothers, 1953.

————. *Growth Toward Freedom*. New York: Harper and Brothers, 1957.

Brunner, Edmund deS. *Community Organization and Adult Education*. Chapel Hill: University of North Carolina Press, 1942.

Community Development Review. Washington, D. C., Community Development Division, Office of Public Services, International Cooperation Administration.

Dickerman, Watson. "Universities Help Communities to Help Themselves." *University of Michigan School of Education Bulletin*, Vol. XXVI (January, 1955), 51-54.

English, Mildred E. *College in the Country*. Athens: The University of Georgia Press, 1959.

Hillman, Arthur. *Community Organization and Planning*. New York: Macmillan Co., 1950.

Lippitt, Ronald, Watson, Jeanne, and Westley, Bruce. *The Dynamics of Planned Change*. New York: Harcourt, Brace and Co., 1958.

McClusky, Howard Y. "Community Influences and Adult Learning." *Adult Education*, VIII (Winter, 1958), 103-6.

McClusky, Howard Y., and Jensen, Gale E. "Community-Adult Education at The University of Michigan," *University of Michigan School of Education Bulletin*, XXIX (October, 1957), 1-6.

McKee, Elmore M. *The People Act*. New York: Harper and Brothers, 1955.

Ogden, Jean Carter and Jess. *Small Communities in Action*. New York: Harper and Brothers, 1946.

————. *These Things We Tried*. Charlottesville: University of Virginia, 1947.

Poston, Richard W. *Small Town Renaissance*. New York: Harper and Brothers, 1950.

————. *Democracy Is You*. New York: Harper and Brothers, 1953.

Ross, Murray A. *Community Organization: Theory and Principles*. New York: Harper and Brothers, 1955.

Sanders, Irwin T. *Making Good Communities Better*. Lexington, Kentucky: University of Kentucky Press, 1950.

Thelen, Herbert A. *Dynamics of Groups at Work*. Chicago: The University of Chicago Press, 1954.

Warren, Roland L. *Studying Your Community*. New York: Russell Sage Foundation, 1955.

CHAPTER 36

CREATIVE ARTS IN ADULT EDUCATION

MAX KAPLAN
Director, The Arts Center
School of Fine and Applied Arts
Boston University
and
CAROL L. PIERSON
Doctoral candidate
Division of Social Studies
Harvard University

INTRODUCTION

As adult education finds itself rethinking its directions, the creative arts have become an expanding interest. Among the reasons for this interest are these:

1. There is a growing recognition that the arts and creative activity somehow contain the possibility of becoming instrumental in counteracting social and personal disorganization, often traced to cultural dislocations, social change, and the weakening of social controls.

2. The "new leisure," which has been gained by a decline of work hours from over seventy in 1850 to thirty-seven in 1960, provides new cultural opportunity. This new time (George Soule calls it the "fourth economic dimension")[1] reaches deeply into issues concerning basic values of work, family, style of life, individual resources, nature of the community, and conceptions of the "good life." A growing conviction has arisen in some quarters that the new increment of leisure can become a powerful factor in achieving a more mature society. The relation of the creative arts to retirement and aging is receiving particular attention and provides a fresh area for experiments in program planning and research.

3. The fine arts, perhaps the central illustration of creative activity, have reached new high levels in the past few decades, with respect to the numbers of participants and size of audience. Figures tell only part of the story—sales of classical records, growth of symphony orchestras, com-

428

munity theatres, opera companies, and so on. The quality of activity is often high, but a vigorous discussion goes on as to the nature and ultimate significance of these trends—a discussion well summarized in the volume *Mass Culture*.[2]

The concern of adult educators with creative activity can become more significant if several basic questions are asked, among them: How do creative activities in adult education affect or provide personal and social satisfactions? How can teachers of the creative arts in adult education deal with "amateurism" and "professionalism" with reference to objectives, methods of teaching, and standards of performance? Why and in what way do they suggest constructive direction in retirement and the "new leisure"?

Among the difficulties to be met in answering these questions is the scattered interest of the social sciences in the nature of creativity and the lack of a conceptual framework within which an artistic activity may find its orientation. Such a framework is presented below, not as model, but as a working device against which the descriptive materials later in this chapter fall into some perspective.

1. *Functions of the creative arts*
    a. Aesthetic (emphasis on inherent or internal elements: form, style, etc.)
    b. Social (emphasis on personality, therapy, group solidarity, recreation, etc.)
2. *Relations to art as a social institution*
    a. To external elements (social class, nature of community, mass media, economic conditions, age, education, etc.)
    b. To internal elements
       (1). Production of art (creating and performing)
       (2). Distribution of art (making it available)
       (3). Consumption of art (becoming an audience)
       (4). Training (for any of the three above)
3. *Social Roles in the creative arts*
    a. Roles in creating or performing (composer, player, actor, director)
    b. Roles in promoting or distributing arts (library, union)
    c. Roles in consuming (listener to music, viewer of drama, etc.)
    d. Roles in training (teachers for any of the above)

The materials for the present chapter were obtained by a questionnaire mailed to several hundred persons active in adult education, as follows: (1) the departments of fine arts of all state universities and several private universities, (2) all state offices of education, (3) about fifty leaders of national agencies or associations, (4) over a hundred "front line" agencies involved directly in teaching or administering education for adults, and (5) other persons or groups recommended by these respondents. At the time of writing about 40 per cent had responded.

GENERAL CONTENT OF THE SUBJECT AREA

We find no clear agreement on what is to be listed under the term "creative arts." The questionnaire listed "graphic arts, music, drama, dance, handicrafts, and writing," and invited other listings. The following additions were suggested by one or more respondents: architecture, speaking, listening, gardening, cooking, flower arranging, folklore, archaeology, genealogy, and "creative thinking". The Camp Fire Girls use the word "handcraft" to suggest the interrelationship between art and craft. Examination of numerous catalogues reveals neither a uniform classification of courses and activities nor a consistency in what is provided under "creative, artistic, recreational, or practical arts." Selected at random from the numerous catalogues received, one listing from an eastern community included the following courses under some art heading: cake decorating, creative writing, basic drawing, fancy food preparation, gardening, guitar playing, painting in oils, piano, and sculpturing. On the periphery, depending on one's catholicity, the same catalogue also lists: dressmaking and tailoring, interior decorating, photography, public speaking and personality, rug hooking, serving, and social dancing.

In view of the lack of agreement on terminology, therefore, we suggest that creative art activity is distinct from those forms of adult activity in which the emphasis is on vocational improvement, civics, or recreation (in the limited sense of passing time, seeking companionship, amusement or entertainment). We submit, as a basis for discussion, that the creative arts within the adult education framework include those in which: (1) there is no clear conception of the resultant form or end of the experience, for these take shape in the course of the experience; (2) the participant contributes to the shaping of the material or medium so that its final result includes an effect upon *him*; and (3) participation may take place on the many dimensions of skills, standards, tastes, or traditions, each of which may provide a degree of creative fulfillment which is to be judged in the context of the situation rather than by professional standards.

The questionnaire posed the question, "What are some of the elements of creativity you would emphasize as particularly pertinent to working with adults?" The variety of replies included: "introduction to new genres," "self-discovery," "voluntary commitment to a disciplined study," "creative discovery," "sense of perspective on art as life," "hidden hunger satisfaction," "creative function in everyday activities rather than in a vacuum," "making things for the home." In no cases were these mentioned by more than one respondent. Several longer statements are given in full:

Virginia Musselman, National Recreation Association:

"Free choice of subject matter; freedom to experiment with various media with orthodox or unorthodox materials and techniques; no element of competition;

freedom to progress at one's own rate, in terms of one's own degree of capability and interest; emphasis on inner self-development rather than on degree of perfection of finished product."

Alfred Bleckschmidt, Supervisor, Fine Arts Education, State Department of Education, Missouri:

"The elements of 'creativity' for adults should be the same as for any student. However, since adults may not have had the privilege of acquiring a broad, general knowledge of the true meaning of 'creativity,' the approach must be a gradual, carefully planned sequence of experiences that would not frighten or discourage mature people. Creativity simply means that one takes ideas, from past and present experiences, reorganizes and crystallizes them into new concepts to fit a need. This, of course, is accomplished much easier in younger students, especially if they are in class daily. Adults, having rather fixed habits of life, are more inclined to want to do something exactly as they observed it being done by others, and of course, this is not creativity."

David Rauch, Director, The Adult Program, Public Schools, Great Neck, New York:

"Adults, as different from children, require an approach that will loosen them up, free them of restraints and reduce their blocks before they can be exposed to any highly disciplined approach. Children need to learn proper disciplines to permit them to be creative. To release creativity in adults one must begin by throwing them into the subject area immediately and give them theory at whatever point they are puzzled by what they are doing and ask about the theory. If you start them with theory you lose them, and make it more difficult for them to release creativity."

OBJECTIVES

Responses given on the objectives of the creative arts programs in adult education were divided into three types: *individual*-centered, *socially*-centered, and *arts*-centered. Emphasis on the first far outweighed the others. Individual-centered objectives were stated by some in such terms as: the "natural urge to create," "self satisfaction and pleasure," "release of creativity," "stimulate latent talent," "art as a medium of self expression." Some statements emphasized the *therapeutic* effects: "a feeling of accomplishment," "art for mental health," "energy outlet," "release from tension." Art for personal improvement was implied in such statements as: "using leisure time constructively," "bring out hidden or unused powers to enhance the personality and character."

Two replies were socially centered: "to develop community interest" and "to encourage more intelligent and active support of the arts on all levels—family, community and national."

Only a few replies placed the emphasis on the production of art *per se*, i.e., "give sound art principles on constructive projects . . ."

However, among those who believe that the social, personal, and aesthetic aims of art are inseparable is Professor Henry Schaeffer-Simmern of the Institute of Art Education, Berkeley, California. His volume, *Unfolding Artistic Activity*, details his work with four groups in art education: mental defectives, delinquent youths, refugees, and business people. He relates that they gradually became conscious of "a unique cultivation of disciplined feeling and thinking, of an intimate coordination of mind, eye, and hand, as well as manual skill. They felt the formative effect which genuine artistic activity had upon them as assisting towards a more harmonised, more balanced personality."[3]

INSTITUTIONAL AUSPICES

Several of the eighteen institutional settings in Part III of this *Handbook* provide examples of sponsorship under which the creative arts take place.

Business, Industry, and Unions

The past quarter century has brought a virtual revolution in managerial philosophy, so that the welfare of the "whole" worker and his family and community are now legitimate concerns of employers. This has been translated into an estimated twenty million dollars spent annually by industry for recreational activity. Dow Chemical Company of Midland, Michigan, for example, maintains a major program of symphony orchestra, chorus, and other musical activities. Chicago's Western Electric Company—famous through the studies of Elton Mayo and others —recently distributed many thousands of booklets on art to its employees. In most cases, the recreation program is initiated, supported, and administered by employees organized for such purposes, or through labor unions. Within our conceptual framework, business and industry are concerned with social functions, such as maintenance of high morale. Educators will find that their offerings in creative activities may be supported in whole or part by subsidies from industry, especially where young executives are involved. In cases where an adult education program includes the sponsorship of a producing or performing art group, local business and industry have often proved financially helpful.

Colleges, Universities, and Extension Services

A growing concept within the American university is that of service to community adults on a degree or non-degree basis. However, as noted in the introduction to the Brighton Canyon Conference (July 3-5, 1958) "If the term 'under-developed' applies to any aspect of adult education in American universities, it applies to education in the 'arts'."[4]

At least forty universities of the National University Extension Association offer art programs for adults. According to the editor of the report of the above conference, Bernard J. James, "Some of these are notable in size; others are extraordinary as imaginative new developments, yet little information is as yet available on such developments, and little critical discussion of theories that underlie adult art education has been published." The importance of this development warrants a listing of projects reported at the conference.

Painting

University of Mississippi: art courses in several state centers.

Kansas State College: circulates paintings; organizes exhibitions of amateur painting, drawings, sculpture. Seven hundred persons annually take fourteen courses in appreciation.

University of Washington statewide association encourages production of art with "market potentialities"; develops community self-studies and action programs in art.

University of Wisconsin Agricultural Extension: state-wide amateur art shows.

University of Michigan: supervisor of social projects organizes state-wide amateur art shows.

New York University Division of General Education: sponsors "studio visiting" and "museum visiting" course.

University of Chicago Downtown Center: lectures at Art Institute, Lyric Opera Company, and Chicago Symphony concerts.

Richmond Museum of Virginia: travelling "artmobile" from museum, accommodates fifteen persons at a time.

Theatre

Wisconsin Idea Theatre: trains community theatre groups; publishes folklore research; produces and sends plays into the state; is launching a National Center for Community theatre.

State University of Iowa: annual Play Production Festival and Community Theatre Workshop.

Hunter College: course in theatrical mime and movement.

University of Tennessee: loan collection of five thousand plays.

Queens College: seminars on "Living Theater," radio and television workshop.

Music

University of Michigan: extension orchestra for adults.

University of Wisconsin: workshops and projects for church music improvement.

University of Illinois: publications for community music leaders.

Hunter College: opera workshop.

University of North Carolina: "Opera Film Forum"—four discussion meetings.

U. C. L. A.: "Spotlight on Opera" television course.

Creative Writing and Literature

New York University and Hunter College: courses in short story writing, novel, etc.

University of Utah: two-week writer's conference.

University of Wisconsin: 1500 persons now active in "Rural Writers' Association"; quarterly publication, "Creative Wisconsin."

Dance

The Brighton Canyon summary notes that dance is the least developed area within university adult art programs. "It virtually has been ignored."

Additional forms of art education under university sponsorship are noted as follows: lectures, public concerts, week-end conferences away from the campus, (Syracuse University); European summer tours on the arts (University of Southern California); film societies (University of Wisconsin Extension and Portland Extension Center of Oregon State System of Higher Education).

The wide range of emerging university interest in the creative arts for adults touches upon all categories of the framework outlined earlier. The emphasis depends in part upon the art philosophy within the university as it applies to the regular student; in part (as in the important Wisconsin development) upon a long tradition of service to the state with the Scandinavian concept of grass-roots participation; in part on the personal positions of strong leaders. In few cases do the professionally-minded faculty see in adult art activities a potential source of careers for these students or a base for building large audiences for professional artists.

Tax-supported Agencies: Federal, State, Municipal

Important work in the creative arts is carried on by the Federal Extension Service of the United States Department of Agriculture. These programs vary widely, depending upon the interests of people who develop the program in various states and communities. In the field of music, a number of states have fine rural groups; among them are Indiana, Iowa, Oklahoma, and North Carolina.

In the field of handicrafts many men and women find that hooking rugs, weaving on a handloom, turning a potter's wheel, or making articles from metals, wood, or other available materials, answers a creative need. Handicrafts in the Extension Service has had two major objectives: (1) to encourage people to make use of leisure time to develop creative skills that may contribute to good mental health, and (2) to aid families to increase their incomes through the sale of quality crafts at roadside markets and through the craft shops.

While the major function of the extension service has been to help in locating craft teachers for special interest groups of men and women, several states have employed specialists in handicrafts. Home demonstration agents have taught craft work in the following states: Georgia, North Carolina, Tennessee, Mississippi, Florida, and Kentucky. In other states local resource persons, many of them former art teachers, have been enlisted as instructors.[5]

On the local level of government, the Post-War period has been marked
by a growing acceptance of tax-financed recreation activities under professional leadership. The recreation movement, for its part, has steadily
enlarged its range of interests and skills, as documented in such volumes
as *The Recreation Program* and *Community Recreation*.[6] Illustrations
can be drawn in which tax supported agencies—or some combination of
public-private administration—sponsor performing groups, make art available to the public in such ways as summer park concerts, and establish
classes. For example, the Los Angeles Bureau of Music administers the
weekly activities of more than 40 choral and community-sing units and
presents over 100 band programs per year. Denver has a well-established
program in the arts, and the Flint, Michigan, Community Music Association has long been a model for middle-sized communities. Boston's
new Charles River art center is being constructed with a quarter-million
dollar allocation of the Metropolitan District Commission, together with
private contributions.

According to the conceptualization presented earlier in this chapter,
performing groups may be legitimately classified under the creative arts
in adult education. Indeed, to do otherwise would eliminate the heart
of "creative" activity and unnecessarily narrow the concept of education.

Voluntary Organizations

Within the community setting there often arises a voluntary group
which organizes creative activities, helps to keep an orchestra going, or
in other ways contributes to the welfare and education of adults through
the arts. Whether or not such activities fall into "adult education," the
adult educator is well-advised to become aware of significant work carried
on by these voluntary associations. The American Symphony Orchestra
League[7] illustrates a national association established to help community
groups. Leadership training courses for adult work may also be directed
to the needs of persons who function in these voluntary settings. It appears clear, further, that the present concern with the meaningful use of
leisure time will result in more volunteer groups from whom leadership
will emerge.

Health and Welfare Agencies

Agencies discussed in Chapter 21 and 31 center their objectives on the
welfare and rehabilitation of people. Their interest in artistic activity
is almost always as a means to group experience (whether for social or
therapeutic reasons), and as a carry-over from a hospital or other artificial
situation into the home or community. Such agencies (settlement houses,

prisons, homes for the aged, hospitals of various kinds) have scarcely caught the interest of teacher-training institutions in the arts. However, with the growing demand for therapists, we might predict a growing demand for art educators in these fields for several reasons: (1) concern of the art graduate for more stable economic support, (2) closer rapport of social sciences and art teaching and the influence upon the art world by such a national group as the Society for Functional Music, and (3) inevitably increased attention to the "aging process" and the nature of creative activities.

Libraries, Museums, Art Institutes

The notable change in library philosophy noted in Chapter 25 has been of direct help to the creative arts by providing lectures, concerts, film programs, records, and scores. The American Library Association tabulated the services offered to the arts by fifty-nine libraries. The type of service offered is arranged by communities under 25,000, 25,000-100,000, and over 100,000 in population. While the general services (acquisition of special materials, information services, reader guidance, etc.) apply to all ages, services to organizations is perhaps most appropriate to adults. Eighteen out of fifty-nine libraries reported major attention to this activity in the past decade, eleven of these were in the largest cities. The availability of books, records, films, slides, and pictures is of significance to adult art interest, and aside from the 11 percent which provided slides, the other services were reported in almost half of the libraries.

A constructive suggestion is made by Basil Langton, director of the reading series, "Poets and Playwrights," in The New York Public Library: "Adult reading groups, and particularly in the field of poetry, need to be encouraged—where adults read aloud to each other and share and experience the sensation of the poetic ideas and emotion which touches or comes close to some hidden and unexpressed experience of their own."[9]

In reference to the framework at the beginning of this chapter the library is essentially a "distributing" agency for books, records, and music. However, enterprising libraries are going much further, sponsoring programs which involve the public more directly with the arts.

Museums, and art institutes have also undergone an enlargement in their functions. For instance, the People's Art Center of the Museum of Modern Art in New York provides art classes for those who wish to pursue art for their personal pleasure as a leisure time activity, "to make them aware of the fundamentals of line, texture, structure, color and composition." The Toledo Museum of Art offers adult classes in design, drawing, painting, crafts, ceramics, sculpture, graphics, art history and appreciation; but in addition, the museum offers music classes, free concerts, a circulating library of 3,000 records, a reference library of 12,000 books on art and music, and 23,000 slides. Similar services are provided by museums and art institutes in the major cities across the country.

Mass Media

As Chapter 26 indicates, there is considerable debate as to the responsibilities of the mass media for the education of its viewers. There is general agreement that educational TV stations are increasingly important in their impact. The services of the National Association of Educational Broadcasters should therefore be known to adult educators. Its listings of taped programs (1951-1958) included 67 series about literature and 91 on music; some of these series consisted of as many as 52 separate programs.

Public Schools

A large number of local school systems, with or without state assistance, carry on an evening curriculum for adults. A small sample of the offering in the creative arts in this setting was obtained in a tabulation of eleven communities of New Jersey for 1958-59: Millburn, Demarest, Red Band, East Orange, Montclair, Ewing, Hanover, Haddonfield, Morristown, N. Hunterdon, and Parsipanny. Of a total of 611 courses listed by these adult schools, eighty-six or 14 percent are in the area of the creative arts. The distribution by schools in Table 1 provides a view of how the courses or activities are grouped.

TABLE 1

TOTAL COURSES IN ARTS, TWELVE NEW JERSEY COMMUNITIES

COMMUNITY Total Courses	A 35	B 54	C 38	D 41	E 67	F 27	G 35	H 33	I 38	J 59	K 24	L 62	Total 611
Music appreciation	1		1	1	1					1			5
Music instrument	5	4			3		2	1		2		2	19
Chorus							1	2					3
Orchestra								1				1	2
Drawing or painting	2	3	1	2	3	2	2	1	4	2	1	1	24
Sculpturing	1	1		1									3
Jewelry making									1				1
Writing		2	1	1	1				2	1			8
Literature appreciation					1		1					1	3
Theatre appreciation					1				1				2
Modern dance, ballet					1	1							2
Ceramics			1		1							2	4
Flower arrangement	1												1
Photography	1	1		1	1		1		1	1		1	8

It is to be noted that all phases of the conceptual outline above are covered in the tabulation, although only three schools have performing groups. The Montclair program presents some offering in all the major arts, and every school has one or more courses in painting or drawing. The Parsippanny school also offers a lecture series covering several arts.

Until a larger study is made we cannot say how these programs in New Jersey compare with those of other states. A statistical report from the State Department of Education in Michigan indicates, however, that in that state during the year ending June, 1958, enrollment in courses in practical arts and crafts increased 16 per cent while it decreased from 5 per cent to 80 per cent in several other categories. It decreased 31 per cent in drama and fine arts—which accounted, however, for 7.9 per cent of the total enrollment in all courses, representing 15,000 individuals.

MAJOR CURRENT PROBLEMS AND ISSUES

The experience of the present authors in this report points to the need for a central clearing house and research agency which can gather and interpret materials of the kind begun here. Eventually, this would serve as a consulting agency which might explore such issues as the following:

1. The relation of the creative arts to other meaningful activity in the light of the "new leisure," characterized by technology, "open class" behavior, trends toward conformity, and the search among educators for sources of constructive values.

2. The relations of amateur to professional activity as well as of the "elite" to the "popular" taste and audience.

3. The dynamics of how choices for leisure activities are made and modified. (An ethical problem precedes this: upon what justification do the leaders of opinion seek or unintentionally bring about change in the tastes or the behavior of other adults?)

4. The training of teachers in the creative arts who are concerned with social as well as aesthetic values, and who can build upon the existing value systems of their students.

5. The significance of the creative arts in a society which becomes increasingly scientific in its outlook.

Footnotes

1. George Soule, *Time for Living* (New York: Viking Press, 1955).
2. *Mass Culture, The Popular Arts in America*, edited by Bernard Rosenberg and David Manning White (Glencoe, Ill.: The Free Press, 1957).
3. Henry Schaeffer-Simmern, *Unfolding Artistic Activity* (Berkeley: University of California, 1950), p. 194.
4. *University Adult Education in the Arts.* A working paper for the Brighton Canyon Conference, July 3-5, 1958. Bernard J. James, editor (Chicago: Center for the Study of Liberal Education for Adults, 1958).

5. From a letter by Mrs. Lillie M. Alexander, Program Leader, Southern States, Federal Extension Service, U. S. Department of Agriculture, May 11, 1959.
6. *The Recreation Program.* 6th Workshop, Athletic Institute, 209 S. State St., Chicago, 1954 and H. D. Meyer and C. K. Brightbill, *Community Recreation* (Boston: D. C. Heath and Co., 1948).
7. Write to Miss Helen Thompson, Executive Secretary, American Symphony Orchestra League, Inc., Box 164, Charleston, W. Virginia.
8. *Northland Recreation Laboratory,* Silver Anniversary Issue, April, 1959, 3100 West Lake Street, Minneapolis.
9. For program descriptions of poetry and play readings, lectures, film showings, chamber music concerts, recitals, and record programs, address The Office of Adult Services, Donnell Library Center, New York Public Library, 20 W. 53rd St., New York 19, N. Y.

Selected Readings

Brightbill, C. H. and Meyer H. D. *Recreation; Text and Readings.* New York: Prentice-Hall, Inc., 1953.

Brownell, Baker. *The Human Community.* New York: Harper & Bros., 1950.

Hauser, Arnold. *The Social History of Art.* New York: Alfred A. Knopf, Inc., Vol. 1-4, 1957-1958.

Kaplan, Max. *Music in Recreation: Foundations and Practices.* Champaign, Ill.: Stipes, 1955.

Kohn, Bernard. "Interrelation of the Arts," *Adult Leadership,* VI (September, 1957).

Kriesburg, Irving. "Art in Adult Life," *Adult Leadership,* IV (December, 1955).

Larrabee, Eric and Meyersohn, Rolf (ed.). *Mass Leisure.* Glencoe, Ill.: The Free Press, 1959.

Machover, Karen, *Personality Projection in the Drawing of the Human Figure* (A Method of Personality Investigation). Springfield, Ill.: Charles Thomas Co., 1949.

Parnes, Sidney J. (ed.). *Compendium of Research on Creative Imagination.* The Creative Education Foundation, University of Buffalo, 1958.

Read, Herbert. *The Meaning of Art.* New York: Penguin Books, 1947.

Rosenberg, Bernard and White, David Manning, (ed.). *Mass Culture: The Popular Arts in America.* Glencoe, Ill.: The Free Press, 1957.

Schaeffer-Simmern, Henry. *The Unfolding of Artistic Activity.* Berkeley: University of California Press, 1950.

Soibelman, Doris. *Therapeutic and Industrial Uses of Music.* New York: Columbia University Press, 1948.

Wasserman, Burton. "The Role of Art Education in Public School Programs for Adult Learning," *Art Education,* XI (May, 1958).

CHAPTER 37

ECONOMIC EDUCATION FOR ADULTS

ALBERT L. AYARS
Director
Education Department
Hill and Knowlton, Inc.

THE NEED FOR ECONOMIC EDUCATION*

When American education was in its infancy, our world was a simple one. The typical child who mastered his three R's and who was blessed with a normal supply of common sense and physical strength could expect to work out his economic destiny with little help or interference from anyone. But the simple life and pioneer isolation have passed. Economic problems, both personal and political, crowd upon all of us—a maze of them, bewildering, and complex. The satisfaction of economic wants no longer lies within the power of the individual's arm or the resources of his family tract.

As a producer and wage earner, the citizen's welfare is closely tied to the program of the government—its fiscal and monetary policies and its social philosophy. The citizen in our society is asked to make political choices that are also economic. The issue may be local—a raise in property taxes, for example. The issue may be national, such as legislation on minimum wages and hours. Even more perplexing, our era has experienced the interknitting of the American economy into an international fabric. So the issue we face at any given time may be international—should the United States participate in giving technical assistance to underdeveloped areas in the rest of the world, distribute surplus cereal grain abroad, make international loans, or establish new trade policies?

Even decisions on personal problems have a bearing on the total health of our economy and our world. Most people manage budgets and buy a lot more than food. Through their composite decisions the people can

---

*Portions of this section have been adapted from an article, "Economic Education and Your School," by the author in the November, 1953, issue of *Business Teacher*.

make or break markets, speed up or slow down the flow of consumer goods, influence tax policy, stimulate or curtail the flow of capital funds, and decrease or increase employment and wages.

The period in which we live is dominated by the prolonged and bitter struggle between two opposing concepts of life and social organization. In the final analysis, our democracy will triumph over communistic totalitarianism only if we prove democracy workable and capable, even under strain, of supplying the common needs of our own people and of undergirding the economic structure of the entire world. The decisions to be made give increasing importance to the insights of the average citizen in relation to our economy.

Another development of recent decades is the growth of lobbies and other vested-interest groups at the local, state, and national levels. The dairy farmer, the businessman, the laborer, and the physician not only have economic opinions but make them felt through organizations powerful enough to require being reckoned with on any questions of national policy. Since the opinions of such organizations often conflict, it is obvious that if sound policies are to be effected the average citizen must make his choices and decisions on the basis of unselfish and thorough-going understanding of the economics involved.

The development of economic understanding is complicated by an almost hopelessly intertwined mixture of social, ethical, moral and political concepts. Our view on federal support for education is tinctured by our attitude toward states rights. Our opinion about public power is influenced by the intensity of our feeling as to the efficiency of private enterprise in promoting the general welfare. Our view of labor legislation depends on our concept of unions either as legalized instruments of interference with the rights of management or as exemplifications of the right of free people to join together to promote the common good.

Managing our economy efficiently implies that we shall have to pursue public and private policies that promote high levels of employment and a continuing high standard of living. In the private sector, this means spending, saving, and investing with due consideration for the general welfare as well as for the immediate gain of the individual or firm. In the government sector, this means that the public must be well enough informed to support measures that tend to stabilize economic activity and avoid extreme fluctuations between inflation and deflation.

To the people are posed the difficult questions: At what point does the disadvantage of curtailment of freedom outweigh the resulting advantages to the general welfare? How can we establish that intricate balance between regulations required to maintain the vitality and equilibrium of the economy and freedom of individual choice and initiative? The answers to such difficult questions can come only from an informed public.

So numerous and so fundamental are our economic problems, and so intertwined are they in the success of democracy, that understanding of economics—its terms, its working patterns, its significance—has become a prerequisite to successful citizenship.

MATERIALS AND PROGRAMS TO MEET THE NEEDS

During recent years there has been a flowering of economic education materials and programs for adults. It is impossible in one chapter to describe even a small segment of the publications and activities in the field, but the listing of a representative sample of them below illustrates their range.

Each year there is a veritable avalanche of publications distributed. These take many forms: magazines and articles, booklets, films, filmstrips, graphs, charts, maps, cartoon stories, pamphlets, annual reports, statistical compilations, books, and advertisements, to mention some of the most common. Programs developed also take many forms: formal classes, field trips, seminars, workshops, discussion groups, lectures, demonstrations, and counseling services.

The economic literature has been greatly enriched by a wide variety of research studies conducted by independent research organizations. Some examples of groups which conduct such research are: The Brookings Institution, The Twentieth Century Fund, Stanford Research Institute, Opinion Research Corporation, the National Bureau of Economic Research, Manpower For The Future, the National Manpower Council, the Rockefeller Foundation, the Sloan Foundation, the National Industrial Conference Board, and the National Planning Association. These and many other organizations carry forth scholarly investigation on our economic frontiers and help to provide resources needed in developing understanding of economic issues and problems. A large number of universities now have bureaus for economic, business, and social research. From these sources, also, come materials of great value.

Many free and inexpensive materials on a broad variety of economic topics come from the federal government and its agencies. The Bureau of Labor Statistics, the Department of Commerce, the Joint Economic Committee of the Congress, the Social Security Administration, and the President's Council of Economic Advisors are examples. The Federal Reserve System, through its regional banks, provides a constant flow of materials of value in understanding the special economic problems of any region of the country.

In preparing this chapter a questionnaire was sent to over one hundred and fifty adult educational leaders to get an overview of what is now going on in economic education for adults. The results of this sample survey are summarized below, providing a broad view of the types of organizations, programs, and materials upon which adults may draw to provide the background for the tremendously consequential economic decisions that are theirs to make.

SOME REPRESENTATIVE PROGRAMS OF ECONOMIC EDUCATION FOR ADULTS

Name of Organization	Purpose of Program and/or Materials	Types of Publications Produced	Types of Activities Developed	Special Emphasis	Groups to Whom Prog. is directed	Date Org. Became Active in Econ. Educ.
AFL-CIO	to develop understanding of labor union movement and role of unions in economy	books, pamphlets, filmstrips, films, newsletter, reports	workshops, conferences	economic principles	union members, public	1881
American Home Economics Association	to develop more efficient home management and family economics	magazine and articles	conferences	home management	home makers	*
American Iron and Steel Institute	compilation of industry-wide statistics and information and distribution to public; report research results	magazine, statistical reports, films, filmstrips, booklets, public information advertising	conferences, seminars, discussions, workshops	economic problems related to industry & free enterprise system	members, editors, teachers, public	1912

*Date not supplied.

Name of Organization	Purpose of Program	Publications	Activities	Emphasis	Audience	Date
American Labor Education Service	cultivate sound human relations through helping workers develop understanding of problems, confidence, sense of social responsibility	newsletters, movies, pamphlets	institutes, courses in labor economic & social problems; field trips, conferences, discussions, lectures	community economic needs	union members	*
American Library Association (Portland, Ore., Denver & Cuyahoga County, Ohio libraries)	to promote better adult understanding through the utilization of library materials and services	books, pamphlets, book lists, recordings, films, slides, pictures	speakers, exhibits, discussions, symposiums	investment services, taxation, economic principles	public	*
The Brookings Institution	to aid in the development of sound public policies through research and to provide advanced training in the social sciences	books, pamphlets reporting research	discussion, speakers	economic analysis & reasoning	public	1927

Name of Organization	Purpose of Program	Publications	Activities	Emphasis	Audience	Date
Brotherhood of Railroad Trainmen	to keep members informed of economic and social issues of importance to the country and to individuals as citizens and union members	newspaper, pamphlets, magazine	speakers, conferences	money management, economic issues, operation of free enterprise system	members	*
Central Y.M.C.A. Chicago	provide formal and informal education needed by members and public	discussion guides, pamphlets	counseling center, classes, speakers, discussion groups	money management, business operation, vocational guidance	members, public	1946
Chamber of Commerce of the United States	develop understanding and appreciation for free enterprise system	books, pamphlets, discussion guides, program guides, filmstrips, films, economic quizzes	discussion groups, plant tours, employee meetings	economic principles, community relations, money management, economic systems	employees, public	*

Name of Organization	Purpose of Program	Publications	Activities	Emphasis	Audience	Date
Cooperative Extension Service, U.S. Dept. of Agriculture	to aid in the achievement of efficient agricultural production, adequate incomes and prosperous communities; to provide practical education for agriculture through demonstration	bulletins, pamphlets, articles, moving pictures, visual aids	discussions, conferences, TV & radio programs, speeches, demonstrations	home management and economics; agricultural economics	farm families	1914
The Committee For Economic Development	to conduct studies into the principles of business and public policy to foster full contribution of business and commerce to general well-being; to promote public consideration and understanding of economic problems	books, pamphlets	discussions, conferences	economic principles, public economic policy	the public	*

Name of Organization	Purpose of Program	Publications	Activities	Emphasis	Audience	Date
Cooperative League of the USA	to encourage the growth of co-operatives and to increase member and public understanding of co-operatives	books, pamphlets, magazines, films, filmstrips, advertising	speakers, seminars, conferences, consultation service	economic principles, free and democratically controlled economy	members & the public	1916
Council of the Southern Mountains, Inc.	to promote community self analysis and improvement within the total economy; to develop a satisfying life pattern for people of Southern Appalachians	magazine, pamphlets	field counselor, speakers, seminars, conferences, group discussions	economic principles as applied to satisfying living, conservation, industrial development	southern mountain families	*
Credit Union National Association	to promote economic democracy through promoting understanding and development of credit unions	booklets, pamphlets, films, filmstrips, group leader's guides	workshops, discussions, speakers, institutes	thrift, saving, money management, economic principles	members, public	1934

Name of Organization	Purpose of Program	Publications	Activities	Emphasis	Audience	Date
National Farmers Union	to develop understanding of farm problems and contributions and legislation favorable to the farmer—to raise farm income and production	booklets, leaflets, discussion guides, action guide newsletters	speakers, discussions, conferences, bus trip campaigns	economic principles, operation of the free enterprise economy	members, public	1902
The Federal Reserve System	to promote better understanding of the Federal Reserve System, the nation's credit and monetary machinery, and ways of maintaining stable economic progress	books, booklets, pamphlets, bulletins, charts, special studies, reprints	speakers, conferences	economic stability, role of money and banking	public	*
Florida Federation of Women's Clubs	develop understanding of economic problems	leaflets, program guides	seminars, speakers, reading & discussing books, articles, etc.	money management, economic principles	members, teachers	1958

Name of Organization	Purpose of Program	Publications	Activities	Emphasis	Audience	Date
The Fund For Adult Education	to expand opportunities that contribute to the continuing development of the mature individual in the responsible exercise of freedom	speech reprints, pamphlets, discussion guides and materials	study-discussions, support of worthwhile adult education programs, awards for articles, speeches	economic principles as related to leadership development, education, & world affairs	the public	1951
Industrial Corporations *Illustrative Examples* Republic Steel Corp. General Electric Co.	to develop greater understanding and appreciation for the problems and contributions of industry and of the free enterprise system	newsletters, magazines, books, pamphlets, films, filmstrips, recordings, flannel boards, demonstration kits	classes, lectures, discussions, panels, radio & TV shows	operation of free enterprise economy	employees (some materials & activities for public)	*

Name of Organization	Purpose of Program	Publications	Activities	Emphasis	Audience	Date
Metropolitan Life Insurance Company	to disseminate information on economic matters of timely import	advertisements, articles, leaflets	employee discussions	economic principles & trends	company employees & public	*
National Association of Manufacturers	to develop understanding and appreciation of the free enterprise system. To preserve freedom of opportunity and enterprise	books, pamphlets, reprints of speeches, films, filmstrips, discussion guides	workshops, conferences, discussions	economic principles, the free enterprise system, productivity	members, employees, the public	*
National Council of Churches of Christ in the U.S.A.	to develop understanding of the relationship between religion, ethics, and economics	films, filmstrips, booklets, pamphlets, sermon materials	workshops, seminars, lectures	fund raising, investment, wage policies, economic principles & ethics, free enterprise economy	clergymen, religious leaders, church members, the public	1947

Name of Organization	Purpose of Program	Publications	Activities	Emphasis	Audience	Date
Philadelphia Museum of Commerce (Franklin Institute)	to develop an understanding and appreciation of trade and commerce	curriculum materials, discussion guides	tours, discussions, lectures	comparative economic systems, international relations	students, teachers and the public	1900
Rural Church Center, Green Lake, Wisconsin	to acquaint rural clergymen with the field of agricultural economics and rural economic institutions	leaflets, program guides	lectures, class study, discussion groups	economic principles	clergy	1947
Public Affairs Committee, Inc.	to popularize economic research and develop understanding	pamphlets, filmstrips	conferences	money management, economic principles	students, public	1936
St. Paul Public Schools (adult program)	to develop better use of money in the family budget	pamphlets, program & curriculum materials	classes, speakers, workshops	money management, family finance, consumer education	teachers, the public	1950

Name of Organization	Purpose of Program	Publications	Activities	Emphasis	Audience	Date
Twentieth Century Fund	to conduct research and public education on economic and social problems	books, pamphlets, charts, clip sheets, newsletters, films, filmstrips	speakers, conferences, radio & TV programs	economic principles, free enterprise system, comparative economic systems, international relations	students, adult study groups, the public	1919
University Adult Education Programs *Illustrative Examples:* University of Akron University of Florida University of Washington Syracuse University Wayne State University Earlham College Program of Community Dynamics	to provide general education in economic problems and nature of the economy	booklets, pamphlets, leaflets, discussion guides	workshops, seminars, conferences, speakers, field representatives, classes	economic principles & practices; free enterprise economy, investment, financial management	business and industry people, women in business, the public	*

Helping adults gain economic competence is a relatively new and recently very active frontier in civic education. The materials and programs cited above give some impression of the effort being expended to meet the need.

It should be recognized, however, that the multiplicity of materials and programs, while serving to point up the need for and interest in economic education, does not necessarily insure easy achievement of its purposes. Broad economic understanding still cannot be acquired like a grocery order.

Among the groups offering the adult economic information there are obvious disagreements in points of view. The eager learner finds himself struggling for understanding in the face of a crossfire of pressures and, sometimes, emotional thinking. Much of the material and many of the programs have focus and utility in developing sound and practical economic insights.

The adult interested in gaining important economic understandings is challenged to identify basic assumptions, compare contradictory evidences and arguments, and exercise his powers of critical analysis. In this way he may benefit richly from the materials and programs available to him not only in the knowledge gleaned but in the development of the skills essential to enlightened civic and economic competency.

Selected Readings

Adult Education Towards Social and Political Responsibility. A report prepared by the UN Educational, Scientific and Cultural Organization Institute for Education. New York: Columbia University Press, 1953.

Ayars, Albert L. "Economic Education and Your School," *Business Teacher,* November, 1953, 7-8.

Brown, H. G. "Foundations, Professors and Economic Education," *American Journal of Economic Sociology,* January, 1958, 145-155.

Bryson, Lyman. *The Drive Toward Reason in the Service of a Free People.* New York: Harper & Brothers, 1954.

Carroll, Thomas H. "Continuing Education and Individual Responsibility," *Adult Education,* Vol. IX, No. 4, 239-243.

Chalmers, J. and Leamer, L. E. "A Philosophy of Economic Education," *Atlanta Economic Review,* Vol. IV, No. 6, 11-16.

Education for the Economic Challenges of Tomorrow. A Report of a Symposium in Conjunction with Tenth Anniversary Observance of the Joint Council on Economic Education, New York, 1959.

Education for Public Responsibility. A Statement by the Directors of the Fund for Adult Education. White Plains, N. Y., 1959.

Gemmell, James, et al., *Economics in General Education.* Proceedings of the Riverdale Conference. New York: Joint Council, 1954.

Hill, Wilhelmina. *The Three R's and Resources,* National Wildlife Federation, 1959.

Houle, C. O., and Nelson, C. A. *The University, the Citizen and World Affairs.*

A report prepared for the Carnegie Endowment for International Peace and others. Washington: American Council on Education, 1956.

Mercer, Blaine E., and Carr, Edwin R. *Education and the Social Order.* New York: Rinehart & Co., 1957.

Merrifield, C. W. "Economic Competence: New Frontier in Civic Education," reprint from *Social Education,* February, 1959.

Murray, E. B. *Some Economic Fallacies and the Citizen.* Utah State University Monograph Series, 5:3, 1957.

Nourse, E. G. "Looking Ahead in Economic Education," National Planning Association, *Looking Ahead,* September, 1958, pp. 1-3.

The Challenge to America: Its Economic and Social Aspects. Special Studies Report IV, Rockefeller Brothers Fund, America at Mid-century Series, 1958.

The Story of Greater Toledo's Economic Education Program. A report prepared by the Toledo Area Chamber of Commerce, Toledo, 1957.

Thomassen, Henry. *Trends in Economic Education.* Washington: Public Affairs Press, 1956.

CHAPTER 38

FUNDAMENTAL AND LITERACY EDUCATION FOR NATIVE AND FOREIGN-BORN ADULTS

ANGELICA W. CASS
*Associate in Americanization and
Adult Elementary Education
Bureau of Adult Education
New York State Education Department*

AN OLD CONCERN WITH A NEW URGENCY

One of the oldest and largest areas of adult education provides fundamental and literacy education for native and foreign-born adults. The large number of adults whose educational preparation for life in a space age is pitifully inadequate is causing increasing concern among leaders of the national program to build and strengthen our reserve pool of manpower. Interest in elementary education for adults has never been as high as it is today. Communities and states are becoming increasingly aware of their responsibility to help foreign-born adults remove the handicaps caused by lack of knowledge of the language, history, and customs of the country in which they live and to help native adults remove the fetters of total or functional illiteracy.

Many evidences of this rising interest can be cited. In 1957 a National Commission for Adult Literacy, composed of thirty-four outstanding citizens of the nation representing labor unions, business, agriculture, government, public schools, universities, mass media, and religious, women's, racial, and civic groups was established by the Adult Education Association. Its objectives are to alert the public to this great need, to collect facts about it, and to stimulate more action to eliminate illiteracy among the adults of our nation.

In 1959 two Presidential committees specifically referred to this field. The President's Committee on Education Beyond the High School reported that "adult education should serve the aspirations of the more mature for literacy, for learning more and more remunerative skills, for a higher degree of culture, for understanding the social, physical and economic environment, for fulfilling the role of responsible citizenship."[1] . . . The President's Science Advisory Committee reported the need for adults to "understand science in order to have a wide and intelligent, democratic participation in many national decisions—the decisions that must be made NOW—not postponed for 20 years—there is no escape from the urgency of providing adult education in science now—*planned for those who are unprepared even in the fundamentals.*"[2]

SCOPE AND DEFINITIONS

General

Fundamental and literacy education divides itself into two parts— programs for foreign-born adults and programs for native adults. Leaders in the field are not fully agreed upon any single term which clearly designates the two parts of this educational offering. Many programs provide offerings for both types of adults and report them under a single heading of "Citizenship" or "Literacy Education." Usually, however, native and foreign-born adults are not taught in the same class or group.

Fundamental education helps adults (native or foreign-born) who have had little or no formal education to understand the problems of their immediate environment. It involves the learning of basic knowledge and skills that are required for day-to-day living.

Literacy education teaches adults (native or foreign-born) to read, write, and figure with ease and comprehension at the level of the fifth grade and to improve their lives so as to benefit the community in which they live.

Fundamental and literacy education does not confine itself to providing instructions in subjects required for citizenship—English language, history, and government. Adults must be "literate" in the basic essentials of living. The purposes and objectives of fundamental and literacy education can be summarized as follows:

1. To provide instruction in the basic, fundamental skills and subject matter of elementary education.
2. To increase ability and skill in participation in community life and government.
3. To provide experiences which will enable the adult to become an interested, alert, socially contributing member of his community.
4. To encourage the concept that naturalization is not the end but just the beginning of full citizenship.
5. To instill a desire for citizenship and active participation in community life.

6. To create an awareness of the duties and responsibilities of citizens and non-citizens in the community, state and nation.

7. To foster the belief that citizenship is not to be held lightly by virtue of birth; that it is a priceless possession containing a dual heritage of privilege and responsibility.

In this chapter the term "fundamental and literacy education" will be used to denote both parts of this type of adult education unless otherwise indicated.

The Foreign-Born

Terminology has changed in the last decade. We have passed through the stage of using such terms as "D.P.," "refugee," "escapee," and "parolee" to that of using such terms as "new Americans" and "new-comers." Seldom to do we hear "immigrant," "Americanization," "melting pot," and similar terms of a quarter century ago. The concept of orientation and cultural pluralism is coming to the foreground.

The term "foreign-born" designates those adults now in the United States who were born in other countries, including both aliens and naturalized citizens.

"Non-English-speaking" is a term used to designate adults who are United States citizens by right of birth, but in whose birthplace English was not the language of communication—Puerto Ricans, for example.

In the last decade the flow of immigration has been tightly regulated by quotas set at a rate that authorizes an annual influx hovering around 150,000 persons. To this should be added additional thousands authorized each year to enter under special legislation, such as the Displaced Persons and Refugee Relief Acts, and those persons who have had their status in the United States adjusted.

Changes in legislation affecting aliens have influenced the nature of the educational program for them. In 1952 the necessity for filing a declaration of intention or "first paper" was eliminated under the provisions of the McCarran-Walter Act. Such a declaration of intention may still be filed by an alien who, for example, may require it for purposes of employment, but a first paper is no longer mandatary.

The McCarran-Walter Act also made an addition to the educational requirements for naturalization. An applicant for citizenship is now required to demonstrate an understanding of the English language which includes the ability to read, write, and speak words in ordinary usage, unless he is physically unable to do so, or unless he was over fifty years of age on December 24, 1952, *and* had been living in the United States for periods totalling at least twenty years as of that date. The requirement that he demonstrate a knowledge and understanding of the fundamentals of the history and the principles and form of the government of our country remains unchanged.

Authorization of the Alien Address Report, in 1952, required all aliens to report their present address during January of each year. Forms for this purpose are provided by and must be returned to local post offices. The number of aliens reporting under this Act has risen from 2,348,881 in 1953 to 2,948,694 in 1959. These figures are offset by the numbers of persons naturalized in that period—92,051 in 1953, increasing to 119,866 in 1958. Many of the nearly 3,000,000 known aliens have had less than five years of schooling, and a large number of naturalized citizens have not availed themselves of educational opportunities other than mere preparation to pass the examination on history and government required for naturalization.

Native Adults

Educational programs for native adults for whom English is the mother tongue but who have had little or no schooling are described by such terms as "basic," "fundamental," "literacy," and "adult elementary." The term "illiterate" is used to designate a person who cannot read, write, and figure at the level of the first grade and has had no formal schooling or its equivalent. "Functional illiterate" is the term used to designate a person who has completed less than five years of formal schooling.[8]

There are approximately 10,000,000 adult citizens over twenty-five years of age in the United States today who are functionally illiterate. This group is composed of 4,000,000 native whites, 3,000,000 foreign-born whites, and 3,000,000 Negroes.

A high proportion of illiterates is concentrated in the ages over forty-five. *Nearly 60,000 new functional illiterates reach the age of fourteen each year.* The number of adult functional illiterates was reduced only about one million during the past decade in spite of adult education activities.

While the rate of illiteracy in several northern and western states is relatively low, as compared to that of southern states, the actual number of functional illiterates in those states is high. The rate in New York, for example, is less than 10 per cent, but the number is nearly a million. The rates in Illinois and California are 7.8 per cent and 6.8 per cent, respectively, but the number of persons in each state is over 400,000. The corresponding number in Massachusetts, Michigan, New Jersey, and Ohio is approximately a quarter of a million. In Connecticut, Indiana, Missouri and Wisconsin the numbers range from 100,000 to about 200,000.

The present high rate of adult illiteracy in the United States is not limited to any particular area. In a typical community of 1,000 persons there will be found 19 illiterates, 37 others who have not completed the fifth grade (functional illiterates) and about 20 aliens. Many communities have more illiterates than college graduates.

INSTITUTIONAL PROGRAMS OF FUNDAMENTAL AND LITERACY EDUCATION

The Public Schools

The most widespread and long established programs are conducted by or sponsored by the public school systems of the nation. The public school is the one agency in every community best equipped with facilities and staff to operate educational offerings designed to meet the citizenship preparation and fundamental and literacy needs of native and foreign-born adults.

There are citizenship and fundamental and literacy education programs in every state of the nation and the District of Columbia. Many of these offer classes and activities both day and evening. In more than three-fourths of the states, the programs are offered by the state education departments through local public schools.

The concern and need for this type of adult education is deep-rooted and has been an ongoing part of the offerings of public schools for many years. For example, programs have been conducted for over 100 years in Maryland, California, New York, and Rhode Island. Other states have offered programs for from 10 to 90 years—the majority for approximately 40 to 60 years. Our newest states have been offering these educational opportunities—Alaska for 4 years and Hawaii for 12 years.

The Immigration and Naturalization Service

The Immigration and Naturalization Service of the U. S. Department of Justice works in partnership with public schools and other organizations concerned with the preparation of aliens for citizenship. The INS is authorized by law to assist and promote instruction and training in citizenship responsibilities of applicants for naturalization, to send the names of candidates for naturalization to the public schools, and to prepare and distribute citizenship textbooks to persons receiving instruction under the supervision of the public schools. It encourages applicants to attend classes in the public schools and informs them of such classes.

The INS provides, upon request, a series of textbooks written on three levels of difficulty which cover the history and government requirements for the preparation for naturalization. Naturalization examiners and officials visit schools and classes, upon invitation, to talk with and answer questions of teachers and students to promote understanding and allay fears concerning requirements for naturalization.

The Office of Education

Invaluable services have been provided for many years in the education of both foreign-born and native adults by the Office of Education,

United States Department of Health, Education and Welfare. These services have been greatly expanded in recent years. In 1955, the Adult Education Section was established with Dr. Ambrose Caliver as its chief, and since then several staff members have been added. Of special interest is the recent appointment of a Specialist in Fundamental and Literacy Education.[4]

Other Agencies

Although the agencies listed above are the principal ones in fundamental and literacy education, a number of other agencies are operating significantly in this field and deserve at least the mention they are given below.

Correctional institutions across the country are engaged in conducting programs for native and foreign-born adults taught by trained teachers with curriculum, methods, and materials much the same as those in the public school programs.

Business and industrial concerns frequently have special classes for employees who need training in fundamental and literacy education. Their more general practice, however, is to refer employees who need elementary education to the public school and other programs in the nearest city or town.

The Bureau of Indian Affairs, U.S. Department of The Interior conducts adult education programs for adult Indians who reside on reservations—mostly rural people in the southwestern states and Florida. The teachers work closely with the tribal councils, use a comprehensive curriculum and prepare their own materials which are specifically geared to the needs and low literacy level of these adults.

United Hias (Hebrew Immigrant Aid Society) Service has conducted classes for many years for the foreign-born adults who enroll in its co-operating agencies across the country. Special classes and programs teach English and citizenship preparation to adults living at "depots" in ports of entry.

Public libraries across the country offer facilities for classes, counseling, referrals to nearby classes, and books and materials.

A Materials Center for teachers of foreign-born adults was established in co-operation with the AEA Section on Non-English-Speaking Adults at the Donnell Library of the New York Public Library. The center contains a collection of reading and workbooks, courses of study, and related materials.

The National Council on Naturalization and Citizenship works with sixty national and local organizations in this field, publishes bibliographies on materials and films, and does research on the integration of the foreign-born.

The National Council of Jewish Women, through its Committee on

Service for Foreign Born, conducts classes where no public school classes are available and offers services which local schools may not be able to provide.

Trade unions often provide programs tailored to meet the very specialized needs of the union members. In the International Ladies Garment Workers Union, for example, in-service training for the teachers is provided and much of the material used in the classes is specially written and prepared by the teachers and supervisors.

The Department of Defense, Office of Armed Services, Information and Education provides classes in basic elementary education in most of the major military installations in the nation. At present approximately seventy thousand adults are enrolled in these classes.

Jewish Community Centers under the auspices of the National Jewish Welfare Board conduct programs for foreign-born adults in many cities of the country, with a primary concern for literacy.

The National Tuberculosis Association conducts classes in fundamental and literacy education for TB patients throughout the nation. Materials relating to health in general and this disease in particular are developed to meet the literacy level of the patients, 50 percent of whom read below a fifth grade level (young and old alike) and 24 percent of whom are functionally illiterate.

Adult education councils are actively engaged in providing services to native and foreign-born adults through referrals to nearby public schools and other elementary education offerings. The Adult Education Council of Greater St. Louis has directly conducted classes in literacy education for five years, since no other program is offered locally.

Colleges and universities, through extension courses and schools of general studies, and junior and community colleges frequently offer classes in citizenship and English and literacy education.

The Junior League conducts classes in this field of adult education in some cities.

Churches of most denominations offer classes to reach adults who are not able or willing to go to public classes.

The Y's in many cities are active in providing classes and programs to fill the unmet needs of the native and foreign-born adults.

THE CURRICULUM

Curriculum content must include those areas basic to achieving competence in community living and fulfilling responsibility in this fast-moving world—health and safety education, consumer education, science, home and family life education, earning a living, government and history, citizenship skills, and the skills of communication.

For foreign-born students the curriculum includes the above areas, with emphasis upon learning to speak, read, and write the new language and preparing to meet the naturalization requirements in literacy, history, and government. For naturalized citizens the curriculum contains the above areas, increasing in depth and level of difficulty to fit their specific needs. For native students the same areas are included, with emphasis upon communication and basic educational skills in addition to training in the ability to speak, listen, and think.

This type of comprehensive curriculum for both foreign-born and native adults is being offered in about one-quarter of the states of the nation. Nearly a fifth of the states offer nothing beyond preparation for meeting the basic educational requirements for naturalization. The curriculum in other states includes some but not all of the above areas.

METHODS

There is no one method that can be considered "best." In the last decade several methods have received visibility and have been developed more intensively. Teachers of adults should be familiar with and able to use several methods in working with students in fundamental and literacy education. The teacher of foreign-born adults should be familiar with the Gouin Theme method, the community approach method, the Basic English method, English as a Second Language or Linguistic method (to name a few) and be able to use one or another as the ability, background, and level of the students may demand. The use of the "direct method" (teaching in the language being learned) is accepted quite generally. For certain purposes, such as orientation, the translation method is found to be effective. Teachers of native adults should be familiar with the methods of teaching illiterates to read and write, such as the Laubach method, the sentence approach, and others.

MATERIALS

Many new materials of various types, specially prepared for use with native illiterates and foreign-born adults at different levels of difficulty have been published in the past decade. Ten years is about the age limit for the use of materials if adults are to keep up with this fast-moving age. Therefore, there is need for a constant supply to meet the needs of adults as they become increasingly competent in the communication skills.

Homemade materials will always be useful and necessary to insure meeting the everyday needs of adults in their local environment. A wise selection of commercially produced materials will enrich the instruction and hold the interest of the adult student.

The types of material most used are homemade materials, hard cover reading books, work books, materials for citizenship preparation (books, charts, etc.), handwriting books, practice sheets, the pamphlet-booklet type of free materials issued in quantity by many organizations, agencies, and business concerns. A number of publishers have entered this field in the last decade and are providing many worthwhile materials. Most of the items included in the bibliography at the end of this chapter contain lists of current materials presently in use.

Special bibliographies of materials in this area of adult education have been prepared by Indiana University, Ohio State University, the National Council on Naturalization and Citizenship, the U. S. Immigration and Naturalization Service, the Bureau of Adult Education, New York State Education Department, the Adult Education Section of the Department of Health, Education and Welfare, and many others.

TELEVISION IN FUNDAMENTAL AND LITERACY EDUCATION

Television can and will play an important role in fundamental and literacy programs for native and foreign-born adults. This new medium for reaching the adults whom our fundamental and literacy programs are designed to serve has emerged in the last decade.

"Television's future role and contribution are in the provision of educational information to help replace and replenish the existing manpower shortage and to create a reserve pool of trained persons to keep up with technological procedures that are being developed." So spoke William S. Paley, Chairman of the Board of the Columbia Broadcasting System, in referring to this field of adult education. Commercial television stations and broadcasters are interested in and sympathetic toward this type of service to the public. However, programs must be able to meet the commercial standards of programming. One station in New York City has conducted five half-hour programs weekly designed to teach English to Spanish-speaking adults and help them in orientation to a new life.

Educational television programs are making their appearance in several places. KVED-TV in Texas presents a program, "Learning to Read by TV," through the Baylor Literacy Center to reach special viewing centers and groups in homes. WKNO-TV in Tennessee conducts "Streamlined Reading" for 1,000 adults enrolled in viewing centers around Memphis. The Chelsea Closed Circuit Project in New York City presents elementary English lessons three nights a week for the adult students in a nearby school and for 607 family units in the housing project in which the station is located. The closed circuit station at Cortland, New York, began a series of twenty-minute teaching programs in elementary English and citizenship.

The Bureau of Adult Education, New York State Education Department, in co-operation with the Immigration and Naturalization Service, produced a half-hour television program for station use and in classrooms as a film through the Regents Educational Television Project, pointing up the advantages of U. S. citizenship and showing what takes place between the applicant and the examiner at the time of the naturalization examination.

There are many projects in this new medium but as yet their effectiveness has not been evaluated. Adult educators have hardly begun to appreciate the potentials of this medium and are badly hampered by the use of some traditional classroom practices as they approach television.

TRENDS

The emerging trends of the past decade indicate an increased amount of growth, interest, and concern in this type of adult education; better organization and administration of programs; co-operative planning and pooling of resources and information. Some of the most significant developments are:

1. Offering of comparable programs for both native illiterates and foreign-born adults.
2. The use of both teachers and persons trained in other professions to work and teach in programs.
3. Issuing diplomas and certificates which enable the holder to enter a public high school. Fourteen states now offer this type of adult elementary certificate; in others high school placement is automatic. Some states offer elementary diplomas through the public school adult education program similar to the high school equivalency diploma available throughout most of the nation.
4. Requiring special training for teachers in these programs—either pre-service or in-service training.
5. Development of broad, comprehensive curriculum offerings.
6. Encouraging of foreign-born students to continue in school after obtaining citizenship.
7. Use of supervisors specifically assigned in this part of the program. Public schools in twenty-four states report that they use such supervisors or co-ordinators to assist in setting goals, developing curriculum, and providing in-service training.
8. Use of special activities which make use of people, agencies, and organizations in the community as an integral part of the offerings.
9. Recognition of the potentials of television and the increasing number of experiments and projects conducted on commercial, educational, and open and closed circuits.
10. The increase of new materials written and prepared especially for use with foreign-born and native adults.

NATIONAL ASSOCIATIONS

For the more than ten thousand persons engaged in the field of citizenship and fundamental education for adults there are two national organizations which offer consultant services, materials, and the opportunity for professional association.

The Adult Education Association of the U.S.A. has two groups in this area: the Section on Fundamental and Literacy Education and the Section on Education for Non-English Speaking Adults. These two sections establish and maintain contacts among the members and conduct meetings at the national conference held in November of each year. A *Handbook on the Production of Fundamental and Literacy Education Materials* will be published in 1960 by the Section on Fundamental and Literacy Education.

The National Association of Public School Adult Educators, has a national committee in this area of adult education. Each issue of its bi-monthly publication *The Public School Adult Educator* contains a special section devoted to ideas and activities currently in use in teaching foreign-born and non-English-speaking adults.

Footnotes

1The President's Committee on Education Beyond the High School, *Second Report to the President* (Washington: Government Printing Office, 1957) p. 62.

2*New York Times*, May 23, 1959.

3These are the definitions used by the U.S. Office of Education and the Bureau of the Census.

4Dr. Edward W. Brice, to whom belongs the credit for much of the material on definitions, facts, and figures in this chapter. For a detailed description of the services of the new section, see Chapter 20.

Selected Readings

Caliver, Ambrose. "Needed: Another Crash Program." *Adult Leadership,* VII (October, 1958) , 104-16.

Cass, Angelica W. *Adult Elementary Education.* New York: Noble and Noble, 1956.

Suggestions for a Program for the Foreign Born. Washington: Citizens Committee of the NEA, 1954.

Essert, Paul L., Lourenco-Filho, Y.B., and Cass, Angelica W. "Developments in Fundamental Education for Adults." *Review of Educational Research,* XXIII (June, 1953) .

Goldberg, Samuel. *Army Training of Illiterates in World War II.* New York: Bureau of Publications, Teachers College, Columbia University, 1951.

Griffin, Ella W. *Let's Help the Ten Million.* New London, Conn.: Educators' Washington Dispatch, 1950.

Ginsburg, Eli. *The Uneducated.* New York: Columbia University Press, 1953.

Kempfer, Homer. *Adult Education.* New York: McGraw-Hill, 1955.

Adult Literacy Education in the U. S. Office of Education Circular No. 324. Washington: Government Printing Office, 1950.

Eight Measures for Evaluating Educational Programs for the Foreign Born. Washington: Office of Education, 1952.

New York City Board of Education. *Resource Materials in Civic Education for Adult Elementary Classes.* The Board, 1959.

Manual for Teachers of Adult Elementary Classes. The Board, 1950.

Office of Education. *Literacy Education.* Circular No. 376. Washington: Government Printing Office, 1953.

Literacy Education and Reprints. Washington: Government Printing Office, 1953.

Radcliffe, Charles H., and Holden, John B. "Adults in the Public Schools." *School Life,* Vol. XL (1958), No. 7.

Sheats, Paul, Jayne, Clarence, and Spence, Ralph. *Adult Education.* New York: Dryden Press, 1953.

UNESCO. *Inter-American Seminar on Illiteracy and Adult Education:* Summary Report. Paris: Education Clearing House, 1950.

——. *Literacy Teaching: A Selected Bibliography.* Paris: Education Clearing House, 1950.

——. *Literacy Statistics from Available Census Figures.* Paris: Education Clearing House, 1950.

United Service for New Americans. *Organizing a Community Americanization Program.* New York: United Hias, 1953.

University of the State of New York. *Education for Citizenship.* Albany, N. Y.: State Department of Education, Bureau of Adult Education, 1953.

CHAPTER 39

HEALTH EDUCATION OF THE PUBLIC*

BERYL J. ROBERTS
Associate Professor

and

WILLIAM GRIFFITHS
Professor
School of Public Health
University of California, Berkeley

Organized community health education in the United States, as it is presently practiced, does more than educate people about health. Owing to the very nature of the methods utilized, which are based upon the best current understanding of the educational process, the people themselves are required to assume responsibility for their own and their community's health through understanding their health problems, planning for prevention, eradication or control, and acting on their plans. This approach necessarily guides people into a consideration of health in its broadest meaning, because emerging and existing health problems in this country are multifaceted in both origin and solution. The problem-solving approach applied to these current health problems, which have many roots, has a real potential for deepening and developing the public's experience in democracy and, at the same time, focusing their interest and concern on the total development of their communities rather than upon health alone. Viewed in this way, health education is adult education in the most fundamental sense.

HEALTH EDUCATION IS ACTION ORIENTED

Health education consists of two interrelated parts, i.e., school and public. School health education takes place primarily through the efforts of the school, is within the total school health program, and addresses

---

*With a special description of safety education prepared by Thomas Fansler.

itself principally to school-age persons. Public health education, on the other hand, is that carried on outside the school, encompassing the efforts of individuals and agencies who attempt to educate people in health. School health education is basic to public health education, but it is the latter which is directed more specifically to adults. It is this part of health education with which this chapter is concerned.

Health education is a highly personal change process which takes place within the individual, whether consciously or not; and in an interplay between new and existing cognitive and affective structures and cultural factors, there occurs a reorganization which is meaningful for the individual and results in healthful action through the development of new, or the reinforcement of existing, appropriate action patterns. Guidance from outside the individual may sometimes aid the change process. Adult educators, including health educators, are agents aiding this process by creating or utilizing situations with an educational potential.

Emphasis is placed today upon the action outcome of health education, for it is the application of what is known in daily personal and community living that renders success in health education. Attitudes and knowledges engendered are intermediary outcomes; action is the criterion against which progress and attainment ultimately are evaluated.

HEALTH EDUCATION EMANATES FROM MANY SOURCES

Education of the public about health emanates from many sources, both public and private, organized agencies and individuals. Several types of workers are involved, ranging from volunteers assisting in agency programs to professional workers in related fields such as agriculture, and professional staff in health. Illustrative of those contributing to the education of the adult public in health are practicing physicians and dentists, nurses, nutritionists, dietitians, social workers, sanitarians, engineers, health educators, classroom teachers, agency executives and program development staff, agricultural extension workers, and persons working in community organization. Among the agencies and organizations engaged in this work are official health and welfare departments; voluntary health groups such as those dealing with tuberculosis, cancer, mental health, heart, and safety; industry and labor in their concern for the health of the employed; medical care centers including rehabilitation centers; professional groups such as medical and dental societies; health and social welfare councils; insurance companies; museums; and groups organized around special industrial interests such as dairy products.

Health education offers the basic approach to the solution of public health problems, and within this, specific methods are selected according to the problem, situation, and people to be affected. Considered thus, public health education is a component of many programs as, for instance, those designed to promote mental health, dental health, nutrition, safety, or environmental health, or to control problems of cardiovascular disease, tuberculosis, and other communicable diseases, chronic diseases, or geriatrics.

When health education is seen as proceeding from so many sources and as basic in so many types of programs, the need of integrating efforts and effecting co-ordination, with the "consumer" as the focus, is made patent. The overlapping as well as the gaps in efforts contribute to present-day problems, however, not just in health education but in the whole field of health, education, and social welfare. The need of integration becomes especially clear if health education is viewed broadly as including the efforts of any person, agency, or group that assists individuals and communities in solving health problems through education. For some, this is a planned, consciously examined part of their approach and function; for others, it is more a by-product of services rendered or of a program in a related field.

STATUS AND DEVELOPMENT OF HEALTH EDUCATION

The educational approach to public health problems is not new, but the present concept of an organized community effort in health education is relatively new. In this country, there was an early belief in educating people in order to promote community health, indeed, a plea for this was made by Lemuel Shattuck in his now famous "Report of the Sanitary Commission" of 1850 and was restated by others over many years.

With the emergence of voluntary health agencies, beginning with the tuberculosis associations in 1904, a real impetus was given to organized effort in public health education. Official health agencies intensified their educational work, over the years, and recognized it in their structure in 1914 when a bureau devoted to health education was created in both the New York City and the New York State Health Departments. The health education aspects of programs related to health were also developing, and as early as 1914 a bureau of health instruction was established in the Extension Division, University of Wisconsin, thus presaging the increasing attention given health in university extension programs.

By 1916 Winslow said, "Education is indeed the keynote of the modern campaign for public health," but while revealing his farsighted leadership, his belief had yet to be translated into any widespread program of health education in 1916.[12]* Emphasis increased gradually, however, as the understanding of the educational process grew and as the nature of public health problems changed, and today the educational approach is the predominant one in public health in the United States.

A sufficient number of workers were involved in public health education by the 1920's so that a Public Health Education Section was formed

---

*References in this chapter are according to bibliographical items in the order listed in the "Selected Readings" at the end of the chapter.

(1923) in the American Public Health Association. Health education workers were recruited then from medicine, nursing, publicity, teaching, and other professions, and there were no formal programs of study in health education. About 1935, professional preparation in health education was first offered at Massachusetts Institute of Technology, and beginning in 1943, public health educators were prepared in schools of public health.** The Committee on Professional Education of the American Public Health Association developed a statement on the functions of and suggested graduate preparation for public health educators, first in 1937 and most recently in 1958.[1] The group of professional health educators grew from 44 in 1942 to about 1,200 trained specialists today.[10] In 1950, the Society of Public Health Educators was formed to assist the sound development of public health education and, thus, contribute to the advancement of health of all people.

LEVELS OF HEALTH EDUCATION

Concern in this chapter is with planned community programs of public health education and with health education as an integral part of all of public health. For purposes of viewing health education within this framework, the "levels of prevention" proposed by Leavell and Clark are useful, viz., health promotion, specific protection, early recognition and prompt treatment, disability limitation, and rehabilitation.[7] Barriers can be set up at any or all "levels" to prevent the original occurrence or continuance of a disorder. Health education comprises an important element at each level in that it leads to the individual, group, or community action which will create the barriers.

Health education in "health promotion" aids by guiding people into such measures as adequate nutrition, for example, to prevent the original occurrence of a disorder. It is illustrated in cancer control in "specific protection" by its use in effecting such actions as will remove known carcinogens from the environment or lead to treatment of pre-cancerous conditions. In "early recognition and prompt treatment," health education brings about self-examination of the breast or, for example, normal vigilance for the early discovery of deviations from the normal, prompt action for diagnosis and follow-through on treatment so that furtherance of the disorder is prevented. Health education in "disability limitation" motivates action for diagnosis and treatment when it was not produced earlier because education was inadequate or lacking, or diagnostic and/or treatment procedures and facilities were not available for action to be taken. Here action, though not early, prevents the disorder from continuing and leading to disability. Education of patient and family aids the acceptance of rehabilitation, the utilization of services, and the estab-

---

**Seven such schools in continental U.S.A. today are accredited by the APHA to prepare public health educators in graduate programs.

lishment of such personal and family behavior as will assist the rehabilitated individual to lead a useful, satisfying life.

The general objective of health education—personal and community action for health—is illustrated by this example. Implied is the public's utilization of private or public services and facilities essential to the action and, sometimes, the creation of needed facilities, such as a particular type clinic, medical care facility, or a health department. As it is illustrated here, health education may be directed toward people in general or toward selected target groups, such as community leaders or certain age groups, depending upon the health problem. The "people" are never an amorphous mass but, rather, a group of "publics" for whom a special program and special actions in health must be made meaningful if a particular health problem is to be solved.

Education is a major component not only of the extramural programs that extend an agency into the community, but also of the intramural staff activities which underlie these. Here are meant especially such activities as staff meetings, in-service education, and the program planning process, for in the light of present-day knowledge about learning, the educational approach is the chief one utilized in the staff-centered activities within a program as well as in the effort to influence the adult public outside the agency.

AGENCY PROGRAMS

This chapter does not permit full discussion of the work of all agencies but is limited to three focal points for public health education: official health departments, voluntary health agencies, and agricultural extension.

Official Health Agencies

Public health education was established as a bureau in the United States Public Health Service in 1936. All fifty-three state and territorial health departments and many local health departments now have bureaus, and most of these are headed by professionally trained public health educators. In addition to the director of health education, in the larger agencies there are frequently other staff public health educators assigned to the bureau of health education or to other bureaus.

In official agencies, practically all programs have objectives which are attained by educational means. Since public health education is a function of all staff members—health officers, dentists, nurses, sanitarians, nutritionists and others—the health educator works with them on ways in which to achieve their educational objectives in their home visits, clinics, and other community contacts. Public health educators at times work directly with community groups, but since the population covered by health departments is often large and the geographic area extensive, a few health educators can reach but a fraction of the population; thus, their time is spent more effectively in helping other staff members become more proficient as educators and in stimulating the assistance of other groups and adult educators in health education of the public.

The programs in which health educators are involved depend upon the needs and problems of the areas in which they work and the priorities given programs by their health departments. Today, some of the programs which public health educators are emphasizing are chronic disease, home safety, alcoholism, mental health, migrant workers, industrial health, and air pollution. In each of these, the educational approach plays an important part in changing health behavior and practices.

Voluntary Health Agencies

Voluntary health agencies have played an active, significant role in the health education of the public. A number of the larger agencies now have full-time, trained educational or program development directors, and in some agencies the executive director is also a trained health educator.

For the most part, the voluntary agencies carry on educational activities relating to their special interest, but tuberculosis associations in recent years have embarked on broad, general health education. Many permit staff to work on any health activity about which people in the community express a need.

Each of the voluntary agencies has made some unique contributions to public health education. Heart associations have been effective in identifying and working with groups having special needs. They have, for example, organized sodium-restricted classes, worked with rest-home personnel on adequate, low-cost diets, and with labor and management on procedures for the employment of cardiacs. Cancer societies have successfully promoted general public education on cancer. The danger signals of cancer are well known, the breast self-examination program has reached thousands of women's organizations, and presently cancer societies are studying decentralization of services to reach a wider population. Cerebral palsy societies have led in establishing rehabilitative services, while mental health societies have promoted legislation to improve mental hospitals and institute preventive mental health services.

Voluntary agencies, free from many restrictions placed on official agencies, have been able not only to supplement the work of official agencies, but also to adventure into new programs, many later being absorbed by health departments.

Agricultural Extension Services

Agricultural extension workers were among the pioneers in public health education, and have regarded health as a major component of their work with rural families. They developed demonstration techniques to a high degree of success, and these have been borrowed by other professions employing community organization methods of working with small groups.

Farm safety, brucellosis eradication safety, and nutrition are just a few of the areas in which health education is sponsored by extension workers. Health has also been an important constituent in 4 H activities.

SAFETY EDUCATION*

Health education and safety education are often treated as separate, albeit related fields. It is the point of view of this chapter that health education is a broad area encompassing the educational component of many health programs, as for example, nutrition, cancer control, or accident prevention. Safety education, in this concept, is within health education and is one aspect of a broadly conceived accident prevention program.

Safety programs in the United States have developed steadily over many years, being formally organized nationally in 1913. A comprehensive effort has evolved which includes the education of adults and embraces activities in accident prevention at work, at home, at play, and on the highway. The National Safety Council and its affiliated groups provide strong leadership, and other groups also further safety education as, for instance, fire and police departments, chambers of commerce, industry, schools, the American Red Cross, health departments, departments registering motor vehicles, agricultural extension services, and parent-teacher associations.

Increased impetus was given safety programs in industry by the widespread passage of workmen's compensation laws. Safety programs, including worker education as well as the guarding of machines, were found to cost less than compensation claims, and today industry recognizes that accidents exceed accident prevention in cost.

Education for industrial accident prevention includes activities such as apprentice and "corridor training" for new workers, classes for supervisors and workers, and "family nights" when workers' families attend safety programs. Classes may include education for traffic, home, and recreational safety as well as industrial safety. Tools such as motion pictures are regarded only as adjuncts to, and no substitute for, day-to-day, face-to-face instruction by the alert foreman.

The sound mental health and educational doctrine underlying safety education for workers is not found in traffic safety teaching where many agencies use varied methods. The policeman who cautions a driver about traffic laws and dangerous practices rightly feels that he is engaging in

---

*This section was prepared by the late Thomas Fansler, Director, Home Safety Division, National Safety Council.

safety education, although the education is often obscured by the issuance of a summons. There are, of course, adult driving schools, and many cities maintain schools for traffic violators which give instruction in laws, driving practices, and pedestrian behavior.

Mass communication media have been extensively used in education for traffic safety, though not usually in a co-ordinated, systematic way. With justice, critics question whether this approach, often ending in pious slogans, results in changed behavior. Traffic experts are aware of their shortcomings which, in part, are due to inadequate financial support and little money until quite recently for fundamental research and demonstrations.

Other groups working on traffic safety include farm groups, led by agricultural extension agents who attempt, for example, to eliminate hazards, such as unlighted farm vehicles on the road at night, through the application of specific remedies. Women's organizations often select targets in traffic safety; and, after learning about the problem, they work for the necessary measures, as for example, a bicycle inspection program, a driver-education program, a city-wide youth conference on traffic safety, the control of "drag strip" racing, or a vehicle inspection program. Such activities might be labeled correctly "adult education for a social purpose." Beyond these groups, in-service training is offered to supervisors and drivers by companies operating fleets of vehicles, and universities often conduct one-week institute type courses for fleet supervisors.

Home safety has received increased attention from public health departments recently. In in-service training, staffs are acquainted with the necessary information which they pass to the public through their face-to-face contacts in clinics, home visits, and group meetings. Another official agency, the local fire department, uses personal visits to educate home owners against loss from fires. In many communities, the department's fire prevention unit conducts programs for school and adult audiences, and National Fire Prevention Week and Clean-up Week are periods when special attention is given hazards.

In rural areas, youth groups and home demonstration clubs frequently use home safety for discussion or demonstration. Youth groups in urban centers may undertake a hunt to mark and report dangerous community hazards, or groups like scouts may distribute literature in house-to-house campaigns. The PTA, women's clubs, service clubs, and civic organizations may undertake education of their members and the general public.

The Red Cross has an extensive program in water safety, including instruction in swimming and in the handling of small boats. The U. S. Coast Guard Auxiliary and outboard motor manufacturers have issued literature and established classes for small boat owners. Increased interest in water sports has necessitated educating the public in safe practices in and near recreational waters.

In summary, the field of safety education is as comprehensive as all of modern living, and with the growth in attention given to accident prevention nationally, is becoming more extensive and intensive.

MAJOR METHODS IN PUBLIC HEALTH EDUCATION

Mass Media Method

Prior to the last ten or fifteen years, the major emphasis was placed on the mass media method. Agencies spent vast sums of money in the production and distribution of health pamphlets, posters, exhibits, films, radio scripts, and other audio-visual materials. They assumed that individuals were interested in health, held health as a value of high priority, and that facts and information would change their health practices. In view of research in the behavioral sciences, undertaken especially since World War II, these assumptions seem naive today. In the last decade, mass media have been utilized more realistically; health workers have learned to use them effectively in presenting basic facts and know that when individuals are instructed toward achieving specific health goals, mass media can be effective in giving them the needed information. They realize that mass media alone will not change attitudes toward health, or health practices. When the attitudes or practices of individuals run counter to those promoted by health workers, mass media must be reinforced or supplemented by community organization and face-to-face methods.

Face-to-Face Method

Public health workers, viewing the community as the patient, naturally use the traditional face-to-face method of clinical medicine, with physicians and nurses imparting information to patients on an individual basis. Public health nurses, sanitarians, and others have relied heavily on individual contact with citizens. Public health nurses, in home visits, discuss with mothers and family all subjects relating to their general health. Sanitarians spend a good deal of time talking with restaurant owners, industrial personnel, and others on ways of improving sanitation.

In the communication of facts and information, the face-to-face method has one distinct advantage over the mass media method in that it is an active interaction process. The public health worker, as a change agent, can question and elaborate and observe numerous clues which point out the direction in which he should proceed.

The face-to-face method has only limited persuasive power, for research shows that the group situation provides superior stimulation for change. An individual as a member of a group faced with common problems, provided with opportunities for exploration of facts and freedom for decision making, is more likely to accept a new health practice than an individual who does not have this group experience. In public health, therefore, the face-to-face method is constantly being reinforced by the community organization method.

Community Organization Method

Community organization is employed when community needs can be met most effectively through joint or co-operative effort. The principle of participation provides the basis of this method; its underlying assumption is that if people concerned with a need are given opportunities to learn the facts about it, they will eventually formulate the best possible solution of the need.

Since many health problems in America today are ones which cannot be solved *for* people, the community organization method is used increasingly. The passing of a referendum for fluoridation, the organization of parents' discussion groups, or working with weight reduction classes are illustrative.

Heavy reliance is now placed upon the behavioral sciences in order to gain greater insights into and understanding of the complexities of the community organization method. Greater knowledge of such areas as motivation, learning, leadership, decision making, power, and status is needed. The key to successful application is a thorough understanding of the interaction process involved in joint or co-operative effort. How can one identify the informal networks within a community? What are the dynamics of the various steps of the decision-making process? What are the effective ways of working with power forces within the community?

PROBLEMS IN HEALTH EDUCATION

There are numerous problems that arise when educators work with adults in attempting to change health behavior and practices. Only four of these will be mentioned.

1. *Reaching the hard core.*—Even after expending a great deal of time and effort, health workers find that they fail to affect some 15 per cent of the population. Either this segment has not been reached, or it has been reached but has not taken the desired action. Community mass X-ray campaigns illustrate this point well, for there is always a "hard core" that does not participate. Public health workers are concerned about this because the hard core might be the group which should be reached most of all from a public health point of view.

It is possible that there are different hard cores for different types of public health problems. The identification of these groups is not an easy task. It has been proposed that to reach the hard core, new techniques in community organization must be devised.

2. *Utilizing informal groups.*—Because formal groups and organizations and their leaders are easy to identify, they have been used frequently by public health workers in the promotion of community health. Formal organizations, even though they have been of value in public health education, do not reach a large part of the population. It is the informal groups—clubs, friendship groups, cliques, and others—that must be reached if many public health programs are to be successful. Within these groups are leaders, sometimes called "opinion leaders," who are influential in the communication of ideas, and the changing of opinions and behaviors. How to reach informal groups, how to utilize them in public health education, remain problems that must be solved.

3. *Power and status in agencies.*—If health agencies and organizations in a community worked truly co-operatively, public health education could be advanced immeasurably. An agency's need for power and status frequently interferes with its entering into co-operative, supportive work relationships with other agencies. For continuous community support, financial and otherwise, agencies feel that they must achieve recognition and hold a certain distinction in the eyes of the public. To share honors is often perceived as a threat to distinction.

If some public health objectives can be achieved more readily and satisfactorily through agency co-operation, how can this problem be resolved? How can agency leaders have a feeling of personal power, see their agency as one of status within the community, and yet work effectively with others? This remains a most important problem to be solved.

4. *Improving understanding of how people learn.*—Health workers in all types of agencies and positions need a more basic understanding of how adults learn. The idea is still too prevalent that correct facts induce change. Moreover, public health workers receive satisfaction from their role of teacher, and it is not easy to convince them that indirect teaching methods, especially when the principle of self-discovery of facts is employed, sometimes produces more effective learning even though consuming more time initially.

A propitious trend has been the increasing number of public health workers who enroll in group development laboratories. Many of these people have radically changed their ways of working with groups and have also stimulated their colleagues to try new teaching methods.

CONCLUSION

Health education has been viewed in this chapter within the context of organized community efforts in health and not as a program in itself. It is a basic approach used today in a wide variety of health programs, the objectives of which can be attained wholly or in part only by individual or concerted community action by people.

Professional workers who direct their efforts toward the education of the adult public about health are engaged in one special field of adult education. Public health educators are thus adult educators, and many other health workers contribute also to adult health education as they carry out their responsibilities. Conversely, adult educators not employed by health organizations often integrate health education into their work when it fits appropriately. There is, then, a two-way street between adult education, generally speaking, and health education.

Health education of the public is a dynamic field of endeavor wherein workers are constantly utilizing relevant research findings from the behavioral sciences in order to increase the effectiveness of their efforts. Moreover, they are suggesting questions that arise out of their practice and require solution and are offering researchable situations which have a potential for illuminating some of the problems that vex those concerned with individual and community action and the whole change process.

Selected Readings

1. Committee on Professional Education, A.P.H.A. "Educational Qualifications of Health Educators," *American Journal of Public Health* (New York), XLVII (January, 1957), 112-19.
2. Derryberry, Mayhew. "Health Education in Transition," *American Journal of Public Health* (New York), XLVII (November, 1957), 1357-66.
3. Editorial. "A New Bureau of Public Health Education," *American Journal of Public Health* (New York), IV (July, 1914), 618.
4. Emerson, Haven. *Local Health Units for the Nation.* New York: Commonwealth Fund, 1945.
5. Griffiths, W. "The Educational Approach to Public Health Work," *Health Education Journal* (London), XV (March, 1957), 13-25.
6. Jean, Sally Lucas. "The Development of Health Education in the U.S.A.," *Health Education Journal* (London), XVII (March, 1959), 36-48.
7. Leavell, Hugh R., and Clark, E. Gurney. *Textbook of Preventive Medicine* (rev. ed.). New York: McGraw Hill Book Company, 1958.
8. Nyswander, Dorothy B. "The Dynamics of Planning in Health Education," *California's Health* (Berkeley, California), XIII (Oct. 1, 1955).
9. Patterson, Raymond W., and Roberts, Beryl J. *Community Health Education in Action.* St. Louis: C. V. Mosby and Company, 1951.
10. *Report from the United States of America in Preparation for Technical Discussions on Health Education of the Public at the Twelfth World Health Assembly.* (Unpublished manuscript). Geneva: World Health Organization, 1959.
11. Rosen, George. *A History of Public Health.* New York: MD Publications, Incorporated, 1958.
12. Winslow, C.E.A. "Organizing a State Campaign of Public Health Education," *American Journal of Public Health* (New York) (August, 1916), 805-13.
13. World Health Organization. *First Report, Expert Committee on Health Education of the Public.* Geneva: World Health Organization, 1953.

CHAPTER 40

HOME AND FAMILY LIFE EDUCATION

MARY S. LYLE
Professor of Home Economics Education
Iowa State College

VARIETY OF TERMS USED

Diversity is an outstanding characteristic of adult education in home and family life in the U.S.A. today. Such a wide variety of organizations, agencies and institutions provide guidance in learning in so many ways, to so many different individuals and groups, and with such a variety of objectives and emphases that it is difficult to portray in concise form the extent and nature of adult education in this field. Even the terms used to identify the different enterprises vary widely. "Parent education," "adult homemaking education," "family life education," "education for family living," and "home and family life education" are all terms frequently used. Each suggests a particular preoccupation but at the same time the definite possibility of great similarity in content.

"Parent education" deals with the understandings and skills needed by parents in guiding the development of their children, including the understanding of themselves as well as of the physical, mental, emotional, and social development of children at each stage of their growth. Being an effective parent also involves co-operation with schools, consequently the term "parent education" is often used when school and home relationships are studied. This is the term used by the National Congress of Parents and Teachers since 1897 for its study groups and also commonly used by public schools and other agencies when parent-child or parent-parent or parent-teacher relationships are the major considerations.

Since 1917 "homemaking education for adults" has been the term used, interchangeably with "home economics for adults," by public schools for the classes and informal types of education that are reimbursed from federal funds provided under the Vocational Education Acts. Skill in being a parent as well as in performing all the manifold responsibilities required to make a house a pleasant, healthy, financially sound, and emotionally satisfying home, have been subjects of study under this title. In addition, classes have been offered for young adults and for the elderly in such subjects as nutrition, financial management, the art of entertaining, and many other topics of concern to them.

"Family life education" throughout the years has meant many things to different people. To some it has been nearly synonymous with parent education. To others it has meant almost entirely husband-wife relations, especially the physical and emotional aspects of these relationships. Others have used it as a label for any adult education that deals with situations affecting the whole family, be they financial, nutritional, recreational, or family and community relations. Today this term, or "education in family living," is commonly used by churches, welfare agencies, the Cooperative Extension Service, and other agencies for any broad educational program that is centered around family problems.

"Home and family life education" is the term adopted by the section of the Adult Education Association as an all-inclusive term for any adult education that deals with the home or the family. Public schools often use this term so that classes for business girls in home furnishings, sewing, nutrition, or classes for men and women in consumer problems, or parents' groups studying the guidance of teenagers, might all be included under it.

DEVELOPMENT SINCE 1948

In 1948 opportunity for adults to study some phase of home and family living was available in every state and territory of the United States. The two great tax-supported agencies providing such opportunities were the public schools and the Cooperative Extension Service. Some membership organizations, churches, and welfare agencies also were providing some education for their members or clients. But many more organizations have initiated or expanded programs in the past decade, and new private and public agencies—such as medical clinics, marriage counselling services, credit unions, consumer leagues, and child study or family living associations, have begun educational programs for various groups of adults.

In the Public Schools

In 1948 reports to the U. S. Office of Education on federally-aided classes in public schools showed adult classes in all the states, the District of Columbia, Puerto Rico, and Hawaii. The enrollment was 570,207, of whom 42,295 were men. By 1958 the enrollment had risen to 617,800 and included classes in the Virgin Islands. At the same time the number of men enrolled in such classes dropped sharply to 24,194. The number of teachers of these classes increased from about 7,000 in 1948 to 12,236 in 1957.

These figures do not tell the whole story, for many adult classes of the public schools are not reported to the U. S. Office of Education because they are supported entirely from local funds. Also public schools in some of the states have been emphasizing informal education which is not reported as classes. Neighbors' clubs, mothers' clubs, family life clubs, individual counselling, radio and television programs, consultation services, and cooperative nursery schools have all been used by some public schools to extend family life education to adults. No reports of such activities are sent to a central office, so enrollment figures are not available.

In Agricultural Extension

The Cooperative Extension Service,[1] also tax supported, had developed an educational program in co-operation with the land-grant colleges in every state. This program in 1948 was reaching 56,151 groups with an enrollment of 3,157,030 adults studying some phase of family living under the guidance of 2,965 county home economists along with 20 state specialists in parent education, 71 in home management, and 83 in nutrition. By 1957 this program had grown to the point that 4,001 county home economists, 39 state specialists in parent education, 102 in home management, and 99 in nutrition were serving 65,519 groups with an estimated enrollment of 6,873,000 adults.

In the past ten years increasing emphasis has been given to the study of family economics, home management, consumer education, child development, human relations, business and legal affairs of the family, citizenship and public affairs. Some attention is also given directly to education concerning the physical and mental health of family members. Continuing emphasis is given to finding and training competent lay leaders to aid in extending the educational program and to provide leadership in action for community improvement.

In the P.T.A.

The National Congress of Parents and Teachers has from its beginning included in its program study groups in parent education to implement its second objective, "to raise the standards of home life." In 1948 almost 14,000 local P.T.A.'s, or 42 per cent of the 33,000 units, were carrying on study groups of parents with an approximate enrollment of 365,000. In 1957-58, 20,500, or about 46 per cent of the 44,000 local P.T.A. units, maintained study-discussion groups. The total enrollment in such study-groups was then approximately 472,000. The ultimate aim of the organization is for "every local association to have an effective parent education study-discussion group participated in equally by parents and teachers."[2] To implement this aim the training of lay leaders of high caliber from the membership has become an important part of the total program.

Emphasis in this program is upon concentrated study of specified ages and stages in the growth cycle of children and their parents in an intensified effort to raise the standard of family life toward one in which "the human spirit thrives best."[3] The theme of the entire program of this organization for all its activities for 1959-1961 is "Strengthening the Home: Source of our Nation's Greatness." The study groups, the official magazine, and other activities will all give emphasis to education to this end.

In the Women's Clubs

Among the departments of the General Federation of Women's Clubs is one created in 1924, known as the "American Home Department," through which informal education of its members is provided. No statistics are available for the number of women engaged in this study either for 1948 or 1957 but the potential is indicated by the existence of 15,000 clubs in 47 states with some 900,000 dues-paying members. If each local club has a Home Department, many women are receiving some education of this sort. Through study and action the American Home department tries to help its members " (1) adjust their living to changing economic and social conditions and improve these as they affect the home; (2) increase pride and respect for homemaking; (3) foster appreciation and skill in the creative phases of homemaking; (4) create an environment in the home which will provide family members the opportunity for wholesome family relations; and (5) enhance the moral, spiritual and aesthetic values of the home and in homemaking."[4] Much emphasis has been given since 1948 to a study of economic problems of families, consumer interests, physical and mental health of family members, and family responsibility for the quality of community life.

In Welfare Agencies

Welfare agencies also make an extensive contribution to adult education. For example:

> For more than a decade, family service agencies—designed primarily to give casework services to families and family members troubled by problems in social and emotional functioning—have been providing group educational services, usually called family life education. In 1957, approximately ninety family service agencies reported to the national organization, the Family Service Association of America, that they were giving this service. Although such services may be given to groups meeting only once, the trend is toward holding several group discussions sessions—from three to ten or more—with

parents of preschool age children, with husbands and wives concerned about their marital relationship, with adolescents, and so forth. In content, family life education is typically concerned with various aspects of family adjustment, the emphasis being on the normal range of family experience rather than on the more disturbed or pathological extremes.[5]

Data on educational activities of these agencies are being collected on a national basis for the first time in 1959. No comparisons can thus be made with the program in 1948. Welfare agencies, both public and private, are finding it necessary to expand their efforts in the education of adults. They accompany their service in helping to solve an immediate family problem with education to prevent problems from recurring or arising in the future.

In Religious Institutions

Churches of many denominations are taking an increasingly active role in education for family life. Illustrative of the effort being expended by churches can be found in a report of the Family Life Bureau of the National Catholic Welfare Conference. Priests are serving as family life directors in 130 of the 138 archdioceses and dioceses of the United States. Pre-marriage courses of instruction of eleven lessons each, marriage conferences from two to ten lessons in length, family week ends and other experimental programs are being used. Figures are not available on a national scale, but the estimates of 25,000 adults studying these phases of family life in 1948 and 200,000 in 1957 suggest the rapid growth of this program. In the Chicago area alone, 33,000 adults in 275 groups were studying family life in Cana Conferences in 1957. Much attention is said to have been given in this program since 1948 to education for mental health of family members, wholesome family relations, management for better use of human resources, and family responsibility for the quality of community life. Some attention has been given to economic problems and physical health of families.[6]

Many Protestant denominations as well have instituted educational programs to educate parents to the end that family life will be strengthened. As one example, the Office of Family Education Research of the United Presbyterian Church of the USA has started a comprehensive research plan to discover how the church can best educate its people for Christian family life. By the end of 1960 reports of the activities of the 8,000 parishes and proposals for extending the program should be available.[7] At present there are no statistics showing the coverage of the churches in parent education, although it is known to be extensive. Most of the major Protestant denominations have family life education commissions, or divisions.

The Jewish welfare groups and settlement houses are also contributing to the education of their people in family living, but no collection of statistics at a central source has been made for these groups.

In National Voluntary Organizations

The National Conference of Christians and Jews has sponsored a nationwide program on the theme "Rearing Children of Good Will" which stresses the role of parents in establishing positive attitudes toward intergroup relations in their children. Institutes for parents have been held in about fifty cities.[8]

A number of other national associations sponsor or promote some education in home and family life as a part of their total program. For example, The National Association of Mental Health, through its 750 affiliate local associations helps parents through "one night stands" or group procedures to understand themselves and their children. It is hoped that this knowledge can be "comfortably utilized in every day relationships" in the family.[9]

The Child Study Association of America, working co-operatively with many other national and state organizations, encourages rather than sponsors parent education groups. Only in the metropolitan area of New York is there a limited program of parent-group education offered by this association. Six to eight groups annually enrolling roughly twenty-five parents each, are offered for demonstration purposes, as a means of training professional persons in parent-group leadership. The development of training programs for professional workers from different disciplines—such as social workers, nurses, religious educators and teachers —for leadership in parent and expectant parent discussion groups has been the significant emphasis since 1958. It also conducted a regional training program for nurses in the southwest region of the U.S. Children's Bureau in Dallas in 1958. Thirty parents groups were guided in study by these nurse trainees who each led two supervised series of parent meetings. Consultation service in programming, and publication and distribution of literature for leaders and adult students are other educational activities of this association.

The American Social Hygiene Association has focused on problems of the family and social health since its inception in 1914. But its emphasis has been turned to a preventive program of family life education since 1953. It is the belief of ASHA leaders that a most effective way to reach young people of all ages is to work with the persons who have an especially intimate out-of-the-home influence upon children and youth; namely, the teachers in schools and colleges. Using annual grants from the Nancy Reynolds Bagley Foundation, a series of regional projects has been inaugurated and supported to further the education and activities of teachers in the family life area. To date ASHA has stimulated many types of programs in nineteen states and the District of Columbia. Means used at the adult level have been institutes and workshops for teachers for the purpose of encouraging integration of family life study in regular curricular materials of schools and colleges and meetings of professional education associations, school board groups, and parent-teacher associations.[10]

In Local Organizations

Local groups likewise have developed special programs of education and counselling to fit the unique needs of their communities. One example of these is the Association of Family Living in Chicago. Financed in part by regular and supporting members and in part by the Community Fund, this association is a member of the Welfare Council of metropolitan Chicago. Organized in 1925 as a non-profit organization to help persons acquire the knowledge and to develop the understanding required for satisfying relationships in the family, it has served many hundreds of individuals and groups in the last ten years. It provides group leadership by professional members of its staff for parents' and young people's groups who wish to study child guidance, family relationships, youth problems, or preparation for marriage. Advice on program planning is provided for clubs or organizations desiring it. Individual counselling by psychiatric social workers and a consulting psychiatrist on pre-marital, marital, personal, or child guidance problems are available also, for a fee.

In Libraries

Libraries, too, have contributed to adult education for home and family life in the past ten years. In a survey of a sample of 110 libraries, 59 responded that they had actively co-operated in educational programs in this field. About 75 per cent had worked with other community organizations. For example, in Philadelphia the Free Library and the Family Service Association co-operatively planned three of six sessions each for parents. These were discussion groups for which the library provided books and films and arranged an exhibit of library materials at each meeting. Similar groups have been developed in branch libraries and a Family Book Fair is in prospect for October, 1959. A large number of city libraries reported some type of activity in family life education, such as assigning a staff member to assist in planning or giving programs, reader guidance, or providing study material. But many libraries in the smallest communities had also given similar service. Acquiring special materials, such as books, pamphlets, films, recordings, and slides was reported by nearly half of the libraries replying in the survey.[11]

In Universities

Universities have also developed programs of education for adult family members. One especially significant program in this category is supported by the Fund for Adult Education at the University of Chicago. The Parent Education Project was initiated in April 1953 by a grant from the Fund and has been maintained by successive grants. Its director reports that:

> The purpose of the project is to develop and try out, in experimental programs, materials and methods of presentation which will help parents to bring up children who will become mature, responsible citizens, able to function in and maintain a free, democratic society. The materials are designed for ultimate use as a mass medium of education, utilizing study-discussion group methods, with considerable responsibility placed upon volunteer leadership and upon all members of the group.
>
> Materials have thus far been prepared for three courses to be used by study-discussion groups: a Basic Course, a course on Middle Childhood, and a course on Later Childhood. Materials for a course on Early Childhood and one on Adolescence are now in preparation. To April 15, 1959, there have been 913 groups using "Parenthood in a Free Nation" courses. These have been located in 170 communities, in 28 states and 3 Canadian provinces. In 1958 about 3500 adults studied one of these courses. The groups have been led by 576 leaders, most of them lay leaders, who were given special leadership training for this program. In all, 111 Leadership Training Courses have been led by 63 professional leaders.[12]

PRESENT STATUS AND TRENDS

From the preceding descriptions it is evident that a tremendous growth in variety and scope of adult education programs in home and family life has taken place since the last *Handbook of Adult Education* was published in 1948. Today there is great interest and activity on the part of many laymen, as well as on the part of professional educators and professionals from many disciplines who work with families in some capacity.

Objectives

To assist adults to understand themselves and others so they can function adequately as family members in today's world is the current conception of a major objective of these activities. Some institutions and agencies see their role as primarily that of disseminating information for adults to use as they see fit. Others believe their role is to stimulate adults to information-seeking and problem-solving. Most of the organizations and agencies have some particular area of concern. Some busy themselves mainly with helping family members understand economic principles, the economic system, and the decision-making processes needed to function adequately in the rapidly changing economics of the home and community. Others take as their specific task helping parents to solve a wide variety of practical day-to-day problems of living. Still others pay particular attention to helping family members understand their own needs as people, their own spiritual goals, and their relationships with others. Yet all share the same major objective of building stronger families in a changing world.

Program Development

The approaches to program development differ widely. Some institutions and agencies offer well-outlined preplanned courses for adults—community colleges, parent-teacher study groups, and the Parent Education Project of the University of Chicago use this approach. Others build a curriculum from the askings of the adults—some public schools and YWCA's use this approach. Others organize a group with a general concern about a subject, such as being a good parent, then plan the particular study from the questions and problems of the group. The content varies greatly depending on whether the group is largely expectant parents, or parents of school-age children, parents of adolescents, or grandparents seeking to develop a new relationship with their married children. Some public school programs, mothers' clubs, and the Cooperative Extension Service programs use this approach.

Program development based largely on helping individuals solve their own problems is characteristic of many programs, such as the marriage counselling of the American Institute of Family Relations in Los Angeles, or the prenatal and infant care program for expectant mothers of the Clara Elizabeth Fund for Maternal Health Program in Flint, Michigan.

Still other institutions and organizations are trying to reach individuals, many of whom are never reached by group education, through extensive use of the mass media. Examples include the TV classroom program "Family Life Series" of the San Diego Public Schools' Home Economics Department and a new "Tea at Three" program over KTCA-TV in St. Paul, conducted by the adult homemaking division of the St. Paul Public Schools. The Cooperative Extension Service also uses the mass media approach through radio and TV programs, and by supplying information feature stories to newspapers.

Some of the institutions and agencies use only professionally trained leaders. Some make extensive use of lay leaders who have been given lay leadership training and who then work under supervision of professionals. Some use public school or college teachers with specialized preparation for work with adults as well as preparation in some phases of home and family life.

Methods

All the methods of teaching used in any other kind of adult education are used in education for home and family living. Lectures, especially illustrated lectures, demonstrations, and field trips are used particularly as information-giving methods for groups. Group discussions are used for developing understanding and change of attitude. Films, slides, flannel board presentations, and other visual aids are commonly used to make the teaching vivid and interesting. For some of the homemaking

skills or for developing a better understanding of child behavior, laboratory work or assistance in co-operative nursery schools are especially
effective teaching methods.

Financial Support

Sources of financial support are likewise varied. Sometimes membership fees to an organization, such as the National Congress of Parents
and Teachers, the General Federation of Women's Clubs, the American
Association of University Women, the Young Women's Christian Association, or the Child Study Association, are the source of support. Sometimes, as with public schools, the Cooperative Extension Service, and
community colleges, the activities are tax supported in whole or in part.
Community chest funds support some of the welfare agencies, which
include education in some phase of home or family living as part of their
program. The diversity in sources of financial support is very great but
support is not sufficient to meet the need.

Training

Professional training for leaders and teachers has grown by leaps and
bounds since 1948 but is still inadequate to meet the needs. All the
land-grant colleges and universities and many others require courses in
developmental and educational psychology, sociology, child development, family relations, and special preparation for working with adults
in the professional preparation of teachers for vocational homemaking.
Special preparation at the graduate level for teaching adults in parent or
family life education is also available at many colleges and universities.
Workshops to train lay leaders in the techniques of group discussion and
in the subject matters they propose to use have flourished mightily. Similarly, institutes and workshops for nurses, social workers, health educators, psychologists, and other professionals as preparation for curriculum
planning and group work with adults have been numerous. Nevertheless, at the present time, the specialized training for each of the major
professions that contribute significantly to family life education provides
only part of the preparation needed by a competent family life educator.
A pooling of the resources of many disciplines is very much needed.

CURRENT PROBLEMS AND ISSUES

Just as inter-disciplinary co-operation is needed in training programs,
so too is co-operation on an inter-disciplinary and inter-agency basis
needed in local communities. There are problems in family living faced
by adults whose adequate solution calls for the knowledge and educational guidance of persons of differing professional backgrounds. Local

educational programs could be greatly strengthened if the organizations and institutions could pool their efforts.

Financing and suitable housing for adult education programs in the area of family living are two other major problems. Finding adequately prepared leaders and administrators with vision of what might be are continuing problems.

There is a tremendous range and a great quantity of printed material available to meet a wide variety of needs, but a dearth of material similar to the curriculum guides provided for public school teachers. Administrators, teachers, and leaders of adults are continually asking where to find suggestions for group study. The lack of uniformity among groups and programs is highly desirable and allows much innovation, but it also makes the task of providing study guides extremely difficult.

In relation to these problems there are likewise unresolved issues. Some of them are illustrated by the following questions: How much professional training is a *must* for a parent education study-group leader? What is the place of the specialist in family life education for adults? What agencies and organizations are best prepared to do what types of education with which groups of people? Who should pay what expenses for this kind of education? Who should provide training needed by leaders? Should colleges and universities do the leader training or should the organizations train leaders for their own programs? How can the standards for preparation of leaders be raised? Who should provide what kind of information and study guide materials?

In the next ten years some solutions will have to be found to these problems and issues as well as to others that will arise. The task ahead seems to be to stimulate thought by a larger number of adults about the vital issues of family living and the relation of family life to our democratic way; to stimulate adults to re-examine the goals and values they hold and the procedures they use to achieve them; to develop understandings basic to satisfying relationships within families and with other families around the world.

Footnotes

[1]See chapter 18 for further discussion of this agency.

[2]Report to the author by the Administrative Assistant to the President, National Congress of Parents and Teachers.

[3]Ibid. Private letter.

[4]Report to author from chairman of the Education Department, General Federation of Women's Clubs.

[5]Quoted from a personal letter to the author from the Assistant Director, Publications Service, Family Service Association.

[6]Reports to author from the Assistant Director, National Catholic Welfare Conference and Assistant Director, Cana Conference of Chicago.

[7]Report from Office of Family Education Research, United Presbyterian Church in the USA.

[8]Letter to author from the Director, Commission on Community Organizations, The

National Conference of Christians and Jews, Inc.

[9]Letter from the Education Specialist, The National Association for Mental Health, Inc.

[10]Report from the Director of Education, American Social Hygiene Association.

[11]Report from the Deputy Executive Director, American Library Association.

[12]Letter to the author from the Director, Parent Education Project, University of Chicago.

Selected Readings

Brown, Muriel. *With Focus on Family Living.* Vocational Division Bulletin No. 249. Home Economics Education Series No. 28. Washington: Government Printing Office, 1958.

Chadderdon, Hester, and Lyle, Mary S. *Reasons Given by Iowa Women for Attending Homemaking Classes for Adults.* Special Report No. 12. Ames, Iowa: Agricultural Experiment Station, Iowa State College, 1955.

Cohen, Pauline. "Better Education for Families", *Adult Leadership,* VII (January, 1959), 197-99, 211.

Goller, Gertrude. "Family Life Education," *Adult Leadership,* VII (October, 1958), 96-98.

Hendrickson, Norejane Johnston. "Parent Education Practices in Ohio's State-supported Colleges and Universities," *Educational Research Bulletin,* XXXVIII (March 11, 1959), 57-65.

Home Economics Education for Out-of-School Youth and Adults. Washington: American Vocational Association, 1954.

Homemaking Education Programs for Adults. Vocational Division Bulletin No. 268. Home Economics Education Series No. 30. Washington: Government Printing Office, 1958.

Lyle, Mary S. "Cooperation in Family Life Education for Adults," *Adult Education,* VII (Winter, 1957), 116-19.

Lyle, Mary S., and Kehm, Freda A. "Parent Education and Home and Family Life," *Adult Education,* II (September, 1952), 197-201.

Patterson, Irene. "Trends in Adult Education," *Journal of Home Economics,* XXXXV (June, 1953), 383-86.

Rugg, Priscilla. "Teaching by Tea-V (at 3)," *American Vocational Journal,* XXXIV (March, 1959), 26-27.

Williamson, Maude, and Lyle, Mary S. *Homemaking Education for Adults.* New York: Appleton-Century-Crofts, 1949.

CHAPTER 41

HUMAN RELATIONS AND LEADERSHIP TRAINING

LELAND P. BRADFORD
Director
National Training Laboratories and Division of
Adult Education Service
National Education Association

THE EMERGENCE OF A NEW SUBJECT FIELD

The emergence of the field of human relations and leadership training as an important area of adult education has taken place during the past fifteen years. While this emergence has been contributed to by several groups in adult education, such as university extension and public school programs and many organizations concerned with informal adult education, the adult educational organization most specifically active in this development has been the National Training Laboratories of the Division of Adult Education of the National Education Association.

The field of human relations and leadership training has gone far beyond inspirational courses on how to influence people or institutes on techniques of conducting meetings. The National Training Laboratories, and the regional laboratories and university centers growing out of its activities, attempt to bridge between the emerging social science research findings about human and social behavior and the growing complexity of human and social problems.

These human and social problems within organizations and communities require more than good intentions for solutions. Only as the growing stockpile of knowledge from the social sciences is utilized adequately by leaders and members in a variety of social groupings will the dislocations resulting from technological advances be remedied or prevented.

This is why a variety of organizations in many social fields are turning to adult education in the form of human relations and leadership training. For example, American industry spends many millions of dollars annually in programs of management development. National and local organizations in the field of health, education, service, welfare, and religion are initiating programs of development of professional and volunteer workers on a vastly increased scale. Government agencies on all levels are today deeply concerned with the development of more effective leadership. The broad scope of this development is indicated by the fact that the National Training Laboratories is engaged in training programs involving school teachers; college professors; union officials; corporation executives; personnel directors; training directors from industry, government and national organizations; armed forces personnel; health officers; community counselors; Red Cross workers; ministers; Girl Scout and Camp Fire Girls officers; adult education leaders; conference directors; hospital executives; nurse educators; YMCA directors; researchers; and many others.

Not only have the efforts to bridge between social science and social practice stimulated a vast amount of leadership training here and abroad, but they have also led to the development of new concepts and methods of teaching adults and expanded understanding of the processes of human learning and social change. The results of social science research and the process of scientific experimentation are opening up new areas of adult learning and teaching.

It is not accidental that this development in the area of leadership and human relations training and the emergence and further development of new approaches to teaching took place in the last fifteen years. Historically, during the twenties and thirties, the method of group discussion expanded and developed in the field of adult education. At the same time, the workshop method developed in the field of education as an approach toward conferencing and in-service growth of teachers. Simultaneously, social case work and group work developed in the social work field. With the war, and its pressures for rapid social change, other forces were pressing toward development in the area of human relations and leadership training. Identification of a few of these forces is helpful in getting a background for those new developments in adult education:

1. The acceleration of the spread of human, social, and technological change has perhaps been the most outstanding characteristic of the first half of the twentieth century; and there is every indication that the acceleration will be greater in the second half. The rapidly increasing social and geographical mobility of our population, great increase in population itself, increasing breakdown of existent cultural patterns and community organization, the increasing technology and consequent complexity of our society, and the increasing interdependence of the world have combined to rush us into a new civilization creating new social human problems and demanding new attempts to solve new problems through more effective participation of all people.

2. Perhaps no time in history has shown as much unfreezing of the barriers of cultural patterns. The world is ripe for change and factors resisting change are weakening. Normally change in any area faces the resistance of stabilized forces in other areas. Today, with the acceleration of change so apparent—not only in technical areas, but also in political and social areas—there is more readiness and acceptance of change.

3. For the past two decades there has been a flowering of volunteer social agencies concerned with the many complex problems of our society, including health, education, welfare, and other aspects of community living. These agencies, endeavoring to maintain the concept of volunteer and private responsibility for social problems, have faced highly complex problems demanding complex leadership and membership. The move from bandage-wrapping as almost the sole task of volunteer workers to the many complex organizational and community tasks volunteers now carry on, has been a profoundly significant one.

4. In the past two decades in this country, we have been blessed with a great richness of human ability available for community and organizational leadership. Technological and educational progress has produced a vastly greater number of women whose home responsibilities enable them to devote time to community organizational affairs and whose high degree of education makes them capable and desirous of doing so.

5. With the increase in education of people and the growing complexity of the social problems to be solved, the traditional authoritarian pattern of group leadership has been increasingly less acceptable. Rigid parliamentary procedures and rules of order are less useful than in the past. The very complexity of the problems faced require more flexible participation of all concerned and more diagnostically sensitive leadership.

6. There have probably been few times in history when the forces of change have created so much personal uncertainty. The increase in social mobility has left fewer stable posts to which people can hold. People need increasingly to find satisfying membership in groups while finding and preserving their own individuality.

These forces, as well as others, have led to the need for an adult education movement directed toward aiding individuals and social groupings in gaining understanding and skill in dealing with the increasingly complex human and social problems faced today. Thus the field of human relations and leadership training, starting as it did in some instances with superficial techniques and inspirational panaceas, has developed into a highly respectable substantive field with a growing stockpile of social science knowledge about individual, group, organizational, and community behavior. At the same time, the action requirements of leadership and social change have helped to bring about a further development of the processes and methods of adult education.

With this background, the development of the National Training Laboratories can more adequately be understood.

History of the Development of the National Training Laboratories

In 1944 Professor Kurt Lewin established the first research center for the study of group dynamics in the world at the Massachusetts Institute of Technology and effectively launched the study of the dynamics in group behavior as an important segment of social psychology. He drew upon other fields of social science in accordance with his concept of inter-disciplinary research.

In 1947, the National Training Laboratory in Group Development opened its first session in Bethel, Maine. At that time it was sponsored jointly by the Division of Adult Education of the National Education Association and the Research Center for Group Dynamics at MIT. Concerned with utilizing new knowledges of individual and group behavior in a laboratory approach to learning which would help in the development of more effective leadership and membership, the "NTL" program endeavored to bridge between science and action through leadership training. From this first session in 1947, the laboratories of NTL have grown to where close to a hundred laboratory sessions of two to three weeks' duration are held in all parts of the country each year.

NTL's staff is composed of over a hundred leading social scientists located in over thirty universities and service organizations throughout the country. They provide an interdisciplinary approach to both training and research. During the past thirteen years over sixty research programs in the area of group behavior and individual learning have been conducted.

In addition to the work of NTL, a number of regional laboratories under university sponsorship have been established in various parts of the country. Among them are the Western Training Laboratory at the University of California, the Pacific Northwest Laboratory under the auspices of the Seattle Board of Education, the Intermountain Laboratory centered at the University of Utah, the Human Relations Training Laboratory at the University of Texas, and the Human Relations Center at Boston University.

The Process of Leadership Training

The process of laboratory learning developed through NTL represents an advance in the process of teaching-learning. Based on concepts of experiential learning combined with opportunities for analysis and feedback and supported by generalization from social science knowledge, the laboratory method systematically utilizes group forces supportive of learning. The following are characteristics of a laboratory approach to teaching and training:

1. In any laboratory program of whatever length (usually of a few

weeks) major emphasis is given to designing a total program in which each part of the day's and week's activities is carefully planned to support and integrate with other aspects of the program. There is no series of courses, but rather a tightly planned program designed to maximize learning.

2. Laboratory situations are created to give maximum experience to the trainee as a participant-observer. Each training experience makes it possible for every individual to participate actively in various types of interactive experience, and simultaneously or almost immediately analyze the consequences of his interaction behavior and to become diagnostic about the situation of which he is a part. The heart of a laboratory program is the diagnostic group. Several adults (from ten to sixteen, typically) are put together in a group situation for a number of hours a day over a period of days in which they face the task of creating a group with common purposes, effective communication, leadership and membership structure, mores, norms and common expectations, and appropriate methods of problem solving. None of these characteristics is supplied by the trainer; he does not assume a leadership role. The group itself, struggling to reconcile a variety of motivations, purposes, feelings, and patterns of personal behavior, each day creates a rich, vivid, living, and personal curriculum content about individual, interpersonal, and intragroup behavior. The task of the trainer is to help the group members analyze the behavior. In addition to creating vivid living data about human behavior, the diagnostic group enables each individual to become both a more effective observer and a more sensitive participant. As the diagnostic group develops in group intensity, opportunities are present for varying types of problems on various levels of sophistication to emerge and be solved. Within the flexible framework of the diagnostic group opportunity is given for individual and group experimentation (the heart of effective learning) in a climate where experimentation is always subject to analysis.

Other laboratory processes of a more structured nature are part of the total laboratory design. During other parts of a typical day, participative cases are utilized in which specific aspects of human and social behavior are created and analyzed.

3. Socal science theory and research findings systematically examined are a necessary part of a laboratory design for leadership training. Such knowledge about social systems, whether individual, group, or organizational, illuminates and supports experiential learning and enables the individual to generalize from experience.

Because the emphasis is upon growth in diagnostic sensitivity, in ability to test assumptions about social organizations and human values, in improvement in the individual's ability to be helped in social situations, and not on rigid techniques of conducting meetings or manipulating people, the new approach to human relations and leadership training produces adults who are better fitted to deal with the complex social problems of our time.

Selected Readings

Books

Benne, Kenneth D., and Muntyan, Bozidar, (eds.). *Human Relations in Curriculum Change.* New York: Dryden Press, 1951.

Cartwright, Dorwin, and Zander, Alvin, (eds.). *Group Dynamics Research and Theory.* Evanston, Ill.: Row, Peterson & Co., 1953.

Chase, Stuart. *Roads to Agreement.* New York: Harper & Bros., 1951.

Gibb, Jack R., and Gibb, Lorraine M. *Applied Group Dynamics.* Washington: National Training Laboratories, 1955.

Gouldner, Alvin W. (ed.). *Studies in Leadership.* New York: Harper & Bros., 1950.

Guetzkow, Harold (ed.). *Groups, Leadership and Men.* Pittsburgh: Carnegie Press, 1951.

Hare, Paul, Borgatta, E. F., and Bales, R. F. *Small Groups: Studies in Social Interaction.* New York: Alfred A. Knopf, Inc., 1955.

Knowles, Malcolm S., and Knowles, Hulda F. *Introduction to Group Dynamics.* New York: Association Press, 1959.

Lewin, Kurt. *Field Theory in Social Science.* Dorwin Cartwright, ed. New York: Harper & Bros., 1951.

––––––. *Resolving Social Conflicts.* Gertrude Weiss Lewin, ed. New York: Harper & Bros., 1948.

Lippitt, Ronald. *Training in Community Relations.* New York: Harper & Bros., 1949.

––––––, Watson, Jeanne, and Westley, Bruce. *The Dynamics of Planned Change.* New York: Harcourt, Brace & Co., 1958.

Miles, Matthew B. *Learning to Work in Groups.* New York: Bureau of Publications, Teachers College, Columbia University, 1959.

Ross, Murray G., and Hendry, Charles E. *New Understandings of Leadership.* New York: Association Press, 1957.

Stock, Dorothy, and Thelen, Herbert. *Emotional Dynamics and Group Culture.* Washington: National Training Laboratories, 1958.

Thelen, Herbert A. *Dynamics of Groups at Work.* Chicago: University of Chicago Press, 1954.

Pamphlets

Adult Education Association of the U.S.A.
    Leadership Pamphlets Nos. 1 to 16.
    Leaders' Digest Nos. 1 to 3.

National Education Association, Division of Adult Education Service
    "Educational Dynamics: Theory and Research," by Herbert A. Thelen.
    "Explorations in Human Relations Training: An Assessment of Experience, 1947-1952."
    "Report of the Summer Laboratory Sessions" for 1955 to 1959.

CHAPTER 42

LIBERAL ADULT EDUCATION

HARRY L. MILLER
Assistant Director
Center for the Study of Liberal Education for Adults

There is probably no area in adult education about which there is so much vagueness, ambiguity, and controversy as the liberal arts. In part this reflects a confusion about liberal education in its original home, the liberal arts college. But in a more important sense, adult education has shaped itself historically to relatively well-defined tasks, based on pressing needs in society. The proudest boast of the adult educator is that he builds his program on the needs of the individual, or the needs of the community. The United States during the first half of the twentieth century was deep in the historical task of metamorphosis: from a rural to an urban society, from an agricultural to a giant industrial economy, from isolation to the source of world power. Inevitably, these changes required training in new economic and social skills.

The fifteen years since the end of World War II has seen the rise of a concern for another mission for adult education, liberal education, whose causes are easy to cite but difficult to rank. Some are: the enormous increase in leisure, the spread of middle-class habits and values, the absence of major war or depression, the increasing professionalization of the field of adult education and the greater sophistication of the questions adult educators ask each other, and the reaction among the adult population to the styles of life of the new consumption economy they themselves created. Perhaps, more simply and most significantly, we are as a total culture turning away at last from the image of work as the cultural ideal to an acceptance of play and to the cultivation of the individual, not for the purpose of productive work, but for its own sake.

Whatever their differences, all advocates of liberal education appear to agree on one postulate. Herberg states it clearly: "Liberal education I would define as education held to be worthwhile on its own account, education designed primarily not to further an extrinsic end . . . but to bring about results somehow terminating in and intrinsic to the one being educated, the kind of education that (roughly and inaccurately put) aims to make one not merely a better doctor or engineer but in some sense a better human being."[1]

Beyond some rather general agreement to this sort of statement, views of what the ends of liberal adult education ought to be or how its curriculum should be shaped tend to be almost as diverse as the number of people willing to write about it. I do not propose, however, to deal with the variety of possible positions in any systematic fashion, but much more simply to approach the problem empirically by describing the major existing programs and their underlying premises.

THREE MAJOR MODELS[2]

1. The Disciplines

The most common model for liberal education for adults is either the curriculum of the undergraduate college program or some adaptation of it. The underlying assumptions of this model run something like this: the liberal arts consist of bodies of knowledge which the academic tradition has codified into a series of scholarly disciplines—the sciences, the social sciences and the humanities; new knowledge and insights into relationships in these disciplines are constantly being added to as a result of scholarly effort; the disciplines can be taught in the form of courses, each of which consists of selections from the available organization of knowledge and principles, graded as to complexity and difficulty; a liberal education consists of a judicious and fair selection from among the lower level—introductory courses transmitting these disciplines with some exploration in depth of one of them.

The most extreme example of this model is the undergraduate curriculum for adults at Rutgers' University College. Until very recently, University College was a separate college of the university, with eleven traditional academic departments staffed with full-time faculty and a department chairman responsible to the Dean of University College. Standards for admission and matriculation into the college are carefully set, and make few if any concessions to the maturity of the students. Policies on absences, grading, and examinations are spelled out by the administrative staff for all part-time instructors.

In most matters of form the Rutgers program resembles a rather traditional day college. "It is quite authentically a college education in the evening—a Rutgers education—and through its experience it has come to reject the superficial, the novel, and the merely functional and to stand on traditional subject matter, established purposes, and conventional forms."[3] But the interesting aspect of Rutgers is that it takes a deliberately traditional definition of liberal education and attempts to offer it to adult students in a context which makes allowance for their maturity. To a certain extent this is achieved by discounting the "sacred sequence hypothesis" of education—for example, students are not required to begin their work at any stated place. But, in a larger sense, the Rutgers plan lays claim to being especially for adults by maintaining a core faculty whose major concern is with the adult student body.

The significant characteristic of this whole type, of which Rutgers is an extreme, is the transmission of bodies of important knowledge and principle within the recognized boundaries of the liberal arts without regard to the variations in selection, methodology, presentation, or format. The following programs, despite great differences in these variables, have in common the same assumption:

1. The modal pattern of credit offerings in evening colleges, extension centers, and liberal arts colleges. Like Rutgers, these programs repeat at night the traditional A.B. courses; unlike it, they are taught by part-time instructors whose loyalties are usually firmly fixed elsewhere and who seldom make any noticeable concession to the different context in which they teach.

2. Discrete, non-credit courses, often called "short courses," sometimes, disparagingly, "cafeteria programs." These are characteristically given not only by a considerable proportion of the universities engaged in adult education, but by YMCA's, high schools, junior colleges and other institutions. These courses are likely to be vocational or purely recreational. The format is a magnificently flexible one, and any group desiring a particular course can usually persuade a nearby institution to offer it. An increasing number of these courses, however, consist of selections from one or another of the arts and sciences, often achieve seriousness, complexity, and brilliance.

3. Many informal, lay-led discussion programs, despite their apparent total dissimiliarity from our model, are nevertheless the same basic version of liberal education. The discussion packages issued by the Fund for Adult Education, for example, are excitingly, sometimes superbly, packaged versions of basic principles of anthropology, economics, political science, and so forth. The programs are successful if, through discussion of the material, the participants grasp the principles explicated by the materials.

4. Probably the widest variation in format is the rise of the residential liberal education institute.[4] Many of the special programs for business executives take their students off to a retreat for periods ranging from a week end to several months. Steelworkers, college deans, or businesswomen similarly have participated in such retreats from the world of work and routine. The popularity of combining liberal studies with a total withdrawal from the work context is interesting confirmation of the thesis linking liberal education with the shift to a leisure culture.

2. The Skills of the Free Man

A second type of program emphasizes intellectual skills rather than the understanding of knowledge and principles. These programs might state a series of assumptions of this order: knowledge in the fields of the liberal arts grows so rapidly that no adult can keep up; the only permanently useful learning he can do is to acquire basic skills of analysis, criticism, and judgment appropriate to particular fields or to certain persistent life situations. The selection of materials for these programs is a matter for serious thought, to be sure, and are taken from the liberal disciplines, but the criterion is what is the most appropriate and useful material to develop a certain skill.

The extreme model of this general type is the Basic Program of Liberal Education for Adults, developed by the University of Chicago's University College.[5] It is an intensive four-year program meeting six hours a week with formal admission requirements, no examinations, and no grades other than pass or fail. Upon graduation, the student is awarded a Certificate in the Liberal Arts.

The Basic Program accepts as reasonable the traditional division of human knowledge into the sciences, the social sciences, and the humanities. But it asserts that, in relation to these areas of knowledge, the liberally educated person should be able to judge the beauty of a work of art, the credibility of the results of scientific research, and the desirability of social and political institutions. "Obviously he cannot be an expert in all these fields; yet it is unwise to leave the judging of these matters in the hands of those who are experts. His education, without making him an expert, trains him in judging the work of experts. For this purpose it is not sufficient for him merely to assimilate the main ideas and conclusions of the various fields through generalized surveys This is because liberal education is a special kind of education, as distinct from the accumulation of general information as it is from training for expertness. Its central concern is the interpreting of the work of experts and the making of judgments respecting them."[6]

Students attend each year a tutorial in each of the three curriculum areas. Outside preparation for these very small classes is light, because the tutorial concentrates on careful and detailed analysis of small parts of difficult and crucial texts. The student also is required to attend an interdisciplinary seminar which demands a great deal of outside reading and is concerned with major texts in the social sciences and with primary poetic, historical, and philosophical works. Textbooks are avoided, "on the ground that they oversimplify and distort ideas by isolation and summary, that conclusions cannot be understood apart from the arguments whereby they were reached, and that greatness of mind and spirit can be communicated only through the original work."

The Basic Program's kinship to some of the other adult programs listed below may not be immediately clear, but all have in common a primary concern with the development of liberal skills, however different their formulation of these skills may be.

1. The Great Books and World Politics programs in their separate ways provide materials which in their judgment will create an opportunity for participants to develop skills of thinking. Of equal importance is the discussion situation; people must be confronted with the necessity of engaging in a dialectic not only with the materials, but with a group of peers, in order to practice the skills they are developing.

The Basic Arts Program of Cleveland College, at Western Reserve University, is no longer operating but deserves mention here because it so clearly reveals the essential characteristic of this general type. The curriculum was based on a core conception: that the various arts require quite different kinds of decisions on the part of the practitioners—that the novelist, for example, proceeds through a series of decisions in the process of writing a work very different from the series of decisions the scientist makes in setting up an experiment. The skills involved in judging any finished product, whether it is a novel, a scientific generalization, or a political policy, depend on a thorough understanding of the criteria for good decision-making in these various realms. The program was taught by highly competent faculty people through a series of seminars.

3. Because the skills of the various arts *are* different, the field has displayed some tendency to develop programs which concentrate on one area. The World Politics program has been already cited; another example is the Fine Arts Program at the University of Chicago, whose objective is to develop a loyal and sophisticated audience for the arts.

4. An interesting experimental variant of this type is still in the drawing-board stage, though it has had one tryout at Northwestern University. It is the proposed Laboratory College for Adults, which builds a curriculum not on the traditionally defined areas of the several arts, but on an analysis of the life situation of the American adult. Its objective is to teach the skills of learning from experience, and it makes the assumption that most adult experience takes place in the context of urban life—a relatively new factor in American culture—and that a number of psychological and social blocks stand between most people and the rich resources available to them in the cities they live in. The curriculum consists of controlled exposure to the resources—museums, mass media, politics, important institutions—and the construction and discussion of the kinds of generalizations one can validly draw from the experience, as well as the theoretical constructions which can help one understand it.

An issue related to this general type of liberal education appears with some frequency and deserves mention here. As part of the humanities, the fine arts present a special problem: is training in the *skills* of these arts itself liberal education? Are courses in how to paint, how to write novels, and so forth, liberal, or merely avocational, like courses in ballroom dancing, bridge, or fly-tying? There is a school of thought which insists that the best way to learn the analytic, cognitive skills of aesthetics is through actual practice of one of the fine arts; the thorough academics would rather leave the doing to the artists and insist that the liberal skills are those of the mind. The issue is nowhere near being resolved.

3. The Liberating Experience

The first two models explored are relatively clear-cut, have obvious connections with the traditional materials of the liberal disciplines, and rationales which tend to be spelled out more or less explicitly. The third model includes programs of which none of these is true but which base the claim to being liberal education on the assertion that the meaning of "liberal" is liberating. Ralph Barton Perry states the position this way:

> Education is liberal insofar as it invites and qualifies men to choose deeply and fundamentally, to choose ends as well as means, to choose remote as well as immediate ends, to choose from many rather than from few possibilities. Liberal education, so construed, makes successive generations of men aware of the widest range of possibilities by the discovery of new possibilities, and by reminding them of old possibilities forgotten. It does so in order that men may choose with the utmost amplitude of freedom—in order that their lives may be filled to the maximum extent by what they thoughtfully and wittingly choose them to be . . . As the professional or vocational school may be liberal, so the so-called liberal arts college may be illiberal, and will be illiberal in so far as it is pervaded with a narrow sectarian bias, or employs methods of mass appeal, or reduces study to the level of drudgery and routine . . .[7]

If one defines "liberal" as "liberating," the first question to be answered is what is the nature of the chains? In a sense, the first type described assumes that the major bondage is ignorance, and that education liberates by communicating knowledge; the second type, that the bondage is habit, and that education liberates by teaching skills of judgment. The third type tends to select from a range of significant bondages, most of them socially induced. The restricted life of the rural family, the narrow training and environment of the professional and technician, the blinders of personal psychological need or social structure, are examples of some assumed bondages underlying special adult programs of this type.

The model program of this type is also the largest and most successful of all adult education enterprises, agricultural extension. The history and general program of this enormous institution is detailed in Chapter 18 of this *Handbook,* it is only necessary here to discuss the extent to which it may be considered liberal education. The claim is often made that it has been truly liberal in a sense in which traditional liberal arts education often has not been.

For example, the extension service has made considerable progress over the past quarter of a century in teaching conservation practices. Aside from the tremendous consequences of such changed attitudes on the future economy of the continent, the educational question is: were American farmers used merely as means to this social end, or were they, in the process, themselves changed as persons? Those who see extension as liberating argue that it has changed people as well as land practices. The basic method of extension is demonstration carried on by controlling significant variables and comparing the end results. If tradition-oriented rural people change toward basing action on the results of experimental inquiry one could scarcely argue that the education producing this change has not been liberating. If people who previously were psychologically as well as spatially isolated now begin to be aware of the impact of the larger world in their lives, and become willing to accept some of the values of that world, it is surely a liberation in some sense. These are changes in values, attitudes, and sensibilities well within the normal range of educational objectives.

But, even assuming that many of these changes can be directly related to extension rather than to the parallel revolution in social communication, there is a significant value question involved in this third type of liberal education. The first two types have about them a sort of neutrality; no one disputes the desirability for example, of having an understanding of the major historical forces leading to the rise of present American civilization, or an understanding of historical method sufficient to judge historical generalizations. Agreement about liberating someone, however, implies that people agree on the particular bondage in question, and on the desirability of the specific direction of liberation. An abiding faith in sheer change may lead to liberating people from a reading of the Bible and open them to the sophisticated delights of Edgar Guest, or from anachronistic but at least consistent conceptions of parent-child relations to a bewildered conformity to the latest psychological fads.

Because the bulk of adult education is vocational at base, the proportion of liberal education is depressingly small unless one accepts this view that liberal influences can infuse the vocational orientation. The great variety of programs makes difficult a selection of models to exemplify the range, but the following are some important focal points:

1. The Federal Executive Program of the University of Chicago is an unusually well thought through attempt to make a vocational program liberating. Most of the participants are at middle-management levels in the federal service and the training programs ordinarily developed for them tend to concentrate on helping them move paper around more efficiently than they do. This is not meant invidiously; most management jobs in a large bureaucracy inevitably become so. Chicago's program goes far beyond this by confronting the students with all of the complex factors which affect the making of decisions in such an organizational context, through discussion of organizational structure, the social psychology of work, communications and the meaning of meaning, political behavior, and the value consequences of decision-making.

2. A major issue in adult education since the forties has involved the

growth of educational programs whose subject matter is group development and whose methods range from fairly ordinary instruction techniques to adaptations of some forms of group psychotherapy.[8] In a society in which planning and decision-making must increasingly take place in groups, an understanding of how to make more effective the behavior of individuals in groups becomes of considerable importance.

Programs of education in group dynamics have tended to standardize in format as residential institutes, although one finds them occasionally taking the form of regular courses as well. Are they liberal? One could persuasively argue that they liberate from the bondage of subconsciously motivated behavior, by bringing such behavior out into the open in the course of training. By learning the ways in which non-rational elements affect the work of a group, people are able to proceed more rationally, the argument runs.

3. All of the program examples mentioned so far are systematic and institutionalized. Yet, in their sum they affect proportionately a tiny part of the population, when compared with the non-systematic educational resources of the society which we might consider to be liberating in the broadest sense. Libraries, art and natural history museums, symphonies, theaters, movies, magazines, newspapers, television are all surely adult education media of enormous size and importance. If indeed they operated effectively and consistently as liberalizing instruments, there would be little use in organizing special programs. It is unfortunate that we know so little how they might be made more effective instruments of education.

PROBLEMS AND ISSUES

It is difficult to define systematic relationships among the major types described, and since they were developed empirically any attempt to impose a real system on them might be spurious. They do form a rough continuum, however, in relation to some important educational variables. Thus:

Vocational			*Liberal*	
Man as Instrument			*Man as Human*	
		I	II	III
		Transfer	Development	Liberation from
Specific Skill	Total Role	of Major	of Intellec-	Social or Self-
Training	Training	Disciplines	tual Skills	imposed Bond-
				ages

No value judgment is intended in the placement of these various types of adult educational enterprise. If a man needs to learn how to operate a lathe, there is no sense in his enrolling in a Great Books group, or an institute on human relations. It is interesting and perhaps useful to note, however, that as one moves to the right along the continuum, the following requirements change:

1. *Constantly decreasing rigidity of material and content in general.* To teach a person to drive a car one needs not only a car (an oxcart or an airplane won't do) but it is useful to have the particular car he will be driving. And accountants had better be familiar with the tax laws of the state they are going to practice in. Under the liberal rubric, text books in the various disciplines differ, to be sure, but they cover essentially the same topics, though the instructor of Sociology 101 is permitted rather more latitude than are instructors of Introductory Accounting. In teaching skills of critical judgment in the social sciences, however, any number of possible texts or cases might be useful. And, as for the third group, it is presumably possible to teach any content or subject in a way that makes it liberating in its effect.

2. *Constantly increasing emphasis on methodology and learning process.* People can learn to tie knots from a good training film, but as one progresses along the continuum more attention must be paid to a deliberate manipulation of elements of the situation. By the time one reaches the third type, learning devices such as complex demonstration and elaborate role plays become common.

3. *Increasing demands on teaching skill.* Much of the teaching of specific skills is still conducted by people communicating by example to others, but the ability to teach what is essentially the scientific method in the course of instructing people how to raise more corn per acre is a high art indeed. The effectiveness of the third type, consequently, depends so clearly and directly on the skill of the instructor that one should like proof, for example, that all the county agents employed by extension are indeed the remarkable breed of teacher that the accomplishment implies.

Appropriateness for Adults

Each of the three general types makes a different adaptation to the special clientele represented by the adult. The disciplinary approach assumes generally that adult liberal education is remedial, that if a person has reached mature adulthood without a knowledge of the fundamentals of history, literature, sociology and the other disciplines, he has a clear-cut deficiency which can be remedied by giving him what he missed. It really does not matter very much how old he is, if he missed one of the formally defined steps of education in the stately progression from grammar school through college, he can hardly be considered educated.

Many of the informal programs developed specially for adults are as remedial in intention as the full-scale college baccalaureate programs. But they do select the most significant areas in the various disciplines, or cut the pieces so small that people can select ones relevant to immediate interests. The colleges and universities, however, apply the same criterion of 120 or so credit hours to the adult as to the undergraduate.

One of the most interesting experiments in liberal adult education in recent years involved an attempt to deal directly with the rigidities of this view. Is it not conceivable, the experimenters asked, that in the course of a full life, or even half-life, the alert and intelligent adult has learned many of the things the college would grant him credit for learning in the classroom? If he starts late to seek a degree, must he sit through courses whose content he already knows, or can we give him, in Diekhoff's phrase, "time off for good behavior?" Within its regular evening B.A. credit program, Brooklyn College set up an experimental program intended to discover whether a college can equate life experience with classroom experience.[9] They contrived an elaborate system of tests and interviews to evaluate the experience of the student, and granted him credit for whatever areas of knowledge and competence he could prove possession of.

This highly successful venture resulted not only in an established program, but in some findings of general interest. One is, on the surface at least, somewhat contradictory; most of the applicants who were granted credit toward the B.A. had knowledge of a highly specialized kind, and needed remedial work in the general, introductory phases of the particular area. The college found itself, consequently, insisting that all those admitted to the special program take a series of general education seminars developed specially for the group.

Ironically, the success of the Brooklyn College project has confirmed many of rigidities of university liberal education, by its evaluation of experience *not* against some desirable image of the liberally educated person, but against the specific courses in the college catalog. Nevertheless, it stands as a signal effort to solve one of the realistic problems of the above-average adult seeking remedial college education.

Programs of the second type, which concentrate on the development of intellectual skills, pay considerably more attention than the first group to the question of the appropriateness of their programs for adults. Some argue that it is not indeed until people have matured and dealt directly with life and the human condition that they are able to appreciate the meaning of significant concepts.

Such considerations lead to the notion that the colleges have reversed the reasonable curriculum order by concentrating general or liberal education in the first two years, before permitting the student to specialize in what is likely to be his vocational field. The youth, the argument runs, is preoccupied with the problems of mating and of gaining vocational competence, and is understandably impatient with the necessary speculation and spirit of inquiry. Nor has his experience yet raised for him the shattering questions for which there are no immediate or easy answers. Why not recognize this reality, and arrange the educational sequence so that vocational education comes first and liberal afterward?[10] Some commentators suggest that the last years of college might concentrate on liberal sudies, others that they be postponed until the career has already been well started, and then undertaken in some form of guided continuing education.[11]

It is hardly necessary to mention that for the third type of program appropriateness for the adult is a meaningless question. The adult clientele is taken for granted, and the only context in which group dynamics, for example, appears in the adolescent classroom is as special classes in social psychology.

Why Liberal Education?

Empirically, our three types seem to be interested in producing rather different human results: the Cultural Literate, the Renaissance Man, and the Problem Solver. But each assumes that to some degree, it subserves the purposes of the other two in its own.

The advocates of the traditional disciplines assume that sufficient exposure to the total range will equip students with the important intellectual skills, and provide them with the ability to approach rationally any problem they are likely to encounter. With somewhat less certainty, those who concentrate on developing skills assume that, equipped properly, the student will explore for himself the significant concepts of the various disciplines, and will be able as well to transfer the intellectual skills of judgment to the solution of practical problems. The liberators, alone, might suggest that the problems of democracy and a viable world order are so pressing that we had better not be found "studying navigation while the ship is going down."

THE INSTITUTIONAL SETTING

The institutions which organize and operate programs of liberal adult education are even more diverse than the programs themselves and by no means demonstrate a straight-line relationship to them. But before proceeding to the operating institutions, it is necessary to note the influence on this particular area of adult education of the active foundations.

Fund for Adult Education (FAE)

During the period covered by the previous *Handbook*, foundation support for adult education had come mainly from the Carnegie Foundation, whose interest was in the general field, with some emphasis on publication and research. The recent period has been dominated by two facts: the establishment of the FAE has led other foundations to consider adult education as out of their field; and the FAE has concentrated on encouraging liberal adult education, to the virtual exclusion of other activities.

Because innovation in education often depends on the availability of extra-institutional risk capital, a considerable proportion of the novel developments in the field during this period have been in liberal education. The Fund itself undertook a series of interesting and bold experiments directed at testing the possibility that liberal education could be made a mass phenomenon.

The details of these experiments may be found elsewhere in the *Handbook*. We need to note here that one of the major findings as a result of these efforts was that some form of institutionalization appeared to be necessary to the maintenance of liberal programs in a community. The earlier attempts to base the programs on a specially created community agency were succeeded by a decision to put them under the control of local or regional colleges and universities.

Universities and Colleges

This decision indicates the central importance of these institutions to adult liberal education. Yet their structure and value system create considerable difficulties and cause the purists in adult liberal education to prefer to try building a separate organization.

The institutions of higher education have:

1. Virtually a monopoly on the easily accessible highly trained people in the liberal arts.
2. A considerable prestige, at least among those who value learning.
3. Resources covering the entire range of the liberal arts, and all the types of curricula we cited as significant. They program the bulk of the first type, and a considerable proportion of the second, agricultural extension operates from state universities, and with one single exception, the programs of group development and human relations are under university auspices.

The problems involved in utilizing these enormous resources are many:

1. Adult education is a marginal activity in an institution which perceives its primary role as the preparation of the young for life and the advancement of knowledge through research.
2. The faculty image of the liberal arts tends to be static and fixed. As specialization in the academic world grows, it will become more so.
3. The level of teaching ability is exceedingly uneven, and the modal teaching style is one that is only irregularly appropriate to some of the aims of adult liberal education.
4. The adult education divisions of the universities are commonly constrained to conform to one or another of two major institutional imperatives: service and profit. In the one case, the service response to any stated need not only places the total responsibility for educational policy in the hands of those who least know about it, but in practice restricts programs to vocational and recreational

offerings; in the other case, the profit motive often discourages any risky experimentation with liberal programs.

The difficulties, however, cannot successfully outweigh what appears to be a major fact of life for liberal adult education—that, if it grows and improves in any permanent sense, the institutions of higher learning must be a major host for it. All the evidence of experience and experimentation supports such a belief.

One agency established and supported by the FAE is committed to the task of helping the colleges and universities become more effective instruments for the liberal education of adults—the Center for the Study of Liberal Education for Adults. Established in 1951, the center is, uniquely, supported by the FAE but independent of it; closely related to the major associations in the field of university adult education, but not officially responsible to them. It is not committed to any one view of liberal education for adults, and sees its major task as the encouragement of experimentation and innovation.[12] The Center in general operates by accelerating promising trends in the field, by helping to set up experimental program models, by diffusing ideas and experiences, and by conducting and aiding others in research into important problems.

The Public Schools

Of the major agencies in adult education, the public schools are perhaps the most committed to a pure service orientation. The institution generally has for decades dedicated itself to meeting the most strongly-felt needs of all American youth, and concentrated, therefore, on the skills of social and economic adjustment. Its most difficult and largely unsolved problem has been the development of a viable general education program, and this difficulty has been demonstrated in its adult programs as well.

Lacking the philosophical commitment of the colleges to liberal education, the high school's service orientation has resulted in a drift toward a curriculum which, when liberal at all, has trivialized the disciplines. There are a few high school adult programs that have developed interesting and significant projects in world affairs, in community problems, and in the arts—mainly in upper-middle-class suburban areas. And, in recent years, through the National Association of Public School Adult Educators, many of the leaders in high school adult education have become concerned with the desirability of doing more in liberal education. This concern may be the beginning of a trend.

TRENDS AND THE FUTURE

The future of liberal adult education is difficult to assess, in large measure because of the ambiguity about its aims which this chapter has anatomized. The term is not so much vague as it is ambiguous; that is, it is given different meanings by different people, who often enough see quite clearly what *their* particular interpretation involves in terms of program directives. Ambiguity presents different problems than vagueness does; it poses a need to recognize that people march to different drums and that perhaps all we can do on a philosophical level is to make certain that each of the interpretations is as clear as we can make it. It is unlikely that this diversity will, in the future, melt into a common purpose, but tolerance for ambiguity in the profession seems to be rising.

A more important and less easily remedied problem is the influence of the enrollment economy so characteristic of adult education generally. Whatever the particular goals of liberal education, they are less immediately practical than other forms of study and more difficult to achieve. When we try to convince a pragmatic population of the necessity of having thinking, well-informed citizens in a healthy democracy, the rhetoric often sounds remote. Yet, so long as expensive liberal programs must be self-supporting, a workable rhetoric must be found.

Future growth of liberal adult education as a real possibility depends to some extent on the development of a conviction among those responsible for educational policy that it is important enough to subsidize. It is a truly astonishing feature of present educational policy that public funds may be used to subsidize vocational training enabling individuals to benefit personally by increasing their incomes, but not for education devoted to raising either the cultural level of the society or the available and dangerously low supply of thoughtful citizens trained to make independent judgments on important public matters.

The crystal ball is not so clouded, however, that some likely directions cannot be described. Some present activities which might well influence the future are discussed below.

FAE and Public Responsibility

The Fund, as the major source of experimental risk capital may have a considerable effect on future trends. The effect of its recent decision to commit a considerable proportion of its resources to the development of programs aimed directly at education for public responsibility is difficult to assess as yet.[13] Indications are that its new direction will involve programs of all three types discussed earlier in this chapter, with an empirical dependence on the field to come up with a variety of curricula aimed at a wide range of audiences.

The Fund has always been interested in the question of how liberal education of individuals can be made to have direct relevance for the application of intelligence to the social order and to the extent that its new emphasis aims to reach future power elites, it is the most daring of its attempts.

Special Adult Degrees

There is presently a scatter of interest in developing two-year and four-year liberal degree programs especially constructed for adults and restricted to the relatively mature and intellectually able. The Brooklyn project encouraged the general interest, and at the moment new curricula of this type are being considered at the University of Oklahoma, University of Pittsburgh, Syracuse University, and New York University. All of these programs represent an attempt to depart from the purely remedial emphasis of the day undergraduate degree program replicated at night, and their tendency is to move toward the intellectual skill development of the second type.

The movement, if it becomes one, represents an ingenious attempt to deal with the problem of financial support. Degree programs, by and large, can support themselves, because a degree is a social and economic symbol of considerable power. The solution of retaining the degree, but changing the substance into true adult liberal education has a beautiful simplicity to it. Its major difficulty as a general solution lies in the possibility that the inertial force of tradition will succeed in slowly changing any new curriculum pattern back into its old forms. Future developments in this new attempt are thus worth watching not only for their effects on the shape of liberal adult education generally but for what may be learned about educational change.

Evaluation

A current effort to develop criteria and instruments for evaluating liberal adult education may, if successful, have some long-range effects of some magnitude. In 1958 representatives of about eighteen separate programs of special adult education met at the invitation of the Center for the Study of Liberal Education for Adults to identify learning objectives common to all or most of them. They succeeded surprisingly well in agreeing on nine important objectives, generally stated, and agreed to continue working, with the aim of specifying them in terms that made measurement of their achievement feasible.[14] If the project continues, the field will eventually have available highly specific statements of its most important learning goals as guides to curriculum development and instructional patterns, and a series of instruments for evaluating the effectiveness of learning experiences in relation to those goals.

Research

The field as a whole, and liberal education most strikingly, seems ready to take a broad forward leap into more effective research activities relating to its pressing problems. The year of preparation of this *Handbook* also saw the release of a perceptive and thoughtful review by Brunner of research in adult education, and a special issue of the *Review of Educational Research* devoted to adult education. The first large-scale study of liberal education in the universities that went beyond a status survey was also completed by CSLEA.[15]

A number of serious research studies are already underway. As the result of Fund grants, special research projects into problems of liberal education have begun at California, Syracuse, and Western Reserve. CSLEA has begun to systematize its research efforts, and is ready to begin studies of motivation, teaching style, adult learning, and other focal problems of adult liberal education.

Footnotes

1. Will Herberg, "Toward a Biblical Theology of Education," *Religious Education,* XLVIII (November-December, 1953), 374-79.
2. Peter E. Siegle and James B. Whipple. *New Directions in Programming for University Adult Education* (Chicago: Center for the Study of Liberal Education for Adults, 1957).
3. G. Stuart Demarest. *Faculty Organization at Rutgers* (Chicago: Center for the Study of Liberal Education for Adults, 1955), p. 21.
4. Royce S. Pitkin. *The Residential School in American Adult Education.* (Chicago: Center for the Study of Liberal Education for Adults, 1956).
5. Peter E. Siegle and James B. Whipple, *op. cit.*
6. Galway Kinnel, "The Basic Program at Chicago," *Notes and Essays* No. 11 (Chicago: Center for the Study of Liberal Education for Adults, 1955), p. 26.
7. Ralph Barton Perry, "When Is Education Liberal," *Modern Education and Human Values* ("Pitcairn-Crable Foundation Lecture Series," Vol. III [Pittsburgh: University of Pittsburgh Press, 1950]).
8. *Cf.* The publications list of the National Association of Public School Adult Educators.
9. Bernard H. Stern. *How Much Does Adult Experience Count? A Report of the Brooklyn College Experimental Degree Project* (Chicago: Center for the Study of Liberal Education for Adults, 1955); and Bernard H. Stern, *Adults Grow in Brooklyn: the Brooklyn College Experimental Degree Project for Adults* (Chicago: Center for the Study of Liberal Education for Adults, 1955).
10. John B. Schwertman, *I Want Many Lodestars* (Chicago: Center for the Study of Liberal Education for Adults, 1958).
11. Margaret Mead, "Thinking Ahead: Why is Education Obsolete?" *Harvard Business Review,* (November-December, 1958), p. 23.
12. The center has attempted to develop a literature for the field of university liberal adult education; see its publication list for general references to this section.
13. The Fund for Adult Education, press release, June 17, 1959.
14. *The Evaluation of Liberal Adult Education; Progress Report: Princeton Conference* (Chicago: Center for the Study of Liberal Education for Adults, 1958).
15. Edmund deS. Brunner, and others, *An Overview of Adult Education Research* (Chicago: Adult Education Association, 1959); *Review of Educational Research,* June, 1959; and James T. Carey, *AUEC-NUEA Study* (Chicago: Center for the Study of Liberal Education for Adults, April, 1959). Preliminary draft.

Selected Readings

For relevant readings, see pp. 402-3.

CHAPTER 43

PUBLIC AFFAIRS EDUCATION

ABBOTT KAPLAN
Director, University Extension
University of California, Los Angeles

Educational programs in public affairs are those that are designed to develop understanding and knowledge of public issues and problems facing the country and its citizens domestically and internationally in political, economic, and social areas. While some are more consciously designed than others to stimulate action, implicit in all such programs is the aim of developing more intelligent citizenship and public decision-making.

All the methods common to other phases of adult education are utilized in public affairs education: classroom instruction, lectures, informal discussion groups, conferences, seminars, residential programs, printed materials, and the mass media. The latter are probably more extensively used in public affairs education than in any other adult education programming.

HISTORICAL BACKGROUND

From the very founding of the Republic it was recognized that the health and well-being of a democratic society must rest upon the education, intelligence, and civic responsibility of its citizens. And as Chapter 2 of this *Handbook* documents in detail, a large part of the education of adults ever since has been concerned with public affairs. Many of the early adult educational institutions, from the Junto through the lyceums and Chautauqua, emphasized the study of public issues. The evening schools and university extension programs early in their development sponsored citizenship classes and courses, lecture series, and forums on public affairs. A number of voluntary associations came into being expressly for this purpose, and others pursued it secondarily.

Since World War II the expansion of this aspect of the curriculum of adult education has greatly accelerated. The establishment of the United Nations and the world-wide political, economic, and military commitments of the United States have prompted greater concern with world affairs than ever before. Problems of population growth, urban development, inflation, federal spending, taxation, defense, uses of atomic energy, agricultural surpluses, integration, mental health, civil rights, teacher shortages, and many others, have prompted the launching of a large number of special educational programs to study these problems. Many of these were sponsored by educational institutions, but as many or more were initiated by other organizations. A number of the latter were established since the war and in some instances are exclusively devoted to public affairs education. Among the new organizations concerned with the study and discussion of public issues and international affairs are: the U.S. National Commission for UNESCO, the American Association for the United Nations, the American Foundation for Continuing Education (recently changed from The American Foundation for Political Education), the Fund for Adult Education, the American Assembly, the American Heritage Foundation, and Residential Seminars on World Affairs.

PROGRAMS IN PUBLIC AFFAIRS EDUCATION

This section will attempt to present a brief over-view of Public Affairs programs for adults sponsored by educational institutions and voluntary organizations. It is based on: (1) a questionnaire sent to extension divisions, evening colleges, and national organizations; (2) published programs and brochures; (3) Morton's study of university extension; (4) the N.E.A.'s study of public school adult education programs; and (5) a questionnaire sent to libraries by Mrs. Grace T. Stevenson. Examples cited are primarily for illustration; they are not necessarily unique. Obviously in so brief a space they must of necessity be limited.

Universities and Evening Colleges

There is some difference of opinion among university extension, evening college, and public adult school administrators as to whether courses carrying credit toward a degree or a diploma properly fall in the category of public affairs education. Many tend to think of public affairs programs as only those programs which are non-credit and focus attention on specifically current public issues. This may well be a false distinction, however. If the concern of public affairs education for adults is the development of an intelligent and responsible citizenry, whether such development results from credit or non-credit courses is clearly irrelevant. The vast majority of the clientele in these programs are past twenty-one years of age—the median age for extension students nationally, for example, was thirty-four years of age in 1953 and is probably higher today. Furthermore, many of the adults enrolled in credit courses are not concerned with credit. Actually, it is more than possible that many of the credit courses for adults in the social sciences do the most serious educational job in the area of public affairs in that they are more likely to provide the background and context in which current issues and problems arise. The greatest weakness of public affairs programs generally is their fragmentary nature; the tendency to cover complicated issues in single lectures, the absence of depth and background, and the lack of adequate reading in connection with the problems discussed. Included for our consideration, then, are all courses and programs, credit and non-credit, formal and informal.

The following table from Morton's *University Extension in the United States* reports the number of persons served by university extension activities in the fields of World Affairs, Economic Understanding and Political Understanding as reported by twenty-eight universities.[1]

Extension Activities	Number Reporting	World Affairs	Economic Understanding	Political Understanding
Extension classes	25	9,249	18,450	9,753
Correspondence study	19	8,006	10,572	9,914
Audio-visual aids	16	919,665	603,662	615,409
Library services	11	37,352	19,107	88,986
Conferences	25	21,534	36,967	12,739
TOTAL		995,806	688,758	736,801

By far the greatest number reached in each activity were through audio-visual aids, which included films and television. These figures are probably not as reliable as those for the other activities. The amount of actual time varies considerably among the different extension activities.

Of the 2,471 courses offered by the reporting institutions in the social sciences which could be considered public affairs education, 91.4 per cent were for credit and only 8.6 per cent were non-credit or informal programs. Comparable courses offered through correspondence numbered 1,107. Of these, 12.5 percent were non-credit or informal programs.

Approximately 16 per cent of all university conference activities concerned questions dealing directly with the public interest and welfare. Twelve per cent were concerned with the improvement of government services. In university broadcast programs, current events programs were second only to music in frequency.

The Morton study provides the most comprehensive data available on university extension nationally. It was published in 1953, however. To obtain more recent data, and some indication of current trends for this chapter of the Handbook, a brief questionnaire was sent to educational institutions and national organizations. Of the eighty-six reporting universities or colleges, sixty-three indicated that they offered educational programs for adults in public affairs. But even among the twenty-three answering in the negative, the majority offered some evening courses in economics, world affairs, or politics, the reason for the negative response being the confusion alluded to above as to what constitutes public affairs education. These were all credit courses and were therefore not considered by the respondents to fall into the category of public affairs education. Only forty-two of the institutions regarded the sponsorship of public affairs educational programs as one of their primary objectives.

As to the areas of public affairs in which the institutions were most interested and to which they paid most attention, the replies were as follows:

Public Affairs Area	Number of Reporting Institutions
International Affairs	38
Political and Legislative Problems (National and Local)	37
Social Problems (Delinquency, mental health, civil rights, housing, community development, etc.)	30
Citizenship and Leadership	28
Economic Issues	23

The following type and number of programs per year were offered:

Type of Program	No. of Institutions Reporting Them	Average Number of Programs Annually			
		Up to 10	10 to 50	Over 50	Varies Yr. to Yr.
Classes	52	16	17	9	10
Conferences or Workshops	45	20	13	5	7
Lectures	43	14	11	8	10
Television or Radio	26	13	4	5	4
Correspondence	23	9	4	4	6
Residential	19	11	2	1	5
Other (including discussion groups)	13	3	3	3	4

There was great variation in the number of adults reached, depending on the size of the institutions, the population centers in which they operated, and whether or not radio or T.V. was used. Twenty-one reported under 1,000 enrollments or participants in their public affairs programs. Nineteen reported from 1,000 to 5,000; seven from 5,000 to 10,000, and ten institutions reported that they served over 10,000 adults annually. Among the latter were four which reported over 100,000 reached annually. Excluding T.V. and radio programs, few of the universities reached more than 10,000 persons in their total public affairs programs and the majority served less than 5,000.

Of the sixty-two institutions which provided information on the financing of their adult programs in public affairs, twelve reported that the participants pay the entire cost and six reported that they pay none of the costs. Fifteen reported that direct costs only were paid by participants; thirteen reported that they paid up to 50 per cent of the costs, and sixteen that the adult paid from 50 per cent to 95 per cent of the costs. Where the entire costs were not borne by the students, institutional budgets and local or state appropriations financed the programs in most cases. Seventeen institutions also received foundation grants or other contributions for their public affairs programs.

Asked to indicate the programs in which there had been the greatest interest, the institutions replied as follows:

Public Affairs Area	No. of Institutions
International Affairs	26
Political and Legislative Problems	24
Economic Problems and Issues	18
Social Problems	17
Citizenship and Leadership	12

Although there was considerable range of opinion among the respondents as to which subjects in public affairs would be most crucial in the coming years, and to which they would most like to devote attention, were adequate financing available, there was a fair degree of unanimity as to the major areas. These were:

Public Affairs Area	No. of Institutions
U.S. National and Local Political Affairs	46
International Affairs	35
Social Problems	24
Economic Problems	21
Community Development and Urban Problems	21

Those universities having specialized institutes, centers, or bureaus in particular public affairs areas, such as world affairs, industrial relations, citizenship, community development, etc., tend to do an especially good adult education job in those fields. This is undoubtedly due in part to the fact that the administrators of these programs tend to be subject-matter specialists in the fields being offered, as well as in adult education. The extension division at the University of Minnesota, for example, through its State Organization Service, administers the Minnesota World Affairs Center which is composed of more than two dozen state associations. The center is a clearing house for organizations interested in world affairs. It stimulates them to more and better-planned activities and supplies them with program services, speakers, pamphlets and visual aids. The center takes no position on issues, although many of its members do so. The staff of the center, headed by a professor of political science in the university, works closely with the officers of its member organizations, which carry on a wide variety of programs and services, such as reception of foreign visitors, exchange of pen-friends, lecture series, education about the United Nations, and promotion of foreign trade. For the most part, the center works through existing organizations in the state, but from time to time arranges special programs and institutes when it appears there is interest in a subject which can only be met through the resources of the university. The center also operates a pamphlet shop which in the year 1958-59 distributed or sold 36,449 pieces of literature on world affairs.

In addition to the activities of the World Affairs Center, the extension division offers credit and non-credit courses, institutes, and lectures on world affairs and distributes hundreds of films. Through the university's radio and television station five programs are broadcast each week on world affairs, exclusive of news broadcasts, reaching an audience of approximately 50,000.

Another example of specialized programs are those offered by the institutes of industrial relations which have been established at more than a dozen universities since the war. In addition to their research projects, most of these institutes offer educational programs to management groups, labor unions, and the general public on labor-management problems, grievances and arbitration, the state of the national economy, and other related subjects.

Still a third area is community development. A number of universities, such as Washington, Nebraska, and Illinois, have established special bureaus in their extension divisions, where services are provided to help communities study, identify, and solve local problems.

A significant development in university public affairs programs in recent years has been co-operative programs with such organizations as the Fund for Adult Education, the U.S. National Commission for UNESCO, the American Foundation for Continuing Education and the Foreign Policy Association. In co-operation with the American Foundation for Continuing Education and the Fund for Adult Education, for example, several dozen university extension divisions and evening colleges have developed adult discussion groups on foreign affairs, economic problems, educational issues, and national political problems. University

Extension, University of California, has developed the largest of these programs. In 1958 it conducted more than 200 discussion groups with enrollments exceeding 5,000 in such subjects as World Politics, American Foreign Policy, Russian Foreign Policy, American Democracy, Great Issues in American Politics, Economic Reasoning, and others. Five groups were also developed for labor union members, with a total enrollment of 136. These discussion groups were in addition to other University of California extension programs in public affairs, including 75 classes, 50 conferences, 10 television programs, 35 correspondence courses, and 35 residential programs. These programs reached hundreds of thousands of California citizens.

Public Schools

Public school adult programs are so numerous and widespread it was not possible to secure up-to-date, representative data on their current public affairs offerings. The most comprehensive data available are provided in *A Study of Urban Public School Adult Education Programs* published by the National Education Association in 1952. The study reported that in the five-year period, 1946 to 1951, there had been an average increase for all reporting schools of 428.1 per cent in civic and public affairs activities in public school adult programs. This was the largest increase reported for any field. The increase was largest in the large cities, 597.6 per cent. It was 193.7 per cent in middle-sized cities and 70.9 per cent in small cities. "This may be indicative", states the study, "of a nation-wide swing toward an enlarged concept of adult education which would embrace community, national, and world affairs. It may also point to national acceptance of a new responsibility for public school adult education—helping adult American citizens achieve greater competency in their activities as citizens and leaders in the world community."

Thirty per cent of the cities reported classes or activities in the category "Civic and public affairs forums, informal classes, other groups." In this study too, however, as the authors indicate, there was some confusion as to what constituted public affairs education. Sixty-five per cent of the cities reported classes in "general academic education," which included social science courses dealing with public affairs. The number of classes and activities in the "civic and public affairs" area constituted 4.6 per cent of the total number of classes and activities offered in sixteen curriculum areas. On the other hand, the enrollments in this area were 22.4 per cent of all enrollments, the largest of any of the sixteen areas. Nor did they include the enrollments in the social science courses reported in the "General Academic Education" curriculum area. It must be remembered, however, that forums accounted for a considerable percentage of the "civic and public affairs" area enrollments. The number of contact hours per enrollee in forums is normally less than in classes, nor are there required readings.

The data reported above clearly indicate a great increase in public affairs programming in public school adult education. While it was indubitably due in part to the increased interest in public affairs in the country, it is also a reflection of the increased importance which public school adult educators attach to public affairs education. Respondents in the study indicated that they considered "civic responsibility" one of the three major goals of adult education. "To make adults aware of their civic responsibilities to one another and to the community, the nation and the world," was reported in 26.6 per cent of the replies as the one major goal of adult education; and as one of the three most important goals in 61.1 per cent of the replies.

Although more current data are not available, examination of a sampling of public school adult education brochures indicates that public affairs offerings have continued to increase since 1951, in some cities by as much as 200 per cent.

Space permits but two brief examples of public school programs in public affairs. Both are in average-size American cities. One is the Springfield Public Forums sponsored by the Springfield, Massachusetts, Public Schools. These forums have been conducted continuously since 1934. They have been notable for the distinguished lecturers they have brought to Springfield and the co-operation of the public library, which has regularly provided reading lists and special book shelves. In 1958 their speakers included Senator Fulbright, Ambassador Abba Eban, Congressman Judd, Professor Hans Kohn, Randolph Churchill, Victor Reisel and Norman Cousins. The subjects included "Where Do We Stand in Our Domestic Policy?," "Issues of American Foreign Policy," "Britain and the World Today," and "Must We Conform?" Attendance at these forums frequently exceeds 5,000 annually.

The Santa Barbara, California, Public Schools sponsor especially imaginative classes and lecture programs in public affairs. In a recent year their classes included "Transition and Tension in Southeast Asia," "The New Industrial Revolution," "Great Issues in American Politics," "Ethics in a Business Society," and "Local Affairs Are Your Affairs."

Public Libraries

Public libraries have long played an important role in public affairs education. In a document setting forth the aims of public librarians in the United States as reported in the Social Science Research Council study, *The Public Library in the United States*, "Public Affairs; Citizenship" is listed first among the "Fields of Knowledge and Interest to Which the Public Library Should Devote Its Resources." The objectives of the public library in this area, states the document, are:

a. To awaken interest, stimulate reading and discussion on crucial problems.

b. To improve people's ability to participate usefully in activities in which they are involved as citizens of their communities, the United States, and the world;

c. To help people develop a constructively critical attitude toward all public issues and to remove ignorance regarding them;

d. To promote democratic attitudes and values, i.e., sensitivity toward people of other backgrounds by knowledge concerning them and by appreciation of the dignity of the individual person; preservation of the precious heritage of freedom of expression; and understanding of the democratic processes of group life.

In terms of future emphasis, the document recommends that "librarians should change the intensity, the duration, and even the nature of their services so that they will contribute directly to the solution of the crucial problems of our time."

To obtain current data on the adult education activities of public libraries, Mrs. Grace T. Stevenson, Deputy Executive Director of the American Library Association, sent questionnaires to a selected group of 110 libraries. Fifty-nine of these were returned. Approximately a third were from communities with populations under 100,000. More than half the reporting libraries provided books, materials and booklists on public affairs. Twenty-five offered group programs including lectures and discussion groups. Eight sponsored radio or television programs on public affairs and nineteen provided films. Forty-four libraries co-operated with and provided services to outside groups and organizations.

Many libraries across the country have sponsored discussion groups on public affairs utilizing the materials of the American Foundation for Political Education, the Foreign Policy Association, the Fund for Adult Education, and the Public Affairs Committee. The New York Public Library, to cite but a single example of these programs, offered in co-operation with the Foreign Policy Association, a lecture and discussion program on India. Special materials were acquired and special staff were assigned. Books, pamphlets, booklists, films, slides, and pictures were used. In addition to lectures and panel discussions, small group discussions were held in connection with the subject. Similar programs on Africa and China were requested and are being planned.

Voluntary Organizations

Many national and local voluntary organizations sponsor public affairs educational programs for adults. In some instances these activities are their primary goals, in others they are part of a larger program of social, economic, civic, or fraternal purposes.

Sixty-eight national organizations returned brief questionnaires inquiring about their public affairs programs. These included educational, civic, women's, religious, labor, minority-group, business, farm, and health organizations. More than two-thirds of those replying (48) indicated that they offer educational programs for adults in public affairs. Forty stated that the sponsorship of such programs is one of their primary objectives.

The following are the areas in which the responding organizations were most interested:

Public Affairs Area	No. of Organizations
Social Problems	32
International Affairs	29
Economic Problems	25
Citizenship and Leadership	22
Political and Legislative Issues	18
All areas	6

The types of programs offered were as follows:

Conferences or Workshops	45
Television or Radio	31
Lectures	29
Classes	12
Residential Programs	5
Correspondence Courses	2
Others (including discussion groups)	10
Publications	6

Eight of the organizations having public affairs programs reported that they either had no records or could not estimate the number of adults reached by their programs. Fourteen indicated that they reach under 5,000 adults annually. Six served between 5,000 and 25,000; nine between 25,000 and 100,000; eleven organizations reported serving over 100,000 adults annually through their public affairs programs. These usually included television or radio programs.

Methods of financing these programs varied considerably. Ten organizations reported that the participants paid the entire costs; thirteen that they paid none of the costs. Among the remainder, participants paid part of the costs. In those cases where the organizations paid all or part of the costs, they received their funds from dues or donations or, in the case of seven organizations, from foundation grants.

The areas in which greatest interest was demonstrated by participants were:

Public Affairs Area	No. of Organizations
International Affairs	18
Social Problems	18
Economic Problems	14
Citizenship and Leadership	10
Political and Legislative Problems	5

The respondents viewed the following areas as those most likely to be crucial in the coming years and to which they would most like to devote attention were adequate financing available:

Public Affairs Area	No. of Organizations
Social Problems	39
International Affairs	36
U.S. National and Local Political Problems	35
Economic Problems	12
Community Development and Urban Problems	7

There were more replies to the latter question in the different categories than to the previous one because most of the organizations tend to offer programs in but one or two areas, and they were there reporting on actual programs in which there was the greatest interest. The significant proportionate difference is the large number of organizations (35) reporting that they believed political problems would be most crucial in the coming years, in contrast to only five reporting that area as one in which the greatest interest had been demonstrated by participants. It was in this area too, that there was the greatest difference in the replies of the universities to the two questions. The other difference between interest of participants and the issues viewed as crucial by both the responding universities and the national organizations was in the area of community development and urban problems. No university or voluntary organization reported this as one of the greatest areas of interest on the part of participants; but twenty-one universities and seven organizations viewed this as one of the crucial public affairs areas in the future.

The following are some of the major national organizations engaged in public affairs education for adults and a brief description of their activities:

American Association for the United Nations.

Offers educational programs on the United Nations and the role of the United States in the U.N. Provides speakers and sponsors workshops. Reaches a membership of approximately 40,000 throughout the country, as well as many times that number of nonmembers.

American Association of University Women.

Provides programs on international affairs, economic and social issues, educational problems, mass media, and legislative issues. The programs are offered through A.A.U.W.'s 1,500 branches to a membership of approximately 145,000.

American Federation of Labor-Congress of Industrial Organizations.

Conducts programs for labor union members dealing with public education, political issues, farm problems, conservation, power, etc. Many of the affiliated international unions also offer educational programs to their membership dealing with public affairs, notably the International Ladies' Garment Workers Union, the United Auto Workers, and the United Steel Workers of America.

American Friends Service Committee.

Sponsors lectures, conferences, and workshops devoted to peace and international relations, race relations, and civil liberties. These programs reach approximately 40,000 adults throughout the country.

Council for Christian Social Action, United Church of Christ.

Provides lectures and conferences on race relations, international affairs, economic issues, civil liberties, and social welfare to approximately 25,000 adults.

Foreign Policy Association.

The oldest and largest national organization concerned with education in world affairs. Has branches in a number of cities and helped form more than 60 independent World Affairs Councils across the country. It publishes semi-monthly the *Foreign Policy Bulletin*, an eight-page analysis of current international affairs, and bimonthly Headline Series pamphlets on foreign policy problems. Its Speakers' Bureau provides program counsel and outstanding speakers on world affairs. In a recent 18-month period the Bureau supplied 746 speakers to as many audiences in 32 states. The F.P.A. also provides program materials and guides.

In 1955 the Association launched the "Great Decisions" program. It is a program to focus citizen attention, for an eight-to-nine-week period, on the principal current issues of foreign policy. Pamphlets, materials and bibliographies are supplied to self-organized adult discussion groups. Materials are also supplied to the local newspapers, radio and television stations. With the help of opinion ballots, individuals are encouraged to express their own views. These ballots are tabulated locally and forwarded to Congress and the State Department. Approximately 425 communities in 34 states participated in 1958. Over 40,000 individuals in approximately 2,400 community discussion groups were involved.

The F.P.A. estimates that it reaches, through all its activities, including radio and television, 100,000 adults directly, and from five to ten million indirectly.

League of Women Voters.

Has chapters throughout the United States. Primary purpose to stimulate interest and keep women informed on political problems, legislative affairs, and other public issues. It is non-partisan and educational. Most chapters sponsor serious study groups in various political and public affairs areas.

National Association of Educational Broadcasters.

Numbers among its membership over 300 educational radio and television stations, production centers and closed circuit TV installations, as well as over 300 individuals engaged in educational broadcasting. Most of the member stations offer programs on public affairs. Some of these are distributed by NAEB Radio Network, which distributes over 1,000 taped educational radio programs a year. Included among the program series produced and distributed by the Association are:— "People Under Communism," "Document: Deep South," "Are National Security and Civil Rights in Conflict," "Atoms for Power," "Voices of Europe," and "Great Lakes: Pathway to Progress." Hundreds of thousands of adults are reached through these programs.

National Association for Mental Health.

Seeks to help people recognize and understand mental illness. Sponsors dozens of conferences and workshops on mental health through state and local associations. It also conducts radio and television programs. It has approximately 500,000 members in state and local associations and many more are reached through mass media.

National Educational Television and Radio Center.

Develops and produces educational television programs on film. Many of these are in the public affairs area. Among the program series recently produced are:— "Decision: The Constitution in Action," "Hats in the Ring" (concerned with election campaigns), "National Agricultural Policy," "America Looks Abroad," "Foreign Aid," "Briefing Session" (A series focussing on significant issues relating to U.S. domestic and foreign policies), and "United Nations Review."

National Farmers Union.

Conducts workshops, television and radio programs on farm policy, international affairs, economic policy, legislative issues, and community problems. Reaches approximately 50,000 adults.

National Grange.

Conducts 150 educational conferences or workshops within states and nine regionally each year. Subjects or areas include local and national governmental problems, farm problems and legislation, foreign aid, power, and trade relations. The Grange estimates 400,000 members attend local meetings and conferences. Their workshop training schools reach approximately 42,000 local officers and leaders.

Public Affairs Committee.

Publishes public affairs pamphlets, approximately sixteen titles a year, on economic problems, social and political organization, intergroup relations, health and welfare, community organization, and civil liberties. The committee reports that it distributes a million and a half pamphlets a year.

Residential Seminars on World Affairs.

Residential Seminars on World Affairs held its first seminar in 1954. Since then 41 seminars have been held which included foreign participants representing 52 countries. More than 25 educational institutions throughout the country have co-sponsored seminars for regional leaders. The seminars are residential in nature and run from three to seven days. They deal with current international issues and require extensive reading in advance of and during the seminar. Each seminar is devoted to a single major issue or subject. Among those dealt with in the recent past are:— "Evaluation of U.S.—U.S.S.R. Relations," "Indian-American Relations," "Rising Influences in Tropical Africa," and "Sovereign Germany Between East and West."

United World Federalists.

The purpose of the organization is to achieve world peace through such amendments of the United Nations Charter as will develop the United Nations into a world federation with necessary power limited to the establishment and maintenance of law and order throughout the world. It has more than 200 chapters throughout the country. Lectures, study groups, and conferences are conducted through the chapters on the strengthening of the United Nations, the World Court, foreign aid, and disarmament. The organization estimates that it reaches approximately 50,000 adults annually through these programs.

CONCLUSION

It is obvious from the above that there has been a great increase in public affairs education for adults during the past ten years. More adults are being reached by these programs than ever before. At the same time, there is little question but that the domestic and foreign issues which will confront this country in the coming years are likely to be more complex and difficult than in the past. The need for a well-informed citizenry will, therefore, be greater than ever.

Great as the growth in programs has been, it is still apparent that public affairs programs represent but a small percentage of the total offerings of adult education institutions and agencies. Furthermore, many of the statistics reported represent brief and frequently superficial contact with adults. They are often single lectures or broadcasts unaccompanied by serious study or reading. Comparatively little research is being done on the quality and impact of public affairs programs for adults. The few studies that have been undertaken are not especially complimentary to the effectiveness of adult education agencies in this area. The study of "A Midwest World Affairs Audience," for example, reports:

> Our findings reveal that interest in world affairs is initiated by a multiplicity of factors, most important of which seems to be an intellectually stimulating family life, and the least important, adult activities or exposure to the mass com-

munications media. To differing degrees, beginning with range of civic interests reflecting a feeling of responsibility to be well-informed, our respondents gradually developed an interest in world affairs. In the process, they became unusual members of their communities, for a majority of Americans, including business and civic leaders, exclude international relations from their range of major interests . . .

Teachers had relatively little influence in creating an interest in world affairs among our respondents; less than 15 per cent could trace their initial interest to an educational institution or stimulating teacher. The mass media and adult meetings and classes were even less effective.[2]

While the growth of public affairs education, then, is heartening, greater emphasis in the future must be placed on its quality, depth, and impact. At the same time, controlled experimentation, research, and evaluation are essential if public affairs programs are to grow in quality and effectiveness as well as in numbers.

Footnotes

[1] John R. Morton, *University Extension in the United States* (University, Ala.: University of Alabama Press, 1953), p.118.

[2] Robert W. and Carolyn P. Hattery, William C. Rogers, and Barbara Stuhler, *A Midwest World Affairs Audience* (Bureau of Government, University Extension, University of Wisconsin, 1959) .

Selected Readings

Almond, Gabriel. *The American People and Foreign Policy.* New York: Harcourt Brace, 1950.

Bailey, Thomas A. *The Man in the Street: The Impact of American Public Opinion on Foreign Policy.* New York: Macmillan Co., 1948.

Barbash, Jack. *Universities and Unions in Workers' Education.* New York: Harper & Brothers, 1955.

Cohen, Bernard C. *Citizen Education in World Affairs.* Princeton: Princeton University Center of International Studies, October, 1953.

Dalgliesh, W. H. *Community Education in Foreign Affairs.* New York: Council on Foreign Relations, 1946.

Grattan, C. Hartley. *In Quest of Knowledge.* New York: Association Press, 1955.

Hattery, Robert W. and Carolyn P., Rogers, William C., and Stuhler, Barbara. *A Midwest World Affairs Audience.* Bureau of Government, University Extension, University of Wisconsin, 1959.

Houle, Cyril O., and Nelson, Charles A. *The University, the Citizen and World Affairs.* Washington: American Council on Education, 1956.

Morton, John R. *University Extension in the United States.* University, Ala.: University of Alabama Press, 1953.

Powell, John Walker. *Learning Comes of Age.* New York: Association Press, 1956.

Urban Public School Adult Education Programs. Washington, D.C.: National Education Association, 1952.

The United States Public and the United Nations. New York: Carnegie Endowment for International Peace, 1958.

CHAPTER 44

ADULT RECREATION EDUCATION

JOSEPH PRENDERGAST
Executive Director
National Recreation Association

INCREASING INTEREST IN RECREATION EDUCATION

Increasing thousands of adults are daily seeking out opportunities to engage in recreation education. They are the young homemakers interested in child care, in interior decoration, in learning sewing, cooking, woodworking. They are adults who have missed the chance of learning how to play golf or tennis, bridge or bowling, or who wish to learn the latest dance step, or to take off weight, or learn to ski, sail or fly cast. They are the middle-aged, whose children have grown up, and who now have the time to discover new interests or re-discover old ones. They are the men and women who find that retirement without inner resources is deadly. They are people who would like to make new friends, to take more of a part in community life, to learn new skills, and to enjoy new activities both as participants and as spectators. They make their own choice, and they participate of their own free will. Their motive is not a point of credit, a certificate, or vocational advancement.

What do these groups select? They choose a choral group, or other music ensemble. They join painting classes, classes in ceramics, in conversational French, in flower arranging, in model building, in music and art appreciation, in acting, poetry, world events, gardening, bridge, golf and tennis instruction, dog obedience classes, and hundreds of other subjects.

Where do they go for such activities? They go where it is convenient to go, where the atmosphere is friendly and informal, where the leadership is stimulating, where the group is congenial, and where the activity is free, or inexpensive. They care very little whether the location is a school, a private agency, a museum, a library, a recreation building, a church, a union hall, or other location.

A QUESTION OF SEMANTICS, MOTIVE, OR SPONSORSHIP

Are such groups recreation or education? In my opinion, they are basically recreation, but this question has become one largely of semantics. Perhaps the distinction between adult education and adult recreation now lies not in the activity but in the sponsorship by school or recreation agency. It is generally accepted now that education need not be formal and dull, or for academic credit, and that recreation does not mean merely games and parties. The objective of each is to add new dimensions to living, to open new doors, to increase capacity for a rich, meaningful life.

The fact that adult recreation education has been allotted seven pages in this book is in itself an indication that the lines between adult recreation and adult education have become increasingly tenuous and flexible.

This point of view was not absent in the 1948 edition of this Handbook. Thomas E. Van Sant, in his chapter, "Public School Adult Education Programs," implied it in his statement:

> . . . For public school adult education leaders realize today more fully than ever before that adult education has become so terrifically consequential that there are literally thousands upon thousands of agencies and organizations that have adult education either as their primary purpose or as a considerably important part of their objectives. And fruitful experience has shown that public schools, while never shirking their ultimate responsibility for the preparation of an informed and trained citizenry, are strongest when they recognize that they are but one of the many fine educational agencies serving the adult public in our democracy.[1]

Malcolm Knowles, editor of this edition of the *Handbook of Adult Education in the United States,* amplified and emphasized this philosophy in a magazine article in 1955:

> . . . I find that in 1950 I wrote, 'A recreational activity is distinguished from an adult educational activity by the purpose of the participant. If an individual participates in an activity for the purpose of learning, for him it is an educational activity; if he participates in it for the purpose of enjoyment, it is recreational.
> . . . I no longer believe this is the difference. I have come to have too much respect for the power of secondary learnings that occur almost without relationship to the primary purpose of an activity.
> . . . I would like to go further, and say that ideally there should be no difference between adult education and adult recreation. My reasoning is that adult education ought always to be recreational, in the sense that it should result in 'genuine satisfaction, creative expression, and the development of powers.' And recreation ought always to be adult education, in the sense that it should yield the highest enjoyment of all, the enjoyment of self-improvement.
> . . . While adult education and recreation may always have some distinguishing difference in flavor, the evidence seems clear that they are closer and closer together in aims and methods.[2]

IMPORTANCE OF COMBINED EFFORTS

The "explosion" in the birthrate of children and the "explosion" of rapidly increasing leisure time of adults are factors that are having and will continue to have tremendous effects upon the schools and all other public and private agencies that have the welfare of the people at heart. Add to these the increasing costs of labor and construction, the mounting public resistance to increased taxation, the problems of land encroachment and increased automation in industry, and it becomes self-evident that duplication of education and recreation services on all levels must be avoided. This means co-operative planning in terms of land acquisition, construction, equipment, facilities, leadership, and program content. No one agency in any community can hope to meet the educational or recreational needs of the community alone. It has become a case of work together and succeed or work alone and fail. The time for quibbling over definitions, the time for arguing over who does what, has already passed. The need is so great that only by combining forces can it be met intelligently and adequately.

Sherwood Gates, Chief of Education, Libraries and Community Services Branch, U.S. Department of the Air Force, emphasized this when he made the following statement:

> . . . As the tidal wave of younger students advances over the next decade, as younger students stretch the capacity of educational facilities to the breaking point, as the growing demand for future technical specialists accelerates, the formal educational opportunities for adults to prepare for and to put their brains to work in the radically new age mankind is entering will become fewer and fewer.
> . . . I suggest to you that many of the lines heretofore drawn between so-called adult education and recreation are false and costly ones. Cooperatively, adult education and adult recreation need to attempt much more serious development of the faculties of our adults.[3]

CO-OPERATIVE PLANNING OF RECREATION AREAS AND FACILITIES

As often happens, co-operative planning between school and municipal authorities on the acquisition, planning, construction, and maintenance of areas and facilities designed for school and community education and recreation use has developed earlier and faster than co-operative planning in terms of leadership and program content. No set, formalized pattern has evolved, but noteworthy methods and results have been obtained in such cities as Minneapolis, Minnesota; New York, New York; Seattle, Washington; Denver, Colorado; Austin and Dallas, Texas; Richmond, Virginia; Oakland, San Francisco and Los Angeles, California; Detroit, Michigan, and many others. Details of such planning have been compiled by George D. Butler, Director of the Research Department of the National Recreation Association.[4]

CO-OPERATIVE PLANNING OF ADULT RECREATION EDUCATION PROGRAMS

Very interesting techniques have been devised in a number of communities whereby programs for adults have been co-ordinated and cooperative action has been delineated. As in the case of areas and facilities, these plans vary, their success hinging upon the imagination and insight of the sponsoring agencies.

In Denver, Colorado, for example, three types of procedure are in effect.

(1) An Opportunity School, managed by the Denver Public Schools, sends teachers into the recreation centers operated by the Department of Parks and Recreation, for classes in sewing, cooking, and the like.

(2) The county agent works under the supervision of the director of recreation, and he sets up extension services for gardening, homemaking, etc., sending leaders into recreation centers to conduct such courses.

(3) A supervisor from the Park and Recreation Department is on the Advisory Committee of the Adult Education Council, which cuts across all agencies.

In addition, in Denver—a very musical city—a Mayor's Advisory Music Committee represents all music interests in spreading the city's music opportunities both by participation and in union contribution. This agency grew directly out of the recreational music program. A Mayor's Advisory Sports Committee accomplishes similar co-ordination in that area. Its constitution provides that the executive secretary of this committee must be appointed by the director of recreation, and is always a supervisor of the Department of Parks and Recreation.

In Waterloo, Iowa—a smaller city—the plan is more informal, but is effective. The Recreation Commission conscientiously tries to avoid competing with either public or private agency programs. For example, it has evolved a policy with its local public school adult education program whereby school offerings tend toward the more formal, academic classes, and its courses more toward the informal, hobby activities. Facilities, too, are a factor. The schools have excellent home economic facilities, so the commission stays away from sewing, cooking, and other such courses. The schools also have better equipped woodworking and metal shops, so the commission stays out of those activities, but offers jewelry-making, pottery, painting, weaving, and other skill and cultural activities. Whenever a question arises, the Recreation Commission and the Board of Education get together and decide who is in the better position to serve the public.

The commission has similar unwritten agreements with the YMCA and YWCA. For example, it does not enter the adult softball and basketball program because the YMCA does a very effective job, but it provides the Y with facilities and maintenance service for this program.

The commission also tries to provide background support to strengthen existing, autonomous hobby groups without interfering with their autonomy. It does this by providing meeting places and workshop facilities, as well as assistance in mimeographing, storage, drayage and the provision of specialized equipment. It also assists in leadership costs, especially when such a group is getting started. It has just helped the Waterloo Arts Council to get launched, and will provide it with leadership and basic house-keeping services as needed. It also is winning the role of the co-ordinating organization for the community, issuing a Special Events Calendar covering the programs of all the community groups.

In Arlington County, Virginia, the mutual respect and appreciation of each other on the part of the Board of Education and the Department of Recreation and Parks has resulted in very harmonious co-operation. As each department expanded over the years, some borderline cases of duplication began to exist. The supervisors in both departments recognized this, and brought it to the attention of the Superintendent of Education and the Director of Parks and Recreation. It was then decided that the supervisors with their staffs should sit down together, discuss both programs, and decide where each activity offered should be placed. As an example of a recent conference of this sort, it was decided that sewing classes should be offered in both, but that the school should offer the Bishop system, the recreation department the standard method, so that the public could have a choice. In art, the school agreed to offer a course in art appreciation for credit; the recreation department would offer all phases of art instruction. In language, the school would offer night courses; the recreation department, day courses for non-working adults. In crafts, the school would offer woodworking and jewelry-making because of special equipment in the school shops, and the recreation department would offer all crafts except those two. In real estate, the school would offer classes designed for persons wishing to pass real estate board examinations, while the recreation department would offer a class primarily for prospective home owners. In creative writing and music appreciation, the school would offer courses for academic credit, and the recreation department would develop interest groups, such as writing clubs, music clubs, and the like.

At the combined staff conferences, besides such decisions, other areas of co-operation are considered, such as standards for instructors, salaries, fees (if any), facilities to be used. Both departments issue attractive brochures about their available programs, and each brochure carries information about the other department's programs. The personnel of each department is trained to answer questions concerning the program of the other.

The basic factor used in Arlington is a simple one. Courses offered by the Public School Adult Education Department are basically for scholastic credit or job improvement. Those offered by the Department of Recreation and Parks are primarily leisure-time activities.

Miami Beach, Florida, has a somewhat similar plan. To avoid duplication, the Recreation Department channels all details through one of its supervisors, who is in constant consultation with the Dade County Board of Public Instruction. This board has a wide program of adult education, but is hampered by lack of funds. In Miami Beach, the Recreation Department supplies the facilities and recruits the classes, while the Board of Public Instruction supplies and pays the instructors. All other adult courses, such as discussion groups, music, sports, art and the like, are conducted by members of the Recreation Department. As the Superintendent of Recreation puts it, "the overall program of adult education and adult recreation is so closely co-mingled that it is difficult to know where one leaves off and the other begins."

ON THE NATIONAL LEVEL

This concern over, and interest in, the cultural life of the nation has finally culminated in a new act of Congress (Public Law 85-874), authorizing a National Cultural Center as a Bureau of the Smithsonian Institution. It will be constructed through funds raised by voluntary contributions, on a site made available in the District of Columbia.

The center will be directed by a Board of Trustees made up of three senators, three representatives, nine public officials and fifteen general trustees appointed by the President.

The act provides that the board shall:
1. Present classical and contemporary music, opera, drama, dance and poetry from this and other countries.
2. Present lecture and other programs.
3. *Develop programs for children, youth and the elderly and for other age groups as well, in such arts designed specifically for their participation, education and recreation,* and
4. Provide facilities for other civic activities at the Cultural Center.

An advisory committee appointed by the President consists of persons who are recognized for their knowledge of, and experience or interest in one or more of the arts.

This official recognition of the arts on the highest governmental level is a momentous event that will have a dramatic effect throughout the nation. Its challenge will reach into every community.

MEETING THE CHALLENGE

The field of adult recreation education is expanding rapidly. Besides the schools, recreation departments, other public and private agencies such as libraries, churches, labor unions, industry, YM and YWCA's, YM and YWHA's, extension departments and the like, it is now branching out into hospitals and institutions, and reaching out to the handicapped and homebound. Its ultimate success will depend largely upon active co-operation and correlation between all the agencies, in order to provide the widest and best service to the public. Its success will also depend upon how intelligently all the agencies can provide depth, as well as breadth to their programs—quality as well as quantity. A public growing rapidly in taste and discernment will not long put up with waste, duplication, and bickering. It will support wholeheartedly, however, those programs based on mutual understanding and planned co-operatively to meet the challenge of modern life. The National Recreation Association has urged this co-operative effort during its past fifty years, and will continue to do so.

Footnotes

[1]Mary Ely, (ed.). *Handbook of Adult Education* (New York: American Association for Adult Education, 1948), pp. 199-200.

[2]Malcolm S. Knowles, "Recreation and Adult Education," *Recreation* (February, 1955).

[3]Sherwood Gates, "Recreational Leaders as Talent Scouts," *Recreation* (June, 1958).

[4]George D. Butler, *School-City Cooperation in the Planning of Recreation Areas and Facilities* (New York: National Recreation Association, 1953).

Selected Readings

Butler, George D. *Introduction to Community Recreation.* New York: McGraw Hill, revised edition, 1959.

————. *Recreation Areas—Their Design and Equipment.* New York: Prentice-Hall, revised edition, 1958.

Dewhurst, J. Frederick and Associates. *America's Needs and Resources.* New York: Twentieth Century Fund, 1955. Chapters 11 and 12.

Neumeyer, Martin H. and Esther S. *Leisure and Recreation.* New York: A. S. Barnes & Company, 1949.

Recreation and Park Yearbook. New York: National Recreation Association, 1956.

School-City Cooperation in the Planning of Recreation Areas and Facilities. New York: National Recreation Association, 1953.

School Grounds Designed for Community Use. New York: National Recreation Association, 1949.

Use of School Buildings for Recreation. New York: National Recreation Association, 1950. (A 1950 study of the experience of 105 cities.)

Zelomek, A. Wilbert. *Changing America, A.* New York: John Wiley and Sons, 1959.

CHAPTER 45

SCIENCE FOR ADULTS

THURMAN WHITE
Dean of Extension
University of Oklahoma

with the collaboration of

HARRY C. KELLY
Associate Director
National Science Foundation

It is now abundantly clear that our lives have entered into a science-based civilization. Swiftly and quietly our environment has become the province of the scientist. What we eat, where we sit, how we travel, and when wars shall end are gifts of science. Better health, more industrial production, satellites, thermo-nuclear weapons, and an incredible array of inventions are the products of science. We like them and we somehow expect science to keep making changes in our environment which, we believe, will improve our lot in life.

The change to a science-based civilization has come with startling suddenness. Forty years ago automobiles were just getting started; airplanes were a novelty; radio and television hadn't been born; homes had no electricity; antibiotics were undeveloped; mass production was mostly just an idea. All of these things are commonplace today and most people seem to assume quite simply that they are a mere prologue to a fantastic shower of new developments during the next forty years.

With so recent an explosion in scientific knowledge, two things seem almost self-evident. The first is that a popular understanding of science is required for the further development of civilization and the other is that adults do not have this understanding.

If scientific discovery had no universality or if it were intrinsically either benign or malignant, the need for an immediate popular understanding would be vitiated. But Conant well makes the case:

> There is an immediate reason for desiring a wider understanding of science in the United States. And if this reason is cogent, we should be concerned with

pedagogic problems of adult education quite as much as with those at the college level. For the argument is a highly practical one related to issues now before the nation.

In a democracy, political power is widely diffused. National policy is determined by the interaction of forces generated and guided by hundreds of thousands if not millions of local leaders and men of influence. Eventually within the limits imposed by public opinion decisions of far-reaching importance are made by a relatively few. These men are almost accidentally thrown into positions of temporary power by the forces working throughout our benignly chaotic system of political democracy. Because of the fact that the applications of science play so important a part in our daily lives, matters of public policy are profoundly influenced by highly technical scientific considerations. Some understanding of science by those in positions of authority and responsibility as well as by those who shape opinion is therefore of importance for the national welfare.[1]

With the yet unsolved riddles of international control of atomic energy and inter-space development hanging ominously above us, such a statement is forceful in the extreme.

The fact that there is no widespread assimilation of scientific discoveries and their application may be directly attributed to the shocking swiftness with which events have come to pass. In the normal course of assimilation, it may take generations for an idea to become a part of the school curriculum and thence a part of people's lives. We need not be surprised if only the career scientists can identify and explain such complex matters as $E = MC^2$. In this equation we see a theory which became an intellectual resource in 1905. In its application, we have seen a war abruptly terminated and more recently we have seen the possibility of commercial application for peace-time prosperity. Its usefulness is the special privilege of the scientist and the technologist; an understanding of its usefulness, of what can and cannot be accomplished with it, is the need of the intelligent citizen. But to suppose that adults generally have a helpful understanding of this and similar matters of science is an obvious absurdity.

A review of current activities in science education must necessarily be impressionistic. No large-scale survey has been made to determine what is being done. Furthermore, such a survey is of doubtful value. The activities are multiplying and diversifying at such a pace that within six months a single survey would be at complete odds with the new situation. There are, however, clearly discernible directions which the brush of social effort has boldly outlined as the primary concerns of the day.

Literally millions of dollars are being spent in the preparation and development of career scientists. Industry is widely aware of the acute need to "hot house" the scientific talent which is presently among its personnel. Most of these efforts have been in the area of applied science where the commercial value makes avid pursuit both profitable and possible. Many companies have working relationships with nearby colleges and universities for graduate programs in engineering, mathematics, and natural sciences. Westinghouse is an example of this approach. Others have developed broadly conceived curricula of their own, but very similar to the usual college and university programs. Western Electric is an outstanding example of this approach. In the case of military installations with tremendous scientific missions, the pattern has usually been for programs with nearby universities. Examples are the arrangements between the Red Stone Arsenal and the University of Alabama and between the Tinker Air Force Base and the University of Oklahoma.

A very considerable effort is underway to find and bring gifted youngsters into science careers. Industry has long been engaged in a variety of isolated projects designed to stimulate interest in science among high school and college students. One of the most effective has been the Westinghouse Talent Search. Only recently has the government seen fit to attack the problem. On September 2, 1958, President Eisenhower signed into law the National Defense Education Act of 1958 which was passed by the 85th Congress. Among its most important provisions, the act makes funds available for the purchase of equipment and provision of facilities for science teachers. This has been hailed as one of the greatest challenges and opportunities in the history of science education. It means that the next generation of adults will not only have a greater number of career scientists but also that most people will have an experimental background in science. The act is a long step toward the assimilation of science into our culture.

By far the most far-reaching governmental effort in the fields of research and the development of scientific personnel was launched with the establishment of the National Science Foundation by Act of Congress on May 10, 1950. This act put the American taxpayer in the position of the world's largest supporter of fundamental, uncommitted research. In describing the functions of the foundation, the Congress made clear its intent as to the type of scientific work to be supported. Among other things, the foundation is authorized and directed:

> to develop a national policy for the promotion of basic research and education in the sciences;
> to support basic scientific research and to appraise the impact of research upon industrial development and the general welfare;
> at the request of the Secretary of Defense, to support specific defense research activities;
> to award scholarships and graduate fellowships in the sciences;
> to foster the exchange of scientific information;
> to maintain a register of scientific and technical personnel and to serve as a central clearinghouse for such personnel;
> to evaluate scientific research undertaken by Federal agencies and to correlate the Foundation's research programs with other such programs;
> to cooperate in international scientific research activities.[2]

Even in the absence of specific data, it is clear that there is an enormous boom in the efforts by industry and government to prepare and develop career scientists. Even so, many fear that the effort is inadequate. If such be the case, it may be attributed to the lack of a general public understanding of science. It is distressingly apparent that no appreciable effort has been made to develop that understanding among the general adult population. For the most part, people have been neglected who are at the heart of a unified, coherent culture—the businessman, executives of industry, lawyers, writers, teachers, clergymen, public servants, mothers, and others of responsible function. Only the faint beginnings can be discerned of what will doubtless become a major segment of the popular adult education movement. A few paperback books have been published; a national TV program for science teachers has been viewed by thousands of non-academic but curious people; public symposia have here and there brought additional thousands into a better understanding of science, and at least one excellent study-discussion guide has been prepared on "Scientists at Work."[3]

While it is impossible to project these extremely sparse data into the specific dimensions of future programs, it is possible to construct a general picture. The principal characteristic of the picture can be predicted with a considerable degree of confidence. It is: there will be a rapid expansion both in the kinds of science education opportunities for adults and in the number of people who participate in them. The burgeoning interest in science careers among young people will catch the attention of parents; the new industrial productions made possible by scientific discovery and application will capture the fancies of financier and wage earner; the social and economic dependency of an enormous working population in science-based industry will lead the population engaged in services and professions to an appreciation of the significance of science; and the public expenditure of vast sums on scientific effort will arouse the interests of taxpayers. Natural curiosity will lead others to learn more about science, the desire to be helpful in a world chiefly responsive to the forces of science will move others; the chain-reaction set off by "everybody's doing it" will account for the participation of others. And the sustained alertness of adult educators to the needs and desires of their communities will everywhere make opportunities where none existed before.

What will the opportunities be? What will the people learn?

For our purposes, let us attempt an answer to these questions without dwelling on how the opportunities will be structured. We can undoubtedly assume that programs will employ all the well-known and customary methods, with appropriate experimentation with novel approaches. Classes, correspondence study, television, laboratory experiences, and discussion (including some dialectical) will most surely be among the more frequent methods. The choice of method is an important problem but can hardly be successfully attacked in the space of this essay. Let us limit our concern here to the problem of objectives.

The principal proposition of this essay is that, generally speaking, a popular understanding and appreciation of science will occur when adult educators provide opportunities which develop:

(1) A feeling for the historian's story of science.

Science began with the Greeks at about 600 B. C. During the next 300 years, this ancient civilization pursued the invention of science with great vigor. Science historians report that the Greeks invented every major branch of science and every major mode of working in science. For 2,500 years scientists have been working on problems which were invented by the Greeks. These intellectual adventures in science provide a continuous thread of activity throughout Islam and modern Western Christendom.

Conant has proposed the use of historical incidences as a fruitful approach to the scientific education of laymen. He has written:

> Let me now be specific as to my proposal for the reform of the scientific education of the layman. What I propose is the establishment of one or more courses at the college level on the Tactics and Strategy of Science. The objective would be to give a greater degree of understanding of science by the close study of a relatively few historical examples of the development of science. I suggest courses at the college level, for I do not believe they could be introduced earlier in a student's education; but there is no reason why they could not become important parts of programs of adult education. Indeed, such courses might well prove particularly suitable for older groups of men and women.
> The case histories would almost all be chosen from the early days in the evolution of the modern discipline. Certain aspects of physics in the seventeenth and eighteenth centuries, chemistry in the eighteenth and nineteenth; geology in the early nineteenth; certain phases of biology in the eighteenth; others in the nineteenth. The advantages of this method of approach are twofold; first, relatively little factual knowledge is required either as regards to the science in question or other sciences, and relatively little mathematics; second, in the early days one sees in clearest light the necessary fumblings of even intellectual giants when they are also pioneers; one comes to understand what science is by seeing how difficult it is to carry out glib scientific precepts.[4]

(2) An appreciation for the method of science.

This is more than the traditional teaching of steps in problem solving or techniques of research. It is more nearly what Duane H. D. Roller has said in some unpublished lecture notes. With a real feeling for the broad understanding which most adults would find intellectually useful, he said:

> As for methodology, the Greeks gave us four ideas that remain the four major methodological ideas in science. The first of these is the emphasis that science is concerned with natural phenomena, that is that science is concerned with sense experiences with the objects in the world around us. Science then is an activity which always ties itself very closely to the things in this world. Second, science is an attempt to seek beyond the things themselves into the kind of view that we can call abstract today. Thus although science is concerned with explaining the roses that grow on a bush, it tends to explain them by thinking of an ideal rose, that grows not on a bush but in the mind, after which the roses on the bush are patterned.
> The third important element of scientific methodology that came from the Greeks—and this is perhaps the most important of all—is logic. Logic is what enables one to blend together the two views of realism and nominalism into a coordinated whole. Starting with concepts, in a man's possessive mind, one can use logic to derive from these concepts of theories statements that are concerned with the world of nature.

The fourth major scientific tool that comes to us from the Greeks is the belief that mathematics is important in attempting to explain phenomena. Notice I do not say that the tool is "mathematics"; the tool is the *belief* that mathematics is important. We now know, for example, that mathematics existed thousands of years before the Greeks. Indeed we have a clay tablet written in about 1800 B. C., over a thousand years before Pythagoras, with the Pythagrean theorem on it. But what the Greeks do introduce is the belief that mathematics is important and that one should therefore seek mathematical relationships in phenomena, that one should be impressed with certain kinds of things that may pop up in the phenomena, and that one should use mathematical logic in making deductions in the theoretical framework of a science.[5]

(3) A working vocabulary of scientific terms.

It seems likely that scientists speaking two different languages have less trouble communicating ideas than an American scientist speaking to a meeting of company stockholders. This is due in part to the astonishing amount of symbolism in the reports of scientific discovery which provides a universal language in the international community of scientists.

It is also due in part to the lack of a popular experience with the language of science. How do you suppose most stockholders would react to an announcement that "Dr. Proto Type has been voted a 30 per cent increase in salary for his extrapolations on the polymer and cosmic plasma markets."

There is nothing obviously weird about this announcement. Most stockholders would find the reference to markets a sufficient justification for an increase in salary. But with just a small understanding of scientific terms, stockholders would be able to raise questions about the competition in plastics and ask when did the company develop the capability of building fusion plants?

So fundamental is the problem of scientific literacy that adult educators may be well advised to tackle it first. Unless the words make sense, people cannot follow the dialogue of history, read the literature of methodology, or intelligently participate in the public decisions of our time. Considerable imagination for the creation of interesting opportunities in vocabulary growth is called for.

(4) A reasonable amount of scientific knowledge.

No great specialization is contemplated in this proposition. A "reasonable amount" means enough knowledge to applaud and support efforts leading to major break-throughs in the frontiers of science and enough knowledge to deal effectively with the day-to-day contacts with science. In the area of fusion, scientists are making a substantial effort to provide mankind with safe and inexpensive power from hydrogen. This will be a major break-through. The excitement of the chase and the thrill of the capture can be shared by men of good will everywhere with no more than a simple awareness of what is now known, what is sought, and how the scientists have attacked the problem. What is true of fusion in this respect is also true for dozens of major frontiers in science. The task of the adult educator is to give people a chance to learn about these frontiers.

In our day-to-day contacts with science, a reasonable knowledge of science will serve to protect and promote our general welfare. Television ads assure us that the sponsor's product is four times better than brand X and this has been proved by laboratory tests. A broker assures us that we should buy a particular stock because the company has recently leased several thousand acres of potash. A neighbor cautions us against planting a garden until the moon is where the almanac says it should be. The editorial writer arouses our indignation against atomic tests because the fall-out threatens our survival. And so on ad infinitum. What and who shall be believed?

It is not enough for adult educators to aspire to programs which develop critical thinking. This is only one-half of the objective—the behavioral half. The other half is the subject about which people are to do critical thinking. All of the decisions called for in the preceding paragraph are in the natural science area. A lifetime of practice in the subject matter represented by the social sciences and the humanities will not be sufficient to a wise decision on any one of the problems. Knowledge of the natural sciences—not very much, to be sure, but some—is required.

Fortunately, suitable materials for this kind of adult learning are on the increase. Look through the racks of paperback books in almost any drug store and at least a dozen readable volumes on as many different science subjects will be found. Look through the new film catalogues and a similar situation will be found in educational film production. Talk with publishers and producers of educational materials and an impression will grow that an enormous number of items designed for popular consumption are projected. Probably the major task of the adult educator is to design learning opportunities which will exploit the materials at hand and to abet preparation of others.

In this account of science for adults, we have been less factual than impressionistic, and our predictions have a slight exhortative tinge. This reflects the state of science in adult education today. Only during recent decades has science been a necessary learning for all men, to the end that civilization may be advanced. The field has matured so rapidly and become so unbelievably complex in so brief a span that its introduction as a liberal subject into the adult education movement is admittedly a complicated matter. It follows naturally after the introduction of science education on a massive scale into the lives of young people and after an accelerated program of professional development for adult career scientists, mathematicians, and engineers. As a matter of popular continuing education, the understanding of science seems destined to be of major significance. The reasonable expectation is that there will be an explosive expansion in the kinds of programs and in the number of participants. It is expected that the programs most frequently offered will, in one way or another, attempt to develop:

A feeling for the historian's story of science
An appreciation for the method of science
A working vocabulary of scientific terms
A reasonable amount of scientific knowledge

Footnotes

1James B. Conant, *On Understanding Science* (New Haven: Yale University Press, 1947), pp. 3-4.

2*The First Annual Report of the National Science Foundation: 1950-51* (Washington: Government Printing Office, 1952), p. 2.

3Prepared by and available from The Center for the Study of Liberal Education for Adults, Chicago, Illinois.

4James B. Conant, *Op. cit.*, pp. 16f.

5Duane H. D. Roller is professor of the history of science at the University of Oklahoma.

CHAPTER 46

ADULT OCCUPATIONAL EDUCATION

HERBERT M. HAMLIN
Professor of Agricultural Education
University of Illinois

Havighurst has written: "In American society, lifework is the most important single thing about a man. He has been taught to evaluate his worth to society, and sometimes his worth in the sight of God, by the level of his occupation and the quality of his performance in it."[1]

Legal provisions for vocational education were the first educational arrangements the colonies provided. It was required generally in the colonies that children be taught to work productively. Apprenticeship was the medium through which vocational education was provided. The development of mechanics and manual labor institutes to supplement apprenticeship paralleled the development of the American high school. Provisions for education in the professions of the ministry, law, and medicine were made in the earliest American colleges.

As research bearing upon the various occupational fields developed, provisions for teaching the resulting science and technology were made. New professions arose for which education was provided. Technical education was needed. Occupations such as farming, hitherto regarded as unskilled, came to require elaborate training facilities. It was found that private enterprise alone could not provide all of the training needed; the public entered the field with colleges of agriculture and mechanic arts, technical schools, extension services, and programs of vocational education in the public schools.

SCOPE

The continuing education of adults for occupational adequacy is a part of almost every institutional program for adult education. Chapter 16, for example, indicates the broad scope of the educational programs of business and industry, which include in-serve training for the continuous

542

up-grading of the competencies of workers and managers and the provision of special schools for new employees. Chapter 17 shows the colleges and universities offering extension courses and short-term institutes for almost every type of technical and professional worker, including business administrators, engineers, doctors and dentists, lawyers, and teachers. Chapter 18 portrays the massive program of the Cooperative Extension Service in improving the technical competence of farmers and rural homemakers. Chapter 20 points out that the in-service training activities of the local, state, and national governments are so vast that they can only be sampled and that they provide opportunities for occupational education through the entire range of vocational, technical, and professional endeavors. Chapter 24 describes the impressive offerings by labor unions and their allied institutions in the field of occupational education. The comprehensive coverage of occupations by private business and technical schools, correspondence schools, and other proprietary schools in providing education suited to individual occupations is described in Chapter 28. In Chapter 29 the role of the public schools in offering education related to agricultural, business, distributive, and industrial occupations is portrayed. This chapter also indicates that education for the "white collar" occupations is becoming increasingly important in the public schools and that women as well as men are being prepared for occupational responsibilities. Chapter 32 suggests that wide scope of occupational education by the professional societies and other voluntary organizations. Almost every other chapter of the *Handbook* mentions education designed for workers in particular occupations.

We shall always have relatively adequate provisions for occupational education in this country because of the American emphasis upon useful work and the obvious advantages of providing this kind of education. We have not had, and we may never have, equally good provisions for education for citizenship, home and family life, health, and use of leisure.

From the beginning of the growth of science and technology, it has been apparent that their advantages should accrue to adults as well as to children. Vocational educators have nearly always taught adults; bias toward teaching only children and youth has never been strong in this field.

ORGANIZATION AND ADMINISTRATION

Like other forms of organized education, occupational education began as private education. There are still segments of American society who do not regard vocational education as a public responsibility. However, the reasons for public participation in providing it have become increasingly clear:

1. All of us benefit from the productivity and efficiency of workers in

any useful occupation and suffer from their lack of productivity and efficiency.

2. National security and defense require specialized kinds of occupational competence, which are provided readily at public expense in times of crisis.

3. Only the largest corporations provide organized vocational and technical education and they are likely to expect that the schools and colleges will supplement their efforts. They are inclined to object to the expense of preparing workers who can be hired by other concerns which have no training programs. The majority of the workers of the country are employed in homes, on farms, and in small businesses and industries which provide no organized training programs or meager programs.

4. The American people are demanding that their schools be useful and practical. Usefulness and practicality are often interpreted in terms of the increased earning power of those who have been enrolled in the schools. A Roper poll, released to the press on February 2, 1958, when the full effects of the Russian sputnik upon thinking about the schools were being felt, showed that 39 per cent of those polled favored increased emphasis on job-training subjects and technical skills and that only 29 per cent favored increased emphasis upon "broader subjects like English, history, and social studies."[2] Other polls corroborate the Roper findings.

5. Professional education was long ago accepted as a public responsibility. For more than a century the injustice of providing vocational education for one kind of workers, the professional workers, and not providing it for other workers has been argued with telling effects. Gradually the public is extending its concern to the education of all useful workers.

The educational institutions the public has provided have been unready to accept and discharge their enlarged responsibilities in the field of vocational education. The local public schools have been geared to persons under eighteen years of age. Until recently the public institutions for education beyond the high school have largely been four-year colleges and universities. Public junior colleges are increasing rapidly, but they have seldom been set up to provide vocational and technical education. One of the major educational issues facing the American public is: What kind or kinds of institutions are to be set up to provide for those of college age who do not belong in four-year colleges and for adults generally? A major sub-division of this problem is: What provisions for vocational and technical education are to be made in these institutions?

Both the elementary schools and the high schools have important roles in educating for useful work, but they can offer little specialized education for particular occupations. High school students are immature and uncertain regarding their future occupations and often lack opportunities for practical experience related to their training in theory. Exceptions are carefully selected students in agriculture and home economics who often do serious work in the vocational subjects and lay good foundations for success in their life careers. Even in these fields, most vocational education must be provided for persons beyond high school age.

Changes in science and technology bring about apparent and striking changes in the ways in which occupations are conducted. It is usually conceded that vocational, technical, and professional education must be continued as long as workers are active. Many of the most vital and appreciated programs of adult education are programs which assist full-time workers in adapting to change, including change from one occupation to another occupation.

The initiative in introducing public vocational education came from scattered school districts. Some states introduced state-wide programs. The national government assisted first in extending professional education through aid to the land-grant colleges and universities. In 1914 and 1917, national aid to extension in agriculture and home economics and to public school programs of vocational education was provided. In the past thirty years many other national provisions for occupational education have been made. There are now about 300 programs of education in about 200 agencies of the national government, a large part of them providing or aiding some form of adult vocational education. The armed forces have become a major agency for adult vocational and technical education. There are extensive programs for the education of the civilian employees of the national government. Nearly all of the national programs are separately organized and administered. Distinct policies for the various agencies cover their relationships with the states when there are state relationships.

The organizational picture in adult occupational education is one of almost complete confusion. Vocational and general education are not well related. The line between public and private enterprises has not been drawn. Communities, states, and the nation have not worked out arrangements for co-operative sharing of the task. As a result of these confusions, we have many good programs of vocational, technical, and professional education, but they are confined to localities or to particular occupations, while many other localities and many other occupations are unserved. There are many superficial programs, few programs which provide the depth and detail required if workers are to become prepared, and stay prepared, for effective work in modern occupations. As the demand for more and more highly skilled workers grows, and as unskilled workers become less and less in demand, the seriousness of the problem grows.

National studies of manpower needs have drawn attention to the inadequacy of our provisions for occupational education. A new emphasis upon developing all of our human resources is appearing. If our human resources are to be fully developed, a large part of the development will occur in occupational life, which has a first claim upon the time of a large part of our population. We shall be forced to give up our idea that our human resources can be fully developed before individuals reach the age of eighteen or twenty-two years. Development must occur throughout adult life.

PUBLIC POLICY FOR ADULT OCCUPATIONAL EDUCATION

There is obvious need for the development of consistent and sound public policies for adult vocational, technical, and professional education. The basic policy questions, which only the public can answer, are the same for this form of education as for other forms:

1. How is public policy to be made? Who are to participate? How are they to participate? How is policy to be interpreted? How to insure that policy will be executed? How is policy to be publicized?
2. Who are to be served? How? How much? When?
3. What public purposes are to be served?
4. How is the public to determine whether its purposes are being served adequately?
5. What provisions is the public to make for organization, administration, program-planning, staff, funds, and facilities?

These are the questions which must be answered locally and at state and national levels. As much consistency as possible among the answers given at these three levels must be obtained.

The Smith-Hughes Act and the related national vocational education acts are relatively sound policy enactments resulting from long deliberation and much public discussion. They are, however, largely unrelated to other acts of Congress and encourage special and separate organization and administration of vocational education. States participating in the national program of vocational education are required to have state plans consistent with the national vocational education acts. Local policies for vocational education are often nebulous, unorganized, or unwritten.

We shall not have better public policies for occupational education until the policy-making process is greatly improved. The Congress of the United States is not an adequate national board of education; it has too many other concerns; in its long history it has not been able to enact a consistent national policy for education. Much of the policy-making for which Congress is responsible has been delegated to agencies Congress has created. The meaning of national policies often depends upon the interpretations given by minor functionaries. The situation is similar in some of the states. State legislatures are not satisfactory boards of education. State boards of education have better opportunities to develop state policy, but they cannot go beyond the policies for which there is adequate public support and there is often no arrangement for involving the public in decisions about public education. Boards of education in the largest school districts have been forced by the scope and complexity of their operations to have organized policies. Usually, however, their policies for adult education are less satisfactory than their policies for the education of children and youth and often policies for these two areas are inconsistent. In a high percentage of the smaller school districts of the country, the boards of education have not yet realized that their primary function is to make policy and see that it is executed.

We are coming gradually to see that official policy-making bodies, however adequate they may be, are not enough to insure that we shall have adequate public policy for education. The public must support the actions of its official agencies. Policy enactment is a short and easy process. It is the development of policy to enact that is difficult. Policy development requires the participation of many lay citizens other than the members of official bodies and the help of professional educators. Citizens committees are being used increasingly in the development of public policy. School staffs and professional consultants are being involved. Only with wide participation can we get policies which will be accepted, maintained, and defended by the public and the educational profession.

It is quite as important that those who develop and enact policy have and use the facts and considerations which they need. Enduring public policy cannot be based upon opinion and prejudice.

It may be expected that there will be increasing attention to public policy for education arising from two related issues: How are the schools to be financed? How good are our schools? The American public is currently excited about both of these issues. Basic policy questions are often settled in this country when we decide how much money is to be spent and how it is to be spent. All of us have opinions about the worth of the schools. They influence our attitudes toward public policy for them.

We may hope that the present ferment regarding public education will lead to consideration of the basic policy issues which affect adult occupational education, though it may not. Too many citizens still think of public education as the general education of children and youth conducted in and by local school districts. They do not accept a definition of public education as education of the total public. They are unaware of or indifferent to the vast development of adult vocational, technical, and professional education under state and national auspices. We must have an adequate number of citizens who see public education whole and who recognize and attempt to correlate its local, state, and national phases. We must come to realize that adult vocational, technical, and professional education is conducted by the public primarily for the benefit of the public and not for the benefit of individuals, and we must see that it is conducted so that the primary benefits are public benefits. As we develop these attitudes and insights, we shall press for the development of policy for education which makes adequate provision for adult occupational education.

PRIVATE VOCATIONAL, TECHNICAL, AND PROFESSIONAL EDUCATION FOR ADULTS

Dr. Harold F. Clark has shown that expenditures for education outside the regular schools and colleges are greater than the expenditures for the schools and colleges. A high percentage of the expenditures by agencies other than schools and colleges is for adult vocational, technical, and professional education.

Our country and our life would be very different if these agencies did not exist. They translate research into efficiency in production, distribution, and management. They up-grade our workers. They assist workers to adapt to change and to retain and increase their earning power.

We shall always need and always have these agencies outside the schools and colleges. We should, however, recognize their limitations. They do not often provide for an individual a balanced program of adult education. They are necessarily designed for the benefit of the business, the industry, or the organization of workers which provides the education. They must be supplemented by education designed to be in the interest of the general public and the individuals undergoing education.

THE PROSPECTS OF ADULT OCCUPATIONAL EDUCATION

No form of education is growing more rapidly than adult vocational, technical, and professional education. In a recent, unpublished survey by Dr. John Coster of Purdue University, five hundred carefully selected leaders in American life indicated overwhelming support of this type of education. The American people as a whole have been for it. A group who might be classed as "pseudo-intellectual" has been apathetic about education for work or scornful of it. Many of these pseudo-intellectuals have recently appeared in minor positions of leadership in education, on boards of education, and in public discussions of education. Their influence will be transient, for we cannot do without education for work.

Commonly, the enrollments of adults in vocational and technical schools are two to three times the enrollments of the younger, full-time students in the same schools. Vocational education for adults is faring so well that the Ford Foundation has seen fit to limit its subsidies to liberal education for adults.

CURRENT NEEDS

Some of the major current needs have already been indicated. We must have school people who understand the importance of education for work as a part of the total educational program and vocational educators who understand the school systems of which they are a part. There is need for carefully developed, consistent, long-term public policy for vocational education. There must be more rigorous evaluation of the vocational education now provided in terms of the changed conditions in which we now find ourselves. Adequate institutions, well financed and staffed, must be set up generally to provide for the educational needs of older youth and adults, including their needs for vocational education. We dare not leave this kind of education to be an incidental and minor concern of a high school or a business or industry. Occupational counseling for adults must be more general and more thorough. Occupational training must be brought into line with manpower needs. Workers must not be cheated of general and liberal education while their needs for vocational education are provided.

NEW EMPHASES IN ADULT OCCUPATION EDUCATION

The pioneers in vocational education (Prosser, Wright, Cooley, and others) tended to emphasize a narrow, specialized type of vocational education, largely segregated from other forms of education. This emphasis may have been suited to the times, but the times have changed. The modern vocational educator emphasizes the need of workers for broad and basic education, for adaptability, for continued growth through a long working life. He deplores any arrangement which leads a worker into a "blind alley," or narrows his vision, or prostitutes him for others' purposes. He has given up the idea that pre-employment education is all that is necessary and has turned his attention to continuing education. He wants to operate in the main tent, not in a sideshow.

Some of the most realistic thinking and some of the most vital programs of adult education that we have are in occupational education. Other educators need the stimuli and the ideas that are now too often confined within the field of occupational education.

We may anticipate in the next generation a fusion of vocation and general adult education to the benefit of all concerned, but particularly of benefit to the clientele served and the American public.

Footnotes

[1]Robert J. Havighurst, *Human Development and Education* (New York: Longmans, Green and Co., 1953) , pp. 129-130.

[2]National Education Association, *Public Opinion Polls on American Education* (Washington: The Association, May, 1958), p. 13.

Selected Readings

Byram, Harold M., and Wenrich, Ralph E. *Vocational Education and Practical Arts in the Community School.* New York: The MacMillan Co., 1956.

Emerson, Lynn A. *Vocational-Technical Education for American Industry.* Washington: U. S. Office of Education, 1958.

Gold, Milton J. *Working to Learn.* New York: Bureau of Publications, Teachers College, Columbia University, 1951.

Hamlin, H. M. "All Students Benefit from Education for Work," *Nation's Schools,* LXIV (August, 1959), 47-49.

————. "Needed More Than Ever: Vocational Education," *Nation's Schools,* LXI (March, 1958), 44-46.

Hawkins, Layton S., Prosser, Charles A., and Wright, John C. *Development of Vocational Education.* Chicago: American Technical Society, 1951.

Keller, Franklin J. *Principles of Vocational Education.* Boston: D. C. Heath and Co., 1948.

McCarthy, John A. *Vocational Education: America's Greatest Resource.* Chicago: American Technical Society, 1951.

Prosser, Charles A., and Quigley, Thomas H. *Vocational Education in a Democracy.* Chicago: American Technical Society. Revised, 1949.

Roberts, Roy W. *Vocational and Practical Arts Education.* New York: Harper and Bros., 1957.

Vocational Training Directory of the United States. Arlington, Virginia: Potomac Press, 1958.

PART V

THE FUTURE OF ADULT
EDUCATION IN AMERICA

CHAPTER 47

PRESENT TRENDS AND FUTURE STRATEGIES IN ADULT EDUCATION

PAUL H. SHEATS
Dean
University of California Extension

Trend analysis and prognostication, especially in the field of adult education, are fraught with considerable risk and peculiarly subject to human error and personal bias. Editors of earlier *Handbooks,* perhaps wisely, contented themselves with descriptive entries—leaving to the reader the task of synthesis and extrapolation.

Despite these considerations, the writer has undertaken the assigned task with a view to stimulating what has been called in this book "the continuous philosophizing" about adult education—its purposes, its organizational characteristics, its programs, and its methodology. This process, which has characterized the field throughout its history, must continue as the only truly reliable instrument for determining future trends and strategies. The day may come when adult education will be comfortably institutionalized, generously financed, and securely established in the hearts and minds of a definable constituency. But, in spite of the impressive evidence of quantitative growth and diversification of programs which this *Handbook* reveals, this day has not yet arrived. The dialogue must continue, the debate must go on in the faith that from this sharing of ideas and experience, from this application of creative intelligence to the issues before us, will emerge "the wise leadership of the wise" upon which the future of adult education and our social system depends.

AIMS AND OBJECTIVES

There seems relatively little risk that practitioners in the field of adult education will be seduced from their preoccupation with the day-to-day business of "getting on with the job" by the siren call of the philosopher.

Preoccupation with the "urgent" often forecloses consideration of the "important"—a distinction which Lyman Bryson made in the 1948 *Handbook*.

There is little evidence in the pages of this book of dissatisfaction with this state of affairs, but observers from related fields have been more critical. The marginality of adult education in the established institutional structure of our society has been ascribed in part to its "aimlessness," to its open-ended and opportunistic "service" approach, to its "cafeteria" offerings of whatever the public demands, to its policy of drift and the absence of goal-directedness. Educational objectives, when stated, are expressed in such general terms as to be meaningless or at least beyond the reach of scientific evaluation and measurement.

Even a less critical view would have to take cognizance of the multiplicity of purposes which motivate the diverse programs and activities described herein. And yet, in spite of this diversity, a comparison of the contents of this *Handbook* with its predecessors discloses, by implication at least, a growing awareness of the philosophical choices now before us.

By way of example, there appears to be some realignment of views on the historical issue over whether adult education should be focused on the meeting of individual needs or developed as an instrument of national policy. Author after author in the preceding pages testifies as to the growing strength of community-centered adult education, as to the need for a union of education and action, and as to the importance of using the resources of adult education agencies to improve the quality of decision-making. The concept of adult education as an instrument of planned social change is heralded as the sign of a new era. A survey is reported in which two out of three respondents see a swing toward community and family improvement as the chief characteristic of the current movement.

It is important to emphasize that this philosophical shift is primarily a rejection of subject-centered instruction rather than of the values of individuality or the importance of personal growth. In fact, by emphasizing behavioral change in the individual as a measure of effective learning it might be argued that individualism is enhanced rather than diminished. Education is a means not an end. Improvement in communication, it is argued, will facilitate personal growth as well as raise the level of problem-solving and citizen decision-making by reducing resistance to new knowledge and social change.

One illustration will have to suffice. Publicly supported agencies of adult education, and many voluntary associations as well, have carefully avoided partisan affiliations, have prided themselves on their ability to avoid entangling alliances which might corrupt the purity of the offerings which they sponsor. Yet, the party system in the United States is the cornerstone of our elective system. Unless the political process can in fact be made an educative process as well, there seems little hope of modifying the current stereotype of "politics" and the "politician" and even less chance of channeling into our party system desperately needed knowledge on both the political process itself and on the national and local issues which party leaders must interpret and explain.

If the shift of emphasis toward adult education for social change does in fact represent a trend, it would be interesting to speculate further as to the cultural and environmental influences which may have effected this result. There is clear evidence, for example, that the newly developing countries of the world are giving central, not peripheral, attention to adult education as a major instrument for achieving national goals and implementing national policies. So-called advanced countries may, in this respect, be more backward than their newer contemporaries, through failure to utilize effectively the instruments of popular education.

Moreover, reluctant as most of us are to use the Soviet Union as a whipping boy for our own mistakes, and inadequate though existing data may be, there seems to be no problem of marginality for adult education enterprises in that country. Admittedly, as has been pointed out in an earlier chapter of this *Handbook,* adult education can be used as an instrument of national control and enforced uniformity. Whether, in a free society, it can be used to implement planned social change without destroying creative initiative and individual responsibility would thus seem to be one of the major issues of our time.

ORGANIZATION AND FISCAL SUPPORT

Few social movements in this country's history have established so important a role and involved so many people in the scope of its activities as has adult education. This has come about in spite of the absence of an institutional structure specifically designed for the operation of an adult education enterprise and without benefit of a clearly definable constituency. Fragmented, unco-ordinated, deprived of adequate fiscal support, low on most lists of educational priorities claiming national attention and causing public concern, the field of adult education is an anomaly in American society. It flourishes in the face of adversity, it grows on a starvation diet, it thrives even on barren soil.

It has been alleged that half of the people engaged in adult education work don't even know it by that name. The great bulk of adult education activities occur under the auspices of institutions created for other purposes. Only a few universities and colleges recognize adult education as an area for which professional preparation should be provided. Even within the educational family it is often regarded as a stepchild of somewhat questionable status. For thirty years it has been the object of pious hopes and wishful declarations in official reports on education in the United States, but even today it receives only .03 per cent of the gross national product.

What then are the trends and issues with which we are confronted?

1. *Can adult education achieve anything like its full potential in American life without the creation of more institutions specifically designed to meet the educational needs of adults?* Or stated in another way, is there any justification for the hope that existing agencies whose primary responsibility is to other constituencies will accept responsibility for adult education on other than a marginal basis?

The evidence in the preceding chapters suggests that while we have some pessimism as to the answer to the second question, no noticeable trend toward the creation of new institutions can be identified. Moreover, there is little comfort in the record of the past ten years for those who believe that until a large and unified constituency for adult education is created, the organizational problems of the field cannot be resolved.

This situation is in marked contrast with developments in certain other countries. For example, in the State of Victoria, Australia, a deliberate effort to create such a constituency within a specially designed institutional framework has achieved considerable success, including direct fiscal support to a statutory body known as the Council of Adult Education. The council is broadly representative of both public and private adult education interests in Victoria and maintains liaison with its constituency through the Adult Education Association of Victoria which is represented on the council.[1] In the field of university adult education there is the further example of the role played by the Workers Education Association in winning public support for adult education both in Britain and in a number of the Commonwealth countries.

May not one of the possible strategies for the future be the exploration of and experimentation with a new organizational approach to the provision of educational opportunities for adults? Granted that by tradition we are skeptical of efforts to provide public support for private bodies (as is the common practice in the Scandinavian countries, for example) a combination of public and private funds might be possible at least for a trial effort, possibly along the lines of the Victoria model referred to above.

The alternative is to seek a more central role for adult education in existing institutions. In two of these, the public schools and the universities and colleges, the pressures induced by the growth in the number of school and college age youth will make this task difficult in the decade ahead.

2. *Is there a trend toward more effective co-ordination of effort in the field of adult education?*

This question requires analysis on three dimensions. It includes co-ordination between and among adult education agencies at the local, state, and national levels. It involves co-ordination between professional and lay personnel within the field. And it should include the problem of co-ordination between professionals in the field of adult education and their colleagues in related disciplines, particularly the social sciences.

Whether, on the basis of discussions in previous chapters, one considers the trend favorable or unfavorable in respect to this problem is a kind of Hobson's choice. There seems to be general agreement on the desirability of these objectives and some evidence of progress, at least for the national level, on all three fronts. However, any realistic appraisal of progress would have to include the judgment that movement toward co-ordination is slow, that competition for the clients' leisure hour is more characteristic of the local scene than co-operation in the development of a well-rounded total program consistent with the ideal of an educative community. It is doubtful if much more can be expected without a clarification of goals and more fiscal support for unified planning and co-operative programming.

3. *Is the fiscal base for adult education activities being improved?*

Those who wish may take such comfort as they can find in the evidence of increasing dollar support for adult education. But even the confirmed optimist must admit that dollar-wise the field has a low level of priority in the competition for both public and private funds. Moreover, past gains offer no security. Few indeed are the communities where a committed and powerful constituency speaks with a loud clear voice at budget-making time in behalf of the required investment in adult education.

Organized attacks on public support are usually oblique: adult education is always a good thing—in fact it is so good that the consumer should be willing to pay for it. This, in spite of the studies which show a direct relationship between the level of public support and the size of the clientele reached and the realtively low average income levels of the population served.

Even more remarkable is our failure to capitalize on the classic case of agricultural extension. Approaching as we are the one hundredth anniversary of the Morrill Act, with almost half a century of experience behind us with the Cooperative Extension Service, the dramatic evidence of what this investment in adult education has done for agricultural production is common knowledge. In fact, the demonstration has been so successful that it is now costing the taxpayer half a million dollars a day just to store the fruits of our increased productivity.

Yet, the lesson has remained unlearned. The perception of public expenditure for adult education is still primarily a negative one: Funds so spent are a drain on the public treasury rather than an investment in human resources which will be repaid a thousand fold. It would be comforting to report that this problem of fiscal support is being resolved or that private agencies are taking up the slack. No such conclusion seems warranted. Without additional support, the American dream of opportunity for every one to develop his potentialities to their maximum simply cannot be fulfilled.

PROGRAMS AND METHODOLOGY

The roll call on institutional programs in adult education as set forth in the table of contents of this *Handbook* is impressive. The only group which might conceivably feel slighted is the "Beatniks." A reading of the chapters seems to suggest that over the past decade there has been increasing attention to the areas of home and family life education, health education, and religious education. There has been a sizeable expansion in the adult education activities of governmental agencies, in business and industry, and in trade unions.

Progress in the use of the mass media to undergird face-to-face methods has been made and the limitations of the former more clearly described. The hottest issue in this area arises in connection with the educational use of television and the extent to which it may be used to supplant the more traditional methods of instruction and the face-to-face relationship between teacher and learner. Encouraging in this connection are the results of recent experimentation in several areas with multiple use of media to reinforce learning in small groups. Here again, those who believe the central purpose of adult education is to bring about behavioral change in the learner rather than to impart information as an end in itself are most reluctant to replace face-to-face methods with mass communication techniques.

Considerable optimism is reported as to the progress being made in narrowing the gap between vocational and liberal education for adults— an optimism not entirely shared by this writer. Whether we may in fact anticipate "a fusion of vocational and general education" and a new approach "to continuing education in its broadest terms" seems doubtful in view of the increasing domination of science and technology in our national life. The sheer magnitude of the task which adult education must undertake of developing the technical and professional skills which will be required if projected manpower needs are to be met seems to insure that vocationally and professionally oriented programs will continue to expand often at the cost of opportunities designed to take advantage of increased leisure and longevity for the cultivation of the individual.

Most hopeful in this situation is the evidence of growing public interest in the liberal arts, growing awareness of the superficiality of a predominantly work-oriented culture. It may be too early to call this development a trend, but the corrective to increasing specialization, to "otherdirectedness," to the "organization man," may well come through an expansion of offerings in the arts and humanities where the wellsprings to nourish man's search for meaning and significance are to be found.

Paralleling this trend and motivated by many of the same considerations is the growing interest in and support for community development programs. From a stage in which operations were limited to small and predominantly rural communities, procedures have been improved and refined for effective use in urban settings as well. Here again, a central purpose is to counteract citizen apathy and withdrawal from civic responsibility by teaching the skills of fact-finding, analysis, and action required for efficient problem-solving and effective participation in community life. Community development programs, like liberal adult education, will depend for their expansion in the years ahead on the discovery of a more adequate fiscal base and conceivably upon the invention of new institutional structures unhampered by the trappings of formal instructional agencies.

A major break-through has occurred in the field of learning theory since the last issue of the *Handbook*. The chapters on program development and methods as well as the chapter on learning theory attest to this and, even more surprisingly, reflect a degree of unanimity which most certainly would not have existed a decade ago. Central in this agreement is the importance of the learner in program development and methodology. The learner participates in the setting of learning goals, his needs and experience must be related to the learning process and program plan, a favorable climate must be created in which the learner will find acceptance and recognition, and there must be learner participation in the evaluation of outcomes.

Apparently the ball is now passed to the program administrator—who more likely than not will be attached to an agency the power structure of which is geared to a learning theory evolved for children or adapted to goals which have little relevance to adult education. The resulting incompatibility will certainly not add to the attractiveness of the administrative role and could lead to some early retirements, both voluntary and enforced, in the years ahead.

At least two alternative strategies for the future appear possible. On the hypothesis that learning theory which is good for adult education might have some desirable effects on other segments of education, we can continue to work within the framework of existing institutions, blunting the resistances to change as best we can. Or, alternatively and perhaps simultaneously, we can accelerate the slow process of designing and building the kind of institutional structures in which the knowledge we now have about adult learning and program building can be put to maximum use.

Writers in this volume attest to the growing body of research and to the improvement over the past decade in both the quantity and quality of new knowledge in the field of adult education. The question has been raised as to whether operational assumptions and procedures are being influenced by these new data and some support expressed for the view that "the use of the literature has not kept pace with its development." Similarly, with respect to the training of professional and lay leaders, some improvement is noted; but the total effort is still woefully inadequate and far short of the progress existing knowledge and skill would permit.

There seems no escape, therefore, from the necessity of reviewing critically the nature of the institutional facilities and agencies which have assumed or have had imposed on them the functions of adult education. It may well be that institutions developed many years ago to meet needs unrelated to the requirements of modern society for continuing education have become so rigid and formalized that a remodeling job will not suffice. Should this be the case, new instrumentalities will have to be forged—calling for all the inventive genius of which we are capable. It is an interesting paradox that this dilemma should be unique to the nations with the longest history of adult education. The newly developing countries, on the other hand, are free to start with a clean slate and the experimentation now going on in many of these nations should be part of our own data as we approach this important task.

CONCLUDING OBSERVATIONS

The twelve years which have elapsed since the last edition of the *Handbook* have been productive and exciting ones in the adult education movement. The range of choices open to the individual citizen in occupational selection, in architecture, in mobility, in the communication media, and in artistic experience has been broadened through scientific advance and technology. But only through education can the individual be equipped to choose more wisely from among these multiplied alternatives those activities which will lead to the fulfillment of the potentialities within him.

To this end, the opportunities for personal growth and development have been increased, and the ranks of those who study, organize, lead, and participate in adult education activities have been expanded. Yet, there is a feeling of impatience bordering on frustration which permeates many of the preceding chapters. Perhaps it is characteristic of the field that the leaders in it so frequently reveal this sense of urgency stemming both from social need and the limitations of mortal man. The magnitude of the task to be done and the depth of personal commitment to the importance of the task make us dissatisfied with the rate of progress toward the goal of "a learning society" and "an educative community."

There are respected members of our profession who see the door to a new age opening before us—an age of maturity, a golden age, an age of learning in which by the application of knowledge and critical intelligence the obstacles to social advance can be removed. A distinguished anthropologist has recently called for a whole new approach to education in which the vertical approach to the transmission of knowledge will give way to the lateral sharing of information and skills between and among individuals at all age levels and at various stages in their attainment of a formal education: "We are now at the point where we must educate people in what nobody knew yesterday, and prepare people in our schools for what no one knows yet, but what some people must know tomorrow."

The fate and future of adult education in the United States are inextricably linked with the fate and future of democracy. If democracy is to survive, the concept of lifelong learning must prevail. And so, as has been the case before in the history of adult education, we face the future with a combination of faith, knowledge, and experience; faith in the perfectibility of man and in his ability—despite the increasing complexity of modern life—rationally to control his destiny; knowledge, new and old, from the vast storehouses and laboratories in which our cultural inheritance is preserved and extended; experience with the adult education enterprise in its multiple forms and variations. Thus armed, we approach the tasks before us with confidence, united in the conviction that the lamps of learning must be kept burning brightly if man's upward struggle toward self-realization and social order is to proceed.

Footnotes

[1]For a more detailed report on this program see the author's "A Report on University Adult Education in Australia and New Zealand" (Chicago: Center for the Study of Liberal Adult Education for Adults, 1959).

PART VI

NATIONAL ORGANIZATIONS, ASSOCIATIONS, AND AGENCIES IN ADULT EDUCATION

DIRECTORY OF NATIONAL ORGANIZATIONS, ASSOCIATIONS, AND AGENCIES IN ADULT EDUCATION

Among the many agencies providing services of some kind related to the education of adults, those listed below have been selected to appear in this directory on the basis of the following criteria: (1) relative historical and contemporary significance in the education of adults, (2) demonstrated concern, interest, and involvement in adult education as an organized movement, (3) national scope of activities, (4) provision of direct services or programs in the education of adults, and (5) desire to be listed. Starred organizations participate in the Council of National Organizations of the Adult Education Association. Data regarding membership, purpose, program, and publications are as of October, 1959. The titles of the officers from whom further information can be obtained are given in preference to personal names in order to avoid the confusion that might result from changes in personnel.

ADULT EDUCATION ASSOCIATION OF THE U.S.A. (1951); 743 North Wabash Avenue, Chicago 11, Ill.; Executive Director.

Membership: 5,500 individuals.

Purpose: To further the concept of education as a process continuing throughout life by developing unity of purpose in the adult education movement, by helping individuals engaged in the education of adults increase their competencies, by bringing the agencies of adult education into closer relationship, by making the public more aware of the need and opportunities for adult education, and by serving as a voice for the adult education movement.

Adult Education Program: The association serves as a clearing house of information about adult educational activities throughout the country, and as a referral center for persons or organizations seeking consultation from its members in solving adult educational problems. Its annual conferences every autumn bring together adult educators from the fifty states and many foreign countries to share experiences, work on common interests, and plan for the future. Through its commissions and sections it conducts research and sponsors conferences and workshops on specialized problems. It interprets adult education through the mass media, provides speakers for organizations, encourages meetings with government agencies and other educational organizations, and assists in the organization and development of state adult education associations.

Publications: Adult Leadership, monthly (except July and August), $5.00 a year; Adult Education, quarterly, $5.00 a year; Leadership Pamphlets, 60c each; Adult Education Monographs, $1.00 each; Leaders' Digests, $2.00 each; miscellaneous books and special reports.

* * *

*ALTRUSA INTERNATIONAL (1917); 332 South Michigan Avenue, Chicago 4, Ill.; Publicity Director.

Membership: 16,000 individuals; 500 clubs.

Purpose: Community service by women leaders from diversified businesses and professions, to help solve community and world problems and promote understanding among all people.

Adult Education Program: Service projects are set up for two years at a time and channeled through these committees: international relations, public affairs, and vocational information. Local clubs are urged to sponsor senior citizens' centers, career clinics, forums, traffic safety drives, and programs in nursing homes, hospitals, and homes for the aged. Activities for the public include sponsorship of United Nations Day, Pan American Day, entertainment for international visitors, job forums for older workers, and job counseling by members. Altrusa co-operates with other organizations on the local level in sponsoring community surveys to determine adult educational needs, and on the national level in promoting educational television, citizenship classes for immigrants, and finance forums.

Publications: International Altrusan, September through June.

* * *

AMERICAN ALUMNI COUNCIL (1913); 1785 Massachusetts Avenue, N. W., Washington 6, D. C.; Assistant Director for Type A.

Membership: 942 institutions; 16 other educational organizations.

Purpose: To mobilize behind education the full strength of organized alumni support in all its spiritual, moral, and practical manifestations.

Adult Education Program: Publications and conference programs for the guidance of colleges, universities, and independent secondary schools in developing activities in continuing alumni education.

Publications: American Alumni Council News, eight times yearly; Continuing Education for Alumni, 1958.

* * *

*AMERICAN ASSOCIATION FOR THE ADVANCEMENT OF SCIENCE (1848); 1515 Massachusetts Avenue, N. W., Washington 5, D. C.; Director of Education.

Membership: 58,057 individual members; 285 affiliates; Alaska, Pacific, Southwestern and Rocky Mountain Divisions.

Purpose: To further the work of scientists; to facilitate co-operation among scientists; to improve the effectiveness of science in the promotion of human welfare; to increase public understanding and appreciation of the importance and promise of the methods of science in human progress.

Adult Education Program: A number of sessions at the annual meeting of the association are open to the public. In the past year AAAS has sponsored a national TV series with the National Academy of Science. It now has under consideration plans for the development of a public information service.

Publications: Science (weekly); The General Program Directory (annually); some 50 technical symposium volumes, ranging broadly through the various field of science.

* * *

AMERICAN ASSOCIATION OF LAND-GRANT COLLEGES AND STATE UNIVERSITIES (1887); 1785 Massachusetts Ave. N. W., Washington 6, D. C.; Executive Secretary.

Membership: 70 institutional members.

Purpose: Concern with national policies affecting higher education generally and land-grant and state universities specifically.

Adult Education Program: The association as such is concerned with policies in adult education rather than programs. The adult education programs are carried on entirely by the 70 member colleges and universities. The association maintains national committees in the fields of (a) general or university extension work and (b) co-operative extension work in agriculture and home economics.

Publications: Proceedings, annually.

* * *

AMERICAN ASSOCIATION OF MUSEUMS (1905); Smithsonian Institution, Washington 25, D. C.; Director.

Membership: 2,500 individuals, 800 institutions.

Purpose: Dedicated to the service of all museums and the museum profession.

Adult Education Program: Consultation services to museums of all kinds; annual meetings; regional conferences; and a Documentation Center which maintains a comprehensive current file of all museums in the United States and Canada.

Publications: Museum News, Museum

Registration Methods, Museum Buildings, College and University Museums, So You Want a Good Museum, Museum Security, Index to Special Articles.

* * *

AMERICAN ASSOCIATION FOR THE UNITED NATIONS (1923 as League of Nations Association; name changed to present one in 1945); 345 East 46th Street, New York 17, N. Y.; Executive Director.

Membership: 40,000 individuals, 200 chapters.

Purpose: To distribute as widely as possible information about the work of the United Nations and the Specialized Agencies; to recommend and support those policies that will help to make United States membership in the United Nations effective; to study those means by which the United Nations may be further developed to meet the needs of an ever-changing world.

Adult Education Program: The AAUN carries out its program by supplying educational material, speakers, and program suggestions to its chapters and to other groups; by arranging conferences of organization representatives to discuss problems facing the United States in the United Nations; by supplying such special services as the Business Fact Sheet which is sent monthly to businessmen throughout the country, and which contains UN news of interest to them; and by co-operating with other organizations on special projects such as United Nations Week in October.

Publications: AAUN News (ten times a year).

* * *

*AMERICAN ASSOCIATION OF UNIVERSITY WOMEN (1882); 1634 Eye Street, N. W., Washington 6, D. C.; General Director.

Membership: 141,000 individual members affiliated with 1,438 local branches.

Purpose: Practical work in education.

Adult Education Program: The association provides program guides, study guides, and bibliographies for study groups of the branches in the following fields: education, international relations, social and economic issues, status of women, the arts, and mass media.

Publications: Journal (four times a year); General Director's Letter (three times a year).

*AMERICAN AUTOMOBILE ASSOCIATION (1902); 1712 G Street, N. W., Washington 6, D. C.; Educational Consultant, Traffic Engineering and Safety Department.

Membership: 6,171,272 individuals, 745 clubs, 4 state organizations.

Purpose: A non-profit organization established and maintained in the interest of the users of motor vehicles. Among its purposes are promotion of traffic safety education among pedestrians of all ages and promotion of driver education for both youths and adults.

Adult Education Program: The association carries on its educational program by the following means: preparation and distribution of safety education materials; assistance in preparation of driver education teachers in college and state department of education teacher preparation programs; AAA Pedestrian Program Appraisal, records and analysis of pedestrian activities and programs in states and cities; assistance in adult driver and pedestrian education research; public education in traffic safety through news releases, articles, radio and TV materials; and an annual convention.

Publications: Sportsmanlike Driving (text-book for driver education); Teachers Manual for Sportsmanlike Driving; Project Workbook for Sportsmanlike Driving; How to Drive (manual for adult courses and driver improvement programs); Planned Pedestrian Program (guide for pedestrian improvement program); News Review (monthly); The Motorist; research reports on accident causes and remedial programs.

* * *

AMERICAN BAR ASSOCIATION (1878); 1155 East 60th Street, Chicago 37, Ill.; Chairman, Committee on Continuing Legal Education.

Membership: 95,000 individual members.

Purpose: To uphold and defend the Constitution of the United States and maintain representative government; to advance the science of jurisprudence; to promote the administration of justice and the uniformity of legislation and of judicial decisions throughout the nation; to uphold the honor of the profession of law; and to correlate and promote such activities of the bar organizations in the nation and in the respective states as are within these objects, in the interest of the legal profession and of the public.

Adult Education Program: In co-operation with the American Law Institute, the American Bar Association encourages and assists in the organization of state and local practicing law institutes and other regional agencies of post-law-school legal education, and it maintains a national publications program.

Publications: Practical monographs on specific legal subjects, through the American Law Institute, 133 East 36th Street, Philadelphia 4, Pennsylvania.

* * *

*AMERICAN CAMPING ASSOCIATION (1910); Bradford Woods, Martinsville, Ind.; Executive Director.

Membership: 7,756 individual and camp members.

Purpose: To further the welfare of children and adults through camping; to extend the recreational and educational benefits of out-of-doors living; to provide for exchange of experiences and successful practices, and for development of materials, standards and other aids for the progress of camping; to serve as the voice of camp leaders in national and local affairs; to interpret camping to related groups and to the public; to stimulate high professional standards of camp leadership; to give emphasis in camping to citizenship training in keeping with the principles and traditions of American democracy.

Adult Education Program: The program for camp directors, counselors, and lay committees is carried out through leadership courses, institutes, workshops, consultations, regional and national conventions.

Publications: News Letter, semi-annually; Camping Magazine, monthly, except summer; Camp Reference Issue and Buying Guide, annually; leaflets, pamphlets, and reports on camp standards, camp practices, camp program, camp leadership courses, legislation, research, and other materials.

* * *

*AMERICAN CANCER SOCIETY (1913); 521 West 57th Street, New York 19, N. Y.; Vice President for Public Education and Information.

Membership: 60 divisions, 3,033 units.

Purpose: Voluntary national health agency engaged in a comprehensive program of cancer research, education and service, with the goal of bringing to every person in the country sufficient knowledge about cancer so that he will not lose his life needlessly.

Adult Education Program: Leadership training courses for volunteers within the society; co-operation with medical profession and official public health agencies in public education concerning yearly health checkups and seven danger signals that might mean cancer. Pamphlets, films, exhibits, posters, speakers, radio, television, and press are widely used to put cancer facts before the public.

Publications: Cancer News, quarterly; Cancer, a bimonthly journal. CA, bimonthly; Medical Affairs Newsletter; Signals, public education quarterly newsletter; PR, monthly bulletin.

* * *

*AMERICAN CIVIL LIBERTIES UNION (1920); 170 Fifth Avenue, New York 10, N. Y.; Associate Director.

Membership: 47,000 individuals; 27 affiliates, which have 50 chapters.

Purpose: To defend the civil liberties of free inquiry and communication, due process, and equality under law.

Adult Education Program: ACLU carries on its educational activities in behalf of civil liberties through open local membership meetings, publication of pamphlets and reprints, consultation with individuals and organizations on civil liberties issues, and news releases. Emphasis is also placed on annual Bill of Rights Day celebration, in which national office and local affiliates co-operate on special programs, which include radio-TV appearances, newspaper publicity, public meetings, and official proclamations.

Publications: Annual Report, monthly bulletin to members, some 50 pamphlets on civil liberties topics.

* * *

*AMERICAN DENTAL ASSOCIATION (1859); 222 East Superior Street, Chicago 11, Ill.; Director of Bureau of Dental Health Education.

Membership: 94,386 individual members; 54 constituent societies; 443 component societies.

Purpose: To encourage the improvement of the health of the public and promote the art and science of dentistry.

Adult Education Program: Through meetings and scientific sessions opportunities are made available to the members of the dental profession to learn new techniques and methods of providing the best dental care to the public. In addition, the association provides educational materials geared to improve public understanding in the area of dental health, to encourage the prevention and control of dental disease, and, in general, to promote the dental health of the public.

Publications: Newsletters, bulletins, pamphlets, and other educational aids related to dental health.

* * *

*THE AMERICAN DIETETIC ASSOCIATION (1917); 620 North Michigan Avenue, Chicago 11, Ill.; Continuing Education Services Director.

Membership: 13,800 individual members.

Purpose: To improve the nutrition of human beings; to advance the science of dietetics and nutrition; and to promote education in these and allied areas.

Adult Education Program: The association sponsors committee activities in the areas of Community Nutrition, Diet Therapy, Education, and Food Administration; cooperates in curriculum planning for nursing students and for vocational training of food service supervisors; cooperates with the American Hospital Association in conducting institutes on hospital dietary administration; prepares educational materials on food administration and nutrition. At state and local levels workshops are conducted; individual members contribute services to nursing homes, homes for the aged, etc., in an effort to improve the nutrition and food services, and give lectures and courses on adequate nutrition to organized groups on request.

Publications: Journal of the American Dietetic Association; Food Facts Talk Back; Curriculum Guide for Dietetic Interns; Eating Is Fun For Older People Too; Handbook of Diet Therapy.

* * *

AMERICAN FARM BUREAU FEDERATION (1919); 2300 Merchandise Mart, Chicago 54, Ill.; Director of Program Development.

Membership: 1,576,462 farm families at the end of 1958.

Purpose: A free, independent, non-governmental, voluntary organization of farm and ranch families united for the purpose of analyzing their problems and formulating action to achieve educational improvement, economic opportunity, and social advancement, thereby promoting the national welfare. Farm Bureau is local, national, and international in its scope and influence, and is non-partisan, non-sectarian, and non-secret in character.

Adult Education Program: Farm Bureau's program stems from policy and program resolutions developed and approved by the membership. Members meet in many thousands of community and county groups to participate directly in organization affairs to develop solutions to problems and to secure widespread support for policies, many of which relate to legislative issues. A broad program of activities relating to farm safety, citizenship, leadership training, education, and social and community betterment is carried on.

Publications: The Nation's Agriculture; AFBF Official News Letter.

* * *

THE AMERICAN FEDERATION OF ARTS (1909); 1083 Fifth Avenue, New York 28, N. Y.; Director.

Membership: Over 2,000 individuals, institutions, and corporations.

Purpose: To encourage the production and cultivate the appreciation of art in America.

Adult Education Program: The federation supplies traveling art exhibitions and color slide lectures to museums, art centers, and educational institutions throughout the country.

Publications: Who's Who in American Art, The American Art Directory, A F A Newsletter, exhibition catalogs.

* * *

AMERICAN FEDERATION OF LABOR AND CONGRESS OF INDUSTRIAL ORGANIZATIONS (1955—AFL founded in 1881; CIO founded in 1936); 815 16th Street, N. W., Washington 6, D. C.; Director of Education.

Membership: 136 national and international unions, 52 state central bodies, 853 local central bodies, and 502 directly affiliated local unions.

Purpose: To improve wages, hours, and working conditions; to bring benefits of free collective bargaining to all workers; to achieve equality of opportunity for all workers, regardless of race, creed, color, or national origin; to support legislation favorable to workers and oppose that harmful to them; to protect and strengthen democratic institutions and preserve America's democratic traditions; to aid in promoting world peace and freedom; to protect the labor movement against corruption and racketeers; to safeguard it from communists, fascists or other totalitarians; to encourage workers to register and vote and exercise fully their responsibilities as citizens; to encourage the sale of union-made goods.

Adult Education Program: Through its Department of Education the AFL-CIO encourages, assists, and supports educational programs of local unions, trades councils, city central bodies, state central bodies, regional agencies, and national and international unions. The department provides organizational support, administrative experience, staff assistance, speakers, and resource persons from its own and other headquarters departments; prepares and distributes publications, plans, materials, audiovisual aids; and assists in co-ordination of resources. Subjects studied under various programs include labor history, collective bargaining techniques, economics, NLRB procedures, civil rights, community participation, housing problems, unemployment compensation, civil defense, and international affairs. Department representatives co-operate with many educational, church, civic, and other community groups by speaking before them, giving an explanation of the American labor movement and its attitude on many subjects. The department maintains a film library and distributes its films and filmstrips to labor organizations and community organizations such as schools, churches, service groups, etc. The AFL-CIO educational program is conducted at resident summer schools and special institutes, in conferences and classes, at regular meetings of unions, at workshops and seminars.

Publications: AFL-CIO Education News and Views (monthly); Shop Steward's Manual, How to Run a Union Meeting, and teaching guides for these; Films for Labor (list of films in film library); film discussion guides.

* * *

*AMERICAN FOUNDATION FOR THE BLIND (1922); 15 West 16th St., New York 11, N. Y.; Director of Public Education.

Membership: Lay persons and professionals in work for the blind.

Purpose: To help those handicapped by blindness achieve the fullest possible development and the utilization of their capacities and the maximum integration into the social, cultural and economic life of the community.

Adult Education Program: The foundation serves as a clearing house for the direct service agencies for the blind. It conducts surveys of facilities and programs for the blind, engages in research in all phases of work for the blind, manufactures Talking Books (complete from original reading of books onto tape by professional readers, through making master records, pressing and plating same, then shipment to 30 branch regional libraries for the blind) under contract with the Library of Congress which finances the program. The Talking Books are distributed, through the regional libraries, *absolutely free* to all blind persons registered with their library. In addition, the Department of Public Education works with all avenues of mass media to create a more realistic attitude toward blindness and blind people, by producing radio and TV programs, posters, exhibits, and by furnishing speakers for interested groups. The foundation's Library and Publications Department publishes books and loans books and other material on various phases of work for the blind.

Publications: New Outlook for the Blind (in inkprint, braille and on Talking Book records); AFB Bulletin; Talking Book Topics (semi-monthly); The Enlightener (house organ, bi-monthly); Braille Book Review (semi-monthly); Touch and Go (for the deaf-blind) in braille and inkprint—monthly. The foundation also publishes a Directory of Activities of Agencies Serving the Blind—now in its 11th edition.

* * *

AMERICAN FOUNDATION FOR CONTINUING EDUCATION (1947); 19 South La Salle Street, Chicago 3, Ill.; Executive Director.

Purpose: To develop materials of liberal education for use by adults in study discussion programs; to offer assistance to organizations, agencies, and institutions of all kinds interested in adult education through consultation, program development, and leadership training; to prepare special materials on liberal arts and politics for business and industry.

Activities: The staff is available for consultation and leadership training with all groups concerned about adult education. The foundation also operates special programs of liberal education for business and industry. The foundation is constantly engaged in research on new materials and is currently at work on programs in the fields of the fine arts and science.

Publications: Available from Oxford University Press—Readings in World Politics, Readings in American Foreign Policy, Readings in American Democracy, Readings in Russian Foreign Policy, Economics and Politics; in addition, several case problems for stimulating discussion on current issues, and a discussion leader's manual are available directly from the foundation.

* * *

AMERICAN FRIENDS SERVICE COMMITTEE (1917); 20 South 12th Street, Philadelphia 7, Pa.; Director, Information Service.

Purpose: To relieve human suffering and to work for non-violent solutions to conflicts between individuals, groups, or nations.

Adult Education Program: AFSC organizes conferences and discussions and provides literature for general community groups, for organized labor, and for councils of churches, on peace problems; helps communities work at equal opportunities for minority groups in housing, jobs, and education; provides education in English, citizenship, and community organization for Latin Americans; helps American Indians on reservations and in cities to develop physical and human resources; brings together government officials (parliamentarians, diplomats, United Nations representatives, etc.) for specialized discussions of international relations; arranges affiliations between U. S. and overseas schools, including international teachers' conferences and ex-

change of teachers; organizes volunteer service projects with educational programs for the students and adults in U. S. and overseas.

Publications: Quarterly bulletin, pamphlets and study materials, some exhibits and films.

* * *

AMERICAN HEART ASSOCIATION (1924); 44 East 23rd Street, New York 10, N. Y.; Medical Director.

Membership: 20,516 medical and 15,378 lay members; 55 state and regional associations, and 298 local chapters.

Purpose: To conduct a program of support for basic and applied research, professional and public education, and community services; to reduce death and disability due to heart and blood vessel disease.

Adult Education Program: Scientific meetings are held for professional people to review recent research advances; symposia, institutes, seminars, and workshops are also held for physician and paramedical groups; handbooks, manuals, and other materials are published to help physicians in diagnosis, treatment, and prevention; many other educational aids, including heart models, professional films, and heart sound tapes are made available to physicians. An extensive program of public education includes pamphlets, books, exhibits, posters, heart diagrams, and films, as well as press materials released to all media.

Publications: For physicians: Circulation, Circulation Research, Modern Concepts of Cariovascular Disease, the Heart Bulletin. For laymen: The American Heart Quarterly. The Heart Research Newsletter.

* * *

THE AMERICAN HERITAGE FOUNDATION (1947); 11 West 42nd Street, New York 36, N. Y.; Executive Director.

Purpose: To develop a greater awareness and a keener appreciation of the advantages we have in this country, emphasizing the relationship of our hard-won liberties to our development as the greatest nation of free people in the world's history; and to persuade all Americans that only by active participation in the affairs of our nation can we safeguard our freedoms, preserve the liberties from which all these advantages flow, and continue to demonstrate to ourselves, and to the whole world, that the way of free men is best.

Adult Education Program: Through its Nonpartisan Good Citizenship Program, the foundation co-ordinates "Register, Vote, and Contribute to the Party of Your Choice" activities of community, civic, and educational organizations. It also promotes nonpartisan practical politics programs of community, business, and labor organizations.

Publications: Good Citizen; How to Get People to Register and Vote; 1960 Nonpartisan Good Citizenship Program.

* * *

*AMERICAN HOME ECONOMICS ASSOCIATION (1909); 1600 Twentieth Street N. W., Washington 9, D. C.; Executive Secretary.

Membership: 25,102 individuals, 49 affiliated state associations, the Puerto Rico and the District of Columbia Home Economics Associations.

Purpose: To provide opportunities for professional home economists and members from other fields to co-operate in the attainment of the well-being of individuals and of families, the improvement of homes, and the preservation of values significant in home life.

Adult Education Program: The association plans, co-operatively with other groups and related disciplines for projects, programs, and conferences in home economics; co-operates with other agencies, groups, and individuals in activities designed to safeguard homes, to improve conditions affecting families, and to protect the economic interest of the family as a consumer of goods and services; promotes education specifically designed to assist employed homemakers better to meet their home and job responsibilities; encourages experimentation with new educational tools and devices to meet the demand of the future for more and better education.

Publications: Journal of Home Economics (monthly, September through June); Home Economics in Higher Education; The AHEA Saga.

* * *

*AMERICAN HOSPITAL ASSOCIATION (1899); 840 North Lake Shore Drive, Chicago 11, Ill.; Secretary, Council on Research and Education.

Membership: 5,000 individuals, 7,300 institutions.

Purpose: To promote the public welfare through the development of better hospital care for all the people.

Adult Education Program: The AHA is concerned with the development of educational programs in all aspects of hospital care for the improvement of hospital services and for development of citizen support for hospitals. It conducts a national program of institutes furthering the in-service education of hospital personnel in its Chicago headquarters and key cities throughout the nation. This program is co-ordinated with the educational programs of allied hospital associations, at regional, state, and metropolitan levels, and of related health organizations; it is continually revised to meet changing educational needs. The association also conducts workshops and conferences for workers in the hospital and health fields; publishes periodicals, manuals, and other materials; and maintains a film library for use by hospitals and health groups in training and recruiting personnel and in community relations activities. Its annual convention offers a balanced educational program for some 12,000 workers in the hospital and health fields each year; its library, the largest collection of hospital literature in the world, is available as an educational resource for members.

Publications: Periodicals: Hospital Auxiliary Newsletter (monthly); Hospitals, Journal of the American Hospital Association (twice monthly); Public Relations Newsletter (monthly); This Month (monthly); This Month in Washington (monthly); Trustee, the Journal for Hospital Governing Boards. Other publications: various manuals; index of hospital literature; public information materials.

* * *

AMERICAN INSTITUTE OF COOPERATION (1925); 744 Jackson Place, N. W., Washington 6, D. C.; President.

Membership: 2,500 farmer co-operatives.

Purpose: To promote an understanding of the place of farmer co-operatives in our private enterprise system.

Adult Education Program: The institute works with other educational organizations and institutions in developing teaching aids, encouraging research to improve the understanding of the public on how our competitive economy operates, and getting the facts about the business life of the community into the classroom. It produces films, flannel-graphs, and slides, and conducts clinics on member responsibility, manager and director improvement, public relations, community improvement.

Publications: American Co-operation (annual yearbook); How we Organize to do Business in America; Business in our Community; Knowing Your Community.

• • •

*AMERICAN IRON AND STEEL IN-STITUTE (1908); 150 East 42nd Street, New York 17, N. Y.; Education Director.

Membership: 2,700 individuals, 101 companies.

Purpose: To collect and disseminate information connected with the iron and steel industry and to provide a forum for the discussion of problems related to the industry.

Adult Education Program: Provides interpretive displays, teaching and study guides, informational booklets and audio-visual materials related to the industry and its problems for members, schools, and the public; helps to organize and conduct special seminars and workshops for company employees, clergymen, teachers, editors, and other interested groups; provides statistics and research results on such subjects as industrial health, safety, insurance problems, industrial processes, and product standards.

Publications: Steelways Magazine, Steel Facts.

• • •

*AMERICAN JEWISH COMMITTEE (1906); 165 East 56 St., New York 22, N. Y.; Educational Consultant.

Membership: 27,200 individual members in 600 communities; 45 chapters.

Purpose: The AJC is a nation-wide educational and community relations organization which seeks to combat bigotry, protect the civil and religious rights of Jews here and abroad, and promote the advancement of human rights for all peoples.

Adult Education Program: The AJC carries on educational programs for its members by means of speakers, turn-over talks, discussion materials, courses on civil liberties and civil rights, Jewish education, community relations, etc. Materials available for the membership

are also available to the general public. Special materials are prepared for school systems and universities in the area of community relations, inter-group relations, civil rights, etc. These include original pamphlets and books, and bibliographies of all descriptions. Specialized library resources, films, pamphlet materials, and consultation services on community relations are generally available for other organizations.

Publications: American Jewish Yearbook; Commentary (magazine); pamphlets on civil rights, civil liberties, inter-group relations, immigration, public education.

• • •

*AMERICAN LABOR EDUCATION SERVICE (1927); 1776 Broadway, New York 19, N. Y.; Director.

Purpose: To co-operate with local and international trade unions in stimulating educational programs among trade unionists, emphasizing demonstration and experimentation in the field of labor education; to develop leadership for the assumption of active union and community responsibility at the grass roots level. The programs are based on the belief that widening and deepening the workers' understanding of our society contributes to more effective participation in domestic and world affairs.

Adult Education Program: American Labor Education Service sponsors conferences for trade unionists on public issues, establishes and directs labor education demonstration centers, conducts summer schools for the study of current economic and social problems, and works in consultation with government and other agencies on educational programs for visiting workers from abroad. In the past its program emphases have included the development of study materials for adult workers, the establishment of resident schools, research and experimentation in educational methods, the study of international affairs and combatting discrimination through union education, the promotion of better farmer-labor relationships, and the development of the study of economic and social problems by white collar workers. At present its program emphases include the interrelation of this country with other parts of the world, the meaning and influence of democracy, the impact of science and technology in the modern world, the effective participation of labor in community life, the importance of understanding social attitudes today, the art of communication, and the learning process. Long term functions include field advisory service to unions, labor education bodies, and community organizations concerned in workers' education; educational counseling and counseling services to individuals interested in entering the field or in serving as teachers; informational and clearing house activities; leadership training; conferences, national, sectional, and local; bibliographical services; special studies.

Recent Publications: Focus on the U. N.—Study Notes for Workers (periodical); World Affairs and Your Union Education Program; History of an Idea, 30th anniversary Journal of the American Labor Education Service; annual reports, articles, studies, and bibliographies.

* * *

*AMERICAN LIBRARY ASSOCIATION (1876); 50 East Huron Street, Chicago 11, Ill.; Executive Secretary, Adult Services Division.

Membership: 18,000 individual members; 4,000 institutional; 55 chapters; affiliated with 9 other national library organizations.

Purpose: The purpose of the ALA is to promote library service and librarianship. The purpose of the Adult Services Division is to provide for those activities of the ALA which stimulate and promote library services for the continuing educational, recreational, and cultural development of adults. This includes the identification, evaluation, and stimulation of the production and use of library materials (book and non-book).

Adult Education Program: Through the work of members and of the headquarters staff, the division studies and reviews library adult services in all types of libraries, conducts projects and research, represents library adult services outside the profession, and stimulates the development of librarians in this area of service through conferences, workshops, publications, and committee work. It provides liaison between librarians and such groups as publishers and the mass media, and is responsible for the choice of the Notable Books of the

year. It also works with special groups such as labor groups, and the various groups responsible for service to the aging. The areas in which the Adult Services Division is directly concerned include: academic education, aging and retirement, community development, fundamental and literacy education, intercultural education, leadership training, liberal education, and public affairs.

Publications: ALA Bulletin, monthly to members; various reprints, manuals, books and pamphlets on library adult education, community study, program planning, etc.

* * *

AMERICAN MANAGEMENT ASSOCIATION (1923); 1515 Broadway, New York 36, N. Y.; Director of Divisions.

Membership: 28,500 individual members.

Purpose: To provide continuing management education for its members and other executives interested in personal and professional development.

Adult Education Program: The association conducts many seminars, courses, conferences, and meetings on all phases of business, management, and executive development, in several sections of the country.

Publications: The Management Review (monthly), Personnel (bi-monthly), Management News (monthly); about 6 research studies per year; about 20 booklets of meeting proceedings per year; about 6 hard-cover books per year.

* * *

AMERICAN MEDICAL ASSOCIATION (1847); 535 North Dearborn Street, Chicago 10, Ill.; Secretary, Council on Medical Education and Hospitals (professional education); and Director, Health Education Department (non-professional education).

Membership: 178,000 physician members; approximately 2,000 component county medical societies and 53 state and territorial constituent societies.

Purpose: To promote the art and science of medicine and the betterment of public health.

Adult Education Program: AMA holds two postgraduate education meetings for its members annually, in addition to many conferences and symposia on specific subjects. At its two annual conventions information is relayed via lectures, scientific exhibits, color TV, and motion pictures. AMA furthers public health education through the monthly health magazine for the public, through exhibits, films, and TV programs, and through the development and distribution of pamphlets on health subjects.

Publications: Journal of the AMA (weekly); 10 monthly journals, each dealing with a special field of medicine; AMA News (every other week); Today's Health (monthly, for the public); American Medical Directory; other books and pamphlets on medicine and health.

* * *

*AMERICAN NATIONAL RED CROSS (1881); 17th & D Streets, N. W., Washington 6, D. C.; National Training Director.

Membership: The activities of the Red Cross are carried on primarily through local chapters which derive their authority from the national organization. Membership is on an individual basis.

Purpose: The American Red Cross is a nation-wide voluntary organization through which all people may serve. It provides emergency relief for disaster victims and needed assistance in restoring them to normal living. It gives personal assistance to members of the armed forces and acts as a means of communication between them and their families. To perform these and other functions designed to prevent or alleviate suffering caused by family, community, national, and international emergencies, the Red Cross carries on a number of service programs in the field of health, education, and welfare. In co-operation with the Red Cross societies of more than eighty other countries, it conducts an international relief program. The American Red Cross also is required to help fulfill the obligations of the United States under certain international treaties.

Adult Education Program: Provides a variety of specific courses, available to the general public, in the fields of nursing, first aid, and water safety; conducts courses, conferences, and institutes in the fields of leadership training and community development; trains volunteers to perform a variety of services in connection with its program activities, through specified courses as well as in-service training; makes available certain kinds of training for volunteers working

with other organizations as well as for volunteers working with the Red Cross.

Publications: Text books related to courses provided for general public; manuals, guides, miscellaneous pamphlets in connection with training for both volunteer and career staff; magazines distributed through schools for use of teacher and junior Red Cross members; monthly newsletter for chapters; miscellaneous interpretive pamphlets and films.

* * *

AMERICAN NURSES' ASSOCIATION (1896); 10 Columbus Circle, New York 19, N. Y.; Executive Secretary.

Membership: 54 state and territorial associations; 831 district associations.

Purpose: To foster high standards of nursing practice, to promote the professional and educational advancement of nurses and the welfare of nurses to the end that all people may have better nursing care.

Adult Education Program: ANA conducts workshops, provides speakers and consultants for conferences, conventions and meetings of constituent associations, and allied health organizations; provides visual displays, produces discussion guides, reports, and pamphlets for members and the public on nursing and association programs and activities. ANA gathers and publishes statistical "Facts About Nursing" each year; publishes and distributes statements of functions, standards, and qualifications for practice in each area of nursing; and conducts and supports research in the profession. ANA also produces and distributes releases, feature articles, and other material to mass media concerning the status of nursing in the United States.

Publications: American Journal of Nursing, ANA in Review, ANA Guide Lines (monthly planning guide), Facts about Nursing; pamphlets, study guides, and 16 mm films both for the public and for the profession.

* * *

AMERICAN PERSONNEL AND GUIDANCE ASSOCIATION (1952); 1605 New Hampshire Avenue, N. W., Washington 9, D. C.; Executive Director.

Membership: 10,000 individual memberships, through affiliation with one or more of the six divisions of the association.

Purpose: To promote and stimulate the

exchange of professional experience through national and regional meetings, to co-ordinate research and other professional activities, and to publish reports on studies, practices, and other pertinent subjects; through united action of the membership, to promote the general understanding and acceptance of the principles, practices, and professional standards of the guidance and personnel movement.

Adult Education Program: The association provides for its members convention programs, specific interest groups, and articles in its journal. In addition, each of the six divisions publishes materials pertinent to its specialty.

Publications: Personnel and Guidance Journal (monthly, September through May); Membership Directory; Directory of Approved Counseling Agencies.

* * *

*AMERICAN PHYSICAL THERAPY ASSOCIATION (1921); 1790 Broadway, New York 19, N. Y.; Executive Director.
Membership: 8,853 individuals, 58 chapters, 48 districts.
Purpose: To foster the development and improvement of physical therapy service and physical therapy education through co-ordinated action of physical therapists, allied professional groups, citizens, agencies, and schools to the end that the physical therapy needs of the people will be met.
Adult Education Program: The association promotes physical therapy education by stimulating the development of programs, guiding and evaluating the organization and administration of curricula, and directing the maintenance of standards. The association also conducts an annual conference for its members, and distributes pamphlets, filmstrips and films.
Publications: The Physical Therapy Review (monthly); pamphlets, films, and filmstrips describing physical therapy.

* * *

THE AMERICAN PUBLIC HEALTH ASSOCIATION (1872); 1790 Broadway, New York 19, N. Y.; Executive Director.
Membership: 12,497 individual members, 52 sustaining members, 48 affiliated societies and branches.
Purpose: To promote personal and public health, to serve as spokesman for the people's health and for health agencies,

to encourage programs for the improvement of public and professional education, to encourage public health research; to seek the establishment of standards and methods of program evaluation.

Adult Education Program: Educational services for members consist of presentation of speakers at the annual meeting of the association, publication of a monthly journal in which scientific and news articles appear, publication of standards in several fields related to public health, publication of a series of educational qualifications for different categories of public health workers, and promotion and sponsorship of short-term educational meetings. The association makes available to the public its publications on activities in public health and on the categories of public health workers. Officers and staff members of the association frequently serve as speakers before public groups. This association is the authorized accrediting agency for university schools of public health.

Publications: American Journal of Public Health (monthly); numerous books, pamphlets, and reprints.

* * *

*AMERICAN SOCIAL HYGIENE ASSOCIATION (1912); 1790 Broadway, New York 19, N. Y.; Director of Education.
Membership: 1,000 individuals; 33 institutions; 33 chapters; 33 affiliates.
Purpose: The strengthening and preservation of the family through demonstration projects in family life education, through investigation of community conditions for living, and through behavioral research.
Adult Education Program: Works with adult and parent groups in states and communities, with schools and colleges, and with community agencies to further family life education programs.
Publications: Social Hygiene News, monthly; Social Hygiene papers, annually; pamphlets and brochures.

* * *

AMERICAN SOCIETY OF ASSOCIATION EXECUTIVES (1920); 805 Associations Building, 2000 K Street, N. W., Washington 6, D. C.; Executive Vice President.
Membership: About 2,000 individual members, 23 affiliated groups.

Purpose: To provide opportunity for exchange of experiences and opinion through discussion, study, and publications on all phases of association activities, to make recognition awards, to conduct courses of study for the benefit of members, to broaden public understanding, to develop and encourage high standards of service, and to co-operate with local groups.

Adult Education Program: The association acts as co-sponsor with affiliated groups of regional conferences and meetings of an educational nature for members and prospective members; co-operates with the Institute Department of the U. S. Chamber of Commerce in their program for the Institute for Organization Management; and presents educational programs at its annual meeting.

* * *

THE AMERICAN SOCIETY OF TRAINING DIRECTORS (1945); 2020 University Avenue, Madison 5, Wis.; Executive Director.

Membership: 3,866 individuals and 68 chapters.

Purpose: To provide effective and continuous leadership in the field of development and training to assure a competent management and work force; to promote acceptance and understanding of development and training; to further the professional education and development of members; to foster the interests of youth in the training profession as a career; to assist in the extension of chapter organizations and to provide continuing help in order to improve chapter performance and operation; to provide for effective co-operation and exchange of information and ideas between chapters; to make studies in the training field and to issue reports to members; and to provide a clearing house of training information for members and management.

Adult Education Program: The ASTD provides for its members a library, training materials exchange service, and a directory. Its annual conferences, basic and advanced institutes, regional conferences, chapter meetings, and seminars and workshops serve both its members and the public.

Publications: The Journal of the American Society of Training Directors; directory; committee and research reports.

AMERICAN VOCATIONAL ASSOCIATION (1926); 1010 Vermont Avenue, N. W., Washington 5, D. C.; Executive Secretary.

Membership: 35,000 individual members in 72 affiliated state associations.

Purpose: To establish and maintain active national leadership in the promotion of all types of vocational and industrial arts education, including guidance services for youth and adults; to render service to state and local communities in promoting and establishing vocational education; to provide a national open forum for the study and discussion of all questions involved in vocational education; to unify all the vocational education interests of the nation through representative membership; to cooperate with other nations in the further development of vocational education; to encourage further development of programs of education related to vocational education, including industrial and other forms of practical arts; to emphasize and encourage the promotion and expansion of programs of vocational education for youth and adults on a part-time basis.

Adult Education Program: The AVA conducts national conferences and studies in the areas of the following eight divisions: Agriculture, Trades and Industry, Home Economics, Business Education, Distributive Education, Vocational Guidance, Vocational Rehabilitation, and Industrial Arts Education.

Publications: American Vocational Journal and bulletins from time to time.

* * *

*ANTI-DEFAMATION LEAGUE OF B'NAI B'RITH (1913); 515 Madison Avenue, New York 22, N. Y.; Director, Department of National Organizations.

Membership: 350,000 individuals, 26 regional offices.

Purpose: To encourage the development of community and organization programs designed to deal constructively with problems of religious and racial bigotry through the democratic processes of education, public opinion, and law.

Adult Education Program: ADL resources are publications, graphics, and films. Trained personnel provide consultative services to B'nai B'rith members and to public and private community agencies.

Publications: ADL Bulletin, Facts, Rights.

ASSOCIATION FOR EDUCATION BY RADIO-TELEVISION—merged January 1, 1957 with the National Association of Educational Broadcasters.

* * *

*ASSOCIATION OF THE JUNIOR LEAGUES OF AMERICA (1921); The Waldorf-Astoria, 301 Park Avenue, New York 22, N. Y.; Consultant on Education.
Membership: 194 leagues.
Purpose: To foster interest among its members in the social, economic, educational, cultural, and civic conditions of the community, and to make efficient their volunteer service.
Adult Education Program: Educational program for members includes continuing education for participation in community life and active citizenship; study and action groups in public affairs; leadership training institutes and workshops. The leagues promote projects to extend and improve educational services, and conduct training institutes for board members and other volunteers, often open to the public and to other organizations.
Publications: Junior League magazine (6 issues per year); manuals on community study, public affairs, and organization leadership.

* * *

*ASSOCIATION OF UNIVERSITY EVENING COLLEGES (1939); Brooklyn College, School of General Studies, Brooklyn 10, N. Y.; Executive Secretary.
Membership: 28 individual and 128 institutional members.
Purpose: To study the problems of evening colleges, to interchange information and ideas among the members, to conduct other activities beneficial to the members, and to continuing education.
Adult Education Program: For its membership the AUEC conducts regional workshops, leadership training institutes, and an annual national conference to study and discuss the problems of administration, organization, and operation of evening colleges. Committees on television education, education-industry relations, research, and liberal education provide members with information and ideas which can be used in their respective institutions. Committees of the AUEC have conducted numerous studies, furnishing data for the improvement of instruction, teacher selection and training, curriculum building, services to the community, and the promotion of evening education.
Publications: Newsletter (eight times a year); Proceedings (of national convention, annually).

* * *

B'NAI B'RITH DEPARTMENT OF ADULT EDUCATION (B'nai B'rith, 1843, Department of Adult Education, 1954); 1640 Rhode Island Avenue, N. W., Washington 6, D. C.; Director.
Membership: 2,000 chapters and lodges.
Purpose: By providing platforms where all significant viewpoints in Jewish life may be heard and discussed, the department seeks to widen and deepen the interests of adults in Jewish learning.
Adult Education Program: Through summer Institutes of Judaism, year-round discussion groups, numerous publications, and programmatic guidance, it offers to help individuals and groups plan programs on the religious and cultural heritage of the Jewish people.
Publications: Jewish Heritage (quarterly); Great Jewish Books (a series of basic adult education texts on Judaism); Adult Study Groups; The Enduring Heritage and other study guides, book lists, and program suggestions.

* * *

*B'NAI B'RITH WOMEN (1909); 1640 Rhode Island Ave., N. W., Washington 6, D. C.; Assistant Executive Director.
Membership: 135,000 individuals, 830 chapters.
Purpose: To give service and support to philanthropic, humanitarian, educational, and patriotic programs.
Adult Education Program: Three areas of adult education are emphasized: training institutes and workshops for national, district, council, and chapter leaders; a Program for Older Adults; and adult Jewish education. Guidance and consultation are given through correspondence and materials. The organization sponsors and participates in national conferences. Local programs are open to the community at large.
Publications: Women's World and a variety of other printed materials.

* * *

*CAMP FIRE GIRLS, INC. (1910); 16 East 48th Street, New York 17, N. Y.; National Director.

Membership: Over one-half million in 336 chartered councils and 49 independent leaders' associations.

Purpose: To provide an educational-recreational leisure-time program for all girls from 7 to 18 years of age.

Adult Education Program: The national organization develops standards, curricula, and materials for use of local councils in the training of leaders, sponsors, board and committee members; prepares for and conducts in-service training for local professional staff through regional and national courses, conferences, and workshops; offers advice and consultation to volunteer and professional personnel through correspondence and field service; publishes a monthly magazine for leaders and a quarterly guide for professional workers and administrative volunteers.

Publications: The Camp Fire Girl (leaders' magazine, monthly except July and August); program books for girls; guides and training manuals for adult leaders.

* * *

CENTER FOR THE STUDY OF LIBERAL EDUCATION FOR ADULTS (1951); 4819 South Greenwood Avenue, Chicago 15, Ill.; Director.

Purpose: The center was established through a grant from the Fund for Adult Education to help American higher education develop a greater effectiveness and deeper sense of responsibility for the liberal education of adults.

Adult Education Program: The center, in close co-operation with universities and colleges, works in three major areas of interest: improving university programs of liberal education for adults, developing improved methods of teaching and discussion leadership for adults, and building a climate of understanding and support for liberal adult education in the universities and in the general public. Four instrumental activities support the center's program operations: a research program conducted by the staff, a clearinghouse for collection and distribution of information, a series of publications, and field work and consultation.

Publications: Notes and Essays (series of pamphlets on problems and issues in liberal adult education); Reports (including research studies, surveys, and program descriptions); Clearinghouse Bulletin; offprints of pertinent articles from various journals; discussion guides.

* * *

*CHAMBER OF COMMERCE OF THE UNITED STATES (1912); 1615 H Street, N. W., Washington 6, D. C.; Manager, Education Department.

Membership: 22,000 business members, 3,400 organization members.

Purpose: To protect, strengthen, and improve the private business system, and to translate economic growth into human progress.

Adult Education Program: The national chamber develops special projects, sequences for study groups, and other activities for local and state chamber of commerce consideration. Many departments of the national chamber hold regional workshops or seminars to motivate voluntary use of national programs in local communities. In addition, summer institutes are held for executives of local chambers at six universities each year. Over 2,000 local chambers have standing committees on education. Particular events or programs, such as Business-Education Days, career planning programs for teen-agers, teacher recognition events, seminars on economics, political action courses, and a wide variety of study groups in other fields are sponsored by these local committees or by other special committees appointed by local chamber boards of directors.

Publications: Nations Business (monthly), Washington Report (weekly), other periodicals with special emphases; pamphlets on Chamber of Commerce organization and management, on chamber activities and special fields of interests, such as education, industrial relations, economic understanding, natural resources, transportation, etc.; motion pictures.

* * *

*CHILD STUDY ASSOCIATION OF AMERICA (1888); 132 East 74th Street, New York 21, N. Y.; Executive Director.

Membership: Individual professional and lay members.

Purpose: To promote positive mental health work through educational services, specifically parent education; to strengthen parent-child relationships and family life through increasing parents' understanding of children's growth, development, and emotional needs; and to help parents to reach a better understanding of their own attitudes, feelings, and behavior.

Adult Education Program: Parents meet in groups at CSAA headquarters to discuss their common concerns and to consider helpful ways of approaching problems with their children. In addition, a personal counseling service is available to parents. Professional social workers, educators, nurses, religious educators, and those from similar fields acquire new skills through CSAA training programs in the leadership of parent discussion groups in their own communities. Through correspondence, consultation, and field service, the program advisory service offers assistance to community groups and agencies in the planning of programs of parent education. The Book Review Committee reviews books in the field of child development and family relationships and publishes annotated lists. CSAA conducts research studies to evaluate the effectiveness of parent discussion groups and leadership training programs.

Publications: Child Study (quarterly); Parent Education Exchange Bulletin; publications for parents as well as professional workers in parent and family life education, on child development and parent-child relationships.

* * *

CIVITAN INTERNATIONAL (1920); 115 North 21 Street, Birmingham 3, Ala.; Executive Secretary.

Membership: 29,000 individuals, 825 clubs, 25 districts.

Purpose: Organized primarily for the purpose of promoting good citizenship, the aim of Civitan International is to develop in its members, in their associates, and their communities a high sense of responsibility toward common problems.

Adult Education Program: The members of Civitan International meet regularly to have fellowship together, to acquire a broader knowledge of public affairs and community needs, to become better prepared for intelligent leadership and co-operation in the solving of civic problems through study and instruction, and to seek out opportunities to render altruistic service to mankind. The purposes and programs are carried out through committees organized on an international, district, and club level.

Publications: Civitan Magazine (11 issues per year).

* * *

*THE COOPERATIVE LEAGUE OF THE U.S.A. (1916); 343 South Dearborn Street, Chicago 4, Ill.; Educational Director.

Membership: 39 regional, state and other national organizations representing all types of co-operatives.

Purpose: The growth of co-operation and co-operative business enterprise to a point where the people's own business (accounting for perhaps 15% to 20% of important lines of commerce) can become an effective balance wheel of a just and truly free economy.

Adult Education Program: The league conducts institutes, seminars, and conferences for members, officers, and employees of member organizations to increase understanding of co-operative principles and to improve their skills in performing specific tasks as members, directors, and employees. Services include publications, films, radio programs, and news service. Most service activities are directed toward achievement of greater understanding of co-operatives on the part of both members and non-members of co-operatives.

Publications: Co-op Report (monthly); Fact Book about Co-operatives (1958, then every other year); First 125 Years—A History of Distributive and Service Cooperation in U. S., 1829-1954 by Florence E. Parker; Story of Toad Lane by Stuart Chase; and History of Cooperation (with questions for discussion) by E. S. Bogardus. Free catalog of publications and films available on request.

* * *

CORRECTIONAL EDUCATION ASSOCIATION (1938), Affiliate of the American Correctional Association; Room 502, State Office Building No. 1, Sacramento 14, Cal.; President.

Membership: 600 individuals.

Purpose: To promote the cause of education in penal and correctional institutions throughout the country; to work for the development and adequate support of correctional education; and to develop relationships with other professional educational organizations and agencies.

Adult Education Program: The association stimulates the organization and professional advancement of educational programs for the inmates of correctional institutions.

Publications: Journal of Correctional Education (quarterly).

* * *

*COUNCIL OF LIBERAL CHURCHES (Universalist-Unitarian) (1953); 25 Beacon Street, Boston 8, Mass.; Director of Adult Programs.

Membership: 180,000 individuals in 1,000 churches and fellowships.

Purpose: To promote the principles of religious liberalism through an educational program for children and adults.

Adult Education Program: The Department of Adult Programs develops and publishes curriculum materials for adults in Unitarian and Universalist churches. Such publications include those designed for discussion groups, forums, and classes. It sponsors seminars on topics of concern to religious liberals. The department maintains representations at the United Nations and national capital and it provides appropriate representation to other national organizations seeking compatible goals. It provides field consultation for groups who plan programs for adults in Unitarian and Universalist churches.

Publications: The Unitarian Register (monthly), The Universalist Leader (monthly); books, manuals, "The Beacon Twenty-five" series for discussion groups; audio-visual materials on related subjects of Unitarian and Universalist concern.

* * *

COUNCIL OF NATIONAL ORGANIZATIONS OF THE ADULT EDUCATION ASSOCIATION (1952); 150 East 35th Street, New York 16, N. Y.; Executive Secretary.

Membership: 92 participating national organizations.

Purpose: To afford an opportunity for national organizations voluntarily to confer, plan, or work together more effectively on problems of common concern in adult education.

Adult Education Program: CNO provides a resource and referral service on adult education problems and issues at the request of participants, works with participating organizations to carry out projects in adult education of benefit to several or all.

Publications: CNO News (quarterly, to participating organizations); occasional special reports, studies, directories, etc.

* * *

*CREDIT UNION NATIONAL ASSOCIATION (1934); 1617 Sherman Avenue, Madison 1, Wis.; Director, Education Department.

Membership: Institutional members.

Purpose: To service credit unions which provide thrift and lending facilities to members on a mutual self-help basis.

Adult Education Program: The Education Department of CUNA assists local credit union leagues by providing educational and training materials, by co-sponsoring management and leadership training sessions, and by promoting programs of family financial counselling. Other departments provide instructional materials for teachers in junior and senior high schools, sponsor overseas training schools, and conduct conferences on economic, legal, and public relations matters.

Publications: The Credit Union Bridge (monthly), Organization News, Education News, CUNA Briefs (weekly), CUNA Yearbook, several pamphlets.

* * *

DALE CARNEGIE ALUMNI ASSOCIATION (1949); 5420 North College Avenue, Indianapolis 20, Ind.; Executive Director.

Membership: Nearly 400 chapters.

Purpose: To improve members' ability to think clearly and to speak more effectively, both in private interviews and before groups; to prepare them for positions of leadership in their business, professional, social, religious, and community activities; to improve their ability to win friends, influence people, and lead richer and happier lives; to enable them to gain courage and self-confidence in all their business and social contacts; and to afford opportunities to make new friends.

Adult Education Program: The activities of the association include chapter programs on how to give a talk and opportunities for speech practice; chapter programs on how to serve others in the community and to initiate projects to improve the community; social programs for the members; speech contests; and experience in leadership activities in the club and in the community. The association conducts training conferences on leadership techniques, and workshops and clinics in other phases of education.

Publications: The Carnegian (monthly); pamphlets on leadership.

* * *

*FOREIGN POLICY ASSOCIATION (1918); 345 East 46th Street, New York 17, N. Y.; Secretary.

Purpose: To advance public understanding of foreign policy problems through all appropriate educational processes, including the provision of non-partisan information, stimulation of discussion and similar activities, co-operation with other groups and agencies of national, state, and local character, and program services to community organizations for world affairs education.

Adult Education Program: The program of adult education includes assistance and information to national, state, and local organizations, information media, and institutions engaged full or part time in world affairs education. These services include publications, program materials for discussion groups and classroom use, speakers, manuals on the organization and conducting of educational programs on world affairs, and professional assistance through field staff on organizing and conducting world affairs programs. The FPA co-operates with the World Affairs Center for the United States in providing films, information, reference services and bibliographies, program consultation, and book, pamphlet, or document sales.

Publications: Headline Series (bi-monthly); Foreign Policy Bulletin (semi-monthly); Speakers Advisory Service (10 per year); "Great Decisions" fact sheets (annually); Clip Sheet (annual series).

* * *

FRIENDS GENERAL CONFERENCE OF THE RELIGIOUS SOCIETY OF FRIENDS (1900); 1515 Cherry Street, Philadelphia 2, Pa.; General Secretary.

Membership: Friends General Conference is an association of seven Yearly Meetings of the Religious Society of Friends.

Purpose: To strengthen the Religious Society of Friends through conferences, intervisitation, publications, and assistance to local Meetings.

Adult Education Program: Activities include a biennial conference with a program for adults of worship groups, round table discussions, and evening lectures on religious and socially significant topics; other shorter, smaller conferences, such as a two-day conference at the United Nations, and a Family Institute devoted to such topics as religious education in the family. The Conference's publications of study courses for adult classes in Sunday schools, and of miscellaneous leaflets about the Society of Friends, are available for use not only by members but by other groups wishing to use them.

Publications: The Religious Education Bulletin (quarterly).

* * *

THE FUND FOR ADULT EDUCATION (1951); 200 Bloomingdale Road, White Plains, N. Y.; The Secretary.

Purpose: To give aid and encouragement to the idea and practice of continuing liberal education.

Adult Education Program: The FAE's interests and activities include the following program areas: creative arts, economic education, general personal development, home and family life, leadership training, liberal education, public affairs, political affairs, international affairs.

Publications: Annual reports, study and discussion programs, lectures, speeches, occasional papers and books.

* * *

*GENERAL ALLIANCE OF UNITARIAN AND OTHER LIBERAL CHRISTIAN WOMEN (1880); 25 Beacon Street, Boston 8, Mass.; Executive Director.

Membership: 20,000 individuals in 426 branches.

Purpose: To foster an association of liberal religious women devoted to the realization of those ennobling ideals to which Unitarians aspire; to strengthen Unitarianism through the local church and by co-operation with other Unitarian groups; to exemplify religious principles in all personal relationships; to strive for the fulfillment of a human brotherhood of justice and peace.

Adult Education Program: The General Alliance provides bibliography and program aids in the area of resolutions which are passed at Annual Meeting;

conducts leadership training seminars and workshops on national and regional levels for its members.

* * *

*GENERAL FEDERATION OF WOMEN'S CLUBS (1889); 1734 N Street N. W., Washington 6, D. C.; Chairman of Education Department.

Membership: 15,000 clubs in the U. S., 60 in other countries; 50 state federations.

Purpose: For the purpose of mutual benefit of members and for the promotion of their common interest in education, philanthropy, public welfare, moral values, civics, and fine arts.

Adult Education Program: The departments of work of GFWC include American home, conservation of natural resources, education, fine arts, international affairs, and public affairs. Each club undertakes a program of study and activities. Conventions are held at the county, district, state, and national levels, designed to inform and to create interest in programs of specific and general purposes. Exhibits, institutes, forums, panels, symposia are held at various times, the time, locality, and nature of these varying with the needs and desires of the members. In most cases there is co-operation with other community groups to promote their projects.

Publications: G.F.W.C. Clubwoman; program pamphlets in each of the eight departments.

* * *

GERONTOLOGICAL SOCIETY (1945); 660 South Kingshighway Boulevard, St. Louis 10, Mo.; Secretary.

Membership: 2,199 individuals.

Purpose: To promote the scientific study of aging; to foster the growth and diffusion of knowledge relating to the problems of aging; to provide a common meeting ground for scientists interested in such problems and those responsible for the care and treatment of the aged.

Adult Education Program: The society holds annual scientific meetings at which members representing biological science, medicine, psychological and social science, and social welfare present papers and symposia on scientific and professional service aspects of aging. Through affiliated organizations it attempts to interest the general public, as well as the scientific and professional community, in problems of aging and in the welfare of the aged. Through standing committees the society attempts to stimulate and develop research and training in gerontology.

Publications: Journal of Gerontology, Newsletter of the Gerontological Society.

* * *

GIRLS CLUBS OF AMERICA (1945); 265 State Street, Springfield 3, Mass.; Executive Director.

Membership: 50,600 girls, 73 chapters, 13 extension programs.

Purpose: To strengthen the Girls Club movement through a continuous program of service and study aimed to assist member clubs, non-member clubs, and all citizen groups interested in forming Girls Clubs.

Adult Education Program: Since Girls Clubs are aimed primarily to serve girls from 6 to 16, the greatest emphasis is on working with growing girls and training them for their future roles of homemakers, mothers, and citizens. Supplementary to this, many Girls Clubs do conduct activities for adults when there is need and interest in the particular neighborhood in which the Girls Club is located. Some clubs conduct classes in such areas as cooking and sewing for parents of girl members and other interested adults.

Publications: Bulletin (5 times per year), Program Handbooks, other educational folders.

* * *

*GIRL SCOUTS OF U.S.A. (1912); 830 Third Avenue, New York 22, N. Y.; Training Development Director.

Membership: 3,000,295 members, including 765,000 adults; 1,099 local councils; 12 regional offices.

Purpose: To inspire girls with the highest ideals of character, conduct, patriotism, and service that they may become happy and resourceful citizens. The Girl Scout program is based on an ethical code, to which all members subscribe, and is carried out in small groups with adult leadership. The democratic process guides all activities and the motivating force in the Girl Scout movement is a spiritual one.

Adult Education Program: The training and development of all adults in the organization is an integral part of Girl

Scouting. The purpose of the training is to improve knowledge of the Girl Scout program, its aim and philosophy; to improve competency for a particular job; and to help adults render effective service in the movement. National, regional, and local training programs are conducted. Courses, workshops, discussion groups, and conferences comprise the main types, and various study guides, manuals, and audio-visual aids are produced to supplement the training program. The national organization maintains a residential summer school (Edith Macy Training school) for over 750 volunteers and professional staff members annually. It also maintains three training centers (East, Mid-West, and West Coast) for professional job training and workshop for administrative volunteers. Special projects in the training of adults are planned from time to time, such as Camping Caravan or Arts Caravan, mobile units that travel throughout the country giving short-term training and demonstrations. The International Friendship Program of the Girl Scouts is furthered by an exchange of adult visitor-observers who participate in workshops and conferences during their stay in the United States.
Publications: The Leader Magazine (to all adults); The American Girl (to all girls); Professional Newsletter; Annual Report to Congress, National Training Catalog, Grants for Study Program, Bulletin on Personnel Administration, and others.

* * *

*GOODWILL INDUSTRIES OF AMERICA (1902); 1913 N Street, N. W., Washington 6, D. C.; Executive Vice President.
Membership: 120 local Goodwill Industries.
Purpose: To provide employment, training, rehabilitation, and opportunities for personal growth for the handicapped and disabled.
Adult Education Program: The major emphasis is on providing vocational training and employment for handicapped persons and such other cultural and special educational services as are required in order to assist disabled people to achieve a maximum of vocational and social adjustment.
Publications: News Letter, Training Man-

uals, promotional pamphlets, annual reports.

* * *

THE GREAT BOOKS FOUNDATION (1947); 37 South Wabash Avenue, Chicago 3, Ill.; President.
Membership: More than 2,200 discussion groups with around 35,000 leaders and participants.
Purpose: To help individuals form groups to read and discuss the Great Books; to further the cause of adult liberal education; to explore and develop the techniques of the study-discussion program.
Adult Education Program: The foundation gives leader training courses and other forms of leader training, provides free publicity material, consults with and advises sponsors of Great Books groups, and makes available to interested parties the services of its professional staff.
Publications: Boxed paperbound sets of readings for the Great Books program (1st through 7th year); Readers' Aids (for each reading); Guide for Leaders of Great Books Discussion Groups; The Gadfly (monthly magazine).

* * *

INSTITUTE OF INTERNATIONAL EDUCATION (1919); 1 East 7th Street, New York 21, N. Y.; President.
Purpose: To increase international understanding through the promotion of all aspects of international exchange.
Adult Education Program: Develops and administers programs of educational exchange of students, teachers, leaders, and specialists between the United States and 80 other countries. Administers exchange programs for the United States and foreign governments, foundations, universities, corporations, and individuals. Serves as a clearing house on all phases of international education.
Publications: Open Doors (a yearly census of foreign students studying in the U. S. and of Americans studying abroad); Handbook on International Study; many other publications.

* * *

*IOTA PHI LAMBDA SORORITY (1929); 1337 North 57th Street, Philadelphia 31, Pa.; National Liaison Officer.
Membership: 1,000 individuals, 80 chapters.
Purpose: To unite in a sisterhood qualified women in related fields of business;

to promote interest in business education among high school and college girls through planned programs and scholarships; to encourage development of personalities for all areas of leadership; and to urge further intellectual development of members through higher education.

Adult Education Program: The sorority's national program consists of the observance of American Education Week, Negro History Week, Iota Phi Lambda Business Week, and Founder's Day. Services for members include planning and conducting leadership clinics and workshops, showing educational films, providing demonstrations of business machines and equipment, conducting tours of business concerns. Among the services for the public are providing "canteens" for young people, citing the outstanding business woman locally, regionally, and nationally, promoting job guidance clinics, holding annual scholarship contest for senior high school students, conducting public celebrations of American Education Week.

Publications: Iota Phi Lambda Journal; "Every Iota a Voter"; Post-convention Newsletter.

* * *

JOINT COUNCIL ON EDUCATIONAL TELEVISION (1951); 1785 Massachusetts Avenue N. W., Washington 6, D. C.; Executive Director.

Membership: American Association of School Administrators, American Association of Land-Grant Colleges and State Universities, American Council on Education, Council of Chief State School Officers, Educational Television and Radio Center, National Association of Educational Broadcasters, National Association of State Universities, National Citizens Committee for Educational Television, National Congress of Parents and Teachers, National Education Association of the United States.

Purpose: The JCET is concerned with the preservation and utilization of educational television channels. The council represents the educational television movement before the Federal Communications Commission, Congressional committees, and other government agencies.

Adult Education Program: The JCET performs the following functions: serves as a source of information on TV channel allocations and government regulations and actions relating to ETV, in particular those of the FCC; publishes regular reports on status of ETV and prepares and distributes material on special aspects of ETV development; provides speakers and field workers for groups planning to establish stations; supplies information on legal, technical, and engineering matters while the station is still in the planning stage; maintains legal representation for ETV in the nation's capital; provides a consulting service on legal and engineering aspects of the construction and operation of ETV stations; represents educational television in matters concerning the total national development of the television art.

Publications: JCET Educational Television Factsheet (monthly except June, July, and August).

* * *

KIWANIS INTERNATIONAL (1915); 101 East Erie Street, Chicago 11, Ill.; Director of Program Development.

Membership: 4,700 chapters.

Purpose: A service organization with high ideals, worthy objects, and challenging objectives, which are realized through the activities of its member clubs in their respective communities.

Adult Education Program: Kiwanis International operates a program of leadership training to develop adults in their ability to handle specific assignments in their local communities. Local clubs carry out activities in two main areas, Youth Service and Citizenship Service. Youth Service consists of Boys and Girls Work committees and vocational guidance. Citizenship Service includes agriculture and conservation, public and business affairs, and support of churches in their spiritual aims. The program brings to the attention of the membership the broad responsibilities of citizenship in a democracy, stimulates individuals in the local community to understand economic, political, social, and religious issues of the day, and encourages projects consistent with the objectives of the organization.

Publications: Kiwanis Magazine, Keynoter, Circle K Bulletin, Bulletin for Kiwanis Officers.

LEAGUE OF WOMEN VOTERS OF THE UNITED STATES (1920); 1026 17th St., N. W., Washington 6, D. C.; President.

Membership: 127,000 individual members, affiliated with 1080 local leagues.

Purpose: To promote political responsibility through informed and active participation of citizens in government.

Adult Education Program: The league provides background materials and study outlines on certain public issues selected by the membership for concerted attention. These materials are available at low cost to the public and other organizations. Local leagues sponsor many programs of information and study on issues of local, state, and national interest.

Publications: The National Voter (10 issues a year); pamphlets and books on public issues such as water resources, international relations, etc.

* * *

LIONS INTERNATIONAL (1917); 209 North Michigan Avenue, Chicago 1, Ill. Executive Administrator.

Membership: 592,404 individuals, 14,357 clubs, in 101 countries.

Purpose: To determine community needs and develop means of meeting them, either through its own efforts or in cooperation with other agencies.

Adult Education Program: There are ten suggested classifications for major activities which Lions Clubs may adopt: agriculture, boys and girls, citizenship and patriotism, civic improvement, community betterment, education, health and welfare, safety, sight conservation and work for the visually handicapped, United Nations. Each local Lions Club is free to choose the activities in which it will engage.

* * *

MUSCULAR DYSTROPHY ASSOCIATIONS OF AMERICA (1950); 1790 Broadway, New York 19, N. Y.; Director of Public Information.

Membership: 360 chapters.

Purpose: To foster scientific research into the cause and cure of muscular dystrophy; to render patient services locally through MDAA Chapters, and nationally by the establishment of clinics and the initiation of pilot-experiments and conferences.

Adult Education Program: MDAA carries on a program of education about muscular dystrophy among physicians, professional people, and the public.

Publications: Muscular Dystrophy News (bi-monthly); Annual Report; various pamphlets on muscular dystrophy.

* * *

*MUSIC EDUCATORS NATIONAL CONFERENCE (1907); NEA Education Center, 1201 Sixteenth Street, N. W., Washington, D. C.; Executive Secretary.

Membership: Over 32,000 individual members in 51 federated state units.

Purpose: The advancement of music education.

Adult Education Program: Promotes improvement of instruction of music in school and community through conferences, workshops, and clinics.

Publications: Music Educators Journal (6 issues per year), Journal of Research in Music Education (twice yearly), Music for Everybody; other publications covering various areas and levels of music education.

* * *

*NATIONAL ACADEMY FOR ADULT JEWISH STUDIES OF THE UNITED SYNAGOGUE OF AMERICA (1940); 1109 Fifth Avenue, New York 28, N. Y.; Director.

Membership: Approximately 650 Conservative congregations affiliated with the United Synagogue of America.

Purpose: To encourage and promote adult learning both formal and informal in the synagogue and in the general Jewish community.

Adult Education Program: The academy carries out its purposes by the following means: preparation and publication of texts, pamphlets, brochures, syllabi, and courses of study for use in adult institutes, home study, and discussion groups; distribution of films on Jewish themes; guidance and information on resources, courses, classes, and over-all programs in adult Jewish education; stimulation and fostering of Laymen's Institutes and the development of new ideas and techniques in adult Jewish education; operation of Cavalcades of Conservative Judaism, offering a series of integrated lectures by visiting speakers to affiliated congregations.

Publications: Adult Jewish Education (quarterly); texts, syllabi, study guides, brochures, etc.

*NATIONAL ASSOCIATION FOR THE ADVANCEMENT OF COLORED PEOPLE (1909); 20 West 40th Street, New York 18, N. Y.; Activities Co-ordinator.

Membership: 400,000 individual members.

Purpose: Achievement of full equality of citizenship for Negro Americans; modification of racial attitudes in the interest of sound and democratic human relations.

Adult Education Program: The association's education program is chiefly directed towards improving the knowledge and skills of leaders of local units about civil rights and techniques for advancing them in such areas as housing, education, political action, voting, access to public accommodations, etc. National staff experts on housing, labor, public relations, youth, etc., serve as consultants to local units. The organization furnishes speakers on civil rights topics.

Publications: The Crisis (monthly); pamphlets, leaflets, reprints in civil rights field, handbooks and manuals for leaders.

* * *

*THE NATIONAL ASSOCIATION AND COUNCIL OF BUSINESS SCHOOLS (1912); 2400 16th Street N. W., Washington 9, D. C.; Executive Director.

Membership: 450 institutions.

Purpose: To serve both the public interest and this branch of specialized education through supervision, development of standards and programs, and maintenance of proper standards of operation; to serve as a national center for the dissemination of information related to programs of business education; to improve the quality and scope of business education; to conduct research programs; and to provide centralized professional leadership on a national level.

Adult Education Program: Services to members include development and maintenance of standards, general guidance on problems of operation, analysis of educational needs and opportunities, distribution of information and materials. The association seeks the adaptation of programs to community and national needs, and the development of new programs of study to meet changing demands and conditions. Records and information on business education are available to other organizations, particularly in connection with their own educational program.

Publications: Annual Directory of Business Schools; Business School Newsletter, Business School Executive Digest; brochures on secretaryship, business administration, and accountancy; reprints.

* * *

*NATIONAL ASSOCIATION OF COUNTY AGRICULTURAL AGENTS (1916); Postoffice Building, Greensburg, Pa.; Secretary-Treasurer.

Membership: 5,700 individuals; 48 affiliated state associations.

Purpose: To assist member state associations and district associations in securing additional opportunities for furthering educational advantages; to encourage a high standard of professional performance among our extension field workers; to promote a high degree of co-operation and loyalty among extension people; to assist in the furthering of the ways and means of improving the effectiveness of co-operative extension work; to advance the basic importance and position of American agriculture and the farming public in our national economy; and to co-operate in carrying out the policies and programs of the land-grant colleges and the Federal Extension Service in the United States.

Adult Education Program: The association promotes professional improvement through both in-service training and graduate work, as well as the annual meetings for the members; conducts national, state, county, and community programs, using demonstrations, meetings, circulars, magazines and newspapers, radio and television; co-operates with other organizations in the areas of agriculture and home economics.

Publications: The County Agent (quarterly); annual reports of each of the county associations.

* * *

*NATIONAL ASSOCIATION OF EDUCATIONAL BROADCASTERS (1925); 14 Gregory Hall, Urbana, Ill.; Executive Director.

Membership: 460 individuals, 324 institutions.

Purpose: The professional association for men and women engaged in educational broadcasting production and teaching; a programming network, distributing tape recorded programs to member stations; the trade association of educational institutions operating radio and television stations, closed-circuit television operations, and radio and television production centers.

Adult Education Program: NAEB operates a network which distributes radio programs designed to improve general adult education and cultural understandings; conducts seminars, workshops, and conferences, and offers scholarships to improve qualifications and status of educational broadcasters; co-operates with many other adult education organization to improve co-ordinated efforts and understanding; undertakes, underwrites, and reports on research in the field of educational broadcasting; provides consultation services, not only to educational broadcasters, but to other adult education organizations needing advice and assistance in the area of broadcasting activities; exchanges personnel, programs, and materials with the broadcasting systems of several other countries.

Publications: Newsletter, Journal; reports and studies in the field of educational broadcasting.

* * *

NATIONAL ASSOCIATION OF HOUSING AND REDEVELOPMENT OFFICIALS (1933); 1313 East 60th Street, Chicago 37, Ill.; Associate Director.

Membership: 3,600 individuals, 700 agencies.

Purpose: To better public administrative practices in housing and community renewal; to foster national leadership in the campaign to achieve a decent environment for all Americans.

Adult Education Program: Through publications, conferences and workshops, and research and information services, the association provides resources for education in the fields of housing and urban renewal for members of the organization, for other organizations, and for the public. Citizen participation and community organization are points of emphasis.

Publications: Journal of Housing (11 issues a year); Housing and Urban Renewal Directory (every two or three years); other pamphlets, reports.

NATIONAL ASSOCIATION OF INTERGROUP RELATIONS OFFICIALS (1947); 426 West 58th Street, New York 19, N. Y.; Executive Secretary.

Membership: 550 individuals.

Purpose: To improve the standards of professional intergroup relations practice, and advance intergroup relations knowledge and skills.

Adult Education Program: The association sponsors national and regional conferences, local groups, study commissions, functional departments, a professional training program, and publications, all designed to help professional intergroup relations workers and others improve the performance of their duties.

Publications: Reporter (bi-monthly bulletin), Journal of Intergroup Relations (quarterly magazine), bi-monthly newsletter, special reports and directories.

* * *

*NATIONAL ASSOCIATION OF MANUFACTURERS OF THE UNITED STATES OF AMERICA (1895); 2 East 48th Street, New York 17, N. Y.; Director, Education Department.

Membership: 21,000 company memberships.

Purpose: To formulate policies and objectives based on the enduring economic, social, and governmental principles embodied in the Constitution of the United States, and without regard to partisan political considerations or the fortunes of any political party or candidate; to provide leadership in bringing about steady improvement: (a) in the economic strength of the nation in order to safeguard peace and the national security; (b) in the contribution of industry to the public welfare, (c) in the operation of the American system of free capital and free labor so as to afford opportunity and incentive for the individual to progress and provide for the well-being and security of himself and his family; to assist manufacturers in appraising the significance of social, legislative, and economic trends as they affect industry, people, the community and the nation; to contribute to a continuing improvement in the relations and co-operation between employer and employee, between government and industry, and between the public and industry; to join with others in bringing to the public and to government the viewpoint of manufacturers as to how national and international issues affect industry and future of every citizen; to help create understanding of how the American capitalistic system works for the benefit of every individual; to formulate its policies and conduct its operations so as to merit the respect and support of the American people.

Adult Education Program: The NAM sponsors meetings between manufacturers and educators to consider common concerns in the education of adults, especially in the vocational and economic areas.

Publications: Career pamphlets, Research studies, Industry and American Economy Series (16 booklets), HOBSO, NAM News (weekly, to membership), 10 Part Program for Better Labor Legislation, Political Education Seminars.

* * *

*THE NATIONAL ASSOCIATION FOR MENTAL HEALTH (1950; successor to the National Committee for Mental Hygiene, founded in 1909); 10 Columbus Circle, New York 19, N. Y.; Director of Education Services.

Membership: 800 state mental health associations.

Purpose: To develop a co-ordinated citizens' voluntary movement to work toward the improved care and treatment of the mentally ill and handicapped; to improve methods and services in research, prevention, detection, diagnosis, and treatment of mental illnesses and handicaps; and to promote mental health.

Adult Education Program: The program of the association aims to reduce fear and prejudice about mental illness, to win public interest and participation in programs to combat mental illness, and to help people recognize and understand mental illness and the principles of good mental health. Educational activities are carried on through literature, posters, exhibits, meetings, conferences, seminars, the press, radio and television, and magazines, at national and local levels.

Publications: Mental Hygiene (quarterly), NAMH Reporter (monthly); Annual Report; other books and pamphlets on mental health.

*NATIONAL ASSOCIATION OF PUBLIC SCHOOL ADULT EDUCATORS (1952); 1201 16th Street, N. W., Washington 6, D. C.; Executive Secretary.

Membership: 2,845 individuals.

Purpose: To extend and enrich opportunities for adult education through local school systems.

Adult Education Program: With the assistance of a grant from the Fund for Adult Education, NAPSAE provides fund grants and consultative services to state departments of education to establish positions of state directors of adult education; in-service training programs for local directors of adult education; employment of a specialist to interpret public school adult education to the educational field and the lay public. In addition, NAPSAE serves as a centralized information service for all public school adult education. News service concerning public school adult education in the form of magazines, pamphlets, newsletters, books, direct mail, displays, brochures, and through such related media as the Press and Radio Service of the NEA is provided. A national conference is sponsored annually by NAPSAE to which all teachers and administrators of adult education are invited.

Publications: Public School Adult Educator; Swap Shop for Administrators; Directory of Administrator Members; Civic Education; Public School Adult Education: a Guide for Administrators and Teachers; When You're Teaching Adults; The Case for Adult Education.

* * *

NATIONAL CITIZENS COUNCIL FOR BETTER SCHOOLS (1956); (formerly National Citizens Commission for the Public Schools, founded in 1949); 9 East 40th Street, New York 16, N. Y.; Director, Communications Division.

Membership: 80 individuals. Members not professionally identified with religion, education, or politics.

Purpose: To help arouse widespread interest in education throughout the United States; to convert that interest into action; and to provide state and local school improvement groups with information helpful in the solution of their local school problems.

Adult Education Program: The NCCBS promotes the improvement of schools and education through conferences, publications, and use of the mass media.

Publications: Better Schools (monthly, except July and August); other publications on wide range of educational issues.

* * *

*NATIONAL CONFERENCE OF CHRISTIANS AND JEWS (1928); 43 West 57th Street, New York 19, N. Y.; Director, Commission on Community Organizations.

Membership: 200,000 individuals, 137 chapters and 64 regional offices.

Purpose: To promote justice, amity, understanding, and co-operation among Protestants, Catholics, and Jews; to analyze, moderate, and finally eliminate intergroup prejudices in religious, business, social, and political relations.

Adult Education Program: NCCJ is engaged in civic education via existing organizations in principal social institutional "trunklines" of society. It emphasizes leadership training in workshops, institutes, and seminars; sponsors Brotherhood Week annually.

Publications: Books, pamphlets, reprints, films, and records, about intergroup relations.

* * *

*NATIONAL CONFERENCE ON SOCIAL WELFARE (1874); 22 West Gay Street, Columbus 15, Ohio; Executive Secretary.

Membership: 5,500 individuals, 1,000 agencies.

Purpose: A voluntary association of individuals and organization members who have joined the conference to promote and share in discussion of the problems and methods identified with the field of social work and immediately related fields.

Adult Education Program: The major activity of the NCSW is to conduct an Annual Forum for the critical examination of basic social welfare problems and issues. This is a service for members, the social welfare field, national organizations in the social welfare field, and the general public. All other NCSW activities grow out of, or are directly related to, this major activity.

Publications: Social Welfare Forum (annually, the official proceedings of the Annual Forum); selected papers in Case Work, Group Work, and Community Organization (annually); Conference Bulletin (quarterly); and volumes of papers from Annual Forum.

* * *

*NATIONAL CONGRESS OF PARENTS AND TEACHERS (1897); 700 North Rush Street, Chicago, Ill.; Administrative Assistant to the President.

Membership: More than 11,500,000 members belonging to 45,200 local parent-teacher associations (P.T.A.'s).

Purpose: To promote the welfare of children and youth in home, school, church, and community; to raise the standards of home life, to secure adequate laws for the care and protection of children and youth; to bring into closer relation the home and the school, that parents and teachers may co-operate intelligently in the training of the child; to develop between educators and the general public such united efforts as will secure for every child the highest advantages in physical, mental, social, and spiritual education.

Adult Education Program: Adult education through parent education is one of the primary activities of P.T.A.'s in carrying out this purpose. A national chairman of Parent and Family Life Education guides and encourages local programs in this specific field through state chairmen, while other national chairmen promote adult education similarly in such areas as health, juvenile protection, legislation, recreation, and safety. Conferences and study groups, both within the National Congress of Parents and Teachers and in co-operative meetings with other organizations, are concerned with awakening in all adults an awareness of their responsibility for the welfare of children and youth. This concern is also reflected in the theme and program developed each year for the national convention. Lay leadership training has an important place in the over-all program.

Publications: National Parent-Teacher: The P.T.A. Magazine (monthly, September through June); National Congress Bulletin (ten times a year); Guiding Children as They Grow; Study-Discussion Group Techniques for Parent Education Leaders; What P.T.A. Members Should Know About Juvenile Delinquency; other pamphlets for parent-teacher education.

*NATIONAL COUNCIL OF CATHOLIC MEN (1920); 1312 Massachusetts Avenue N. W., Washington 5, D. C.; Director, Development and Training.

Membership: 16 national organizations, 54 diocesan councils, 9,000 local organizations.

Purpose: To serve, co-ordinate, and represent Catholic men's organizations.

Adult Education Program: Provides information and program materials in a variety of religious, social, and civic fields; conducts leadership training programs for leaders of member organizations; produces all regularly scheduled Catholic programs on national radio and television networks.

Publications: Monthly newsletter magazine, monthly program publication, miscellaneous manuals, pamphlets, and other publications; 16 mm. film library.

* * *

NATIONAL COUNCIL OF CATHOLIC WOMEN (1920); 1312 Massachusetts Avenue N. W., Washington 5, D. C.; Executive Secretary.

Membership: 22 national and state and approximately 12,000 local organizations; 60 organizations in American military posts overseas.

Purpose: To unite the Catholic organizations of women in the United States in religious, educational, social, and economic fields; to render assistance to these organizations and to stimulate them to greater service in these fields; to represent Catholic women in national and international meetings; to establish relations with national and international organizations to the end of working on common problems.

Adult Education Program: Through 17 national committees, headed by volunteers, suggested committee programs are sent out in the fields of civil defense, charitable work, religious education, family and parent education, foreign relief, home and school association, immigration, international relations, inter-American relations, citizenship education, libraries and literature, public relations, rural life, social action, spiritual development, youth organization, and development of groups and programs. Leadership training institutes are held biennially in various parts of the country. National conventions are also held biennially with inspirational and informa-

tional speakers, and committee workshops. Assistance is given through correspondence, program suggestions, bibliographical references, suggestions for speakers, field services, both in organization and leadership training, reports, and exhibits.

Publications: Monthly Message to Affiliated Organizations, Women in Catholic Action (quarterly), Women at Work (manual for local organizations).

* * *

*NATIONAL COUNCIL OF THE CHURCHES OF CHRIST IN THE UNITED STATES OF AMERICA (1950); 475 Riverside Drive, New York 27, N. Y.; Director of Adult Work.

Membership: Protestant denominations serving approximately 35 million individuals.

Purpose: To continue and extend the work of the merging agencies by the creation of an inclusive co-operative agency of Christian churches in the USA; to bring churches into further united service for Christ and the world; to strengthen the spirit of fellowship, service, and co-operation among them; to promote the application of the law of Christ in every relation of life; and to encourage and further the achievement of such purposes in local communities and throughout the world.

Adult Education Program: The Department of Adult Work assists the denominations and state councils in the development of objectives, standards, resources, research, and experimentation. It provides consultation services, conferences and workshops, institutes for training workers with adults, and a mail information service.

Publications: Information Service, International Journal of Religious Education, City Church, Christian Scholar; Planning for Young Adults, The Fulfillment Years.

* * *

*NATIONAL COUNCIL OF JEWISH WOMEN (1893); One West 47th Street, New York 36, N. Y.; Head, Public Affairs.

Membership: 110,000 individuals and 235 chapters.

Purpose: To promote education, social action, community service, and overseas services.

Adult Education Program: The Council

sponsors programs in social legislation, contemporary Jewish affairs, and international relations; study groups in these fields for council local groups; public forums and conferences to reach the community.

Publications: Council Woman, Council Platform, New Horizons in Community Services, Overseas.

* * *

*THE NATIONAL COUNCIL OF NEGRO WOMEN (1935); 1318 Vermont Avenue, N. W., Washington 5, D. C.; Executive Director.

Membership: 500 life members, 96 chapters, 22 organization affiliates.

Purpose: Functions as a clearing house for national organizations; unites women's organizations for effective study and action at the national and local levels on matters affecting the social, educational, economic, and cultural welfare of women.

Adult Education Program: The National Council of Negro Women provides leadership training institutes, conferences, and seminars at national, regional, and local levels. It services its councils and affiliates with program guides and resource materials. It promotes programs and projects which serve community needs. It functions in a representative capacity at national and international conferences.

Publications: Periodicals, manuals, reports, pamphlets.

* * *

*NATIONAL COUNCIL OF WOMEN OF THE UNITED STATES (1888); 345 East 46th Street, New York 17, N. Y.; Executive Vice President.

Membership: 1,200 individuals, 23 national organizations; affiliated with 44 national councils in the International Council of Women.

Purpose: The council believes that women have a responsible role to play in their own communities and that they should be informed about domestic affairs and international issues in order to contribute to world understanding. Its basic purpose is, therefore, to advance the democratic way of life.

Adult Education Program: The council carries out its educational purposes through lectures, conferences, workshops, and study courses.

Publications: Bulletin of National Council; occasional reports; monthly U.N. Calendar.

* * *

NATIONAL EDUCATION ASSOCIATION, DIVISION OF ADULT EDUCATION SERVICE (1945—successor to Department of Adult Education, established in 1921); 1201 16th Street, N. W., Washington 6, D. C.; Director.

Purpose: To work with educators in seeking ways and means of continuing to broaden the scope of adult education as carried on in the public schools.

Adult Education Program: Its services include consultation, membership on national committees, publications, meetings, conferences.

Publications: Various books, pamphlets, and reprints on public school adult education.

* * *

NATIONAL EDUCATIONAL TELEVISION AND RADIO CENTER (1952); 10 Columbus Circle, New York 19, N. Y.; Vice President in Charge of Programming.

Membership: 44 non-commercial television stations.

Purpose: The National Educational Television and Radio Center is the network headquarters for non-commercial television broadcasting in the United States. Its primary functions are to provide its member stations with cultural informational programs; to disseminate the aims, purposes, and benefits of educational television on a national and international basis; to initiate and co-ordinate developmental activities that will bring substantial financial underwriting both to the center's operations and those of the stations.

Adult Education Program: More than 350 hours per year of educational TV programs for adults are broadcast by more than 40 educational television stations in the United States. Further, many of these programs are used by schools and adult study groups as substantive resource materials on film.

Publication: Educational Television Today.

* * *

NATIONAL FARMERS UNION (1902); 1575 Sherman Street, Denver 3, Col.; Director of Organization and Education.

Membership: Individuals, local and state unions.

Purpose: To promote the welfare and economic well being of the family-type farmer.

Adult Education Program: The organization's activities include national conferences, state and regional conferences, seminars, workshops, camps for both youths and adults. It provides informational and educational services for its members and for the public.

Publications: National Union Farmer (monthly to membership), Action Letter (monthly to leaders), Washington Newsletter (weekly); miscellaneous books, periodicals, and pamphlets.

* * *

THE NATIONAL FEDERATION OF BUSINESS AND PROFESSIONAL WOMEN'S CLUBS (1919); 2012 Massachusetts Avenue N. W., Washington 6, D. C.; Staff Director of Career Advancement.

Membership: 174,000 individuals, 3,400 clubs.

Purpose: The improvement of conditions in all businesses and professions; the extension of opportunities to better the business and professional status of women; the preparation of women for leadership in their communities, their states, and the nation; and the advancement of women in their respective fields of work so that they may make their greatest contribution to the common good.

Adult Education Program: The program promotes study in five major fields: Career Advancement, Health and Safety, International Relations, National Security, Public Affairs. Programs for older women workers, reorientation, and "brush-up" courses are offered through local clubs in co-operation with other organizations and civic groups. Career Advancement programs for members stimulate specialization, further training, and self-development. The federation supports current legislation safeguarding the rights of women, discouraging discriminatory practices, and improving the status of women.

Publications: The National Business Woman (monthly).

* * *

*NATIONAL FEDERATION OF SETTLEMENTS AND NEIGHBORHOOD CENTERS (1911); 226 West 47th Street, New York 36, N. Y.; Secretary, Social Education and Action.

Membership: 268 agencies.

Purpose: To improve neighborhood life through support of legislation, through services to neighborhood agencies, and exchange of information and experience among them.

Adult Education Program: The national office supplies information and ideas on neighborhood work, conducts studies of neighborhood social conditions, holds conferences, provides field and office consultation to settlements and neighborhood centers, and maintains a personnel referral service. It maintains relationships with settlements in other countries.

Publications: Round Table (8 issues yearly); pamphlets on subjects relating to work in settlements and trends in community life, such as "Neighborhood Goals in a Rapidly Developing World" and "Dynamics of Citizen Participation."

* * *

*THE NATIONAL FOUNDATION (originally The National Foundation for Infantile Paralysis, Inc.) (1938); 800 Second Avenue, New York 17, N. Y.; Division of Scientific and Health Information.

Membership: 3,100 chapters—county basis.

Purpose: To be an organized force for medical research, patient care, and professional education for attack on health problems on a broad front. Initial targets are birth defects, arthritis, polio and other viruses, central nervous system disorders.

Adult Education Program: The National Foundation maintains a year-round information program through all media to acquaint the public with facts about the disease areas covered, and developments in medical research. Free teaching materials are offered schools and colleges and program material provided organizations interested in health. Professional groups are reached through regular releases by exhibiting at conventions. Scholarships and fellowships are offered for training in a number of health professions.

Materials: Pamphlets, booklets, reports, newsletters, films, filmstrips, exhibits.

* * *

THE NATIONAL 4-H CLUB FOUNDATION OF AMERICA (1948); 7100 Connecticut Avenue, Washington 15, D. C.; Executive Director.

Purpose: Established by the Cooperative

Extension Service of the state land-grant colleges and universities and the U. S. Department of Agriculture to develop and use private support for educational purposes that will best meet the needs and advance the interests of extension youth work.

Adult Education Program: The foundation provides consultant and training services to the extension service for professional personnel; promotes leadership development for volunteer adult leaders, and citizenship training for young people; conducts an international exchange of persons program, and owns and operates the National 4-H Center.

Publications: Pamphlets, studies, manuals, and reports for professional extension workers; journal reporting on the program of the foundation.

* * *

THE NATIONAL GRANGE (1867); 744 Jackson Place, N. W., Washington 6, D. C.; Lecturer.

Membership: 850,000 individual members in 7,000 chapters.

Purpose: A rural family fraternity, seeking to improve the lot of rural Americans, and to develop a "higher manhood and womanhood among our members."

Adult Education Program: The National Grange conducts conferences for state and local leaders and serves as a resource on program ideas and materials. At the local level the program is mainly concerned with home and farm, and community activities, employing courses, lectures, discussions, demonstrations, etc.

Publications: National Grange Monthly.

* * *

NATIONAL HEALTH COUNCIL (1921); 1790 Broadway, New York 19, N. Y.; Executive Director.

Membership: 67 national organizations, including 48 active professional and voluntary members, 7 advisory (governmental) members, 7 associate members, and 5 sustaining (business) members.

Purpose: To help the national health agencies work more effectively together and with others in the cause of health improvement of the nation.

Adult Education Program: The council stimulates interest in, and utilization of, existing health resources and available health knowledge, for the improvement of personal, family, and community

health, by means of forums, conferences, publications, and visual aids.

Publications: Forum reports, Health Careers publications, study guide and other materials for community health planning, and special activities publications.

* * *

*NATIONAL HOME DEMONSTRATION AGENTS' ASSOCIATION (1933); 504 Court House, Birmingham 3, Ala.; President.

Membership: 3,494 individuals.

Purpose: To foster professional improvement of home demonstration agents.

Adult Education Program: The association promotes the improvement of the adult educational skills of the membership through workshops and conferences.

Publications: H D A Reporter (quarterly).

* * *

*NATIONAL HOME STUDY COUNCIL (1926); 800 18th Street, N. W., Washington 5, D. C.; Executive Director.

Membership: 58 institutional members.

Purpose: To serve as a professional association and accrediting agency for private home study schools as designated by the U. S. Office of Education under the terms of Public Laws 82-550 and 85-864.

Adult Education Program: The council performs the following services: accrediting private home study schools which offer over 400 different adult education courses; providing consultation services for improvement of both business and educational functions of the schools; publishing a list of schools which have been found to meet ethical and educational standards. In addition, the council acts as a clearing house of information on private home study schools and courses, advises prospective students which schools are believed to be reputable and which are not, and informs students where they may obtain the courses they desire. It works with other educational associations, state departments of education, etc., in helping to establish legislation to control and limit the operation of disreputable and unethical private home study schools.

Publications: Annual Statistics on Enrollments in Home Study, Home Study Blue Book, Directory of Approved Home Study Schools, List of Accredited Private Home Study Schools, other miscellaneous publications.

NATIONAL INDUSTRIAL CONFER-
ENCE BOARD (1916); 460 Park Avenue, New York 22, N. Y.; Director, Public Information and Education Division.

Membership: 3,700 subscribing associates.

Purpose: To promote the prosperity and
security of the American people by assisting in the effective operation and
sound development of voluntary productive enterprise in the United States and
Canada; to conduct research in the fields
of economics, business management, and
human relations, and to publish the
findings of such research.

Adult Education Program: During each
year, The Conference Board brings together business, labor, and industrial executives in conferences on economic affairs in leading cities throughout United
States and Canada. It serves as a source
of facts and figures bearing on all aspects of economic life.

Publications: Weekly and monthly publications supplying facts on all phases of
current business, industrial, and economic developments; periodic reports of
studies in personnel policy, business policy, labor statistics, and business economics; special publications of statistical
data, analyses of economic problems, etc.

* * *

NATIONAL INSTITUTE OF LABOR
EDUCATION (1957); 1303 University
Avenue, Madison 5, Wis.; Executive Di-
rector.

Purpose: To serve as a framework for co-
operation in the field of education between labor and non-labor agencies.

Adult Education Program: NILE origi-
nates programs in the field of labor education primarily on subject matters of
liberal education. Projects are usually
conducted as a joint co-operative undertaking of several universities and other
non-labor agencies on the one hand and
unions on the other, with NILE providing the over all co-ordination and direction.

* * *

*NATIONAL JEWISH WELFARE
BOARD (1917); 145 East 32nd Street,
New York 16, N. Y.; Director, Adult
Program Services Department.

Membership: 350 Jewish Community Centers and Y.M. and Y.W.H.A.'s.

Purpose: As the national association of
Jewish Community Centers and Y.M.
and Y.W.H.A.'s, the JWB provides guid-

ance in setting goals, in assisting local
program efforts, in recommending and
training personnel, in interpretation, in
stimulating joint regional and national
program projects, and in assisting in the
planning of physical facilities and operational methods.

Adult Education Program: Local centers
engage in family life education, Jewish
cultural activities, formal classes, forums,
concerts, public affairs activities, and
leadership training institutes. Through
its Adult Program Services Department
the JWB assists local centers in planning
and evaluating their adult programs, in
locating program resources, in highlight-
ing current needs, and in determining
local interests. It also conducts a lecture
and concert bureau which arranges for
tours of outstanding authorities in specific topical areas and for tours of artists
in dramatic, dance, and musical presentations.

Publications: The Circle, Jewish Community Center Program Aids, the Adult
Program Services Newsletter, and a variety of studies, manuals, and pamphlets.

* * *

THE NATIONAL MANAGEMENT AS-
SOCIATION (1925); 333 West First
Street, Dayton 2, Ohio; Manager of Edu-
cation.

Membership: 70,000 individuals in 320
chapters.

Purpose: To foster leadership development, to work for unity in management,
and to promote management as a profession.

Adult Education Program: The association's activities include study-discussion
programs, seminars, speakers, and leadership training programs.

Publications: Manage Magazine, Club Education Bulletin, research studies.

* * *

NATIONAL RECREATION ASSOCIA-
TION (1906); 8 West Eighth Street, New
York 11, N. Y.; Executive Director.

Membership: 4,037 individuals and 1,724
organizations.

Purpose: That every child in America shall
have a chance to play; that everybody in
America, young or old, shall have an
opportunity to find the best and most
satisfying use of leisure time.

Adult Education Program: The association sponsors national and regional conferences for recreation leaders and agen-

cies; maintains consultation and correspondence service; conducts training workshops; makes community surveys and studies of recreation areas, facilities and program; maintains consultant service on recreation for the ill and handicapped, field service for recreation departments, and a placement service for recreation personnel.

Publications: Recreation (monthly), newsletters, Playground Summer Notebook (annually); numerous books and booklets on all phases of recreation.

* * *

NATIONAL SCHOOL BOARDS ASSOCIATION (1940); 1940 Sheridan Road, Evanston, Ill.; Executive Director.

Membership: 50 state associations and District of Columbia Board of Education, 1,000 local boards, 7 sustaining members.

Purpose: To promote the general advancement of education for the youth of the United States and its territories.

Adult Education Program: NSBA conducts an annual convention and special projects and workshops; provides consultative services by staff members and officers; issues special releases through the press, magazines; furnishes a film, *School Board in Action,* for local showing and for television. It co-operates with other groups to inform them about NSBA activities as well as to secure information for distribution to NSBA membership.

Publications: School Boards (monthly), Yearbook (annually); special pamphlets, booklets, reports, etc.

* * *

NATIONAL SOCIETY FOR CRIPPLED CHILDREN AND ADULTS (1921); 2023 West Ogden Avenue, Chicago 12, Ill.; Executive Director.

Membership: 52 state and territorial societies and 1,600 local societies are affiliated.

Purpose: To help the crippled through programs of care and treatment; rehabilitation; research into causes, prevention and improved treatment; and education of the public, professional persons, parents, and employers.

Adult Education Program: The society provides consultation services to affiliated societies and other interested organizations; sponsors institutes and workshops for professional personnel, officers and board members; gives scholarships

and research grants for advanced training and approved research projects; maintains a nationwide library service available to any responsible person or agency; sends free literature to anyone seeking information; publishes and distributes technical and non-technical materials; produces audio-visual aids for use before small groups and for mass media outlets. Affiliated societies provide educational, recreational, and therapy services for the homebound, and sponsor parent groups.

Publications: Rehabilitation Literature (monthly); Easter Seal Bulletin (monthly); parent pamphlet series; miscellaneous publications including annual reports, reprints, bibliographies, booklets and leaflets; audio-visual materials, including films.

* * *

NATIONAL TRAINING LABORATORIES (1947); Division of Adult Education Service, National Education Association, 1201 16th Street N. W., Washington 6, D. C.; Director.

Purpose: To develop and conduct training programs for leadership in all types of occupations in the area of human relations, group relations, community and occupational leadership; to conduct research in human relations and the process of training; to publish books and pamphlets.

Adult Education Program: Its services include consultation, publications, research, training workshops and conferences.

Publications: Books, pamphlets, reports in the area of human relations and leadership training.

* * *

*NATIONAL TUBERCULOSIS ASSOCIATION (1904); 1790 Broadway, New York 19, N. Y.; Director, Education and Public Relations.

Membership: 5,000 individuals, 57 Constituent associations, 2,750 affiliate associations.

Purpose: To study, to disseminate knowledge concerning, and to encourage the prevention and scientific treatment of tuberculosis and related diseases; to stimulate, unify, and standardize the work of affiliate associations; to co-operate with medical societies and with other nonofficial and official organizations interested in tuberculosis and related health problems; and to promote international relations in connection with the control of tuberculosis and related diseases.

Adult Education Program: The program of a tuberculosis association has as its objectives the education of the individual and of the community to the end that tuberculosis be prevented and adequate provision be made available for diagnosis, treatment, and rehabilitation of the tuberculous. Tuberculosis associations may engage in any activity in the fields of respiratory diseases, promotion of health departments and school health programs, as well as in any health education programs in connection with any local public health problem.

Publications: Newsletter (bi-weekly), Bulletin (monthly); miscellaneous pamphlets, reports, posters, guides; exhibits; 16 mm. films, 35 mm. filmstrips; Health Education Opportunities for Tuberculosis Association; annual report.

* * *

*NATIONAL UNIVERSITY EXTENSION ASSOCIATION (1915); 152 Nicholson Hall, University of Minnesota, Minneapolis 14, Minn.; Secretary.

Membership: 80 institutions.

Purpose: The establishment of an official and authorized organization through which colleges and universities engaged in extension may confer and co-operate for the development and the promotion of the best ideals, methods, and standards.

Adult Education Program: NUEA sponsors an annual conference, a number of committees working on problems common to university extension, and periodically produces research reports and other publications.

Publications: Spectator; Proceedings (of annual meeting); occasional studies, reports, manuals.

* * *

NATIONAL URBAN LEAGUE (1910); 14 East 48th Street, New York 17, N. Y.; Executive Director.

Membership: 25,000 individual memberships, 63 affiliates.

Purpose: To organize effective community interest toward the solutions of community problems resulting from inequality of opportunity in employment, education and training, family welfare, and housing.

Adult Education Program: The National Urban League provides management and labor leaders with educational materials to assist in the utilization of the skills of Negroes; provides information on economic trends and occupations to encourage Negro workers and youth to take fullest advantage of training and educational opportunities that will qualify them for the best possible jobs; organizes and conducts training institutes for league community leaders and staff to help obtain adequate housing, health, and cultural opportunities; offers consultation services to community organizations interested in developing better racial understanding in their communities; develops materials and guides to build a higher level of understanding and co-operation between whites and Negroes; conducts an annual forum on race relations and periodic seminars on employment, housing, and education.

Publications: Newsletter (bi-monthly); pamphlets, studies, reports on the economic and cultural conditions of the Negro population.

* * *

NATIONAL WOMAN'S CHRISTIAN TEMPERANCE UNION (1874); 1730 Chicago Avenue, Evanston, Ill.; President.

Membership: About 8,000 chapters. Organizations in 70 countries of the world, including every state and territory of the United States.

Purpose: To disseminate information as to what alcohol is and what it does and the impact which the use of alcoholic beverages has upon the social and economic life of the nation today.

Adult Education Program: A program guide and material for monthly meetings are provided for local unions. The national president and department directors provide recommendations, plans of work, and guide sheets encompassing all permanent projects, and current emphases for the year. An Abstinence Information Service is provided for church and civic leaders, and one 16 mm film is produced each year in addition to film strips and other visual aids. A semi-monthly magazine brings current information on alcohol and its related problems. A summer course for teachers is conducted.

Publications: The Union Signal, The

Young Crusader, Annual Report, Hand Book, Program Guide, The Christian Case for Abstinence, etc.

* * *

*OFFICE OF CIVIL AND DEFENSE MOBILIZATION (1958); (Formerly Federal Civil Defense Administration); Operational Headquarters, Battle Creek, Michigan.

Purpose: The mission of OCDM is the protection of life and property by preparing for and by carrying out nonmilitary functions to prevent, minimize, repair, and recover from injury and damage; and mobilization and management of resources and production.

Adult Education Program: OCDM teaches the principles of individual, family, and community protection against enemy-caused disaster through existing adult education programs.

Publications: Various booklets prepared in co-operation with national educational organizations to delineate areas of civil defense participation and action of their membership.

* * *

*PLANNED PARENTHOOD FEDERATION OF AMERICA (1922); 501 Madison Avenue, New York 22, N. Y.; Director of Information and Education.

Membership: Affiliated committees.

Purpose: To provide leadership for the universal acceptance of family planning as an essential element of responsible parenthood, stable family life, and social harmony, through education for family planning; to provide necessary services; and to promote research in the field of human reproduction.

Adult Education Program: Provides and arranges talks, exhibits, radio programs, etc., on various aspects of family planning including birth control, the population problem, and marriage education. Publishes pamphlets and books for those interested in family planning and for professionals working in this field. Holds symposia and workshops for physicians, social workers, and others. Prepares material for magazines and newspapers to extend general public knowledge about planned parenthood.

Publications: Periodicals, pamphlets.

* * *

ROTARY INTERNATIONAL (1905); 1600 Ridge Avenue, Evanston, Ill.; Head, Program Department.

Membership: 481,000 individuals, 10,302 clubs in 114 countries.

Purpose: To encourage and foster the ideal of service as a basis of worthy enterprise and, in particular, to encourage and foster: (1) the development of acquaintance as an opportunity for service; (2) high ethical standards in business and professions, the recognition of the worthiness of all useful occupations, and the dignifying by each Rotarian of his occupation as an opportunity to serve society; (3) the application of the ideal of service by every Rotarian to his personal, business, and community life; and (4) the advancement of international understanding, good will, and peace through a world fellowship of business and professional men united in the ideal of service.

Adult Education Program: Rotary International provides information, motivation, techniques, and training to club leadership. Rotary clubs are autonomous but suggested programs fall generally into four categories of service: club, community (including youth), vocational, and international. Scientific surveys of community needs, vocational information for youth, projects aimed toward understanding employer-employee relations, international exchanges of students and correspondence are common examples of Rotary Club programs. It carries on continuous research of world-wide activities in adult education.

Publications: Periodicals: The Rotarian (monthly); Revista Rotaria (monthly, in Spanish); R. I. NEWS (monthly to all club and international officers, in four languages); General Secretary's Letter (monthly to all international officers); Program Ideas and Timely Tips (to specific club committee chairmen on scheduled basis). Books: Adventure in Service; Service is My Business; Seven Paths to Peace. Pamphlets and leaflets: Education is Your Business; New Horizons through Adult Education; Discussion with a Purpose; A Buzz Session at the Weekly Meeting.

* * *

*THE SALVATION ARMY (1865); 120 West 14th Street, New York 11, N. Y.; The National Commander.

Membership: Individual.

Purpose: To promote through the means

of education the basic purpose of the organization: the spiritual, moral, and physical reformation of man.

Adult Education Program: Promotes programs for adults through church and institutional groups; through national committees and advisory councils stimulates the development of standards and programs; sponsors counselling for young adults and senior citizens; cooperates with other groups in the development of community programs.

Publications: War Cry (weekly), Young Soldier (weekly); manuals and pamphlets for study groups; program services folders.

* * *

SOCIETY FOR ADVANCEMENT OF MANAGEMENT (1936); 74 Fifth Avenue, New York 11, N. Y.; Executive Director.

Membership: 7,500 individuals, 75 chapters.

Purpose: To develop efficiency through the study and application of scientific principles and methods of management; to promote and accomplish the various mutual interests of management, investors, labor, government, and the public in improved management; to provide direct means whereby executives, engineers, teachers, public officials, and others concerned, are aided in applying scientific methods to management problems, and promoting this common interest; to inspire in manager and employee a constant adherence to the highest ethical standards for their individual and social responsibilities within their companies and in their communities.

Adult Education Program: The society's program includes numerous conferences, seminars, study groups, on all phases of management. It maintains a reference library for use by members; provides consultation and information services for members, for other organizations, and for the public; conducts research on management problems.

Publications: Advanced Management (monthly), S. A. M. Newsletter, Proceedings; reports of surveys and projects; articles and reprints.

* * *

*SOCIETY OF PUBLIC HEALTH EDUCATORS (1950); Secretary, Charlotte Leach, National Tuberculosis Association, 1790 Broadway, New York 19, N. Y.

Membership: 347 fellows.

Purpose: To promote, encourage, and contribute to the health of all people by encouraging study, improving practices, and elevating standards in the field of public health education.

Adult Education Program: The society holds a two-day annual meeting, with program content focussed on health and education. During the year, fellows may meet in local groups to share information and ideas. Fellows represent the society in work with other national and international groups. Interest is promoted and inquiries answered regarding health education as a career. A study is now in progress on the functions, training, and in-service education needs of professional health educators.

Publications: Quarterly Newsletter; Annual Meeting Proceedings; brochure describing the Society; several monographs a year on health education.

* * *

SPEECH ASSOCIATION OF AMERICA (1914); Louisiana State University, Baton Rouge 3, La.; Executive Secretary.

Membership: 5,000 individuals, 1,200 institutions.

Purpose: To study oral communication as an instrument of thought and social cooperation, to promote high standards in the teaching of the subject, to encourage research and criticism in the field of speech, and to publish information and research studies.

Adult Education Program: The association publishes three quarterly journals in the field of oral communication; holds annual conventions; maintains nineteen interest groups in the various areas of speech; promotes and encourages research, criticism, and publication in oral communication; and lends its support and co-operation to a variety of activities designed to improve oral communication in all facets of life and inter-personal relations.

Publications: Quarterly Journal of Speech, The Speech Teacher; Speech monographs; Annual Directory of Speech Association of America.

* * *

TOASTMASTERS INTERNATIONAL (1932); Santa Ana, Cal.; Executive Director.

Membership: 3,050 chapters.

Purpose: To improve the personality, leadership ability, and general usefulness of members, through practice and development of ability in speech.

Adult Education Program: Provides speech training, instruction and experience in parliamentary procedure and conference techniques, leadership training; encourages participation by members in group and community activities; provides speaking opportunities with outside organizations.

Publications: The Toastmaster magazine, Amateur Chairman, Speech Evaluation, Speechcraft, various pamphlets and manuals for officers.

* * *

*UNITED STATES ARMED FORCES INSTITUTE (1941); 102 North Hamilton Street, Madison 3, Wis.; Director.

Purpose: To offer civilian-like courses for men and women on active duty with the United States armed forces.

Adult Education Program: USAFI, an activity of the Office of Armed Forces Information and Education, offers approximately 204 courses at the elementary, high school, and college levels to military personnel through correspondence or group study.

Publications: U S A F I Catalog, USAFI Handbook, correspondence courses offered by colleges and universities through USAFI.

* * *

UNITED STATES COMMITTEE FOR THE UNITED NATIONS (1948); 375 Park Avenue, New York 22, N. Y.; Executive Director.

Membership: National organizations.

Purpose: To disseminate facts about the United Nations, to arouse interest in the United Nations, and to promote the observance of UN Day in the United States.

Adult Education Program: Co-operation with member organizations, local UN Committees, state and municipal governments, radio and television outlets, magazines, and newspapers in carrying out the committee's threefold purpose; distribution of literature and program aids; development of projects centering on the United Nations and assistance to citizens in carrying out such projects.

Publications: Books, pamphlets, leaflets about the United Nations; Leaders Guide, Speakers Kit, various program aids.

* * *

*U. S. DEPARTMENT OF AGRICULTURE, COOPERATIVE EXTENSION SERVICE (1914); Federal Extension Service, U. S. Department of Agriculture, Washington 25, D. C.; Administrator, Federal Extension Service.

Membership: A national system of cooperative extension services of the land-grant institutions in 50 states and Puerto Rico, with the Federal Extension Service, U. S. Department of Agriculture, serving as the national headquarters.

Purpose: To aid in diffusing among the people of the United States useful and practical information on subjects relating to agriculture and home economics, and to encourage its application.

Adult Education Program: Provides informal educational activities and services for people who can apply the results of research on subjects relating to agriculture and home economics. Although farm families are the major audience, over the years the Cooperative Extension Service has been called upon to provide educational assistance to a broader audience that includes people in these general groups: non-farm rural residents; farm, commodity, and related organizations; individuals, firms, and organizations which purchase, process, and distribute farm produce, and which provide farm people with essential services and supplies such as credit, fertilizers, feed, and many others.

Publications: Extension Service Review; Review of Extension Research; miscellaneous training materials, reports of educational research, and p r o g r a m guides.

* * *

*U. S. DEPARTMENT OF DEFENSE, NAVY INFORMATION AND EDUCATION PROGRAM (1943); Chief of Naval Personnel, Department of the Navy, Washington 25, D. C.; Head, Information, Education and Overseas Dependents Schools Section.

Purpose: To provide naval personnel on active duty with informational and educational opportunities designed to increase their efficiency, broaden their academic background, build and maintain their morale, and contribute to their well being.

Adult Education Program: An internal information program is provided to assist naval personnel to grasp their mission, understand the importance of the individual in the American way of life, and fulfill his responsibility as a military citizen and an informal ambassador of good will. An academic education program is provided giving each individual an opportunity to participate on a voluntary basis in a broad general education program at a nominal cost to the end that he may perform his assigned duties better, better prepare for career advancement, continue toward a goal the education begun before entry into service, and study courses of special interest to him. Information materials and services consist of Armed Forces Press, Radio, and Television services; pamphlets, posters, maps, motion pictures, pocket guides to foreign lands, foreign language recordings, etc. Education services and materials consist of counseling, class programs, subject and general educational development tests, correspondence courses in elementary, high school, and college courses, and filmed course materials.

Publications: Information and Education Manual; I & E Newsletter (quarterly); Sense pamphlets (Education Sense, Discipline Sense, Conference Sense, etc.)

* * *

*U. S. DEPARTMENT OF HEALTH, EDUCATION, AND WELFARE, OFFICE OF EDUCATION (1867); 330 Independence Avenue S. W., Washington 25, D. C.; Chief, Adult Education Section.

Purpose: The Office of Education seeks to provide national leadership without domination and assistance without interference; to fill gaps in information and services; to stimulate ideas and action. It seeks to encourage citizen understanding of, and responsibility for, education; to focus attention on the value of education to the individual and the nation; to promote agreement among educators and laymen on common goals; and through research and the publication of research findings, to make accurate information available to all.

Adult Education Program: The Adult Education Section conducts programs of research, consultative services, and a clearinghouse of information. These pro-

grams include, among other things, attention to the following: statistics; education of the aging, the foreign-born, young adults, and leaders and teachers of adults; fundamental and literacy education; community development; education for public affairs and leisure time; intergroup education; and citizenship education.

Publications: School Life (monthly); various special reports and publications concerned with statistics, bibliographies, and selected national educational problems.

* * *

*U. S. DEPARTMENT OF HEALTH EDUCATION, AND WELFARE, PUBLIC HEALTH SERVICE (1798); Washington 25, D. C.; Public Inquiries Branch, Public Health Service.

Purpose: Support of state and local health agencies; basic and applied research; foreign quarantine operations; and other interstate and international health activities.

Adult Education Program: Support and technical assistance to state and local health departments in the field of health education and information; production and distribution of lay health information leaflets, and assistance to mass media; publication and distribution of a wide variety of technical journals and publications for all disciplines and specialties relating to the broad field of public health.

Publications: Public Health Reports (monthly); PHS Publications (numbered series of irregular studies and reports).

* * *

*U. S. DEPARTMENT OF THE INTERIOR, BUREAU OF INDIAN AFFAIRS (1824); Interior Building, Washington 25, D. C.; Chief, Branch of Education.

Purpose: The Bureau of Indian Affairs through its Branch of Education provides educational opportunities to meet the needs of Indian children and adults who reside on reservations or restricted trust lands. The adult education program is directed toward assisting Indian adults who desire to advance their general education achievement level, and to improve their individual competencies, so that they may more effectively function in the main stream of American life either as individuals or in groups.

Adult Education Program: The Bureau's adult education program provides educational activities for the following: Indian adults who have never attended school so that they may develop the basic skills of reading, writing, and speaking English, and using arithmetic, may become acquainted with the accepted habits, customs, and manners of American life, and may understand and discharge the civic and governmental responsibilities of a citizen in our democracy; Indian adults who have had less than an 8th grade education so that they may further develop their skills and understanding in order to cope with daily problems of employment, home and family responsibilities, civic participation, personal economics, and health and safety; Indian adults who in their youth completed at least 8 years of school and now desire to continue their formal education in order to acquire a high school diploma or a certificate of equivalency; organized community groups which provide the means for solving local community problems.

Publications: Know The Truth About Indians; other publications on Indian Affairs.

* * *

*UNITED STATES NATIONAL COMMISSION FOR UNESCO (1946); U. S. Department of State, Washington 25, D. C.; Program Officer for Citizen Consultations, UNESCO Relations Staff.

Membership: 100 individuals, appointed by the Secretary of State.

Purpose: To advise the United States Government on matters related to UNESCO; to serve as an agency of liaison between UNESCO and American organizations, institutions and individuals interested in UNESCO and matters relating to it; and to promote an understanding of the general objectives of UNESCO on the part of the people of the United States.

Adult Education Program: The commission supplies printed and visual materials on UNESCO generally and on specific activities within the UNESCO program, such as Human Rights Day observance and International Theatre Celebration. On occasion it assists in obtaining speakers on UNESCO topics. One of its principal domestic activities is its program of Citizen Consultations, initiated for the purpose of broadening

and deepening the commission's relationships with the American people. In this program the commission seeks the advice of representative citizens on programs related to international activities of the United States in the fields of education, science, and culture. The commission supplies background papers and supplementary materials on certain current topics and requests the citizen groups to hold discussion seminars and to report their findings and recommendations.

Publications: National Commission Newsletter (biweekly); UNESCO Basic Documents; pamphlets and booklets on work of UNESCO and the National Commission.

* * *

UNITED WORLD FEDERALISTS (1947); 820 Thirteenth Street, N. W., Washington 5, D. C.; President.

Membership: 14,241 individuals, 167 chapters, 11 branches, and 4 regions.

Purpose: To achieve world peace through such amendments of the United Nations Charter, constitutionally adopted, as will develop the United Nations into a world federation with necessary powers limited to the establishment and maintenance of law and order on the world level.

Adult Education Program: Provides literature, films, and study kits on such subjects as disarmament, the International Court of Justice, nuclear test suspensions, etc.; and operates a speaker's bureau.

Publications: The Federalist Newsletter (monthly except August); pamphlets on international affairs and the United Nations.

* * *

*YOUNG MEN'S CHRISTIAN ASSOCIATION (1851); National Council of the YMCA's of the U. S. A., 291 Broadway, New York 7, N. Y.; Adult Program Secretary.

Membership: 2,427,810 individuals; 1,823 local YMCA's; 18 area and state organizations.

Purpose: "The Young Men's Christian Association we regard as being, in its essential genius, a world-wide fellowship united in common loyalty to Jesus Christ for the purpose of developing Christian personality and building a Christian society."

Adult Education Program: Local YMCA's

sponsor informal adult education programs with courses in a wide variety of subjects; special interest groups in many areas of recreation and education; fellowship groups with some programs of an educational nature planned by members; public affairs programs; health and physical education; workshops, conferences, seminars, and institutes for leadership development. Programs generally include men and women and in most instances are offered to the public as well as to members.

Publications: Several professional magazines for YMCA secretaries. A large variety of adult education books by the YMCA's publishing arm, The Association Press.

* * *

*YOUNG WOMEN'S CHRISTIAN ASSOCIATION OF THE UNITED STATES OF AMERICA (1858); 600 Lexington Avenue, New York 22, N. Y.; Director of Leadership Services.

Membership: 2,000,000 individuals, in 441 community associations, 500 student associations, 273 Registered YWCA's.

Purpose: "To build a fellowship of women and girls devoted to the task of realizing in our common life those ideals of personal and social living to which we are committed by our faith as Christians. In this endeavor we seek to understand Jesus, to share his love for all people, and to grow in the knowledge and love of God."

Adult Education Program: Local associations sponsor informal courses open to members and the public in a variety of subjects, specialized courses for skill training, organized clubs with some educational programs, lecture series, social action projects, and leadership training. Programs are designed especially for employed and young married women as well as co-ed and family groups. The national board develops program materials, provides consultations to local Associations, and conducts leadership training for volunteer and professional workers.

Publications: YWCA Magazine (special section for young adults); The Bookshelf (program bulletin for advisers and leaders of teen-age program); pamphlets.

INDEX*

*In the case of national organizations listed in PART VI, the page number of the listing there is given first.

605